INTRODUCTION TO THE

Old Testament

This volume introduces Israel's Scriptures, or the Hebrew Bible, commonly called the Old Testament. It also traces the legacy of monotheism found in the pages of the Old Testament. Where pertinent to the message of the Old Testament, the book explores issues of history, comparative religions, and sociology, while striking a balance among these topics by focusing primarily on literary features of the text. In addition, frequent sidebar discussions introduce the reader to contemporary scholarship, especially the results of historical-critical research and archaeology. Along the way, the book explores how the Old Testament conceptualized and gave rise to monotheism, one of the most significant developments in history. This work

- pays unique attention to the origins of monotheism, the common heritage of Jews, Christians, and Muslims;
- includes frequent sidebar discussions in each chapter, a generous number of illustrations, and twenty freshly created maps, as well as concise chapter summaries and a glossary of terms;
- has a Web component that includes study guides, flash cards, PowerPoint lecture slides, and a test bank.

Bill T. Arnold is the Paul S. Amos Professor of Old Testament Interpretation at Asbury Theological Seminary. He is the author of numerous books and articles in biblical studies, including *Genesis* (The New Cambridge Bible Commentary Series, 2009) and *A Guide to Biblical Hebrew Syntax* (with John H. Choi, 2003). He is also the coeditor of *Dictionary of the Old Testament: Historical Books* (with H. G. M. Williamson, 2005) and *Readings from the Ancient Near East: Primary Sources for Old Testament Study* (with Bryan E. Bayer, 2002) and the author of *Who Were the Babylonians?* (2004) and *1 and 2 Samuel: The NIV Application Commentary* (2003).

INTRODUCTION TO THE

Old Testament

BILL T. ARNOLD

Asbury Theological Seminary

CAMBRIDGE
UNIVERSITY PRESS

CAMBRIDGE
UNIVERSITY PRESS

University Printing House, Cambridge CB2 8BS, United Kingdom

One Liberty Plaza, 20th Floor, New York, NY 10006, USA

477 Williamstown Road, Port Melbourne, VIC 3207, Australia

314-321, 3rd Floor, Plot 3, Splendor Forum, Jasola District Centre, New Delhi - 110025, India

79 Anson Road, #06-04/06, Singapore 079906

Cambridge University Press is part of the University of Cambridge.

It furthers the University's mission by disseminating knowledge in the pursuit of education, learning and research at the highest international levels of excellence.

www.cambridge.org
Information on this title: www.cambridge.org/9780521705479

© Bill T. Arnold 2014

First published 2014
3rd printing 2016

A catalogue record for this publication is available from the British Library

Library of Congress Cataloging in Publication data
Arnold, Bill T., author.
Introduction to the Old Testament / Bill T. Arnold.
pages   cm – (Introduction to religion)
Includes bibliographical references and index.
ISBN 978-0-521-87965-1 (hardback)
1. Monotheism – History of doctrines.   2. God (Judaism) – History of doctrines.
3. Bible. Old Testament – Theology.   I. Title.
BS1192.6.A76   2014
221.6′1–dc23   2013027349

ISBN 978-0-521-87965-1 Hardback
ISBN 978-0-521-70547-9 Paperback

CONTENTS

List of Illustrations		*page* xii
Preface		xv

1 What Is the Old Testament? 1

Sidebar 1.1. Friedrich Delitzsch's rejection of the
    Old Testament — 2

Old Testament, Tanak, or Hebrew Bible? — 4

The legacy of monotheism — 6

Sidebar 1.2. Israel's God, Yahweh — 6

Sidebar 1.3. "Monotheism" — 11

Your main task in reading the Old Testament — 12

2 Word of Truth – Word of God 16

The power of words — 17

What is a book? — 19

The Old Testament canon — 21

Sidebar 2.1. "Canon" — 21

Sidebar 2.2. Council of Jamnia — 22

Sidebar 2.3. Jerome, also known as Eusebius Hieronymus
    (ca. 347–420 CE) — 25

Copies and translations of the Old Testament canon — 25

The word's influence — 28

3 The Old Testament World 31

Axial Age changes in world history — 32

The stage of the Old Testament drama — 32

Sidebar 3.1. What shall we call the land of the Bible? — 37

World history before and during the Old Testament drama   40
　　Sidebar 3.2. Christian Thomsen and the periodization of history   41
　　Sidebar 3.3. The correspondence of Abdi-Heba of Jerusalem   45
The Old Testament story   46
　　Sidebar 3.4. Highlights of Israel's story   47

4   **The Primary History**   51
The Herodotus, father of history?   52
　　Sidebar 4.1. Antiquarianism versus historiography   53
　　Sidebar 4.2. Herodotus (ca. 484–425 BCE), the father of history   54
Israelite historiography   54
　　Sidebar 4.3. Sources of Old Testament literature   56
The Primary History: From creation to the fall of Jerusalem   58
　　Sidebar 4.4. Spinoza on biblical studies   59

5   **Beginnings** 67
Old Testament reading: Genesis 1–11   67
The Primeval History: Genesis 1–11   69
　　Sidebar 5.1. Historical and priestly traditions of Genesis 1–11   70
　　Sidebar 5.2. YHWH, Yahweh, and "LORD"   71
The concept of "creation," and the need to explain origins   72
Ancient Near Eastern parallels   74
　　Sidebar 5.3. Sources for ancient Near Eastern texts   75
Myth, epic, or history? Something else entirely? A question
　　of literary type   77
Themes of the Primeval History   79
　　Sidebar 5.4. Monotheism and the equality of men and women   82

6   **Ancestors** 84
Old Testament reading: Genesis 12–50   84
Fathers and mothers of faith   85
　　Sidebar 6.1. From where do we get our chapter
　　　and verse numbers?   86
　　Sidebar 6.2. More on the literary sources of Genesis   88
Archaeology and the search for what really happened   89
　　Sidebar 6.3. The rise of archaeological research   90
Life in ancient Israel   92
Religion in the ancestral narratives   94
Abraham's faith and Abrahamic religions   96

7   **Torah Story** 99
Old Testament reading: Exodus and Numbers   99
　　Sidebar 7.1. The Torah's literary sources   100

Israel's story   100

What really happened?   106

    Sidebar 7.2. Excerpt from the Stela of Merneptah   108

Yahweh: What kind of God?   112

8 Torah Instruction... 116

Old Testament reading: Leviticus and Psalms 19 and 119   116

    Sidebar 8.1. Excerpt from Psalm 119   117

Commandments, ordinances, statutes, instructions, laws,
and so forth   117

The core of the Torah, and Israel's "ethics"   120

The Ten Words   121

    Sidebar 8.2. Ten Words? Try counting them!   123

Tabernacle, sacrifice, and priesthood in ancient Israel's worship   124

Law "codes," writing, and monotheism   125

    Sidebar 8.3. How old are the priestly legal materials
of the Torah?   126

    Sidebar 8.4. Ancient Near Eastern law codes   128

9 Torah Revisited 131

Old Testament reading: Deuteronomy   131

Speeches of Moses   132

    Sidebar 9.1. The Shema   134

Covenant renewal and the book's structure   135

    Sidebar 9.2. Treaty of Suppiluliuma, the Hittite "Great King"   136

    Sidebar 9.3. Succession Treaty of Esarhaddon   138

Moses' sermons – the "center of the Old Testament"   138

    Sidebar 9.4. King Josiah and his reforms   140

The death of Moses – the birth of Torah   144

What does "Deuteronomic" mean? What about
"Deuteronomistic"?   145

    Sidebar 9.5. The Deuteronomistic History   146

10 The Religion of Moses 148

Old Testament reading: Exodus 3:1–15, 6:2–9, and 18:1–12;
Psalms 104, 105, and 106   148

Main features of the religion of Moses   149

Moses and Abraham   152

    Sidebar 10.1. Exodus 6:2–9 in light of source analysis   154

    Sidebar 10.2. El in Canaanite religion   154

Moses and ancient Near Eastern precursors   156

    Sidebar 10.3. Excerpt from *The Great Hymn to the Aten*   158

    Sidebar 10.4. The *Baal Cycle*   161

Origins of the religion of Moses   162
    Sidebar 10.5. "Shasu of YHW" in Egyptian inscriptions   163
Legacy   164

11 Was There an "Ancient Israel"? 167
Interpreting text and tell – the example of Jericho   169
    Sidebar 11.1. The tale of a tell   170
Chronology of ancient Israelite history   173
    Sidebar 11.2. High chronology or low chronology?   175
    Sidebar 11.3. Excerpt from the Babylonian Chronicle   177
    Sidebar 11.4. Excerpt from the Cyrus Cylinder   178
History of Israelite religion(s)   178

12 Land 184
Old Testament reading: Joshua and Judges   184
    Sidebar 12.1. Where is the book of Ruth?   185
At long last, the land! Fulfillment of the Pentateuch's promises   185
The books Joshua and Judges   189
    Sidebar 12.2. The role of Joshua and Judges in the
        Deuteronomistic History   189
    Sidebar 12.3. What is "Yahweh War" in the Old Testament?   192
Three views of what really happened   195
    Sidebar 12.4. Israelite architecture and pottery   197
Israelite religion in Iron Age I   201
The problem with the promise – What about the land today?   204
    Sidebar 12.5. Why does genocide play a role in Joshua
        and Judges?   204

13 Kings 207
Old Testament reading: 1 and 2 Samuel   207
"The scepter shall not depart from Judah"   208
The books of First and Second Samuel   209
    Sidebar 13.1. The role of 1–2 Samuel in the Deuteronomistic
        History   209
    Sidebar 13.2. The original source known as David's
        "Court History"   216
What really happened?   217
    Sidebar 13.3. The evidence of the Tel Dan Inscription   219
Religious expression in the United Monarchy   220
    Sidebar 13.4. The strange case of 1 Samuel 28 – Death
        cults in ancient Israel?   222
    Sidebar 13.5. Was Israel an ancient amphictyony?   224

14 More Kings 226
 Old Testament reading: 1 and 2 Kings 226
 The books of First and Second Kings 227
  Sidebar 14.1. The role of 1–2 Kings in the Deuteronomistic
   History 228
  Sidebar 14.2. Excerpts from *The Instruction of Ptahhotep* 229
  Sidebar 14.3. The role of Josiah in Israel's history and in
   Old Testament literature 233
 What really happened? 234
  Sidebar 14.4. Excerpt from the Babylonian Chronicles 235
  Sidebar 14.5. The Black Obelisk 237
 Religious expression embedded in the account of Israel's
  monarchy 237

15 History Revisited 244
 Old Testament reading: 1 and 2 Chronicles and Ezra-Nehemiah 244
  Sidebar 15.1. Where is the book of Esther? 245
 A new history for postexilic times 245
 The books of First and Second Chronicles and Ezra-Nehemiah 248
  Sidebar 15.2. David, Solomon, and the city of Zion 250
  Sidebar 15.3. The evidence of the Moabite Stone 251
 Background of the Chronistic History 254
  Sidebar 15.4. Kings of ancient Persia 257
 Monotheism in the Chronistic History? 259

16 More Books 261
 Old Testament reading: Genesis 49, Deuteronomy 32,
  and Judges 5 261
 All the rest, and how they relate to the Primary and Chronistic
  Histories 262
  Sidebar 16.1. Titles and authors of ancient compositions 264
 The characteristics and qualities of Old Testment poetry 267
  Sidebar 16.2. Is poetry a distinct Old Testament literary
   category? 268
  Sidebar 16.3. Acrostic structures in poetry 273

17 Israel's Wisdom 275
 Old Testament reading: Job and Proverbs 275
 Wisdom literature in the ancient Near East 276
  Sidebar 17.1. Excerpts from *The Poem of the Righteous Sufferer* 279
 The books of Job and Proverbs 280
  Sidebar 17.2. And Ecclesiastes makes three 280

Sidebar 17.3. Job's living redeemer   282
Sidebar 17.4. Excerpts from *The Babylonian Theodicy*   284
Revelation, monotheism, and the problem of evil   286
Sidebar 17.5. Excerpts from *The Instruction of Amenemope*   287

18 Israel's Hymnal 291
Old Testament reading: The book of Psalms   291
The book of Psalms   292
Sidebar 18.1. Where are the books of Ecclesiastes and
    Song of Songs?   292
Sidebar 18.2. The power of music   295
Form criticism and psalm types   296
Sidebar 18.3. Other methods beyond source and form
    criticism   297
Sidebar 18.4. What kind of poem is Psalm 23?   301
Images of Yahweh/God in the book of Psalms   303

19 Israel's Prophets: The Maturing Period 307
Old Testament reading: Amos, Hosea, Micah, and Isaiah 1–39   307
Sidebar 19.1. Writing in ancient Israel   308
What is "prophecy"?   309
Sidebar 19.2. Other designations for Old Testament prophets   310
Sidebar 19.3. Ancient Near Eastern prophecies   311
Israel's books of prophecy   312
The books of Amos, Hosea, Micah, and Isaiah   315
Sidebar 19.4. The history of prophecy in ancient Israel   319
Religious contributions of the eighth-century prophets   323

20 Israel's Prophets: The Crisis and Beyond 326
Old Testament reading: Jeremiah, Obadiah, Nahum, Habakkuk,
    Zephaniah, Ezekiel, and Isaiah 40–66   326
The books of Jeremiah, Obadiah, Nahum, Habakkuk, Zephaniah,
    Ezekiel, and "Isaiah of the exile"   327
Sidebar 20.1. Where is the book of Lamentations?   328
Sidebar 20.2. The prophetic struggles against Zion theology   330
Sidebar 20.3. The production of a biblical book   331
Sidebar 20.4. Sequence of events defining "the exile"   335
Religious contributions of the prophets of the crisis   339

21 Israel's Prophets: The Restoration 342
Old Testament reading: Haggai, Zechariah, Malachi, Joel,
    and Jonah   342

The restoration of Jerusalem and Judah (Yehud) in the
  Persian period   343
    Sidebar 21.1. Sequence of events defining the postexilic period   343
The books of Haggai, Zechariah, Malachi, Joel, and Jonah   346
Use and/or abuse of the Old Testament prophets   351
Religious contributions of the prophets of the restoration   352

22 Israel's Apocalyptic Message 355
Old Testament reading: Daniel   355
What does "apocalyptic" mean?   356
Where did apocalyptic literature come from?   357
The book of Daniel   358
    Sidebar 22.1. Apocalyptic texts from ancient Mesopotamia   359
    Sidebar 22.2. Maccabean period history   364
Contributions of Israel's apocalyptic message   366

23 The Scrolls 370
Old Testament reading: Song of Songs, Ruth, Lamentations,
  Ecclesiastes, and Esther   370
The Megilloth, or the five scrolls   371
    Sidebar 23.1. Egyptian parallels to the Song of Songs   373
    Sidebar 23.2. Mesopotamian parallels to Ecclesiastes   377
Contributions of the Megilloth to Old Testament faith   381

24 The Old Testament Today 383
Anatomy of the Old Testament   384
Enduring contributions of the Old Testament   386

Glossary   391
Bibliography   397
Index   401

ILLUSTRATIONS

PLATES

Plates follow page xvi

    I. Hieroglyphics from Egypt

    II. Astrological calendar from Mesopotamia

    III. Egyptian creation

    IV. Clay tablet reproducing an episode of the Gilgamesh Epic
       (Old Babylonian period, ca. 1800 BCE)

    V. The Western Wall with the Dome of the Rock

    VI. Mount Nebo

    VII. Glazed brick relief of dragon from the gates of Ishtar
       at Babylon, ca. 570 BC

VIII. Beth-shan

    IX. Tower of Lachish under siege

    X. Page from the Book of the Dead, Thebes, Nineteenth
      Dynasty (ca. 1275 BCE)

    XI. Jehu, king of Israel, prostrating himself before King
      Shalmaneser III of Assyria

    XII. The Dead Sea

FIGURES

1.1. Assyriologist Friedrich Delitzsch, portrait 1903	*page* 2	
1.2. Stele of Qadesh	8	
1.3. Scroll of Isaiah	13	
2.1. Ahiram sarcophagus inscription	18	
2.2. Torah scroll	19	
2.3. The Old Testament canon	24	

2.4.	Caves near Qumran	27
3.1.	The Pyramids of Giza	42
3.2.	Amarna Letter	45
4.1.	Hittite Treaty	52
4.2.	Herodotus	54
4.3.	Spinoza, 1632–1677	59
5.1.	Michelangelo's *Creation of Adam*	68
5.2.	The Ziggurat of Ur	72
5.3.	Cuneiform tablet relating the Epic of Creation	76
5.4.	The "Baal of Lightning" found in a sanctuary at ancient Ugarit	78
6.1.	Sir Flinders Petrie, 1853–1942	90
6.2.	William F. Albright, 1891–1971	90
6.3.	Julius Wellhausen, 1844–1918	91
6.4.	The Standing Stones of Gezer	95
7.1.	Pharaoh Ramses II, ca. 1279–1213 BCE	102
7.2.	Saint Catherine's Monastery at the base of Jebel Musa	104
7.3.	Gold-plated calf from Byblos in ancient Phoenicia	105
7.4.	Merneptah victory stela	108
8.1.	The tabernacle in the wilderness	119
8.2.	The Iron Age sanctuary from Arad	125
8.3.	Detail of the Code of Hammurabi	127
9.1.	Mounts Ebal and Gerizim, viewed from the east	135
9.2.	Priestly benediction on a silver amulet	141
10.1.	Michelangelo's *Moses*	150
10.2.	The Canaanite god El	153
10.3.	The god Baal of the thunderstorm	160
11.1.	Ancient Jericho	172
11.2.	Nabonidus Chronicle	177
12.1.	Jericho, with the Mountains of Moab in the background	191
12.2.	Artist's rendition of the courtyard of an Israelite four-room house	196
13.1.	Michelangelo's *David*	210
13.2.	Portrait of a captured Philistine	212
13.3.	Caravaggio's *David*	214
13.4.	The Tel Dan Inscription	219
14.1.	Seal inscribed with "[Belonging] to Shema, the servant of Jeroboam"	232
14.2.	The Black Obelisk of Shalmaneser III of Assyria (858–824 BCE)	234
14.3.	Execution of Israelite prisoners of war at Lachish	235
15.1.	View of the City of David, with the Old City of Jerusalem in the background	246

15.2. Victory Stela of Mesha, King of Moab   251
15.3. Cyrus Cylinder, from Babylon, southern Iraq, ca. 539–530 BCE   258
16.1. Cylinder seal depicting "contest scene"   263
17.1. The goddess Ma'at   277
17.2. Mesopotamian Leviathan (third millennium BCE)   283
18.1. Jug with lyre player and cymbals   295
18.2. Hermann Gunkel, 1862–1932   298
18.3. The Psalms at Qumran cave 11   300
19.1. The Khirbet Qeiyafa Inscription (tenth century BCE)   309
19.2. Rendition of the Khirbet Qeiyafa Inscription   309
20.1. Exile scenes from Sennacherib's palace in Nineveh   327
21.1. Darius I, also known as Darius the Great (522–486 BCE)   344
21.2. Yehud coin   346
22.1. *Belshazzar's Feast* by Rembrandt, about 1635   362
22.2   Antiochus IV Epiphanes (175–164 BCE)   365
23.1. Megillat Esther   372
23.2. Ruins of Apadana Palace, Persepolis, Iran   381
24.1. Old Testament   389

MAPS

3.1.   Geography of ancient Israel   33
3.2.   The ancient Near East   35
3.3.   Ancient Egypt   36
3.4.   The Levant   38
3.5.   Highways of the ancient world   39
6.1.   Journeys of Abraham according to Genesis   87
7.1.   Initial route of the exodus   109
12.1. Initial campaign (Joshua 1–8)   186
12.2. Ideal northern and southern borders of the promised land   188
12.3. Southern campaign   198
12.4. Northern campaign   199
12.5. Israel in the land after conquest (Iron Age I)   203
13.1. Saul's kingdom   213
13.2. David's kingdom   215
13.3. Solomon's kingdom   221
14.1. Israel and Judah in the Southern Levant   231
15.1. Extent of the Persian Empire   255
15.2. Persian district "Yehud" in the satrap "Beyond the River"   256
19.1. Southern Levant during the eighth-century prophets   316
20.1. The world of the seventh- and sixth-century prophets   329

PREFACE

The Old Testament is a complex collection of literary works from a wide range of periods spanning centuries of history. We have many options for launching into the study of the Old Testament. One may take an essentially *historical* approach, which is helpful because so much of the Old Testament is embedded in history. But this may give the impression that learning Israelite history, or ancient Near Eastern history, is the same thing as learning the Old Testament. Clearly, acquiring an understanding of history is not the same as learning what the Old Testament says.

One could take a *theological* approach. But as we shall see, the message of the Old Testament has been taken in different ways in Judaism, Christianity, and Islam. These religious traditions sometimes agree on the meaning of the Old Testament, but not always. And today's secularist reader will also need a basic understanding of the Old Testament.

One may take a *comparative* approach, studying religious practices and expressions of the Old Testament with other world religions. But much of the Old Testament has little connection with non-Abrahamic religions, and such an approach would move us off the main task of learning the basic message of the Old Testament itself.

In contrast to these approaches, I have taken in this textbook a *literary* approach since the Old Testament is, after all – although it may sound silly to say this – literature. So this book can be taken as an entrée into the literature of ancient Israel as it has been preserved in the pages of the Old Testament. At the same time, I have focused on the Old Testament's unique contribution to the history of religious ideas in human civilization. The Old Testament has left an enormous legacy in the history of ideas, which naturally leads to connections in theology and philosophy. This introduction to the Old Testament as literature will therefore trace the single most important contribution of the Old Testament – that of monotheism – as a theme throughout this book.

A word about the title, *Introduction to the Old Testament*. The term "introduction" is not intended in the technical, scholarly sense (German *Einleitung*), which would imply that the volume discusses all the critical issues for every biblical book. Rather, this is a textbook, introducing the literature and legacy of the Old Testament for the beginning student.

The book will focus on monotheism as the legacy of ancient Israel's Scriptures, providing a subtheme running alongside and parallel to the general discussion. As we will see, the Old Testament itself is not uniform in its understanding of the singularity of God. Only certain portions contribute to that legacy, and so we will not take up the question of monotheistic faith in every chapter along the way. This subtheme will highlight the Old Testament's enduring legacy in the three monotheistic faith traditions, Judaism, Christianity, and Islam, which is a topic of renewed interest in our world today.

You will need a translation of the Old Testament close by as you read through this textbook. I recommend a recent translation in colloquial English, the best of which are the New Revised Standard Version (NRSV), the Common English Bible (CEB), and Today's New International Version (TNIV). Every translation is itself an interpretation. Translations from the Old Testament in this textbook are from the NRSV, although I have occasionally made slight changes in order to illustrate my points (such as "Yahweh" for "the LORD" with small caps, and "enduring covenant" instead

of "everlasting covenant"). I have provided my own translation at other times and will mark with "my translation" where I have done so (e.g., Psalm 1 in Chapter 16).

All dates in this textbook are "BCE" for Before the Common Era, unless otherwise indicated. Most of the chapters include a header with the designation "Old Testament Reading." I suggest you read the portions of the Old Testament assigned there before reading the chapter, or at least along with the chapter, in this textbook (perhaps taking breaks in the OT readings to study this book).

And finally, it is a joy to express appreciation to the Association of Theological Schools in the United States and Canada, and its Lilly Theological Research Grant. I was awarded the Lilly Faculty Fellowship for fall semester 2010, which made it possible for me to devote focused attention to this project. I am also grateful to Asbury Theological Seminary for a study leave in spring semester 2011. To my former students Mark Awabdy, Deborah Endean, Jason Jackson, and James D. Wilson I owe a great debt of gratitude, as well as one to Andy Beck, formerly of Cambridge University Press, and to Dr. Asya Graf, currently assistant editor for humanities and social sciences at the Press, who was extremely helpful at several points along the way. Jim Holsinger was a good advisor and friend during the time I worked on this project. As always, I owe most to Susan.

Plate I. Hierglyphics from Egypt. The Greeks called Egyptian writings "holy carvings" (hieroglyphics) because of their perceived sacred character. This is an inscription dedicated to Amon-Min, a fertility god, from the time of Sesostris I (1950 BCE). (Photo: Erich Lessing / Art Resource, N.Y.)

Plate II. Astrological calendar from Mesopotamia. The distinctive cuneiform ("wedge-shaped") script seen in this first-millennium text from ancient Uruk is the first attested writing system in world history. Cuneiform writing was adapted for use with many languages and exported widely thoughout Mesopotamia, Syria-Palestine, and Asia Minor. (Photo: Erich Lessing / Art Resource, N.Y.)

Plate III. Egyptian creation. In this Egyptian version of creation from approximately 1000 BCE, the sky-goddess Nut, extends over the created order and is generated by Geb, god of earth. This version is reconstructed from a fresco from a tomb at Thebes, Valley of the Kings. (Photo: © DeA Picture Library / Art Resource, N.Y.)

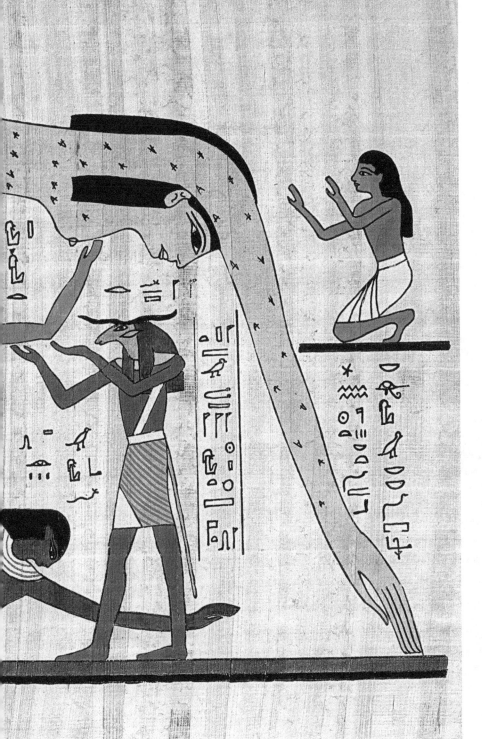

Plate IV. Clay tablet reproducing an episode of the Gilgamesh Epic (Old Babylonian period, ca. 1800 BCE). The Yale Gilgamesh Tablet is one of the most important copies of this epic poem from ancient Iraq. (Photo: Yale Babylonian Collection)

Plate V. The Western Wall with the Dome of the Rock, Jerusalem. The Temple Mount in Jerusalem is revered as sacred by Jews, Christians, and Muslims. The Dome of the Rock was built over the traditional site where Abraham is believed to have offered his son Isaac as a sacrifice (Genesis 22). Additionally, Islamic tradition holds that Muhammad was miraculously transported here in a night vision, and from this place toured heaven and spoke with Abraham, Moses, and Jesus. The Western Wall (*foreground*) contains portions of a retaining wall built by Herod the Great for the expanded temple platform. (Photo: © Peter Spirer / Dreamstime.com)

Plate VI. The view of the northern Dead Sea and the Jordan Valley from Mount Nebo, the top of Pisgah (see map 3.1). God showed Moses the promised land from this vista before Moses' death (Deuteronomy 34:1). (Photo: Courtesy of Bill T. Arnold)

Plate VII. Glazed brick relief of dragon from the gates of Ishtar at Babylon, ca. 570 BC. The surface of the entrance into Babylon by way of the Ishtar Gate was covered with blue enameled bricks, serving as background for alternating red-and-white dragons, symbolic of the god Marduk, chief deity of ancient Babylon. (Werner Forman / Art Resource, N.Y.)

Plate VIII. The mound known as Tell el-Husn has been identified as ancient Beth-shan, also spelled Beth-shean, viewed here from the south. Later Roman and Byzantine ruins are in the foreground. The impressive mound itself preserves evidence of occupation from the Neolithic period in the lowest layer (stratum XVIII) all the way to Byzantine remains in the uppermost level of the tell (stratum I). (Photo: courtesy of Bill T. Arnold)

Plate IX. Tower of Lachish under siege. The stone panels from the southwest palace of Sennacherib in Nineveh contain numerous relief sculptures depicting the capture of Lachish in 701 BCE. This image shows the tower of the fortified city of Lachish under attack. The artwork imitates the violence of ancient warfare, showing the Assyrians, supported by archers, maneuvering siege engines up ramps, while the Israelites inside the city hurl torches and stones from the tower and walls against the Assyrians below. (Photo: Erich Lessing / Art Resource, N.Y.)

Plate X. Page from the Book of the Dead, Thebes, Nineteenth Dynasty (ca. 1275 BCE). The funerary papyrus shows the weighing of the souls (psychostasis). *Reading from the left*, the god Anubis, jackal-headed god associated with mummification, brings the deceased to the place of judgment, where Anubis supervises the judgment scales. The heart of the deceased is being weighed against a feather, the symbol of the goddess Ma'at, cosmic order, truth, and righteousness. (Photo: © The Trustees of the British Museum / Art Resource, N.Y.)

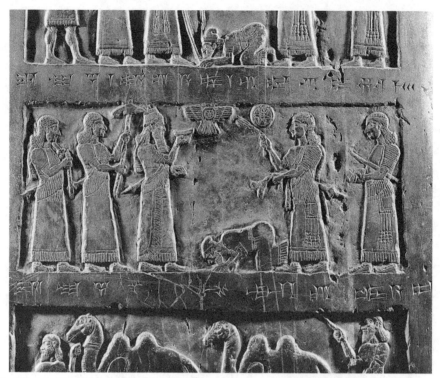

Plate XI. In this detail from the Black Obelisk, Jehu, the king of Israel, is seen prostrating himself before King Shalmaneser III of Assyria; see Sidebar 14.5. (Photo: ErichLessing / Art Resource, N.Y.)

Plate XII. The surface of the Dead Sea, or "Salt Sea," is 1,388 feet below sea level, which is earth's lowest elevation on land. The Dead Sea is also earth's deepest hypersaline lake, making it inhospitable to most life forms. Yet the Old Testament prophet Ezekiel envisions a day when the Dead Sea will become Life Sea, the source of life-giving water for nearby Jerusalem. (Photo: courtesy of Bill T. Arnold)

What Is the Old Testament?

The significance of the Old Testament for human history and culture is undeniable. Whatever our personal convictions regarding its content, the OT contains the origins of nearly everything we think about God. Variously labeled as the Hebrew Bible, the Tanak, the First Testament, and the Old Testament, among others, this library of texts from ancient Israel has been preserved for more than two thousand years.

Emerging from the polytheistic context of the ancient world, the enduring significance of the OT is to be found in the concept of monotheism. Indeed, Judaism, Christianity, and Islam share in this unique religious legacy. We will discover in this chapter what lies behind the terminology we use when we speak of monotheism, and how the OT perceives and develops the understanding of a singular God. Known to ancient Israel as Yahweh, Israel's God came to be understood as Creator, source of all, and sovereign over all. Only in time would Israel come to believe that Yahweh was not only its God, and the God Israelites were called to worship, but the one and only God.

What you think about God – if you think about God at all – affects nearly everything else you believe to be true. Wars have been fought and nations divided based on what people think about God. On a more individual level, important personal and ethical decisions are often made based on what we think about God.

While you're thinking about God, consider this. Nearly everything we think about God has been expressed first in the Old Testament. A great many other assumptions about God, that God is vengeful

SIDEBAR 1.1. FRIEDRICH DELITZSCH'S REJECTION OF THE OLD TESTAMENT

One of the leading professors of Europe at the turn of the twentieth century, Friedrich Delitzsch (1850–1922) created a sensation with his "Babel und Bibel" lectures. In a series of three lectures delivered in 1902, 1903, and 1904, Delitzsch championed Babylonian religion and culture as superior to that of the Israelites of the OT. He argued that the Israelites were an unfortunate regress in the history of religion; that the OT became increasingly law centered, resulting in the lamentable legalism of Judaism; and that first-century Samaria and Galilee were essentially Babylonian with Aryan racial stock, suggesting that Jesus was Aryan rather than Jewish. In the midst of international uproar, Delitzsch refused to recant. In his final publication, a two-volume work in 1920 and 1921 called *The Great Deception* (*Die Grosse Täuschung*), he sought to expose the OT as fraudulent, proposed that German Christians cut it from their Bibles, and warned that the Jewish people posed a threat to the future of Germany.

Delitzsch was preceded in his extreme views by the theologian and historian Adolf von Harnack (1851–1930). Harnack had similarly argued that Christians in the nineteenth century should reject the OT in the name of progress. Such rank nationalism and anti-Semitism contributed to the historical and ideological foundations of the young German state and the rise of Nazism later in the 1930s.

1.1. The Assyriologist Friedrich Delitzsch. Delitzsch posed for this photograph in 1903, a few months after giving his first public lecture, "Babel und Bibel," in Berlin in January 1902. (Photo: Yale Babylonian Collection)

or wrathful, for example, are *thought* to be in the Old Testament but are not, at least not as many assume. There are certainly exceptions to my assertion that everything we think about God comes from the Old Testament, such as the much later beliefs that Jesus is the incarnation of God or that God sent a final and definitive revelation to Muhammad. Yet even these have origins in the Old Testament. As a result, it's a pretty good idea to learn what the Old Testament has to say about God.

People have not always thought highly of the Old Testament. One famous intellectual in the 1920s argued that the Old Testament was no longer necessary for further human progress. In fact, Friedrich Delitzsch wanted to do away with the

Old Testament altogether. He was not alone. Many have attacked the writings of the Old Testament in different ways and for a variety of reasons, and they have done so for many centuries. Yet the contributions of the Old Testament to human history and culture cannot be denied. Consider its impact on philosophy, for example, from the perspective of the "history of ideas" over the past three thousand years, and you will find that few ancient writings have had a greater influence. In addition, consider that millions of readers today still find in its pages a source of inspiration and faith. The purpose of this textbook is not to argue for the continuing value of the Old Testament, nor to convince you of either the truthfulness of its religious claims or the untruthfulness of those claims. This volume seeks rather to introduce you to the Old Testament's content, structure, and central messages, and to do so by focusing on what it says about God. Its significance for you today will be left to you to decide.

This textbook is about a library. Like most libraries, this one houses different types of literature — history, songs, parables, prayers, and many others. As a collection of books and writings, this library tells of nations and empires, of tribes and families, of war heroes and crimes, of tragedies and triumphs, and above all, of the religious convictions of its authors.

But we're not talking about your average library here. This collection of writings, most often known as the "Old Testament," is the legacy of an ancient people from the Middle East — the Israelites. Many other groups of people just like the Israelites existed during that period of history. By contrast, for most of those other groups, we know little more than their names and for some, their approximate geographical homeland. Yet these writings of ancient Israel have been preserved for well over two thousand years, translated into all primary languages and many obscure secondary dialects, and have made a contribution to human history that is impossible to calculate. Everyday expressions you use instinctively, philosophical concepts you probably assume, and perhaps even faith you express have all been influenced to some degree by this ancient library.

Why? Why have Israel's writings left such an indelible mark on the world? The literature of most other peoples of the ancient world before Greece and Rome often vanished, leaving only traces here and there. Why did this singular collection

of writings now contained in the Old Testament survive through the ages, and why has the Old Testament left such an impact on human history and civilization?

Many answers to these questions may occur to us when we think of sociology, history, or cultural studies. But I offer one particular answer here that commends itself through the heirs of the Old Testament itself. What I mean by this is that it is the distinctively *religious* contributions of the Old Testament that are continued in Judaism, and later in Christianity and Islam as well. These three so-called monotheistic religions have a common origin in the religious and theological writings of this library, specifically the Old Testament's conviction about the nature of God. Israel routinely refers to its national God as the sovereign Lord of the universe, and in a few contexts, even the *only* God of the universe. Indeed, the defining characteristic of the Old Testament is what I will call "Israel's gift to the world," the **monotheism** defined and propagated in its pages.

Not all will agree that monotheism is a "gift." In fact, monotheism itself is not even defined clearly in the Old Testament. Others contend that monotheism, whether defined clearly in the Old Testament or not, has a violent history and is certainly no "gift," whatever its origins. But this is getting ahead of our story. At this point, it is enough to know that ancient Israel's library — read and studied for centuries by countless believers as the "Old Testament," or the Hebrew Scriptures — is distinctive in the ancient world for its convictions about God and its profound expressions of God's nature, but especially of God's singularity or sole existence. For this and other reasons, Israel's library has survived and has influenced the world dramatically. As the religious and literary foundation of the world's three monotheistic religions, Judaism, Christianity, and Islam, this library bequeathed by ancient Israel continues to be an important topic for us to explore.

OLD TESTAMENT, TANAK, OR HEBREW BIBLE?

We begin by asking in this chapter a question: What is the Old Testament? At first glance, we might assume that this would be a simple question to answer. But you may have noticed that the library of ancient Israel goes by many different names. Besides "Old Testament," it is also known as the Hebrew Bible, the First Testament, the Older Testament, the Hebrew Scriptures, the **Tanak**, the Miqra, and others. In fact, the label we use for this body of literature reveals what we think of it, to some degree. But deciding what to call the Old Testament is not the only problem when trying to explain exactly what it is. We also have different collections of books and writings to be included in Israel's library, and differences in how they should be arranged. Some ancient traditions include more books, while others have fewer, and the order of the books varies as well. Here I will explain the various labels used for the Old Testament, and in the next chapter, I will turn to the question of the number and arrangement of its books.

The names we use for the Old Testament stem for the most part from the various faith traditions reading it. For Jewish readers, the writings of ancient Israel are known as the *Tanak*, an acronym

based on the first letters of the three subdivisions according to their Hebrew names.[1]

T = *tôrâ* (anglicized as *Torah*), "law, instruction"
N = *nĕbîʾîm* (*Neviim*), "prophets"
K = *kĕtûbîm* (*Ketuvim*), "writings"

Thus the T(a)n(a)k refers to the Old Testament simply as "the Bible." Jewish readers sometimes also call the Old Testament by another name, *Miqra*, meaning "reading" or "selection read out loud." This term is related to the Arabic word *Qurʾan* (anglicized as Koran), which means "recitation."

The earliest Christians saw themselves as part of the Jewish community and assumed that the Scriptures of Israel were central to their own faith. Thus the New Testament often refers to the Old Testament partially using the subdivisions of the Jewish arrangement, "the Law and the Prophets," or simply as "the Scriptures," "the Holy Scriptures," or some variation. When Christianity emerged beyond its Jewish roots and became largely a gentile faith, its adherents began to struggle over the question of just how Christians were to relate to the Old Testament. Christianity slowly came to embrace a two-part Bible, of which the Scriptures of Israel were the first and largest part. The early Christian writer Tertullian (ca. 155–230 CE) applied the Latin labels *Vetus Testamentum*, "Old Testament," and *Novum Testamentum*, "New Testament," to the two separate portions of a new Christian Bible. Thus, "Old Testament" implies a distinctly Christian and theological interpretation

---

1 We will return to these subdivisions, and to other arrangements and sequences of the books of the Old Testament, in the next chapter.

of Israel's sacred writings. Yet the problem of how Christians read the Old Testament has never really gone away. Some Christians assume that the New Testament supersedes or replaces the Old. Others apply a rigid prophecy-fulfillment pattern between the testaments or otherwise a simplistic preparatory or so-called Christological reading. Because of these problems, some Christians prefer names such as *First Testament*, and *Older Testament*. But then readers are left with the awkward and misleading labels *Second Testament* (how many are there?), and *Newer Testament*. Most Christian readers continue to use "Old Testament" because of subtle uses of "new covenant" and "old covenant" in the New Testament itself (see Luke 22:20; 2 Corinthians 3:14).

For Muslim readers, the Old Testament, or at least its various parts, constitutes the first of a series of revealed sacred texts given to a sequence of God's legislative prophets: Adam, Noah, Abraham, Moses, Jesus, and Muhammad. These six were envoys or messengers who heard directly from God and bore a special burden of divine revelation over thousands of other prophets who did not hand down sacred texts. The Qur'an uses the term *kitāb* (pl. *kutub*) for "book" or, better, "scriptural text" to refer to divine revelations given to these six prophets. The Qur'an especially highlights and honors the revelations of the *Tawrāt* (Torah) given to Moses and the *Injīl* (Gospel) to Jesus. Yet each new and successive divine revelation or book surpassed the preceding one. In this way, the Qur'an, given to the world through Muhammad, is the final and definitive revelation of God to humanity.

So this problem of what we should call the Old Testament has not been resolved. In order to avoid privileging one faith tradition over others, scholars in interfaith or secular contexts often use "Hebrew Bible" for Israel's Scriptures. This designation has the advantage of avoiding non-English-sounding labels like *Tanak* or *Miqra*. More importantly, it avoids pejorative-sounding labels like *Old Testament*, which might imply that ancient Israel's library is outmoded and in need of replacing. Indeed, for most Christians, "Old Testament" is a theological assertion about the way Israel's Scriptures relate to Jesus, although there is disagreement about the details of that relationship. For this reason, "Hebrew Bible" is widely used today in many contexts. Nonetheless, this label also has its shortcomings. First, "Hebrew" is misleading because two books of Israel's library contain Aramaic, a closely related language to Hebrew.[2] Second, the adjective "Hebrew" may imply the existence of many other Bibles. Actually, we will see in Chapter 3 that there *is*, in fact, a Greek Bible, an Aramaic Bible, a Latin Bible, and so on, unfortunately suggesting an equal status to them all. People who use "Hebrew Bible" certainly understand the differences between all these, but the inadequacy of the label is clear.

The long-standing "Old Testament" is recognized the world over as a conventional designation for the books that make up Israel's ancient library. It is used in this textbook for convenience only in light of the inadequacy of the other designations and is abbreviated "OT." Whether Jewish, Christian, Muslim, or secularist, what you actually believe about the OT will be entirely up to you to decide.

---

2 Ezra 4:8–6:18 and 7:12–26, and Daniel 2:4b–7:28, plus one verse at Jeremiah 10:11.

SIDEBAR 1.2. ISRAEL'S GOD, YAHWEH

The term "God" is from Old English, probably derived from the adjective "good," and is used in the OT for a number of different Hebrew terms for God, such as *El, Eloah,* and *Elohim.* These Hebrew terms for God are somewhat impersonal. Yet Israel did not perceive God as an impersonal, detached being. Like other peoples of the ancient world, Israelites had a distinctive personal name for God. Israel's God was known as "YHWH," usually pronounced "Yahweh." The origins, meaning, and even exact spelling of this name are uncertain. For now, it is enough to know that the OT originally used only the four letters of YHWH for the name, so that it is sometimes called the *tetragrammaton* (Greek, "four letters"). It occurs almost seven thousand times in the OT. The vowels used in "Yahweh" are something of a scholarly guess as to its original pronunciation.

Names in the ancient world were thought to reflect the nature and character of the name bearer, and so the name of Israel's God may reveal much about how Israelites perceived him. Unfortunately, we simply cannot trace its origins. Most scholars assume that it relates to the Hebrew verb "to be" and has a causative meaning such as "he causes to be," "he brings into being," or "he creates." If correct, the name is probably an abbreviation for something like "He who creates (the winds, or the universe, or Israel)," or more likely, "He who creates (the heavenly armies)." This last option would be the meaning of the OT's "LORD of Hosts," or YHWH Sabaoth.

> Who is this King of glory?
> The LORD (YHWH) of hosts (Sabaoth),
> He is the King of glory. (Psalm 24:10)

Yet the name may also be the Hebrew verb "to be" without the causative idea, meaning "He is" or "He reveals himself and is there (for you)." In this case, the original pronunciation would have been more like "Yihweh" than "Yahweh." Still others assume that the name identifies Israel's God as a storm god and think it means "He who drives the wind." Regardless of where the name came from originally, it came to mean for ancient Israelites the deeply personal God who lives in **covenant** relationship with them, as we shall see.

THE LEGACY OF MONOTHEISM

Having explored the various names for the OT, we return now to the question of why it has left such a lasting legacy in world history. You will recall that my answer is its religious contribution, especially the monotheism that found articulation in its heirs in Judaism, Christianity, and Islam. No matter what we call it, the OT has clearly changed the world by inspiring its readers to believe in only one God. Just as what you believe about God affects everything else you believe, so the OT's views of God have changed the history of ideas in human civilization.

Monotheism as defined in the OT is one of the most significant developments of history.

But it may surprise you to learn that the OT is not uniform in its views of God. It contains texts that assume polytheism (belief in many gods), in addition to passages that claim that ancient Israel's God, whose name is **Yahweh**, is the only deity. We *may* conclude that these are contradictory views, but Israel's authors and scribes appear to have worked from a developmental model. They assumed that God had progressively moved their ancestors away from polytheism through a concept of God's universal sovereignty and eventually to an entirely new understanding of God as singular. In this way, they could retain the different views of God without fear of contradiction.

And here we have a danger. To avoid this danger I need to explain a difference between history and literature. I am not primarily exploring in this textbook what the ancient Israelites believed about God. That would be a *historical* question, relying on archaeology, socioanthropology, and so forth. I will eventually summarize what we can know about their religious beliefs based on a reconstruction of their history as best as we can know it (Chapters 10 and 11). But instead, we are primarily exploring what the OT claims about God, which is a *literary* and *ideological* question rather than a purely historical one. My task in this volume is to introduce you to the literature of the OT itself. So the more pertinent question is what these texts say individually about God, and what overarching concepts they claim when taken as a collective whole. As we walk through the OT together, you will see that the answer is not a simple one. Much of the OT assumes that Israel's God is sovereign over the nations or the universe, but it seldom articulates clearly that Yahweh is the only deity in existence. The expression of monotheism in the whole of the OT is greater than the sum of its parts.

Atheism

An idea gaining popularity in our day is that of atheism, the position that no deities exist. "Wide atheism" holds there is sufficient evidence to conclude that no gods exist, whereas "narrow atheism" may deny the existence of a particular deity or conception of deity. Generally today, however, most people use "atheism" for the position that no supernatural beings exist.

The OT never entertains this possibility. In fact, atheism is a relatively recent development, and it would be most unusual for anyone of the ancient world to consider it. All ancient peoples assumed the existence of divine forces in the cosmos; any other possibility was unthinkable. The assumption of the ancient Israelites may be summarized by the words of the Psalmist: "Fools say in their hearts, 'There is no God'" (Psalm 14:1). The OT makes no attempt to prove God's existence. None was needed. Its authors perceived God at work in the universe and in the affairs of the nation Israel. To say otherwise was sheer folly. Accordingly, the opening words of the OT, "In the beginning when God created the heavens and the earth,"[3] sets aside the possibility of atheism.

Polytheism

The default position of all ancient peoples was the idea that many gods exist, all independently and coeternally. Egyptians, Babylonians, Assyrians, Canaanites, and many others all believed in numerous deities. Most organized the various greater and lesser gods in a *pantheon*, in which highest rank was most often attributed to deities of cosmic dimensions, such as the sun or moon, or to powerful forces of nature, such as a storm god. Other important gods were associated with earthly governance, so that the chief deity of a particular city or region may rise to preeminence in the pantheon,

---

3 Or, according to some translations, "In the beginning God created."

1.2. Stele of Qadesh. Qadesh, a Syrian goddess of sacred ecstasy and sexual pleasure, came to be incorporated into the Egyptian pantheon in New Kingdom times. Here she stands on a lion, accompanied by her consort, another Asiatic god, Reshep (*to the right*), and by the Egyptian fertility god Min (*to the left*). Approximately 1295–1069 BCE. (Photo: Erich Lessing / Art Resource, N.Y.)

such as Marduk of Babylon. The most important deities of a pantheon were often perceived as meeting in assemblies or divine councils for discussion of essential business and decision making.

The pages of the OT preserve relics of these beliefs for ancient Israel, although in most cases, later editors have suppressed the polytheistic bits. So, for example, Psalm 82 seems clear enough: "God has taken his place in the divine council; in the midst of the gods he holds judgment" (v. 1). In this case, the author perceives God as taking his place among other gods in their divine assembly and condemning them for their failure to help the poor. Ultimately, God pronounces a death sentence on the other gods for their failure to provide justice (vv. 6–7), and the psalm ends with a call for God to reign supreme over all nations of the earth (v. 8). Some readers take these other gods as angels or spirits, but this text seems to preserve an ancient belief in a pantheon in which Israel's God was one member and rose to supremacy among the rest. Similarly, the "sons of gods" or "heavenly beings" of Psalm 29:1 must have originally referred to a divine assembly. But now those other deities are called on to praise Yahweh, Israel's God of glory and strength.

The OT has other passages that reflect an early belief in a divine assembly (consider Psalm 89:5–6, Job 1–2, or 1 Kings 22:19–22). One particularly important and interesting passage illustrates how the lesser gods have all been subsumed under the authority and supremacy of Yahweh. When Yahweh first came from Mount Sinai to become Israel's God, the "myriads of holy ones" became "a host of his own" and all the "holy ones" were given to his charge (Deuteronomy 33:2–3). Although the

texts of these older poems are difficult to interpret, it appears that Deuteronomy 32:8–9 expresses the idea that each people group of the ancient world was allotted its own deity, just as Israel has been allotted Yahweh.

Be careful not to conclude that these few passages reveal widespread polytheism in early Israel. These texts are relatively few in number, are often open to various interpretations, and are certainly the exception rather than the rule. Polytheism was not the norm in the OT.

Henotheism and Monolatry

I want you to consider henotheism and monolatry together because they are so close in meaning. In fact, many assume that these two concepts mean the same thing. Generally speaking, they both refer to the belief in one god without denying the existence of others. Only one god really matters; the rest exist but are for someone else.

For our purposes, I want to suggest a subtle distinction between these two. We'll take henotheism as a philosophical belief, specifically an ontological belief. By this I mean henotheism is a cognitive *acceptance* of one god, while also admitting the existence of others. Everything else in the universe, including other deities, is thought to depend on one god. Monolatry holds the same belief but also makes the commitment to serve and be loyal to the one deity, especially as related to supporting the cult system of the one deity and sacrificing to that god. The deity is considered to be the one and only god at the time of worship. This is really only a matter of perspective and emphasis: henotheism relates to philosophical conviction, and monolatry relates to worship. Both consider only one god as important.

The OT suggests that other deities – wherever they are thought to be real – are perceived as members of Yahweh's attendants or entourage. In this way, early Israel has been thought to hold to a "**monolatrous henotheism**," meaning Israelites are committed to worshipping the one God they believe is supreme over all others without denying the reality of the others.[4] Ancient Israel defines itself as loyal only to Yahweh as the incomparable God, although not the only god. It holds to Yahweh alone in belief and practice, without assuming the nonexistence of other deities. This is essentially the meaning of the **Ten Commandments**, when the text says famously, "I am Yahweh your God, ... you shall have no other gods before me" (Exodus 20:2–3). The command does not deny the existence of "other gods," only that Israel must not be devoted to them.

Monotheism

Simply stated, monotheism is the belief that there is only one God. Yet that is entirely too simply stated. The concepts expressed in the OT are much more complex, and so the term is often modified by adjectives. For example, *explicit* monotheism includes a specific denial of the existence of any other deity, whereas *implicit* monotheism functions as though there is only one God but does not specifically deny that others exist. Or, *emergent* monotheism refers to the gradual appearance of beliefs

about the singularity of God; the concept is emerging in Israel's thinking but is rarely articulated fully. Another example is *affective* monotheism, assuming that Israel prefers a single deity, Yahweh, not as an expression of dogma or theology but as an expression of devotion.

The truth is, strict and philosophically expressed monotheism is a recent development and does not apply neatly to OT faith. Rather than a definition that expressly denies the existence of all other deities, something like the following is often given as a definition of biblical monotheism.

> *The mark of monotheism is ... the idea of a god who is the source of all being, not subject to a cosmic order, and not emergent from a pre-existent realm; a god free of the limitations of magic and mythology.*[5]

This might be called *implicit* monotheism, in that it contains no precise denial of the existence of other deities. Yet it captures the OT's fixation on Yahweh, the God of Israel, as supreme over all beings, the source of all, and sovereign over all. The scholar who wrote that definition argues further that this type of monotheism is absent elsewhere in the ancient world except Israel. Maybe. But as we shall see, the Egyptian worship of Aten, and Mesopotamian hymns to the moon god and myths about the storm god Marduk came close.

Though we will be exploring the rise of monotheism in the pages of the OT, please remember that, as a philosophical assertion denying the existence of other deities, "monotheism" is far from adequate to describe OT faith. It is not

---

4 For "monolatrous henotheism," see the work of Baruch Halpern in "Where to Find More" at the end of this chapter."

5 For this definition, see Kaufmann (p. 29) in "Where to Find More" in this chapter.

SIDEBAR 1.3. "MONOTHEISM"

"Polytheism," "monotheism," and other terms like them discussed here do not occur in the Bible itself. In fact, they are relatively modern terms used by philosophers and theologians to explore the species and subspecies of ancient (and modern) religions, and they are not always helpful in a discussion of the OT. The use of the term "monotheism" in this textbook is not meant to imply such philosophical precision, either for the OT itself or for the faith of the ancient Israelites.

The first occurrence of "monotheism" was in the writings of the British philosopher Henry More (1614–1687), who used it initially as an antonym not to "polytheism" but to "atheism."* More first claimed that polytheism is really nothing more than materialistic atheism and then spoke of monotheism or the belief in one singular and personal God as superior to atheism (and, by implication, polytheism). After More, the term came to be used more narrowly as a way of organizing different religions, while defending the superiority of belief in one God. In other words, it came to be used as it is today: a simple proposition denying the existence of multiple deities while expressing belief in only one God.

* *Oxford English Dictionary*, 2nd ed., s.v. "monotheism."

---

that "monotheism" says the *wrong* thing about the OT's beliefs about Yahweh, only that it does not say *enough*.

The OT, then, preserves individual texts that hint at polytheism, but as a whole, the OT is monolatrous with monotheistic features. This implicit monotheism is the OT's legacy handed down through Judaism, Christianity, and Islam. The Israelites rarely if ever defined their ideas of God as today's philosophers do in some strict monotheism that denies the existence of other deities. Yet, as I have suggested, the whole of the OT is greater than the sum of its parts.

While the OT itself is *implicitly* monotheistic, there is no agreement today on precisely how and when this monotheism developed in ancient Israel. In general, there are two schools of thought. The first assumes a dramatic, even revolutionary expression of the singularity of Yahweh early in Israel's history, which was then nuanced and developed further over time. Most in this camp focus on Moses as the revolutionary agent. The second school of

thought assumes an evolutionary development from polytheism early in Israel's history to expressions of monotheism only late in Israel's history, most likely in the exilic period (586–539 BCE;[6] see Chapter 3). The focus in this explanation is on the anonymous prophet often referred to as **Deutero-Isaiah**, or Second Isaiah (ca. 540 BCE), who clearly affirms the belief that only Yahweh exists.

The problem, of course, is that we do not have enough evidence to settle this dispute. And yet, studies of society and human culture have shown that simple evolutionary explanations of religion are not adequate. Theories that assume a straight-line progression from primitive to advanced religion have proven unhelpful. So, for example, we should no longer assume a simple development from animism, the worship of countless spirits inhabiting natural objects, to polytheism, to henotheism, to monotheism. Anthropologists have shown that

6 "BCE" is Before the Common Era, which is nonsectarian. All dates in this book will be "BCE" unless otherwise indicated.

many cultures, both primitive and modern, often hold monotheistic and polytheistic ideas simultaneously, existing side by side in a single society. Thus the OT is not the culminating advancement of monotheistic impulses found elsewhere in the ancient world. Rather, the OT reflects a society in which monotheism eventually won the day as the best explanation, the most consistent belief system. As such, the OT is not a uniformly monotheistic book but rather a monotheizing document.

For the purposes of our introduction to the literature of the OT in this textbook, I will assume that most of these texts are monolatrous and henotheistic, or at times implicitly monotheistic. The view in most of the OT is that Yahweh is the only God *for Israel*. In addition, we will have occasion to explore certain texts, especially in the books of Deuteronomy and Isaiah, that are explicitly monotheistic. In these texts, the author is clear that Yahweh is the only God *period* – for Israel and for everybody else. When we turn to the historical questions, my assumption will be that early Israel was at least monolatrous and perhaps even monotheistic although not self-consciously so. Israel self-identified as monotheistic only later in its history, as we shall see.[7]

Your Main Task in Reading the Old Testament

The OT is not an easy read. People read or study it for many different reasons. But one reason that affects all of us around the globe – and in some ways, unites us as readers – is this question of monotheism. Why did monotheism emerge in and from the pages of the OT? Why did it not take root and thrive among Israel's neighbors in the ancient Near East, even as they experimented with monotheism here and there?

We may never be able to explain how or why monotheism emerged in ancient Israel while it did not emerge at the same time among Israel's neighbors. But we can assert simply *that it did appear* in the OT and that it changed the world. This introduction to ancient Israel's library will highlight those first monotheistic impulses in the pages of the OT while introducing you to those pages themselves.

And so I offer this as your main task for reading the OT along with this textbook – to consider the significance of the OT's monotheism, especially in light of the polytheisms all around ancient Israel. This has, in fact, been called the primary task for scholars of the OT – to attempt to explain the rise and development of Israel's monotheism, especially in view of the enveloping polytheism around Israel in the ancient world. But this is also an important objective for you as you launch into this study. Whether you are Jewish, Christian, Muslim, a reader from another faith tradition, or a secularist reader, consider the impact monotheism has had on the world of religion and philosophy, and indeed, the whole world to this day. These three faith traditions, Judaism, Christianity, and Islam, fall into the genus of religion and form a single subspecies of all theistic religions: the so-called monotheistic religions. These three have a unique relationship to each other because they share a common conviction in the personal Creator God who first made himself known to ancient Israel's ancestors.[8]

7 Again for these terms, see Halpern in "Where to Find More" in this chapter.

8 For more on this unique relational bond between the three monotheistic faiths, see Neusner, Chilton, and Graham in the "Where to Find More" list in this chapter.

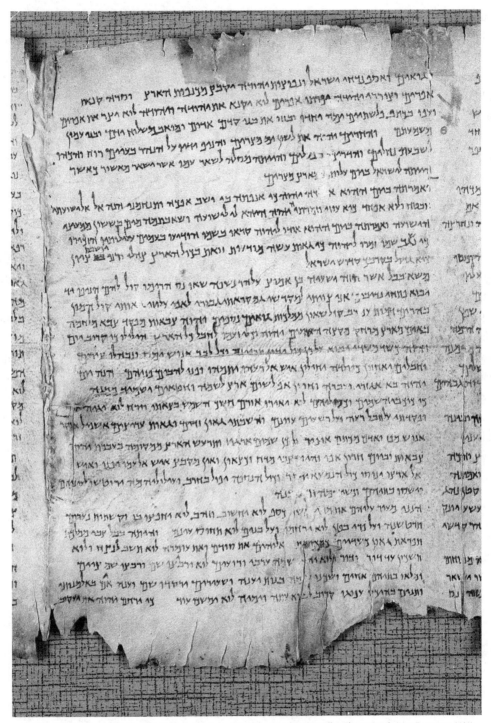

1.3. Scroll of Isaiah. A page from the scroll of Isaiah, one of the Dead Sea Scrolls. (Photo: Snark / Art Resource, N.Y.)

Their earliest, classic sources and founding documents share a belief in one singular God, Creator of heaven and earth. They each develop that conviction along different paths, but they share at least this much in common. This introduction highlights those first monotheistic impulses in the pages of the OT, while also highlighting the way these three traditions concur in general and in particular ways. They tell stories of the same type, and they cover some of the same ground. By exploring the origins of monotheism and the role of monotheism in religion, this textbook expores this nexus between Judaism, Christianity, and Islam.

What then is the OT? It is the literature of ancient Israel, compiled by the Israelites and then collected and preserved through the centuries by their heirs. This "library" is most profound for its convictions about the nature of God and God's relationship with Israel. Those convictions are expressed in ways that are monolatrous and henotheistic, and at times even monotheistic. And since the whole of the OT is greater than the sum of its parts, this conviction of monotheism became the heartbeat of Judaism, Christianity, and Islam. The OT's monotheism changed the world, and for this reason, a basic understanding of the OT is critical for understanding the world in which we live.

Yet your task is a bit more complex than this. The fact is that the OT is less concerned with explicitly defining monotheism, which is, after all, a simple proposition about the number of deities and the proper object of worship. The proposition "monotheism" negatively asserts Yahweh's singularity by denying the existence of other deities. But this minimizes the message of the OT, which makes numerous positive assertions about the nature of Yahweh and his attributes. Your task will be to explore the importance of the OT's monotheism as a gift to the world of religious ideas and the history of philosophy. But your task will also be to listen carefully to the voices of the ancient Israelites as they teach, narrate, exhort, and sing about Yahweh.

WHERE TO FIND MORE

Assmann, Jan. *Of God and Gods: Egypt, Israel, and the Rise of Monotheism*. Madison, Wisc.: University of Wisconsin Press, 2008.

Explains the significance of monotheism, not simply as the oneness of God, which is a philosophical idea, but as the difference of God, which is a "narrative truth" at the very foundation of Israel's identity. The "Mosaic distinction" is the idea of an exclusive and emphatic Truth that sets God apart from everything that is not God and therefore must not be worshipped.

Halpern, Baruch. "'Brisker Pipes than Poetry': The Development of Israelite Monotheism." Pages 77–115 in *Judaic Perspectives on Ancient Israel*. Edited by Jacob Neusner, Baruch A. Levine, and Ernest S. Frerichs. Philadelphia: Fortress Press, 1987. Reprinted in Baruch Halpern, *From Gods to God: The Dynamics of Iron Age Cosmologies* (Matthew J. Adams, ed., FAT 63; Tübingen: Mohr Siebeck, 2009), 13–56.

Not for the faint-of-reading hearts! This chapter is perhaps the best explanation of early Israel's conception of God as monolatrous henotheism, or an unself-conscious monotheism.

Halpern traces Israel's narrowing tendencies during the Axial Age to a self-consciously defined monotheism in the late seventh century BCE (especially in the time of the prophet Jeremiah). Halpern also claims that this development is unique to ancient Israel.

Kaufmann, Yehezkel. *The Religion of Israel, from Its Beginnings to the Babylonian Exile.* Translated by Moshe Greenberg. Chicago: University of Chicago Press, 1960.

MacDonald, Nathan. *Deuteronomy and the Meaning of "Monotheism."* Forschungen zum Alten Testament II/1. Tübingen: Mohr Siebeck, 2003.

Chapter 1 (pp. 5–58) has a survey of the use and understanding of "monotheism" from Henry More to its current usage in OT studies.

Neusner, Jacob, Bruce Chilton, and William A. Graham. *Three Faiths, One God: The Formative Faith and Practice of Judaism, Christianity, and Islam.* Boston: Brill Academic Publishers, 2002.

The first chapter (pp. 1–35) explores the foundational documents of the three so-called monotheistic faiths and how they relate to the OT; chapter 2 (pp. 36–98) has an equally helpful study of ways the three religions concur on the personhood of God, even as they each claim uniquely true knowledge of God as revealed to humankind.

Smith, Mark S. *The Origins of Biblical Monotheism: Israel's Polytheistic Background and the Ugaritic Texts.* New York: Oxford University Press, 2001.

Introduces many of the topics discussed here, including the idea of a divine council in the ancient Near East (pp. 41–53), and the definition of "monotheism" (pp. 151–54).

CHAPTER 2

Word of Truth – Word of God

In this chapter, we will examine the OT's role in religious communities as an authoritative revelation from God – the concept of "scripture" common to the three monotheistic religions: Judaism, Christianity, and Islam. These texts hardly began as the books that now comprise the Bible; rather, what we will discover is a lengthy, complex development of authoritative texts from oral to written to canon.

This chapter will take us inside the ancient world of the OT's formation. Words, considered powerful, were painstakingly preserved through centuries in the hands of anonymous authors and editors, scribes and scholars. Texts were collected into books and went through a process of use and standardization by the ancient Israelites, beginning as early as the tenth century BCE and lasting through the Babylonian exile and beyond – emerging finally in the canonical form we know today as the OT.

*M*illions of believers around the globe consider the Old Testament the "word of God." Of these, many study and read it looking for divine direction or comfort. Other believers don't read it at all even though they consider it God's word in some manner; they value it but don't read it. For all these, the OT is in some way religiously authoritative. It somehow stands as inspired, or inspiring, as a word of truth or a word that has its origins in God – the word of God. As such, the OT is a living tradition that shapes communities and provides inspiration for believers within those communities.

For countless other readers, the OT is of interest for reasons other than religious authority. For these readers, the OT does not represent God's authority or word of truth but is of interest for its insight into history, sociology, philosophy, or the history of religion. Whatever your reason for studying the OT, it is without doubt one of the most important documents ever preserved from antiquity, and one that has changed the world immeasurably.

How is it that these ancient texts, collected as they are into "books" and cataloged into different lists, have come to be so venerated by so many readers? And especially how has this happened so many centuries after these texts were written? The answer to this question is found partly in the previous chapter's survey of what we called the "legacy of the Old Testament" – monotheism. But this answer skips several steps. We might just as easily ask how it all began. Why originally were these texts considered so important to the people who wrote and preserved them? For this, we must go considerably further back to a primal instinct.

The Power of Words

Writing was a mystical thing in the ancient world, nearly magical. The first written texts were mnemonic tools; they were a means for aiding the memory instead of for communicating something entirely new. We have reason to believe that most ancient texts were not written in a way that could be understood except by someone who already knew the text well. The first scripts were extremely complex, and could be read and written only by well-trained specialists. The alphabet as first invented had no way of indicating vowels and so did not reflect spoken language closely. Instead, we might think of written texts as a musical score for a musician who knows the piece well. Some musicians

can sight-read better than others, but most would need to know the music well before "reading" the score.[1] Thus, long and religiously important compositions like the ones eventually preserved in the OT were nearly memorized by those who recited them, and the written text merely aided them in the recitation.

Even behind a written text, which seemed mysterious and wonderful in its own way, the words themselves were thought to have their own power in the ancient world (see Plates I and II). Israel during most of the biblical period was largely an oral culture; few Israelites had the ability to read or write. The written word seemed powerful to them partly because it was inaccessible. And in such oral cultures, spoken words too had power. The religious practices of polytheism in both Egypt and Mesopotamia routinely assumed the reality of performative magic. Such magic sometimes involved a physical action but usually also included the recitation of words. Spoken incantations, spells, charms, and curses were central to ancient Near Eastern magic. Magicians were thought to have extraordinary powers related to their use of audible pronouncements, which were believed to work automatically. By contrast, the OT prohibited the use of magic (e.g., Deuteronomy 18:10–11). Yet the emotional power of the spoken word was quite real in Israel. For example, the verbal naming of a child at birth was perceived as revealing profound truth about the new child (Genesis 4:1). Similarly, the pronunciation of God's name was not to be taken lightly (Genesis 32:29; Judges 13:17–18).

1   For this metaphor, see Carr (pp. 4–5) and Barton (p. 129) in the list of resources in "Where to Find More" in this chapter.

2.1. Ahiram sarcophagus inscription. This alphabetic inscription found written across the lid of the limestone coffin of Phoenician King Ahiram (tenth century BCE) included a curse against any who would raid the coffin. (Photo: Erich Lessing / Art Resource, N.Y.)

At some point in Israel's history, an important transition occurred from the power of speech to the power of the written word. As important as monotheism was in Israel's thinking (or monolatry, or henotheism), the advent of the written word as a source of authority was also transformative. Now a recorded text could be just as authoritative and powerful as a spoken word. We have no way of knowing precisely when this idea first began to take root in ancient Israel. It seems entirely likely that both ideas — monotheism and textual authority — are related. I will suggest in the next chapter that the rise of an urban elite in Jerusalem in the eighth and seventh centuries was a likely time when changes in the culture and society generally saw the rising importance of literacy, the written text, and monotheism. But for now, it is enough to know that at some point in Israel's history, the people came to value the authority of written texts as few cultures before them ever had.

This helps us understand why the concept of "Scripture" or the "word of God" is so powerful even today. When God speaks with Moses on Mount Sinai, he writes the ten most important things he wants to say on stone tablets with his own finger (Exodus 31:18; Deuteronomy 9:10). The OT claims to be the revelation of God himself to ancient Israel, the powerfully spoken word now written for Israel's future generations. As "Scripture," it is still today the focus of intense interest for diverse faith communities. And this transition from the power of speech to that of written text, now recognized as having religious authority, provides insight into the very origins of the OT itself.

What Is a Book?

You might think it a strange question, but we begin by asking, "What is a book?" We have, after all, called the OT a library. And presumably the library is full of books. Yet these books are different from what you probably have in mind. Our word "book" implies a single physical entity, a volume, with pages bound between covers, which is the result of a "work" of an author or authors (editor or editors). But the OT's word "book" (*sēper*) means no such thing. In fact, the Hebrew word refers to anything written down and is usually much smaller, closer to what we would call a "text," and eventually preserved in scrolls.[2] What we now have in the Bible are collections of these written texts in larger compositions, often with less expectation for unity of theme, structure, or closure than you and I might expect for "books." So even though I'll be using "book(s)" in this chapter, you need to think in terms of groups of texts, edited together in special collections, and preserved as religiously authoritative for early Israel. These books were collected, copied, and preserved because they were thought to be the very word of God.

But who did all this writing, collecting, and preserving? If you glance through your copy of the OT now, you will see that most of its books do

2.2. Torah scroll. For centuries, Jewish believers have preserved the first five books of the Old Testament, the so-called books of Moses, on scrolls of parchment like this one. (Torah scroll [wood and parchment], German School [fifteenth century] / Private Collection / photo: © Zev Radovan / The Bridgeman Art Library)

not identify authors. Some have names of leading characters, like Joshua or Ruth, but most are anonymous. We have later Jewish and Christian traditions assigning authorship to many portions, such as Moses for the Torah, the prophet Samuel for 1 and 2 Samuel, or David for the Psalms. But these traditions viewed authorship in a way very different from ours today, more as authorizing figureheads for the materials in those books. Notice, for example, that Moses is often referred to in the third person in the **Pentateuch** ("Moses went up on the mountain"), or that Samuel's death is recorded in 1

2 For more on this, see Barton (1998) in "Where to Find More" in this chapter.

Samuel 25 making it highly unlikely that he wrote 2 Samuel.

In general, you should be aware of four types of thinkers and scholars who produced these books.[3] The first category is that of anonymous authors, some of whom gave us long stretches of material. One such author probably wrote the story of Joseph's life (Genesis 37–50), and another wrote an account of how Solomon came to succeed David as king of Israel (2 Samuel 9–20; 1 Kings 1–2). A second category is that of collectors or compilers of existing texts. Such individuals updated texts or collected various laws and arranged them in new ways for new situations (as in Deuteronomy 12–26), or combined psalms and wisdom sayings in new collections. These collectors and compilers may also have taken older traditions preserved for centuries by word of mouth and put them in writing as texts for the first time. A third category is that of editors or redactors, who intentionally rearranged existing texts, at times writing new segments and supplements to create whole new compositions. These are likely the individuals who gave us the current book structure of many of the books, such as Genesis, Exodus, and so forth. A fourth and final category is that of scribes and scholars, who meticulously preserved the settled and approved text from one generation to the next. In this last category we will include translators who preserved editions of the OT in many different languages.

The activities of these thinkers and scribes are often overlapping; their work cannot always be distinguished. As a result, we have quite a number of unanswered questions about the authorship and composition of most OT books. It is especially impossible to discern exactly *when* most of these books were written. During the monarchy, before the Babylonian exile began in 586 BCE, scribes in Israel's royal court appear to have collected and edited older materials. This process continued among scribes in the exile itself, at which time many of the OT books were fixed in shapes similar to what we have now. Another set of thinkers among the priests of the temple were writing and editing at the same time. Some of this material, from early oral traditions to formal curriculum, was being collected over a long period for purposes of educating the elite class, perhaps at the royal court. While much of this is speculative and we cannot be dogmatic about how it happened, it seems likely that major components of the OT were compiled into what we will study as the **"Primary History"** (Chapter 4) during the exile in the middle of the sixth century BCE, or shortly afterward. The shapes of many of the prophetic books such as Jeremiah were probably also settled by this time. During and shortly after the exile (i.e., after 539 BCE), new compositions and revisions of older works were produced for the new circumstances. This resulted in several new historical books, such as 1 and 2 Chronicles, and new psalms, works of poetry, and so forth.

So the production of the OT seems to have gone something like this. Portions likely date back to early in Israel's monarchy, perhaps as early as the tenth century BCE. At this early stage, we are unable to reconstruct what those materials were like, poetry or prose, or even written as

---

3 See Vriezen and van der Woude in "Where to Find More" in this chapter.

SIDEBAR 2.1. "CANON"

The word "canon" (with only two *n*'s, please) in this context refers to the list of books officially accepted into the Bible.* It comes from Greek and included an original meaning of "reed staff," with a secondary figurative meaning of "measuring stick, yardstick." As such, it came to be used in religious contexts for the theological "norm" for a particular community of faith (as in Galatians 6:16) or for the "list" of approved books bearing authority for faith and practice for that community. Such a canonical list of authoritative books is assumed to be divinely inspired and is therefore a closed collection. No new books can be added to it, and none can be deleted from it. Thus the OT canon is a fixed list of books approved retroactively by a community of faith recognizing the divine authority of those books for the community's religious beliefs and practices.

* *Oxford English Dictionary*, 2nd ed., s.v. "canon".

opposed to orally preserved. Other portions were written during the eighth, seventh, and sixth centuries BCE, or between the time of Isaiah and running through the last half of Israel's monarchy down to the fall of the city of Jerusalem to the Babylonians (722–586 BCE). The most important prophets active during the writing of these texts were Isaiah and Jeremiah; the most influential kings were Hezekiah (715–686 BCE) and Josiah (640–609 BCE). During the Babylonian exile (586–539 BCE), these texts and collections continued to be developed and others were added to the growing body of Israelite sacred literature. After the exile ended in 539 BCE, the remaining pieces were added, and the whole was combined into something like our OT of today.[4]

THE OLD TESTAMENT CANON

The OT, then, is made up of a list of these books written, edited, and compiled by many people over a long period of time. Such a list of the writings

4 See Freedman in "Where to Find More" in this chapter.

accepted into the OT is known as a "canon." The process by which the list of books was settled, or "canonized," is unknown. But we know at least that this process is based on a new idea: the authority and power of the spoken word has been transferred to the written word. Texts and books have now become authoritative in a process of canonization; the idea of "scripture" is born.

In Chapter 1, you learned that the Jewish Bible has three parts, (1) Torah (Law), (2) Neviim (Prophets), and (3) Ketuvim (Writings), from which we get the acronym Tanak for "the Bible." We used to assume that canonization took place in three successive stages corresponding to the three parts of the Hebrew canon. In this theory, the Torah was formalized around 400 BCE, the Neviim-Prophets around 200 BCE, and the Ketuvim-Writings added to the collection at a rabbinic assembly or council held at the city of Jamnia (Jabneh) near the end of the first century CE. However, it seems unlikely the process of canonization was based on the authority of an assembly. More importantly, we have reason to believe that the books of the OT canon were considered authoritative scripture earlier than the dates of

---

SIDEBAR 2.2. COUNCIL OF JAMNIA

After the destruction of Jerusalem by the Romans in 70 CE, a new Jewish center of learning emerged thirty miles west northwest of Jerusalem at Jamnia (or Jabneh). We know that learned rabbis at Jamnia discussed which of their sacred books "defile the hands," apparently meaning those books that are genuinely sacred and worthy of continued study and reading as part of an approved canon. This process was part of a larger development among a loose assocation of rabbis and disciples in early rabbinic Judaism. Their primary purpose was to redefine and reinvent Judaism in light of the loss of the temple and priesthood. Although the Talmud hints that these rabbis also decided the official Jewish canon, we have no reason to speak of this process as involving a so-called council or synod, and no official rulings were made to determine the canon. The Jewish canon thus developed in a more informal way than we might imagine by the use of the words "council" or "synod."

---

the three stages, and we are not even certain that the so-called Council of Jamnia actually took place.

Instead of a sequence – first the Torah, then the Prophets – the first two portions of the Jewish Bible may have developed canonical status simultaneously, being perceived as authoritative earlier than we imagined. The fall of Jerusalem to the Babylonians in 586 BCE, marking the beginning of the exile, probably initiated the process of canonization. The fall of the capital was a traumatic event in Israel's history, involving the loss of both the temple with its priestly rituals and the palace with its royal court. This watershed event left people with a need to preserve their priestly, prophetic, and historical traditions in new ways and with renewed urgency. Thus as I have suggested already, the books of the so-called Primary History (Chapter 4) were probably in something like their present form during the exile and seem to have become authoritative shortly thereafter.

This early date may also be confirmed by a development among Greek-speaking Jews in Egypt in the mid-third century BCE. The Hebrew original of the Torah was translated into Greek at that time

(we will talk about the "**Septuagint**" later in this chapter). Yet the Torah was undoubtedly thought of as authoritative long before its translation into Greek. In fact, the book of Nehemiah relates an episode in which the venerable scribe Ezra read the "book of the law of Moses" in Jerusalem in 458 BCE (Nehemiah 8). We have every reason to believe this was the Torah nearly as it stands in our Bibles today.

Earliest Jewish and Christian sources mention the Law (Torah) and the Prophets side by side, and it is likely that already as early as the second century BCE the three-part structure familiar now in the Jewish Bible was set. The book of Ecclesiasticus (also known as the Wisdom of Ben Sira, or simply, Sirach) is a second-century book preserved in the Roman Catholic canon, and relying on the Torah, the Prophets, the Psalms, Proverbs, Job, Ezra, and Nehemiah. The author's grandson added a preface referring to "the Law and the Prophets and the others that followed them." Of the three parts – Law, Prophets, Writings – the first two seem to have arrived at canonical status by the second century BCE. The third portion probably had not yet been given a name and likely was not yet a closed list of approved books. Yet we have evidence it was also concluded before the Common Era, nearly a century before the so-called Council of Jamnia.

Thus far I have been speaking generally about three parts to the OT canon. But if you're using a standard Christian Bible, you will see a somewhat different arrangement of the books of the OT. Not only are the books arranged differently, but the list of books is even longer. Rather than the Jewish Bible's three-part structure, the Christian Bible has four parts: (1) Pentateuch, (2) Historical Books, (3) Poetry, and (4) Prophets. The differences can be traced to the ways the different faith traditions developed historically, to different processes of canonization, and to some extent even to the different views they have of the OT itself. Islam has no list of canonically approved books since it is assumed that the OT itself has been superseded by the Qur'an.

The first five books of the Christian canon are the same as the Jewish Bible, although sometimes known instead of the Torah as the "Pentateuch," from the Greek *pentateuchos* (*pente* "five" and *teuchos* "scroll") or a five-book scroll. Beyond the Pentateuch, the Jewish and Christian lists diverge. Most Christians of the earliest church were Greek speakers, and therefore many relied on Greek translations of the OT, particularly the Septuagint (to be discussed shortly). This translation placed the prophetic books at the end, collected the historical books together in a new arrangement after the Pentateuch, and created a new category for books of poetry and wisdom.

But variations in simple arrangement are not the only differences you will notice when comparing

Jewish, Protestant, and Roman Catholic lists. Protestant Christians use the same thirty-nine books as the Jewish Bible, although arranged in the four-part presentation of the Septuagint: Pentateuch, Historical Books, Poetry/Wisdom, and Prophets. Most Jewish traditions count twenty-four books, because the following are considered one book each: 1–2 Samuel, 1–2 Kings, 1–2 Chronicles, the Twelve (so-called minor prophets), and Ezra-Nehemiah.

Beyond these twenty-four books, early Judaism valued a number of other books as well. We must consider seven such books here because they are included in the canon by some: Tobit, Judith, 1 Maccabees, 2 Maccabees, Wisdom of Solomon, Ecclesiasticus (also known as Jesus Sirach), and Baruch.[5] The earliest sources show that there was some fluidity to whether these books should be thought of as canonical. Most understood them as valuable and useful for study, but early Jewish interpreters considered them postprophetic in their origins and did not include them in the Hebrew canon. The early Christian scholar Jerome (ca. 347–420 CE) agreed, insisting on a return to the Hebrew canon (see Sidebar 2.3). Jerome, also known as Eusebius Hieronymus, was the first to apply the term "**Apocrypha**" to these books (Greek *apokrypha*, "hidden things"), separating them from the canon officially but including them as additional books valuable for devotional use.

Despite Jerome's objections, most Christians continued to use the additional books and included them in the canon. This continued to be the case

5 In addition to these seven, the books of Esther and Daniel have expansions in the Septuagint included in their Roman Catholic versions.

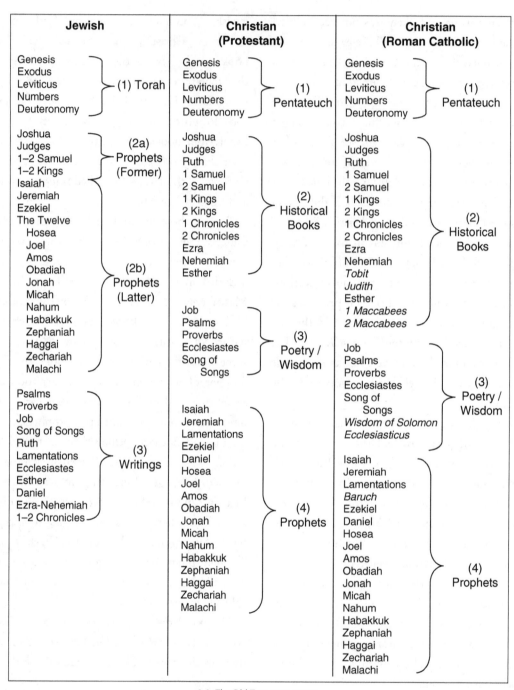

2.3. The Old Testament canon

SIDEBAR 2.3. JEROME, ALSO KNOWN AS EUSEBIUS HIERONYMUS (CA. 347–420 CE)

Jerome was born into a Christian family and received a classical education in Rome. He is most noted for his translations and expositions of Scripture. After a period of time in Rome as papal secretary to Pope Damasus I (bishop of Rome, 366–384), he moved to Bethlehem and cofounded a double monastery for men and women. He engaged in a great deal of scholarly activity at this time, including translating the Bible into Latin from the Septuagint which he considered inspired. He eventually came to believe that only the original Hebrew was inspired, and so he learned Hebrew from several Jews in Palestine. Jerome was a gifted linguist and Latin stylist. His translations of the entire OT and at least the Gospels of the New Testament were collected by his friends into one volume, which later became known as the **Vulgate**.

until the sixteenth-century Protestant Reformation, with its principle of "sola scriptura" (Scripture alone). The Protestants revived the objections of Jerome and others, and therefore considered the additional books and expansions valuable but separated them as "Apocrypha" or left them out of the list altogether.

In response, Roman Catholic Christians, meeting at the Council of Trent in 1546, accepted the wider canon with the seven additional books and expansions to Esther and Daniel. Instead of "Apocrypha," they preferred the designation "deuterocanonical" (or "second canon"). The seven deuterocanonical books are in italics in the Roman Catholic column of Figure 2.3. Christians of the Eastern Orthodox tradition further include 1 Esdras, 3 Maccabees, Prayer of Manasseh, and Psalm 151.

Despite the appearance of complex differences between the canonical lists of Jews, Protestants, and Roman Catholics, they share in common a large library of sacred books. For a number of reasons, we will use in this textbook the Jewish and Protestant canon.[6]

---

6 For more on the Deuterocanonical/Aprocryphal books, see deSilva in "Where to Find More" in this chapter.

COPIES AND TRANSLATIONS OF THE OLD TESTAMENT CANON

The Old Testament canon has been treasured as the "word of God" by countless believers through the ages. The status of these books as sacred word resulted in copies of the Hebrew texts for future generations. And as believers in those later generations came to speak different languages, translations were needed for purposes of up-to-date study. These copies and translations – preserved through the centuries – make it possible for us today to understand the history of the text, although we have gaps in our understanding.

We have in our possession none of the original Hebrew manuscripts of OT books, which are known as "autographs" (from the Greek *autographos*, "written in one's own hand"). Yet we have evidence that the text of the OT itself was settled by the beginning of the second century CE, followed by an elaborate guild of professional scribes and technical specialists who preserved the Hebrew text in meticulous detail and for many centuries. Faithful Jewish scribes maintained the consonantal text proper (since Hebrew originally had no vowels), devised a complete set of vowel points and accents, and added marginal and final notes. This was an elaborate system of checks and balances yielding a remarkable quality control, preserving the text of the OT with care and precision for centuries, and all without computers! The last group of these scribes was active from approximately 500–1000 CE and are known as Masoretes (Hebrew *māssôrâ*, for "transmission [of tradition from one generation to another]," or simply, "sign"). Thus, the best-preserved Hebrew tradition of the OT is called the *Masoretic Text*, complete copies of which come from the tenth century CE.

So the Masoretic scribes preserved the Hebrew text with remarkable care and precision. Still, until 1947, our oldest Hebrew manuscripts were approximately one thousand years removed from the original texts. Then from 1947 to 1962, roughly eight hundred manuscripts were discovered in eleven caves near Qumran along the northwestern coast of the Dead Sea. Of these so-called *Dead Sea Scrolls*, roughly one-quarter are manuscripts of the OT, mostly in fragmentary form.[7] With the discovery of these invaluable texts, our closest manuscript witness to the Hebrew texts jumped backward in time a thousand years to the first century BCE. Though they add variants to OT texts here and there, they also confirm the accuracy of the Masoretic Text.

Such scribal work and scholarly devotion have also left us translations of the OT from antiquity. Shortly after the Babylonian exile, Hebrew slowly became more of a literary language and was used less and less for everyday speech. Over time, Jewish and Christian readers of the OT naturally came to speak a wide variety of languages known from world history generally: Aramaic, Greek, Latin, and many others. So the OT was translated into a number of languages, all of which are useful today for understanding how the OT was interpreted in antiquity. These translations are also important for scholars who study the textual transmission of the OT, comparing and contrasting the various texts — both in Hebrew and in other languages — in an effort to understand the process of text transmission, as well as to reconstruct as much as possible the literary product standing at the beginning of the text transmission. This scholarly work is known as *textual criticism*, and it is an important component of OT interpretation.[8]

The oldest and most important translation of the OT is the Greek *Septuagint*, beginning with the Pentateuch translated by Jewish scholars in Alexandria, Egypt, in the third century BCE. In the following two centuries, translations of most of the other books of the OT were added. The name *Septuagint* comes from a legend preserved in the Letter of Aristeas from the second century BCE asserting that seventy-two scholars translated the Pentateuch into Greek. The number was later rounded down to seventy to yield the name "Septuagint," meaning "seventy," sometimes represented by the Roman numeral LXX. This name is used now somewhat imprecisely for all Greek translations of OT books. The early Christians were predominantly Greek speaking, and most OT quotations in the New Testament come from the Septuagint. As a result, the Protestant and Roman Catholic canon adopted the four-part structure of the Septuagint, and many of the names of the OT

---

7 Called the "Dead Sea Scrolls," these texts and manuscripts are more accurately the Discoveries in the Judean Desert, since they come from a wider geographic area than simply the Dead Sea.

8 See Tov in "Where to Find More" in this chapter.

2.4. Caves near Qumran. Some of the caves where the scrolls were discovered along the shores of the Dead Sea, seen from the settlement of Qumran. (Photo: Courtesy of Bill T. Arnold)

books in the Christian Bible come from the Greek names, such as "Genesis," "Exodus," and so forth.

As we have said, Hebrew gradually ceased to be used in everyday speech after the exile, and by the first century BCE, most Jews spoke a closely related international language, Aramaic. In the worship practices of this period, the Hebrew text of the OT continued to be read in the synagogues but interpretations were given in Aramaic so worshippers could understand the text. These orally preserved interpretations and paraphrases became standardized and were preserved in writing as *Targumim* ("translations" or "renditions"; sing. ***Targum***). These Targumim are heavily interpretive, differing

frequently from the Hebrew text. They are of great value for the history of interpretation of the OT but less so for the study of textual criticism.

Latin translations of the OT appeared as early as the second century CE, most of which were based on the Septuagint and differed from each other substantially. Hoping to develop a standard text for Roman Catholics, Pope Damasus I in 382 CE commissioned his secretary, Jerome, a leading scholar in Rome to produce an official translation (Sidebar 2.3). Jerome set out relying again on the Septuagint and completed a new edition of the Psalms. But he eventually became convinced that he needed to work directly from the Hebrew, and so started an entirely new Latin translation of the OT, which he finished in 405 CE. This translation is known as the *Vulgate* (the "common," or "popular [translation]") and became the standard edition of the Bible for a thousand years.

We have several other ancient translations available for study, but most of these others are largely based on the Septuagint or Vulgate. The most important sources for text critics today – both for establishing and interpreting the OT – are the Masoretic Text, the Dead Sea Scrolls, and the Septuagint.

The Word's Influence

As we have seen, religious rituals and spoken words were taken together as having authority in the lives of ancient peoples. In Israel, this powerful authority was gradually transferred from ritual and spoken word to written texts. Such exalted reverence for written texts made Israel distinctive in the ancient Near East. Other peoples of the world had temples and shrines with an image of their deity. But in Israel, the priests ministered before an ark containing a copy of the Book of the Law. And this book-centered religion is a trait of the three monotheistic faith traditions that flow from ancient Israel. Jews, Christians, and Muslims are people of "the book" as no others; it is the common authority of written texts that ties them together.

These three monotheistic traditions bear a unique relationship with each other among all the theistic religions of the world. The narrative they use to understand God and the world shares much of the same story. Judaism begins the story of the one Creator God who lovingly formed the people of Israel as his own possession among all nations. Christianity accepts that story but takes it in a different direction by reading the OT in light of the single representative of God's work in the world, the **Messiah**, and enlarging God's mission to include all peoples. Islam also accepts the story and repeats many of its leading features, affirming portions of God's revelation in Judaism and Christianity but also taking the narrative in a different direction. Although the vast differences between these three are obvious, it is their shared monotheism and metanarrative contained in the OT that binds them together. And each of these traditions has extensive literature depending on and building on the authority of the OT.

The Hebrew term *Torah* ("instruction, law") is used for the law of the first five books, and then for those first five books themselves as a unity (the Pentateuch). In early Judaism, *Torah* was expanded further to refer to the entire OT, as well as to the oral legal traditions first written by the rabbis around 200 CE in the *Mishnah* ("study, repetition"). The Mishnah extended the authority of the OT by applying the biblical laws of the Torah to the new situation after the destruction of the temple in 70 CE. With the spread of Christianity during the Byzantine Empire of the fourth century CE, Judaism expanded the authority of the Torah and Mishnah again. This time, the authority of God's word was continued into commentaries on the Mishnah in the *Palestinian Talmud* around 400 CE and the *Babylonian Talmud* around 600 CE. In these writings, and in many other commentaries and expositions besides, Judaism embraces and continues the authority of the OT.

From the beginning of Christianity, the OT has been considered the authoritative word of God. Doubts were raised about including the OT as Christian Scripture in the second century CE, but the church moved quickly to renounce those doubts. The New Testament was produced in primitive Christianity to defend the identity of Jesus of Nazareth as the Messiah and to encourage faith in him, as well as to explain baptism and worship. Between the second and fourth centuries CE, early Christian scholars such as Irenaeus in France and Origen in Egypt wrote much about the meaning of Christian faith, all while relying on the authority of the Old and New Testaments. After the New Testament was canonized, it seemed only natural to refer to Israel's Scriptures as the "Old Testament."

In Islam, the Qur'an defines itself consciously as "scripture" (*kitāb*, "book, scriptural text"). Islam thinks of divine revelation as a sequential set of disclosures. God's revelation to Muhammad in the Qur'an is preceded by his revelation to Moses in the Torah (*Tawrāt*) and to Jesus in the Gospel (*Injīl*; Surah 3:3). Each in turn was "scripture" in its own right, standing in an honored position in the continuity of revelation (Surah 4:136). Yet the Qur'an's self-referential quality is also clear that it supersedes all other revelations. Other forms of canonical revelation have been corrupted, and the Qur'an alone is preeminent, the climax of God's revelation to humanity. Its relationship to the OT is thus complex because the Qur'an not only confirms the OT but replaces it.

Despite their many differences, this scripturizing tendency in Judaism, Christianity, and Islam is a common feature and distinguishes them from other religions. In a unique way, Judaism accepted the OT as scripture, authorizing beliefs and legitimizing religious practices. Christianity would follow with its own affirmation of the OT, to which was added the New Testament. And Islam would follow with its own scripture, perceived as final and definitive. The idea of "scripture" was born in the monotheistic religions relying on the OT.

WHERE TO FIND MORE

Barton, John. *The Spirit and the Letter: Studies in the Biblical Canon*. Hulsean Lectures 1990. London: SPCK, 1997.

Barton, John. "What Is a Book? Modern Exegesis and the Literary Conventions of Ancient Israel." Pages 1–14 in *Intertextuality in Ugarit and Israel*. Edited by Johannes Cornelis de Moor. OtSt 40. Leiden: Brill, 1998.

Carr, David McLain. *Writing on the Tablet of the Heart: Origins of Scripture and Literature*. Oxford, New York: Oxford University Press, 2005.

DeSilva, David A. *Introducing the Apocrypha: Message, Context, and Significance*. Grand Rapids, Mich.: Baker, 2002.

Freedman, David Noel. *The Unity of the Hebrew Bible*. Distinguished Senior Faculty Lecture Series. Ann Arbor: University of Michigan Press, 1991.

McDonald, Lee Martin. *The Biblical Canon: Its Origin, Transmission, and Authority*. 3rd ed. Peabody, Mass.: Hendrickson, 2007.

Neusner, Jacob, Bruce Chilton, and William A. Graham. *Three Faiths, One God: The Formative Faith and Practice of Judaism, Christianity, and Islam*. Boston: Brill Academic Publishers, 2002.

Chapter 1 has a discussion of the classical sources of Judaism, Christianity, and Islam, and introduces the normative doctrines of each (pp. 1–35).

Niditch, Susan. *Oral World and Written Word: Ancient Israelite Literature*. Library of Ancient Israel. Louisville, Ky.: Westminster John Knox Press, 1996.

Shows that we are mistaken to distinguish too narrowly between oral and written. Oral societies were not unsophisticated or underdeveloped. Far from it. They were, in fact, quite complex, and their oral compositions could be intricate while written texts may be simple and one-dimensional. Even after the advent of writing, orality and written texts existed side by side.

Rollston, Christopher A. *Writing and Literacy in the World of Ancient Israel: Epigraphic Evidence from the Iron Age*. SBLABS 11. Leiden /Boston: Brill/SBL, 2010.

Sæbø, Magne. *On the Way to Canon: Creative Tradition History in the Old Testament*. JSOTSup 191. Sheffield, Eng.: Sheffield Academic Press, 1998.

Schniedewind, William M. *How the Bible Became a Book: The Textualization of Ancient Israel*. New York: Cambridge, 2004.

Schniedewind refers to the transference of religious authority from oral to written as "textualization." He traces the development of written texts as having religious and cultural authority in ancient Israel.

Toorn, Karel van der. *Scribal Culture and the Making of the Hebrew Bible*. Cambridge, Mass.: Harvard University Press, 2007.

Tov, Emanuel. *Textual Criticism of the Hebrew Bible*. Minneapolis, Minn./Assen-Maastricht: Fortress/Van Gorcum, 1992. 2nd ed., 2001.

It was once naïvely thought that textual critics were attempting to reproduce "original" texts of OT books. Now, however, textual critics tend to think only of reconstructing the earliest copies or traditions standing at the end of the composition of a book, and at the beginning of the text transmission of those books. This volume by Emanuel Tov changed the way we think about textual criticism in light of the discovery of the Dead Sea Scrolls. For advanced readers.

Vriezen, T. C., and A. S. van der Woude. *Ancient Israelite and Early Jewish Literature*. Translated by Brian Doyle. Leiden and Boston: Brill, 2005.

For how texts and documents evolved in the ancient world, see the chapter "Authors and Authorship" (pp. 40–49), and for more on text and canon, see pages 53–101. For the Apocrypha, see pages 512–63. For the texts known as the Dead Sea Scrolls, see pages 659–94.

CHAPTER 3

The Old Testament World

Ancient Israel existed in real time and space. In time, we will recall that ancient Israel was preceded by thousands of years of world history, including, for example, the first writing of the Sumerians (third millennium BCE), the Babylonian Empire, and the renowned history of ancient Egypt. In space, Israel was part of Syria-Palestine. Together with Egypt and Mesopotamia, Israel constituted a vast swath of arable land known as the "Fertile Crescent." Syria-Palestine was thus a vital land bridge between three continents and, likewise, highly vulnerable to surrounding power struggles. The latter meant frequent invasions and domination by a succession of world empires.

The primary purpose of Israel's story contained in the pages of the OT is to explore its relationship with God. Yahweh initiated an intimate relationship with a man named Abraham, which was defined by a covenant and by promises of descendants and land. The ensuing history covers an era that left its own mark on world history, in no small part due to Israel's legacy. The age between 800 and 200 BCE (the Axial Age) witnessed the appearance of ethical religion and rational philosophy in human civilization. Israel gave the world the Old Testament and the concept of monotheism emerging in its pages.

*T*he OT comes from a specific time and place, a definite world very different from our own. Don't think of the OT as a holy book dropped from the sky without historical context. Quite the contrary! The OT reflects the world of antiquity rich in literature, in art, and in something we might even call "the sciences," and with elaborate philosophies about the nature of the world. And the world in which the ancient Israelites lived and worked had a history already spanning thousands of years. The first cities of human civilization and first fledgling empires were as distant in time to ancient Israel as the Roman Empire is to you and me.

The OT world is pre-Classical, meaning it comes before the time of the Greeks and Romans, or the so-called Classical period of human civilization. Prior to this Classical period of human history, or at least overlapping with its earliest stages, is a period sometimes identified as the **Axial Age**, from approximately 800 to 200 BCE. This was a decisive moment in human history, a time identified as one of spiritual development in humanity. Civilization before the Axial Age has sometimes been called the Mythical Age.

Axial Age Changes in World History

The origins of monotheism in the OT did not occur in isolation. In fact, we have reason to relate it to other innovations in world history that were taking place at the same time and in different places. Philosophers have identified this period from about 800 to 200 BCE as an era of revolutionary new thinking that changed the world forever, an Axial Age, or turning point in world history.[1] During this time, world traditions developed simultaneously but independently of each other in four locations: China, India, Israel, and Greece. Especially in these last two – the two cultures of the eastern Mediterranean – the revolutionary ideas of monotheism (Israel) and philosophical rationalism (Greece) transformed human civilization. To this day, these Axial Age developments influence the way we think and live.

[1] Especially Karl Jaspers, *Origin and Goal of History* (trans. Michael Bullock; New Haven, Conn.: Yale University Press, 1953). For an introduction to this topic, see Karen Armstrong in "Where to Find More" in this chapter.

Prior to these changes, religion was mostly a matter of ritual and animal sacrifice. Rituals reenacted a cosmic drama in which worshippers experienced the divine, and sacrifices were necessary for perpetuating life as they knew it and for keeping the world in motion. The Axial Age revolutionaries did not completely do away with ritual and sacrifice, but they transformed them with new understandings. The OT gives ritual a new ethical dimension, placing morality at the heart of spiritual life. One's behavior becomes more important than ritual performance. And sacrifice becomes a matter of inward faith, in which one's attitude and submission are more important than the physical act itself.

I could describe these and other profound changes of the Axial Age in a number of ways. But for now, it is enough for you to remember the appearance of ethical religion and rational philosophy for the first time in human history. The world in which Israel first emerged simply did not think of religion as you and I do. It is to a survey of that very different world we now turn.

The Stage of the Old Testament Drama

Ancient Israel was located on the extreme eastern shores of the Mediterranean Sea. Relatively small compared to many of its neighbors, Israel was one part of a larger geographical entity commonly known as the ancient Near East. This region corresponds generally to the modern Middle East, including Iran, Iraq, Kuwait, Saudia Arabia, Jordan, Turkey, Syria, Lebanon, Israel, Palestine, and Egypt. We will consider this vast region as a unity because it shared something of a common culture, despite

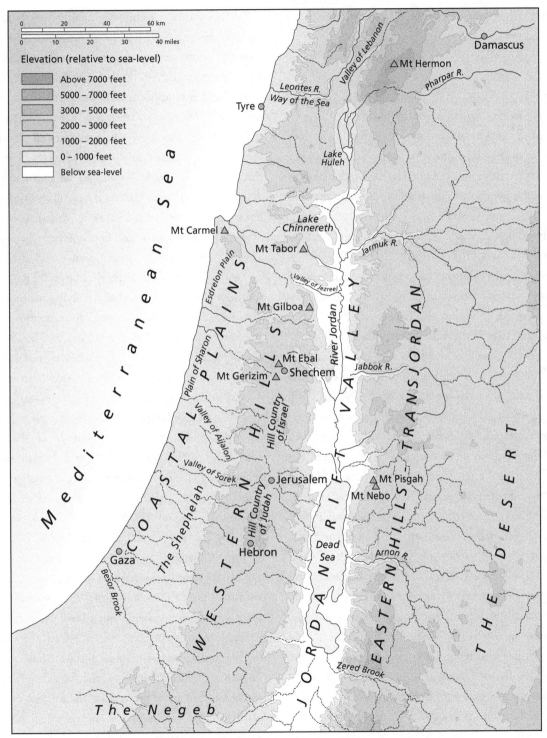

Map 3.1. Geography of ancient Israel

many ethnic and linguistic differences among its subregions.

The Ancient Near East

A glance at any map of the ancient Near East yields a simple observation: geographically, it does not appear to be a unity; no single feature ties the region together. It is bounded by the Mediterranean coastline to the west, the Iranian plateau in the east, the Black and Caspian Seas to the north on either side of the Caucasus Mountains, and the Arabian Desert in the south between the Red Sea and Persian Gulf. The designation is also not very precise since it sometimes includes, in the west, not only Turkey (ancient Anatolia) but also Greece and Italy, and in the east, areas beyond the Iranian plateau.

Yet one feature explains the need to consider this vast territory as a unified entity. A band of arable land stretches from the mouth of the Persian Gulf northwestward in a semicircle image on the map, like a crescent, extending to the southern reaches of the Mediterranean coastline (dark shaded area of Map 3.2). This stretch of arable land is known as the "**Fertile Crescent**." Water was available in this region, from either rainfall or river water used for irrigation. Because an organized labor force first appeared here to develop agriculture, the Fertile Crescent has been identified as the birthplace of human civilization. After the evolution of agriculture, with its domistication of plants and animals, people in this region built the first cities, developed metalworking, and, eventually, built the first empires. Perhaps among the most important developments in this region was the invention of writing and introduction of written documents, which officially marked the beginning of history.

So the story of human civilization begins here in the ancient Near East. We need next to consider three subregions of this vast territory: Mesopotamia, Egypt, and Syria-Palestine. The eastern and central portion of the Fertile Crescent was called *Mesopotamia* (Greek for "between the rivers"), although this subregion extended well beyond the banks of the Tigris and Euphrates Rivers themselves. Ancient Mesopotamia had no natural defenses and was vulnerable at nearly all its borders, resulting in a checkered history as various groups of people came and went. The northern portion of Mesopotamia was mountainous and usually had enough rainfall for successful agriculture. The southern portion consisted of low-lying plains and marshes, and depended on rivers for irrigation for agriculture, as well as for international trade. These north-south distinctions affected Mesopotamia's history, leading eventually to divisions between Assyria in the north and Babylonia in the south.

The second subregion of the ancient Near East was *Egypt*, in the northeastern corner of Africa. The country was essentially equated with and defined by the Nile River. The longest river in the world, the Nile originates in central Africa and flows north through the Sudan and Egypt before emptying its waters into the Mediterranean Sea. Its north-flowing direction led Egyptians to distinguish between two unequal portions of their country. Upper Egypt runs along the narrow river valley as it twists and bends northward through the desert. Lower Egypt is the delta, where the river divided into seven branches in antiquity, although only two of these branches survive. Egypt was largely isolated from the rest of the ancient Near East because it was limited to this narrow band of arable land created by the Nile Valley. The country

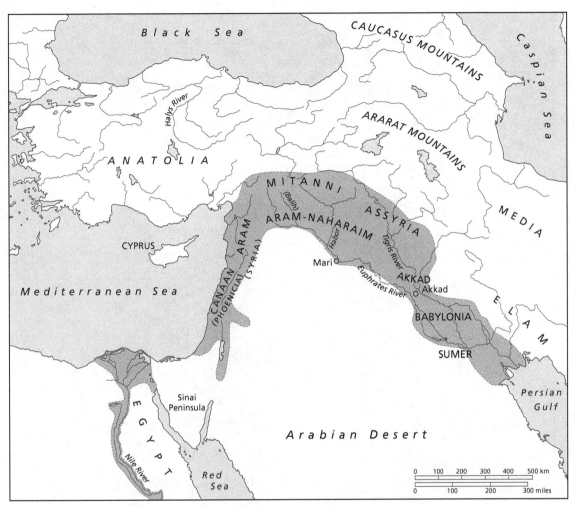

Map 3.2. The ancient Near East

rarely suffered intrusions from different nationalities, except occasionally along the northern shore of its delta and across the Sinai Peninsula. As a result, Egypt tended to retain its distinctive culture throughout most of its history.

A third subregion of the ancient Near East was *Syria-Palestine*, the area extending from the northern bend of the Euphrates River along the Mediterranean coast southward to the Sinai desert. The area around the eastern shores of the Mediterranean specifically is known as the **Levant** and incorporates what is today a portion of Turkey, Syria, Lebanon, Israel, Palestine, Jordan, and portions of Egypt. While both Mesopotamia and Egypt were centered on dominant river cultures – the Tigris-Euphrates and Nile Rivers, respectively – Syria-Palestine has smaller rivers, several mountain ranges, and less uniformity. It most naturally divides into the Northern Levant (modern Syria and Lebanon), marked by mountainous

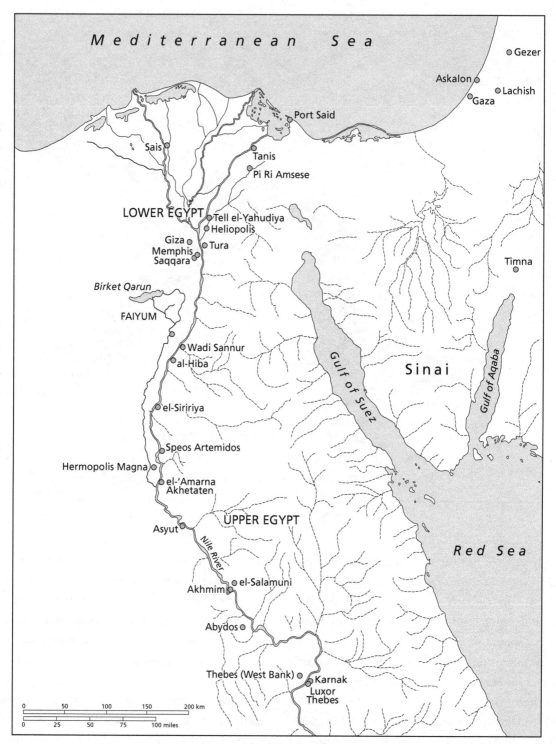

Map 3.3. Ancient Egypt

What we call the land of the Bible today has potential for misunderstanding. This small strip of land in the Southern Levant has been occupied by so many, fought over and carved up so many times, that it is hard to know just what to call it. The use of "Israel" implies to some that all of it belongs today only to the Jews as legitimate descendants of OT Israel. Similarly, "Palestine" has a longstanding usage, but may imply that all of it belongs to Palestinian Arabs exclusively. Both of these terms could be used strictly for geography. But because of the contemporary Israeli-Palestinian conflict, both terms also may introduce misunderstanding. And biblical scholars have no universal agreement on this topic.

"Syria-Palestine" is often used, as here, for geographical precision. But it is only the southern portion of Syria-Palestine that was occupied by ancient Israel, and it does not always communicate sufficiently. "Canaan" is an ancient name, but it also is not exactly conterminous with the land occupied by ancient Israel. I have used "Southern Levant" occasionally here but admit that this is a strange expression. I will most often refer simply to "Israel," by which I mean the territory of national Israel in the OT, but hope the reader will understand no modern political claims by this use.

terrain and natural seaports, and the Southern Levant (Israel, Palestine, and Jordan), the regions of ancient Canaan and Israel, although the boundaries of these two entities were fluid. Historically and socially, the Levant was important as a land bridge at the center of three continents: Africa, Asia, and Europe. Its inhabitants were frequently caught between the great world powers of Mesopotamia and Egypt, perhaps making it something less than ideal as the land promised to Israel's ancestor, Abraham (Genesis 15:18–21).

In addition to these three – Mesopotamia, Egypt, and Syria-Palestine – a few other regions on the periphery of the ancient Near East are of interest in biblical times. Among these are Asia Minor, also known as Anatolia (modern Turkey), where the ancient Hittites ruled. Another is the Iranian plateau east of Mesopotamia, home of the **Persian Empire**.

Ancient Israel

The Levant is marked by four distinct features, all of which become more prominent as one moves

north to south. These topographical features divide Syria-Palestine into four longitudinal zones: (1) a coastal region or shoreline, (2) a western mountainous ridge, (3) a central rift valley, and (4) eastern mountains giving way to an upland plateau (see Map 3.1). These features give the land of the Bible a distinct north–south orientation.

The mountains of the Northern Levant rise close to the shoreline, leaving few coastal plains but many natural harbors. This region is most characterized by impressive mountain ranges and the valleys between them, especially the Lebanon and Anti-Lebanon ranges (see Map 3.4). The western interior is marked by dry plains.

In the Southern Levant, the coastal plains grow wider in the south, leaving few natural harbors in the land that would become ancient Israel. In its southernmost portion, the spreading coastal plain would become home to the ancient Philistines. The western mountains extend continuously north to south, with only the Jezreel Valley to interrupt them, and grow smaller as one progresses north to south. The most important Israelite cities were built

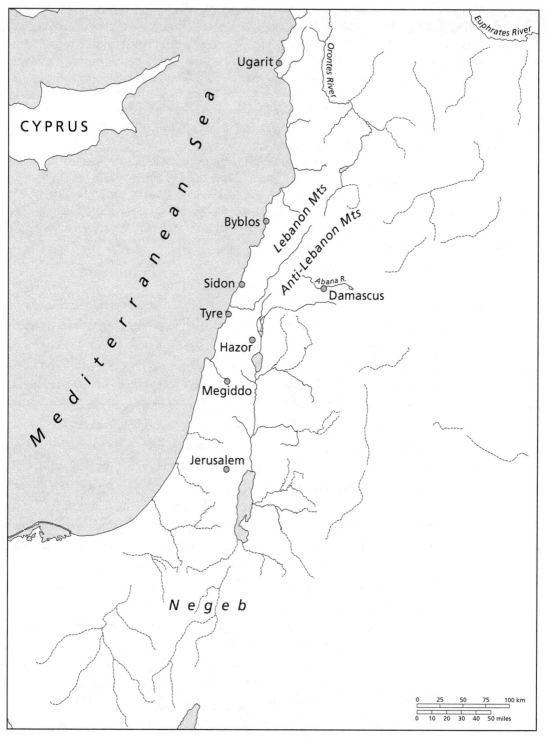

Map 3.4. The Levant

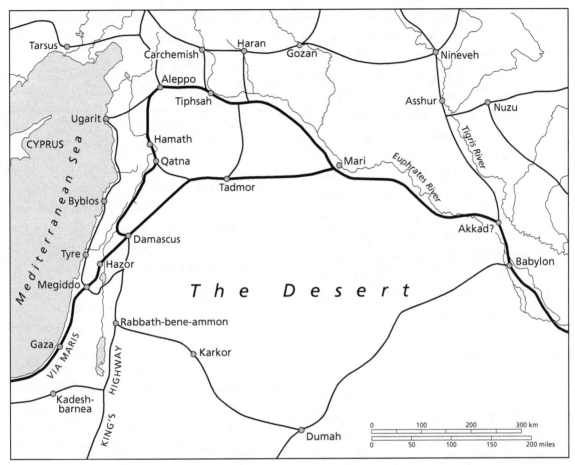

Map 3.5. Highways of the ancient world

along this central mountain range. The Shephelah, or "Lowland," is a separate and smaller ridge of hills between the Philistine plain and the Judean Hills.

The rift valley runs the entire length of the Levant, giving the region its north–south orientation. Several features of this rift play prominent roles in ancient Israel's story: Chinnereth (the Sea of Galilee), the Jordan River, the Dead Sea, and the southern Arabah. Beyond the rift in the so-called Transjordan, mountains rise again from the rift valley, divided naturally by tributaries or similar features, and yielding regions important in biblical times: Bashan, Gilead, Ammon, Moab, and Edom. These hills and mountains were bounded on the west by the Arabian desert plateau.

The steep incline across the Levantine mountains made travel difficult in the ancient world. Roadways used for travel and commerce in this region needed to negotiate the central highlands, the rift valley, and the Transjordanian hills. The main route for traversing the ancient Near East was the "Way of the Sea" (Isaiah 9:1, or *Via Maris*), although it follows the Mediterranean Sea only partially, linking Egypt with Syria and Mesopotamia by passing through the Philistine plain, crossing at the Jezreel Valley, and going on to Syria and Mesopotamia in the east. Another particularly important road system known in the Bible is the King's Highway (Numbers 20:17), which avoided the central hills and rift valley by following the Transjordanian hills north to south from central Syria to the Red Sea.

This sliver of land in the Southern Levant where the biblical drama unfolds could be a precarious place to live. Such a region, without easily irrigable land or natural sources of fresh water, was susceptible to prolonged periods of drought. Israel's obvious dependence on rainfall for agriculture can be seen in the OT's several words for rainfall: "regular rain," "early rain," "latter rain," "heavy winter rain," and "dew."[2] In good years, grain crops were harvested in the spring and summer, and vineyards and orchards yielded fruit in the summer months. Judah in the south was more dependent on animal husbandry, especially goats and sheep. Even when agriculture was flourishing, the land was susceptible to enemy attack from the southern desert (the Negeb), the eastern plains in the Transjordan, or the north and northwest, where there were arteries for imperial armies throughout Israel's history. We may blithely think of this as the "promised land," but it would take a resilient and trusting people to survive there for long.

2 See, for example, Deuteronomy 11:14. Not included in this verse are "dew" (*ṭal*) and "heavy winter rain" (*gešem*).

WORLD HISTORY BEFORE AND DURING THE OLD TESTAMENT DRAMA

For centuries, readers of the OT assumed Israel appeared at the dawn of human history just as civilization was developing. Then in the mid-nineteenth century, explorers began finding evidence of cultures and vast empires in the ancient Near East thousands of years before Israel appeared on the scene. Now we know that long before Israel, the ancient Near East had seen several advanced cultures rise and fall. The first world empires then developed during Israel's existence and had an impact on its national history, as we shall see.

So, for example, if Israel's King David and his son Solomon ruled a united monarchy with Jerusalem at its center about 1000–922 BCE, as the OT suggests, then the world known to David and Solomon had already experienced fifteen hundred years of history. During those many centuries, advanced civilizations in both Mesopotamia and Egypt had long ago established the essential features of human culture that would be the hallmark of civilization for three thousand years until the Greek conquest in the fourth century BCE.

One problem in studying the history of such early times is the lack of a precise chronological system. It wasn't until Roman times and the development of the Julian calendar that anything like an absolute chronology can be established. Authors and scholars of the ancient Near East kept chronological records, but these were always based on some arbitrarily chosen fixed point, such as the start of a ruler's reign or the beginning of a new dynasty. Generally, the further back we go in time,

SIDEBAR 3.2. CHRISTIAN THOMSEN AND THE PERIODIZATION OF HISTORY

The division of history into segments of time based on technology or sociopolitical events is known as "periodization." The three-age periodization of human culture using stone, bronze (an alloy of copper and tin), and iron was first proposed by the Danish scholar Christian J. Thomsen in 1819. Thomsen, while organizing antiquities at the National Museum of Denmark, decided to arrange the artifacts according to this chronological sequence. While it was used widely for European history, it was not until the 1920s that it was adopted to standardize several different systems in use at the time for ancient Near Eastern history. For Mesopotamia and Egypt, it is strictly more accurate and helpful to use cultural or sociopolitical features to periodize history, which is often done by specialists studying these societies in isolation. For overall comparisons across the ancient Near East, the three-age system is still widely used.

the more imprecise our dates will be for events and the more tentative our chronological sequence.

In the absence of a precise system for dating the events of ancient Near Eastern history, we rely on a three-age system of stone, bronze, and iron. This assumes an ever-increasing advancement in tools and weapons technology, using first stone, then bronze, and finally iron. The system unfortunately gives the impression of a neat sequence of three ages in a linear evolution, which is too simplistic when applied to ancient cultures and societies. But the three-age system has been so widely adopted that it remains in use today as the most helpful way to divide history into periods for study. The three primary ages have been subdivided into Early, Middle, and Late **Bronze Ages** and three **Iron Ages**. In addition, a Copper Age (Chalcolithic) has been identified between the Stone and Bronze Ages (see Table 3.1). Each subdivision has distinctive characteristics, culturally, socially, and historically, that justify investigating it separately. The dates given here are, of course, approximate. We will be adding to this chronology and referring back to it frequently as we move along through this textbook.

TABLE 3.1. CHRONOLOGY OF ANCIENT NEAR EASTERN HISTORY (ALL DATES ARE BCE)

Age	Approximate Date
Paleolithic (Old Stone Age)	before 14,000
Epipaleolithic (Final Old Stone Age)	14,000–8000
Neolithic (New Stone Age)	8000–4200
Chalcolithic (Copper–Stone Age)	4200–3300
Early Bronze I	3300–3000
Early Bronze II	3000–2800
Early Bronze III	2800–2400
Early Bronze IV	2400–2000
Middle Bronze Age I	2000–1800
Middle Bronze Age II	1800–1650
Middle Bronze Age III	1650–1550
Late Bronze Age I	1550–1400
Late Bronze Age II	1400–1200
Iron I	1200–930
Iron IIA	930–721
Iron IIB	721–605
Iron IIC	605–539
Persian	539–332
Hellenistic	332–63

Third Millennium BCE

History proper begins with writing. Details about the invention of writing itself are only vaguely known, but by the third millennium BCE advanced

3.1. The Pyramids of Giza. The Pyramids of Giza, approximately 2589–2350 BCE; *from left to right*, Mycerinus, Chefren, and Cheops. (Photo: Erich Lessing / Art Resource, N.Y.)

cultures in both Mesopotamia and Egypt were producing lots of texts. In Mesopotamia, the Sumerians appear to have invented writing. We know little about the origins of the Sumerians, but in Early Bronze Ages I–III, powerful Sumerian city-states in southern Mesopotamia left behind enough writing to show that they had established the cultural, religious, social, and, in some respects, even political foundations of the ancient world for the next thousand years and more. Among these Sumerian city-states were Ur and Uruk, known in the OT as Ur of the Chaldeans (Genesis 11:28) and Erech (Genesis 10:10). A new Semitic group, the Akkadians, rose to prominence during Early

Bronze IV. For centuries the region was known simply as "Sumer and Akkad." But at the end of Early Bronze, the Akkadians ruled most of Mesopotamia, perpetuating the Sumerian culture with, however, a number of Semitic innovations.

Compared to Mesopotamia, Egypt was isolated and relatively secure from hostile intrusions. As a result, its history is organized into thirty-one royal "dynasties" (traditionally marked with Roman numerals), illustrating again the relative consistency and continuity of Egypt's culture. This sequence of dynasties was rarely interrupted in approximately twenty-seven hundred years of history. In the Early Bronze Age, Egypt's Old Kingdom period (dynasties III–VIII) saw the rise of statehood unifying Upper and Lower Egypt. At the center of this administration was a king who was also a god. This god-king combined religion with the state, and governed on his own behalf according to Egyptian ideals of justice and truth (Egyptian *maat*). This is also the period of great royal tombs in the form of pyramids, which continue to amaze and dazzle us today. As ancient architectural accomplishments, the Egyptian pyramids are unsurpassed, although we still have little understanding of their origins or purpose.

Second Millennium BCE

At the beginning of the second millennium, a new people group appears throughout Mesopotamia, Semites known as Amurru, from which comes the term "Amorites" in the OT. They gradually begin to control the old Sumero-Akkadian city-states, and establish new cities as well. One of these, a formerly small and insignificant city in the heartland of southern Mesopotamia, named Babylon, or "Gate of God," became the center for a powerful new Amorite dynasty, most notable for its sixth king, Hammurabi (1792–1750 BCE). Hammurabi unified most of Mesopotamia and expanded Babylon's power in a way that anticipated later empires of the first millennium. He is best known for his law code, which is really more like a list of Babylonian ideals than an actual legal code. Many of the 282 laws of Hammurabi's collection are quite close in content and even in phraseology to the laws of Moses in the book of Exodus (so we will return to this topic later; see Chapter 8). Beyond this important law code, this period, known as the

Old Babylonian period (ca. 2000–1595 BCE), left a legacy of literature, art, mathematics, astronomy, and religion, preserving and adapting the older Sumero-Akkadian culture and establishing the cultural foundations for inhabitants of Mesopotamia for centuries.

Egyptian civilization in the first three centuries of the second millennium BCE achieved its classical phase. Especially during dynasty XII (ca. 1991–1785 BCE), Egypt expanded south into Nubia, and northeast into the Sinai Peninsula to mine turquoise, and further into the Levant for trade and commerce. A new administrative center was established near Memphis at this time, complementing Thebes in the south as the main dynastic capital. Egyptian literature and the arts flourished in this Middle Kingdom period (ca. 2040–1730 BCE), establishing forms and styles imitated in later periods of Egyptian history. Egyptians of the Old Kingdom period had preserved on the walls and chambers of the royal pyramids the rituals needed by the dead to assist them on their journey to a blessed afterlife. During the Middle Kingdom period, these Pyramid Texts were written on burial boxes and were called Coffin Texts; as we shall see, they were eventually preserved as the Book of the Dead in the New Kingdom period.

Sometime during dynasty XIII, probably around 1730 BCE, the central governing authority lost control, and Egypt entered a so-called Second Intermediate period (ca. 1730–1550 BCE). During this time, Egypt was ruled by outsiders known as Hyksos from Avaris, their capital center in the delta. Exactly who the Hyksos were and where they were from is uncertain, although they are often taken as Semites from Syria-Palestine. They controlled

Egypt's commerce and appear to have held most of the country for about a hundred years.

Beginning with dynasty XVIII, the Egyptians managed to overturn Hyksos rule and reestablish an era of stability and strength. New Kingdom Egypt (dynasties XVIII–XX, ca. 1550–1069 BCE) was the height of Egyptian culture in terms of military power, wealth, and prestige. During this time, the king became known simply as the "great house," or pharaoh, because of the enormous wealth of the royal household. This is also the time in which King Amenophis IV established a new royal city in the center of the country near Hermopolis, and a new religious cult for the sun disc, Aten. The king changed his name to Akhenaten and called the new royal city Akhetaten (modern el-Amarna; see Map 3.3). In a revolutionary change, the sun god was thought to absorb features of other deities, so that Aten was perceived as the sole heavenly king, with Akhenaten as his earthly counterpart. Akhenaten's religious innovations did not last long, and the Amarna period (1403–1306) can be said to be an exception to Egyptian religious traditions. Nonetheless, this Amarna experiment with monotheism, or with something close to it, has been compared to Mosaic religion, and we shall return to this topic later (Chapter 10).

The second half of the millennium was a period of internationalism. A balance of power across the ancient Near East saw New Kingdom Egypt matched by the Hittites in Anatolia and the Kassites in Babylonia (among others) during the Late Bronze Age. The use of the Babylonian dialect of Akkadian as a universal language made commerce and diplomatic relations possible across the Fertile Crescent. An archive of 382 texts was found in 1887 at el-Amarna, mostly in Babylonian, containing letters between the Egyptian pharaohs (Amenophis III and Akhenaten) and the various rulers of Syria-Palestine and Mesopotamia over a thirty-year span (ca. 1352–1322 BCE). This so-called Amarna Age was a remarkable period of wealth and prosperity among the great powers of the ancient Near East. But it was short-lived.

The ancient Near East witnessed dramatic political changes around 1200 BCE, the time of transition from Bronze Age to Iron Age. For reasons not completely clear to us, the dominant nation-states of the Mediterranean rim – the Egyptians, the Hittites of Anatolia, the city-states of the Levant, and even the Mycenaean civilization of Greece – all collapsed within about fifty years of each other. The Iron Age marks the beginning of hundreds of years of political struggle in the Levant, along with many cultural changes. The age of internationalism ended, and new political systems and people groups appeared in the Levant. In addition, the alphabet was invented, changing the accessibility of written texts. The Israelites arrived in the central highlands as part of these changes, along with several other new people groups, which we will discuss later.

We are unable to determine precisely why all these changes took place. Was it the result of natural catastrophe? Earthquakes? Drought or famine? Were new technologies involved, such as the invention of iron-working? Was some dramatic climate change responsible? Or some combination of these? Although we cannot answer these questions satisfactorily, we are aware, based on Egyptian inscriptions referring to

The Amarna archive contains six letters from Abdi-Heba, ruler of Jerusalem, to the Egyptian pharaoh, Ameno-phis IV, also known as Akhenaten.* These letters reflect the role of Jerusalem in the history and culture of Canaan in pre-Israelite times, particularly in the mid-fourteenth century BCE. Although the archaeological evidence from Jerusalem is not available to us because of the continuous occupation of the city for nearly six thousand years, these letters show Jerusalem to have been a regional center with considerable influence hundreds of years before it became David's capital.

Late Bronze Age Canaan was governed at this time by a network of local rulers. The pharaoh considered them to be municipal rulers or mayors, while local Canaanites perceived them as kings of city-states. Each such ruler commanded agricultural holdings in the surrounding peripheral areas of his city, sometimes extending into nearby villages and towns. The letters of Abdi-Heba refer to the "land of Jerusalem" and its "towns," re-flecting its status as an Egyptian vassal city-state. One of these letters (EA287) mentions Abdi-Heba's "house," or palace, for the ruling family, which probably also served as the seat of government. Jerusalem at this time may also have had a temple and presumably had houses for the necessary bureaucracy and the local elite.

* William L. Moran, *The Amarna Letters* (Baltimore: Johns Hopkins University Press, 1992), Letters 285–90, pages 325–34.

3.2. Amarna Letter (E29793). A letter addressed to Pharaoh Amenho-tep III from Tushratta, king of Mitanni. The letter sends greetings to his daughter, who had become one of Amenhotep's wives. The tablet has three lines of Egyptian in hieratic script written in black ink, proba-bly an archiving notation added when the letter arrived. (Photo: © The Trustees of the British Museum / Art Resource, N.Y.)

peoples "of the countries of the sea," that groups were on the move across the Mediterranean. These sea-borne groups of displaced peoples, the so-called Sea Peoples, were likely from the islands of the Aegean Sea along the shores of Greece to the west and Anatolia to the east. They were probably not the first cause of the collapse of Late Bronze cultures, but likely were victims of some unknown catastrophe. Yet as one of the most important domino effects, the arrival of the Sea Peoples was part of the changing face of the ancient Near East.

First Millennium BCE

The entire eastern Mediterranean coastline was affected by the changes taking place in Iron I. The power balance of the Late Bronze Age was gone. Egypt would never again be the same dominating presence in the Levant that it had been. The Hittite kingdoms of Anatolia and the powerful city-states of Syria-Palestine were slowly replaced by new polit-ical entities and social structures. Mesopotamia was less affected by these changes, and as a result, the region's center of power shifted to the east. The relative stability of the region led in time to the emergence of the world's first real empires, all from a base in Mesopotamia. Ancient history during this time may be summarized as a series of imperial powers, first Assyria, then Babylonia, and finally, Persia.

The rise of the *Assyrians* in the early first millennium BCE is a story of at first recovery and then expansion across the Fertile Crescent. Assyrians grew in strength until they gradually asserted themselves over northern Mesopotamia from roughly 950–745 BCE. Then, under powerful King Tiglath-pileser III (745–727 BCE), the Assyrians came to control all of Mesopotamia and Syria-Palestine, even holding Egypt for a time. Assyria's dominant imperial strength across the entire Fertile Crescent lasted roughly from 745 to 610 BCE. As part of their continuing efforts to take and hold Syria-Palestine, the Assyrians captured Samaria, the capital of northern Israel, in 722 BCE, and surrounded and besieged Jerusalem in 701 BCE, although the city did not fall at that time.

After the fall of the Assyrian Empire, power shifted to the south to the *Babylonians*. (Review Map 3.2 for the general location of Assyria and Babylonia.) A new dynasty was founded in Babylon, whose most notable king, Nebuchadnezzar II (604–562 BCE), restored the old city to a spectacular period of strength and prosperity. This Babylonian Empire was brief (604–539 BCE) – a mere interlude between the Assyrians and Persians. Yet Babylon's renewed grandeur, impressive architecture, and legacy in the Bible and other Classical sources represent something of a climax in ancient Near Eastern imperial strength. Jerusalem once again became embroiled in international politics, and the city fell to Nebuchadnezzar's army in 586 BCE.

The *Persians* were the last native Mesopotamian empire. From the Iranian mountains in the eastern extremes of the Near East, the double Medo-Persian Empire, also known as the Achaemenid Empire (ca. 550–330 BCE), was the largest the world had seen. (See Map 15.1.) King Cyrus II ("the Great," 559–530 BCE) captured the city of Babylon in 539 BCE, releasing the Jews in Babylonia and allowing them to return to Jerusalem, officially ending the exile. His successors expanded the empire to Egypt and Anatolia, coming to a famous standoff with the Greeks. The Jews who returned from Babylonia joined those who had never left the region and formed a modest community around Jerusalem, the Persian province of **Yehud**. Beginning in 334 BCE, Alexander the Great marched through the Levant, Egypt, and Mesopotamia, capturing Babylon in 331 and bringing the Persian Empire to an end.

Throughout this long history, through the rise and fall of kingdoms and empires, the religious traditions of the ancient Near East were remarkably consistent. Some have speculated that early religions developed in an evolutionary pattern from animism to **pantheism** and polytheism. But from earliest times, we have evidence only of a complex polytheism as the dominant conviction of ancient peoples. Egyptian and Babylonian experiments with monotheism, or at least a monolatrous henotheism, occurred in the Late Bronze Age (Egypt's sun disc, Aten and Babylon's storm god, Marduk). But these were relatively short-lived and were abandoned as heretical in both cases. Israel's monolatrous henotheism, developing eventually into genuine monotheism, was unique, as we shall see.

THE OLD TESTAMENT STORY

With this ancient Near Eastern history in the background, Israel gives a surprisingly honest

---

SIDEBAR 3.4. HIGHLIGHTS OF ISRAEL'S STORY

The OT authors of Israel's story present the nation's history in a straightforward manner, focusing on Israel's relationship with Yahweh. The following highlights of the OT account are helpful to remember.

1. Ancestral beginnings: covenant and promises (Abraham, Isaac, and Jacob)
2. Deliverance from Egypt and covenant at Mount Sinai (Moses)
3. Conquest of the promised land (Joshua)
4. Tumultuous period of judges rule prior to the monarchy
5. **United Monarchy** (Saul, David, and Solomon)
6. Two kingdoms, Israel and Judah
7. Exile and restoration

This general outline is the OT's presentation of Israel's history. The actual historical details are much more complicated. We have a great many controversies and debates to discuss as we move through the OT itself. But this seven-point outline should be consulted as the OT's summary of Israel's history. I will return to these highlights, especially in Chapter 11.

---

account of its own history. Beginning with wandering ancestors in far off Mesopotamia, the OT tells of slavery in Egypt, deliverance, occupation of a new land promised to them by God, emergence of statehood and monarchy, sin and loss, exile and restoration, and much more besides. The account is generally national in scope but with many individual vignettes as well. The OT makes no attempt to whitewash Israel or hide its shortcomings. Through it all, the driving purpose of the OT account is to explore Israel's relationship with God in all its complex and intimate details. In this way, the OT is first and foremost a theological statement told as a story. We will have several occasions later to explore historical reconstructions of the events. You will see that today's scholarship is much divided about the historical reality. For now, it is important that you have an overview of Israel's account of itself contained in the OT.

The first eleven chapters of the OT tell the universal story of all humans. Then Israel's national history begins, with the ancestors Abraham and Sarah, Isaac and Rebekah, and Jacob and his wives, Rachel and Leah. (We'll get to the idea of polygamy later.) Abraham enters into an intimate relationship with the God, Yahweh, which is described as a covenant. Associated with this covenant are divine promises of children and land. Isaac is the miraculous gift of God to Abraham and Sarah in their old age, and through him numerous descendants are promised. Abraham also has a secondary wife, Hagar, who gives birth to Ishmael. Thus Abraham is the father of Jews and Muslims alike. Christians consider him their father in faith, making Abraham the father of Judaism, Christianity, and Islam, the so-called Abrahamic religions. The OT continues by tracing a line of descent through Isaac, for whom Rebekah bears twins, Jacob and Esau. Jacob, who is also named Israel, becomes the father of twelve sons, the ancestors of the twelve tribes of Israel.

Jacob/Israel and his twelve sons live in the land promised to them by God, Canaan, in the

Southern Levant. But because of drought, they are forced to relocate to Egypt. They settle in northern Egypt indefinitely and grow so large in number, the Egyptians fear and distrust them. The pharaoh feels compelled to enslave them, and the Israelites remain in the land as slaves for centuries.

In Egypt, the Israelites cry out to Yahweh for deliverance from their oppressive slavery. God graciously prepares and sends a savior named Moses to deliver the people from their slavery. Yahweh sends miracles against Egypt through Moses, ten plagues, that prove the superiority of Yahweh over the Egyptian gods. The Israelites escape their bondage and suffering in Egypt because of Yahweh's intervention and Moses' leadership. The Israelites are brought to an especially important mountain in the Sinai Peninsula, Mount Horeb/Sinai, where Yahweh enters into a covenant relationship with the nation similar to his covenant with their patriarch, Abraham. Yahweh and Moses provide the people with Ten Commandments and other laws and instructions to ensure the future of this intimate covenant relationship.

But the Israelites rebel against Yahweh and Moses almost immediately. As a result, instead of making the journey to the promised land straight away, which should have taken no more than eighteen months, they languish in the desert for forty years. This first generation of Israelites dies in the desert, and their leader, Moses, dies before crossing over into the promised land. A new generation, led by the general Joshua, enters the land promised to the ancestors. Yahweh again performs great miracles of deliverance to provide the land of Canaan as his gift to the Israelites.

Even after settling in the new land promised to their ancestors, the Israelites repeatedly rebelled against Yahweh and his appointed leaders. For about two hundred years or so, the people lived in a cycle of breaking their covenant with Yahweh, then changing their minds and asking forgiveness, then finding deliverance through a temporary leader or "judge," and once again finding themselves at peace in the land. This long line of judges ruled the tribes of Israel and might have continued to provide inspired leadership. But Israel's constant rebellion and lawlessness resulted in threats within and without, invaders from outside the borders as well as tribes turning on each other in fratricidal war. Everyone seemed to do whatever they liked, and there was no moral compass among the people.

The answer was for one of these judgelike rulers to become a king, establish royal authority throughout the land, and maintain a standing army to defend the people. The first king was Saul, of the tribe of Benjamin. He was divinely appointed and publically acclaimed. But he was also tragically flawed, and eventually he disqualified himself as king. He was replaced by David, of Judah. Together with his son, Solomon, they governed over a **united monarchy**, with a capital in Jerusalem; during their reign, Israel enjoyed its greatest period of success and prosperity. Yet even David and Solomon were imperfect in their devotion to Yahweh, and Solomon's crimes and pride eventually resulted in the dissolution of the kingdom.

After Solomon's death, the United Monarchy broke into two separate kingdoms, Israel in the north and Judah in the south. The northern kingdom grew rich and prospered, although it was politically unstable and had nine separate royal dynasties in just two hundred years. Moreover, the northern kingdom compromised its covenant with Yahweh, and suffered the consequences when its capital city, Samaria, fell to the Assyrian Empire. The southern kingdom, Judah, maintained a single dynasty, the sons of David, on the throne in Jerusalem for four hundred fifty years. Yet it, too, gradually compromised Yahweh's covenant, failing to heed the warnings of the prophets. Sadly, Jerusalem fell to the Babylonians, the great temple of Solomon was destroyed, the city's leadership was dragged away into captivity, and the people of God dispersed.

Even while the people were in exile, Yahweh was gracious to them. A remnant remained faithful, crying out to him, and longing for the day of their return to the fallen city of Jerusalem. Finally, Cyrus the Persian liberated them and allowed large numbers to return home, where they slowly and with great sacrifice rebuilt the temple and city walls. As in days of old, Yahweh performed miracles for his people, provided for their needs, and established them securely in the promised land. They were not a great nation as in the days of David, but the people of God preserved the sacred traditions, maintained regular temple worship, and awaited a coming messiah, a descendant of David, to make all things new and restore Israel to its intended grandeur.

The monotheism preserved in pages of the OT is what makes Israel unique. Otherwise, this little people group in the Southern Levant is very much like others of the ancient Near East. In fact, by leaving us the texts that became our OT, Israel has disproportionately influenced world history. By means of this religious contribution, Israel has had an impact on human civilization, philosophy, and literature far beyond expectations for a nation its size in antiquity. Israel's contribution to world thought is a direct inversion of its historical significance in the ancient Near East.

WHERE TO FIND MORE

Armstrong, Karen. *The Great Transformation: The Beginning of Our Religious Traditions*. New York: Knopf, 2006.

Beitzel, Barry J., and Laurie Whiddon, eds. *Biblica: The Bible Atlas; A Social and Historical Journey through the Lands of the Bible*. Hauppage, N.Y.: Barron's Educational Series, 2007.

Golden, Jonathan M. *Ancient Canaan and Israel: An Introduction*. Oxford and New York: Oxford University Press, 2009.
For details of the physical landscape of ancient Israel, see pages 15–27.

Jaspers, Karl. *The Origin and Goal of History*. New Haven, Conn.: Yale University Press, 1953.
The first seventy pages gave definition to the "Axial Age."

King, Philip J., and Lawrence E. Stager. *Life in Biblical Israel*. Library of Ancient Israel. Louisville, Ky.: Westminster John Knox Press, 2001.

Kuhrt, Amélie. *The Ancient Near East, c. 3000–330 BC*. London: Routledge, 1994.

Best source for more on the historical background information covered in this chapter.

Mazar, Amihai. *Archaeology of the Land of the Bible, 10,000–586 B.C.E.* Anchor Bible Reference Library. New York: Doubleday, 1990.

Rainey, Anson F., and R. Steven Notley. *The Sacred Bridge: Carta's Atlas of the Biblical World.* Jerusalem: Carta, 2006.

Chapter 3, pages 30–42, gives details for several of the geographical features discussed in this chapter.

Stern, Ephraim. *Archaeology of the Land of the Bible: The Assyrian, Babylonian, and Persian Periods, 732–332 BCE.* Anchor Bible Reference Library. New York: Doubleday, 2001.

CHAPTER 4

The Primary History

All historiography or history writing is done with a purpose, and the purpose of Israel as expressed in the OT was clearly religious and theological. The Israelites sought to record their relationship with God in the past – to express their unique understanding of God, his universe, and his relationship to Israel. Additionally significant is the fact that Israel was among the first in the ancient world to write history.

This chapter will take us into the library of ancient Israel to get a better look at how the books of the OT narrate history and how these books have been organized. Specifically, we will investigate the sources that appear to have been interwoven to create the so-called Primary History. These sources are characterized by their distinctive ways of referring to God and by their themes and literary techniques. We will observe that the OT presents the Primary History in such a way as to provide a framework for understanding the historical contexts of all the rest of the OT books.

Not everyone sees the OT's legacy of monotheism as a good thing. The belief in only one God is necessarily exclusive, defining itself over and against belief in many gods. This exclusivity may lead to intolerance of other views and eventually to violence against others. Some therefore connect monotheism to violence. Others blame monotheism for centuries of mistreatment of women, arguing that the feminine aspects of the divine were suppressed in the process of reducing all divine aspects to only one God.

I will return to these questions later. For now, it is enough to know that the concept of the oneness of God as expressed in Israel's library was the first time in human history that ancient thinkers formulated a consistent and integrated view of reality – of life in the universe. It is true that Israelite monotheism did not suddenly bring an end to the violence already widespread in the ancient Near East. Yet monotheism as a new understanding of God transformed Israel's thinking about nature, culture, and gender, and also resulted in a new value for human life. It changed everything. This is why Israel's monotheism is one of the most important developments of the Axial Age, what I called "Israel's gift to the world" in Chapter 1. I hope to show later in this textbook that OT monotheism eventually made modern science possible, as well as equality among men and women, and many other benefits we take for granted.

Before we get to all that, I want you in this chapter to consider the origins of history and history writing. When you look at Israel's library, one of the surprises is just how much history is found there. The OT contains many types of literature – songs, prayers, sermons, and many others. But narratives of past events are the largest portion by far, and this historical narrative frames the whole OT. In Israel's case, it seems the art of writing history is in some way connected to monotheism. And Israel was perhaps the first, and certainly among the best, at writing good history.

HERODOTUS, FATHER OF HISTORY?

The OT is full of history. In fact, the entire collection is something of a grand sweep of history – a metanarrative – beginning with the creation of the universe and concluding with Yehud, the Persian province around Jerusalem. Additional books of hymns, sermons, wisdom lessons, and so forth, are tied to that history, fleshing out the details.

4.1. Hittite Treaty. Treaty concluded between Pharaoh Ramses II and the Hittite King Muwatalli II, approximately 1286 BCE after the battle of Kadesh. This Akkadian-language version of the Hittite Treaty is a rare example of a parity treaty between two partners acknowledging each other as equals. The treaty itself was signed as many as ten years later by Ramses II and the new Hittite king, Hattusili III. (Photo: Erich Lessing / Art Resource, N.Y.)

Why was Israel so focused on history writing? Other peoples in the ancient Near East showed relatively little interest in writing an account of the past. The Hittites of Anatolia in the second millennium demonstrated a historical awareness and wrote historical prologues in their accounts of treaties with other nations. Later Mesopotamian authors kept elaborate lists and annals that reflected at least a modest interest in the past. History writing probably had its origins in the imperial propaganda written on royal victory monuments set up in the Levant by conquering Assyrian kings and later imitated by kings of smaller city-states in the Levant. But in a way more elaborate than previous history writing, Israel's narratives have features we usually think of as real history writing, or historiography. For the first time, Israel's history has (1) evaluation and use of older sources, (2) selection and arrangement of events along a chain of cause and effect, (3) elaborate characterization and plot development, and (4) presentation of events as having a purpose, explaining the historian's present.

In our effort to explain why Israel's library is so full of history, the question of motive is helpful. Israelites simply were motivated to write history in a way others were not. The Hittites were interested in using the events of the past for political purposes, as introductions to diplomatic treaties in order to coerce weaker nations into keeping their commitments. Mesopotamian authors seem to have

been inspired by a general antiquarian interest and by an impulse to organize data. Inscriptions written on victory monuments clearly also had the political motivation to intimidate. All these early examples of history writing have a historical consciousness. But the historical narratives preserved in the OT go much further. Here we have a penetrating religious and theological motivation. We might hesitate even to call this historiography, because it is so singularly focused on narrating the past as a religious account. But all history writing has a purpose, and in Israel's case, we can discern that purpose clearly. They were recording their relationship with God in the past.

Furthermore, it is just possible that Israel's distinctive history writing is a result of its monotheism (remembering that it began as monolatrous henotheism; see Chapter 1). The common literary genre in the ancient Near East for speculating about the gods and reflecting on life was mythology.

SIDEBAR 4.2. HERODOTUS (CA. 484–425 BCE), THE FATHER OF HISTORY

It was apparently the Roman philosopher Cicero (104–43 BCE) who first called Herodotus the "Father of History," and justifiably so. Herodotus wrote his masterpiece, *Histories* (*Inquiries*, which gives us the word "history"), or *History of the Persian Wars*, in the 440s BCE, after traveling widely in the Persian Empire. While some doubt the authenticity of his account, most acknowledge Herodotus as our best source for Persian history, as well as for valuable details about ancient Egypt and Mesopotamia. He was the first historian to conduct research for the task, visiting actual sites, interrogating eyewitnesses where possible, and carefully tracing a cause-and-effect continuum. A gifted storyteller, Herodotus combines history, geography, and anthropology in his work in a lively manner and with dramatic flair. While he allows for the miraculous, his *Histories* have a more secular and political tendency than Israelite historiography.

4.2. Herodotus. Head of Herodotus – a second-century AD Roman copy of a Greek original; on display at the Stoa of Attalus in Athens. (Photo: Scala / Art Resource, N.Y.)

Egyptians, Mesopotamians, and others produced numerous myths explaining how the gods related to each other, how humanity was created, and how life works. And the OT itself preserves vestiges of early Israelite mythology. But history has replaced mythology in ancient Israel as the way to talk about God, and this is likely related to monotheism. There being only one God, the Israelites were not interested in speculation about Yahweh's relationship to other gods, or about the forces of nature as reflections of other gods. Instead, the relationship of Yahweh to Israel – his intervention in the past, his management of history, and his use of reward and punishment as part of an overarching plan – contributed to a new way of thinking about and writing history. History was not an entirely new literary genre, but it was sufficiently transformed by the Israelites to yield a new way of explaining God, his universe, and his relationship to Israel.

Your elementary school teachers probably taught you that Herodotus was the "Father of History." The Greek explorer wrote extensive accounts of wars between the Greeks and Persians, gathering and investigating various sources, testing where possible the views of those sources, and writing the results of his "researches" (or "histories") in a unified narrative. Later historians and philosophers too were justified in calling him the "Father of History." And yet Israelite authors were writing history at about the same time as, or even a little before, Herodotus. Their histories clearly have a religious motivation, but Israel was nevertheless among the first to write history.

ISRAELITE HISTORIOGRAPHY

Many OT books that you don't normally think of as "historical books" still have sections of narrative.

So, for example, books of prophecy often have historical accounts that provide background for that particular prophet. Jeremiah has long stretches of narrative interspersed with the prophet's sermons. To a lesser degree Isaiah, Amos, and others also have history mixed in with their sermons. Sometimes psalms have historical titles attached to give the reader context, or a psalm may spend long verses recounting Israel's history.

Beyond these bits and pieces of history writing dispersed in the OT, we turn now to consider Israel's first works of history that provide the majority of the historical narrative in the OT. There were originally three large complexes of historical narrative. Two of these expansive histories have been interwoven in the books of the OT and make up the Primary History. This nine-book continuous account of Israel's story from creation to the exile may be called "The First Bible," containing Genesis, Exodus, Leviticus, Numbers, Deuteronomy, Joshua, Judges, 1–2 Samuel (as one book), and 1–2 Kings (as one book, following the Jewish canon; see Chapter 2). The third historical work stands independent of these and is preserved in the books 1–2 Chronicles and Ezra-Nehemiah.

The Yahwistic History

Israel's first history is likely the world's first work of prose. Later in Israel's history, scribes and editors broke it apart and used it for compiling several of our current books of the OT. So we are left with reconstructing its contents from Genesis, Exodus, and Numbers, and some say several of the historical books have parts of it as well. This history was essentially an epic narrative, tracing Israel's national origins and early years. It begins with the creation of the world as a paradise, Eden. The historian explores the unfortunate choices of the first humans in Eden; Yahweh's decision to start over with a single righteous person, Noah; and Yahweh's need to start over yet again with another single righteous person, Abram, who becomes Abraham, the father of the Israelite nation. But the nation, like all humans before them, tended to rebel against Yahweh. The history tells of their struggles, enslavement, and deliverance, and of Yahweh's fresh start (again!) with Moses and a covenant with the people. Where exactly this national epic history ended, we do not know. Some assume that the history continues with the Israelites entering the promised land, where they survived for two centuries without a king but then enthroned Saul, David, and Solomon.

This first narrative history is distinctive because of its particular words and phrases, continuous account with an intricate plot and characterizations, parallel stories across vast narrative stretches, and characteristic literary techniques and themes. Its most distinctive feature, however, is the way it uses the sacred name for God, "YHWH," or "Yahweh." We refer to this author as the **Yahwist**, and to his or her work as the Yahwistic History.[1] This first Israelite historian, the Yahwist, lived and wrote at a point in time impossible for us to determine. Most scholars believe that the Yahwist was a historian of the southern kingdom of Judah in the eighth or ninth century BCE.

---

1 I say "his or her" because a number of studies have explored the possibility that the Yahwist was a woman in view of the work's sympathetic portrayals of women despite the male-dominated society.

SIDEBAR 4.3. SOURCES OF OLD TESTAMENT LITERATURE

The Five Books of Moses, the Pentateuch, are comprised of at least four older sources. The earliest of these documents come from Israel's historical traditions and have been introduced in this chapter. The work of *source criticism* starts with the assumption that ancient literary compositions often combined or absorbed other, older texts. Indeed, we have numerous examples from the ancient Near East of precisely this process of combining older texts into a new literary work. Many OT books were produced in this way, so that source criticism divides the book into its component parts and attempts to identify the relative dates of these parts (see Sidebar 18.3). This process is a little like an archaeologist exposing the various dateable layers of an ancient site.

OT scholars discovered these sources hidden in the Pentateuch by means of centuries of study and debate. The French physician Jean Astruc in 1753 made the first observations that led eventually to the sources' discovery (although he had lesser-known predecessors, like the German minister H. B. Witter in 1711). Astruc's work was developed further by a German professor, Johann G. Eichhorn, in a three-volume introduction to the OT in 1781–1783. OT scholars and literary specialists have refined our understanding of these earliest Israelite documents over the last two hundred years. For convenience, the sources are abbreviated by a single letter.

J – The first and the oldest, this source freely used the divine name Yahweh, which is sometimes spelled Jehovah, and thus designated J. This document is the Yahwistic History covered in this chapter.

E – A second early history, this one from the northern kingdom, referred to God as Elohim, and is therefore designated E. These first two documents were edited and merged as JE sometime shortly after 722 BCE.

P – The largest of the sources, it collected the legal and priestly traditions of ancient Israel and is therefore known as P. This document was subsequently adapted and expanded by a holiness school of priests (H). We will return to this topic later (Chapter 8).

D – A seventh-century source found only in the book of Deuteronomy is designated D. Our discussion here of Israelite history writing relates mostly to J, E, and the use of D in the writing of the **Deuteronomistic History**. We will return to D later and explore further how the Pentateuch was written (Chapters 6 and 7).

Nineteenth-century OT scholars assumed that P was the last of these sources, and so their classic theory of the composition of the Pentateuch was the now-famous JEDP Hypothesis, otherwise known as the **Documentary Hypothesis**. But this sequence of the sources is open to discussion. The precise chronology is still debated today, and a sequence of JEP(H)D is preferable.

Some object to this kind of source analysis altogether. We do not have copies of any of these old sources, and their existence is purely theoretical. So, the argument goes, this kind of research is in fact foreign to the way the OT was written. However, empirical studies of the way similar literature was composed in the ancient Near East have confirmed the use of such sources by ancient authors and scribes. In fact, the actual process of composing such large texts as the Pentateuch has now been essentially confirmed by such comparative studies. Scholars make no claim to understand every feature (or verse!) of the Pentateuch in this way. Yet the basic outline of this source analysis is established.

Our story gets a bit complicated at this point. It is entirely possible that this Yahwistic History was itself combined or joined with another historical account of Israel, this one coming from the northern kingdom of Israel at about the same time. This historian wrote with quite different themes and literary techniques, and refers to God not by the personal name, Yahweh, but simply as "God," or *Elohim* in Hebrew. For this reason, we call this northern historian the **Elohist** author, although some today doubt this narrative ever existed as an independent document or source. At any rate, these historical sources were woven together into a continuous history at a point in time impossible for us to reconstruct. Most likely it was soon after the fall of the northern capital of Samaria to the Assyrians in 722 BCE. Thus, this first history of Israel was Yahwistic, but it may also have been a compound Yahwistic-Elohistic continuous narrative with a distinctive worldview and theology. Still later, this history was combined with priestly and other sources to make up our current Pentateuch. But here we are covering only Israel's histories, so I will reserve that story for later.

The Deuteronomistic History

The second extended history begins with Israel encamped on the plains of Moab ready to cross the Jordan River into the promised land. Moses delivers farewell addresses to the nation and then dies just east of the Jordan. From there the history traces Israel's conquest of the promised land, the judges settlement period, the rise of the monarchy, the divided kingdoms, and the eventual collapse and ruin at the hands of first the Assyrians and then the Babylonians. Unlike the cropped and rearranged use of the Yahwistic History in the various OT books in which it is preserved, this second history has come to us essentially in the series of books Deuteronomy, Joshua, Judges, 1 and 2 Samuel, and 1 and 2 Kings. The first of these, Deuteronomy, stands at its head and establishes themes and a theological

agenda that stretches across the entire narrative. Thus we call this narrative the "Deuteronomistic History" (see Chapter 9).

This history was likely written in two phases, first in the late seventh century BCE before the fall of Jerusalem, and second during the Babylonian exile that followed. The purpose of this second edition written during the exile was to explain why the catastrophe occurred, why the Babylonians were used by God to destroy Jerusalem. The Deuteronomistic History is based on the book of Deuteronomy's covenant theology, which states that obedience to God and to Israel's covenant with God results in life and wholeness. Rejection of God and failure to keep the covenant results in death and despair. This concept, known as *retribution theology*, becomes the foundation for the editors and authors of the history's narrative. The conquest of the Southern Levant (Joshua), the premonarchic settlement period (Judges-Samuel), and the monarchies of Israel and Judah (Samuel-Kings) are all narrated from this perspective. The historian's goal is to explain the collapse of the two kingdoms as the result of the people's failure to be faithful in their relationship to Yahweh. It serves also, of course, to warn the reader not to repeat the Israelites' mistakes.

The Postexilic Chronistic History

The third extended historical narrative comes after the exile and restoration. It consists largely of what we have in the books of 1 and 2 Chronicles, Ezra, and Nehemiah. Like the Deuteronomistic History, this extended narrative has combined and developed sources in a creative new historical narrative. The purpose was to justify the restoration of Israel and to encourage the disheartened inhabitants of the Persian province Yehud. This narrative focuses primarily on the importance of temple worship in the newly rebuilt temple (we will call this the Second Temple period). It also seeks to trace the restoration community to the ancestors and traditions of Israel's most glorious periods of history. The historian wanted to show that the new, restored Israel is a continuation of the old, that it is, in fact, the only legitimate heir and successor of preexilic Israel. The narrative covers the distant past (1 and 2 Chronicles), and the recent past (Ezra and Nehemiah). We will return to this topic in Chapter 15. We turn now to the way the Yahwistic and Deuteronomistic Histories were combined in our current books of the OT.

The Primary History: From Creation to the Fall of Jerusalem

Older historical narratives have been preserved in the OT books in a way that is not always obvious. They are almost hidden there. In fact, learning about how scholars discovered these histories is like reading a mystery novel. First they found that the authors of OT books used sources from different times and places in Israel's history. Then by observing common phraseology and religious convictions they realized that a few of these sources extended over large portions of the Pentateuch, or the Historical Books, and that, at some point in time, these sources must have been independent, self-contained documents. Only over time and with a great deal of cooperation between hundreds of scholars have we been able to identify these three early histories. And the process is still ongoing, as we will see.

For now, consider how these first two historical writings, the earliest in Israel – the Yahwistic History and the Deuteronomistic History – have been preserved in our OT today. For this discussion, you may need to review the list of books in the OT canon in Figure 2.3. The Torah and the Former Prophets of the Jewish canon are the books we will focus on here. Remember that the Christian canons insert Ruth between Judges and 1 Samuel, and collect and arrange the Historical Books in a different way.

The first nine books, comprising the Torah and the Former Prophets, make up approximately one-half of the entire OT (not in book count, of course, but by word and sentence count). These nine are a series of books, intended to be read together, covering a broad historical continuum from creation to the destruction of Jerusalem and its temple (586 BCE) and slightly beyond. In the ancient world, authors usually brought their narratives down to their own time, recording as final episodes events roughly contemporaneous with the writer. If this is true of the Primary History, it was completed sometime in the 550s BCE, approximately the time of the last episode recorded in 2 Kings 25:27–30.[2] This is at least the time of the completion of the Deuteronomistic History, which was folded into the Primary History.

This Primary History is thus a nine-book account of Israel's story from creation to the exile. As we have suggested, this may be considered "The First Bible": Genesis, Exodus, Leviticus, Numbers, Deuteronomy, Joshua, Judges, 1–2 Samuel (as

2 Based on chronological links with Babylonian history. Because the account does not extended to Cyrus's edict of 539 BCE ending the exile, we assume the historian wrote prior to that date.

SIDEBAR 4.4. SPINOZA ON BIBLICAL STUDIES

Benedict (Baruch) de Spinoza (1632–1677) was in many ways the founder of modern biblical studies. His parents emigrated to Holland from Portugal seeking religious tolerance. Influenced profoundly by René Descartes (1596–1650), Isaac La Peyrère (1596–1676), and Thomas Hobbes (1588–1679), Spinoza employed critical discussion of the OT in his own political writings. His 1670 work *Theological and Political Treatise* applied to the reading of the OT methods used to study nature. Spinoza essentially turned Israel's Scriptures into an object for study instead of merely a source of metaphysical knowledge.

4.3. Spinoza. Benedict (Baruch) de Spinoza, 1632–1677. (Photo: The Art Archive at Art Resource, N.Y.)

one book), and 1–2 Kings (as one book). More than three centuries ago, the Jewish philosopher Benedict de Spinoza observed an intentional interconnection and unifying theme in these books. Each book of the Pentateuch begins with a link to the previous book, and such connecting links continue into the Former Prophets. So, as Spinoza observed, the death of Moses, recorded at the end of Deuteronomy, opens Joshua, with "after the death of Moses …" And the death of Joshua opens Judges, "after the death of Joshua …" The book of Judges concludes with the repeated note that Israel had no king in those days, which prepares the reader for the narrative in which a king is demanded and provided in 1 Samuel.[3] The story of David is not finished in 2 Samuel but leads on to 1 Kings, completing the unity of the nine books.

As Spinoza observed, these nine books have no particular titles of their own, and are therefore not self-contained documents with their own internal plot and unity. Instead, they are intentionally linked or edited together to provide a continuous unity in the telling of Israel's history. The theme that holds the Primary History together is the covenant that Yahweh made with Israel at Mount Sinai and the Ten Commandments.[4] The book of Deuteronomy, which reemphasizes the covenant and repeats the Ten Commandments, is deliberately placed at the center of the Primary History as the pivot for the entire work.

So this great work is a symmetrical whole, with Deuteronomy's covenant at its center. The historian in this case has woven together Israel's two earliest historical complexes – the Yahwistic History and the Deuteronomistic History – and combined

3 Benedictus de Spinoza, *Complete Works* (ed. M. L. Morgan; trans. S. Shirley; Indianapolis, Ind.: Hackett Publishing, 2002), 477–78. Spinoza included Ruth in his series, which I believe is mistaken.

4 This particular theme is the focus of David Noel Freedman's definition of the Primary History; see Freedman in "Where to Find More" in this chapter.

them with additional priestly legal and other materials to write the First Bible. It tells the story of Israel's four major covenants, with Noah, Abraham, Moses, and David. And it presents the historical framework around which the rest of the OT is written. Since the series contains nine books, it is sometimes known as the **"Enneateuch,"** from the Greek *enneateuchos* (*ennea* "nine" and *teuchos* "scroll"), or nine-book scroll. The books are arranged strictly according to content.

Genesis

The first book in the series is Genesis and, of course, a good place to begin. (Have a contemporary translation of the OT nearby for this section, and skim the occasional references.) As a book of "beginnings" (Greek *genesis*, "birth, beginning"), this book recounts the beginning of the universe, and then of national Israel's ancestry. The first portion of Genesis tells of the creation of the universe in a way that explains for Israel why things are as they are (Genesis 1–11). The world is wonderful because God created it as a perfect paradise. But human rebellion ruined paradise. God flooded the world to give humans a second chance. But the second chance also didn't solve the problem, which is humankind's apparently limitless capacity for wrongdoing. No matter how gracious or patient God is with humans, they find a way of rebelling or of trying to usurp his authority.

The second portion of Genesis opens with yet another second chance (Genesis 12–50). God forges a new and intimate relationship with Abram and Sarai, who become Abraham and Sarah because of their unique covenant bond with Yahweh. This covenant with Israel's ancestors is marked by promises of land and descendants, and it becomes the foundation for future Israel's relationship with God. But the book also tells of a detour in this plan. The grandchildren and great-grandchildren of Abraham and Sarah leave the land promised to them and live in Egypt, through circumstances narrated in the Joseph story at the book's conclusion (Genesis 37–50).

Exodus

The second book opens with Abraham's grandchildren hopelessly enslaved in cruel bondage in Egypt. In response to their cry for help, Yahweh prepares and sends Moses to deliver them from slavery. By means of ten spectacular interventions in nature, the "ten plagues," Yahweh delivers the Israelites and guides them across the Re(e)d Sea, again miraculously, into the safety of the Sinai Peninsula. The first portion of the book of Exodus relates this deliverance ("departure, exit"; Greek *exodos*) from Egypt and Israel's safe passage to Sinai (Exodus 1–18).

The book of Exodus is about more than salvation from Egypt. In fact, over half the book is about the covenant relationship that Yahweh establishes with Israel at Mount Sinai, including the Ten Commandments and their explanations (Exodus 19–24), and the construction of a tabernacle as an appropriate place of worship (Exodus 25–40). Since Israel is not yet a settled people living permanently in the land, they are not ready for a temple, a permanent building for Yahweh's presence. Instead, Yahweh will reside in a tent, or tabernacle, similar to their own family tents. Yahweh's tent-tabernacle will be placed in the midst of the twelve tribes, and serve as the focal point of their worship. At the conclusion of the book, the covenant is established, and Yahweh's glorious presence fills the newly constructed tabernacle. (See the theoretical reconstruction of the tabernacle in the Sinai Desert in Figure 8.1).

Leviticus

The third book of the Bible suspends the narrative of Israel's history long enough to establish the rituals and regulations for the proper worship of Yahweh. Yet even here, the historical narrative of the Primary History is nearby to provide context. The entire book is presented as the instructions for righteous living given by Yahweh to Moses during the fourteen-month period when they were encamped at Mount Sinai.

The conclusion of the book of Exodus establishes a proper tabernacle for worship. It explains *where* Israel is to worship Yahweh, but not *how*. Leviticus (Greek *leuitikos*, "concerning to the Levites") is so named because it provides for Israel all things relating to the Levitical priesthood and other issues concerning worship. Acceptable forms of various sacrifices open the book (Leviticus 1–7), followed by acceptable priestly representation (Leviticus 8–10). Together these instructions make it possible for the people of Israel to have their sins atoned for, or forgiven, so they may live in harmony with Yahweh. This is followed by instructions for cleanness in order for Israel to avoid impurities harmful to the nation (Leviticus 11–16). Finally, the book closes with more instructions to ensure the holiness of the people and priests, and

on numerous other topics related to the nation's life with God (Leviticus 17–27). The theme of this concluding portion is that Israel must have a character reflecting Yahweh's own holy character (Leviticus 19:2). So the book of Leviticus is about becoming holy (Leviticus 1–16) and staying holy (Leviticus 17–27).

Numbers

The fourth book of the Primary History has a rather unfortunate name, "Numbers" (Greek *Arithmoi*). The book has this name because it contains two census reports, in which the people of Israel are numbered (Numbers 1 and 26). In reality, the book of Numbers is about far more than this, as it follows the Israelites geographically from Mount Sinai to a location known as Kadesh Barnea on the southern border of the promised land, and finally to the plains of Moab on the eastern border of the promised land.

The opening chapters take up where the book of Exodus leaves off, providing more laws and instructions for the Israelites before their departure from Mount Sinai (Numbers 1–10). Along the journey, however, the Israelites reject Yahweh's leadership and rebel against him in ways that make it impossible for them to succeed. They fail to maintain the covenant relationship with God and, as a consequence, that generation of Israelites is not permitted to fulfill the promise of the covenant. Instead of entering the promised land, they wander in the desert for forty years until the generation dies out (Numbers 10–20). The closing chapters relate their journey to the plains of Moab, across the Jordan Valley from the promised land, and narrate their final preparations and provisions for inheriting the land (Numbers 20–36). Unlike most biblical books, this one has a mixture of literary types, mixing laws with historical narrative but yielding a compelling portrait of Israel's sinful failure mixed with glorious potential and hope.

Deuteronomy

The fifth book of the Bible is unique. Its location at the center of the symmetrical Primary History makes it the final book of the Torah/Pentateuch, the books of Moses, but also the introduction and lead book of the Deuteronomistic History. It is both the culmination of the Torah and the foundation of the Historical Books.

The name is an unfortunate story. The Greek translators mistakenly took the phrase in Deuteronomy 17:18, "a copy of this law," as "a second law" (*deuteronomion*), which was then applied to the book. Yet oddly enough, the title is somewhat appropriate since the book is a recapitulation of Yahweh's covenant with Israel in the plains of Moab in addition to the original covenant of Sinai (Deuteronomy 29:1). It is truly a Second Law in that it repeats much of Exodus through Numbers.

This book presents farewell speeches of Moses in a literary outline known from ancient Near Eastern treaties. The great lawgiver first summarizes the relationship between Yahweh and Israel up to the people's presence on the plains of Moab (Deuteronomy 1–4). The law is then updated for a new generation of Israelites, in general terms, first (Deuteronomy 5–11) and then, in specific (Deuteronomy 12–26). Finally, the covenant is renewed, and the book closes with various related summarizing items such as the death of Moses (Deuteronomy 27–34).

Joshua

The sixth book of the **Enneateuch** is named after the leading character, Joshua, son of Nun, who had been Moses' assistant and was now his successor. Joshua is essentially a military general who leads the Israelites across the Jordan Valley and into the promised land.

The book of Joshua has roughly equal halves. The first portion narrates the conquest of the promised land (Joshua 1–12). Yahweh miraculously provides victory for Israel in central and southern campaigns, and then in a northern campaign that puts the entire Southern Levant in the hands of Joshua and the Israelites. The second portion of the book describes the allotment of the land to the different tribes of Israel, various other issues related to settlement, and a covenant renewal at Shechem (Joshua 13–24). This is no great accomplishment of military strength. Their covenant with Yahweh reminds the Israelites that the promised land is exactly what was promised in God's covenant with their ancestor Abraham. Failure to maintain that covenant relationship will result in failure to live in the land.

Judges

Book seven in the series continues the story but in a surprising way. The book of Judges covers the period from Joshua's death to the birth of Samuel, roughly Iron I (1200–1000 BCE). Here we have a different perception of the settlement period, one that seems almost to contradict the book of Joshua's portrait of miraculous conquest and settlement. The book is named after the military leaders who deliver the people of Israel from oppressors. Since these "judges" are rarely legal arbitrators, the English term is somewhat misleading.

In the book of Judges, Israel is organized as a confederation of tribes without a centralizing authority. It is a time of escalating religious unfaithfulness and social decay. The tribes repeatedly rebel against Yahweh and suffer the consequences in the form of invading enemies on all sides. When the people cry out for salvation, Yahweh raises individuals ("judges") from within the tribes to deliver them, and then peace is restored. Yet they go through a recurring cycle of rebellion, oppression, repentance, and deliverance. This cycle provides the literary structure for the book, which follows especially the actions of Othniel, Ehud, Deborah, Gideon, Jephthah, and Samson (the most prominent of the thirteen judges in the book). Gradually, the cycle illustrates the ever-escalating moral decline of the tribes of Israel, who are languishing without royal leadership. In this way, the book of Judges prepares the way for the establishment of kingship in ancient Israel and shows the kind of royal leadership needed for the nation.

Rather than contradicting each other, the books of Joshua and Judges are intended to be read side by side. Together, they present a well-rounded view of the settlement period. The people of God triumphantly took possession of the land and assigned allotments to the various tribes (Joshua), but they also failed to maintain Yahweh's covenant and struggled to occupy the land successfully (Judges). They conquered but failed to occupy the land.

1–2 *Samuel (as one book)*

The eighth book of the Bible introduces a new character, Samuel, for whom the whole composition is named. The books of Samuel begin with his leadership of Israel, in which he functions first as a prophet, but occasionally also as a judge and even a priest. His most important role is as a transition figure, guiding Israel from **theocracy** (tribal structure under the kingship of Yahweh alone) to monarchy. He becomes the "kingmaker," as the prophet responsible for anointing the first two kings of Israel.

The opening portion of the books of Samuel show again the need for a monarchy, as was clear from the book of Judges (1 Samuel 1–7). The priestly leadership is immoral, and the Israelites suffer terrible military losses to the Philistines. In this crisis, the Israelites request a king like that of other nations around them. Yahweh responds by providing a military leader who is like the previous judges. This time, however, he directs the prophet Samuel to anoint the new leader as a "prince," whose royal dynasty will lead Israel into the future.

The book then narrates the rise and fall of the first king of Israel, Saul (1 Samuel 8–15). A complex character, Saul begins well, but he tragically and inexplicably fails to grasp the nature of Israel's new monarchy. God, through the prophet Samuel, limits the power of Israel's kingship, making Israel's king quite different from the typical ancient Near Eastern ruler. Samuel anoints a second king, David, who is also imperfect as king (1 Samuel 16– 2 Samuel 24). The extended narrative of the rest of the books of Samuel illustrate that despite King David's personal failures, he is capable of grasping the limited nature of Israel's new monarchy. The books of Samuel, relying on the covenant and retribution theology of Deuteronomy, demonstrate what kind of monarchy is acceptable in ancient Israel, and who may serve suitably as king. In a word, Yahweh must remain Israel's true king, and the human king must always be the second in command, king in name only. The books of Samuel illustrate this principle (and warning) for all future kings of Israel.

1–2 Kings (as one book)

The ninth book of the **Enneateuch** continues the narrative from David's son, Solomon, through the destruction of northern Israel (722 BCE) and Judah (586 BCE). It gives an account of all the kings of Israel; hence the name. Each king is introduced by literary formulas, and each in turn is evaluated based on the Mosaic ideal of kingship (Deuteronomy 17:14–20).

Sadly, the people of God experience few good kings; most of their rulers do not live up to the ideal. The account opens with the impressive beginnings of the reign of Solomon, a king who nevertheless failed to worship Yahweh exclusively (1 Kings 1–11). His failure resulted in the division of the kingdom into two new entities, Israel in the north and Judah in the south. The remainder of the books of Kings detail the gradual decay of both nations, with only brief interludes of hope. Kings of Israel and Judah are presented in review, like participants in a parade passing before the grandstands (1 Kings 12–2 Kings 17). After the fall of Samaria in the north, the account continues with the kings of Judah alone, until the fall

of Jerusalem (2 Kings 18–25). Through the entire composition, a gradual sense of increasing apostasy becomes inevitable. The historian is convinced of the Deuteronomic teaching of retribution: obedience to God's covenant brings success and disobedience brings failure. In this way, the historian explains the failure of Israel and Judah, but hopes to ensure a future for God's people.

Finally, let us return to Spinoza for one final observation. As we said, he noted the careful way in which these nine books are connected by narrative links into a continuous narrative thread. They have no separate individual titles, or, as they are sometimes called, superscriptions. Interestingly, Spinoza also observed that most of the other OT books *do* have a variety of such superscriptions, or labeling titles, marking each book as a self-contained unit. These other OT books may be read independently. Yet because of their superscriptions, they may also be read in conjunction with the Primary History. Its title or superscription gives each book a certain context from the perspective of Israel's history.[5] Two examples of such links to the Primary History are the book of Ruth, which opens with "in the days when the judges ruled," and the book of Ecclesiastes, which begins with "the words of the Teacher, the son of David, king in Jerusalem." Most of the books of prophecy open with similar links, associating a particular book with some specific moments in Israel's history narrated in the **Enneateuch**. There are a few exceptions, but the idea is simply that the Primary History provides the historical framework for the entire OT.

5 The books of Ezra, Nehemiah, and 1 and 2 Chronicles may be exceptions, partly because they themselves are historical books.

This is a helpful way to understand the books in Israel's library. The Primary History provides a metanarrative for the whole. The books of hymns, prophecy, and poetic wisdom are in most cases intentionally hooked into this grand narrative sweep provided by the **Enneateuch**. Thus, in a most general sense, the entire OT has a simple two-part design based on history writing. On the one hand, we have the broad historical sweep of the Primary History, which combines all of Israel's earliest historical traditions with the priestly law. On the other hand, this Primary History, or **Enneateuch**, provides an entrée to all the rest of the books of Israel's library by establishing the historical context.

WHERE TO FIND MORE

Amit, Yaira. *History and Ideology: An Introduction to Historiography in the Hebrew Bible*. Biblical Seminar 60. Sheffield, Eng.: Sheffield Academic Press, 1999.

Argues that Israel's choice of history writing as a literary genre is related to the nature of monotheistic faith. The rejection of mythological explanations of the divine resulted in learning about God by means of his connection with his people, Israel. The past became the platform for observing and studying God.

Freedman, David Noel. *The Unity of the Hebrew Bible*. Ann Arbor: University of Michigan Press, 1991.

A most creative way of understanding the Primary History (pp. 1–39). Freedman's use of "Nine Commandments" to explain the unity of the books in the Primary History is unconvincing, but his point about unity is established without that particular argument.

Friedman, Richard Elliott. *Who Wrote the Bible?* San Francisco: HarperSanFrancisco, 1997.

Overview of many topics covered in this chapter.

Friedman, Richard Elliott. *The Hidden Book in the Bible*. San Francisco: HarperSanFrancisco, 1998.

Explains the possibility that a single author, often known as the Yahwist and living in the ninth century BCE, wrote a continuous story from the creation of the world to the Davidic kingdom to David's successor, Solomon.

Frymer-Kensky, Tikva. *In the Wake of the Goddesses: Women, Culture, and the Biblical Transformation of Pagan Myth*. New York: Free Press, 1992.

Explains how features of other deities of antiquity were combined and absorbed in the image of Yahweh in the OT. Chapter 8, pages 83–99, is especially helpful in showing how Israel's belief in the oneness of Yahweh transformed its thinking about nature, culture, gender, humanity, and so on. The author shows how Israel's monotheism made possible a surprisingly egalitarian view of men and women.

Halpern, Baruch. *The First Historians: The Hebrew Bible and History*. San Francisco: Harper & Row, 1988.

Sparks, Kenton L. *Ancient Texts for the Study of the Hebrew Bible: A Guide to the Background Literature*. Peabody, Mass.: Hendrickson Publishers, 2005.

Contains useful discussions of both myth (chap. 10, pp. 305–43) and history (chap. 12, pp. 361–416).

Van Seters, John. *In Search of History: Historiography in the Ancient World and the Origins of Biblical History*. New Haven, Conn.: Yale University Press, 1983.

CHAPTER 5

Beginnings

OLD TESTAMENT READING: GENESIS 1–11

The first eleven chapters of Genesis – and of the OT – constitute the Primeval History. This carefully arranged collection of traditions detail God's good creation of the cosmos, the nature of humanity in the created order of the universe, and God's relationship with humans. In this chapter, we will explore various genres such as cosmogony, theogony, myth, and history, all of which will help to demonstrate ways in which Israel's Primeval History resembled the traditions of its ancient neighbors and ways in which Israel's form and content were completely unique.

Importantly, Genesis 1–11 prepare the reader for the rest of the Bible. They also function as an explanation for Israelite readers of why things are the way they are. Furthermore, they introduce themes that will be central throughout the remainder of the OT: the concept of creation, the unchallenged sovereignty of God, the central role of humanity, and the first mention of covenant.

What would you expect to find at the very beginning of Israel's library? If Israelite authors had been focused primarily on writing a national history, we might have expected them to begin straightaway with an account of their ancestors, the patriarchs and matriarchs who became the great-grandparents of all Israel. We'll get to that story later (Genesis 12–50). But here, in the opening chapters of the Bible, we learn that Israel's interests are broader and deeper than that. What we have here might surprise you.

Israel was not one of the great powers of the ancient Near East, as you will remember from Chapter 3. In fact, Israel's legacy and its influence

5.1. Michelangelo's *Creation of Adam*. Painted around 1511 on the ceiling of the Sistine Chapel, Michelangelo's *Creation of Adam* has become one of the most iconic images of world art, depicting God and Adam at the moment of humanity's creation. (Photo: Alinari / Art Resource, N.Y.)

on world philosophy and theology are out of proportion to the relatively insignificant role the nation played politically. And so, the OT opens, not with an account of Israel's ancestors, but with God and with a theological claim that Israel's God created the entire universe. The chapters in Genesis 1–11 are a collection of traditions about God's creation of the cosmos, the nature of humans in the created order of the universe, and God's relationship with humans. All of these are arranged carefully, with intentional detail.

What gives Israel the right to speak about such grandiose and sweeping topics? The Egyptians and

Mesopotamians had their own accounts of cosmic structure and order. Yet their creation stories were not presented in such an all-encompassing and inclusive manner as Genesis 1–11. And their explanations were lost in the sands of time, to be rediscovered only relatively recently. Egyptian and Mesopotamian theories of cosmic origins had little impact on world thought and philosophy. They have been rediscovered and deciphered and interpreted by scholars only over the past one hundred fifty years.

It may seem audacious for Israel to have offered explanations for …, well, for everything! But with bold confidence, the OT opens with precisely such explanations. Israel's God is and acts completely alone, without help from the gods of Egypt or Mesopotamia. In fact, those other gods aren't even present. Israel's God creates a good universe without any divine competitors, and he sets out to have a relationship with the human beings he created for the world. We have identified Israel's monotheism as one of the most important Axial Age developments of human civilization. But that monotheism is not explicitly stated in these opening chapters of the Bible. Instead, we encounter here something more like monolatrous henotheism, as we said in Chapter 1. Yet this exclusive commitment to the one Creator God of the universe gives the opening chapters of the OT a unique cohesiveness. And these first eleven chapters of the OT have had unprecedented authority in world thought; they present us with a truly remarkable beginning.

THE PRIMEVAL HISTORY: GENESIS 1–11

We cannot cover in this textbook all the materials of the OT in depth. My purpose in this chapter is to introduce you to the highlights, pointing out a few important issues for interpretation. If you haven't yet read Genesis 1–11 carefully, please stop now and read it to prepare for this discussion. You will find in these chapters a mixture of narrative and genealogical-type lists, with an overarching thematic unity imposed on the whole.

The book of Genesis has two portions. First comes the **Primeval History** (Genesis 1–11) and then the ancestral narratives (Genesis 12–50), which we will discuss in the next chapter. By using "primeval" in the title for this first portion, I don't mean that it is primitive in any way. I mean, instead,

that this part of Genesis is about the first or earliest eras of the universe and of human civilization. These chapters are really about the beginning of everything. The use of "history" for these chapters is also tricky, but we'll come to that later.

The second portion of Genesis – the ancestral narratives – tells of Abraham, Isaac, and Jacob, and includes the story of Joseph embedded near the conclusion. These accounts prepare for what follows in Exodus, Leviticus, Numbers, and Deuteronomy (Exodus 2:24; Deuteronomy 1:8 and 34:4). By contrast, the first portion of Genesis – the Primeval History – is hardly mentioned in the rest of the Torah at all. Yet these chapters are also preparing you as a reader, not just for the Torah but also for the rest of the Bible. The themes of the Primeval History are central to the message of the remaining parts of the OT.

The first chapter of the Bible is one of the most profound texts you will ever read. It isn't poetry, but the prose of Genesis 1 is so graceful and lilting that it reminds you of poetry. It doesn't begin by arguing for the existence of God or by defending Israel's God as supreme over other gods. Instead, it simply assumes God's singular existence and quickly shows what kind of God we're dealing with by describing his actions and the universe he creates. This God creates by simple command, without effort or exhaustion: "God said, … and so light appeared" (Genesis 1:3). After calling light into existence, God then systematically creates everything else. He adds symmetry and beauty to the cosmos, and seems deeply pleased with his work. Everything God does is "good." Humankind is especially good. God creates the first human couple as the climactic conclusion to the rest of the work. He finishes the work on the seventh day and makes that day holy for all

SIDEBAR 5.1. HISTORICAL AND PRIESTLY TRADITIONS OF GENESIS 1–11

In the previous chapter, we discussed the oldest sources of the Pentateuch, designated by the letters J, E, P, H, and D. The first of these sources comes from Israel's historical traditions, the Yahwistic History (J), and possibly an Elohistic History from northern Israel (E), although we have less confidence in what we know about this one. These two were combined into a unified narrative, JE, probably soon after the fall of the northern capital, Samaria, in 722 BCE.

What we have now in the book of Genesis is a combination of these historical traditions from early Israel with priestly materials. These are usually designated with P for "priestly." So Genesis 1, for example, has distinctive priestly phraseology, as well as themes important to the priests: Sabbath keeping; specifics of the animal kingdom as preparation for Israel's dietary laws; and specifics of the sun, moon, and stars as markers of times and seasons for Israel's sacred festivals. Similarly, the genealogies of the Primeval History have priestly origins (Genesis 5 and 10, as well as Genesis 11:10–26). There was a separate priestly flood account, which has been melded into the current flood narrative (see Sidebar 6.2).

Today's scholars are not agreed about how and when these priestly materials were combined with the Yahwistic History into Genesis 1–11. Some believe much of what we have in P has been expanded and edited by holiness authors, and thus "H" is sometimes used. But in general, this gives you an idea how Israel's historical and priestly materials were blended. We will return to this topic later (in Chapter 8).

time. Every week in human history is like a stroll through God's wonderful creation.

After this, we have several narratives that were once part of Israel's first great historical work, the Yahwistic History introduced earlier (see Chapter 4). This includes the Eden narrative (Genesis 2:4–3: 24), the Cain and Abel story (Genesis 4), the flood story now combined with other materials (Genesis 6–9), and the Tower of Babel episode (Genesis 11:1–9). These have been combined with other sources in Genesis 1–11, mostly priestly materials.

The Eden narrative (Genesis 2:4–3:24) is a story of tragic loss. Yahweh fashioned a beautiful home for the first humans, Paradise Garden. The name "Eden" represents pleasure and luxury. The first human couple, known simply as Man (or Every-Man, "Adam") and Life-Giver ("Eve"), had a perfect existence surrounded by luxury. They also enjoyed

easy familiarity and acceptance before Yahweh and with each other. All was perfect. But their refusal to allow Yahweh to be God alone ruined it all. They listened to the serpent in Paradise Garden (no attempt is made to explain why the serpent was permitted entrance) and decided to become like Yahweh. Their decision to disobey Yahweh's one simple command was a rebellious action that cost them everything, including access to Paradise Garden forever. Were it not for the gracious actions of Yahweh to protect and provide for them after they were banished from the garden, they would not have survived at all.

Outside Paradise Garden, life begins to take shape as the Israelite authors know it (Genesis 4). Adam and Eve's children quarrel, and violence ensues. Cain kills his brother Abel. The first act of murder illustrates just how far the humans have come from Paradise Garden, and how

We saw in Chapter 1 that Israel's name for God was YHWH, perhaps pronounced "Yahweh" (see Sidebar 1.2 for theories about this name). At some point early in Israel's history, this name for God was considered so holy, deemed so sacred and blessed, that it was thought best not to utter it aloud. The scribes who preserved the Hebrew text provided marks and signs for pronunciation of other words but made an exception for the name YHWH. Rather than guide the reader in a way to vocalize the name, they came up with an ingenious way of highlighting the name's importance. They superimposed the signs and marks for a different word, *adonai*, "the Lord," over the letters for YHWH. Their suggestion for Jews reading the text was simply to say "adonai" ("my lord") when reading the text aloud instead of actually saying God's name.

The Septuagint translation followed this lead, frequently using the Greek word "lord" (*kyrios*) to translate YHWH. Most of today's English translations also follow this lead, using "LORD" (note the small caps) for the sacred name YHWH in the OT. Take a moment now to see how the translation you're using handles Genesis 2:15: "The LORD God took the man and put him in the garden of Eden." Whenever you see "LORD" with small caps you will know that the original Hebrew text has YHWH.

quickly. In a world quite different from Paradise Garden, other sons and daughters of Adam and Eve establish the religious, cultural, and social institutions of human existence. These include urban dwellers and tent-dwelling nomads, musicians, metalworkers and herdsmen, and religious innovators (Genesis 4:17–26). These narratives have the purpose of explaining for Israelite readers why things are the way they are (known as "etiologies," explaining the causes or origins of something).

The priestly genealogy of Genesis 5 breaks the primeval period into ages, from Adam to Noah in the tenth generation. This genealogy is picked up again at the conclusion of the Primeval History to trace the descendants of Noah through ten more generations, from his son Shem to Abram (Genesis 11:10–26). While genealogies may seem boring to read, they play a central role in the literary structure of the Primeval History. They probably also played an important role in the social and cultural context of ancient Israel.

The pattern of the genealogy changes with Noah, where for the first time it segments at his generation, listing his three sons Shem, Ham, and Japheth (Genesis 5:32). It serves then to introduce the story of the great flood, which is a complex narrative combining historical and priestly traditions into a unified account (Genesis 6–9). The rebellion of Adam and Eve, Cain, Lamech, and indeed of all humanity has escalated beyond control: "The LORD saw that the wickedness of humankind was great in the earth, and that every inclination of the thoughts of their hearts was only evil continually" (Genesis 6:5). Heartbroken, Yahweh regrets making humanity and determines to annihilate them and everything else he had created (Genesis 6:6–7). Noah's singular righteousness changes Yahweh's plan. Noah, his family, and the animals were saved from the great flood in a specially crafted vessel of Yahweh's own design. After the flood, God blesses Noah and his family, and establishes a covenant with him. This is the Bible's first use of "covenant" (*bĕrît*), which will be one of the most important topics we cover.

5.2. The Ziggurat of Ur. The reconstructed northeast façade of the ziggurat, from approximately 2100 BCE. Most such stepped towers of southern Mesopotamia were of three to seven stages. A famed ziggurat of Babylon was likely the inspiration for the account of the Tower of Babel in Genesis 11. (Photo: © World Religions Photo Library / The Bridgeman Art Library)

The Table of Nations (Genesis 10) picks up with the sons of Noah again and sounds at first like a typical genealogy. But in a way quite different from Adam's genealogy of Genesis 5, this one presents a snapshot of the entire human race in the post-flood era. Descendants of Noah's sons are listed according to their families, languages, lands, and nations. Sometimes the names in this list are individuals, as we would expect in a genealogy. But at other times they are locations (Egypt, Canaan, etc.) or whole people groups (Jebusites, etc.). In this way, the Table of Nations provides a kind of ethnic map of the world for Israelite readers.

After the flood, Noah's sons grow into the peoples and nations described in the Table of Nations, and spread out over the earth (Genesis 10:32). The Tower of Babel (Genesis 11) is out of place

chronologically because it explains how humanity came to be displaced. It has been put after the Table of Nations most likely to illustrate the continued problem of human rebellion. The mutinous tendencies of pre-flood humanity have exited the ark with Noah's family and now continue among his descendants. Unified in their rebellion, the humans build a city and tower as symbols of their human pride. Yahweh introduces distinct languages as a way of dispersing and fragmenting wayward humanity.

THE CONCEPT OF "CREATION," AND THE NEED TO EXPLAIN ORIGINS

We humans instinctively ask questions about the origin and nature of the universe. Life on planet earth arouses such awe and curiosity. It naturally raises questions, and this inquisitiveness is part of what it means to be human. How did this amazing universe come into existence? Why is it here? What sustains it and keeps it running? A theory answering these questions is called a "**cosmology**," a specific model for understanding the structure and dynamics of the physical universe. These questions lead to still others about human life. Why are we here? Why do we act and live as we do? Why do we relate to each other as we do, sometimes in fulfilling and healthy relationships but sometimes in violence and discord? Why is death inevitable? What divine forces are at work in it all?

Israel's Primeval History in Genesis 1–11 provides answers to these questions. This is Israel's cosmological answer. Beyond its creation accounts, this first portion of Genesis sets up other essential ideas as background for the rest of the OT, as we shall see. But Israel was not alone in answering such questions. The great civilizations of the ancient Near East had their own cosmologies, their own theories for explaining the universe and the way things work in the world. These theories were complex and multifaceted because of polytheism. The presence of multiple divine forces in nature requires an explanation of the universe that makes sense of the diversity and complexity of the world. By contrast, Israel's implicit monotheism – or at this stage, monolatrous henotheism (see Chapter 1 on these terms) – sets off the OT's cosmological beginnings as unique.

In the next section, I will introduce a few of the most important creation accounts of the ancient Near East. For the meantime, think of them as two types: **theogony** ("origin of the gods") and **cosmogony** ("origin of the universe"). These are somewhat overlapping, so it is a matter of emphasis. The theogony explains the universe by recounting the birth and succession of the gods (Greek, *theos*, "god," plus -*gonia*, a suffix from the root *ginomai*, "be born, come about"), especially of those gods perceived as ancient and influential at the beginning. Theogonies use language of time, primordial long-age days, at the beginning. Such bygone epochs are the source of the structures of reality, establishing for all times the dynamics of the universe, to which gods and humans alike are subject. Theogonies also explain the gods as living in families, usually led by pairs of gods coupled in opposite realms (e.g., sky and earth), who procreate and become parents of other gods.

The second type of creation account in the ancient Near East is the cosmogony (Greek, *kosmos*, "world," plus the same suffix -*gonia*). Cosmogonies locate the origin of the universe in a great conflict between old and young gods. The young gods win this colossal battle. Afterward, kingship is established among the gods and the cosmic order is set for all time. The institution of human kingship is modeled after cosmic government. In this way, human kingship is justified and sustained by religious rites and practices. Most ancient Near Eastern creation accounts combine the two types – theogony and cosmogony – using the theogony as a prologue to the cosmogony. So pairs of ancient gods give birth to younger gods in bygone primordial days (theogony), which sets up the conflict between gods of different generations (cosmogony). The universe is then born as a result of this conflict (see Plate III).

As you can easily see, the contrast with Israel's creation accounts is pretty dramatic. Take for example, Genesis 1. There is no cosmic battle here. God does not emerge victorious after struggling against older deities, eventually to become king of the universe. It has little in common with ancient Near Eastern cosmogonies. On the other hand, if you look closely, it *does* have literary features in common with the ancient theogonies. It opens with the language of time, which we will see later is characteristic for many creation acounts: "When God began to create …" The coupled gods in the ancient Near Eastern stories have become simple objects present at creation: heaven and earth, wind and water, darkness and light. No longer deities, these old venerated gods of the ancient myths have been demoted to simple natural objects. Israel has modified the literary theogony because of monolatrous henotheism.

In a sense, Genesis 1 is Israel's theogony literarily, serving as a prologue to a larger story. But this only highlights another difference. Genesis 1 does not introduce a different type of creation literature, a cosmogony with its titanic conflict. Instead, it prepares for and introduces Israel's grand epic history – Paradise Garden, the flood, the ancestors, and beyond. Instead of using the literary category theogony to introduce a conflict between the gods (cosmogony), as happens in other ancient Near Eastern creation accounts, Genesis 1 is a modified theogony used to introduce *a story* – Israel's story. The theory of cosmic origins is related briefly and only as a prologue to Israel's national history.

In our survey of the Primeval History, we noted the importance of genealogies in this first portion of Genesis (Genesis 5, 10, 11:10–26). But there's more. The author/editor of Genesis has adapted a type of genealogy to link Israel's theogony in Genesis 1 to the historical narratives. The expression "these

are the generations of the heavens and the earth" in Genesis 2:4 is used with little variation eleven times in Genesis to bring order to the whole book.[1] After this first example of the expression in 2:4, all the rest have to do with the descendants of a character in the narrative: Adam, Noah, Noah's sons, Shem, and so forth. In other words, the divine coupling, birthing, and parenting of younger gods in ancient theogonies has been replaced in Genesis with the coupling, birthing, and parenting of the leading characters in Israel's story. In the Primeval History in Genesis 1–11, theogony has been transformed into a genealogy of humanity's earliest ancestors. And it doesn't introduce a divine conflict to explain the origins of the universe but instead introduces Israel's historical traditions.

ANCIENT NEAR EASTERN PARALLELS

Israel's neighbors in the ancient Near East also gave answers to the cosmological questions. We have numerous literary traditions from across the Fertile Crescent concerning creation and early human history. Here I can introduce you to only the most important of these. We will focus on the ones most helpful for comparison with Israel's Primeval History in Genesis 1–11.

From Egypt we have an inscription on a monument placed in the temple of the god Ptah at Memphis. It is most likely from the thirteenth century BCE and is known as the *Memphite Theology*. In this text, the god Ptah created other deities by the simple expression of his heart and tongue. That which Ptah planned in his heart was commanded

---

1 Genesis 2:4, 5:1, 6:9, etc.

SIDEBAR 5.3. SOURCES FOR ANCIENT NEAR EASTERN TEXTS

The OT was preserved in Hebrew and translated into many ancient languages down through the ages. It has a continuous history. By contrast, sources for texts from the ancient Near East were for the most part completely lost in antiquity. Once explorers to the Middle East began finding the texts, it was decades before anyone could read them. Egyptian **hieroglyphics** and Mesopotamian **cuneiform** were deciphered only about a century and a half ago. Since then, thousands of texts have been discovered in archaeological excavations.

Translations of these texts are often available only in obscure scholarly venues, and sometimes in languages other than English. Fortunately, the ones considered especially helpful for comparisons with the OT have frequently been collected in English translation. An older work that is still helpful at times and was originally published in 1950, significantly expanded in a third edition in 1969, and released in a new format in 2011, is James B. Pritchard, ed., *The Ancient Near East: An Anthology of Texts and Pictures* (Princeton, N.J.: Princeton University Press, 2011). The best source for most of the texts discussed here is the three-volume William W. Hallo and K. Lawson Younger, eds., *The Context of Scripture* (3 vols.; Leiden and New York: Brill, 1997–2002). The historical sources have been collected and translated in Mark W. Chavalas, ed., *The Ancient Near East: Historical Sources in Translation* (Malden, Mass.: Blackwell, 2006). Popular translations are available in Victor H. Matthews and Don C. Benjamin, *Old Testament Parallels: Laws and Stories from the Ancient Near East* (fully rev. and exp. 3rd ed.; New York: Paulist Press, 2006), and Bill T. Arnold and Bryan E. Beyer, eds., *Readings from the Ancient Near East: Primary Sources for Old Testament Study* (Grand Rapids, Mich.: Baker Academic, 2002). If you are interested in reading any of the texts we have covered here, use one of these translations. For bibliography on them, you should also see Sparks in the "Where to Find More" section at the end of this chapter.

by his tongue in divine speech, and thus the creation of other deities was accomplished. Ptah's creation by divine decree is similar to "God said, ... and it was so" (Genesis 1:9). After his creative work, Ptah "rested," also reminiscent of God's Sabbath rest (Genesis 2:2–3).

Another fascinating text from ancient Egypt is the *Instructions to Merikare*, a composition of wisdom literature that may be as old as the twenty-first century BCE. Here the creator deity (*ntr*, "god"), who in these wisdom texts is often unnamed as an abstract general concept, performs creative and protective actions for humanity. The following excerpt has so many similarities to Genesis 1 that it has been called "the little Genesis."

Well tended is humankind — god's cattle,
he made sky and earth for their sake,
he subdued the water monster,
he made breath for their noses to live.
They are his images, who came from his body,
he shines in the sky for their sake;
he made for them plants and cattle,
fowl and fish to feed them.
He slew his foes, reduced his children,
when they thought of making rebellion.[2]

From Mesopotamia, we have the *Epic of Atrahasis*, which can be dated to around 1700 BCE but may

2 Adapted from Miriam Lichtheim, *Ancient Egyptian Literature: A Book of Readings* (3 vols.; Berkeley: University of California Press, 1973–1980), 1:106.

have been composed much earlier. The text opens with conflict between the high gods and the lesser deities who were forced to dig irrigation canals by their superiors. The lesser deities complain and demand release from their menial labor. As a solution, the high gods create humankind to assume responsibility for doing undesirable physical work and providing for the gods. In time, humans multiply to such an extent that their raucous noise irritates the high gods, a few of whom devise a plan to exterminate humanity in a great flood. One of the humans is warned in advance of the flood, and he survives in a boat, together with his family and all species of animals. This survivor, Atrahasis, whose name means "ultrawise," is the hero of the epic. A feature of this text making it especially instructive for comparison with the OT is the combination of creation and the great flood in a unified narrative, so that it is similar to the Primeval History not only in themes but also in basic structure.

Perhaps the best-known text from Mesopotamia is the *Epic of Creation*, also known by its Akkadian title **Enuma Elish**. The text was probably composed around the eleventh century BCE. Although we refer to the *Enuma Elish* as a creation myth, the central theme is the rise of Marduk, chief deity of the city of Babylon, and a defense of his supremacy at the head of the pantheon. This seven-tablet composition begins with a coupling and the birthing of the high gods, which prepares for the cosmic battle between Tiamat, the monstrous goddess of ocean water, and Marduk. Victorious Marduk kills Tiamat and creates the universe from her carcass. This epic best illustrates the use of theogony (birth of gods) to prepare for cosmogony (birth of the universe).

5.3. Cuneiform tablet relating the Epic of Creation. Dated to the seventh century BCE, this tablet was excavated at Nineveh. (Photo: © The Trustees of the British Museum / Art Resource, N.Y.)

The twelve-tablet masterpiece, the *Gilgamesh Epic*, is comparable in scope and literary grandeur to Homer's *Odyssey*. It is the longest, and usually considered the greatest, literary composition from Mesopotamia (see Plate IV). Copies have come to us from nearly every period of history, including the early second millennium, which even had Sumerian precursors. The epic tells the account of ancient king Gilgamesh of the city of Uruk and of how he rebelled against death when he saw his friend, Enkidu, experience it. Through many twists and turns, the epic follows Gilgamesh through numerous adventures and travels, meeting and conquering distant regions, fighting monsters, but slowly coming to realize that death is inescapable. At one point, he listens to the advice of a barmaid, who reminds him that because eternal life has been reserved for the gods, the best thing he can do is to appreciate fully the joys of life, such as food and family, as long as life lasts. Gilgamesh returns to his city, takes pride in its splendor, and accepts his fate.

The quest for eternal life is answered in the Primeval History when Adam and Eve are locked out of Paradise Garden, with its lifegiving tree (Genesis 3:22–24). But the most striking parallel of the Gilgamesh Epic is its story, on tablet eleven, of a great flood. While on his quest for immortality, Gilgamesh learns of only one immortal man, Utnapishtim, sometimes called the "Babylonian Noah." When Gilgamesh finds him, the king is surprised and disappointed to find an elderly man instead of someone young and vigorous. Utnapishtim had discovered immortality but not eternal youth. He explains to Gilgamesh how he had been forewarned of a divine plan to flood the world. He survived the deluge in a large reed boat accompanied by his family and pairs of all animals. But this event is unrepeatable, and gives Gilgamesh no hope for his own immortality. Several parallels with Genesis 6–9 demand explanation, and many think that the Israelite account is in some way or another dependent on the Mesopotamian story. For example, after Utnapishtim's boat came to rest on a mountain, he let loose a dove and then a swallow but both returned indicating that the birds could find no dry land. Finally, he let loose a raven, which did not return (Genesis 8:6–19). So Utnapishtim opened the boat and made sacrifices to the gods on the mountain (Genesis 8:20).

Finally, from Syria-Palestine, we have the *Baal Cycle*, written in a language called Ugaritic because it came from the Levantine city of Ugarit (see Map 3.4). This cycle of episodes from the fourteenth century BCE relates the struggles of the storm god, **Baal**, who gains the right to succeed the older deity, El, establishing supremacy in the pantheon. The collection explains how Baal defeats Yamm, the sea god, and Mot, the god of death, to secure kingship for himself. Baal's conflict with Yamm has similarities with the battle between Marduk and Tiamat in the *Enuma Elish*. One may be dependent on the other, but we at least have a common mythological theme at work here.

MYTH, EPIC, OR HISTORY? SOMETHING ELSE ENTIRELY? A QUESTION OF LITERARY TYPE

Exactly what kind of literature do we have in Israel's Primeval History? This is a question often addressed but difficult to answer. Most of the ancient Near Eastern texts we've just compared

5.4. The "Baal of Lightning" found in a sanctuary at ancient Ugarit. Often linked with features of the natural world central to agriculture, the West Semitic deity Baal was viewed as a storm god and especially associated with clouds, thunder, lightning, and rain. In this depiction, he brandishes a battle-mace overhead, while in his left hand, he holds a thunderbolt ending in a spearhead thrusting toward the ground. (Photo: Scala / Art Resource, N.Y.)

to Genesis 1–11 may be categorized as "myth" or "epic." Yet I have called these chapters the "Primeval *History*" and presented them as the first portion of the OT's Primary *History*. So which is it – myth, epic, or history?

The term "myth" is difficult to define, especially as a literary type. The ancient Near Eastern myths are stories told in a primordial otherworldly time, a time before history, when foundational events (usually actions of the gods) set in motion certain cosmic, cultural, and social institutions for all (real) time. So myths are usually stories about the gods and are intended to explain origins. God is certainly *the* lead character of Genesis 1–11 but not the *only* character. One need only review Genesis 5 to discover how many human characters we have here. And the Primeval History certainly explains the origins of things, such as why we have to work for sustenance, why women have pain in childbirth, why we don't like snakes, why we live in cities, why Israelites observe Sabbath, and many others. But we will see that the ancestral narratives in the rest of Genesis also share this interest in origins.

More importantly, remember that the Primeval History has been quite deliberately structured and then linked with the rest of Genesis by the use of genealogical notations, such as "these are the generations of the heavens and the earth" (2:4), or "this is the list of the descendants of Adam" (5:1), or "these are the descendants of Noah" (Genesis 6:9), and so forth. Rather than timeless events set in a primordial realm, these stories are quite intentionally tied to Israel's world all the way down to the ancestors, Abraham, Isaac, and Jacob. Whatever else the materials of Genesis 1–11 may be, they are not "myth."

Nor is "epic" entirely satisfactory. This term is used for traditional narrative collections relating events that are "normative," or give meaning to its readers. Such narratives in antiquity relate deeds of both gods and humans in a way that shape a national entity providing cultural foundations. "Epic" is appropriate in many ways for the Yahwistic History. But as Genesis 1–11 now stands, it has combined the Yahwistic (and perhaps Elohistic) epic strand with priestly materials. Genesis 1 and portions of the flood story in Genesis 6–9 are not narrative traditions in the same vein as the Eden narrative or Cain and Abel accounts. The use of "epic" is more appropriate for earlier Israelite narrative traditions, such as the Yahwistic History.

Nor is "history" strictly appropriate, even though I use it in "Primeval History" (stay with me here). Genesis 1–11 relates events that are unconnected to history itself. They cannot be so connected. This is so not only because they cannot be traced by archaeology or verified by references in other contemporary sources, as we might do in historical investigation. Beyond that, we have too many hints in the text of Genesis 1–11 that we are reading here about a time and place different from our own, detached from all historical moorings. There is a distinct "otherness" about a narrative whose characters are Everyman and Everywoman ("Adam" and "Eve"), who live in a garden named Paradise, with a tree of life and a tree of moral responsibility, and with talking serpents. This is not to mention the genealogy of Genesis 10, which includes among the descendants of Noah not only individuals but also peoples, nations, and geographical locations. These are not the tools of someone writing "history." That is not to assume none of these things

happened, which is a matter of personal opinion and faith.

I prefer to think of Genesis 1–11 as a unique type of literature. It serves the foundational function of myth in other ancient Near Eastern texts, but it also arranges things along a continuous chain of cause and effect, like history. It tells of beginnings and origins in primordial time like myth, but does so in a kind of historical chronicle. This is Israel's version of myth, but one presented in history-like form. The hyphenated label "mytho-historical" is the best way of thinking of Genesis 1–11.[3] But this would have been torturous and confusing in my headings, "the Primeval Myth-History." And so, Israel's version of cosmic beginnings uses a history-like chain of cause and effect like a historical chronicle; and thus, the "Primeval History."

THEMES OF THE PRIMEVAL HISTORY

Whatever label we use for the literature of Genesis 1–11, and however it may compare to ancient Near Eastern parallels, it nevertheless has a clear and unmistakable message. This first portion of the OT moves beyond a simple impulse to explain cosmic origins. The Primeval History has a distinctly religious intent. Here are a few of the most important themes you need to remember from the Primeval History before we continue with other portions of Israel's library.

First is the rather obvious importance of the concept of *creation*. The Primeval History has three

---

3 And has been proposed; see both Jacobsen and Miller in "Where to Find More" in this chapter.

accounts of creation, although the third presents the creation of humankind only.

> Genesis 1:1 – "When God began to create the heavens and the earth"
> Genesis 2:4b – "When the LORD God made the earth and the heavens"
> Genesis 5:1b – "When God created humankind"

Each introduces a new thread in the text and has its own distinctive way of emphasizing the various themes I want you to consider here. (Interestingly, they all have something else in common: each begins with a temporal clause, much like the *Enuma Elish* and the Atrahasis Epic. Apparently, ancient Near Eastern creation accounts begin with temporal clauses.) The OT will return to the creation story in different ways, emphasizing divine power, divine wisdom, or divine presence.[4] But nowhere else will we find such a systematic and inclusive treatment of creation than here at the beginning of the OT.

A second theme to remember from the Primeval History is the unchallenged *sovereignty* of God. Not only does the God of Genesis 1–11 have no rivals among other deities, he is no match for nature or humanity. Israel's conception of the cosmos in Genesis 1 is structured and orderly, the express thoughts of the mind of God, and spoken effortlessly into existence by God's decree. Genesis knows no impersonal, ultimate power

4 On these three models of creation in the OT, see Mark Smith in "Where to Find More" in this chapter.

beyond God, and therefore the cosmos is secure and whole. This also clarifies why the frequently cited difference between myth and history is inadequate to explain the distinctiveness of Israel in the ancient Near East. The idea of the singularity of God, his supreme reign as king (many royal images are also included here) over the universe, and his uncontested power is enough to explain Israel's distinctiveness. We have in these opening chapters the monolatrous henotheism we discussed in Chapter 1. These first chapters of the Bible inspire and invite a singular devotion to the creating and sustaining God, even though we have no explicit denial of the existence of other deities.

On this last point, consider the word "God" used here and elsewhere in the OT. The opening words, "When God began to create," uses *ʾĕlōhîm*, the most common word for God in the OT (occurring more than 2,500 times). In form and occasionally in meaning, it is plural, "gods," but oddly enough, it routinely takes singular verbs in the OT (as "create" in Genesis 1:1). In such cases, even the word selected for "God" indicates, at least implicitly, a singular quality about God. So without an explicit denial of other gods, the Primeval History opens the OT with a positive assertion about the singularity of God, which we may call implicit monotheism.

This conviction about God's nature gives Israel's cosmology a definite one-dimensional quality compared to the *Enuma Elish*, and other accounts from the ancient Near East. Devotion to only one God simplifies things considerably. Nature itself is objectified. The sun, moon, and stars, important deities in other cosmologies as high gods, become objects of God's creation, markers of times and seasons. There is no room for pantheism here, no simple equation of God with the universe itself. God is wholly separate from the universe, above and over it as its Creator and sustainer. Simplification may also be seen in the plurals used in divine deliberation: "Let us make humanity in our image" (Genesis 1:26, and compare 11:7). Other deities have been reduced to a sort of divine council, which God consults in the process of deciding something important. This illustrates the process by which Israel eventually comes to deny the other gods' existence altogether.

Third is the central importance of *humanity* in Genesis 1–11. Other creation accounts of the ancient Near East portray the creation of humans almost as an afterthought, to provide a needed work force to help with undesirable physical labor after lesser gods complained. But in the Primeval History, humans are the centerpiece of the created order. Adam and Eve do not live in a world of competing deities. Humans are created to inhabit a space and time expressly made for them, which is "good" in every respect, and which makes it possible for them to relate rightly to God, trusting without manipulating. The "image" and "likeness" of God (*imago Dei*, Genesis 1:26–27) is royal terminology used in the ancient world to portray a king or pharaoh as the divinely appointed representative of the kingdom. Humans are created to exercise God's dominion over creation, as God's representatives, reinforced by "and let them have dominion over." God's rulership over creation has been democratized in humanity. Even after humans forfeit this privileged status in the created order, rebelling against God and stooping to become like other creatures, God refuses to abandon them entirely. Throughout the Primeval History, their stubborn rejection of God is matched only by God's gracious and determined persistence to preserve them and give them more chances to get it right.

The final theme to keep in mind as we move further into the OT can only be mentioned in passing. The idea of *covenant* is first introduced in the flood story (Genesis 6:18; 9:8–17). We will return to Noah's covenant with God later, because it will become a model for the covenant with Israel's ancestors and then with Israel at Mount Sinai and much later with King David. Unfortunately, our word "covenant" fails to convey the OT's concept. It has a basic understanding of a binding relationship between two parties. But as it develops in the pages of the OT, it takes on rich significance defining the way Israel understands what it means to live in relationship with God. In the flood story, God's covenant with Noah is his commitment to save him and his family from the floodwaters, while it implies certain obligations on Noah's part as well (such as following instructions for building the ark). And this one is an "enduring covenant" (Genesis 9:16), a designation used for the most important covenants of the OT (compare Genesis 17:7, Exodus 31:16, and 2 Samuel 23:5). While some covenants require periodic renewal and upgrading, these are indefectible covenants. They have no expiration dates.

SIDEBAR 5.4. MONOTHEISM AND THE EQUALITY OF MEN AND WOMEN

At creation, God created humans to enjoy perfect companionship,intimacy between two humans unmatched in the rest of creation. The animals provided companionship, but all of them fell short in some way, so God creates a "woman" perfectly suited to Adam's "manhood" (Genesis 2:18–23). These two have a flesh-and-bones intimacy without equal elsewhere in creation (2:23). In the creation account of Genesis 1, the human is created as *male and female* "in God's own image," resembling God as his representatives over creation (1:26–27). Since both were created in God's image, they share an essential similarity that is characteristic of Israelite understanding.

In the ancient Near East, by contrast, the closest bond possible – the most intimate human relationship – is between friends of the same gender. Gilgamesh is considered far superior to other humans. When the deities set out to create someone who is his equal, someone to interact with him on an equal footing, they create Enkidu, another male. The closest similarity possible and therefore the closest friend for Gilgamesh was considered to be another male. This is not likely a sexual intimacy (although some think so), nor is it simple male bigotry. Enkidu is not male because it is assumed females are inferior. They are simply different, and in the ancient Near East intimacy is assumed to require similarity.

Why does Israel assume differently? Why is true human intimacy associated in the OT with male-female companionship? It seems likely that the equality of men and women – their essential alikeness – is another result of Israel's monotheistic impulses.* To the Israelite way of thinking, there are no goddesses to represent "womanhood." All the roles and functions of female deities have been absorbed by Yahweh. And gender among humans is simple biology, not a question of nature or identity, and certainly not an issue of superiority or inferiority. The loss of gender among the gods has also resulted in a new understanding of equality among men and women.

* For more on this argument, see Frymer-Kensky (pp. 141–43) in "Where to Find More" in Chapter 4.

WHERE TO FIND MORE

Commentaries: The best technical and advanced commentary on **Genesis** is the three-volume work by Claus Westermann, *Genesis* (trans. John J. Scullion; Minneapolis, Minn.: Augsburg, 1984–86). For more recent treatment, see Bill T. Arnold, *Genesis* (New Cambridge Bible Commentary; Cambridge and New York: Cambridge University Press, 2009).

Blenkinsopp, Joseph. *The Pentateuch: An Introduction to the First Five Books of the Bible.* New York: Doubleday, 1992.

Helpful discussion of many topics covered in this chapter; see pages 119–20 for the "indefectible covenant" language.

Cross, Frank Moore. *Canaanite Myth and Hebrew Epic: Essays in the History of the Religion of Israel.* Cambridge, Mass.: Harvard University Press, 1973.

A classic study that establishes among many other important topics a distinction between theogony and cosmogony in ancient Near Eastern creation accounts (p. 120). This author elaborates the two types further in a later work, From Epic to Canon: History and Literature in

Ancient Israel *(Baltimore: Johns Hopkins University Press, 1998), 73–83, and makes the case for the use of "epic" for early Israelite narratives in that volume as well (pp. 22–52).*

Hiebert, Theodore. *The Yahwist's Landscape: Nature and Religion in Early Israel.* New York: Oxford University Press, 1996.

Pages 78–80 for an introduction to the topic of literary type, whether the Primeval History is myth, epic, history, or something else.

Jacobsen, Thorkild. "The Eridu Genesis." Pages 129–42 in *I Studied Inscriptions from Before the Flood: Ancient Near Eastern, Literary, and Linguistic Approaches to Genesis 1–11.* Edited by Richard S. Hess and David Toshio Tsumura. Sources for Biblical and Theological Study 4. Winona Lake, Ind.: Eisenbrauns, 1994.

Miller, Patrick D., Jr. "Eridu, Dunnu, and Babel: A Study in Comparative Mythology." Pages 143–68 in *I Studied Inscriptions from Before the Flood.* See under Jacobsen in "Where to Find More" in this chapter.

Oswalt, John N. *The Bible among The Myths: Unique Revelation or Just Ancient Literature?* Grand Rapids, Mich.: Zondervan, 2009.

Smith, Mark S. *The Priestly Vision of Genesis 1.* Minneapolis, Minn.: Augsburg Fortress, 2009.

On the question of the literary genre of Genesis 1, see pages 139–59. For priestly phraseology and themes of Genesis 1, see pages 117–38.

Sparks, Kenton L. *Ancient Texts for the Study of the Hebrew Bible: A Guide to the Background Literature.* Peabody, Mass.: Hendrickson Publishers, 2005.

Contains useful discussions of ancient Near Eastern creation myths (chap. 10, pp. 305–43).

Walton, John H. *The Lost World of Genesis One: Ancient Cosmology and the Origins Debate.* Downers Grove, Ill.: IVP Academic, 2009.

CHAPTER 6

Ancestors

OLD TESTAMENT READING: GENESIS 12–50

The three major sections of Genesis 12–50 focus on the ancestral narratives of Abraham, Jacob, and Joseph. We know little of the historical details, although archaeological data suggests a plausible context for these stories in the Middle Bronze Age. We will see that the narratives themselves hint at such early traditions, suggestive of oral traditions preserved and woven into the texts. In these narratives we will also encounter the social structure of kinship-based tribal societies. The "father's house" and the larger clan formed the subunits of the geographically based organization of the tribe.

This portion of Genesis narrates Yahweh's provision of hope for the divine-human relationship so tragically marred by human rebellion (Genesis 1–11). Moreover, God chooses an individual, Abraham, to partner in a covenant. This covenant, shaped by God's promises of land, descendants, and worldwide blessing, is the lasting hallmark of Israelite religion. Abraham's descendants include not only those named in the OT but those in the three monotheistic religions for which Abraham is acknowledged as the "father of faith."

Now we come to that portion of the OT that binds Jews, Christians, and Muslims together more than any other — and sadly also divides them. Judaism, Christianity, and Islam are known as Abrahamic religions. They share Abraham as a common ancestor, but they also disagree about his significance. In this chapter, we will talk about why this is the case. We will explore how Abraham became the father of faith for millions of believers around the world.

The remainder of Genesis introduces Israel's ancestral family. Here we read Israel's ancient traditions about Abraham, Isaac, and Jacob (Genesis 12–36), as well as the Joseph narrative at the book's conclusion (Genesis 37–50). The stories of three generations of ancestors, the patriarchs, center on divine call and covenant. The story of Joseph is about providential guidance and protection. In this way, the ancestral narratives of Genesis serve both to teach readers about Israel's ancestors and to call readers to live faithfully in their footsteps. They are founders and examples of faith (see Plate V).

This account of Israel's ancestors is masterfully tied to what came before it in Genesis with genealogical links, using the "these are the descendants of X-ancestor" catchphrase. In the Primeval History of Genesis 1–11, God created the universe and set up a covenant with a single righteous person, Noah, in order to save humankind from the floodwaters. In Genesis 12–50, God creates a nation, Israel, and sets up a covenant with a single righteous person, Abraham, to save humankind from its own self-destructive patterns.

FATHERS AND MOTHERS OF FAITH

So far, we have seen that the OT opens with nine books (following the Jewish canon; see Chapter 4) telling Israel's story in broad outline. We called these nine books the **Enneateuch**, or more simply, the "Primary History." This overarching story of Israel is "primary" because it will be supplemented later in the OT with additional historical books, as well as with books of poetry, wisdom, and prophecy, filling out Israel's library.

In this nine-book Primary History, the first literary unit is Genesis 1–11, which works as a prologue for the rest of the OT. We called these chapters the "Primeval History" because they introduce characters and events of primeval or primordial times, and

yet they do so in a history-like narrative. The editors of these chapters have used genealogies especially to tie these accounts together in a way that gives them this history-like quality. And yet the Primeval History of Genesis 1–11 functions as myth in other ancient Near Eastern cultures. Framed as it has been by distinctive Israelite ideology, this first unit of the Bible, the Primeval History, serves a number of functions in Israel's library.

One of those functions of Genesis 1–11 is to illustrate the problem of the human condition, as we discussed in the previous chapter. God created the universe perfect in every way, but the humans rebelled against all authority and moved quickly from eating forbidden fruit to murder to universal evil. There seemed no limit to humankind's wickedness. They ruined God's perfect order. No matter how gracious and forgiving was God's response, the humans continued to rebel against him. Even a great flood failed to solve the problem. Humanity was on a self-destructive course. The Tower of Babel episode raised doubts about whether there could be any hope for the divine-human relationship. Finally, the answer comes in God's covenant relationship with a single individual and his family, the ancestors of ancient Israel, and ultimately with Israel itself. The ancestral narratives of Genesis 12–50 introduce the beginning of that solution to the universal problems of humanity. This is what makes Abraham the father of faith for millions.

The OT counts three fathers of Israel: Abraham, Isaac, and Jacob, the patriarchs (Exodus 2:24; 3:6, 15, etc.). But the ancestral narratives introduce us to quite a number of women too: Sarah, Hagar, Rebekah, and many others. While the underlying structure of the society was "patriarchal" (see the

---

SIDEBAR 6.1. FROM WHERE DO WE GET OUR CHAPTER AND VERSE NUMBERS?

We saw in the previous chapter that Israel's first creation account is found in Genesis 1:1–2:3. Now we have to begin our discussion of the Abraham cycle at 11:27 instead of at a clean break at the beginning of a new chapter. These chapter breaks are not very precise. What gives?

Chapter and verse numbers were added quite late to the OT. The chapter breaks in our English Bibles are from the manuscript tradition of the Vulgate dating to the thirteenth century CE. Numeration of the verses was added even later, although these follow the markings used by Jewish scribes to distinguish the verses. The verse distinctions are almost always helpful. Unfortunately, the chapter distinctions are often in awkward and unhelpful locations. Sometimes scholars and commentators on the biblical text will refer to a unit extending across these chapter divisions, as we did for Genesis 1:1–2:3.

Both the beginning and conclusion of the Abraham cycle are imprecisely marked by chapter divisions. The cycle really begins at 11:27 and ends at 25:18. To simplify things, I will refer to the Abraham cycle as Genesis 12–25, but please remember that, technically, it is 11:27–25:18. Similarly, the Isaac interlude, and therefore the Jacob cycle, begins at 25:19. So I will refer to the Jacob cycle as Genesis 25–36 but, technically, it is 25:19–36:43.

---

section "Life in Ancient Israel" later in this chapter), this does not mean that only the men matter in Israel's story. Quite the contrary. The Israelites give a more central and important role to women in their literature than did most other groups in the ancient Near East.

The ancestral narratives of Genesis 12–50 cover a lot of territory. You should think in terms of three subsections:

1. An Abraham cycle of stories and traditions (Genesis 12–25)
2. A Jacob cycle (Genesis 25–36)
3. A short story about Joseph (Genesis 37–50)

The traditions about Abraham took place mostly in the southern region of what became the promised land, while those of Jacob are mostly set in Mesopotamia and the central promised land. The Joseph narrative takes place mostly in the promised land and in Egypt. The Jacob cycle begins with an

Isaac interlude that explains Jacob's role and places him in historical and literary context (Genesis 25:19–26:35).

Abraham Cycle

The Abraham cycle begins with the genealogy of his father, Terah, as we have come to expect in the book of Genesis: "these are the descendants of Terah" (11:27). Abram (his original name) is the tenth generation from Noah, just as Noah was himself the tenth generation of humanity (5:32). The world's beginnings and Israel's beginnings are tied together as one story of salvation. Noah's covenant seals salvation for a suffering cosmos; Abram's covenant (through Israel) offers hope to a suffering humanity.

After a few family details in Genesis 11:27–32, all of which become important later in the story, we read that Yahweh spoke to Abram, and called him to leave his "father's household" and journey to a

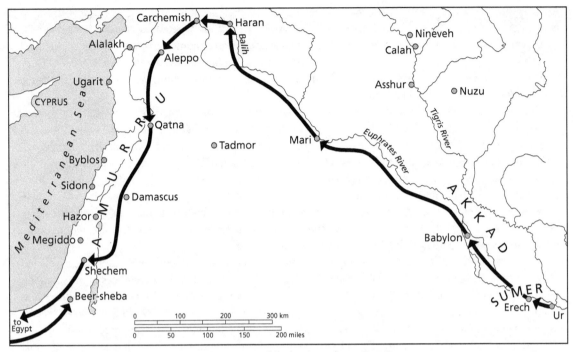

Map 6.1. Journeys of Abraham according to Genesis

different land. That new land was Canaan (12:5). The call to follow God is marked by divine promises, which are stated both generally (12:1–3) and specifically as land and children, or "seed" (12:7). Tying these promises together – land and seed – is God's plan to make Abram a means of blessing for the entire world. The concept of God's "blessing" recurs in the ancestral narratives, as God's plan to bless the world through Israel's ancestors (12:3): "in you all the families of the earth shall be blessed." And God's promises of land and seed drive the narrative forward into the rest of the OT.

A covenant between God and Noah was at the center of the Primeval History, marked by a rainbow as a perpetual sign (review Genesis 9:8–17). Here in the ancestral narratives, God establishes a similar covenant with Abram, signifying the

intimacy of their relationship, which increases as the narrative progresses. Like Noah's covenant, this one also is an "enduring covenant" (17:7), needing no periodic upgrading or renewal. And this covenant too is sealed with a powerful sign: circumcision of every male on the eighth day (17:10–12). A hollow religious ritual has been transformed into a powerful reminder of the promises of God's covenant. Abram's name becomes Abraham and Sarai's name becomes Sarah, signaling a new era and a new status for Israel's ancestors.

Jacob Cycle

The Jacob cycle begins with the *Isaac interlude* (Genesis 25:19–26:35), in which Isaac is shown to be a true patriarch, the son of Abraham and father of

In previous chapters, we have seen how the Pentateuch is composed of numerous older sources, designated by the letters J, E, P, H, and D (review Sidebar 4.3). And we also explained how the Primeval History of Genesis 1–11 appears to be a combination of a unified JE narrative blended with materials written by priests, usually designated with P or H (Sidebar 5.1).

Early on, readers realized that Genesis was originally composed of distinct narrative threads. These threads were most obvious in their use of different names for God, Yahweh and Elohim, as we have seen. Readers also puzzled over duplicate and triplicate accounts of certain events, such as two accounts of creation (Genesis 1 and 2). More complicated still were times when competing narrative plotlines cross each other in the same text, such as the flood narrative's account of how many animals entered the ark (two of every kind or seven pairs of clean animals) or of how long the flood lasted (a year or 40 days). Once these distinct narrative threads were observed, their differences were confirmed further by differences in phraseology and theology. Most scholars speak of JE narratives and P narratives in Genesis. Others prefer to be less specific, referring simply to priestly traditions (P or H), and nonpriestly traditions (non-P).

The ancestral narratives have a similar type of literary history. Several duplicate accounts are explained as variations of original sources, usually JE and P variations. For example: three occurrences of the so-called wife–sister theme (Genesis 12:10–20, 20:1–18, and 26:1–11), two explanations of the covenant with Abraham (Genesis 15 and 17), and two accounts of Jacob's name change (Genesis 32:27–28 and 35:9–10). Most of the material in the ancestral narratives can be identified as originally coming from these priestly (P and H) and nonpriestly sources (J and/or E), with minor editorial connections tying them all together. In the next two chapters on Torah history and Torah instruction, we will return to this topic.

Israel. His son, Jacob, however is an entirely different character – conniving and deceitful. The divine promises of Abraham's covenant are threatened by the questionable character of this grandson. He does not seem to merit God's continued grace. After stealing his brother's birthright and deceiving his father, Jacob runs for his life to Mesopotamia. There he settles with relatives, acquires wives (the future mothers of Israel), and has eleven sons and one daughter. More than once along the way, Jacob encounters the God of his fathers, Abraham and Isaac, and gradually is transformed into Israel. Again, a name change signifies a change of character and status. Later, a twelfth son is born, and we have the heads of the twelve tribes of Israel. Jacob returns to Canaan, makes peace with his estranged brother, and settles in the land of promise once again.

The Jacob cycle is characterized by the promises of the Abrahamic covenant, which seem to be in jeopardy at every step along Jacob's journey. The promise of seed – countless descendants like the stars of heaven – begins to become a reality in Jacob's children. The promise of land – a permanent settlement for Abraham's many children – seems nearly lost when Jacob runs away to Mesopotamia but is regained when he returns. The promise of blessing – the assurance of God's guidance and protection – seems forgotten when each character reflects a cursed nonblessing. Yet the main character's desperate plea at a critical juncture, "I will not let you go, unless you bless me" (32:26), is a turning point. God does, in fact, bless him, and in that moment, Jacob becomes "Israel" (32:28–29).

Joseph Story

The last genealogical notation of Genesis introduces the story of Joseph: "this is the story of the family of Jacob" (37:2). Genesis 37–50 is not a "cycle" of traditions like the Abraham and Jacob cycles. Reading these chapters feels more like reading a suspenseful novel with an elaborate story line, rapid scene changes, and an amazing ending. Besides, the character Joseph is not a patriarch in the same sense as Abraham, Isaac, and Jacob. He is not the ancestor of the future kings of Israel, which all come through the tribe of Judah instead of through Joseph's tribes, Ephraim and Manasseh. More than an ancestral "cycle," this is just a great story that was too good to leave out of the OT.

The story itself is ageless, filled with jealousy, intrigue, and suspense. Joseph was the favorite of his father, Jacob, who brazenly showed his favouritism by giving Joseph fancy clothes. (And no, we have no idea what made Joseph's robe so special, whether it was its length, design, color, or some combination of features.) Joseph's jealous brothers kidnap him and sell him into slavery in Egypt. But Joseph is an industrious and gifted young man; "the Lord was with Joseph" (39:2). Though betrayed and abandoned more than once, Joseph overcomes all odds and eventually rises to the second highest rank in all Egypt. With several dramatic and surprising twists along the way, Joseph

becomes the means of deliverance from drought and saves his own family and countless others from starvation in Canaan. Thus Joseph brings Jacob and his family to live in northern Egypt, where they settle permanently. In this way, the Joseph story explains how the children of Israel came to dwell in Egypt instead of in the promised land of Canaan.

The Joseph story is united by a penetrating theological conviction. God's purposes are not limited by human malevolence; indeed, they are advanced by it because of God's good graces. Joseph twice says as much, when he tells his brothers, "you sold me. ... God sent me" (Genesis 45:5) and "even though you intended to do harm to me, God intended it for good" (50:20). In the Joseph story, God perceives the unethical behavior of humans as an opportunity for good, and transforms it.

ARCHAEOLOGY AND THE SEARCH FOR WHAT REALLY HAPPENED

Archaeology is a relatively recent field of scholarship. It seeks to recover and study the material remains of the past, that is, physical objects such as household vessels, tools, weapons, buildings, sculpture, and written texts left behind by humans. It began in the nineteenth century with explorers who were trying to find as many artifacts as possible. But as the discipline of archaeology matured, it became a complex scientific field of study in its own right. For readers of the OT, it has also made innumerable contributions to our understanding of the biblical world. We will have many opportunities to turn to archaeological evidence throughout this textbook, to show how it has contributed to OT studies.

SIDEBAR 6.3. THE RISE OF ARCHAEOLOGICAL RESEARCH

6.1. Sir Flinders Petrie, 1853–1942. British Egyptologist and pioneer of systematic methodology and preservation of artifacts. (Photo: © Bettmann / CORBIS)

6.2. William F. Albright, 1891–1971. American archaeologist and Bible scholar, who can reasonably be said to have founded a school of thought, sometimes known as the American School of "Biblical Archaeology." During his professorship at Johns Hopkins University (1930–1958), he trained an entire generation of scholars in biblical studies, archaeology, and philology. (Photo: Sheridan Libraries; Johns Hopkins University)

Archaeological research of the lands of the Bible has occurred in three phases.* First, the period before World War I witnessed the earliest scientifically controlled excavations (1838–1914). Many of the biblical locations were identified during this period. Sir Flinders Petrie first appreciated the nature of an ancient *tell* (mound or ruin), the artificial hills left behind by ancient cities. Petrie also established the importance of pottery for determining relative chronology. Excavation techniques were primitive, and the goal was often the simple retrieval of artifacts; little attention was given to study or interpretation.

Second, the period between the world wars (1918–1940) saw the first large-scale excavations. Advances were made in methods and in the recording of the discoveries. W. F. Albright pioneered the comparative study of pottery and stratigraphic research, and he integrated archaeological findings with OT studies and ancient Near Eastern scholarship generally. The period between the wars also saw the rise of international schools devoted to archaeological research in biblical lands.

After World War II, a third phase of archaeological research began (1948–present). The international schools began to decline, and "national schools" were born. For example, today, leading universities in Israel and Jordan have responsibility for excavations, with the approval of departments of antiquities in both states. Methodologies have continued to be refined, and volunteers are now used, turning some excavations into virtual schools for field archaeology. Since the 1970s, fieldwork has become more deliberate because of financial constraints, and at the same time, the work has become more complex and interdisciplinary. A veritable information explosion has resulted in a lively and dynamic field of study.

* For more, see both Dever and Mazar in "Where to Find More" in this chapter.

When it comes to Israel's ancestors, however, archaeology is of little help. In fact, the historical search to find evidence that Israel's ancestors even existed has turned up nothing. Some claim this should not be surprising in light of the kind of life described in the ancestral narratives: roaming seminomadic tribes, living in tents without permanent structures and leaving no trace of their lives. Still, as important as these Israelite ancestors were, they are not referred to in any other ancient text beside the Bible; we have no trace of them in historical sources. As OT scholarship began to come of age in the nineteenth century, many researchers began to suspect that none of this had really happened and to question whether Abraham, Isaac, and Jacob were historical figures. This culminated in the famous opinion of Julius Wellhausen that the figure of Abraham is "a free creation of unconscious art." He concluded that we can know nothing historical about the ancestors. We can only hope to learn about the time when these stories were created by later Israelites, a picture of the ancestors that was then projected into antiquity and "reflected there like a glorified mirage."[1]

All of this changed with the rise of archaeology. William F. Albright and his numerous students and colleagues approached the ancestral narratives in light of an explosion of new information from archaeological research. No explicit connections were found to Israel's ancestors. Yet their work reconstructed what was believed to be a plausible context for the lives of Israel's ancestors, especially among the social and legal institutions of Mesopotamia in the second millennium BCE (such as from the cities of **Mari**, Nuzi, and others). A general consensus emerged in this school of thought in the mid-twentieth century that Abraham and his family lived during the Middle Bronze Age (2000–1550 BCE).

6.3. Julius Wellhausen, 1844–1918. German professor who became the most famous Old Testament scholar of the nineteenth century. Wellhausen is most notable for his source-critical investigations of Pentateuchal origins, culminating in the well-known Documentary Hypothesis. (Photo: Archives of the Mathematisches Forschungsinstitut Oberwolfach)

The pendulum swung again in the opposite direction beginning in the mid-1970s. It was discovered, first, that most of the social and legal parallels from Mesopotamia were not really relevant to Israel's ancestors, or at least that their relevance had been exaggerated. The second development was a growing skepticism about the OT text itself. Gradually, by the close of the twentieth century, many scholars had returned to the nineteenth-century opinions about the lack of any historical reality behind Israel's ancestral traditions.

Today's opinions swing between two extremes. Some take Abraham, Isaac, and Jacob to be real historical individuals and think the events happened just as described in Genesis. Others believe they are fictional and that nothing described here actually took place. These extremes reflect two methodological ideologies. On the one hand, some readers simply accept what is described as historical because it is written in the OT, while on the other hand, other readers do not accept anything as historicial unless proven by sources or archaeological evidence

1 Julius Wellhausen, *Prolegomena to the History of Israel* (Atlanta, Ga.: Scholars Press, 1994 [originally published in translation in 1885]), 319–20.

outside the OT. One position assumes that the OT is right until proven wrong, while the other assumes that the OT is wrong until proven right. The truth lies somewhere between these extremes.

Whatever we conclude, we should remember certain clues buried in the ancestral stories that hint at genuine memories from the past.[2] For example, the personal names of Israel's ancestors are for the most part not the names that were used by later Isaelites. Also, even though the social and legal customs of the ancestral stories may not be precisely paralleled in ancient Near Eastern texts, they certainly weren't common in later Israel. And above all, the religious practices and beliefs of the ancestors are remarkably different from those of later Israel, as we well see. Some argue that these features were intentionally created by later Israelite authors in order to make their literary inventions *appear* old and important. But it is more likely that these are authentic glimpses into Israel's earliest ancestors.

Certain geographical hints in the Genesis narratives may also point to distinct ancestral groups. For example, the Abraham cycle may reflect a group that settled in the hills around the city of Hebron, worshipping Yahweh at an open-air sanctuary adorned with "the oaks of Mamre" (Genesis 13:18, 14:13, and 18:1). Abraham's nephew Lot, of course, is identified with the area around the western and southern Dead Sea (Genesis 13:5–13). Isaac lived in the region of Gerar, around Beer-sheba (Genesis 26:6,33). And the Jacob cycle traces those ancestors dwelling in the north-central hills, primarily near Shechem.

We will not settle soon whether the OT's ancestral narratives preserve genuine history or not. Whatever our assumptions about such things, we should consider the possibility of oral traditions from Israel's earliest periods. Oral tradition of ancient literature is a topic studied by form critics (on *form criticism*, see Chapter 18). We should allow for the possibility of certain genuine memories from the past for early Israel, which found their way into the current ancestral narratives. For this reason, it may be best to think of these portions of Genesis as Israel's "protohistory."[3]

Life in Ancient Israel

These ancestral narratives introduce you to a world very different from the one we know every day. While we can't answer the question of how much history we have in these stories, we can know quite a lot about the basic family structures reflected here. Several features of ancient Israel's society assumed in these narratives are known to us from studies of other traditional societies.

For example, the genealogies of Genesis trace the characters through direct lines of sons; daughters are hardly mentioned in these lists. And, as we have said, later references in the OT have a standard list of "patriarchs": Abraham, Isaac, and Jacob. This reflects an inheritance practice in which a family's accumulated wealth and status is passed down to the eldest son, a practice known as *primogeniture*. Although in the OT the eldest son is often, surprisingly, replaced by a younger brother (Jacob instead of Esau), the principle remains in place, which is what makes the rise of a younger brother

2 See Pitard in "Where to Find More" in this chapter for more details on these comments.

3 See Malamat in "Where to Find More" in this chapter.

so surprising. Because of this dominance of the oldest male in Israel's cultural conventions, which is so different from what occurs in our own culture, we often make the mistake of simply assuming that OT Israel was "patriarchal." Let's examine that assumption.

We live in a society in which "family" can be defined in many different ways. No such cultural assumptions are made about inheritance practices or genealogies. And our high value on equality between men and women makes some of these narratives of the OT hard to understand. We have many social differences from ancient Israel. At the heart of those differences is Israel's tribal kinship structure based on a hierarchy from top to bottom: from (a) the tribal federation or monarchy, to (b) the tribe, to (c) the extended family, to (d) the "father's house" (more on these in a moment). Many assume that this hierarchical "top-to-bottom" power structure continues in the family household itself, with men holding dominance over women. And so ancient Israel is often called a "patriarchal" society, although that term is not easy to define. We most often mean it to be a male-dominated society, in which men hold authority in social, political, and economic institutions in a way that is oppressive to women.

Yet we have evidence in the OT that women had their own groups of professionals in fields like funerary services, prophecy, music, and health care, as well as more informal networks for the production of bread, textiles, and the like. Ancient Israel was not likely a simple hierarchical or patriarchal society, which would not have allowed women to rise to such powerful jobs. We should think of its organizational structures laterally or horizontally, which explains the flexibility in rank or status we

see for some women in Israelite culture.[4] So Israel's overall organization was hierarchical. But this was not a gender-based hierarchy in the family unit. Israel's social structure was much more complex. Although it was not a simple egalitarian culture, men and women shared power in ways that makes "patriarchal" somewhat misleading.

The kinship structure of tribal societies is especially important background for reading the OT. And this framework *is* hierarchical, each unit embedded in the next higher organizational unit in the society. This family arrangement was basically the same throughout the OT, so it will be important to keep the following social structure in mind.

First, the primary unit of society was the "house" (*bayit*) or "father's house" (*bêt 'āb*). Think of this as an "extended family" or "family household." Instead of today's nuclear families of one couple and their children, these "joint families" were made up of a couple, their grown sons and the sons' wives, and their grandchildren, all living in a compound of two or three connected dwellings. Members of this family unit could even come from outside the immediate kinship structure, related as debt servants, slaves, day laborers, orphans, and so forth. This joint-family unit was the most important feature of Israelite society, providing the center of religious, social, and economic life, and it partly explains what was at stake in Yahweh's call for Abram to leave his "father's household" to travel on his own (Genesis 12:1).

These family households were connected to others like them locally, usually in villages, in what is often called a "kinship group" or sometimes a

---

4 For more on this, see Meyers in "Where to Find More" in this chapter.

"clan" (*mišpāḥâ*). This second structural unit enabled households to join together in village life and to share farming space, working the fields, orchards, and vineyards around the village cooperatively.

Households and clans related to each other in larger kinship organizations geographically as a "tribe" (*šēbeṭ* and *maṭṭeh*), the third societal unit. Tribes were joined by language, legal practices, and religion, and they provided a judicial system for deciding disputes between the clans, as well as a means of rapid response for military defense. Israel is conceived ideally as twelve tribes that are named for the household of Jacob/Israel; in later Israel, each tribe is associated with a specific territory. The tribe of Levi, however, became a priestly tribe without a land allotment and is sometimes left out of the list. To maintain the ideal number of twelve tribes, the two sons of Joseph, Ephraim and Manasseh, are counted in place of Levi (compare the lists in Genesis 49 and Numbers 26).

The twelve tribes of Israel made up the "people, kindred" (*ʿam*) or nation of Israel, first as a tribal federation (Joshua and Judges), and later as a monarchy (1–2 Samuel and 1–2 Kings). The ancestral narratives of Genesis 12–50 explain that father Abraham established the original household, from which the twelve tribes issued through Jacob, whose name became Israel. In the Joseph story, the household came to reside in Egypt, where it would gradually grow into a great people. But for that, we will await the book of Exodus.

RELIGION IN THE ANCESTRAL NARRATIVES

You may have noticed when reading Genesis 12–50 that its religious concepts are quite different from those found elsewhere in the OT. We have nothing here of Jerusalem with its great temple, the official place of an elaborate sacrificial system in the hands of a guild of priests. We have no mention here of great religious observances like Passover, the Day of Atonement, or the Festival of Tabernacles. Nor is there any mention of Sabbath keeping or dietary restrictions. The concept of "holiness" is central to Moses' understanding of God (from Exodus 3:5 on), yet it is also missing entirely in the ancestral narratives.

But there's more. Besides being surprised – from the perspective of the rest of the OT, that is – by what is missing from it, you might wonder about certain things that *are* present in this narrative. We have here a bewildering number of names for God, most beginning with *El*, the general Hebrew word for "god": El Shaddai (Genesis 17:1, 28:3, 35:11, 43:14, and 48:3), El Elyon (14:18), El Roi (16:13), El Olam (21:33), El Elohe Israel (33:20), or simply "El" (46:3 and 49:25). (Most modern translations give footnotes indicating what we think these names mean.) Abraham most often relates to El, but the God he worships is also El Shaddai or El Elyon. The names El Olam and El Roi are most often associated with the southern portions of the promised land, sometimes connected with Isaac, whereas Jacob is thought to relate to a deity named Pahad ("Fear"), found primarily around the city of Shechem (Genesis 31:42,53).

Also, Israel's ancestors build altars and offer sacrifices whenever and wherever they feel led to do so. More shockingly still – again, from the later OT perspective – is the role of trees and standing stones in Israelite worship. Abraham worships Yahweh at an open-air sanctuary at the "oak of

6.4. The Standing Stones of Gezer. Religions of the ancient Near East routinely included the veneration of stones. Rows of standing stones, such as these found at Gezer, have been found also at Ugarit, Hazor, and elsewhere, and were probably connected to ancestor worship. (Photo: Erich Lessing / Art Resource, N.Y.)

Moreh" near Shechem (12:6–7), and again at the "oaks of Mamre" near Hebron (13:18). Isaac builds a similar open-air shrine at Beer-sheba (26:25), as does Jacob at Shechem and Bethel (33:20 and 35:7–8). Any green tree in such sacred shrines held meaning in the ancient world as physical symbols of divine presence. Sacred standing stones also were sometimes used in these outdoor sanctuaries. Jacob sets up such stones at Bethel and Gilead (28:18,22; 35:14; and 31:45). Ancestral religion, similar to Canaanite religion, worshipped God in the form of an El-type name and did so in open-air sanctuaries. These sanctuaries or holy shrines typically have three elements: an altar, a sacred tree, and often a standing stone.

Such practices are specifically prohibited later in the OT (Exodus 23:24 and 34:13; Leviticus 26:1; etc.). How do we explain these differences between later Israelite religion and the religious practices of Israel's ancestors? Some assume that these narratives are written intentionally to reflect an ancient time, so that these features are deliberately creating an archaic aura about the ancestors. Others assume that they reflect something authentic, something genuinely ancient about these narratives. We cannot be certain which it is, but we will return to this question in Chapter 10.

ABRAHAM'S FAITH AND ABRAHAMIC RELIGIONS

The ancestral narratives portray a growing intimacy between Abraham's family and God. This intimacy starts with the "Divine I" of God's self-revelation:

"*I will bless*" (Genesis 12:3)

"*I give this land*" (12:7)

"*I am your shield*" (15:1)

"*I am the Lord*" (15:7)

"*I am El Shaddai (God Almighty); walk before me, and be blameless*" (17:1), and so forth.

Such intimacy between God and Israel's ancestors results in a covenant, a binding relationship that becomes the hallmark of Israelite religion.

This covenantal intimacy also reflects the monolatrous henotheism we defined in Chapter 1, which is an *implicit* monotheism. The nonexistence of other deities is nowhere stated in Genesis 12–50. Yet among the three leading faith traditions emerging from the OT, genuine monotheism is central to what it means to be a follower of Abraham. This is the single conviction binding Judaism, Christianity, and Islam together. On this foundation – Abraham as the father of faith – there is agreement.

Jewish, Christian, and Muslim believers understand themselves to be descendants of Abraham. Of course, for Jews, their line of descent is quite literal, as described in the pages of Genesis: Isaac and Jacob, who becomes Israel, and the twelve tribes. They are the biological children of Abraham. For Christians, faith determines the true line of descent. Jesus is the faithful child of Abraham, and faith in Jesus makes one a member of Abraham's family (Romans 4:16–25; Galatians 3:29). Christians believe they are grafted into the taproot of Abraham's faith because of belief in Jesus (Romans 11:17–24). For Muslims, the line of descent is through Ishmael, in a story that differs from that of Genesis. Abraham himself, together with Ishmael, (re)built the Ka'ba, the most sacred sanctuary of Mecca, at the site where God appeared to Hagar, instead of along the southern route to Egypt (Qur'an, Surah 2:125–7). And of course, Ishmael's descendants grow into twelve princes in a tribal federation similar to Israel's twelve tribes (Genesis 25:12–18). The text of the OT implies that Abraham is more than the father of Jews, the father of Christians, and the father of Muslims. He is indeed the father of all who believe.

Unfortunately, our world today knows that Jews, Christians, and Muslims are not in agreement about the meaning of Abraham. Each tradition has interpreters who make Abraham the possession of their own particular religion to the exclusion of others.[5] Disagreement arises even over which son Abraham nearly sacrificed in the important passage known as the Aqedah, the "Binding" of Isaac (Genesis 22). Muslims believe that it was at the same location as the Ka'ba in Mecca that Abraham almost sacrificed Ishmael (Qur'an, Surah 37:100–107). And some Christians believe that their grafting into the Abrahamic taproot necessarily implies the rejection of Jewish believers (as some would interpret Romans 11:19–20).

But the text of the OT itself is not exclusive about Abraham. Even though Genesis insists on tracing

---

5 For popular discussion of this problem, see Bruce S. Feiler, *Abraham: A Journey to the Heart of Three Faiths* (New York: Harper, 2002), 113–85.

the line of promise through Isaac, it also retains the line of Ishmael as true children of Abraham and blessed by God. Indeed, Ishmael is the first to receive circumcision as the sign of Yahweh's covenant (Genesis 17:20 and 23).[6] God includes Ishmael in the covenant people, blessing him with numerous descendants as a great nation. Whatever violence and conflict has occurred between the descendants of Abraham over the centuries, this was not the intent of the OT message.

WHERE TO FIND MORE

Commentaries: The best technical and advanced commentary on **Genesis** is the three-volume work by Claus Westermann, *Genesis* (trans. John J. Scullion; Minneapolis, Minn.: Augsburg, 1984–86). For more recent treatment, see Bill T. Arnold, *Genesis* (New Cambridge Bible Commentary; Cambridge and New York: Cambridge University Press, 2009).

Dever, William G. "Archaeological Method in Israel: A Continuing Revolution." Biblical Archaeologist 43 (1980): 40–48.

Finkelstein, Israel, and Amihai Mazar. *The Quest for the Historical Israel: Debating Archaeology and the History of Early Israel*. Edited by Brian B. Schmidt. SBLABS 17. Atlanta, Ga.: Society of Biblical Literature, 2007.

Helpful overview of the current opinions on historical questions, presented from opposite views and convictions.

King, Philip J., and Lawrence E. Stager. *Life in Biblical Israel*. Library of Ancient Israel. Louisville, Ky.: Westminster John Knox Press, 2001.

Malamat, Abraham. "The Proto-History of Israel: A Study in Method." Pages 303–13 in *The Word of the Lord Shall Go Forth: Essays in Honor of David Noel Freedman in Celebration of His Sixtieth Birthday*. Edited by Carol L. Meyers and Michael Patrick O'Connor. ASOR Special Volume Series 1. Winona Lake, Ind.: Eisenbrauns, 1983.

Mazar, Amihai. *Archaeology of the Land of the Bible, 10,000–586 B.C.E.* Anchor Bible Reference Library. New York: Doubleday, 1990.

For more on the history of archaeological research on lands of the Bible, see pages 10–21.

Meyers, Carol L. "Hierarchy or Heterarchy? Archaeology and the Theorizing of Israelite Society." Pages 245–54 in *Confronting the Past: Archaeological and Historical Essays on*

---

6 A point emphasized by John Goldingay, *Old Testament Theology*. Vol. 1, *Israel's Gospel* (Downers Grove, Ill.: InterVarsity Press, 2003), 203 and 225–26.

Ancient Israel in Honor of William G. Dever. Edited by Seymour Gitin, J. Edward Wright, and J. P. Dessel. Winona Lake, Ind.: Eisenbrauns, 2006.

Perdue, Leo G., Joseph Blenkinsopp, John J. Collins, and Carol L. Meyers. *Families in Ancient Israel.* Louisville, Ky.: Westminster John Knox Press, 1997.

Several chapters provide more background information on topics of this chapter, especially on Israelite tribes, clans, and family households.

Pitard, Wayne T. "Before Israel: Syria-Palestine in the Bronze Age." Pages 25–57 in *The Oxford History of the Biblical World.* Edited by Michael David Coogan. New York: Oxford University Press, 1998.

Excellent survey of pertinent ancient Near Eastern materials, explaining also what can and cannot be known about the history of the ancestral period. On the "genuine memories" Pitard explores, see pages 28–29.

Ska, Jean-Louis. *Introduction to Reading the Pentateuch.* Translated by Pascale Dominique. Winona Lake, Ind.: Eisenbrauns, 2006.

On repetitions and duplicate accounts in the Pentateuch, see chapter 4 (pp. 53–75), and on the history of source analysis, see chapters 6–7 (pp. 96–164).

CHAPTER 7

Torah Story

OLD TESTAMENT READING: EXODUS AND NUMBERS

In this chapter we will move into the heart of the Pentateuch and explore narrative highlights from the books of Exodus and Numbers. The story begins in Egypt, where God's people are enslaved. Yahweh reveals himself through a burning bush to Moses and instructs him to confront the pharaoh. Ten plagues challenge the Egyptian pantheon, but they also reveal the unique nature of Yahweh. He delivers his people and leads them into the desert wilderness, en route to the promised land. The journey is punctuated by episodes of Israelite rebellion, Yahweh's responses, and tabernacle plans, but most importantly, by another covenant – Yahweh's covenant with Israel at Mount Sinai.

We will observe that archaeology does not provide answers to many historical questions we might have regarding this ancient people and their wilderness sojourn, but it has brought to light Near Eastern political treaties remarkably similar to those of Israel. In striking contrast, no other nation perceived of its deity as a treaty partner. Yahweh, the all-sufficient covenant-making God, demanded a loyalty and exclusivity that marked the radically new idea of Israel's monolatrous henotheism, and ultimately its concept of monotheism.

The Hebrew term *torah* has a rich assortment of meanings: instruction, law, a scroll of law, wisdom proverb, and many others. In Judaism, it even came to mean divine revelation generally, or the OT itself. We use it most often simply for the first five books of the OT, the five-book scroll, or "Pentateuch," otherwise known as the books of Moses.

Genesis, with its account of beginnings and ancestors, has prepared readers for the heart of the Torah. The middle three books of the

SIDEBAR 7.1. THE TORAH'S LITERARY SOURCES

Previously we saw that the Pentateuch is composed of numerous older sources, J, E, P, H, and D (see Sidebars 4.3 and 6.2). The observation that the Torah as it now stands in the OT is sometimes unintelligible leads us to ask why this is so. Scholars working on the Pentateuch for two hundred years have been like detectives sorting out this mystery. First they observed that the Torah narrative as we have it in Genesis has separate threads, usually identified as J and E (Sidebar 4.2). These originally independent threads are preserved also in Exodus and Numbers, although the distinctiveness between them is less obvious. Then we learned that the Torah's legal portions also have independent threads or separate collections. So we have come to refer to priestly legal traditions (P) and Deuteronomic legal traditions (D). We will cover these in the next chapter in more detail and see how they are related to holiness traditions (H), and even to an earlier Elohistic legal tradition (E).

Eventually it became clear, in the history of interpretation and the study of the Pentateuch, that legal traditions were often the centerpiece of a narrative thread.* The Ten Commandments are presented more than once in the Pentateuch (Exodus 20:1–17 and Deuteronomy 5:1–21), and each list originally had its own narrative context preparing for and framing the laws. Thus the sources behind the Pentateuch were already a blend of narrative and legal traditions. The current arrangement of a five-book Torah sometimes obscures the history of these traditions, but we should not be surprised by the intricate combination of narrative and law that marks the Pentateuch generally. We will cover the narrative portion in this chapter, and the legal portions in the next.

* On the history of this interpretation, see Ska in "Where to Find More" in this chapter.

Torah – Exodus, Leviticus, and Numbers – are a blend of historical narrative and law. While these books have many fascinating accounts of early Israel, they are not written to be read easily and quickly. They invite reflection; they require slow and serious study. In fact, some have concluded that, because of its sometimes disjointed narratives mixed with long stretches of law, the Torah simply cannot be read. But taken together, both narrative and law, the Torah becomes the authoritative and founding text for Israel's religious expression. We will focus on the historical narratives of Exodus and Numbers, and their overarching story of early Israel, in this chapter. The next chapter will cover the so-called legal portions of the Torah.

ISRAEL'S STORY

The narratives of the Torah relate some of the best-known and most-beloved stories of world literature. Here we summarize the essential features of that story as told in Exodus and Numbers. These are only highlights; there is much more here. But you will need to know at least this general outline because this account is so central to the rest of the OT message.

Egyptian Bondage

The ancestral narratives of Genesis concluded with the Joseph story, which explained how Jacob/ Israel and his entire family came to live in the land of Goshen in northern Egypt rather than in the

Canaanite homeland. (On Egypt and its proximity to ancient Canaan, review "The Stage of the Old Testament Drama" in Chapter 3.) This presents a problem that builds suspense: the *promised offspring* of Abraham are not living in the *promised land*. Instead, they appear to be permanently settled in far-off Egypt (Genesis 46:5–7), where they are, however, thriving and growing in numbers (Genesis 46:8–27 and 47:27).

The book of Exodus opens with this problem. The people of God are not living in the land God promised to them. But the problems get worse. After the passage of time, a new pharaoh who did not know Joseph or the children of Israel takes over Egypt (Exodus 1:8). He is distrustful and suspicious of Israel's descendants, who by now have become a significant population group in Egypt. The new pharaoh forces the Israelites into slave labor and uses them to build cities in northeastern Egypt. The OT emphasizes the ruthlessness of this Egyptian oppression, yet all the while, the people of Israel continue to grow in number and strength.

Deliverance from Egypt

Centuries pass. Into this oppressive context, Moses is born to an Israelite family (tribe of Levi). He is rescued from certain death in infancy, and raised in Pharaoh's court, with every privilege of education and culture. Yahweh appears to Moses in the form of a miraculous bush – burning, but not consumed – and calls him to serve as the savior of the Israelites. Yahweh commits himself to Moses and the Israelites by revealing his intimate personal name, YHWH, as distinct from names by which he was known to the ancestors (Exodus 3:13–15 and 6:2–3; see Sidebar 1.2). With the help of his brother, Aaron, Moses is charged with confronting Pharaoh and demanding freedom for the Israelites. After initial missteps and failures, Moses eventually becomes a bold spokesperson for Yahweh in negotiations with the pharaoh.

Of course, the pharaoh and his advisors do not want to let the Israelites go. Why should they? The Israelites have become an effective source of slave labor for building Egypt. Moreover, in the Egyptian worldview, it seems impossible that an otherwise unknown deity of a slave population could demand the attention and respect of the mighty Egyptians. At first, the pharaoh objects: "Who is Yahweh, that I should heed him and let Israel go? I do not know Yahweh" (Exodus 5:2). Pharaoh's question seems to drive the narrative forward: who is this new deity, and what kind of god is he? The events of Israel's deliverance teach Pharaoh, Moses, the Israelites, and the reader about the nature of Yahweh. These are not just interesting narratives; they are intended to reveal something specific about Yahweh.

Pharaoh and the Egyptians agree to Israel's release only after an impressive show of force. This "show of force" is not an overpowering military presence but a series of miraculous interventions in nature. By means of ten "signs and wonders" or "plagues" (Exodus 7:3 and 9:14), Yahweh shows himself superior to any deity the Egyptians had ever seen. No portion of the natural world is beyond Yahweh's control. His plagues command the Nile's waters, frogs, gnats, flies, disease, boils, hail, locusts, darkness, and life itself for Egypt's firstborn sons (Exodus 7–11). This is no direct attack or refutation of individual deities of Egypt's pantheon, but

7.1. Pharaoh Ramses II, ca. 1279–1213 BCE. The specific pharaoh's name is not given in the Old Testament. Evidence suggests, however, that the book of Exodus has in view the Ramside period of New Kingdom Egypt, the most prominent ruler of which was Ramses II. This colossus of Ramses II, with his daughter Meritamun, stands in the temple of Amun in Karnak. (Photo: © Ziga Camernik / Dreamstime.com)

rather an assault on the entire Egyptian world-view. And Yahweh's express motive for these ten plagues is that he might be known: "so that you [Pharaoh] may know that there is no one like me in all the earth" (9:14). The plagues are narrated to show more than simple monotheism (Yahweh is the *only* deity), or perhaps the best deity (monola-trous henotheism). These signs and wonders reveal Yahweh's nature, and as such they teach that there is no other God like this one.

After the Israelites leave Egypt, Pharaoh changes his mind. He pursues the Israelites with the full might of the Egyptian army into the desert in order to bring them back to their former service. When the Israelites find themselves trapped between the Egyptian army and the Red Sea, they panic (Exodus 14:10–12). But Yahweh takes action, driving back the sea and drying its waters. The Israelites cross on dry land. When Pharaoh and his army attempt to pursue them, they are all drowned in the resurg-ing waters. Yahweh declares he will "gain glory" for himself and make himself known by these actions (Exodus 14:17–18). This single act of salvation is celebrated both in narration and in song (Exodus 14 and 15).

Covenant at Mount Sinai

Yahweh made himself known to Israel (and Egypt!) in the plagues. But God's self-revelation doesn't end there. Yahweh's ultimate purpose is to bring the Israelites out of Egypt to a quiet, lonely place in the desert to make himself known to them in a covenant relationship (Exodus 19–24). God leads the Israelites through the Sinai Peninsula to the original spot where he met with Moses at

the burning bush (Exodus 3:12). In a remarkable speech, Yahweh tells the Israelites (through Moses) that their rescue from Egypt had a singular pur-pose: that they might live in intimate relationship with him.

You have seen what I did to the Egyptians, and how I bore you on eagles' wings and brought you to myself. Now therefore, if you obey my voice and keep my covenant, you shall be my treasured possession out of all the peoples. (Exodus 19:4–5)

This covenant then presents the core instruc-tions guarding the relationship, including the Ten Commandments. This is followed by a formal cer-emony, binding Yahweh and Israel together in a blood covenant (Exodus 24:3–8).

Israel's covenant relationship with Yahweh builds on the earlier covenants of Noah (Genesis 6:18 and 9:8–17) and Abraham (Genesis 15:7–21 and 17). (Review Chapters 5 and 6). There are subtle differences between these three covenants. Essentially, the covenant with Israel in Exodus has democratized the relationship. Yahweh is no longer in a binding commitment with an individual like Noah or Abraham, but now with an entire peo-ple. There are also similarities, so that in some ways, you could think of this as one single cov-enant relationship with new iterations. It is also important to remember that covenants are bilateral agreements between two parties. They are not sym-metrical in their requirements; that is, they do not require the same obligations for both parties. But they are nonetheless intended to bind two parties intimately together in a relationship perceived as mutually exclusive.

7.2. Saint Catherine's Monastery at the base of Jebel Musa. The location of *the* Mount Sinai, also known in the Old Testament as Mount Horeb, is impossible to identify. Ancient tradition identifies it with this mountain in the southern Sinai Peninsula, whose Arabic name, Jebel Musa, means "the mountain of Moses." Saint Catherine's Monastery, shown here in the foreground, is one of the oldest working monasteries in the world and has a library with one of the finest collections of ancient manuscripts in the world, second only to the Vatican's. (Erich Lessing / Art Resource, N.Y.)

Tabernacle in the Wilderness

While at the foot of Mount Sinai, and as part of this new covenant relationship, Yahweh gives Israel a detailed plan to build a tent shrine, or tabernacle, as his earthly home (Exodus 25:8). The "tabernacle" (also known sometimes as the "tent of meeting")[1] is simply a portable tent structure, similar to the tent homes of the individual Israelites, except bigger (Exodus 25–31 and 35–40). It houses the ark of the covenant and all furniture necessary for the proper worship of Yahweh. It will be disassembled and moved about with the Israelites wherever they journey during their forty years in the wilderness before entering the promised land, positioned at the center of the people with three tribes to the north, three to the east, three to the south, and three to the west (Numbers 2). It will serve as Yahweh's home until replaced by Solomon's temple. We will return to this topic in the next chapter.

---

1 Although in some passages, the "tent of meeting" appears to be a separate structure (e.g., Exodus 33:7–11).

7.3. Gold-plated calf from Byblos in ancient Phoenicia. Many of Israel's immediate neighbors worshipped the bull as a symbol of physical strength and sexual potency. Theriomorphic depictions, such as the one shown here, have been discovered at Ugarit, Tyre, Hazor, and elsewhere. (Photo: Erich Lessing / Art Resource, N.Y.)

While Moses is on the mountain receiving Yahweh's instructions, the Israelites do something that seems like a good idea at the time. They construct and worship a golden calf, probably as a substitute for Yahweh, violating the first two commandments (Exodus 20:2–6). The episode of the golden calf illustrates the tendency of the Israelites to make their own arrangements (Exodus 32), and it becomes the prime example of their rebellion in the OT. The Israelites are portrayed here as "stiff-necked," or persistently rebellious (Exodus 32:9); their future is thrown into jeopardy by the same sinful impulses that nearly led to the destruction of the human race prior to the flood. But Moses intercedes on their behalf, and the covenant is preserved. Once Moses and the Israelites construct the tabernacle, it is filled with the glorious presence of Yahweh, demonstrating dramatically his gracious forgiveness and acceptance of his people (Exodus 40:34–35).

Wilderness Rebellion and Forty-Year Wanderings

Under normal circumstances, it should take the Israelites around eighteen months to travel from northeastern Egypt into Canaan. In fact, they break camp and set out for the promised land a little over thirteen months after their departure from Egypt (Numbers 10:11–12). If they stay on schedule, they should arrive in a few more months. But they don't stay on schedule. The rebellion of the golden calf episode is a sign of things to come. First the people complain about the privations of travel through the desert (Numbers 11), and then the leadership within Moses' own family complain (Numbers 12). Ultimately, when the people learn that the promised land is occupied by powerful Canaanite city-states who will need to be defeated militarily, they lose heart and decide to turn back to Egypt (Numbers 13–14). The people are then reprimanded for their lack of faith. Yahweh declares that they themselves will never enter the promised land. Their children will be forced to wander in the desert for forty years as nomadic shepherds, until an entirely new generation of Israelites is ready to inherit the promised land in Canaan.

Even these forty years of desert wanderings are not without problems. Through various rebellions (Numbers 16), experiments with prohibited religious practices (Numbers 25), and wars (Numbers 20–21 and 31–32), Yahweh demonstrates his grace and commitment to Israel. The Israelites eventually conquer areas east of the Jordan River and encamp in the plains of Moab, where the new generation of Israelites will prepare for taking the promised land (Numbers 33). The book of Deuteronomy provides the farewell speeches of Moses and closes the Torah with Moses' death (Deuteronomy 34). The Pentateuch narrates Israel's story to the edge of the promised land, but it leaves them there for the book of Joshua.

What Really Happened?

As we have seen, the OT is full of historical narrative (review Chapter 4). The books of Exodus and Numbers continue the history from Joseph and his family in Egypt to the Israelites encamped on the plains of Moab. All of this history raises a question: how much of it really happened? The OT claims to narrate real events from the past, which naturally leaves us with the task of asking, What actually happened?

Readers of the Torah respond to this task in different ways. Consider these two extremes. The first extreme is to assume that everything happened just as described in Exodus and Numbers. The problem with this assertion is that we have no extrabiblical evidence, such as archaeology or Egyptian texts, to defend such a statement. The second extreme is to assume that nothing happened as described in Exodus and Numbers. Readers in this category picture the whole story as a grand religious metaphor fabricated by later authors. The problem with this position is that the Pentateuch has many features that appear to be genuine and ancient, and we have no foundation for assuming that later Israelites or Jews would simply invent these stories.[2]

The problem is made worse by the nature and limitations of archaeology. When it comes to ancient Near Eastern archaeology, our evidence is largely accidental. By this I mean that which periods of ancient history are illuminated by our discoveries have been left to chance. We uncover only

---

2 For an overview of several options between the extremes, see Finkelstein and Mazar in "Where to Find More" in this chapter.

a tiny fraction of life in those ancient periods, and the likelihood of finding confirmation of such ancient traces is minimal. This is especially true of finding evidence of an ancient people group without a national identity, homeland, or settled way of life. Whether we are looking for wandering ancestors living in tents and shepherding flocks, a slave culture living in the northeastern delta of Egypt, or wandering pastoral seminomadic tribes in the desert, we are unlikely ever to find confirmation of early Israel. This leaves us with several unanswered (or *unanswerable*) questions.

The Exodus

So, for example, if we rely only on extrabiblical evidence, we are unable to say when or if the exodus occurred. We do have the victory inscription of Pharaoh Merneptah, from the late thirteenth century BCE, in which he recounts his campaign against the Libyans and closes with a list of conquered foes in Syria-Palestine (Sidebar 7.2). Israel is mentioned seventh in the list of eight enemies, as a distinct tribal entity but not a territorial one. This suggests, at least, that the exodus *may* have occurred earlier in the thirteenth century, as many have argued, and that Israel *may* be identified with peoples attested in the archaeological record as settling in the central hills of the Southern Levant at this time. But this is still only suggestive evidence.

The problem, of course, is that the OT describes the exodus as a dramatic, transitional point in Late Bronze Age history: ancient Egypt decimated by plagues, its mighty army drowned, its economy left in ruins after the escape of huge numbers of Hebrew slaves. How likely is it such

events would leave no extrabiblical record? Nor do we have evidence of a forty-year Israelite wandering in the desert. For example, the site of Kadesh was an important stop along the Israelite journey (Numbers 13:26 and 20:1; see Map 7.1), and yet we have no evidence the place was inhabited between the Middle Bronze Age and the tenth century BCE (modern Tell el-Qudeirat). Surely, we might conclude, such a spectacular event in history would leave some scrap of evidence.

Instead, even the route of the Israelites as they departed Egypt and headed to Canaan is impossible to trace. They may have traveled along a southern route through the Sinai Peninsula, in which case the traditional site of Mount Sinai is Jebel Musa. Or perhaps they journeyed along a northern route, following the Mediterranean coast, which was more often used by travelers to Syria-Palestine from Egypt. In that case, we have no indication where Mount Sinai itself might have been located. It is also possible that the Israelites used one of several east–west routes running along desert wadis (seasonally dry water channels), indicating a more central journey through the peninsula. Whatever the case might have been – assuming a group of Israelites actually *did* escape from Egypt – we cannot reconstruct their route across the Sinai Peninsula.

We can be no more certain about a Red Sea crossing. The Hebrew phrase *yam sûph* has traditionally been translated as Red Sea, but Reed Sea is also possible. Later passages seem to indicate the Red Sea (1 Kings 9:26), and this is supported by the Septuagint and Vulgate translations. Most assume in this case that the Israelites miraculously crossed the saltwater Gulf of Suez, the

SIDEBAR 7.2. EXCERPT FROM THE STELA OF MERNEPTAH

The much-discussed **Merneptah Stela** from approximately 1207 BCE (also known as the "Israel Stela") is the most important piece of evidence we have about early Israel. This is the first and only mention of Israel in Egyptian sources. The epic narrative poem (paralleled in another place by a longer narrative text), begins with the pharaoh's royal titles, followed by a description of the defeat of the Libyans. Then comes a declaration of Pharaoh Merneptah as victor, and a celebration of the return of peace. The text closes with a twelve-line poem of praise, declaring Merneptah's victory over additional enemies of Syria-Palestine.

The princes are prostrate saying: "Shalom!"
Not one of the Nine Bows lifts his head:
Tjehenu [Libya] is vanquished, Khatti [the
     Hittites] at peace,
Canaan is captive with all woe.
Ashkelon is conquered, Gezer seized,
Yanoam made nonexistent;
Israel is wasted, bare of seed,
Khor [Hurru = Syria] is become a widow for
     Egypt.
All who roamed have been subdued
By the King of Upper and Lower Egypt,
     Banere-meramun,
Son of Re, Merneptah, Content with Maat,
*Given life like Re every day.**

The cities of Ashkelon, Gezer, and Yenoam are included, as well as the nation Khatti [the Hittites]. The name Israel is included with a determinative sign indicating "people" or ethnic group, unlike the other entities in the list, who are marked as geographic locations such as a city or nation. This suggests that Israel at this early stage was an important population group in Canaan, though not a city-state polity or nation.

7.4. Merneptah victory stela. Pharaoh Merneptah (reigned approximately 1213–1203 BCE), son of Ramses II, initiated several military campaigns during the first years of his reign. (Photo: © DeA Picture Library / Art Resource, N.Y.)

* Miriam Lichtheim, *Ancient Egyptian Literature: A Book of Readings* (3 vols.; Berkeley: University of California Press, 1973–1980), 2:73–78, esp. 77.

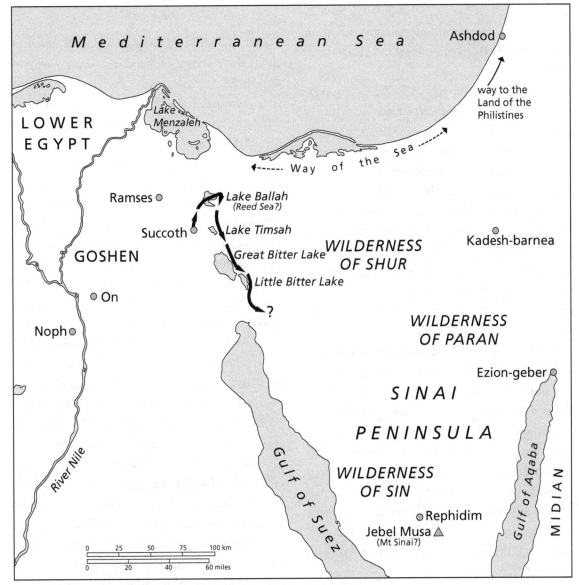

Map 7.1. Initial route of the exodus

Red Sea's northwestern extremity (see Map 7.1). However, the Hebrew term *sûph* itself denotes reeds or rushes (plants growing in water), and so many assume that Pharaoh's army was destroyed in the freshwater reed marshes, one of many lakes located between the Mediterranean Sea and the Gulf of Suez. This position, in fact, better explains the geographical references in Exodus and is more plausible than the Gulf of Suez as the point of crossing. Still others argue that there was no Israelite crossing of *any* sea in escape from the Egyptians.

So was there an exodus? a Red Sea crossing? a wilderness wandering? Part of our difficulty is in assuming that the OT intended to write *history* in our modern sense of the term. The Exodus narrative is not such pure historiography but is more of a religious or theological treatise. Yet behind this theological writing is an assumption of historical events – a conviction that something real happened. This is not pure history, that much is clear. But neither is it pure fiction. We should think of it more like a "docudrama" or historical novel, which combines both types of writing.[3]

And so we are left with vastly different conclusions. Some believe that we have nothing more here than traces of an ancient memory, a distorted and distant reflection of some unreconstructable event. Others argue for at least the *plausibility* of the events largely as narrated in Exodus, and dated roughly in the thirteenth century BCE.[4] Questions about the exodus, the crossing of the Re(e)d Sea, and the wilderness wanderings remain for the meantime unanswerable. How you address each problem personally will depend to a large degree on how you read the OT.

---

3 For Exodus as "docudrama," see Redmount in "Where to Find More" in this chapter.

4 For these conflicting conclusions, see the works of Grabbe and Hoffmeier in "Where to Find More" in this chapter.

The Covenant

Equally difficult to answer are historical questions about the covenant of Exodus 19–24. As we have seen, Israel's covenant with Yahweh at Mount Sinai is an essential feature of OT faith. It was once widely assumed that Israel's theological use of the idea of covenant was a late development, probably appearing first in the eighth-century BCE prophets like Hosea. If this is true – it seems obvious to say it – then there was no covenant between Israel and Yahweh in the thirteenth century BCE at Mount Sinai. In this case, Mosaic covenant religion would be a late invention, one aspect of the revolutionary idea of monotheism as Israel's Axial Age contribution to human civilization. If so, we waste our time raising the historical question.

All of this changed about sixty years ago. That's when scholars discovered remarkably close literary parallels between the OT's covenant passages and Hittite vassal treaties written seven centuries *before* Hosea. Taken together with later Neo-Assyrian treaties, these texts have revealed a previously unknown literary tradition of ancient Near Eastern culture that lasted from the Late Bronze Age well into the Iron Age. When we study the book of Deuteronomy (Chapter 9), you will discover just how closely the OT's idea of "covenant" is related to these ancient Near Eastern political treaties.

Such binding relationships between two parties were not uncommon in the ancient world. The difference is that nowhere else did a people group perceive *its deity* as a treaty partner. Ordinarily, both parties of the treaty/covenant were humans, except in Israel, where such a treaty became the primary means of explaining the relationship with God. So the covenant of Moses at Mount Sinai is an important topic for understanding the OT, and we will return to it many times. But the question for now is – did it really happen? Was the covenant formulation really a feature of early Israel?

After the literary parallels with the Hittite treaties were discovered, numerous students of the Torah argued that the covenant was, in fact, an early feature of Israelite religion. Others believe that the OT covenant passages find closer parallels with the later Neo-Assyrian treaties and have assumed the older view that the idea of covenant was a later development in Israel. Either way, the covenant idea was certainly a part of Israel's Axial Age contribution, from at least the eighth century BCE onward. Whether it goes back to the Late Bronze Age origins of ancient Israel is, for the meantime, one of our unanswerable historical questions.

The Tabernacle

Many have raised similar questions about whether the tabernacle ever existed. The importance of the tent sanctuary is obvious from the number of Torah verses devoted to it, more than to any other single topic. Few raised questions about the facts of the story until the nineteenth century when scholars working on the sources of the Pentateuch began to suspect that the priestly writings, including the elaborate instructions for building the tabernacle, were among the last writings of ancient Israel (see Sidebar 8.3). Famously, Julius Wellhausen concluded that the tabernacle

was "the copy, not the prototype, of the temple at Jerusalem."[5] By this he meant that the tabernacle was a late literary invention, which was projected into the past as a precursor to Solomon's temple. It never existed. Instead, the tabernacle was an idealized fiction designed to glorify the Mosaic age and to unify religion after the destruction of the temple in Jerusalem.

Other readers of the Torah since Wellhausen have drawn on archaeological and comparative evidence to argue that the tabernacle was an actual historical structure. This has included (a) sacred tent shrines from Phoenicia (northern Levant) at the center of a battle encampment with an altar nearby; (b) Egyptian art depicting a mobile tent of the same layout and design as that in Exodus; (c) the Late Bronze Age deity El, chief god of the Ugaritic pantheon, who lived in a tent, while the younger deity, Baal, lived in a temple; and (d) large public tents from the city of Mari on the Euphrates, built with similar wooden frames described with Semitic words similar to those used in the OT to refer to the tabernacle's construction.[6] The Exodus narrative may have embellished the grandeur and opulence of this tent shrine. But we have no reason to doubt that it was real and that it played an important role in the formative period of early Israel's religion.

---

5 Julius Wellhausen, *Prolegomena to the History of Israel* (Atlanta, Ga.: Scholars Press, 1994 [originally published in translation in 1885]), 37.

6 For more on this topic, see Homan in "Where to Find More" in this chapter.

Yahweh: What Kind of God?

Who is Yahweh, and what kind of God is he? The narratives of the Torah raise this question through the words of the Egyptian pharaoh: "Who is Yahweh, that I should heed him and let Israel go? I do not know Yahweh" (Exodus 5:2). Israel's God is formally introduced as Yahweh in the Torah story (Exodus 3:14–15 and 6:2–8), so it is appropriate to ask what kind of God we have here.

The Torah narratives portray Yahweh as the *sovereign Lord of nature*. He easily commands the forces of nature in the ten plagues, ruling the waters of the Nile and the entire animal kingdom. He commands the waters of the Red Sea, provides heavenly bread in the desert (the manna; Exodus 16), and supplies fresh water from a desert rock (Exodus 17 and Numbers 20). Yahweh calls forth earthquakes to punish rebellious Israelites (Numbers 16) and determines the message of foreign prophets (Balaam son of Beor; Numbers 22–24). No power of the universe seems beyond his control.

Yahweh is a *revealing God*. He appears to Moses in the burning bush, to Pharaoh in the plagues, and to the people of Israel at Mount Sinai. Yahweh's express motive for the plagues against Egypt is that he might be known: "so that you [Pharaoh] may know that there is no one like me in all the earth" (Exodus 9:14). In an especially striking and mysterious passage, Yahweh reveals himself to Moses physically, allowing him to see only a portion of his back because, he declares, "no one shall see me and live" (Exodus 33:18–23). Yahweh is not immanent in the created order, as though he inhabits the sun, moon, stars, or any component of nature. Instead,

Yahweh is above and beyond all that, transcending Israel's experience. Paradoxically, God reveals himself to Israel, making himself known as the one and only Yahweh.

Yahweh is a *warrior God*. The freed Israelites were a slave population, with no army and no experience at warfare. When they are caught by Pharaoh's army at the Red Sea, Moses declares, "[Yahweh] will fight for you, and you have only to keep still" (Exodus 14:14). Even the Egyptians realize (too late!) that Yahweh is fighting the war for the Israelites (Exodus 14:25). And in hymnic celebration, Moses declares "Yahweh is a warrior; Yahweh is his name" (Exodus 15:3). Yahweh does not use typical weapons; he uses water as a weapon to destroy his enemy (Exodus 15:4–8). Later, in a skirmish with the Amalekites, Israel prevails as long as Moses holds high the staff of God, and Yahweh declares Amalek his enemy (Exodus 17:8–16).

Yahweh is a *savior*. God heard the groaning of the Israelites who cried out for help because of their Egyptian bondage. He took notice and acted to deliver them, remembering his covenant with their ancestors (Exodus 2:23–25). When he called Moses at the burning bush, Yahweh declared that he had arrived in order to deliver Israel (Exodus 3:8). The narrative summary of Yahweh's miracle at the Red Sea states that Yahweh saved Israel that day from the Egyptians (Exodus 14:30). His continued provisions of quail, manna, and water in the desert were also acts of salvation.

Yahweh is *king*. At the conclusion of the hymn celebrating the defeat of Pharaoh's armies, the Israelites acknowledge that Yahweh "will reign forever and ever" (Exodus 15:18). This attribute of Yahweh becomes more pronounced later in the OT, but even in the Torah, the tabernacle itself and the ark of the covenant imply that Yahweh is king in Israel. Indeed, the ark serves as his footstool, the cherubim above the ark as his throne, and the inner sanctuary of the tabernacle as his throne room (Exodus 25:22).

The Torah narratives also portray Yahweh as a God who *makes his presence known*. As the Israelites depart Egypt, Yahweh guides them along the way physically in the form of a pillar of cloud by day, which turns to fire by night (Exodus 13:21–22; Numbers 14:14). Yahweh's presence at Mount Sinai is evident in fire and smoke, thunder and lightning, violent movement and trumpet blast (Exodus 19:16–18). Once the Israelites complete the tabernacle, the presence of Yahweh in the form of the cloud covers it and Yahweh's "glory" fills it (Exodus 40:34–35; "glory" is *kābôd*, the splendor or majesty of Yahweh's essence or manifestation of power). Indeed, the pillar of cloud or fire – representing Yahweh's own personal presence – attaches to the tabernacle, signaling when to break camp and when to settle down (Exodus 40:36–38). The tabernacle becomes a portable Mount Sinai, housing Yahweh's cloudy-fiery presence and leading the Israelites safely to the promised land.[7] Moses believes it is this very presence of Yahweh that makes Israel distinctive among all nations of earth (Exodus 33:14–16).

As you can see, the Torah narratives emphasize many dimensions and attributes belonging to Yahweh. No single description is adequate. And the legal portions will add even more, which we will cover in the next chapter. But perhaps Yahweh's most important attribute in the Torah is that of *covenant maker*. He is not only a saving, revealing, ever-present deity. Yahweh's purpose for all this activity is to bind himself in a relationship with Israel in the form of a covenant (Exodus 19–24). The exclusive nature of this covenant ("have no other gods before me"; Exodus 20:3), brings us once again to the question of how Israel thought of other deities. At first, Israel did not deny their existence. Other deities simply belonged to other nations; for Israel, there was only Yahweh. But no other gods could compare to Yahweh, who was supreme above all others (monolatrous henotheism; see Chapter 1). Eventually, Israelite philosophers denied the existence of other gods and expanded the concept of Yahweh, who absorbed all the attributes and functions of the other deities. This "monotheist leap," as it's been called, means that Yahweh takes on all the roles served by other, lesser deities in the pantheon.[8]

Other people groups in the ancient Near East had gods for the provision of food, and separate deities for health, fertility, and protection against enemies. But in Israel, all these roles were combined and provided by Yahweh. Near the conclusion of the covenant passage, Yahweh promises the Israelites that he is sufficient to serve all their human needs.

[When you come to the land] you shall not bow down to their gods, or worship them, or follow their practices, but

---

7 See Propp in "Where to Find More" in this chapter.

8 See Frymer-Kensky in "Where to Find More" in this chapter for this terminology.

you shall utterly demolish them and break their pillars in pieces. You shall worship Yahweh your God, and I will bless your bread and your water; and I will take sickness away from among you. No one shall miscarry or be barren in your land; I will fulfill the number of your days. I will send my terror in front of you, and will throw into confusion all the people against whom you shall come, and I will make all your enemies turn their backs to you. (Exodus 23:24–27)

No other gods are necessary; they are in fact prohibited. Yahweh alone is sufficient for Israel. The covenant assumes that Israel can and should be loyal exclusively to Yahweh because he is sufficient to absorb and subsume the features of all other deities. This was a new and radical idea — even revolutionary — as Israel's monolatrous henotheism begins to morph into monotheism proper on the way to changing the world.

WHERE TO FIND MORE

Commentaries: The best technical and advanced commentaries on **Exodus** and **Numbers** are William H. C. Propp, *Exodus 1–18* and *Exodus 19–40* (Anchor Bible 2 and 2A; New York: Doubleday, 1999 and 2006), and Jacob Milgrom, *Numbers: The Traditional Hebrew Text with the New JPS Translation* (JPS Torah Commentary; Philadelphia: Jewish Publication Society, 1990). For briefer treatment, see Carol L. Meyers, *Exodus* (New Cambridge Bible Commentary; Cambridge and New York: Cambridge University Press, 2005), and Gordon J. Wenham, *Numbers: An Introduction and Commentary* (Tyndale Old Testament Commentaries 4; Leicester, Eng., and Downers Grove, Ill.: InterVarsity Press, 1981[2008]).

Finkelstein, Israel, and Amihai Mazar. *The Quest for the Historical Israel: Debating Archaeology and the History of Early Israel*. Edited by Brian B. Schmidt. SBLABS 17. Atlanta, Ga.: Society of Biblical Literature, 2007.

Frymer-Kensky, Tikva. *In the Wake of the Goddesses: Women, Culture, and the Biblical Transformation of Pagan Myth*. New York: Free Press, 1992.

On the "monotheist leap," see pages 83–99.

Grabbe, Lester L. *Ancient Israel: What Do We Know and How Do We Know It?* London and New York: T & T Clark, 2007.

For the possibility that the biblical text preserves only a "distant – and distorted – memory of an actual event," see pages 84–88.

Hoffmeier, James K. *Israel in Egypt: The Evidence for the Authenticity of the Exodus Tradition*. New York: Oxford University Press, 1997.

Culls all available evidence in defense of a thirteenth-century date for a historical exodus. Specifically on the Red Sea versus Reed Sea debate, see pages 199–222.

Homan, Michael M. *To Your Tents, O Israel! The Terminology, Function, Form, and Symbolism of Tents in the Hebrew Bible and the Ancient Near East*. Culture and History of the Ancient Near East 12. Leiden: Brill, 2002.

For complete discussion of the ancient Near Eastern parallels to the tabernacle, see chapter 7, pages 89–128.

Nicholson, Ernest W. *God and His People: Covenant and Theology in the Old Testament*. Oxford/New York: Clarendon Press/Oxford University Press, 1986.

Redmount, Carol A. "Bitter Lives: Israel In and Out of Egypt." Pages 58–89 in *The Oxford History of the Biblical World*. Edited by Michael David Coogan. New York: Oxford University Press, 1998.

For the route of the exodus, see pages 66–69.

Ska, Jean-Louis. *Introduction to Reading the Pentateuch*. Translated by Pascale Dominique. Winona Lake, Ind.: Eisenbrauns, 2006.

For more on the history of the identification of the sources, see pages 96–164.

CHAPTER 8

Torah Instruction

OLD TESTAMENT READING: LEVITICUS AND PSALMS 19 AND 119

In this chapter, our attention will shift from narratives to the law materials present in the Pentateuch. These portions include the Book of the Covenant, tabernacle instructions, purification laws, holiness legislation, and a collection of priestly laws. The laws of Torah, better understood as instruction, represent the central feature of living in covenant relationship with Yahweh. Most notable are the Ten Commandments, whose value has remained virtually unsurpassed in the history of ethics. These "Ten Words" (Hebrew), combined with Israel's narrative story and covenant with Yahweh, set the trajectory for the rest of the Bible.

The form in which the independent lists of laws were originally preserved in ancient Israel closely parallels that of other known law codes in the ancient Near East. Israel's Torah instruction also exhibits certain affinities with later Greek developments, particularly in its expansion and placement within the narrative framework. Importantly, the emphasis on the writing of the covenant law marks a turn from preliterate ancestral religion to a literate Mosaic faith, and helps ensure the preservation of a sacred text for all time.

The Torah – also known as the five books of Moses, or the Pentateuch – is a blend of narrative and law. Israel's story is first recounted in the narrative thread of Exodus and Numbers. Mixed into this narrative, and at times making the thread difficult to follow, is a diverse group of materials we typically call *law*. That term, "law," is an unfortunate English label. A better designation for this material would be something like "instruction" or "direction," since such a term is

The longest hymn in the book of Psalms is Psalm 119, an elaborate poem in praise of God's law. Notice the different words for law in this excerpt, highlighted in roman and underlined.

> *With my whole heart I seek you;*
> *do not let me stray from your* <u>commandments</u>*.*
> *I treasure your* <u>word</u> *in my heart,*
> *so that I may not sin against you.*
> *Blessed are you, O* LORD*;*
> *teach me your* <u>statutes</u>*.*
> *With my lips I declare*
> *all the* <u>ordinances</u> *of your mouth.*
> *I delight in the way of your* <u>decrees</u>
> *as much as in all riches.*
> *I will meditate on your* <u>precepts</u>*,*
> *and fix my eyes on your* ways*.*
> *I will delight in your* <u>statutes</u>*;*
> *I will not forget your* word*. (Psalm 119:10–16)*

You can see that the OT has many words for Torah instruction. Israel's theologians and philosophers explored the richness of God's law. "Open my eyes, so that I may behold wondrous things out of your law" (Psalm 119:18). As you learn about the many complex aspects of Torah instruction, keep in mind its wondrous beauty and grace as celebrated by ancient Israelites.

closer to the Hebrew meaning of *torah*. This portion of the Pentateuch sets down instruction for a fruitful and fulfilling life with Yahweh, Israel's God.

Many people today have a poor opinion of the law, or of anything "legal." Don't let this prevent you from appreciating what a beautiful thing is the OT's law. The ancient Israelites had a great regard for the Torah's instruction. They saw the law as providing all things necessary for a good life. Torah instruction is the gift of God, lovingly provided to guide and direct Israel in peace and security. As we will see later (Chapter 18), Israel's library includes a hymnbook, or collection of songs, and a few of these are songs of celebration of God's law and songs of thanksgiving for its benefits. So, for

example, Israelites sing that the law of Yahweh is perfect, providing life and joy, and making one wise and good. This law is more precious than gold and sweeter than honey (Psalm 19:7–10). As you learn about the Torah instruction in this chapter, remember that the people of Israel saw this law as the path illuminated by Yahweh for a meaningful life. Torah law makes one's life worthwhile and is the source of life itself. This is something to celebrate!

COMMANDMENTS, ORDINANCES, STATUTES, INSTRUCTIONS, LAWS, AND SO FORTH

Jewish rabbis of a much later period counted 613 commandments given to Moses. Of these, 365 were said to correspond to the number of days in the year, and the remaining 248 to the number of bones in the human body.[1] Most of these have nothing to do with what we today call law. Instead, most regulate relationships between humans and God (theology), or describe acceptable behavior between humans (ethics).

When reading straight through the OT, the first portion of law we find is, appropriately enough, (1) the *Ten Commandments* (Exodus 20:1–17, and see the recurrence in Deuteronomy 5:6–21). We sometimes refer to these as the Decalogue, which is Greek for "Ten Words." As a matter of fact, they aren't really called "commandments" in the OT but "Ten Words" (the Hebrew of Exodus 34:28 and Deuteronomy 4:13 and 10:4). These are broadly stated principles that provide context for the more specific laws to follow. Their literary location also makes the Ten Commandments an essential feature of the covenant at Mount Sinai. God himself writes these words with his own finger on two stone tablets (Exodus 31:18).

The next portion of law is (2) the *Book of the Covenant*, which sets out the specific ordinances to be observed (Exodus 21–23).[2] These ordinances, or Mishpatim (*mišpāṭîm*), are detailed as "if ... then ... " cases and are called casuistic laws. This unit as a whole receives its name, the "Book of the Covenant," within the narrative framework (Exodus 24:7), so that it is the written version of the covenant at Mount Sinai. Yahweh says to Moses, "Come up to me on the mountain, and wait there; and I will give you the tablets of stone,

with the law and the commandment, which I have written for their instruction" (Exodus 24:12). Yet the laws in the Book of the Covenant reflect a settled life in the promised land, in which Israelites live in houses, worship at temples, and cultivate crops and fields. These ordinances, then, anticipate life after the conquest of the land, expressing Israel's ideal law rather than preserving any actual law code.

Coming next as we read through the Torah are (3) the *instructions for the tabernacle* and all its furnishings (Exodus 25–31 and 35–40). Yahweh gives Moses a specific pattern for the tabernacle to be built as a sanctuary for his presence in the midst of Israel (Exodus 25:8–9). This plan has three parts: an outer courtyard, a holy place, and, finally, an innermost sanctum of holiness, the "most holy place," which is separated from the holy place by a curtain (Exodus 26:33–35). Included in the instructions are plans for the ark of the covenant and for a table for the bread of Presence, a lampstand, curtains, altars for sacrifice and incense, and an outer court. In addition, Yahweh provides detailed instructions for priestly garments and for the consecration of priests for service in worship at the tabernacle. There is a final reminder to keep the Sabbath (Exodus 31:12–17). These instructions are matched at the conclusion of the book of Exodus with an account of their fulfillment (Exodus 35–40). So these instructions for the tabernacle include the imperative commands (Exodus 25–31) and the indicative fulfillments (Exodus 35–40).

The next several chapters contain (4) the *sacrificial laws* (Leviticus 1–7). While reading these may seem tedious to us, they were critically important (and exciting!) for the Israelites. Animal sacrifices in most ancient cultures were thought to return

1 According to Rabbi Simelai in the Talmud; Jacob Neusner, *Judaism: The Basics* (London: Routledge, 2006), 78–79.
2 Technically, Exodus 21:1–23:19, with a preface (20:22–26) and sermonic conclusion (23:20–33).

8.1. The tabernacle in the wilderness. An artist reconstruction of the tabernacle in the Sinai Desert. The great altar for sacrifices was in the outer courtyard, and the tent housed the holy place and the holy of holies. (Photo: © Balage Balogh / Art Resource, N.Y.)

life or energy to its divine source, restoring the power of that source for the good of nature and humanity. But Israel understood Yahweh as independent and self-sufficient. The sacrifices prescribed here become a means of showing gratitude and of ensuring a right relationship with Yahweh. The assumption in these chapters is that human sin breaks the covenant relationship with Yahweh for both individuals and the nation Israel as a whole. The sacrifices provide atonement (i.e., reconciliation), purging offenders and cleansing the tabernacle and its sacrificial altar of impurities and sins. The cultic instructions for lay people have five types of sacrifices: burnt offerings, grain offerings, peace offerings, purgation offerings, and guilt offerings (Leviticus 1–5). Specific ritual

instructions for the priests conclude this set of laws (Leviticus 6–7).

The sacrificial laws were focused on the tabernacle and the altar. The next set of laws, (5) the *purification laws*, are concerned with purity or impurity in everyday life (Leviticus 11–15). This set of laws culminates in the great Day of Atonement, which prescribes a ritual for cleansing both tabernacle and people (Leviticus 16). Sin and guilt are removed from individuals throughout the year by means of the sacrificial system. But when Yahweh forgives such guilt, his sanctuary continues to bear responsibility. Therefore, once a year, all sin and guilt accumulated over the past twelve months and attached to the tabernacle is purged and physically removed through a scapegoat ceremony. The Day of

Atonement ritual purges the sanctuary and makes it possible for a just and righteous Yahweh to continue to dwell there. Thus, Leviticus 16 is the heart of the Torah, the center point of the Pentateuch. The Day of Atonement is the Torah's "most holy place," a ritual in which the high priest enters the center of Israel's religion and makes it possible for Yahweh to remain with his people.

The next portion of Torah instruction is (6) the *holiness legislation*, punctuated as it is by frequent calls to become holy, as Yahweh is holy (Leviticus 17–27). Indeed, holiness is the theme of the book of Leviticus. Previous legal sections may leave the impression that only priests or sanctuaries are holy. But these laws, which touch on just about every topic of everyday life, democratize holiness; it is the call and privilege of all God's people to be holy. And the entire promised land is to become holy, not just the tabernacle (and, later, the temple). The transcendence, or surpassing separateness, of Yahweh is the model. Israel's life, every aspect of its existence, is called in these laws to be different – like Yahweh – and through that uniqueness, to be closer to him.

Finally, our walk through the legal portions of the Torah concludes with (7) a *collection of priestly laws* in the book of Numbers. Instead of being collected in one location in Numbers, these laws are scattered through the book (Numbers 5–6, 8–10, 15, 18–19, and 27–30). Many of the topics in these laws return to earlier issues – the treatment of those with impurities of various sorts, the coveting of someone else's property, Sabbath keeping, types of offerings and sacrifices, and so on – but they are not merely repetitious. Most add some new detail to previous legal passages in Exodus or Leviticus, or they develop the topic in a more complete fashion.

The Core of the Torah, and Israel's "Ethics"

These various laws of the Pentateuch, what we are calling the Torah instruction, may seem like a confusing hodgepodge of regulations and rules. Think of them, instead, as the core of the Torah, which complement the Torah story (covered in Chapter 7). Most readers are more familiar with the details of Israel's story; they are less familiar with the instructions. But Leviticus is quite literally the core, standing as it does in the symmetrical center of the five-book Torah. Symbolically, these laws of Exodus, Leviticus, and Numbers form the heart of the Torah. They encourage the proper relationship with God and with fellow human beings, which is the ultimate objective of Israel's story.

This brings us to the question of what exactly these "laws" are and what purpose do they serve. The majority of the laws are religious in nature and have little to do with what we more narrowly call "law" in English. Such laws in this narrow definition are rules regulating relationships between humans in the conduct of their everyday lives, protecting their economic, social, physical, and psychological interests. Only about 10 percent of the commandments of the Torah are these kinds of laws, establishing rights and duties between individuals (governing things like marriage, inheritance, property, contract, crime, etc).[3] The rest are rules regulating relations between humans and God, such as instructions related to the tabernacle, the priesthood, and sacrifices. Others encourage

---

3 For more on these definitions and on the estimation of 60 out of 613 commands as everyday law, see Westbrook and Wells in "Where to Find More" in this chapter.

ethical behavior, such as fair and just treatment of one's neighbor or the poor.

So these laws are not an official Israelite "code" of law (a topic we will return to later). In other words, the OT has no comprehensive system for dealing with all behavior throughout Israelite society. Such laws would be *prescriptive*, authoritative laws established by society and enforced by legal officials. They would also quickly become outdated. Rather, the OT's laws are *descriptive*, listing customs and practices that were in force in ancient Israel and were believed to be helpful. And like other ancient peoples, the Israelites attributed their laws to the deity. Their laws were given to them by Yahweh, which gave the ordinances an ethical dimension. Failure to observe the law becomes an offense against Yahweh himself.

And yet, unlike other peoples of the ancient world, Israel linked its laws directly to a covenant relationship with Yahweh. The laws came from Yahweh at Mount Sinai, and in this way the Torah instruction is connected to the Torah story. Israel's laws become the central feature of living in covenant relationship with Yahweh. Israel's understanding of Yahweh as supreme ruler of the universe – the OT's monolatrous henotheism – makes Yahweh the one ultimately responsible for justice. The king of the world ensures justice for all (Genesis 18:25): "Shall not the judge of all the earth do what is just?" Although other peoples of the ancient Near East had what we call "ethics" in today's terminology, they had no similar integrated moral universe. Israel's law, as diverse as it stands in the Torah, represents a unified and unifying moral portrait of life with God.

For most believing readers through the centuries, this unifying moral vision of the Torah is also revelatory. In other words, beyond a list of rules to keep, the Pentateuch's laws are a reflection of Yahweh's nature. This God is one who wants fairness and justice for everyone, including himself. Israel must live in relationship with Yahweh in a way that justly and fairly acknowledges and celebrates God's supremacy. And Israel must also live in a way that celebrates a fair and just society, a society in which one respects one's neighbors and provides for the less fortunate. And this ideal vision of the Torah instruction somehow reflects the nature of Israel's God. Acceptance of this moral vision is almost like a creed of Yahwistic faith.

THE TEN WORDS

This ideal moral vision of the law is perhaps best captured by the Ten Commandments. As you saw in our list of legal materials in the OT, the Ten Commandments, or Decalogue, make up the first portion of law and are found in two places in the Torah: Exodus 20:1–17 and Deuteronomy 5:6–21. These two lists are almost identical. A similar list is found in Exodus 34:11–26, which is however focused on proper worship. This recurrence reflects three origins of the Ten Words, one found in the Yahwist source (Exodus 34), one in an early Elohist source with priestly additions (Exodus 20:1–17), and finally, one in the D source (Deuteronomy 5:6–21). It is possible these last two (E/P and D) go back to a shared earlier source.

The Torah thus emphasizes the importance of the Ten Commandments in a number of ways. The Decalogue is the first portion of legal material, recurs several times, and even is written by the very *finger of God* on stone tablets (Exodus 31:18; Deuteronomy 4:13, 5:22, and 9:10). This list of ten principles becomes the centerpiece of Israel's covenant relationship with Yahweh, placed at the core by the Torah's narrative framework. The other legal materials that follow the Decalogue may be seen as laying out the particulars of its general and universal truths. These ten principles establish a moral arc or trajectory for the rest of the Torah, and indeed for the rest of the Bible. A simple parallel can be seen in the way the U.S. Constitution relates to the explicit cases or case laws that have developed out of it.[4]

Thus these "Ten Words" as they are called in the Bible (Exodus 34:28) encapsulate the moral vision of the OT for all time. Their literary form illustrates the point. The ordinances (*mišpāṭîm*) of the Book of the Covenant detail specific cases by means of hypothetical situations, characterized by casuistic sentences (Exodus 21–23). An opening "when/if/whoever" clause states the legal circumstances of a hypothetical case (the protasis), followed by a second clause detailing the legal consequences (the apodosis). Ancient Near Eastern law codes commonly use this approach: "If a man kidnaps the young child of another man, he shall be killed."[5] By contrast, the Ten Commandments drop the first clause, the specific situation, and simply establish the principle that should (or should not) be done. These ten are different from the ordinances, commandments, and statutes to follow. They are not specific to any particular circumstance but are prescribed for all circumstances. They are not for any one occasion but are for all occasions and for all times. Rather than hypothetical case laws, these are absolute and foundational. They are Israel's nonnegotiable requirements rooted in its covenant with Yahweh.

The Ten Commandments must be taken as a whole. They have a literary and logical progression flowing from one command to the next, each command building on what came before it. The list has two sections. The first details what is required for Israel's relationship with Yahweh, and the second what is required between humans. In order to arrive at ten, the commands have been divided and counted differently by the various faith communities. Essentially, the first four start with a demand for exclusive loyalty to Yahweh alone, and a ban on representing Yahweh with idols. This requires paying proper respect to God's sacred name, Yahweh, and keeping the Sabbath. These first commands are rooted in the very nature of Yahweh, and they are essential before moving on to how to relate properly to one's neighbor. The remaining commands are essentially for maintaining a safe and healthy community. When it comes to ethics, all one needs to know is contained in these Ten Words, whether summed up briefly (as in the Great Commandment to love one's God and neighbor; Mark 12:28–33), or expanded in detail elsewhere in the Torah's legal materials.[6] The value of these Ten Words has not been surpassed in the history of human ethics.

Yet the Ten Words will not suffice as a universal moral code. The Torah instruction, even as crystallized in the Ten Words, establishes a bare minimum standard below which humans must not sink. These laws determine the lower reaches

4 For this analogy, see Miller in "Where to Find More" in this chapter.
5 Law of Hammurabi no. 14, and compare Exodus 21:16.

6 See Miller (p. 4) in "Where to Find More" in this chapter.

SIDEBAR 8.2. TEN WORDS? TRY COUNTING THEM!

The Bible does not make clear how the "Ten Words" are to be counted. They were written on two tablets (Exodus 34:29), supporting the idea of two (perhaps unequal) portions. The first portion addresses one's relationship to Yahweh and the second the relationship to one's neighbor. Beyond that, we have different ways of numbering them. Most Jewish, Catholic, and Lutheran readers take the commands against "other gods" and "idols" as one command. The Jewish tradition takes the prologue "I am Yahweh your God ..." (Exodus 20:2) as the first command, thereby coming to the number ten. Catholics and Lutherans divide the last command, that against "coveting," into two, in order to get ten. This separates coveting the neighbor's wife from coveting other property. Most Eastern Orthodox and Protestants (besides Lutherans) count "other gods" and "idols" as separate commands, and take "coveting" as a single commandment to arrive at ten.

We may assume that the Decalogue was originally a list of brief clauses, some of only two words. This made them easier to memorize. The number ten was probably used to correspond to the digits of one's hands, again as an aid to memory. In the following list, the Jewish counting comes first, followed by the Roman Catholic and Lutheran (in parenthesis), and the Orthodox and most Protestants [in brackets]. References are to the book of Exodus.

1			Prologue: I am Yahweh your God (20:2)
2	(1)	[1]	Have no other gods before me (20:3)
		[2]	Make no idols (20:4–6)
3	(2)	[3]	Make no wrongful use of the name of Yahweh (20:7)
4	(3)	[4]	Keep the sabbath day (20:8–11)
5	(4)	[5]	Honor your father and your mother (20:12)
6	(5)	[6]	Do not murder (20:13)
7	(6)	[7]	Do not commit adultery (20:14)
8	(7)	[8]	Do not steal (20:15)
9	(8)	[9]	Do not bear false witness (20:16)
10	(9)	[10]	Do not covet your neighbor's wife (20:17a)
	(10)		Do not covet your neighbor's other property (20:17b)

---

or limits of acceptable behavior. One reader has observed that most of the Ten Commandments "could be kept by staying in bed all day and avoiding any human contact."[7] Yet taken together, the Torah instruction and the Torah story are calling for much more. These laws are combined in the Torah with Israel's narrative story in order to illustrate Yahweh's ethical ideal, which transcends even the Ten Commandments. It is the Torah taken as a whole – both its laws and narrative – that reveal Yahweh's ethical ideal, sealed with a covenant and setting a trajectory for the rest of the Bible.

7 John Barton, *What Is the Bible?* (2nd ed.; London: SPCK, 1997), 94–95.

Tabernacle, Sacrifice, and Priesthood in Ancient Israel's Worship

The Ten Words embody Israel's ethical ideals. Yet the Torah instruction has more verses on the tabernacle than on any other single topic. And great care is given to defining and prescribing the various sacrifices to be offered at the tabernacle, as well as the priests who offer them. This is hardly "law" as we think of it, but it is Torah instruction. Especially crucial for these topics is the role and nature of worship in Israel's relationship with Yahweh.

The tabernacle creates a new world for the Israelites to live in. Their previous existence as slaves required them to live in submission to a sovereign ruler of Egypt. Israel's reason for being was to serve Egypt exclusively. At Sinai, Yahweh's instructions to build the tabernacle and its furnishings provide Israel with a new category, a substitute world in which Yahweh rules as sovereign over the universe and dwells in a tent home in the midst of the tribes of Israel. Israel now exists in a covenant relationship with Yahweh, living exclusively for him and serving him alone. The sacrifices and priestly system make it possible for the Israelites to preserve and maintain Yahweh's tent home. Otherwise, such a holy and transcendent God cannot dwell in the midst of Israel. His purity and holiness are too much for mortals. The sacrifices function first to purge all impurities from the tent home so that Yahweh may dwell therein, and second to purge and purify the people of Israel so they are acceptable in Yahweh's sight.

All religions have a set of practices designed to produce a proper world, and proper humans in that world. These are usually divided into *ritual* practices for worship and *ethical* practices for behavior. Israel's tabernacle, sacrifices, and priesthood are ritual by definition, but they become ethical by virtue of the Torah story's framing and preparing the reader for the covenant with Yahweh. The new world created by Israel's tabernacle is countercultural; it stands in opposition to any alternative worldview. Its vision of space, time, and status mirrors God's cosmic design, known from the familiar creation account of Genesis 1. In fact, Genesis 1 and the tabernacle laws are linked by themes and terms illustrating that this act of tabernacle building parallels God's act of world building. To take just one example, "God finished the work" has its parallel in "Moses finished the work" (compare Genesis 2:2 with Exodus 40:33). God has designed the cosmos as a place of peace and harmony, and now Israel builds a sacred space on earth where the holiness of Yahweh may live in harmony with humans.

At creation, God established boundaries in the universe between the holy and the common. Likewise, the architectural plan of the tabernacle divides and organizes Israel's new life according to God's design. The three-part pattern of the tabernacle organizes space into ordered and graduated zones of holiness.[8] The tent structure has a concentric series of enclosures with increasing degrees of holiness as one moves from the exterior to the interior; that is, from the common world of the Israelite encampment outside, to the sacred space of the outer courtyard, then to the holy place, and

8 For details, see Menahem Haran, *Temples and Temple-Service in Ancient Israel: An Inquiry into Biblical Cult Phenomena and the Historical Setting of the Priestly School* (Winona Lake, Ind.: Eisenbrauns, 1985), 158–77.

8.2. The Iron Age sanctuary from Arad. Archaeologists have found examples of this three-part structure in sanctuaries such as this one from Arad in the south. The great altar for sacrifices is in the outer courtyard in the foreground, and the holy of holies is the inner cubicle containing incense altars and standing stones. (Photo: Todd Bolen / BiblePlaces.com)

finally to the holiest place.[9] Nearly every aspect of the tabernacle is marked by the graduated zones of holiness. The utensils used by the priests, the materials used to make those utensils, the craftsmanship required, the priestly garments, even the types of fabrics and their colors – all illustrate the gradual increase in holiness as one moves closer to Yahweh's presence. Israelites who are not priests are permitted in the courtyard, ordinary priests are allowed in the holy place, but only the high priest is permitted to enter the holiest place, and then only once a year (on the Day of Atonement; Leviticus 16).

Graduated zones of holiness are required by the very nature of Yahweh, who lives in the tent dwelling and whose essence is defined as transcendent *otherness*: "be holy, for I am holy" (Leviticus 11:44). Moses first encounters Yahweh on "holy ground," which is Mount Sinai, also known as "Horeb, the mountain of God" (Exodus 3:1). Later, when

Yahweh again meets Moses there, this time with the Israelites encamped at the foot of the mountain, God's presence is clear in thunder and lightning, thick fiery cloud, and trumpet blast (Exodus 19:16). The Israelites are required to purify themselves and to set boundaries around Mount Sinai beyond which they are not permitted to cross (Exodus 19:12, 23). Now, as they prepare to leave Mount Sinai and journey to the promised land, the tabernacle essentially replaces the mountain and becomes a portable Sinai.[10] The Israelites will tear down and reerect the tabernacle at each stop along their journey, and they will understand that Yahweh's indescribable presence goes with them. Their mountaintop experience will accompany them through the valleys, until they enter the promised land, bringing Yahweh's presence with them in his own tent dwelling to a new mountaintop in their new world.

LAW "CODES," WRITING, AND MONOTHEISM

As we have seen, the legal material of the Torah is of many types. Some laws are religious in nature, such as the ones focused on the tabernacle, sacrifices, or the priesthood, and others are instructions about everyday life. The way we examined the seven portions of Torah instruction earlier obscures the way independent lists of laws were originally written and preserved in ancient Israel. These originally independent collections of laws are most often called "codes." Such codes are collections of laws arranged systematically and usually intended to be comprehensive. And thus the term is not strictly

9 "Holy of holies" is simply the Semitic superlative for "holiest place."

10 See the commentary by Propp (AB2, pp. 687–88) in "Where to Find More" in Chapter 7.

SIDEBAR 8.3. HOW OLD ARE THE PRIESTLY LEGAL MATERIALS OF THE TORAH?

Previously we have seen that the Pentateuch is composed of numerous older sources, J, E, P, H, and D (Sidebars 4.3, 6.2, and 7.1). The nineteenth-century scholars isolating and identifying these sources at first assumed that the law came early in ancient Israel. Then, in a critical turning point, Julius Wellhausen famously concluded that the law had appeared not near the beginning of *Israelite history* but at the beginning of the *Jewish state*, that is, at the end of the OT period in the postexilic period. Wellhausen also believed that early Judaism was the remnant of Israelite religion after it had died, portraying Judaism as a dead legalism compared to the vitality of Israel's earlier prophetic religion. He has been widely criticized as anti-Semitic for these views.

The picture today is very different. Numerous scholars now believe that the law emerged early in Israel's history. The change has occurred because of fresh studies of the law's language, theology, and especially the way the various legal codes in the OT relate to each other. For example, P nowhere assumes a central location for religious practices, which is a fundamental assumption of D (see Deuteronomy 12:2–7). Today there is no wide agreement about whether the law was among the earliest features of Israelite culture, or the latest. But the dogmatic assertions of the nineteenth-century source critics can no longer be maintained.

accurate for ancient Near Eastern legal materials, which were not intended to be comprehensive, covering all aspects of society. Still, the term is useful for distinguishing these legal materials by their literary characteristics from other types of ancient literature.

Behind the Torah instruction discussed in this chapter, scholars believe that there were originally as many as four separate law codes written in early Israel. The first of these is the *Covenant Code*, containing the list of laws of the Book of the Covenant (Exodus 20:22–23:19). This was apparently the earliest of the Israelite law codes. At some point it was joined to the Ten Commandments and placed at the center of Israel's covenant with Yahweh. Next is the *Priestly Code*, comprised of laws related to the tabernacle (Exodus 25–31 and 35–40), sacrifices (Leviticus 1–7), the priesthood (Leviticus 8–10 and scattered in Numbers 1–10), and purity (Leviticus 11–16). This Priestly Code is not identical with the priestly source (P) that we talked about earlier because it was combined by later priestly authors

with various narratives (especially in Genesis), and edited over a long period of time. The P source incorporated, expanded, and edited the Priestly Code in a way we cannot entirely trace; nor can we date it with certainty. But the Priestly Code seems to have made up a large portion of the priestly source.

The third legal code was the *Holiness Code* (Leviticus 17–26), which relates to the Priestly Code in a way we are not entirely able to explain. It has a different worldview and different theological concerns from the Priestly Code. While it was once thought to be older than the Priestly Code, we are no longer able to speak with confidence about which is older. The fourth and last Israelite code to be mentioned here is the *Deuteronomic Code* (Deuteronomy 12–26), which we will consider in the next chapter. It seems to have built on and developed the Covenant Code, as we will see. Scholars working on OT laws often spend a great deal of energy trying to determine the relationship between these various early codes. But with the exception of the Covenant

Sumerians in Mesopotamia and second-millennium Hittites of Anatolia. We have two such law codes written in Sumerian, four in Akkadian, and one in Hittite. The only thing these cultures have in common is the use of the cuneiform writing system, and yet they have remarkably similar legal traditions.

Philosophers and scholars of early Mesopotamia classified the world around them by making lists of things – almost everything, including words, plants and animals, stars and planets, gods, and kings. It's not surprising then that they also listed legal decisions, which were developed into these law codes. These collections were almost always in the form of the casuistic sentences, as we have seen in the Mishpatim ("ordinances"; *mišpāṭîm*) of the Covenant Code, listing the circumstances of a hypothetical case followed by the legal consequences. Here are two examples.[12]

8.3. Detail of the Code of Hammurabi. The text of Hammurabi's famous law code is inscribed in columns turned horizontal, just below the iconography at the top of the stele. In this image, the sun god Shamash is seated on his altar, while King Hammurabi stands reverentially before him. (Photo: Erich Lessing / Art Resource, N.Y.)

Code, which is probably the oldest, it may be best to assume that they developed simultaneously, side by side as it were, rather than in a strictly chronological sequence. This explains why it is difficult to find hard dates for the law codes in general.

It has been said that these OT law codes have closer parallels to ancient Near Eastern literature than does any other portion of the Bible.[11] Indeed, it appears that ancient Israel shared a common legal heritage with other cultures as diverse as third-millennium

1. Whoever kidnaps a person, whether that person has been sold or is still held in possession, shall be put to death. (Exodus 21:16)

   If a man should kidnap the young child of another man, he shall be killed. (Hammurabi, law number 14)

2. When an ox gores a man or a woman to death, the ox shall be stoned, and its flesh shall not be eaten; but the owner of the ox shall not be liable. (Exodus 21:28)

   If an ox gores to death a man while it is passing through the streets, that case has no basis for a claim. (Hammurabi, law number 250)

11 See Westbrook and Wells (p. 24) in "Where to Find More" in this chapter.

12 Translations of the laws of Hammurabi are from Martha T. Roth, *Law Collections from Mesopotamia and Asia Minor* (2nd ed.; Atlanta, Ga.: Scholars Press, 1997), 84 and 128.

SIDEBAR 8.4. ANCIENT NEAR EASTERN LAW CODES

The closest ancient equivalents to modern law are the so-called law codes. These lists of casuistic examples touch on most topics typically covered by law, although they were not intended to be comprehensive. Most law codes were framed by a prologue and epilogue, claiming divine authority or royal credit for the laws.

Seven ancient law codes preserved in the cuneiform tradition have been discovered. The first two were written in Sumerian, the rest in Akkadian, except for the Hittite laws. (For more on these, see pp. 22–23 of Westbrook and Wells in "Where to Find More" at the end of this chapter.)

1. Laws of Ur-Namma, from the city of Ur around 2100 BCE.
2. Laws of Lipit-Ishtar, from the city of Isin around 1900 BCE.
3. Laws of Eshnunna, from the city of Eshnunna around 1800 BCE.
4. Laws of Hammurabi, from Babylon, dated to approximately 1750 BCE.
5. Middle Assyrian Laws, from the city of Ashur in the fourteenth century BCE.
6. Neo-Babylonian Laws, from the city of Sippar in the seventh century BCE.
7. Hittite Laws, from Anatolia, from approximately the sixteenth and twelfth centuries BCE.

You can see how remarkably close these examples are, even though they are separated by many centuries, different cultures, and different languages. Many explanations have been offered for the parallels. Despite recent claims that Israel's Covenant Code is dependent on the laws of Hammurabi, it seems more likely that Israel participated in a common legal tradition known throughout the ancient Near Eastern world, with the possible exception of Egypt.

Yet Israel's law is different in a way that reflects the Axial Age. The ancient Near Eastern law codes were simple lists arranged in general categories but lacking detailed classifications or abstract definitions. Israel's lists, especially the Book of the Covenant, are similar. But the Bible has affinities also with later Greek development of an advanced legal science, especially in the use of the narrative framework to nuance and define the role of law.

You may also have noticed when reading through the Torah instruction a few references to Moses writing the covenant law (Exodus 24:4 and 34:27–28; Deuteronomy 31:9). The giving of Yahweh's law to Israel is so closely associated with the act of writing that the Ten Commandments are written by the very finger of God (Exodus 31:18 and Deuteronomy 9:10). This act of writing has itself been linked to the new law-based religion of Moses. The Torah brings together various features – the important new role of writing, a (presumably) literate priesthood, and a law-centered covenant with Yahweh – in a religious innovation that will stand throughout the rest of the Bible. The written Torah now characterizes Israel's covenant with Yahweh. Regardless of when this happened (a controversial question, as we shall see), the Torah marks a turn from preliterate ancestral religion to literate Mosaic faith. We will return to this topic in Chapter 10.

It may also be possible that writing and monotheism (or Israel's henotheism) have a reciprocal relationship in the Torah instruction. The Ten Commandments prohibit the making of idols or sculptured images (Exodus 20:4), leaving the divinely written tablets as the new sacred symbol.[13] In this way, the new medium of writing has replaced the physical representation of God, who is invisibly transcendent. The tablets of law were stored in the ark of the covenant (Exodus 25:16 and Deuteronomy 10:2) for future reference. Israelites may not make physical copies of Yahweh, but they are to preserve his words in a sacred text for future generations. This feature of Mosaic religion will become a mark of Israel for all time, and will continue into Judaism, Christianity, and Islam.

WHERE TO FIND MORE

Commentaries: The best technical and advanced commentaries on **Leviticus** are Jacob Milgrom, *Leviticus 1–16, Leviticus 17–22,* and *Leviticus 23–27* (Anchor Bible 3, 3A, and 3B; New York: Doubleday, 1991, 2000, and 2001), and Gordon J. Wenham, *The Book of Leviticus* (New International Commentary on the Old Testament; Grand Rapids, Mich.: Eerdmans, 1979).

Balentine, Samuel E. *The Torah's Vision of Worship.* Overtures to Biblical Theology. Minneapolis, Minn.: Fortress Press, 1999.

Describes the tabernacle and its appurtenances as a "substitute world" for Israel (chap. 5, pp. 119–47), especially as a reflection of God's creation of the cosmos (pp. 136–41), and the Torah as inviting a "counterimagination" of the world.

Demsky, Aaron. "Writing in Ancient Israel and Early Judaism, Part One: The Biblical Period." Pages 1–20 in *Mikra: Text, Translation, Reading, and Interpretation of the Hebrew Bible in Ancient Judaism and Early Christianity.* Edited by Martin Jan Mulder and Harry Sysling. CRINT/ Section 2, Literature of the Jewish People in the Period of the Second Temple and the Talmud 1. Assen/Philadelphia: Van Gorcum/Fortress Press, 1988.

Gane, Roy. *Cult and Character: Purification Offerings, Day of Atonement, and Theodicy.* Winona Lake, Ind.: Eisenbrauns, 2005.

Treats various theories of ritual and purification and compares the Day of Atonement to the inner sanctum or most holy place of the Torah.

Greengus, Samuel. *Laws in the Bible and in Early Rabbinic Collections: The Legal Legacy of the Ancient Near East.* Eugene, Oreg.: Cascade Books, 2011.

Helpful general introduction to a complex issue.

Miller, Patrick D. *The Ten Commandments.* Interpretation. Louisville, Ky.: Westminster John Knox Press, 2009.

---

13 See Demsky (pp. 19–20) in "Where to Find More" in this chapter.

Examination of the Ten Commandments as a comprehensive framework for OT ethics. Includes literary indications in the Torah reflecting the importance of the commandments and suggests ways that today's readers should think about them (pp. 3–9).

Vriezen, T. C., and A. S. van der Woude. *Ancient Israelite and Early Jewish Literature.* Translated by Brian Doyle. Leiden and Boston: Brill, 2005.

Explores the legal portions of the Torah in seven parts, similar to this treatment (pp. 230–52).

Wenham, Gordon J. *Story as Torah: Reading Old Testament Narrative Ethically.* Grand Rapids, Mich.: Baker Academic, 2004.

Explores the Torah instruction as "a minimum standard of behaviour" and shows how its combination with the historical narrative illustrates God's ethical ideal (especially chap. 5, pp. 73–107).

Westbrook, Raymond, and Bruce Wells. *Everyday Law in Biblical Israel: An Introduction.* Louisville, Ky.: Westminster John Knox Press, 2009.

Helpful discussion of the "law code" tradition in the ancient world, counting as many as ten law codes known to date: seven from the ancient Near East and three from the Greco-Roman world. Also explains that only about 60 of the 613 commands of the Torah actually have to do with everyday law and shows how biblical law straddles the era of revolution defined as the Axial Age (pp. 26–27).

CHAPTER 9

Torah Revisited

OLD TESTAMENT READING: DEUTERONOMY

We will now focus our attention on the final book of the Pentateuch, Deuteronomy. We will discover that, even as the book recounts what has come before for the sake of Israel poised to enter the promised land, it does so in a new setting, in an innovative literary format, and with distinctive emphases that speak to generations present and yet to come.

Deuteronomy consists of four collections of speeches given by Moses, set off by literary superscriptions. Scholars have determined that the book is organized in the form of an ancient international treaty. Following a historical prologue, the speeches reiterate and affirm Torah instruction, institute a covenant renewal that links blessings with covenant fidelity, and detail provisions for Israel after Moses' death (recounted in the final chapter of the book). Deuteronomy is distinctive in the Pentateuch for its focus on the centralization of Israel's religious cult at the place where Yahweh will cause his name to dwell, the great statement of faith known as the Shema (6:4), and the first explicit statements of monotheism in the OT.

The fifth book of the Bible is not entirely new. It isn't simple repetition either. The Torah – both its narrative and its law – is revisited in Deuteronomy in a way that renews it for the next generation of Israelites. In doing so, the book of Deuteronomy shows that the Torah is dynamic and renewable for every generation.

You will remember from the Torah story that the Israelites rebelled against Yahweh and were condemned to wander in the desert for forty years.[1] That generation of Israelites died in the desert, and now an entirely new, young generation, unscarred by rebellion, is encamped on the plains of Moab,

1 Review Numbers 13–14.

poised to enter the promised land (the basic thrust of Numbers 22–36). Before they cross the Jordan River and take the promised land, the covenant, with its all-important Torah instruction, is renewed for this new generation of Israelites.

This renewal feature of Deuteronomy has something to do with the unusual name of the book. But only in an indirect way. The core of the book (chaps. 12–26) is legal material, much of it related to the Book of the Covenant in Exodus 21–23. In a passage from this legal section, Israel's future kings are required to keep always handy a "copy of this law" to ensure successful reigns (Deuteronomy 17:18). The Greek translation (the Septuagint) incorrectly but understandably translated "copy of this law" as "second law" (*deuteronomion*) because so much of the law is repeated in the book. This mistranslation gave us the book's English name.

SPEECHES OF MOSES

The figure of Moses towers over the whole Torah. But in Deuteronomy, his role changes slightly. In Exodus, Leviticus, and Numbers, Yahweh delivers his words to Israel *through* Moses: "Yahweh said to Moses" (Exodus 25:1). Yahweh's revelation comes directly to the Israelites with Moses as the mediator. But the book of Deuteronomy is itself the words of Moses to Israel: "These are the words that Moses spoke to all Israel" (Deuteronomy 1:1). Rather than a direct Torah revelation from Yahweh, Deuteronomy is Moses' explanation of the law. The opening paragraph portrays Moses as beginning "to expound" the law to Israel (1:5), and his explanations are contained in the book. In Deuteronomy, Moses becomes a law interpreter instead of the lawgiver. His words and Yahweh's words merge together as one.

Deuteronomy is thus presented as a collection of Moses' speeches. Moses speaks to the Israelites while they are camping along the border of the promised land, on "the plains of Moab" east of the Jordan River. To add to the drama, these are Moses' "farewell speeches" because his death is recorded at the end of the book. These are his final words of wisdom for the Israelites prior to their entrance into the promised land.

The book structure organizes the speeches of Moses into four collections of unequal length, although the speeches could also be divided into several smaller subspeeches. In the book's canonical form, the speeches have been organized along the lines of four distinct superscriptions, or literary titles. The *first* such title – "these are the words that Moses spoke" (1:1) – may be said to introduce a lengthy discourse summarizing events since the departure from Mount Horeb (the name of Sinai in Deuteronomy). This summary recalls the highlights of the Torah story first told in Exodus and Numbers, as a means of putting the moment in proper perspective (Deuteronomy 1:5–3:29). In a way, this speech reviews Israel's relationship with Yahweh as a means of motivating Israel to keep the law that guards that relationship. This is followed immediately by a sermonlike plea for the Israelites to observe the law (4:1–40). You may have noticed when reading these chapters a sermonic, preaching tone that is part of Deuteronomy's unique style. We will return to this literary style later when we consider the adjective "Deuteronomistic."

A *second* title – "this is the law that Moses set before the Israelites" (4:44) – introduces the largest section of the book of Deuteronomy (4:44–26:19).[2] This is the portion of the book that most closely parallels the legal sections of Exodus, Leviticus, and Numbers. It has the role of seconding and reinforcing the earlier Torah instruction. We have two portions of this legal discourse, the first general and the second filled with particulars. The general exhortations of chapters 5–11 introduce and prepare for the specific laws of chapters 12–26. Yahweh's covenant at Horeb (Sinai) was not just for their fathers and mothers but was with the younger generation of Israelites too (5:2–3). The covenant was the means by which Yahweh established an intimate, "face-to-face" relationship with them, using Moses as a sort of translator (5:4–5). Next, the Ten Commandments are repeated to illustrate their centrality for the covenant for all time (5:6–21). The instruction of Yahweh is then crystallized in one of the greatest expressions of faith of all time, the Shema (6:4): "Hear, O Israel: The LORD is our God, the LORD alone." While not an explicit statement of monotheism, the Shema asserts Yahweh's dependable nature. Yahweh is consistent and single-minded in his devotion to Israel. The only logical response to Yahweh's nature follows immediately in a call to love him wholeheartedly and learn his commands (6:5–9). Other sermons and exhortations of chapters 5–11 also call on Israel to love and revere Yahweh, and establish compelling reasons for Israel to obey the commands to follow.

The specific commands of Deuteronomy 12–26 are the legal core of the book. Like previous legal collections in the Torah, these rules provide for proper worship, for institutions such as kingship and prophecy, and for laws of a wide variety of other types. Many of these laws have a particularly close association with the Book of the Covenant (Exodus 21–23), as we shall see later. The legal portion proper is followed by a solemn national assembly near the city of Shechem, between Mounts Ebal and Gerizim, and a list of blessings and curses to illustrate the seriousness of the moment (Deuteronomy 27–28).

A *third* title – "these are the words of the covenant that Yahweh commanded Moses to make with the Israelites" (29:1) – introduces concluding discourses (Deuteronomy 29–32). Moses distinguishes this covenant in the land of Moab from the earlier one of Horeb/Sinai, and a ratification ceremony is followed by more blessings and curses (29–30). The Israelites have a clear choice: life and blessing, or death and curses (30:19–20). This is followed by a description of Moses' activities to prepare Israel for his departure (31), and by the poetic "Song of Moses," which stands as a witness against Israel (32). Several other OT books that are mostly prose also close with poetry (see Genesis 49); in this case, the poem summarizes the content of Deuteronomy. In fact, these chapters, together with Deuteronomy 33–34, make up a concluding epilogue for both Deuteronomy and the whole Torah.

A *fourth* and final title – "this is the blessing with which Moses, the man of God, blessed the Israelites" (33:1) – introduces another closing poem and the narration of Moses' death (Deuteronomy 33–34). The "Blessing of Moses" lists tribal proverbs for the twelve tribes of Israel, similar in fashion

2 Remember that the Bible's chapter and verse numbers do not always stand at the most logical breaks of the material; review Sidebar 6.1.

SIDEBAR 9.1. THE SHEMA

The "Shema" in Deuteronomy 6:4 is so named because of the first word in the expression, the command "hear" (Hebrew imperative, *šĕmaʿ*, pronounced *she-MAH*). As an opening term, "hear" calls the reader or hearer to listen carefully and give full attention to what is about to be said. The line that follows is perhaps the closest thing to a creed of faith in the OT. This verse encapsulates and summarizes the gist of Israel's relationship with Yahweh as called forth in Deuteronomy 5–26. Thus this verse has become central to later expressions of faith in both Judaism and Christianity.

Ironically for a verse as important as this one, we are not entirely sure how to translate the Shema. Without getting too much into the grammatical details, it is enough to know that the Hebrew sentence assumes the verb "is" but does not specify exactly *where* the verb should stand (a verbless clause). To complicate matters, the sentence may be divided into two verbless clauses (option 4). Any of the following four translations is possible.

1. Yahweh *is* our God, Yahweh alone.
2. Yahweh our God *is* one Yahweh.
3. Yahweh our God, Yahweh *is* one.
4. Yahweh *is* our God, Yahweh *is* one.

Whatever we make of the details grammatically, the substance of the sentence is clear enough although the nuances differ with each translation. The Shema is a powerfully *positive* statement about who Yahweh is. It gracefully asserts something specific about the character of Yahweh and about the way that he relates to Israel. Yahweh is singularly – and this can be said only of Yahweh – and consistently dependable! He has initiated communication with Israel ("Hear"), has done so personally ("our God"), and has no ambivalence about relating to Israel ("is one"). This last point is to say that Yahweh is resolved in his devotion to Israel; he has no hesitation or reservations about being Israel's God. Yahweh's singularity likely means he is not distracted by other people groups; he is singularly devoted to Israel. As sovereign Lord of the created order, Yahweh has no competitors who might interfere with his relationship to Israel, no rivals to compete for Israel's attention or affections.

The Shema is not affirming monotheism. It is no strict denial of the existence of other deities. Such a statement is itself inherently *negative* (there are "no others gods"), whereas this is a *positive* assertion about Yahweh. He alone is Israel's God, the *only* God for the Israelites. They cannot worship him alongside other deities (monolatry). Furthermore, Yahweh is one and the same for all Israel. He is consistently the same God, whether worshipped in Samaria or in Jerusalem, Bethel, or Hebron (sometimes called mono-Yahwism). The Shema is focused on the relationship between Israel and Yahweh; it gives no thought to the existence of other gods.

to those of Jacob in Genesis 49. The circumstances of Moses' death and burial distinguish him as a one-of-a-kind leader for all time. The narrative explicitly observes that no prophet of Israel can be compared to Moses (34:10), a remarkable sentiment to which we will return.

The speeches of Moses are thus arranged according to these four titles, grouped loosely

9.1. Mounts Ebal and Gerizim, viewed from the east. At just over 3,000 and 2,800 feet above sea level, respectively, Ebal and Gerizim were prominent features of the central hill country (see Map 3.1). Moses gave instructions for an altar of unhewn stones to be constructed on Mount Ebal, where Israel was to renew the covenant by reciting the curses and blessings of Deuteronomy, presumably in antiphonal responsive readings between Ebal and Gerizim (Deuteronomy 11:29 and 27:5). (Photo: Todd Bolen / BiblePlaces.com)

according to theme: historical reflections, laws, covenant renewal, and various provisions for Israel after Moses' death. The arrangement is comprehensive, since the historical prologue reflects on the past, the laws are for the present, and the covenant and various preparations are for the future.

COVENANT RENEWAL AND THE BOOK'S STRUCTURE

One of the most amazing discoveries of OT studies relates to Deuteronomy. Sometimes biblical scholars are like detectives, poring over evidence trying to solve a mystery. In this case, they had plenty of clues. But it wasn't until unexpected new evidence from outside the Bible itself came to light in the twentieth century that scholars were able to come up with a solution. Deuteronomy, as you have seen, is a curious blend of materials. The Torah story of Exodus, Leviticus, and Numbers provides a narrative framework for the Torah instruction. But in Deuteronomy, the speeches of Moses combine story and instruction in a structure that is hard to explain. What holds these speeches of Moses together?

SIDEBAR 9.2. TREATY OF SUPPILULIUMA, THE HITTITE "GREAT KING"

The general outline of a Hittite treaty was common for centuries. But there was also quite a lot of flexibility among individual treaties. The following excerpts are from a treaty between the "Great King" of the Hittites, Suppiluliuma I (ca. 1370–1330 BCE), and a vassal ruler named Shattiwaza of the kingdom of Mittanni (adapted from Gary M. Beckman, *Hittite Diplomatic Texts* [2nd ed.; Atlanta, Ga.: Scholars Press, 1999], 42–48).

A long historical introduction explains the complicated history between Suppiluliuma and the land of Mittanni. When Tushratta of Mittanni was assassinated, his son Prince Shattiwaza fled for his life and sought refuge with the Hittite king. Suppiluliuma established the reign of Shattiwaza but required of him exclusive loyalty and was attempting by this treaty to ensure future relations between the two countries. The treaty ends with a document clause (deposition of the tablet), a call for future readings of the text, and numerous blessings and curses made before divine witnesses.

"A duplicate of this tablet is deposited before the Sun-goddess of Arinna, since the Sun-goddess of Arinna governs kingship and queenship. And in the land of Mittanni a duplicate is deposited before the Storm-god, Lord of the shrine of Kahat. It shall be read repeatedly, for ever and ever, before the king of the land of Mittanni and before the Hurrians.

"Whoever before the Storm-god, Lord of the shrine of Kahat, alters this tablet, or sets it in a secret location – if he breaks it, if he changes the words of the text of the tablet – in regard to this treaty we have summoned the gods of secrets and the gods who are guarantors of the oath. They shall stand and listen and be witnesses: The Sun-goddess of Arinna, who governs kingship and queenship in Hatti, the Sun-god, Lord of Heaven, the Storm-god, Lord of Hatti, ...

"They shall stand and listen and be witnesses to these words of the treaty. If you, Prince Shattiwaza, and you Hurrians do not observe the words of this treaty, the gods, lords of the oath, shall destroy you and you Hurrians, together with your land, your wives, and your possessions.... And you, Shattiwaza – they shall overthrow your throne. And you, Shattiwaza – these oath gods shall snap you off like a reed, together with your land. But if you, Prince Shattiwaza, and you Hurrians observe this treaty and oath, these gods shall protect you, Shattiwaza, ... And the land of Mittanni shall return to its former state. It shall prosper and expand.... Prolong the life of the throne of your father; prolong the life of the land of Mittanni."

In the 1930s, scholars studying second-millennium BCE treaties between Hittite kings with less powerful rulers noticed a standard literary outline for the treaties: (1) preamble, (2) historical prologue, (3) stipulations, (4) deposition of a treaty document, (5) divine witnesses, (6) curses and blessings. Such political treaties between a powerful overlord (called a suzerain) and subordinate local ruler (or vassal) were an important feature of Hittite rule in the late second millennium. We have more than thirty-five such treaties preserved from Hittite texts,

and others are mentioned in Hittite correspondence. The historical prologue of a Hittite treaty reviews the political history between the two parties as a means of encouraging submission by the vassal. The stipulations detail the requirements imposed on the vassal, including a demand for exclusive loyalty to the Hittite suzerain. The deposition clause stipulates that the treaty document is to be housed in the temple of the vassal's deity.

Soon it was discovered that similar treaties and loyalty oaths were preserved in first-millennium

Assyrian documents, binding kings of the mighty Neo-Assyrian empire to submissive rulers of smaller kingdoms. We have fifteen of these, including one discovered just in 2009. We also have three written in Aramaic, an alphabetic language closely related to Hebrew.[3] Interpretation of the Aramaic treaties is uncertain, but at least we have examples of the same literary phenomenon in Syria, preserved in the local dialect. Once all of these clues were considered together, it was possible to draw an important conclusion: the practice of making treaties and writing documents sealing the political treaties was widespread in the ancient Near East from the Late Bronze into the Iron Age. Although preserved in three different languages and showing some flexibility, written treaties had a common cultural and literary uniformity, and shared some basic content.

Now comes the amazing part. Biblical scholars then discovered, good detectives that they are, that covenant passages of the OT share this same basic treaty structure and even content. By the 1950s, it was shown that the actual origin of this biblical idea can be found in the international treaties of the ancient Near East. The treaty outline was found in Exodus 19–24 and a covenant renewal passage of Joshua 24. But the biggest breakthrough was how this discovery relates to the book of Deuteronomy, which can now be understood as organized according to this treaty structure:

1. Preamble (1:1–5)
2. Historical prologue (1:6–4:49)
3. Stipulations (5–26)
4. Document clause (27:1–10; 31:9–29)
5. Witnesses (32)
6. Blessings and curses (27:12–26; 28)

This is not the whole story, because the book's treaty outline can actually be much more detailed than I'm suggesting here.[4] But the idea is almost beyond dispute: Deuteronomy has been intentionally structured to read like an ancient Near Eastern treaty. What had been a political idea among Israel's neighbors now becomes a religious one.

Now consider further how ingenious Israel's use of the treaty structure is. In the ancient Near Eastern treaties, the gods of the Hittites and Assyrians are called as witnesses to the treaty, so that if needed they may testify later that the treaty is binding (5th item in the treaty outline). But in Israel, the heavens and earth are called as witnesses against Israel (Deuteronomy 31:28 and 32:1). And the concept is perfect for Israel, because Yahweh is a jealous God who allows no rival deities (32:16). The exclusive loyalty demanded in the political treaties is put to good theological use by Israel, for Yahweh demands exclusive faithfulness. Only in Israel is this treaty structure used to bind humans to a diety. All other ancient Near Eastern treaties are between human partners, however unequal they may be in status.

The obvious way in which Deuteronomy has been structured as an ancient treaty also raises a question. Some believe that Deuteronomy is closer to the older Hittite structure, whereas others focus on the Assyrian parallels. It seems likely that the authors and editors of Deuteronomy were

---

3 We will come back to this later because the OT has two large sections written in Aramaic instead of Hebrew (Chapter 22).

4 Check the commentaries in "Where to Find More" in this chapter.

SIDEBAR 9.3. SUCCESSION TREATY OF ESARHADDON

Esarhaddon of Assyria (680–669 BCE) went to great lengths to ensure the peaceful succession of his son, the crown prince Ashurbanipal. The following succession oath is one example of many imposed across the empire, and it is the best preserved of the surviving Neo-Assyrian treaties. It has a much more complex format than the simple six-part structure we have discussed in this chapter, and a text of nearly seven hundred lines, only a small portion of which is excerpted here (adapted from Erica Reiner, "The Vassal-Treaties of Esarhaddon," in *The Ancient Near East: An Anthology of Texts and Pictures* [ed. James B. Pritchard; Princeton, N.J.: Princeton University Press, 2011], 213–22).

"This is the treaty of Esarhaddon, king of the world, king of Assyria, son of Sennacherib, likewise king of the world, king of Assyria, with Ramataya, city-ruler of Urakazabanu …

"This is the treaty which Esarhaddon, king of Assyria, has established with you before the great gods of heaven and earth, on behalf of the crown prince designate Ashurbanipal, the son of your lord Esarhaddon, king of Assyria, who has designated and appointed him for succession. When Esarhaddon, king of Assyria, departs from the living, you will seat the crown prince designate Ashurbanipal upon the royal throne, he will exercise the kingship and overlordship of Assyria over you.

"If you do not serve the crown prince designate Ashurbanipal, whom Esarhaddon, king of Assyria, has presented to you and ordered you to serve, on behalf of whom he has made this binding treaty with you, … If you side with the instigators of a revolt, be they few or many, … If you do not fight for the crown prince Ashurbanipal, son of your lord Esarhaddon, king of Assyria, if you do not die for him, if you do not seek to do what is good for him, if you act wrongly toward him, do not give him sound advice, lead him on an unsafe course, do not treat him with proper loyalty, …

"May Ashur, king of the gods, who determines the fates, decree for you an evil, unpropitious fate, and not grant you fatherhood, or old age, … May Anu, king of the gods, rain upon all your houses disease, … May Sin, the luminary of heaven and earth, clothe you in leprosy, … May the great gods of heaven and earth, who inhabit the world, all those that are named in this tablet, strike you down, look with disfavor upon you, curse you angrily with a baleful curse, on earth, may they uproot you from the living, below, may they deprive your spirit of water, …"

familiar with both.[5] And perhaps the most innovative (and I'll say it again, ingenious!) part of this is the way Israel took Assyria's means for intimidating and controlling lesser powers, the political treaty, and turned it around as a point of defiance of Assyrian might. This was a kind of declaration of Israel's independence from Assyria. It seems subversive. Assyria demands political submission, but Deuteronomy takes that very demand and uses it to articulate Israel's allegiance to Yahweh alone instead. Israel will have "no other gods" before Yahweh, and that includes Assyria!

MOSES' SERMONS – THE "CENTER OF THE OLD TESTAMENT"

Deuteronomy has many features that set it off as unique among the five books of the Torah. Instead of third-person narratives such as we have

5 Weinfeld makes this case; see *Deuteronomy 1–11* (p. 9) in the commentaries in "Where to Find More" in this chapter.

seen elsewhere in the Torah ("Moses was on the mountain for forty days and forty nights"; Exodus 24:18), Deuteronomy is most often narrated in the first person ("I stayed on the mountain forty days and forty nights"; Deuteronomy 10:10). Its laws also have first-person authority ("be careful to obey all these words that I command you today"; 12:28). The combination of narrative and law that we saw in Exodus, Leviticus, and Numbers is here woven together in the farewell speeches of Moses and constitutes, in certain ways, a seconding and affirming of the earlier Torah.

These farewell speeches have a sermonlike quality. Moses' words are repetitious and urgent, pleading with Israel to obey and to keep the covenant with Yahweh. His sermons were delivered in the "land of Moab," just across the Jordan River from the promised land (1:5). Tied together as they are, the sermons take on a unique quality as boundary literature. Deuteronomy stands on the border of a new Israel, surveying past and future and representing the juncture of several critical decision points for Israel.[6] These literary features underscore several other ideas of Deuteronomy that make it distinctive or innovative for the entire OT.

Centralization of Israelite Worship

One such important feature is Deuteronomy's emphasis on the *centralization* of the religious cult (or system for religious worship and ritual). At the beginning of the detailed laws, the Israelites are told to demolish "all the places" they previously used for worship (Deuteronomy 12:2–4). Instead, Yahweh will designate a new "place" to which all Israelites must bring their sacrifices, and only there, at this new location, may they worship Yahweh (12:5–14). This new place for worship replaces all others. Israel is not permitted to worship Yahweh formally in other locations; only the new chosen place will be acceptable. The rest of the legal portions of Deuteronomy assume this centralizing principle (e.g., 14:22–29, 15:19–23, and many others).

Why is this interesting? Because elsewhere in the Torah, worship is not centralized in one location. The ancestors of Genesis were free to build altars and worship wherever the people roamed (a topic for Chapter 10). The Book of the Covenant in Exodus – which is directly related to the laws of Deuteronomy, as we have seen – opens with the assumption that Israel may worship "in every place" where Yahweh's name is remembered (Exodus 20:24). This change relates to another, which requires that all slaughter of domestic animals must take place at a sacred altar (Leviticus 17:1–9). Deuteronomy, instead, provides for secular slaughter, meaning that no altar is needed (12:15–16). These may seem at first glance like minor adjustments in Israel's worship laws. But in reality, this was a revolutionary turning point in Israelite religion, both in practice and in ideology.

Name Theology

In their new form of worship, the Israelites are to destroy any places of worship other than the location designated by Yahweh, blotting out the "name" of any other deities from those "places" (Deuteronomy 12:2–3). A place named for a deity

6 Miller (p. 9) refers to the "boundary character of the book," and Balentine (pp. 178–84) develops the concept; see "Where to Find More" in this chapter for Miller, and in Chapter 8 for Balentine.

SIDEBAR 9.4. KING JOSIAH AND HIS REFORMS

King Josiah of Judah (640–609 BCE) was responsible for a major program of religious reform and national restoration (2 Kings 22:1–23:30; 2 Chronicles 34:1–35:27). During a period of Assyrian decline, he sought to reunite Judah with its neighbor to the north, the kingdom of Israel, in an attempt to revive the nation to its former glory under David and Solomon. He apparently sought to be anointed king (messiah) of the restored united kingdom, with Jerusalem and the temple at its center. His reforms were cut short when he was killed by Pharaoh Neco of Egypt in a battle at Megiddo. After his death, King Josiah became the model for a restored Davidic monarch. The ideal portrait of a unified kingdom ruled by a Davidic king is an important theme in, a variety of books of the OT. This is especially true of the Deuteronomistic History, as well as of Isaiah, Jeremiah, Hosea, Amos, and several other prophets.

makes a claim for that deity. The god is present symbolically in the name, and thus the place has a strong connection with that deity. But the new location for Israelite worship is "the place that Yahweh your God will choose … to put his name there" (Deuteronomy 12:5).

In other Torah instruction, Yahweh actually dwells physically inside the tabernacle (Exodus 25:8) and more precisely, above the ark of the covenant, which serves as Yahweh's royal throne (Exodus 25:22). The "glory" of Yahweh is his actual "body" or "substance," and describes the weight or importance of his presence (Exodus 40:34). But in Deuteronomy's new way of understanding God, Yahweh cannot be conceived as physically dwelling only in a tabernacle or temple. Rather, he has caused the tabernacle/temple to be *called by his name* or *caused his name to dwell* in it. By his "name," Yahweh is present in the tabernacle, but he also mysteriously transcends it.

This is a more abstract theology. Yahweh's presence is not restricted to a building; only his name lives there. Settling his name in a place of his own choosing illustrates Yahweh's sovereignty over that place and removes all other claims on Israel. Since Israel can have only one place, and one name, its

options have been simplified and streamlined. One place for worship, one presence of Yahweh, and one option for loyal service.

Election and Mission

Of all peoples on earth, Israel has a unique relationship with Yahweh. The book of Exodus describes the relationship as intimate ("you shall be my treasured possession") and service oriented; Israel is to become a priestly kingdom and a holy nation (Exodus 19:5–6). Priests will function as go-betweens connecting humans and God, and so Israel will be an intermediary between other nations and Yahweh.

Deuteronomy now, for the first time, addresses the actual "chosen" nature of Israel's relationship: Yahweh chose Israel as his "treasured possession" out of all the peoples of the earth (7:6, and see 14:2). This was not because Israel was bigger ("more numerous") than other nations, for ironically it was among the smallest (7:7). Yahweh's choice was based solely on his love for Israel and his faithfulness to his promises to Abraham, Isaac, and Jacob (7:8). Such a claim of election, however, also assumes a universal perspective for Israel's God.

Yahweh is able to choose and commission Israel from among all nations only if he has sovereignty over those nations and the authority to send Israel to serve (compare Deuteronomy 32:8–9).

Retribution Theology

In the first books of the Torah, divine blessing or favor is a natural part of the creation flowing from the grace of God (Genesis 1:22,28; 5:2; etc.). Israel's patriarchs become the conduit for God's favor to all families of the earth (Genesis 12:3). This blessing, for Israel, is the gift of a gracious God: "in every place where I cause my name to be remembered I will come to you and bless you" (Exodus 20:24). By means of the priesthood, Yahweh provides a specific formula for the blessing.

> *Yahweh bless you and keep you;*
> *Yahweh make his face to shine upon you, and be gracious to you;*
> *Yahweh lift up his countenance upon you, and give you peace.*
> (*Numbers* 6:24–26)

Even when Israel's enemies attempt to curse the Israelites, Yahweh turns their curses into blessings (Numbers 22–24). All of this is based on the covenant between Yahweh and Israel. And yet the emphasis is on God's gracious and unmerited blessing for Israel, and by extension, for the world.

As with other topics of the Torah, Deuteronomy adds a slightly different perspective. In its sermonic structure of the covenant, the speeches of Moses use the potential blessings of Yahweh in the future to motivate the Israelites to keep the covenant. Conversely, their failing to be faithful to the covenant will result in curses. So Deuteronomy lists appropriate blessings and curses near the end of

9.2 Priestly benediction on a silver amulet. This tiny silver plaque from a late-seventh-century burial cave near Jerusalem is one of two of the earliest known fragments of a biblical text, predating the oldest biblical texts from Qumran by more than three hundred years. The inscription contains an abbreviated version of the priestly blessing of Numbers 6:24–26. (Photo: The Israel Museum, Jerusalem)

Moses' speeches as both an inspiration and cautionary warning for the future (Deuteronomy 28). In this way, blessings and appropriately corresponding curses have been used in the ancient Near Eastern treaty structure we discussed earlier, as the sixth and last part of the treaty outline. But the "blessing or curse" dichotomy also summarizes the simple choice before Israel at this critical juncture in the fields of Moab. The Israelites must choose between "life and death, blessings and curses" (30:19); to keep Yahweh's covenant is blessing and life but to break his covenant is curse and death.

Deuteronomy's link between blessings and covenant fidelity defines a new retribution theology: the obedient will prosper, but the disobedient will be cursed. Continued blessing requires covenant faithfulness. Conversely, Israel holds the potential of being cursed by Yahweh if it breaks his covenant. The very possibility of this curse warns of the potential for failure and exile, and so prepares Israel for the future. And Deuteronomy's retribution theology will become an especially important concept throughout the Bible, as we shall see.

Love and Fear: A New Covenant Ethic

We have seen how the great expression of faith known as the Shema culminates in a call for Israel to love Yahweh (Deuteronomy 6:4–5). This is Israel's only logical response to the character of Yahweh – love. The command to love God is only one of several other imperatives sprinkled generously throughout the commands of Deuteronomy 5–11: remember Yahweh and do not forget his covenant, follow him and no other gods, serve and worship Yahweh, cling to him, and perhaps most surprisingly for us today, fear Yahweh.

These words and expressions are characteristics of Deuteronomy's sermonic style. Taken together, the speeches of Deuteronomy 5–11 have been called the first attempt in history to summarize succinctly "the essential substance, the heart of the faith of Yahweh."[7] These chapters stand as the first comprehensive effort to understand Israel's total relationship to Yahweh. And the commands to fear and to love Yahweh converge at the center of all the rest. They complement each other so that love of Yahweh is impossible without reverence, and fear of him is impossible without joy. Placed as they are near the end of the Torah but at the heart of Deuteronomy, the sermons of Deuteronomy 5–11 constitute a new ethical standard for ancient Israel as part of its covenant relationship with Yahweh.

Monotheism or Monolatry?

Deuteronomy has the first explicit statements of monotheism in the OT. In the speech of Deuteronomy 4, Moses asserts first that "other gods" are really no gods at all but only products of human effort, objects of wood or stone that cannot see, hear, eat, or smell (4:28). He next tells the Israelites they have witnessed Yahweh's mighty saving acts in their deliverance from Egypt in order that they might "acknowledge that Yahweh is God; there is no other besides him" (4:35). Finally, Moses challenges Israel: "So acknowledge today

---

7 See von Rad (p. 20) in the commentaries of "Where to Find More" in this chapter.

and take to heart that Yahweh is God in heaven above and on the earth beneath; there is no other" (4:39). This is matched in the poetry of the Song of Moses, when Yahweh declares, "See now that I, even I, am he; there is no god besides me" (32:39).

Some readers believe even this is not genuine philosophical monotheism, asserting that these statements do not explicitly deny the existence of other deities. Instead, these passages are said to be similar to the first commandment and the Shema: they assert the uniqueness of Yahweh *for Israel* and they call for exclusive devotion to him.[8] In other words, in this interpretation, even these passages are monolatrous rather than truly monotheistic.

On the other hand, the "no other" expression seems clear enough. Whether or not this is a strict philosophical denial of the existence of other gods, it is nevertheless a *practical monotheism*. Here Deuteronomy goes beyond calling for the Israelites' exclusive loyalty because of Yahweh's grace and goodness to them. Here they must be loyal because they have nowhere else to go. Yahweh is their only option, their only hope. And so monotheism is stated not for the sake of philosophical speculation about God's character but as a means of motivating Israel to obedience.

It is also possible that Deuteronomy's explicit statements of monotheism are simply different from the priestly materials of Exodus, Leviticus, and Numbers. In this case, the priestly writings may be taken as monotheistic but only *implicitly* so. Priestly authors of earlier portions of the Torah

thought in terms of a progression from *Elohim* ("God") in the Primeval History to *El Shaddai* ("God Almighty") in the ancestral narratives, to *Yahweh* in the time of Moses (Exodus 6:2–3). Without expressly stating as much, these priestly authors may have thought of other deities as acceptable compared to Elohim and El Shaddai before Moses. For these priestly authors, divine revelation was progressive, and their monotheism may be said to be *inclusive*; other peoples worshipped the same God whether or not they possessed the right vocabulary for naming him. That explains why these priestly materials of the Torah have no explicit condemnation of "other gods." None was needed. Deuteronomy, by contrast, is for the first time expressing an *exclusive* monotheism, urging Israel not to worship "other gods," even denying their existence occasionally.[9]

The "Center" of the Old Testament?

The importance of the book of Deuteronomy will be obvious as we move through the rest of the OT. We will have many occasions to refer back to this discussion.

Why? There are several ways to explain Deuteronomy's role in the OT. Its literary style and structure are distinctive, as speeches of Moses with unique expressions and phrases. Its covenant structure gives it a certain weightiness. The profoundness of the themes we have discussed are enough to highlight its role in Israelite religious thought.

8 For example, see MacDonald (pp. 78–96) in "Where to Find More" in this chapter.

9 See Pakkala (pp. 18–19) in "Where to Find More" in this chapter.

Deuteronomy is also transitional, serving as both the end of the beginning and the beginning of the end. It concludes the Torah with Moses' death, and it looks forward to the conquest of the promised land and the rest of the historical books in the Primary History. Deuteronomy is a hinge around which all of this turns.

Scholars working on the basic content and message of the OT often raise the question of whether Israel's library has a "center." Is there one central theme or event that holds all these diverse materials together? Most conclude today that the OT has no one particular center, as such. But one leading scholar famously identified the book of Deuteronomy as "the middle point of the Old Testament," which is certainly true for all these reasons and more, as we will discuss.[10]

The Death of Moses – the Birth of Torah

Deuteronomy's unique combination of features – literary and thematic – raises a question: Exactly what kind of book is it? Scholars working on Deuteronomy have typically described it in one of five ways: covenant, sermon, law code, constitution, or catechesis. This last option comes closest as an authoritative teaching, or Torah, intended for the future religious education for a community of faith.

10 Famously by Gerhard von Rad, "Deuteronomy's 'Name' Theology and the Priestly Document's 'Kabod' Theology," in *Studies in Deuteronomy* (trans. David Stalker; Chicago: Regnery, 1953), 37. For several more similar quotations, see Miller (p. 16) in "Where to Find More" in this chapter.

We have a hint about the nature of the book of Deuteronomy in its last chapter, recording the death of Moses. His death not only provides a logical closure to the Pentateuch but also presents Moses as the primal voice of authority: "never since has there arisen a prophet in Israel like Moses" (34:10). In the closing verses of the book, Moses' acts and accomplishments are compared to the mighty deeds of Yahweh in Egypt when the Israelites were delivered from their bondage. Remarkably, the uniqueness of Moses can be compared only to the uniqueness of Yahweh! So this is a fitting close to the speeches of Moses (obviously) and to the Pentateuch as a whole (see Plate VI).

But there's more. Leading up to Moses' death, Deuteronomy essentially presents itself as a book about the writing of a book. But not the writing of just any book. Deuteronomy points beyond itself to *the* book, the Torah. The narrative portions of Deuteronomy 27–34 gradually emphasize more and more the writing of Moses' words (27:1–3, 31:9–13, and 31:24–26; and compare 31:19,22). And here, too, Moses is unique just as Yahweh is unique. God wrote laws on stone tablets; Moses wrote the Torah in a book. Like the stone tablets, the Torah is deposited with the priests in the ark of the covenant, which means, of course, that it is not available for the average Israelite to read and study. But this book, Deuteronomy, *is* available. In fact, it must be read periodically, every seven years, in the hearing of all the people. A copy must be provided also for Israel's future kings for constant study and instruction (17:18–19). In this way, Moses' speeches are transformed into a book that (pre)determines its own audience and reception among Israel's people and king.

The speeches of Moses written in the book of Deuteronomy have become a surrogate for another book – the Torah. Since the Torah itself is tucked away in the ark, Deuteronomy gives us its basic content without assuming its identity. By closing with the death of Moses, Deuteronomy offers itself not only as a replacement for the inaccessible Torah in the ark of the covenant but also as a replacement for Moses himself (also inaccessible, since he's dead!). Moses the man, the prophet, is replaced by Moses, the book. Almost immediately in the OT writings, Deuteronomy is taken together with other books about Moses (plus Genesis) in place of the Torah itself. The Torah as God's life-giving and life-sustaining instruction is thus preserved for future Israelites as an authoritative text.

What Does "Deuteronomic" Mean? What about "Deuteronomistic"?

The book of Deuteronomy is so central to the way we read the OT that it has become the lens through which we view large portions of the rest of the Bible. Its name has given us adjectives that we will use elsewhere in this book, and you will quickly see them used in other literature about the OT as well.

In the previous chapter, we introduced the legal core of the book as the *Deuteronomic Code* (Deuteronomy 12–26; see Chapter 8). Most readers assume that the laws of Deuteronomy were building on and developing the Covenant Code (Exodus 20:22–23:33), which was probably the first of Israel's legal collections. Roughly half of the material in the Covenant Code reappears here, mostly the religious apodictic laws of Exodus 22:17–23:19, less so from the casuistic civil laws of Exodus 21:1–22:16.[11] So "Deuteronomic" typically refers to the original core of the book of Deuteronomy.

We have also seen how one of Israel's large complexes of historical narrative is called the *Deuteronomistic History* (Chapter 4). This name given by modern scholarship to the history from Joshua to 2 Kings illustrates the towering significance of the book of Deuteronomy for that history. The several innovative themes we have discussed, especially retribution theology, become foundational for the narration of Israel's history. Subsequent characters in Joshua to 2 Kings are judged by the blessings or curses of the covenant as defined here. The kings of 1–2 Samuel and 1–2 Kings are especially evaluated on whether they are blessed under the covenant or cursed because they fail to maintain the covenant. In addition, the rhetorical style and particular phraseology of Deuteronomy is closely related to these books and several others like the prophet Jeremiah. So "Deuteronomistic" refers not only to that particular collection of historical books but also to a distinct literary style and ideology permeating the OT.

---

11 See Weinfeld, *Deuteronomy 1–11* (pp. 19–24) in the commentaries in "Where to Find More" in this chapter.

SIDEBAR 9.5 THE DEUTERONOMISTIC HISTORY

The Deuteronomistic History is a scholarly reconstruction of one of Israel's historical narrative complexes (see Chapter 4 for others). The unified narrative extends from the Israelites in the land of Moab (Deuteronomy), to the conquest of the promised land (Joshua), to the premonarchic settlement period (Judges and 1 Samuel 1–7), and to monarchic Israel (1–2 Samuel and 1–2 Kings). The hypothesis asserts that the theological tenets of the book of Deuteronomy provide the undergirding for the account of Israel's emergence, growth, and maturation, and of its eventual collapse and ruin, first at the hands of the Assyrians and then the Babylonians.

The theory of the Deuteronomistic History (sometimes simply DtrH or DH) first emerged in the mid-twentieth century. The Deuteronomistic Historian, who was combination author and editor, was thought to have used an extesive collection of older source material, combining them with his own distinctive theology and worldview. Scholars quickly discerned two separate editions of the DtrH, the first edition in the time of King Josiah and the second edition in the early exile. The second edition added materials in an attempt to explain the loss of the monarchy, the temple, and the priesthood in light of the failure of Israel to maintain the covenant with Yahweh. This so-called double redaction theory has been elaborated occasionally, such as the possibility of an earlier edition in the time of King Hezekiah. Others have theorized that there were as many as three postexilic editions of the DtrH, each with its own distinct perspective on Israel's history.

WHERE TO FIND MORE

Commentaries: The best technical and advanced commentaries on **Deuteronomy** are Moshe Weinfeld, *Deuteronomy 1–11* (Anchor Bible 5; New York: Doubleday, 1991), and J. G. McConville, *Deuteronomy* (Apollos Old Testament Commentary 5; Leicester, Eng./Downers Grove, Ill.: Apollos/InterVarsity Press, 2002). Weinfeld especially may be consulted for more on the revolutionary nature of Deuteronomy's religious innovations (pp. 37–44) and on the nature of Deuteronomy 4:35,39 as "practical monotheism" (pp. 433–35). For theological insights, see Patrick D. Miller, Jr., *Deuteronomy* (Interpretation; Louisville, Ky.: John Knox Press, 1990), Gerhard von Rad, *Deuteronomy: A Commentary* (trans. Dorothea Barton; Old Testament Library; Philadelphia: Westminster Press, 1966), and J. A. Thompson, *Deuteronomy: An Introduction and Commentary* (Tyndale Old Testament Commentaries 5; Downers Grove, Ill.: InterVarsity Press, 1974).

Kitchen, Kenneth A. and Paul J. N. Lawrence. *Treaty, Law and Covenant in the Ancient Near East.* 3 vols. Wiesbaden: Harrassowitz, 2012.

Levinson, Bernard M. *Deuteronomy and the Hermeneutics of Legal Innovation.* New York: Oxford University Press, 1997.

MacDonald, Nathan. *Deuteronomy and the Meaning of "Monotheism."* Forschungen zum Alten Testament II/1. Tübingen: Mohr Siebeck, 2003.

Olson, Dennis T. *Deuteronomy and the Death of Moses: A Theological Reading.* Overtures to Biblical Theology. Minneapolis, Minn.: Fortress Press, 1994.

Offers a helpful discussion of the ways scholars have defined the genre of Deuteronomy, covenant, sermon, law code, and constitution, and adds catechesis as another (pp. 7–14).

Pakkala, Juha. *Intolerant Monolatry in the Deuteronomistic History*. Publications of the Finnish Exegetical Society 76. Göttingen: Vandenhoeck & Ruprecht, 1999.

Discussion of definitions for monotheism, polytheism, and monolatry (pp. 15–19). Pakkala's "intolerant monolatry" is what I have called "exclusive monotheism" in Deuteronomy.

Sonnet, Jean-Pierre. *The Book within the Book: Writing in Deuteronomy*. Biblical Interpretation Series 14. Leiden and New York: Brill, 1997.

The classic study of Deuteronomy as the surrogate for the Torah (see especially pp. 259–62).

Sparks, Kenton L. *Ancient Texts for the Study of the Hebrew Bible: A Guide to the Background Literature*. Peabody, Mass.: Hendrickson Publishers, 2005.

For discussion of the ancient Near Eastern treaties, and a complete bibliography, pages 435–48. And compare Weinfeld's commentary (pp. 6–9) and McConville's (pp. 23–24).

Sweeney, Marvin A. *King Josiah of Judah: The Lost Messiah of Israel*. Oxford: Oxford University Press, 2001.

Weinfeld, Moshe. *Deuteronomy and the Deuteronomic School*. Oxford: Clarendon Press, 1972 [1992].

A classic treatment of Deuteronomy's literary style and contributions to Israelite literature; for the so-called name theology, see especially pages 191–209.

CHAPTER 10

The Religion of Moses

> **OLD TESTAMENT READING: EXODUS 3:1–15, 6:2–9, AND 18:1–12; PSALMS 104, 105, AND 106**
>
> In previous chapters, we focused on the structure and content of the books in the Pentateuch. Here, we will explore the religion of Moses emerging from these materials. Specifically, we will observe the way in which divine revelation developed from direct communication with individuals such as Abraham and Moses to mediated revelation through a written Torah and the priesthood. We will explore the significant concepts of holiness, covenant, and practical monotheism, particularly as compared to the religion of the ancestral narratives (Genesis) and that of surrounding ancient Near Eastern cultures.
>
> It will be important that we consider the characteristics of Mosaic religion against the backdrop of the ancient Near East at a time when certain polytheistic cultures are known to have elevated a single deity above other gods – known as a "theology of exaltation." Furthermore, we will explore some possible influences and origins for the Yahwistic faith – the religion so foundational for the remaining OT and whose roots belong to monotheistic religions to the present.

The religious ideas attributed to Moses in the Torah changed the world. This chapter places aside for the meantime our walk through Israel's library in order to explore the religion of Moses in more depth. How was the religion of Moses different? Where did it come from? Why and how did it change the world?

Don't expect definitive answers to these questions. We simply do not have enough information to be certain in every case. But the religion of Moses is so important to human civilization and world history that we need to consider these questions.

Main Features of the Religion of Moses

We start with a consideration of the main features of the religion of Moses. What we mean by the "religion of Moses" is, of course, religious expression as preserved in the first five books of the OT – the Pentateuch, or Torah. Precisely how early these features appeared in historical Israel is a separate question and will be reserved for the next chapter.

Divine Revelation

The first thing to note is the way God reveals himself in the religion of Moses. In the Torah, the ideal conduit for divine self-revelation of Yahweh is through an intermediary. The Moses religion of the Torah establishes the official religious cult – a priesthood and sacrificial system at the tabernacle – as the means of mediation for Yahweh's revelation. From this point forward, Israel relates to Yahweh through officially sanctioned priests, the mediators of his grace. Yahweh inhabits a tent dwelling in their midst, and his transcendent holiness is protected from their human frailties and offenses through atonement and cleansing provided by the sacrificial structure.

Yet this elaborate system is only gradually developed in the Torah. At first, Yahweh appears and speaks to Moses at a burning bush. Even here, God appears in a direct way that is nonetheless mediated because he appears in the form of "the angel of Yahweh" (Exodus 3:2). Later, Yahweh speaks directly to Moses on numerous occasions, and in one passage, God permits Moses to see his "glory" and his "goodness," and to hear the name, "Yahweh," pronounced aloud (Exodus 33:17–23).

Indeed, Moses is the only person in history about whom it can be said that Yahweh "used to speak to Moses face to face, as one speaks to a friend" (Exodus 33:11). So *to Moses*, God's revelation may be direct at times, but it is always mediated by Moses to the people (Exodus 19–24). Direct revelation is not considered the norm. The mediated system established by Moses is to be normative for all future Israel: Yahweh communicates with the people through priests and sacrifices, and eventually through prophets who would be recipients of special new messages from God.

The role of Deuteronomy is critical in this progression through the Torah. In its more abstract theology, Yahweh is not restricted simply to his enthroned presence in the tabernacle (and later, the temple), but he has caused his "name" to dwell there (see Chapter 9). And Moses' role changes here as well. As the last book of Moses, Deuteronomy is a deliberate *interpretation* of Torah already revealed (Deuteronomy 1:5). This is an even more indirect means of revelation. With the death of Moses in Deuteronomy 34, the nature of revelation itself changes. Rather than mediating Yahweh's will and presence through Moses the man, now it is the written Torah, Moses the law, that becomes the primary means of revelation, along with priests and sacrifices in the tabernacle.

Holiness

Yahweh's appearance to Moses at the burning bush introduces a new theme in Israelite religion. The first lesson Moses learns from Yahweh comes in the form of this warning:

> *Come no closer! Remove the sandals from your feet, for the place on which you are standing is holy ground.* (Exodus 3:5)

10.1. Michaelangelo's *Moses*. The master's famous sculpture of Moses, housed at the tomb of Pope Julius II at the Church of Saint Peter in Chains, Rome. Why does Moses have horns? Because the expression in Exodus 34:29, "the skin of his face shone," was taken as "his face was horned" in the Latin Vulgate in use at the time of Michelangelo's work. (Photo: Scala / Art Resource, N.Y.)

Sandals are not in themselves unholy or unclean. Rather, the bare feet show respect for the nature of a unique location. Yahweh is in "the place." Immediacy and access to Yahweh's presence bears responsibility. It is dangerous to take his presence lightly. And the reference to "the place" foreshadows the way Yahweh's presence makes another "place" sacred – the central sanctuary of Israel's worship (Deuteronomy 12:2–14), which will eventually become the temple in Jerusalem.

Holiness in Mosaic thought is God's essential nature, and it can be properly attributed to God alone. It involves separation or separateness (transcendence), although it takes on other dimensions as well, such as moral goodness, righteousness, and purity. God alone is holy. And yet, certain things, places, or times may be considered holy by their association with God. The burning bush is holy ground, for example. Similarly, the tabernacle is holy, the priests are holy, and the festivals of Israel's religious calendar are holy. The tabernacle (and later, the temple) is holy in degrees: the outer courtyard, the holy place, and the inner sanctum of holiness (i.e., the "most holy place," Exodus 26:33–34). Israel is called to be a "holy nation" (Exodus 19:6; Deuteronomy 7:6), and Sinai/Horeb is a holy mountain (Exodus 19:23).

Holiness is therefore communicable; it may be transmitted from God to objects, people, places, or times. But it always comes from God alone. Much of the priestly material in the Torah restricts God's holiness to specific persons (priests) and places (the tabernacle). Yet a special feature of the Holiness Code of Leviticus 17–26 is that it democratizes holiness. The ideal in this version of the religion of Moses is that every Israelite is holy, and the entire promised land is holy. So the emphasis on "law" or instruction, as we have seen, is related to this theme of holiness, so that the religion of Moses is a form of *nomism* in the best sense of that word: the establishment of ethics based on moral law.

Covenant

In previous chapters, we have explored how the Torah links these important religious themes to another idea – that of the covenant at Mount Sinai/Horeb. Texts making the connection especially clearly are the Book of the Covenant (Exodus 19–24) and the entire book of Deuteronomy. All of Exodus, Leviticus, Numbers, and Deuteronomy presumes it in many ways. The covenant is something of a linchpin in Torah thought.

The idea of covenant in the religion of Moses takes the widespread ancient Near Eastern political treaty and transforms it into a profound theological statement. The exclusive political loyalty demanded by treaties was a perfect parallel for the exclusivity of worshipping Yahweh. In Mosaic religion, you simply cannot worship Yahweh *plus* another deity, any more than a city ruler in Syria-Palestine could serve both the Assyrian king and the Egyptian king at the same time. The treaty structure was widely known for centuries, as we have seen, and was used to define relationships between two *human parties* in political treaties. In the religion of Moses, however, the treaty structure was co-opted and used to define the relationship between God and Israel. The importance of the Sinai/Horeb covenant is so central to the religion of Moses that it was anticipated in the covenants of Noah and Abraham (Genesis 9:8–17, and Genesis 15 and 17).

The Mosaic covenant ties together the other innovative themes of the new Yahwism of Moses — holiness and mediated revelation. The covenant is the literary and theological context for the tabernacle and the sacrificial service of the priesthood. So the religion of Moses is a unified and unifying system. The covenant is the nexus between Israel and Yahweh. Yahweh dwells peacefully in Israel's midst in the tabernacle, and his self-revelation to Israel is mediated by his priests.

Monotheism

Most readers today assume that monotheism is the primary characteristic of the religion of Moses. As we have explained in Chapter 1, the OT generally expresses something more like monolatrous henotheism, and this is true for the religion of Moses as well. What we mean by this is that the Torah calls for an exclusive commitment to serve one God, Yahweh, while not denying the existence of other dieties. The first commandment, for example, calls Israel to "have no other gods" before Yahweh but stops short of claiming that Yahweh is the only deity available for worship. It implies, in fact, the opposite. The other gods are a temptation for Israel.

A few passages in the Torah, all in Deuteronomy, appear to claim that other deities are not real (Deuteronomy 4:35,39 and 32:39; and discussed in Chapter 9). It is completely understandable why and how the Torah came to be thought of as monotheistic. The faiths of later Jews, Christians, and Muslims share this single feature in common. They are monotheistic religions, assuming a common heritage going back to Abraham and Moses. And this is logical, because Abraham and Moses

took the first steps to genuine monotheism. But the Torah itself is summarized better in the Shema (Deuteronomy 6:4), which asserts the uniqueness of Yahweh and calls for exclusive devotion to him. This *practical monotheism* set the stage for genuine monotheism later. But the heart of the Torah is the call for exclusive devotion to Yahweh as the sole God of Israel, which is something more than monotheism.

MOSES AND ABRAHAM

This summary of the religion of Moses raises interesting questions. First, how does Moses' religion compare to the religion of Abraham in Genesis, the first book of the Torah? Second, how does the religion of Moses relate to other religions in the ancient Near East at the time? And finally, where did the Mosaic innovations come from? Is it possible to trace precursors or origins for the religion of Moses? Let's explore these important questions next, keeping in mind that our answers to the last question are especially tentative because of lack of information.

The religion of Moses is found in the expressions of faith and theology in Exodus, Leviticus, Numbers, and Deuteronomy. How is this similar or different from the faith of Israel's ancestors known from the ancestral narratives (Genesis 12–50) and the Primeval History (Genesis 1–11)?

To answer this question, we start with a passage that points to the differences between Moses and Abraham.

God also spoke to Moses and said to him: "I am Yahweh. I appeared to Abraham, Isaac, and Jacob as God Almighty,

10.2. The Canaanite god El. The chief of the pantheon and father of the gods worshipped by the Canaanites was El, portrayed here in gold-covered bronze. Excavated at Megiddo, and dating to the Late Bronze Age. (Photo: Courtesy of the Oriental Institute of the University of Chicago)

SIDEBAR 10.1. EXODUS 6:2–9 IN LIGHT OF SOURCE ANALYSIS

This text is the cornerstone of the investigation into the original sources behind the Pentateuch. It asserts that God did not reveal himself *as Yahweh* to Israel's patriarchs – Abraham, Isaac, and Jacob. But this raises an interesting question about the book of Genesis. The name "Yahweh" is used in the narratives and speeches about these three patriarchs ninety-two times (Genesis 12–36), including, at times, on the very lips of one of the patriarchs. In one critical juncture in Abraham's life, he names a particular place "Yahweh provides" (Genesis 22:14).

How do we explain this? Why does the name occur so frequently in Genesis when Israel's ancestors were not supposed to have known the name? Although many answers have been tried, the most reasonable explanation is that the ancestral narratives have been heavily edited from the later perspective of the religion of Moses. These ancestral traditions may have been transmitted orally, which is something we are not able to trace. But they were written down and edited at a time when Mosaic religion (i.e., the new religion of Yahweh) was the main explanation of Israel's understanding of God. The ancestral narratives have thus been carefully edited to show the continuity: The Yahweh of Moses is in fact the same God worshipped by Abraham, Isaac, and Jacob.

This explanation takes Exodus 6:2–9 as an intentional link or transition between priestly texts before Moses and those after him. According to the P source (Sidebar 4.3), this is the moment when God revealed his name for the first time in history. While other authors and editors freely used the sacred name in Genesis, the priestly authors of Exodus 6:2–3 were intentionally showing the continuity between the God of Abraham and Yahweh of Moses, while highlighting this moment in revelation history.

SIDEBAR 10.2. EL IN CANAANITE RELIGION

The word *el* or *il(u)* is used in almost all Semitic languages for "god." In the Ugaritic texts from modern Ras Shamra, the noun is used as a personal name for the god El, chief of the Ugaritic pantheon. From the Ugaritic texts, among others, we learn that El was a gray-bearded aged deity, benevolent and wise, father of the gods, and creator of the universe. El resides with the deities on their sacred mountain. His divine wife is Athirat (**Asherah** in the Bible), mother of the gods. The OT has no polemic against El, as it does for the weather god Baal, and more often than not, the OT identifies El with Yahweh.

---

but by my name 'Yahweh' I did not make myself known to them." (Exodus 6:2–3)

The understanding of God as "Yahweh" is new with Moses. While the sacred name, Yahweh, occurs in the narratives and even in the speeches of Genesis, this is not the way Israel's ancestors knew God prior to Moses. Ancient Israelites refer to God by one of several other names, such as Elohim ("God"), El Shaddai, El Olam, and so on.[1] These names reflect a theology that understood the character of God as the source of blessing and the keeper of the ancestral promises. El was the faithful protector of the family and tribal group. The Canaanites prior to the arrival of Israel in Syria-

---

1 And on occasion, the editors of Genesis have used the sacred name in ancestral speeches; e.g., "Surely Yahweh is in this place" (Genesis 28:16).

Palestine also worshipped El as the leading god of their pantheon. El was the creator god and ruler over other gods. He was wise and merciful, exercising power over life and death, and over fertility in one's family. This is compatible with the ancestral view of God, so that Israel's ancestors are portrayed as acknowledging El as their God.

But what about the use of the name Yahweh in Genesis? Why is it used in the book, in light of the assertions in Exodus 3:14–15 and 6:2–3 that the name itself is God's special revelation to Moses? The answer is that Genesis has been edited to make a theological statement. The Primary History and the ancestral narratives are presented deliberately from the perspective of the religion of Moses. In this way, the God known to the ancestors by El-type names is, in fact, the same God who revealed himself to Moses as Yahweh. Israel's covenant God, Yahweh, is the same Creator God of Genesis 1–11, and of the ancestors in Genesis 12–50. Thus the first book of the Torah has a definite continuity with the rest of Torah religion.

And yet the Torah itself is also clear that Moses introduced fundamentally new ideas in Israel's understanding of God. Consider two of the four primary features of the religion of Moses we have discussed in this chapter – revelation and holiness.

Divine revelation is unmediated in Genesis. No priests or sacrifices are needed in the Garden of Paradise, of course, which is prior to human rebellion. But even elsewhere in Genesis, God reveals himself and communicates without need of mediation. He calls Noah in direct speech to prepare for the flood (Genesis 6:13–14), and the call to Abram is similar (12:1). At times God appears in a vision

(15:1) or a dream (28:12), but one gets the sense from the narrative that these were means of catching the ancestors' attention more than anything else. Unlike the later Israelites, who needed Moses to intercede for them, the ancestors received direct communication from God/Yahweh.

The difference in types of divine revelation is most visible in the building and use of altars for worship and the offering of sacrifices. The religion of Moses establishes regulations for such worship, including the nature of specific sacrifices, and the priests authorized to make sacrifices on behalf of the people. By contrast, Noah and Abraham are free to build their own altars and to offer sacrifices themselves without the need of priests (Genesis 8:20; 12:7; 22:13). In general, worship in the ancestral age is not unlike that of Bronze Age Canaan, where altars were freely built in open-air shrines often embellished with standing stones or stela, and trees with special sacred significance. Such practices were condemned in Iron Age Israelite religion, and they are prohibited in the Torah (Exodus 23:24; Leviticus 26:1; Numbers 33:52; Deuteronomy 7:5).

The theme of holiness, so central to the religion of Moses, is completely missing in Genesis. The single exception to this statement is the priestly creation account of Genesis 1, which concludes with God's blessing of the seventh day and making it holy (2:3). This is the only occurrence of the term "holy" in the Primeval History of Genesis 1–11 (in this case, a verb meaning "to make sacred"), or even in the ancestral narratives of Genesis 12–50. In fact, the term does not occur again in the Bible until Moses stands before the burning bush in Exodus 3:5. Something close to holiness in the religion of Moses occurs in Yahweh's charge to Abram, "walk before me, and be blameless" (Genesis 17:1). But this can only be said to anticipate and foreshadow the importance of holiness in Exodus to Deuteronomy.

So then, how *does* the religion of Moses compare to the religion of Abraham? While there is much more we could say on this topic, this is enough to show that the religion of Moses was a genuine innovation. The ideal of a mediated divine revelation of God's holiness is sufficient to illustrate the distinctive traits of Moses' religion. We can also see how unmistakably the Primeval History and the ancestral narratives of Genesis have been edited and framed in light of Mosaic religion. The authors and editors of Genesis were determined to show that the God of Moses is essentially the same God of creation of Israel's ancestors.

One scholar captured the differences between the faith of Moses and that of Abraham by referring to the ancestral narratives as "the OT of the OT."[2] His point is that the differences are similar to the way the New Testament relates to the Old Testament. Abraham's faith and covenant are distinct but are folded into and become part of the new Mosaic religion. Though different, the old is confirmed in the new and becomes part of it.

MOSES AND ANCIENT NEAR EASTERN PRECURSORS

The religion of Moses did not spring up in a vacuum. It might have been possible to think so prior to the discovery of thousands of texts from

ancient Egypt, Mesopotamia, and Syria-Palestine. But now that we have information about religion in the ancient world, the question naturally presents itself: How does the religion of Moses relate to other religions in the ancient Near East at approximately the same period of time?

It may be difficult for most of us in the West to grasp, but polytheism provided a unified and logical religious system for ancient eastern peoples. It was helpful to them to think of the universe as filled with multiple and competing deities in a tiered pantheon. They appear to have thought of the gods in a sort of hierarchy, like people living together in the same society, with the most important and powerful gods at the top and the functionary weaker gods at the bottom.[3] Such a religious system explains the diversity and confusing complexity of the world experienced by ancient worshippers. Polytheism was the default system over thousands of years.

This all began to change in the Late Bronze (1550–1200 BCE) and Iron I Ages (1200–930 BCE). Gradually, across the ancient world, each culture began elevating and promoting one deity to the highest rank among other gods, in what one scholar has called a "theology of exaltation."[4] It is among these theologies of exaltation surveyed here that the closest parallels can be found to Mosaic religion. These developments occurred prior to the Axial Age contributions we mentioned earlier, of

2 R. W. L. Moberly, *The Old Testament of the Old Testament: Patriarchal Narratives and Mosaic Yahwism* (Minneapolis, Minn.: Fortress Press, 1992)

3 Lowell K. Handy suggests they thought in terms of a four-fold hierarchy: authoritative deities, active deities, artisan deities, and messenger deities; see his book in "Where to Find More" in this chapter

4 Karel van der Toorn, "Theology, Priests, and Worship in Canaan and Ancient Israel," in *Civilizations of the Ancient Near East* (ed. Jack M. Sasson; Scribner, 1995), 3:2043–58, esp. 2056.

which Irsrael's monotheism was one part (review Chapter 3 before continuing). In a way, these developments anticipated and prepared for those Axial Age contributions.

Aten in Egypt

Pharaoh Amenophis IV of Egypt (1352–1336 BCE) changed the entire cultural system of Egypt. Or at least he tried to change it. His ideas and reforms were essentially a revolution from the top down. Under his predecessors in New Kingdom Egypt, the sun god Re had been merged with the local god of Thebes, Amun ("the hidden one") to become the most important deity of the land, Amun-Re. Amenophis IV took this a step further by becoming a devotee exclusively of a particular physical image of the sun disc, known in Egyptian as "the Aten." The king thus changed his name from Amenophis ("Amun is satisfied") to Akhenaten ("beneficial for Aten") and elevated Aten as supreme in the pantheon. Aten became the sole heavenly king and Akhenaten, his earthly incarnation. Other deities of the Egyptian pantheon were excluded in Akhenaten's theological innovations.

With Akhenaten, we reach a new development in Egyptian religion. In addition to building a new temple for Aten at Karnak and moving the capital to a new site (modern el-Amarna) north of Thebes, which had been the traditional capital of religion, Akhenaten abandoned the temples of other deities (see Map 3.3). The names of his family members have "Aten" as the divine element, showing how he suppressed the worship of other gods. For example, the famous King Tut, or Tutankhamun, the boy king, probably Akhenaten's only son, was originally named Tutankhaten, "living image of Aten." These religious innovations are usually taken to be an experiment with monotheism because of the ideas elevating the sun disc Aten, especially in hymns to Aten.

Akhenaten's reforms did not survive long. Almost immediately after his death, his Aten worship was branded a heresy, lasting scarcely twenty years. Tutankhaten quickly abandoned el-Amarna, moved the royal court to Memphis, the traditional capital, restored the religious practices of other deities, and changed his name to Tutankhamun, "living image of Amun." Egypt's experiment in monotheism was short-lived.

Since the days of Sigmund Freud, and of his book *Moses and Monotheism* (1939), readers of the OT have speculated about connections between Moses' Yahwism and Akhenaten's Atenism. Freud theorized that Moses was in actuality an Egyptian priest who attempted to save Atenism by attaching himself to a Semitic tribe living in bondage in Egypt at the time. After the priest's death, this new religion was allegedly combined with the Midian worship of a volcanic deity named Yahweh (for the possible origins of Yahwism among Midianite tribes in north Arabia, see "Origins of the Religion of Moses" in this chapter). Freud's reconstruction was filled with historical inaccuracies and naïve in its approach. Nevertheless, scholars working on the OT today still speculate from time to time about the plausibility of a connection between Atenism in New Kingdom Egypt and Moses.[5]

---

5 For example, see William H. C. Propp, *Exodus 19–40: A New Translation with Introduction and Commentary* (Anchor Bible 2A; New York: Doubleday, 2006), 762–94.

SIDEBAR 10.3. EXCERPT FROM *THE GREAT HYMN TO THE ATEN*

The Great Hymn to the Aten was discovered among other hymns and prayers in the tomb of one of Akhenaten's courtiers at el-Amarna. The hymn is an eloquent celebration of the one god, Aten, illustrating the monotheizing doctrine of Akhenaten theology. In a dramatic break from previous Egyptian religion, this hymn asserts that Aten alone created the world and everything in it. Aten alone gives and preserves life for humanity. He alone rules in the sky. The close parallels in wording and ideology have frequently been observed with Psalm 104:10–30, although direct literary dependence is not likely.

The following excerpt is adapted from William Kelly Simpson, "The Hymn to the Aten," in *The Literature of Ancient Egypt: An Anthology of Stories, Instructions, Stelae, Autobiographies, and Poetry* (ed. William Kelly Simpson, 3rd ed.; New Haven, Conn.: Yale University Press, 2003), 279–83.

"When day breaks you are risen upon the horizon, and you shine in the Aten in the daytime. When you dispel darkness and give forth your rays, the two lands are in a festival of light, alert and standing on their feet, now that you have raised them up. Their bodies are clean, and their clothes put on; their arms are lifted in praise at your rising.

"The entire land performs its work: All the flocks are content with their fodder, trees and plants grow, birds fly up to their nests, their wings extended in praise for your *Ka* [life force]. All the flocks prance on their feet; everything which flies up and alights, they live when you rise for them. The barges sail upstream and downstream too, for every way is open at your rising. The fishes in the river leap before your face, when your rays are inside the sea.

"You who places seed in woman, and makes sperm into man, who brings to life the son in the womb of his mother, who quiets him by ending his crying; you nurse in the womb, giving breath to nourish all that has been begotten. When he comes down from the womb to breathe on the day he is born, you open up his mouth and supply his needs. When the fledgling in the egg speaks in the shell, you give him air inside it to sustain him. When you have granted him his allotted time to break out from the egg, he comes out from the egg to cry out at his fulfillment, and he goes upon his legs when he has come forth from it.

"How plentiful it is, what you make, although they are hidden from view, sole god, without another beside you; you create the earth as you wish, when you were by yourself, before mankind, all cattle and flocks, all beings on land, who fare upon their feet, and all beings in the air, who fly with their wings.

"The lands of Khor and Kush [Syria-Palestine and Nubia] and the land of Egypt: you set every man in his place, you allot their needs, every one of them according to his diet, and his lifetime is counted out. Tongues are separate in speech, and their characters as well; their skins are different, for you differentiate the foreigners."

Marduk and Assur in Mesopotamia

We have evidence of something similar happening in Mesopotamia, although much less dramatic than the Atenism experiment in Egypt. Our story begins with the god Marduk, patron deity of the city of Babylon. His name, "calf of the storm," reflects his original nature as god of the thunderstorm, providing abundance by means of rainfall. For much of Mesopotamian history, Marduk was only one god among many. More important deities represented cosmic phenomena; there were gods of the heavens, of lands, of wisdom and magic, of the moon, of the sun, of love and war, to name but a few. Marduk was just one deity in a crowd.

Then, political and religious events combined late in the second millennium BCE (around the twelfth and eleventh centuries) resulting in Marduk's elevation in the pantheon. Most importantly, the city of Babylon rose to prominence in the early part of the second millennium under the powerful kings of the so-called Old Babylonian period. The most important of these rulers was the celebrated lawgiver Hammurabi (Chapter 8). As the city of Babylon emerged politically, Marduk began to accrue characteristics and roles from other deities. Toward the end of the second millennium BCE, Babylon's stature was established as the religious and cultural capital of Mesopotamia, and so Marduk became the head of a prestigious pantheon.

Marduk's exaltation came to its culmination in the Babylonian creation myth, known as the *Enuma Elish* (Chapter 5). We turn to this text often to understand how the Babylonians explained creation. But its central theme is the exaltation of Marduk. In the mythological account, Marduk defeats the coalition of gods surrounding Tiamat, the saltwater deity, and creates the universe and humanity in the battle's aftermath. The myth concludes with the building of Babylon as Marduk's abode, celebrated with a grand feast at his temple complex where other deities acknowledge Marduk's supremacy as king of the gods and master of the universe. They honor him with fifty names, contributing to the perception of Marduk as chief god of the pantheon.

The date of the composition of the *Enuma Elish* is uncertain, and we cannot be sure when Marduk's elevation was complete. But it appears related to a political event in the late twelfth century BCE. The cult statue of Marduk had been taken captive to a neighboring region, but it was retrieved by a new Babylonian ruler and returned to its shrine in Babylon. This event, dated sometime around 1120 BCE, gave Marduk a new level of supremacy in the pantheon, as is clear from numerous texts from the period. One text from that time calls Marduk "king of the gods," and from this point forward, his sovereignty over the gods is standard in Babylonian thinking (see Plate VII).

The elevation of Marduk never led to the denial of the existence of other deities. Yet his rise from a relatively minor status to top deity in the pantheon illustrates the monotheizing tendencies in the ancient world, especially at the beginning of the Iron I period. Later in the first millennium, even the Assyrian god Assur, chief deity of the city by the same name, is depicted in the role of Marduk. In some Assyrian versions of the *Enuma Elish*, the hero of the story was the god Assur, not Marduk. Regardless of which deity was at the top, Mesopotamian religion could perceive all male deities as in some way a manifestation of one chief deity, either Marduk or Assur. Female deities, for a variety of reasons, tended to retain their own characteristics.

El and Baal-Hadad in Syria-Palestine

We believe that a similar development took place in Syria-Palestine, although here we have less evidence. Interestingly, it was again the storm god who

10.3. The god Baal of the thunderstorm. This gilded bronze statue of Baal was found at the nearby port of ancient Ugarit. The interpretation of such figurative representations of Baal are somewhat theoretical. Yet the god often appears with a raised mace or other weapon, as here with an upraised right hand and a thunderbolt in the other hand (compare Figure 5.4). In some periods, the storm god appears in this posture riding on the back of a lion-dragon (see Plate VII) or standing on the back of a bull. (Photo: Erich Lessing / Art Resource, N.Y.)

SIDEBAR 10.4. THE *BAAL CYCLE*

Beginning the 1920s, the discovery of Ugarit and its texts filled a gap in our knowledge of the history and religion of the Levant in ancient times. One of the most important discoveries was a six-tablet mythological composition of approximately fifteen hundred poetic verses, known today simply as the *Baal Cycle*. It was committed to writing in the fourteenth century BCE, although it was likely repeated for centuries prior to this time. In poetry strikingly similar to later biblical Hebrew poetry, the composition tells of Baal's ascent over the other gods. The *Baal Cycle* is a great classic of ancient Near Eastern literature, revealing much about ancient perceptions of El, Baal, Yam, and many others.

For English translations of the *Baal Cycle*, see the resources in Sidebar 5.3. For a critical edition, see Mark S. Smith and Wayne T. Pitard, *The Ugaritic Baal Cycle* (Leiden: Brill, 1994 [vol. 1], and 2009 [vol. 2], a third volume is forthcoming).

eventually ascended to the top of the pantheon. This weather deity was known in some regions as Hadad and in others as Baal. By the first millennium, Hadad was his name among the Arameans, and Baal among the Phoenicians and Canaanites.[6]

Although we have some evidence from the OT itself and from various Syro-Palestinian inscriptions, it is especially from the mythological texts discovered at modern Ras Shamra (ancient Ugarit) that we learn most about Baal (see Ugarit on Map 3.4). His role as the chief weather god changes when he is permitted by the head of the Ugaritic pantheon, the older and wiser father deity, El, to challenge the god Yam, whose domain is the sea. One of these texts, the *Baal Cycle*, describes the conflict, which is at least similar to Marduk's battle with Tiamat in the *Enuma Elish*. And like that outcome, the storm god defeats the sea god, and establishes kingship over other gods. The other deities proclaim Baal's kingship over them, and he takes up

residence as sovereign ruler in a new palace built in his honor, again similar to the *Enuma Elish*.

It would be inaccurate to say Baal simply replaces El as chief deity of the Ugaritic pantheon. El retains his position as the venerated father god, who is portrayed as wise and beneficent. It's as though El simply retires from active service, while Baal becomes the primary force of the universe. Baal has authority over clouds, storms, lightning, wind, rain, snow, and the fertility of the soil. The mythological texts from Ugarit are clear that he rules supreme among the gods.

We should not necessarily think of the religion of Moses as *directly* related to any of these developments. So in answer to the question, How do the Mosaic innovations relate to other religions of the ancient Near East?, we must admit the limitations of our evidence. Yet these religious developments during the Late Bronze Age and Iron I Age do suggest a general theology of exaltation across the entire Fertile Crescent. And the religion of Moses makes sense viewed from this background.

We turn now to our final question for this chapter. Is it possible to speculate even further about

---

6 Although Hadad could also be called Baal, which means "Lord," just as Marduk became known as "Bel" in Babylonia.

the origins of the Mosaic innovations? Can we trace actual precursors or origins of the worship of Yahweh? As we explore these important questions, keep in mind that our answers are especially tentative because of lack of information.

Origins of the Religion of Moses

We described the religion of Moses at the beginning of this chapter in four themes: revelation, holiness, covenant, and monotheism. The Mosaic Torah is more complex than this, of course, but at least these innovations characterize the Torah religion of Exodus to Deuteronomy.

Where do these innovations come from? By this question, I don't mean to imply that Moses — regardless of how much we can or cannot actually know about him historically (see next chapter) — could not have developed these religious innovations himself. Of course Moses could have been a great religious innovator! But we should also ask whether we might discern other influences that contributed to the development of the worship of Yahweh in earliest Israel. What evidence do we have for the origins of Yahwism?

The worship of Yahweh is not original to Syria-Palestine, since Yahweh is not found among the deities of Canaan or of the peoples along the Levant (except Israel). Archaeology and other historical sources are of little help. However, the Torah itself leaves hints. For example, Moses has a father-in-law, the priest of Midian, and by means of this relationship, Moses first encounters the sacred place in Midian named Horeb, "the mountain of God" (Exodus 3:1). The bush at Horeb from which Yahweh first appears to Moses is the desert version

of a sacred tree (3:2), suggesting that Moses' introduction to Yahweh was in a Midianite shrine or holy place. After the exodus from Egypt, Moses and the Israelites return to Midian (for its location, see Midian in Map 7.1). There, presumably at the same shrine at Horeb, Moses' priestly father-in-law asserts that Yahweh is "greater than all gods" and offers sacrifices to him, leading Moses, Aaron, and the elders of Israel in the worship of God (Exodus 18:11–12). Is this when Moses and Aaron learn about the proper sacrifices for the worship of Yahweh?

The oldest portions of the OT are typically poetic strands preserved in narratives. These almost always confirm an origin of Israel's earliest religion in the south. In addition to frequent mention of Sinai/Horeb, these geographical names include Teman and Mount Paran, Cushan and the land of Midian (Habakkuk 3:3,7), and Seir and the region of Edom (Deuteronomy 33:2 and Judges 5:4–5). All indications point to Yahweh's coming from the land of Midian in north Arabia, so we should probably look to the northeastern regions of the Sinai Peninsula or to the southern Negeb.

Such evidence as we have beyond these hints in the OT itself support the hypothesis that the worship of Yahweh originated among Midianite tribes in north Arabia. Egyptian inscriptions from the fourteenth century BCE make mention of "Shasu of YHW." The Shasu appear to have been nomadic or seminomadic people residing in northern Arabia roughly equivalent to Midianite territory. The "YHW" in these inscriptions is a place name, but seems to be related to the divine name YHWH, or Yahweh. Whether the deity took his name from the place, or the other way around, we do not know. Although the evidence is only suggestive, we may

SIDEBAR 10.5. "SHASU OF YHW" IN EGYPTIAN INSCRIPTIONS

The Shasu bedouin are known only from Egyptian texts from approximately 1500 to 1100 BCE, mostly in lists of conquered areas. They appear in these texts as seminomadic pastoralist tribes dwelling most of the time in tents but occasionally also in towns. The term "Shasu" is not an ethnic designation but a general Egyptian term for nomadic pastoralists applied to those living in the Southern Levant.

In one letter, a scribe reports that the Shasu have been permitted to pass an Egyptian fortress in order to water their flocks: "We have just let the Shasu tribes of Edom pass the Fortress of Merneptah-hetephermaat, ... to the pool of Pithom ... in order to revive themselves and revive their flocks."* These Egyptian texts place the Shasu mostly in southern Palestine east of the Jordan River, particularly in Edom and Moab, but they occasionally also appear elsewhere. Whether the Shasu constituted a distinct ethnic group or merely a social class is something we cannot determine. Some scholars believe that the Shasu were proto-Israelites, or at least were related to the early Israelites in some way.

* James P. Allen, "A Report of Bedouin," *The Context of Scripture* (3 vols., eds. William W. Hallo and K. Lawson Younger, Jr. (Leiden and Boston: Brill, 2002), 3:16–17.

tentatively assume that Moses adapted his father-in-law's version of Yahwism in the land of Midian. Even this earliest Yahwism appears to have been monolatrous in that Moses' father-in-law worshipped no other gods (Exodus 18:11–12).

In assessing the evidence, most readers take one of two directions. The first is to assume an evolutionary development from polytheism to henotheism to monotheism, and the second is to assume a religious revolution that occurred more or less suddenly.[7] The *evolutionary* approach typically assumes that Israel was essentially polytheistic early on, worshipping Yahweh, El, Baal, and a goddess known as Asherah (we'll talk about her in the next chapter). Early Israelite religion was essentially Canaanite in this reconstruction. Gradually, during the Iron II Age, Israelite Yahwism broke away from its Canaanite roots, under pressure from prophets such

7 For examples, see the writings of Mark S. Smith (first approach) and Stephen L. Cook (second) in "Where to Find More" in this chapter.

as Hosea, becoming henotheistic. Yahweh absorbed the features of other deities in a sort of "mono-Yahwism" or Yahweh-only form of worship. In the centuries just before the Babylonian exile, older features associated with Baal and Canaanite practices were eliminated from the worship of Yahweh altogether, yielding monotheism in the exile itself.

The *revolutionary* explanation does not deny that Israelite Yahwism had a long and developmental history. People worshipping Yahweh in the ninth century BCE certainly had different ideas from those worshipping in the sixth century. But that history was independent of polytheistic Canaanite religious developments and did not emerge in a single-line evolution from Canaanite polytheism to biblical monotheism. Sociology has had an impact on this debate. Evolutionary theory, it has been argued, may explain the nature of religion in great societies like Egypt or Mesopotamia, the so-called primary religions. But sociologists question whether it is a realistic explanation for biblical Yahwism, which bears the earmarks of a "counterreligion," or a religion that defines itself by opposition to another.[8] Such counterreligions occur more rapidly and are revolutionary in nature, as with Atenism in Egypt, or even with Christianity or Islam.

In this understanding, the religion of Moses emerged more or less internally in early Israel. In some reconstructions, henotheistic Yahwism characterized early Israel and was preserved throughout Israel's checkered history by a minority of social groups, like elders or priests, until it emerged late in Israel's history as the accepted form of worship. All the while, a more popular strain of Israelite religion was practiced in most periods of Israel's history that was more accepting of worshipping Yahweh alongside other deities, especially Asherah. But the minority version of early Yahwism was advocated by lawgivers, prophets, and royal reformers, and eventually it became the hallmark of the OT as we have it today. In this way, as we explained in Chapter 1, the OT is *implicitly* monotheistic, and we may think of the early Israelites as unselfconsciously monotheistic.

LEGACY

I began this chapter with an assertion that the religious ideas attributed to Moses changed the world. What is the legacy of Mosaic Yahwism? Clearly the innovations of Torah religion are the foundation for the rest of the OT. The OT itself is its legacy, and perhaps that is enough of an answer.

But the influence of Torah religion doesn't end there, of course. Through the OT, Torah religion has become the bond holding Jews, Christians, and Muslims together as the so-called Abrahamic

faiths. As we have seen, Judaism considers the Torah the foundation of all authoritative truth, which is therefore expanded in the Mishnah and Talmud (Chapter 2). Christians also hold the Torah as central; as Jesus said, "I have come not to abolish [the law or the prophets] but to fulfill" (Matthew 5:17). While Christians differ on how the New Testament relates to the OT law, Christianity itself does not consider rejecting the OT altogether. Muslims believe that the Torah (*Tawrāt* in Arabic) was unique divine revelation and "Scripture" in its own right. Now, however, the Qur'an has superseded the Torah's authority and stands alone as the climax of God's revelation. Even with all their differences, Judaism, Christianity, and Islam have in common the monotheism that has its roots in the religion of Moses.

Monotheism has been called the single most significant innovation in human history. Israel's monotheism is at least among the most significant contributions of the Axial Age (Chapter 3). The question remains: Is monotheism a blessing or a burden for humanity? Whatever your personal views, it is important to know that ideas of God first taught in the religion of Moses have shaped human history and culture. Some will choose to emphasize the positive, such as monotheism's role in the rise of science or the abolition of slavery. Others will find monotheism to blame for intolerance, violence, and injustice.[9]

---

8 On Mosaic Yahwism as a "counterreligion," see Assmann in "Where to Find More" in this chapter.

9 See Rodney Stark for the first approach (*One True God: Historical Consequences of Monotheism* [Princeton, N.J.: Princeton University Press, 2001], and *For the Glory of God: How Monotheism Led to Reformations, Science, Witch-hunts, and the End of Slavery* [Princeton, N.J.: Princeton University Press, 2003]), and Regina M. Schwartz for the second (*The Curse of Cain: The Violent Legacy of Monotheism* [Chicago: University of Chicago Press, 1997]).

On this last point, we need to ask whether it is in fact the allegiance to the idea of one God that has resulted in intolerance and violence throughout Western history. Or rather, is it the abuse of that idea that has been a burden to humanity? In other words, is the power of this relatively new idea of monotheism innately and inevitably prone to exclusion and violence? Or has it been contorted into a pretext for violence against "the other" by human failure? This question is as deeply personal and intimate as what one believes to be true about God.

WHERE TO FIND MORE

Arnold, Bill T. "Religion in Ancient Israel." Pages 391–420 in *The Face of Old Testament Studies: A Survey of Contemporary Approaches*. Edited by David W. Baker and Bill T. Arnold. Grand Rapids, Mich.: Baker Books, 1999.

Assmann, Jan. *Moses the Egyptian: The Memory of Egypt in Western Monotheism*. Cambridge, Mass.: Harvard University Press, 1997.

As a religion based on the distinction between true and false, monotheism was revolutionary in ancient thought, distinguishing itself from traditional religions, which were branded as paganism, idolatrous, or otherwise "false." Monotheism was thus a counterreligion, opposing and rejecting what went before or what goes outside of itself.

Cook, Stephen L. *The Social Roots of Biblical Yahwism*. Society of Biblical Literature Studies in Biblical Literature 8. Atlanta, Ga.: Society of Biblical Literature, 2004.

Green, Alberto R. W. *The Storm-God in the Ancient Near East*. Biblical and Judaic Studies 8. Winona Lake, Ind.: Eisenbrauns, 2003.

On the emergence of Baal in the Middle Bronze Age (pp. 153–218).

Handy, Lowell K. *Among the Host of Heaven: The Syro-Palestinian Pantheon as Bureaucracy*. Winona Lake, Ind.: Eisenbrauns, 1994.

Hess, Richard S. *Israelite Religions: An Archaeological and Biblical Survey*. Grand Rapids, Mich.: Baker Academic, 2007.

Lemaire, André. *The Birth of Monotheism: The Rise and Disappearance of Yahwism*. Washington, D.C.: Biblical Archaeology Society, 2007.

True universal monotheism is not the religion of Moses, David, or Solomon; nor is it the conviction of the early prophets. Rather, it appeared first in the sixth century BCE in Second Isaiah. On the Midianite origins of Yahwism, see pages 19–28.

Mettinger, Tryggve N. D. *In Search of God: The Meaning and Message of the Everlasting Names*. Translated by Frederick H. Cryer. Philadelphia: Fortress Press, 1988.

The progression of Israelite religion can be seen best, perhaps, in the use of divine names in the OT (see especially Mettinger's conclusion, pp. 201–4); for interpretations of Exodus 6:2–3 and occurrences of "Yahweh" in Genesis, see pages 50–74.

Miller, Patrick D. *The Religion of Ancient Israel*. Library of Ancient Israel. Louisville, Ky.: Westminster John Knox Press, 2000.

Oswalt, John N. *The Bible among The Myths: Unique Revelation or Just Ancient Literature?* Grand Rapids, Mich.: Zondervan, 2009.

Considers today's scholarly explanations for the unique transcendance of God in Judaism, Christianity, and Islam, concluding that all three derived the concept from the OT. Maintains that only a unique divine revelation makes such a philosophical break possible in the ancient world.

Smith, Mark S. *The Origins of Biblical Monotheism: Israel's Polytheistic Background and the Ugaritic Texts*. New York: Oxford University Press, 2001.

One of many important books and articles by this scholar on the topic. See also The Early History of God: Yahweh and the Other Deities in Ancient Israel *(2nd ed.; Grand Rapids, Mich.: Eerdmans, 2002), and* The Memoirs of God: History, Memory, and the Experience of the Divine in Ancient Israel *(Minneapolis, Minn.: Fortress Press, 2004).*

Zevit, Ziony. *The Religions of Ancient Israel: A Synthesis of Parallactic Approaches*. London and New York: Continuum, 2001.

CHAPTER 11

Was There an "Ancient Israel"?

This chapter will lay some historical groundwork in preparation for our consideration of OT books included in the Primary History. As we attempt to reconstruct Israel's history, we will discover several challenges. The first is how best to relate the historical accounts in the biblical texts with the evidence of modern archaeology. One example, excavation at the ancient settlement of Jericho (featured in the conquest narrative of Joshua), will demonstrate the difficulty of the endeavor and the need for a balanced interpretive approach.

A second challenge is that of OT chronology, which must be relative since we lack evidence for fixed dates prior to the seventh century BCE. Only as we move through the OT to later events can we confirm dates of biblical accounts with parallels in ancient Near Eastern sources. Finally, we will consider what we can know of Israel's history of religious ideas. Although biblical texts were written and preserved by members of the "official" religion, we can detect the vestiges of "local" and "family" religion from earlier sources used to compile the OT.

We have come to a turning point in our study of Israel's library. The Torah, or first five books of the OT, make up the books of Moses. We leave Moses behind now and move on to consider the rest of the Primary History: Joshua, Judges, 1–2 Samuel, and 1–2 Kings (review Chapter 4). After these remaining books of the Primary History, we will also consider historical books from the exilic and postexilic periods (Chapter 15), which are grouped together with the Primary History in the Christian canon because of their attention to history.

Before launching into this section of Israel's library containing books focused on history, we need to consider how much or how little we actually know about ancient Israel's past. In Chapter 3, I asked you to become familiar with a simple seven-point outline of Israel's history as summarized in the OT (Sidebar 3.4).

1. Ancestral beginnings: covenant and promises (Abraham, Isaac, and Jacob)
2. Deliverance from Egypt and covenant at Mount Sinai (Moses)
3. Conquest of the promised land (Joshua)
4. Tumultuous period of judges rule prior to the monarchy
5. United Monarchy (Saul, David, and Solomon)
6. Two kingdoms, Israel and Judah
7. Exile and restoration

Our study of the Torah covered only the first two of these: the ancestral period (Genesis) and the events during the life of Moses (Exodus, Leviticus, Numbers, and Deuteronomy). But immediately, we saw how difficult it is to be confident about the details of Israel's early history. We concluded that the text of Genesis contains "clues" that hint at memories from the past about Israel's ancestors. But nothing more (Chapter 6). We then considered central features of Israel's Torah story: the exodus, the covenant, and the tabernacle. We concluded that here, too, we cannot confirm or even date these events with any precision in the history of the ancient Near East, although we need not be especially skeptical about them (Chapter 7).

What about the rest of Israel's history? Beginning with the conquest of the promised land narrated in the book of Joshua, what can we know from external history about ancient Israel?

How does this seven-part story of Israel as told by the authors of the OT relate to what we can reconstruct of actual history? To put this question another way, How does Israel's account of its history in the OT relate to modern research about Israel's history?

To be blunt, scholars working on the OT today have wildly different perspectives on this topic. My title for this chapter raises the possibility that "ancient Israel" never existed as an independent political entity, and alludes to a prominent book published several years ago.[1] In the book, the author asserted that "ancient Israel" is a construct of modern scholars with little foundation in archaeology or history. In his view, the Israel of the OT is a literary creation with no grounding in reality. He believed that Israel is essentially a literary fiction; there simply *was* no "ancient Israel."

His conclusion is the result of an approach that gives preference to archaeology and assumes that all the biblical evidence is late and not to be trusted in matters of history. Archaeology becomes paramount in this approach, and the OT text is considered guilty until proven innocent. Scholars in this camp usually combine archaeological evidence with sociology and anthropology to reconstruct ancient history independently of what the OT says about Israel. Most of these scholars conclude that the OT (or nearly all of it) was composed in the Persian period or later. In this case, we don't really have anything like "ancient Israel" in the Levant in the Iron I and Iron II periods. Central figures like Saul, David, and Solomon are fictional characters.

---

1 See Philip R. Davies in "Where to Find More" in this chapter.

In some ways, this relatively new approach is an overreaction to another approach, which was equally inadequate. Some scholars working on the OT have given preference to the biblical story line. Thus the history of ancient Israel is simplistically repeated from the pages of the OT (along the lines of our seven-part outline), and simply backed up occasionally with archaeology or evidence from elsewhere in the ancient Near East. The Bible is made ruler over archaeology, just as the opposite extreme puts archaeology over against the Bible. What is needed instead is a balance between the Bible and archaeology.

But striking such a balance isn't easy, and not everyone agrees on how to achieve it. Our purpose in this chapter is not to settle such debates between scholars about Israel's history. (As if we could!) Nor do I want simply to tell you what I think you should believe about such topics. What I do want you to think about as you read this chapter are a few key background issues that will be necessary to remember as we move through the OT's historical books. In order to prepare for the next several chapters, we will need to take up again the topic of archaeology. Then we will consider how each of the seven portions of the history of Israel as told in the pages of the OT can or cannot be explored from the perspective of today's historians.

Interpreting Text and Tell — the Example of Jericho

The scientific recovery and study of material remains from the past, or "archaeology," is a relatively recent field of research (compared to the study of languages or of history generally; review Chapter 6, especially the three phases of archaeology, Sidebar 6.3). In its early stages, archaeological research in the lands of the Bible was largely motivated by interest in the Bible itself. Digging and excavating the remains of ancient cities in what is now the Middle East was driven by an intense desire to understand more about the text. In fact, until relatively recent decades, many people practicing "biblical archaeology" were motivated by the naïve expectation that it would one day prove the Bible true.

This early naïveté assumed that the truths buried in a city's ancient "tell," or ruin heap, could verify the truths of the Bible (see Plate VIII). And it is true that some relatively spectacular discoveries have been made. The names of Israelite kings such as Omri, Ahab, and Jehu have been found in Assyrian records, the siege of Jerusalem by the Assyrian king Sennacherib has been illuminated by native sources, and several cultural features of the ancient world have shed much light on everyday life of the Israelites.

Yet archaeology has not succeeded in settling our most penetrating historical questions about ancient Israel, and it is not likely to anytime soon. It has slowly become clear that archaeology, as helpful as it is for illuminating ancient history, simply cannot meet the expectations of the earlier pioneers of the discipline for at least two reasons. First, most archaeological discoveries, even the spectacular ones, prove that a certain historical person existed, but they seldom tell us more than that they existed. Second, we have learned that even archaeological evidence needs to be explained. Tells need interpretation as much as texts do. When reading texts, we study words

SIDEBAR 11.1. THE TALE OF A TELL

Arabic, Hebrew, and other Semitic languages have given us the English noun *tell*, "mound, ruin heap" (also spelled *tel*). Certain geographical names preserve the noun, as in Tel Aviv and Tell ed-Duweir (ancient Lachish). Such artificial hills contain material remains of human occupation accumulated in successive layers over centuries of time. The oldest layers, or strata, are at the bottom of the tell, with each successive stratum moving up the tell representing more recent periods of history. The topographical landscape of the ancient Near East is marked by hundreds of these tells, each bearing witness to an ancient city or village and the people who lived in it (see photograph of the tell at Beth-shan at Plate VIII). In a real sense, these ruin heaps narrate a tale of history.

The location of an ancient city or village was based on easy access to a water source, such as a natural spring or some other source of fresh water, and the ability to defend the site from hostile forces. Most sites in Syria-Palestine had homes, public buildings, and fortifications built of stone and mud brick. After some time (perhaps centuries), the city or village was destroyed or abandoned for whatever reasons, and may have been left unoccupied indefinitely. During this period, wind and rain sometimes washed away portions of the walls and roof structures. But eventually, the features that made the site desirable originally, namely, water and its natural defenses, would attract new inhabitants. Building stones may be reused in new structures. But the rubble of mud bricks and other debris were simply collapsed into a new floor, creating a detailed account of successive layers of occupation recorded in the architecture, in artifacts such as pottery and tools, and in sedimentary records. Such tells may preserve thousands of years of recorded history, with successive strata building one on top of another like the layers of a cake, each stratum marking its own period of history.

The goal of archaeology, then, is to explore the successive layers of these tells in order to learn as much as possible about the history of the site and the people who lived there. Archaeologists have developed an elaborate system for coordinating layers of one tell with those of other tells, most often relying on pottery styles to create a relative chronology. Occasionally, a written inscription or datable artifact, such as an item from Egypt or Cyprus, also makes it possible to synchronize a relative chronology between cultures. Ideally, archaeologists excavate tells exhaustively, dividing the surface of the tell into squares and then digging each square to a certain depth. Once the artifacts of each square are numbered, analyzed, and catalogued, photographs of the remaining walls are taken before the square is completely uncovered. Once a number of adjoining squares have been thoroughly excavated, the next level down may be explored. This process is, however, incredibly slow and expensive. As a result, another approach is to carry out a sounding, digging a trench into the mound at angles to determine as best as possible the history of the site. Surface surveys of large areas and multiple tells may also be helpful in determining settlement patterns or may even occasionally provide information about the ancient identity of a modern tell.

(parsing verbs, nouns, etc.), grammar, and syntax, and carefully place each paragraph in its larger literary context. Similarly, archaeologists study pottery types, analyze stratigraphy, and read artifacts in their context. Unfortunately, scholars disagree about tells as frequently as they do about texts.

Ultimately, however, the religious and spiritual claims of the OT can never be proven by a historical enterprise like archaeology. Both text and tell need careful interpretation. How we read one may affect the way we read the other. But the archaeological tell is rarely capable of helping us reconstruct the history of ancient Israel, and it certainly cannot verify the religious claims of the OT text. Those claims must stand or fall on their own. Archaeology is an important and valuable tool for understanding the culture and history of the lands of the Bible – indispensible, really! But it should not be considered an instrument for proving the Bible. Neither should it be taken as the sole source of our history of ancient Israel. Our study of ancient Israel requires a delicate balance between text and tell.

The city of Jericho is the textbook example of just how difficult this task of finding a balance can be. As one moves westward across the Jordan River from the Transjordan, the city was the first settlement in the valley, representing the gateway for the Israelites into Canaan. It was therefore of tactical importance for them to capture Jericho first (see Map 12.1).

The OT account of the battle of Jericho seems clear enough. The account in Joshua 6 narrates the first military phase of Israel's conquest of the promised land. According to the text, Jericho was a site large enough to have a king and standing army, although they were locked behind the city walls because of the Israelite threat (6:1–2). Yahweh nevertheless promised to give Jericho over to Joshua and the Israelites in a rather unorthodox manner, at least as far as military strategy is concerned. Yahweh instructed Joshua to send the Israelite army marching around Jericho's city walls once a day for six days, led by a small group of priests playing trumpets before the ark of the covenant. On the seventh day, the priests and soldiers were to march around the city seven times. On the final trip around the city, the priests were to give a loud blast on their trumpets, a signal for the Israelites to raise a battle cry, at which time Yahweh promised that the city's defensive walls would simply fall down. At that point, the Israelite soldiers could charge straight into the city unencumbered by fortress walls. And that is what happened, according to the text. The walls fell down, and the Israelites charged into the city and captured it. They then proceeded to burn Jericho and everything in it (6:20 and 24).

So that's what the *text* says. Yet the text needs careful interpretation. Some scholars assume that any narrative with an exciting plot, or with interesting characters described with fictional qualities such as invented speeches, must therefore be unreliable for historical reconstruction. Other scholars argue that such an assumption is too skeptical, and that the OT has numerous such narratives that preserve ancient traditions, especially in the Deuteronomistic History. So we should curb our skepticism when interpreting these ancient texts.

And yet, our interpretation of the *tell* may not be as cut-and-dry as it first appears. Archaeologists discovered occupational remains at Jericho from the Mesolithic period (or Epipaleolithic; see Table 3.1), making it one of the oldest settlements in the world. In the 1930s, evidence was uncovered of a violent destruction layer and fallen walls, both dated to the end of the Late Bronze Age. At first, this was considered confirmation of the OT's account of Joshua's destruction of Jericho sometime in the thirteenth century BCE. Then in the 1950s, other excavations discovered that the destruction layers had been dated incorrectly, and that, in fact, Jericho was destroyed around 1550 BCE, at the end of the Middle Bronze period, probably by an earthquake or by the Egyptians.

11.1. Ancient Jericho. Jericho is one of the oldest known inhabited settlements. The Neolithic-era moat, tower, and fortification wall are visible here. (Photo: Erich Lessing / Art Resource, N.Y.)

This was significantly too early to have anything to do with Joshua's siege of the city. Most archaeologists now agree that the city does not appear to have had defensive walls or fortifications at the end of the Late Bronze Age, when Joshua and the Israelites would have been there. Indeed, few archaeological remains have been found from the Late Bronze Age, leading us to assume that the site was unoccupied until late in the Iron Age I and suggesting that it was already abandoned when the Israelites were said to have captured it.[2]

Thus in the case of Jericho, we appear to be forced to decide between text and tell. Was the city of Jericho well populated and defended by fortification walls at the time of Joshua (the text), or was it basically unoccupied and without defensive walls (the tell)? It helps to remember that both text and tell need careful examination. The text of Joshua does not actually claim that Jericho was necessarily a large and heavily fortified city at that time, and even the term "king" can designate a simple local leader. And we have evidence from other sites that massive Middle Bronze fortifications could be reused by settlers during the Late Bronze Age. Just as the text needs close reading, so the archaeological evidence needs more attention. While we have no evidence of large numbers of inhabitants in the city in the Late Bronze Age, there is nevertheless evidence of at least *some* occupation during this period, although most of the remains appear to have been eroded by natural elements or removed by later human activity.

In other words, in cases where we seem to have significant problems in bringing text and tell together, we need to move cautiously. The lack of direct archaeological confirmation of a biblical text should not necessarily lead us to assert that the OT story of Israel's conquest of Jericho is "a romantic mirage" as some would have it.[3] But the archaeological evidence also leads us to be wary of a simplistic and literalist approach to the text. You will need to keep all this in mind as we move through the rest of the OT historical books.

CHRONOLOGY OF ANCIENT ISRAELITE HISTORY

In my explanation of an archaeological *tell* (Sidebar 11.1), I used the phrase "relative chronology." We are not able to speak of anything like an absolute or fixed chronology for OT history, by which I mean precise dates for the events of ancient Israel. Why not? Because we don't have enough information from either the biblical text or the archaeological tells to be so precise. We have specific dates for few events, and none from the earliest stages of Israel's history. Only at the turn of the seventh century do we begin having a few fixed dates such as 701 BCE, most coming from the Neo-Babylonian and Persian periods. In general, the further back we go through the centuries of Israel's history, the less precise our dating of events. So we are forced to use what evidence we have to create a relative chronology for the history of ancient Israel.

2 For survey of this archaeological evidence, see Thomas A. Holland, "Jericho," in *The Oxford Encyclopedia of Archaeology in the Near East* (5 vols.; ed. Eric M. Meyers; New York: Oxford University Press, 1997), 3:220–24.

3 See Finkelstein and Silberman (p. 82) in "Where to Find More" in this chapter, and for a more balanced approach, see Mazar (p. 331).

Using our seven-point outline of what the OT itself says about Israel's history, let us consider now when these events might have taken place. The first two of these historical periods – the ancestors and the exodus period – have been discussed previously. The others are preparing you for our study of the rest of the OT.

1. *Ancestral Beginnings*

As we saw in our study of Genesis 12–50 (Chapter 6), we have no evidence – either OT text or archaeological tell – to give dates for Israel's ancestors. Opinions vary. Some believe that Abraham and other characters in the narratives were fictitious characters. Others see them as shadowy figures from the past, but see the stories about them in Genesis as being from a much later time and not reliable historically. Still others find reasons to date Israel's ancestors generally in the Middle Bronze Age (2000–1550 BCE). Even if one takes the ancestors as historical, the fact that we can be no more specific than this about their dates shows our problems with chronology for the earliest periods.

2. *Deliverance from Egypt and Covenant at Mount Sinai*

We were also unable to assign precise dates to the events surrounding the exodus from Egypt (Chapter 7). As important as this event was for early Israel, you might think we could know *when* the exodus occurred. What about the Red Sea crossing? The wilderness wandering, or the covenant at Sinai? What of the building of the tabernacle? Again, some readers assume that none

of these stories of early Israel is historical, or that none of them happened in anything like the way they're narrated in the OT. Most who do accept some historical reality behind these narratives date the exodus roughly to the thirteenth century BCE.

3. *Conquest of the Promised Land*

We will see in the next chapter something you have come to expect by now. We are unable to determine the exact nature of Israel's emergence in the central hills of the Southern Levant. Some readers conclude that Israel came into the promised land from outside it, through either military conquest or peaceful infiltration. Others maintain that Israel emerged from within Canaan in a social transformation. Our problem, of course, is that evidence from both text (the book of Joshua) and tells (numerous archaeological sites) can support several theories to explain Israel's presence in Canaan.

For now, it is enough to remember two points related to the question of when Israel appeared in Canaan. First, every theory must take seriously the evidence of the Merneptah Stela (Sidebar 7.2), which suggests that Israel was a settled ethnic group in the Southern Levant by the end of the thirteenth century BCE. Second, the OT text asserts that Israel entered into the promised land forty years after the exodus (Numbers 14:33–34, 32:13; Deuteronomy 8:2). If the exodus was an actual event of some sort and occurred in the thirteenth century BCE, the arrival of the Israelites is relatively easy to place as an event forty years later. Of course, as we shall see, it is not at all as simple as this.

SIDEBAR 11.2. HIGH CHRONOLOGY OR LOW CHRONOLOGY?

The dates of (approximately) 1020–922 BCE for the United Monarchy seem a neat and tidy conclusion. But before we move on, I must tell you about a group of scholars who disagree with this portrait of the reigns of Saul, David, and Solomon. Some have "downdated" archaeological strata at several cities of ancient Israel that have been taken as evidence of imperial expansion under David and Solomon. Especially critical in the debate are the cities of Hazor, Megiddo, and Gezer, which were taken to be administrative centers for the Israelite state (see Map 13.3). But the strata in those cities have been redated from the tenth century BCE, the alleged time of David and Solomon, to the ninth century BCE instead. In other words, levels of remains in these strata, together with architectural styles thought to have been those of David and Solomon, have been moved to the ninth century and the time of King Omri.*

This so-called low chronology places the archaeological evidence for Israel's expansion and statehood nearly a century later and limits it to the northern kingdom of Israel after the division of the United Monarchy into two separate states, Judah in the south and Israel in the north. In this reconstruction, David in Judah becomes little more than a bandit from a small backwater village of Jerusalem, and Solomon little more than a tribal chieftain. It was not until the northern empire of Omri almost a century later that true statehood emerges in ancient Israel.

Scholars continue to debate this low chronology, which puts in doubt the OT's portrait of the United Monarchy. Yet to reassign the physical evidence by downdating it to later strata in numerous tells and to reconstruct David and Solomon in such a way requires at least two questionable assumptions. First, this approach relies heavily on a lack of evidence for a tenth-century state centered in Jerusalem, assuming as it does that Jerusalem was an insignificant village at the time. This ignores the fact, however, that Jerusalem appears already to have been the most important city-state of the Southern Levant in the fourteenth century BCE, as we know from the letters of Abdi-Heba, king of Jerusalem, to the Egyptian pharaoh (see Sidebar 3.3). Furthermore, Jerusalem has been continuously occupied for nearly six thousand years, making it impossible to excavate systematically and leaving the low chronology approach with an argument from silence.

Second, as we have said before, the fact that the biblical traditions about David and Solomon in the Deuteronomistic History are artfully written narratives does not necessarily put them in the category of pure fiction. They contain enough clues in the text to suggest they are at least preserving traditions that have a foundation in history. We will point some of these out in Chapters 13 and 14.

If the archaeological evidence from Hazor, Megiddo, Gezer, and other cities in Israel is from the tenth century, it requires us to construct a unifying political power that made possible such systematic expansion. If we did not have the OT evidence, we would be forced to speculate about an imperial power in the Southern Levant in the tenth century. The OT text gives us the names David and Solomon, and the so-called high chronology is still the best explanation of all the evidence.

* So, for example, see Finkelstein and Silberman (pp. 180–90) in "Where to Find More" in this chapter.

4. Tumultuous Period of Judges Rule Prior to the Monarchy

The book of Judges catalogues twelve judges who led Israel during the period from Joshua's death to the rise of Israel's monarchy. The chronological question for this period is precisely how long it lasted. It isn't as simple as adding up the total years each judge was active to determine how long the Judges period lasted. That would result in a span of more than four hundred years, much too long in almost any reconstruction. Rather, some of the judges lived simultaneously, overlapping chronologically, and active in different parts of the Southern Levant at the same time. Most were only local leaders rather than rulers of the whole people of Israel. In this way, the Judges period should be telescoped into a term of around one hundred fifty years, which took place sometime in Iron I prior to the rise of the monarchy.

5. United Monarchy

Saul, David, and Solomon were the first kings of Israel. We are able to date their successive reigns over a united kingdom of Israel, plus or minus about a decade, because of historical synchronisms with other events in the ancient Near East. We move backward in time to make such synchronisms. Starting with chronological "pegs" in the Persian and Babylonian periods at the conclusion of the OT period, and moving to earlier Assyrian synchronisms as confirmed in the chronologies of the books of Kings, we are able to date the reigns of Saul, David, and Solomon more specifically than anything before them in Israel's history. By this means, most scholars put Solomon's death at 922 BCE with an error factor of about ten years. The beginning of Saul's reign is probably to be placed around 1020 BCE, so that the entire United Monarchy was around one century in length.

6. Two Kingdoms, Israel and Judah

The united kingdom of Israel fell apart at Solomon's death into two separate states, Israel in the north and Judah in the south (see Map 14.1). As we have seen, this would have occurred in 922 BCE, give or take a decade. We cannot be more precise. The northern kingdom, Israel, survived another two centuries. During that time, nine royal dynasties ruled, most from a capital at Samaria, before finally succumbing to the Assyrians in 722 BCE. The southern kingdom, Judah, had only one dynasty, the Davidic dynasty, ruling from Jerusalem, until falling to the Babylonians in 586 BCE. The error factor for these two dates – 722 and 586 BCE – is one year. As you can see, the later in time we progress through Israel's history, the more precise we can date events of that history.

7. Exile and Restoration

With the fall of Jerusalem and the destruction of the temple in 586 BCE, large numbers of Israelites were taken into exile to other places of the ancient Near East, especially Babylonia and Egypt. Finally, at this period in our survey, we are able to confirm precise dates of some of these events with parallels in ancient Near Eastern sources.

The end of the exile may be concretely dated to October 539 BCE, when the Persians captured the city of Babylon. This event is recorded in native Babylonian and Persian sources, as well as by Greek historians like Herodotus and Xenophon, providing us with an absolute chronology. Shortly thereafter, the Persians released the Jews in Babylonia, allowing many to return to Jerusalem. This presumably occurred in 538 BCE (Ezra 1:1–11), although we do not have independent confirmation of that date. This first group of returnees is said to have laid the foundation of the new temple (Ezra 3:8–13). Completion of

SIDEBAR 11.3. EXCERPT FROM THE BABYLONIAN CHRONICLE

In early October 539 BCE, the Persian king Cyrus led his army against the city of Babylon, winning first a major battle against the Babylonians at the city of Opis on the Tigris River. On October 10, another important city in the north, Sippar, fell to the Persians, and Babylon itself fell on October 12.

This excerpt is adapted from Babylonian Chronicle 7, otherwise known as the "Nabonidus Chronicle" after the last king of the Babylonian Empire. This is one type of historical synchronism allowing us to determine fixed dates for OT history.

In the month of Tishri, when Cyrus conducted a campaign at Opis on the banks of the Tigris against the army of the Babylonians, the people of Babylon took flight. He made off with plunder and killed the people. On the fourteenth day [October 10], Sippar was captured without a fight. Nabonidus became a fugitive. On the sixteenth day [October 12], Ugbaru, the provincial governor of the land of the Gutium and the army of Cyrus entered Babylon without a fight. Afterwards, when Nabonidus had withdrawn, he was captured in Babylon.... On the third day of the month of Marchesvan [October 29], Cyrus entered Babylon.

11.2. Nabonidus Chronicle. Cuneiform tablet with portions of Babylonian Chronicle 7. This chronicle covers events from the reign of Nabonidus (556–539 BCE). The first several years of his reign are poorly preserved, but found near the chronicle's conclusion are details of Babylon's fall to the Persians and the capture of Nabonidus himself. (Photo: The British Museum / The Trustees of the British Museum)

* Adapted from Bill T. Arnold, "The Neo-Babylonian Chronicle Series," in *The Ancient Near East: Historical Sources in Translation* (ed. Mark W. Chavalas; Blackwell Sourcebooks in Ancient History; Malden, Mass.: Blackwell, 2006), 420.

the second temple, however, was delayed until the inspiration of the prophets Haggai and Zechariah, and the support of the Persian king Darius. The second temple was completed in either 516 or 515 BCE. Ezra and Nehemiah returned in the mid-fifth century BCE to lead additional reforms, although the chronology for these events is complicated (and will be addressed in Chapter 15).

We summarize the history of ancient Israel as follows:

1. Ancestral beginnings – shadowy figures, perhaps rooted in the Middle Bronze Age
2. Deliverance from Egypt and covenant at Mount Sinai – perhaps thirteenth century BCE
3. Conquest of the promised land – appearance of Israel in late thirteenth century BCE
4. Tumultuous period of judges rule prior to the monarchy – early Iron I, approximately 1200–1025 BCE
5. United Monarchy – approximately 1020–922 BCE

Cyrus II of Persia (539–530 BCE) conquered Babylon and became the founder of the Persian Empire. This inscription, found in the ruins of Babylon in 1879, describes not only his victory over Babylon but also Persian imperial policy toward subject peoples. Here Cyrus explains his rise to kingship over Babylon as the will of the chief deity of the Babylonian pantheon, Marduk, who was unhappy with the previous Babylonian king, Nabonidus.

The OT records a decree of Cyrus granting release of the Jews in exile and authority to rebuild the temple of Yahweh in Jerusalem (Ezra 1:1–4; 2 Chronicles 36:22–23). Claims that the **Cyrus Cylinder** authenticates the OT decree have been exaggerated. The cylinder text is, however, compatible with the biblical decree of Cyrus and at least suggestive of the tolerant policies of the Persian Empire (see Figure 15.3).

I am Cyrus, king of the world, great king, mighty king, king of Babylon, ... After entering Babylon in peace, amidst joy and jubilation, I made the royal palace the center of my rule.... As for the citizens of Babylon, whom my predecessor, Nabonidus, had made subservient in a manner totally unsuited to them against the will of the gods, I released them from their weariness and loosened their burden.... I returned the divine images to the sanctuaries (of cities throughout Mesopotamia), sanctuaries founded in ancient times, whose images had been in them there and I made their dwellings permanent. I also gathered all their people and returned to them their habitations.*

* Adapted from Piotr Michalowski, "The Cyrus Cylinder," in *The Ancient Near East: Historical Sources in Translation* (ed. Mark W. Chavalas; Blackwell Sourcebooks in Ancient History; Malden, Mass.: Blackwell, 2006), 429.

6. Two kingdoms, Israel and Judah – 922 BCE until the fall of northern Israel in 722 BCE and of southern Judah in 586 BCE
7. Exile and restoration – 586 BCE until the returns of Ezra and Nehemiah in the mid-fifth century BCE

So in answer to the question raised by this chapter's title, we may safely say there *was*, in fact, an ancient Israel. It was not the idealized Israel we read about in the OT in every respect. And yet a new entity appeared in the Southern Levant by the name "Israel" in Iron I as proved by the Merneptah Stela. In the tenth century BCE, Israel's United Monarchy was well established, as shown by evidence in both text and tell. The nation divided into separate entities in the late tenth century: Israel in the north and Judah in the south. Both eventually fell to Mesopotamian empires, Israel to the Assyrians in 722 and Judah to the Babylonians in 586. Large numbers of exiles living in Babylonia were released by the Persians and returned to Jerusalem at various times beginning in 538. With Persian support, and together with those who had remained in Jerusalem, they rebuilt the city and temple, and restored the people of God in a new Persian province, Yehud.

HISTORY OF ISRAELITE RELIGION(S)

Our inability to date many events of early Israelite history only illustrates that the OT authors were less interested in writing formal history than they were in expressing their theological and religious ideas. In light of our focus here on the religious contributions of the OT to our day, we turn now to a brief survey of those religious ideas using again our seven-point outline of what the OT itself says about Israel's history.

I begin this survey by inviting you to think in terms of three levels of religion. First, *official religion* may be thought of as endorsed by institutional authority, such as priests in a temple or kings in a palace, and may be advanced by schools or academies. Official religion may take many forms, but it is typically focused on the people of a society as a whole and is oriented toward political experiences. Second, *family religion* is oriented toward the personal piety of the smaller group making up one's family (review "father's house," "kinship group," and "tribe," in Chapter 6). Family experiences such as the parent-child relationship find religious expression in personal piety, comforting and stabilizing members of the society. Third, *local religion*, which is practiced in local sanctuaries or villages, may at times be present in a society. A particular village or region may contribute additional religious ideas or practices to official or family religion, which would otherwise not have such distinct features.

In the study of religion, we used to think that just as there is evolution in the biological world, there had been an evolution of religion from primitive polytheistic religions to ethical monotheism at the apex of religious evolution. Such a simplistic evolutionary approach has been disproven. So-called primitive religions are often quite sophisticated and sometimes reflect multiple layers of official, family, and local practices all at the same time. Also, we shouldn't put too fine a point on these distinctions between official, family, and local. They often overlap at significant junctures. Yet when we consider the history of religious ideas in ancient Israel, we can clearly see how these distinct types of religious practices were at work. The family and local expressions of Israel's religion have more in common with other ancient Near Eastern religions.

In general, the OT has been written and preserved by members of the official religion. But it makes no attempt to cover up or hide the vestiges of local and family religion often showing up in the early sources used to compile the OT.

1. Ancestral Beginnings

Israel's patriarchs, Abraham, Isaac, and Jacob, were free to worship wherever they pleased, and often in open-air sanctuaries. Such sanctuaries were made up of an altar, a sacred tree, and often a standing stone (review Chapter 6 for references in Genesis). Their expressions of faith were a family religion, which however was free to interact with local and regional expressions of Canaanite religion. Thus they knew God by several names and could easily interact with the worship at local sanctuaries at Shechem, Hebron, Bethel, and elsewhere. Abraham's appreciation for the priest and king of Salem, Melchizedek, illustrates the point (Genesis 14:18–20).

2. Deliverance from Egypt and Covenant at Mount Sinai (Mosaic Period)

The Mosaic period begins with a divine revelation to Moses at a local sanctuary in Midian on Mount Horeb, elsewhere also known as Sinai (Exodus 3–4). This open-air sanctuary has no mention of an altar or a standing stone, but the burning bush was the desert version of a sacred tree, making this sanctuary like those of Israel's ancestors. Yahweh appears at this time to have been the deity of a family religion, practiced as the faith of Moses' father-in-law, the priest of Midian (Chapter 9). His father-in-law serves as the priest of the sanctuary, where offerings are made at a sacred feast (Exodus 18:12). Moses serves as "judge" or leader for all Israel (Exodus 18:13), and the establishment of laws in Yahweh's name and a tabernacle for Yahweh's presence reflects the move from family religion to official religion. The relationship between Yahweh and the Israelites is formalized as a covenant, or binding mutual commitment, on the analogy of ancient Near Eastern treaties (Chapter 9). It used to be commonly thought that the decision to define Israel's relationship with Yahweh as a treaty was made late, or at least no earlier than the eighth century BCE (since the prophet Hosea assumes this idea). But as we have seen (Chapters 7 and 9), we have reason to believe that the covenantal relationship with Yahweh was a theological conviction from early in Israel's history.

3. Conquest and 4. Judges Rule

I take the conquest of the promised land and the period of Judges rule – two parts of our outline of Israel's history – together, because their religious expressions are essentially the same. Once the Israelites were in the promised land, a covenant renewal at Shechem continued the process of nationalizing the worship of Yahweh as the official religion. The covenant was ratified in an open-air sanctuary, complete with standing stone and oak tree (Joshua 24:26). Exclusive worship was expected ("put away the foreign gods that are among you"; Joshua 24:23), but again, we have no narrow monotheism here. On the strength of archaeological evidence and parallels with other ancient religions in Canaan, some believe that Israel was polytheistic at this time. In one theory, Yahweh had a wife, or consort, Asherah, and in another theory, Israel worhipped at least four deities. Some readers of the OT, however, assume that Israel's religion was quite distinct from ancient Canaanite religion, emphasizing the latter as a fertility or nature religion marked by myth, whereas Israel's was a historical religion. Such a distinction is overly simplistic. But because of our lack of evidence, we shall have to leave open the precise nature of Israel's religion during this period.

Other sanctuaries were permitted during these years, such as the important one at **Shiloh** where an annual pilgrimage festival was celebrated (Judges 21:19; 1 Samuel 1:3). Here the ark of the covenant was housed in either a tent shrine or a semipermanent building called Yahweh's "temple" (1 Samuel 3:3), and was administered by a line of priests descended from Aaron, the sons of Eli. Prophecy begins to emerge as an important feature of Israel's religion, as the prophet Samuel unifies the people "from Dan to Beer-sheba" (1 Samuel 3:20) in the worship of Yahweh.

5. United Monarchy

With the arrival of the United Monarchy in the tenth century BCE (assuming the traditional high chronology), the religion of Yahweh completes the move from a family religion to an official state religion. If the biblical traditions are correct, Jerusalem becomes a new central capital at this time, and the ark of the covenant is transferred there along with the remnants of the Elide priesthood. A new temple is constructed as a permanent home for the ark. In order to unify the entire country, attributes of local religions with regional variations were assimilated into Yahweh, who becomes now not only the God of Mount Horeb/Sinai but also the warrior God, and the storm God, among others. He is now the "God of Israel." Prophets remain as an important feature of the religion of Yahweh. The focus of their teaching is generally limited to the actions of the kings.

6. *Two Kingdoms, Israel and Judah*

The worship of Yahweh had emerged from a family and local religion to become the official religion of national Israel. Religious practices and divine attributes from various regions had been assimilated under the name Yahweh. With the division of the kingdom into northern Israel and southern Judah, certain religious differences naturally emerge between the two. Older local Canaanite traditions were tolerated in the north alongside the worship of Yahweh. Syncretism, or the assimilation of two competing systems, became the focus of prophetic preaching, reflected in the OT traditions about the prophets Elijah and Elisha in the books of Kings. Under the prophetic critique, religion in northern Israel was changed from a sort of ditheism, or worship of both Baal and Yahweh, back to a version of the earlier monolatry.

During these years, from the late tenth to the early sixth century BCE, the role of Israelite prophecy evolved dramatically. In the eighth century, the prophets ceased addressing primarily the kings, began addressing the people more generally, and also began preserving their preaching in writing. The first written prophets, such as Hosea, Amos, Micah, and First Isaiah (Isaiah 1–39) left us books that are independent of the officially produced historical books of the royal scribes. These prophets believed that faith in Yahweh had ethical implications for all members of Israelite society, and they also believed that Yahweh's power was not limited to the geographical borders of Israel; that is, they believed in the **universalism** of Yahweh's power.

After the fall of the northern kingdom to Assyria in 722 BCE, King Hezekiah of Judah embarked on religious reforms. He banished all remnants of the older local and family traditions, which permitted worship in multiple locations in sanctuaries with trees, standing stones, and altars. These practices had evolved in the popular imagination into a sort of plurality of Yahwehs. Hezekiah centralized all worship at Jerusalem, and the unity of Yahweh as reflected in the Shema, "Yahweh is our God, Yahweh alone" (Deuteronomy 6:4, see Chapter 9), became the official understanding of Yahweh. Hezekiah's reforms were not effective, but they were revived by King Josiah just before the exile.

7. *Exile and Restoration*

Yahweh had emerged from a family religion to become "God of Israel." Yet in the minds of many, Yahweh was essentially bounded by the geographical borders of Israel. The eighth-century prophets had emphasized Yahweh's international power and thereby prepared for the crisis of the Babylonian exile. The prophets of the exile, Ezekiel and Second Isaiah especially, taught that Yahweh was not confined to Jerusalem but was present in the midst of his people wherever they were. This was only one step away from another development, the conception of genuine monotheism. If Yahweh was present in Babylon with his people, and was sovereign over deities of Babylonia, perhaps those deities did not even exist. Thus Second Isaiah especially went beyond the older monolatry and articulated a genuine universal monotheism: Yahweh is God, and there is no other.

WHERE TO FIND MORE

Scholars working on the history of Israel during the OT period are much divided over details. And these scholars are prolific! The books included here merely introduce the topic and are representative of diverse perspectives.

Albertz, Rainer. *A History of Israelite Religion in the Old Testament Period*. Translated by J. Bowden. 2 vols. Louisville, Ky.: Westminster John Knox Press, 1994.

Extensive treatment; see volume 1 (pp. 17–21) for definitions of and distinctions between official religion, family religion, and local religion.

Coogan, Michael D., ed. *The Oxford History of the Biblical World*. New York: Oxford University Press, 1998.

Davies, Philip R. *In Search of "Ancient Israel."* JSOTSup 148. Sheffield, Eng.: JSOT Press, 1992.

Argues for three "Israels": (1) historic Israel, a tiny state in the central hills of the Southern Levant, roughly between 900 and 700 BCE; (2) biblical Israel, the fictitious Israel of the OT, created by authors of the Persian and Hellenistic periods; and (3) ancient Israel, a scholarly construction based on the first two.

Finkelstein, Israel, and Neil Asher Silberman. *The Bible Unearthed: Archaeology's New Vision of Ancient Israel and the Origin of Its Sacred Texts*. New York: Free Press, 2001.

Golden, Jonathan M. *Ancient Canaan and Israel: An Introduction*. Oxford and New York: Oxford University Press, 2009.

For a survey of the history of archaeology, including its techniques, pages 28–44.

Grabbe, Lester L. *Ancient Israel: What Do We Know and How Do We Know It?* London and New York: T & T Clark, 2007.

Lemaire, André. *The Birth of Monotheism: The Rise and Disappearance of Yahwism*. Washington, D.C.: Biblical Archaeology Society, 2007.

The best general introduction to many of the ideas discussed here related to the history of religious expression in ancient Israel.

Lemche, Niels Peter. *Ancient Israel: A New History of Israelite Society*. Sheffield, Eng.: JSOT Press, 1988.

Long, V. Philips, ed. *Israel's Past in Present Research: Essays on Ancient Israelite Historiography*. Sources for Biblical and Theological Study 7. Winona Lake, Ind.: Eisenbrauns, 1999.

Mazar, Amihai. *Archaeology of the Land of the Bible, 10,000–586 B.C.E.* Anchor Bible Reference Library. New York: Doubleday, 1990.

Provan, Iain W., V. Philips Long, and Tremper Longman III. *A Biblical History of Israel*. Louisville, Ky.: Westminster John Knox, 2003.

Rendsburg, Gary A. "Israel without the Bible." Pages 3–23 in *The Hebrew Bible: New Insights and Scholarship*. Edited by Frederick E. Greenspahn. Jewish Studies in the 21st Century. New York: New York University Press, 2008.

Shows what can be known about ancient Israel based solely on the evidence provided by archaeology from both epigraphic and material remains.

Williamson, H. G. M., ed. *Understanding the History of Ancient Israel*. Proceedings of the British Academy 143. Oxford and New York: Oxford University Press, 2007.

CHAPTER 12

Land

OLD TESTAMENT READING: JOSHUA AND JUDGES

In the books of Joshua and Judges, God's gift of land to Israel takes center stage. The first book recounts Israel's conquest and division of the land under the leadership of Moses' successor, Joshua. The book of Judges highlights governance in the land by a succession of twelve leaders. Connected by a recurring cycle – Israel's disobedience to Yahweh, foreign oppression, repentance, and deliverance – the Judges stories narrate the end of one era in Israel's history and serve as introduction to the next.

Alongside these Primary History accounts, we will consider archaeological evidence for a significant population increase in Canaan during Iron Age I and look at three theories that attempt to explain the appearance of new populations in the region at that time. In addition to observing the nature of religion during Israel's early history in the land, we will address the difficult subject of the land today. Jewish, Christian, and Muslim readers all have varying responses. Joshua and Judges should not and need not be used in the debate, but they remind us how very ancient is the issue of land.

The concept of "land" has been a recurring theme in the Pentateuch. At times, the theme has come to the surface as our narrative, such as the account of ⟨⟩stors, Abraham, Isaac, and Jacob, ⟨⟩ land as part of their covenant relationship with Yahweh. At other times, the theme of the "promised land" has been just below the surface, such as during the Israelites' long sojourn in the desert, when they were not permitted to enter it. As we move from the Pentateuch now into the OT's historical books, this theme of Israel's relationship

SIDEBAR 12.1. WHERE IS THE BOOK OF RUTH?

You are probably wondering why I'm not including the little book of Ruth in this chapter. If you're using a standard Christian translation of the OT, you will see that Ruth comes immediately after the book of Judges, and before 1–2 Samuel (review Figure 2.3). So why have we reserved it for Chapter 23?

In the Jewish canon, five relatively short books are placed together near the end and preserved as a collection of "scrolls" (Hebrew *mĕgillôt*). In early Judaism, these books were read in the synagogues at specific times in the liturgical calendar: Passover (Song of Songs); the Festival of Weeks (Ruth); the fast in commemoration of the destruction of the temple, or the Ninth of Ab (Lamentations); the Festival of Tabernacles, or Booths (Ecclesiastes); and Purim (Esther). Their location elsewhere in the standard Christian Bible (following the Septuagint and Vulgate) has perfectly reasonable historical and literary rationales. For a variety of reasons, I find it useful to discuss them together, and so the Megilloth will be treated in Chapter 23.

to the promised land returns as a central component of Israel's story. As readers, it's as though our movement from the Pentateuch to the historical books reflects the Israelites' movement from the desert to the land promised to their ancestors.

After the Pentateuch, the next two books of the Primary History — Joshua and Judges — are historical in nature. This does not mean they are relaying strictly historical events. But they are continuing Israel's story from the plains of Moab (Deuteronomy) into the promised land, and they prepare eventually for the rise of Israel's monarchy. They show how difficult it was for Israel to provide leadership for peaceful governance of the land.

AT LONG LAST, THE LAND! FULFILLMENT OF THE PENTATEUCH'S PROMISES

The Torah story continues here. At the conclusion of the Pentateuch, in both Numbers and Deuteronomy, the Israelites are encamped "in the plains of Moab across the Jordan from Jericho" (Numbers 22:1 and 36:13; Deuteronomy 1:5; see Map 12.1). Israel is perched on the very edge of the

promised land, ready to enter and take possession of the promises of God. In this way, simple geography is linked to the promises of God and the covenant of God with Israel. We cannot overstate the importance of the land in Israel's self-understanding or in the message of the OT that the land is God's gift to Israel.

Land is God's gift from the very beginning. Its appearance as "dry land" at creation is one of God's first acts of order and structure arising from the chaos of primordial waters (Genesis 1:9). Israel's perfect idea for a homeland is a rich agricultural garden — a garden of Eden, or "paradise" — in which there are beautiful trees, luscious fruit, and abundant life-giving rivers (Genesis 2:8–10). Because humans rebelled against God's restrictions, they must now exert great effort to get the land to yield its abundance (Genesis 3:17–19). But a life in the land of Canaan, farming the rich soils of the central highlands, remains Israel's ideal.

After the flood, the land of the entire arable world is said to be divided among the three sons of Noah (Genesis 10). The territory of the Canaanites is given special attention in the list, which describes

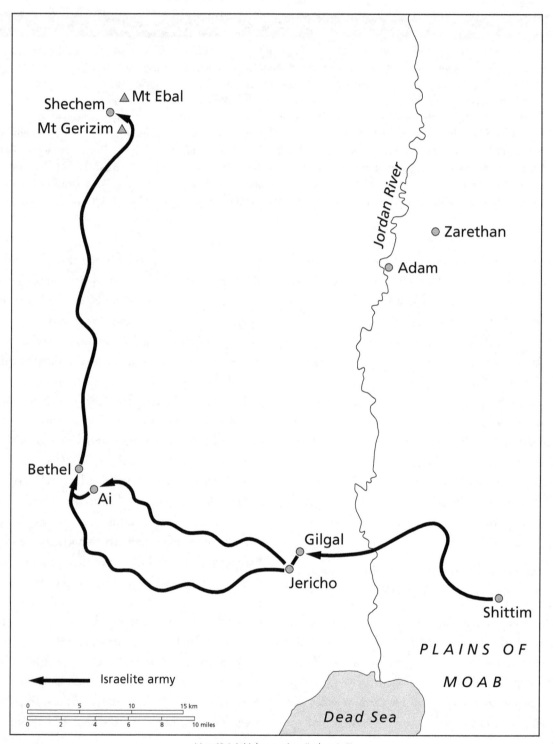

Map 12.1. Initial campaign (Joshua 1–8)

the boundaries of Canaan (Genesis 10:15–19). This is the first description of Israel's homeland, later to be promised to the ancestors. That this homeland is inhabited by Canaanites is a complication that prepares the reader for the books of Joshua and Judges.

Israel's ancestors are described in Genesis as pastoral tribalists who are seminomads (see Chapter 6). They own large quantities of sheep and goats, and so live in temporary settings during certain seasons of the year, but they become tent-dwelling travelers looking for grazing pastures for their flocks at other times of the year. In such a society, if one's family or tribe grows too large, it must be separated into smaller units in order to find sufficient pastureland. The ideal of a rich agricultural homeland is an unrealistic dream. Yet this is precisely what God promises Abraham. The call of Abraham includes the promise of numerous descendants (Genesis 12:1–3), and after the great patriarch obeys God's command, the promise of land is added (12:7). At a critical juncture, Abraham is invited to survey the land itself (Genesis 13:14–17), and God's promise is eventually sealed in a covenant (Genesis 15:18–21). The land promise is repeated to Abraham's sons, Isaac (Genesis 26:2–4), and Jacob (Genesis 28:13–15). The promise of land is the ultimate gift of God's grace to the ancestors, and it drives the narrative of the Pentateuch forward.

The Torah describes the dimensions of this land in various ways. The promised land extends from Sidon in the north to include various locations near the southern end of the Dead Sea (Genesis 10:19). Or, it extends from the Jordan River in the east to the Mediterranean Sea in the west, and from a stream known as the Brook of Egypt[1] in the south to the city Hamath in the north (Numbers 34:1–12). Another passage more generally describes the promised land as extending from the Sinai desert in the south to the Lebanon mountains in the north, and from the Euphrates River in the northeast to the Mediterranean Sea in the west (Deuteronomy 11:24).

Although a precise "map" of the promised land may be impossible to construct from the Pentateuch's references, Israel's future homeland is always described as a wonderful place. It is "a good and broad land, a land flowing with milk and honey" (Exodus 3:8). This was indeed a spectacular picture of abundant dairy products and natural agricultural produce, especially for these former slaves of Egypt traveling many years across a dry and barren desert. Moses describes this promised land in contrast to the land of Egypt, which requires arduous irrigation.

For the land that you are about to enter to occupy is not like the land of Egypt, from which you have come, where you sow your seed and irrigate by foot like a vegetable garden. But the land that you are crossing over to occupy is a land of hills and valleys, watered by rain from the sky, a land that the LORD your God looks after. The eyes of the LORD your God are always on it, from the beginning of the year to the end of the year. (Deuteronomy 11:10–11)

---

1 Or Wadi of Egypt, today's Wadi el-'Arish. A "wadi" is valley stream bed that remains dry until the rainy season. The Wadi of Egypt serves as a natural border between the southern Negeb and the Sinai Peninsula.

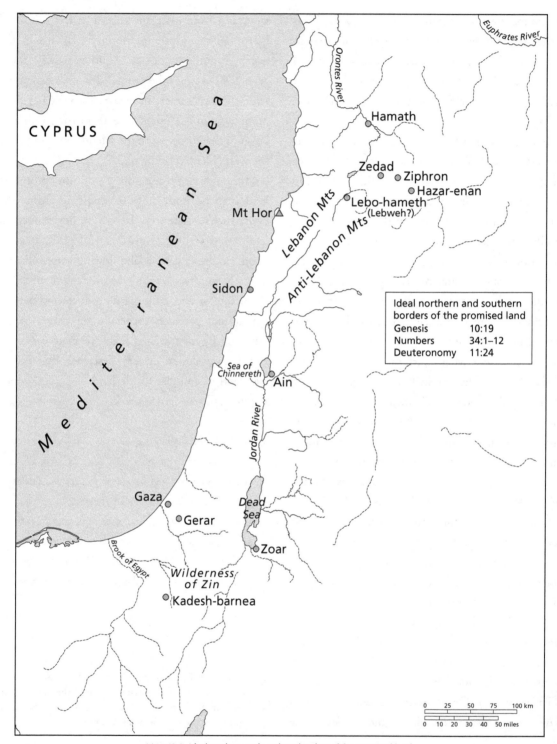

Map 12.2. Ideal northern and southern borders of the promised land

We have seen that the books of Joshua and Judges comprise a portion of Israel's greatest historical narrative complex (Sidebar 9.5). How precisely do these two books fit into that theory? What sources were used in their composition? How were they edited in order to contribute to the Deuteronomistic History?

Some scholars see evidence in Joshua and Judges of the continuation of the sources of the Penateuch (J, E, etc.), especially in Joshua 2–11 and Judges 1. Many scholars have assumed that these sources originally continued into the first half of Joshua in a narrative that described the conquest of the land and logically concluded the narrative of the Torah. This would be more of a Hexateuch, or six-book scroll. Others see more evidence for these two books as sources independent of the Pentateuchal documents, and edited specifically for inclusion in the Deuteronomistic History. This poses a Tetrateuch, or four-book scroll, identifying Numbers 36:13 as the conclusion of a Torah centered on the life of Moses.

These two positions may not be strictly exclusive of each other. It is entirely possible the book of Joshua received its final form as part of the Deuteronomistic Historian's grand rewriting of history, but that it had J, E, and perhaps other sources at its foundation (especially for Joshua 2–11 and Judges 1). In fact, the Bible may have grown first as a Hexateuch in its earliest phases (Pentateuch plus portions of Joshua), then as a Tetrateuch in a second phase (Genesis through Numbers) when Deuteronomy was broken away to serve as the first book of a new historical complex, and finally as an extended Primary History of all nine books (Eannateuch).

It is impossible to reconstruct whatever sources lay behind the book of Joshua before its current Deuteronomistic version. In general, it appears that Joshua 2–11, 13–21, and 24 contain ancient source materials, some of which may have served at one time to conclude a Hexateuch. But these sources have been thoroughly revised in our current book of Joshua in order to be included in the Deuteronomistic History. The book of Judges appears to have had fewer Deuteronomistic editorial changes or insertions, except perhaps for the prologue to the core of the book at 2:6–3:6. To this we add as Deuteronomistic the overall framework provided by the cyclic literary pattern, which was probably superimposed over an older collection of independent narratives without much additional editorial work.

Unlike Egypt with its dependence on the Nile River and its annual floods, the promised land will be watered naturally by rainfall year-round. This passage also hints that life in this land requires faith. Yahweh himself cares for it. Life in the promised land will force Israel to trust in Yahweh to supply their needs.

The Torah understands the promised land as God's gift to Israel (Genesis 12:7; Exodus 6:4). Yet the land rightly belongs only to God and will always remain his possession, even while Israel enjoys life in its abundance (Leviticus 25:23). Harvests of the land's bounty therefore belong also to God, who requires a return gift of first crops in sacrifice (Leviticus 27:30–33; Deuteronomy 14:22). The Israelites are but tenants and sojourners in God's land (Leviticus 25:23), and they must always respect the land as his gracious provision for them.

THE BOOKS JOSHUA AND JUDGES

The first nine books of the Jewish canon, the Primary History (also known as the **Enneateuch**), make up approximately one-half of the OT (review

Chapter 4). Taken together, these nine books present in broad historical continuum Israel's story from creation to the destruction of Jerusalem and its temple in 586 BCE (and just beyond). We take these next two books together because the first one, Joshua, opens a new era in Israel's history and the second, Judges, narrates what happens in that premonarchic period. This is the story of how Israel took possession of the promised land, fulfilling God's promises to their ancestors. It also, however, shows how difficult life was in the land prior to the rise of Israel's monarchy.

Conquest of the Land (Joshua 1–12)

The book of Joshua is named for its leading protagonist. Joshua was a military man. He is the first character in the OT with God's sacred name, "Yahweh," built into his personal name.[2] It was Joshua who was the military hero when Moses and the Israelites first had to defend themselves against the Amalekites as they were trekking across the desert. Moses and Aaron prayed at the mountaintop observatory, while Joshua, down in the valley, did the actual fighting (Exodus 17:9–10). Joshua became the personal assistant for Moses (Exodus 24:13). Eventually, he is commissioned as the successor to Moses, although his role is more that of a military officer, the general of Israel's armies, than that of a lawgiver.

> So the LORD said to Moses, "Take Joshua son of Nun, a man in whom is the spirit, and lay your hand upon him; have him stand before Eleazar the priest and all the

2 The Hebrew form of the name, Yehoshua, begins with the divine element, *yhw*.

congregation, and commission him in their sight.... at his word they shall go out, and at his word they shall come in, both he and all the Israelites with him, the whole congregation." (Numbers 27:18–21)

It makes sense that the book is named after Joshua, but this is no statement about authorship. The book is anonymously written, and the Bible is silent on that topic.

The book of Joshua has a symmetrical arrangement. The first twelve chapters narrate the conquest of the promised land, the second twelve its division among the tribes and a few administrative matters. The big idea in the book is simple: the land promised to Israel's ancestors and longed for in Moses' generation finally becomes the homeland for God's people. Success is not attributed to the Israelites' brilliant military strategy but is a result of their obedience to Yahweh's commands.

The first five chapters of the book tell of preparations for military action. One might expect to find here details of mustering and inspection of troops, making of weaponry, and rehearsal of military strategies. We have hints of these in Joshua 1–5, but the narrative is driven instead by a religious agenda. This agenda opens with a kind of commissioning of Joshua to lead the Israelites in the absence of Moses, and it includes religious observations such as circumcision and Passover. In chapter one, Joshua, who had been personal aide to Moses, is told to be "strong and very courageous" three times. As Yahweh was with Moses, so he will be with Joshua to ensure success (1:5). The key to Joshua's success is his devotion to the law of Moses, which he must meditate on constantly (1:7–8). The new general of Israel's forces has had military training and preparation, as we know from Exodus and Numbers. But the text is here interested only in his religious devotion.

The narrative then recounts how two Israelite spies reconnoitered Jericho, where they were protected by the prostitute Rahab (Joshua 2). She will come into the story again later. The Israelites crossed the Jordan River miraculously "on dry ground," while the priests stood in the middle of the dry riverbed holding the ark of the covenant of Yahweh (Joshua 3–4). In solidarity with their ancestors, this new generation of Israelite males was circumcised, and the nation observed Passover (Joshua 5). In a paragraph that echoes the call of Moses at the burning bush, the "commander of the army of Yahweh" appeared to Joshua and told him to remove his sandals out of respect for "the place" where he stood, which was made holy by Yahweh's presence (Joshua 5:13–15, and on "the place," see Chapter 10). Joshua has become a military version of Moses the lawgiver. Preparations for the conquest are complete.

Jericho was the gateway to the promised land. It would be impossible to enter and possess the whole without taking this first city on the list of strategic objectives (see Map 12.1). And, you will have to admit, Jericho was captured in a most unconventional way! Joshua, at Yahweh's directions, used circuitous marching, priests parading the ark of the covenant while playing trumpets, and loud battle cries to bring down the defensive walls of Jericho (Joshua 6). This was Yahweh's victory in a way no Israelite army could have hoped to accomplish.

12.1. Jericho, with the Mountains of Moab in the background. After years of wandering in the desert, the sight of Jericho situated in the luscious Jordan Valley would have been striking to the entering Israelites. (Photo: Erich Lessing / Art Resource, N.Y.)

In such a religious war, initiated by Yahweh and conducted according to his instructions, the Israelites were not permitted to benefit from the spoils by taking objects "devoted" to Yahweh. Because one of their number, a certain Achan, confiscated a "devoted" object, the Israelites suffered defeat at Ai at first. They then regrouped in order to take possession of it as well (Joshua 7–8). Joshua responded with an act of worship, building an altar and making sacrifices to Yahweh (Joshua 8:30–35), as instructed in the law of Moses (Deuteronomy 27:1–7, and see discussion in Sidebar 12.3).[3] Again, this is not a simple postcombat action report. The book of Joshua is focused on the religious significance of Israel's actions.

The inhabitants of the city of Gibeon escape destruction at the hands of Israel by trickery (Joshua 9). Joshua, who now is obligated to come to their rescue, conquers a five-king coalition in the south and occupies their land (Joshua 10; see Map 12.3).

3 Deuteronomy 27:5–6 is cited directly in the specs for building the altar in Joshua 8:31.

The OT does not really have "Holy War" as such, which implies human efforts to achieve what is thought of as the will of God. By contrast, "Yahweh War" in the OT is a battle in which Yahweh is the prime actor, and humans are sometimes called on to assist. Ancient Israel had a document entitled "The Book of the Wars of Yahweh" (Numbers 21:14–15) that was not preserved intact among the books of the OT, but scraps of poetry here and there may be quotes from that source (e.g., Exodus 15:3–4 or Judges 5:4–11).

While Yahweh is always the one who ensures victory and, in fact, does the actual fighting, the Israelites have clear instructions for their participation in Yahweh War. They must seek God's direction prior to the conflict (Judges 1:1 and 20:18), and they must follow him into battle (Judges 4:14; compare Deuteronomy 20:4). The Israelites must submit to Yahweh's manner of combat, whether marching in circles with battle cries and trumpet blasts (Joshua 6:2–7), hailstorms (Joshua 10:11), flood (Judges 5:21), or lightning (2 Samuel 22:15; Habakkuk 3:11). Their primary responsibility is mopping up afterward, finishing off the panicked and now defeated enemy (Joshua 10:10; Judges 4:15–16). They are not allowed to profit from the plunder or to take any of the conquered foe's possessions (Joshua 7). The acceptable response to Yahweh's victory is either to stand firm in faith and silence, or to sing songs of celebration and praise (Exodus 14:13–14 and 15:1; Judges 7:3). The practice of Yahweh War appears to have disappeared in Israel once warfare became the official responsibility of the monarch and his standing army.

This is followed finally by a northern campaign, in which a four-king coalition of Canaanites falls to Joshua (Joshua 11; see Map 12.4). In this way, the surrounding territories of the leading cities in the promised land come into the possession of the Israelites. The conquest of the land is topped off by an overview of all the conquered kings and their territories (Joshua 12). The conquest of the promised land is complete, and Joshua has finished the task started by Moses.

Settlement of the Land (Joshua 13–24)

It remains now to recount how the Israelites divided the land and settled it. While portions remain unconquered (Joshua 13:1–7), the idea is to grant the various tribes their specific land allotments, some of which must be conquered thoroughly later. Portions east of the Jordan River are allotted to two and one-half tribes, Reuben, Gad, and the half-tribe of Manasseh (13:8–33), and the rest is given to the remaining nine and one-half tribes (Joshua 14–19). Certain cities are designated as cities of refuge, where offenders may seek mediation regarding punishment for manslaughter or homicide (Joshua 20). In this way, a judicial system becomes available to counter the retaliatory justice of Israel's former system of "blood avengers" (Deuteronomy 19:6).

The tribe of Levi was uniquely appointed to serve as ministers of Yahweh. They didn't inherit land as the other tribes did, and in this particular list used in the book of Joshua, the Joseph tribes of Ephraim and Manasseh were counted separately to maintain the number twelve. (Twelve was an important round number for the concept of the unified tribes of Israel.) In order for the Levites to enjoy the benefits of the land with the other tribes, they were allotted forty-eight cities distributed throughout the other tribal allotments (Joshua 21).

Joshua dismisses the eastern tribes – Reuben, Gad, and the half-tribe of Manasseh – allowing them to return to the Transjordan, signaling the official end of the conquest and settlement of the land (Joshua 22:1–9). Trouble arises, however, when the eastern tribes construct an altar near the Jordan, which the western tribes take as an act of rebellion and treachery. Disaster is narrowly averted when the priests clarify the meaning of the altar and negotiate peaceful terms (Joshua 22:10–34). The book closes with Joshua's farewell address (Joshua 23) and a covenant renewal and ratification for the whole nation Israel gathered at Shechem (Joshua 24).

Governance of the Land: The Judges (Judges 1–16)

The book of Judges is so named because of the twelve leaders of Israel during this period, whose activity is described as "judging." The term is somewhat misleading in English. It's true that these leaders bore judicial authority as judges, but their role was more inspirational. They were charismatic rulers devoted to restoring order and peace (*shalom*) for ancient Israel in times of crisis. At times, the restoration of peace and order involved military campaigns as Yahweh's instruments for salvation.

The book lists six major judges: Othniel (Judges 3:5–11), Ehud (Judges 3:12–30), Deborah (together with Barak, Judges 4–5), Gideon (Judges 6–8), Jephthah (Judges 10:6–12:7), and Samson (Judges 13–16). In addition to these, there are brief notations on the activities of six so-called minor judges: Shamgar (3:31), Tola (10:1–2), Jair (10:3–5), Ibzan (12:8–10), Elon (12:11–12), and Abdon (12:13–15).

The first chapter of the book of Judges (technically through 2:5) gives us a different picture of the conquest than that portrayed in the book of Joshua. This is no extermination of the native populations but an expulsion, and even this is only partial. The nine and one-half tribes west of the Jordan River (called **Cisjordan**) enter the land and drive out *some* of the inhabitants. But many Canaanites remain. In some tribes, the Canaanites "lived among" the Israelites (Judges 1:29). In others, the Israelites "lived among the Canaanites" (1:32), implying that the Canaanites are still the majority population. In this way, the book of Judges opens with an assertion that some tribes have a lot of work left to do, and that at this time they are really only one portion of the overall population of their particular territories.[4]

The heart of the book of Judges is a collection of stories held together by a recurring literary formula, a kind of cyclic narrative thread introducing the six major judges (Judges 2:6–16:31). The book's use of this recurring cycle arranges the events along a historical continuum. The cycle generally has six parts, but it is also flexible. As an example of the six components, consider the literary framework in the narration of the first judge, Othniel (3:7–11).

1. Israel does what is evil in Yahweh's sight (Judges 3:7).
2. As punishment, Yahweh delivers the Israelites into the hands of an oppressor; Cushan-rishathaim, in this case (Judges 3:8).

4 It seems likely that this chapter was originally the concluding portion of the ancient J document and was preserved independently of those sources lying behind the book of Joshua.

3. Israel calls out in repentance to Yahweh (Judges 3:9).
4. Yahweh responds by raising up a deliverer (judge) to rescue the Israelites; Othniel, in this case (Judges 3:9).
5. Israel's oppressor is defeated (Judges 3:10).
6. Peace is restored in the territory (Judges 3:11).

This string of narratives is introduced by a prologue (Judges 2:6–3:6), probably added by an editor to clarify the seriousness of Israel's situation.

> In order to test Israel, whether or not they would take care to walk in the way of the LORD as their ancestors did, the LORD had left those nations, not driving them out at once, and had not handed them over to Joshua. (Judges 2:22–23)

The Israelites' struggles with surrounding enemies thus served to determine whether they truly depended on Yahweh for salvation, together with Yahweh's leaders, the judges. Their alternative was to trust in the Canaanite religious customs and practices of the land (Judges 2:11–13).

Under the leadership of Deborah, assisted by Barak, Israel is victorious against Sisera, general of the army of King Jabin of Hazor (Judges 4–5). The poetic version of this account in Judges 5, the Song of Deborah, contains one of the oldest pieces of literature in the OT (vv. 12–30). The account of Gideon illustrates the ideal of theocracy, or God rule, for ancient Israel instead of government by a monarch (Judges 6–9). After victory against the Midianites, the people of Israel offer Gideon kingship. He refuses in a classic statement of Israel's official theocracy: "I will not rule over you, and my son will not rule over you; Yahweh will rule over you" (Judges 8:23). Yet Gideon functions as a king in every respect except in name (8:24–31). His son, Abimelech, becomes king of the city-state Shechem, and the narrative at this point becomes a direct critique of institutional monarchy, especially of dynastic succession.

Things continue to deteriorate in early Israel. The account of Jephthah (Judges 10:6–12:7) traces further religious decline and suffering at the hands of enemies both east and west, Ammonites and Philistines (10:6–9), and the danger that Yahweh will no longer deliver Israel (10:13). Jephthah's terrible vow illustrates the progressive decline of Israelite religious expression from Gideon's idolatry (8:24–27) to Jephthah's manipulative and foolish actions (11:30–40). There is no statement of peace restored to the land at the end of Jephthah's judgeship (12:7).

The Samson account is full of familiar stories (Judges 13–16). His judgeship is perhaps the most tragic because it begins with great promise but fails in nearly every respect. Indeed, Samson, the last of the judges, represents Israel itself. He has the greatest potential, but he does everything wrong. He breaks his vows to God (13:4–5, 14:9, and 16:19); intermarries with Israel's greatest enemy, the Philistines (14:2–3); and, finally, goes into exile in Philistine territory. Yet even in failure and defeat, Samson, like Israel, is not utterly abandoned by Yahweh in the end (16:28–31). As with Jephthah, Samson's death is recorded without a statement of peace in the land. The fact that the Philistines continue as Israel's perpetual enemy into the books of

1 and 2 Samuel show that Samson's final victory was not Israel's final victory.

Anarchy in the Land (Judges 17–21)

Materials in the last chapters of the book of Judges are of a different sort. And they have a different message. Here the list of Israel's judges ends, and we have two separate narratives about events prior to the rise of Israel's monarchy. The first narrative describes the rise of an illegitimate worship site at the northern city of Dan and the relocation of the tribe of Dan to the north (Judges 17–18; see Map 12.4). This story illustrates Israel's religious unfaithfulness. The next story, that of the atrocities at Gibeah, shows Israel's social decline (Judges 19–21). The tragic dismemberment of the woman at Gibeah is symbolic of Israel's social condition (Judges 19:29).

The refrain of this portion of the book highlights Israel's moral and social decay: "In those days, there was no king in Israel; all the people did what was right in their own eyes" (Judges 17:6 and 18:1; and compare 19:1 and 21:25). These chapters aim to show exactly how low Israel stooped before gaining a king to provide central authority and unified religious leadership. These chapters are decidedly in favor of having an Israelite monarchy. In this sense, they serve as an introduction to the books of 1–2 Samuel as much as a conclusion to the book of Judges.

THREE VIEWS OF WHAT REALLY HAPPENED

As we have seen, Israelite history writing has deep roots in the way Israel gave account of its past and its relationship to Yahweh (Chapter 4). Readers

today who are interested in reconstructing what actually happened in ancient Israel have a difficult task. The narratives in the OT oscillate between historiography and imaginative writing. The first type of narrative may throw light on actual events of the past, while the second type reflects on meanings and significances beyond the task of today's historians. And sometimes it's difficult to know which is which. When this is combined with the complicated nature of the archaeological evidence for early Israel, we have trouble discerning how to understand the events described in Joshua and Judges.

At the beginning of Iron I, something new started happening in the central hills of the Southern Levant. Archaeologists have discovered a virtual population explosion in the central highlands, which had not previously been heavily populated. Surface surveys and other archaeological evidence have revealed new village settlements popping up first in the northeastern hills of Galilee and then extending to the southwest into the hill country of Judah and the Negeb. The statistics tell the story. These regions had 88 Late Bronze Age sites with a population of around 50,000 inhabitants. The same regions had 678 settlements in Iron Age I, with a population estimate of 150,000 inhabitants. Perhaps more tellingly, 93 percent of these Iron Age I settlements were new villages.[5] Taking the territory of Ephraim as an example, the earliest settlements appear on the eastern slope of the mountain range in areas along the edge of the

---

5 For these statistics, see Lawrence E. Stager (pages 100 and 129) in Coogan's book in "Where to Find More" in this chapter. Stager concludes, "There must have been a major influx of people into the highlands in the twelfth and eleventh centuries BCE" (p. 100).

12.2. Artist's rendition of the courtyard of an Israelite four-room house. The pillared four-room house could also be enlarged or expanded, and combined with other houses in family complexes. (Photo: © Balage Balogh / Art Resource, N.Y.)

desert where villagers could both graze flocks and plant crops. As the population grew, they spread westward, clearing the forests of the highlands and then settling western slopes.[6]

These new settlements carry over certain features from the Late Bronze Age culture, forming a kind of subset of Canaanite culture. Yet certain other features make them distinctive. Some scholars believe that a combination of unique characteristics among these Iron Age I newcomers creates an archaeological profile for them, including their so-called four-room pillared houses

6 For more on the example of Ephraim, see page III of Rainey in "Where to Find More" in this chapter. He is relying on the surface surveys of Israel Finkelstein.

and their large collared-rim storage jars. One of the most interesting practices of the newcomers in the central hills is terrace farming, needed because the hills did not provide enough tillable land naturally. This practice, together with the use of cisterns to catch rainfall, made it possible for the newcomers to adapt rainfall agriculture, which they combined with traditional herding of goats and sheep to sustain their lives in the central hills. Herding was a way to protect themselves against seasons of drought because herds were less affected by drought than crops were. Other features of a potentially distinctive material culture are suggestive, but these villages shared most of them with other cultures in the Iron Age I

SIDEBAR 12.4. ISRAELITE ARCHITECTURE AND POTTERY

Besides terrace farming and lime-plastered cisterns, two additional features are often identified as characteristic of an Israelite archaeological profile: houses and pottery types. The first is a distinctive four-room pillared house, in which two rows of stone pillars were used in the construction. The building was a rectangular
structure with a broadroom at the back and usually three more rooms extending from it. These three rooms
consisted of a large courtyard with two side rooms separated from the courtyard by the rows of pillars. The
broadroom at the back was used mainly for storage. So far, the four-room pillared house is rarely found in
Bronze Age periods, which has led to speculation that it was an Israelite innovation. Others argue that it follows a Canaanite building tradition. Regardless of its origins, it was the preferred building fashion of Iron Age
I and was adopted by the newcomers in the central highlands, thus contributing to a collection of distinctive
cultural features of the highlands inhabitants in Iron Age I, presumably the early Israelites. The villages have
no monumental public architecture.

With regard to pottery, many Late Bronze types continue into the Iron Age I, but without the decorative
features of the earlier periods. The most distinctive pottery of the central highlanders were a collared-rim
store jar and cooking pots with longer-flanged rims. This assemblage is said to distinguish the newcomers in
the central highlands of Iron Age I, just possibly the early Israelites.*

* For more on these cultural features, see pages 338–48 in Mazar in "Where to Find More" in this chapter.

Levant.[7] In general, the newcomers of the central
highlands in Iron Age I exhibited the same culture
as the Canaanites of the surrounding regions. Few
today deny that these newcomers were Israelites, or
at least proto-Israelites. The mention of "Israel"
in the Merneptah Stela from approximately 1207
BCE seems to confirm the Israelites' presence in
Iron Age I (Sidebar 7.2).

Taking into consideration both text and tell —
that is, the biblical portrait of Joshua and Judges
together with the archaeological evidence — three
theories have been proposed to explain Israel's relatively sudden appearance in the Southern Levant
in Iron Age I.

---

7 Other features, such as collared-rim store jars; pillared
houses; and faunal assemblages of sheep, goat, and cattle
(but of little or no pig), are often discussed, but we have
little consensus on them. See page 102 of Stager under
Coogan in "Where to Find More" in this chapter.

1. *The Conquest Theory*

The conquest theory assumes the essential accuracy
of the book of Joshua concerning Israel's appearance in the Southern Levant. Archaeology is thought
to confirm the military conquest of Canaan by outsiders in the late thirteenth century BCE. Numerous
key Canaanite cities are believed to have been burned
or captured simultaneously, followed immediately
by cultural change. But although the cultural change
from Late Bronze Age to Iron Age I is undeniable,
the widespread and synchronous destruction of
Canaanite cities cannot be supported by the archaeological evidence. Destruction levels at Bethel and
Hazor may support the idea of an Israelite conquest,
but numerous other cities show no occupation levels
at the time or have no evidence of destruction. The
assumption that archaeological evidence confirms
the military conquest is unsustainable.

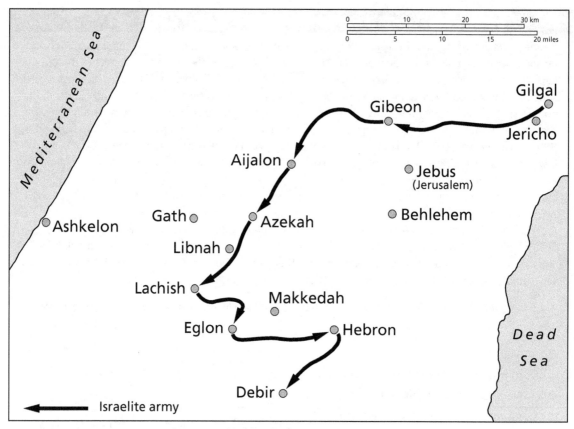

Map 12.3. Southern campaign

On the other hand, the significant increase in population levels in the central highlands suggests a migration of newcomers from outside Canaan, if not a military conquest. And the biblical evidence itself does not require massive burn levels or even destruction levels at all the cities mentioned in Joshua 6–12 and Judges 1. The book of Joshua itself portrays the conquest occurring in three stages. There was first a *central campaign,* in which Israel entered from the east, crossed the Jordan River and established a base at Gilgal before capturing Jericho, Ai, and Bethel, essentially gaining a beachhead in the land (see Map 12.1). The agreement with the Gibeonites resulted in, second, a *southern campaign.* A coalition of five city-state kings besieged Gibeon, and the Israelites rose to their defense. By defending the Gibeonites, Israel thus defeated the kings of Jebus (which would become Jerusalem), Hebron, Jarmuth, Lachish, and Eglon, acquiring their territories and those of Makkedah, Libnah, and Debir. This is followed by, third, a *northern campaign* against a coalition of kings around the upper Galilee, led by the king of Hazor. Joshua and the Israelites defeated these kings and "burned Hazor with fire" (Joshua 11:11).

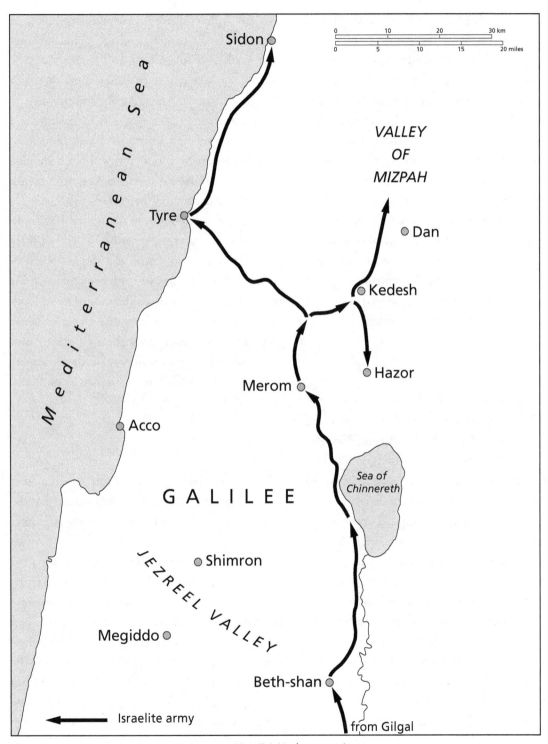

Map 12.4. Northern campaign

Interestingly, the text says that Joshua burned only Hazor and none of the other towns (Joshua 11:13). Nor does it say that the Israelites necessarily inhabited these cities once they captured them. We assume too much when we think of the Israelites as entering and conquering the land. In fact, when they defeated a city-state ruler, the Israelites assumed authority of the region surrounding the city-state. But there is no claim to the burning and occupation of all the cities mentioned in these lists. The conquest theory may have assumed too much from the archaeological evidence. But it also assumed too much from the biblical text. The OT conquest narratives do not claim massive destruction of all these cities. We should not be surprised, then, not to find such evidence in the archaeological data.

2. The Peaceful Infiltration Theory

Also known as the "pastoral nomad theory," the peaceful infiltration approach observes that the central highlands of the Southern Levant had relatively few inhabitants at the time of Israel's arrival. There were no masses to conquer, at least not in the highlands. It assumes that the Israelites were pastoral nomads from the marginal areas in the Transjordan and the south, who settled in the hills and took up farming. They evolved from pastoral nomadism to sedentary agriculture, entering the land peacefully at first and settling in new villages in the hills. The Canaanites inhabited mostly the urban centers in the lowlands. Only later did the Israelites encounter them in military skirmishes, and some of these skirmishes were exaggerated and recorded in the book of Joshua.

This approach has at times reflected a simplistic view of pastoral nomads in the ancient world.

We have little evidence for nomads dependent on sheep- and goat-herding evolving gradually from desert tribes to village farmers to urban dwellers. In fact, we have reason to believe now that such changes occurred rather suddenly, and that aspects of the former way of life such as tribal customs and social and family structures were usually retained in the new situation. But even without a simplistic evolutionary view of these social developments, the peaceful infiltration theory fails to account for the population explosion in the central highlands. It has no answer to the question of why all these pastoral nomads appeared, and did so relatively suddenly. Some readers will also point out that the book of Joshua cannot be discounted as so exaggerated as all this. As we have said, the book is not recording strict history as such, but neither can it be dismissed as pure fiction. Our theories must explain the textual witness of military conflict to some extent.

3. The Peasants' Revolt Theory

The previous two theories agreed in one detail: that Israel came into Canaan from the outside, that the Israelites were not native to the Southern Levant. The peasants' revolt theory, in contrast, assumes that the earliest Israelites were "peasants" who lived under the oppression of Canaanite city-states in the lowland areas of western Canaan. These Canaanite peasants rebelled against their urban overlords and sought refuge in the central highlands. The rebellion was essentially a religious revolution, affirming the liberating faith of the God Yahweh, adapted from a group of escaped slaves from Egypt. This new faith provided the catalyst for revolutionary change in which Canaanite peasants found new identity as

Israelite (or proto-Israelite) settlers. The peasants' revolt theory, unlike the conquest and peaceful infiltration theories, saw these peasants as insiders who rebelled and relocated.

One variation of the peasants' revolt theory emphasizes the egalitarian spirit of the new "free" Israelite society over and against the oppressive hierarchical city-state regimes. Relying partly on a Marxist ideology, this approach imagines a struggle between proto-Israelite peasants (the proletariat underclass) and the powerful bourgeoisie (Canaanite urban overlords), resulting in a revolution. While the Marxist explanations of this process are now considered outmoded, many believe that the earliest Israelites were from the Canaanite lowlands because of the disintegration of Canaanite city-state societies.[8] Instead of invading outsiders conquering or peacefully settling the highlands, it was an inside job.

Everyone is in agreement that the central highlands of the Southern Levant were sparsely populated in the Late Bronze Age but saw rapid population increases in mostly new village settlements in Iron Age I. Most would agree also that these newcomers were the first Israelites, or were, at least, proto-Israelites. Beyond that, we have little agreement. For the meantime, we should probably consider some compromise between the first two theories as the best explanation. It seems likely that there had been a partial Israelite conquest followed by the assimilation of many of the inhabitants of the land in a process that lasted for centuries.

Whether we emphasize the conquest aspects or the peaceful infiltration features, it seems likely that the Israelites were outsiders for at least four reasons.

First, there are simply too few peasants living on the fringes of the Late Bronze city-states in Canaan to account for the rapid population growth in the highlands in Iron Age I. Some of these newcomers may have been native to Canaan. But not the majority of them. Second, we have seen that Yahweh is not a native Canaanite deity (Chapter 10). All indications are that the worship of Yahweh originated in the land of Midian in north Arabia, which casts doubt on the assumed Canaanite origins of early Israel. Third, early Israel shares more in common culturally with the Shasu bedouin society known from Egyptian texts than with the Canaanite culture native to the Southern Levant (Sidebar 10.5). The Egyptian sources place the Shasu mostly in southern Transjordan, particularly in Edom and Moab. Finally, fourth, we should not discount the possibility that the biblical traditions in Joshua and Judges contain vestiges of historical truth, especially those consistent traditions that portray Israel as entering the land from east of the Jordan River.[9]

ISRAELITE RELIGION IN IRON AGE I

The books of Joshua and Judges have been edited to reflect later religious convictions, especially those of the Deuteronomistic History. So, for example, the Deuteronomistic layer portrays Israel's faith as firmly rooted in the book of Moses, even at this early period (Joshua 1:8 and 23:6; and compare 2 Kings

8 The scholars most associated with the theories are William F. Albright and Yigael Yadin (conquest), Albrecht Alt (peaceful infiltration), and George E. Mendenhall and Norman K. Gottwald (peasants' revolt); for details, see Stager in Coogan in "Where to Find More" in this chapter.

9 On the problem of how long the Judges period lasted, see Chapter 11.

23:24–25). Yet the editors left hints in these books that reflect the religious convictions and practices of early Israel in Iron Age I (ca. 1200–930 BCE).

No doubt the most surprising image of God from the perspective of our modern sensibilities is the role of God in Israel's wars. The Israelite authors of the OT thought of these things in a manner much different from that of you and me. To gain understanding into the way they saw such things, it may be helpful to remember that the notion of war as a religious event with divine participation was deeply ingrained in ancient Near Eastern culture. And so it was for Israel. Military victories in the book of Joshua confirm Yahweh's power and love for Israel, and acquire the land as fulfillment of ancestral promises. Yahweh himself ensures victory (Joshua 6:2 and 8:1–2). The spoils of war belong solely to him (6:24, 8:26–27, and 11:14). The book of Joshua celebrates the belief that "Yahweh fought for Israel" (10:14 and 23:3). Similarly, Yahweh is the victor in the book of Judges (4:15 and 7:21–22).

At times, Yahweh is a Divine Warrior, fighting on behalf of his people. He marches forth from southern regions leading a supernatural army, the Yahweh of Hosts (Judges 5:4–5 and 20), and he appears to Joshua as "commander of the army [i.e., hosts] of Yahweh" (Joshua 5:13–15). The ark of the covenant, as a concrete representation of Yahweh's presence, is a powerful symbol when carried into battle before Israel (Joshua 6; and compare Numbers 10:35–36 and 1 Samuel 4–7). Yahweh's victory is miraculous, whether when walls mysteriously collapse (Joshua 6), one's enemies are destroyed in a huge hailstorm (10:10–11), or the sun and moon cease their courses as a sign that one should continue fighting (10:12–14; review Sidebar 12.3).

One of the most important clues to early Israel's religion is found in the covenant renewal ceremony at Shechem (Joshua 24). Joshua calls on the Israelites to serve Yahweh alone, showing again the monolatrous henotheism we have discussed previously in this book: "choose this day whom you will serve, whether the gods your ancestors served …; but as for me and my household, we will serve Yahweh" (24:15). Although this text has been edited from a later perspective, it preserves a genuine constitutional ceremony in which an alliance between various groups or tribes was formed under the common banner of Yahweh worship. That day, a new Israelite confederation was sealed, uniting tribes in a common worship of Yahweh, with statutes and ordinances, at a large standing stone under an oak tree in an open-air sanctuary called the "sanctuary of Yahweh" (24:25–26). These features of the open-air sanctuary were the same as those of the ancestral period (Chapter 6), but they were used now in a new way binding large numbers of Yahweh followers together as one people.

This Israelite confederation at Shechem calling for devotion to Yahweh would not have assumed that worship had ceased at other sanctuaries throughout the land. In fact, the ark of the covenant was housed in the tent of meeting at Shiloh (Joshua 18:1 and 1 Samuel 4:3), and an annual pilgrimage festival was celebrated at Shiloh (Judges 21:19; and compare 1 Samuel 1:3,21). Archaeological evidence suggests that there were local sanctuaries at many other locations throughout Israel. However, Micah's private cult center involved the making of an idol and teraphim (Judges 17:4–5), which were images and figurines clearly prohibited in the Ten Commandments (Exodus 20:4–6, which may have been written later). Such religious

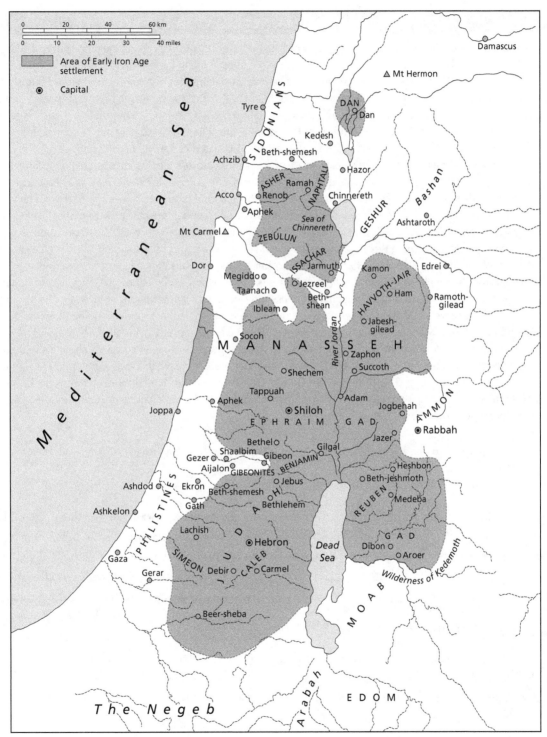

Map 12.5. Israel in the land after conquest (Iron Age I)

SIDEBAR 12.5. WHY DOES GENOCIDE PLAY A ROLE IN JOSHUA AND JUDGES?

Without question, readers of the OT struggle most with the role of violence in the taking of the promised land in Joshua and Judges. And rightly so. The seven people groups living in the promised land will be removed to make room for Israel: Canaanites, Hittites, Hivites, Perizzites, Girgashites, Amorites, and Jebusites (Joshua 3:10). Sometimes the language of expulsion is used (God will "drive them out" before Israel; Joshua 3:10, 13:6, etc.), and at other times the language of extermination (Joshua "devoted to destruction by the edge of the sword all in the city"; 6:21). And this is not an Israelite crusading spirit running out of control. It is not condemned as unethical in the text. Indeed, this violence is initiated as the will of Yahweh!

Other texts in the Pentateuch are at least aware of the need to provide theological explanation, portraying the inhabitants of the promised land as cursed or iniquitous. The curse of the Canaanites may be traced to Noah immediately after the flood (Genesis 9:24–27). In the ancestral promises, Yahweh declares that he will wait hundreds of years to give the promised land to Abraham's descendants because the iniquity of its inhabitants was "not yet complete" (Genesis 15:16; and compare Deuteronomy 9:4–5). The implication is that Yahweh is justified in wiping them out because their sin is so severe. This long-standing tactic is a common rhetoric of war, demonizing and dehumanizing the opponent as a means of justifying acts of violence.

We have no completely satisfactory answer to this issue.* The best explanations go a long way to understanding the problem. But it must be admitted, these offer no complete resolution. At least we can say this much: culture plays a role. Yahweh's revelation condescended to the cultural understanding of the ancient Near East, in which warfare and military conquest symbolized divine strength and affection. Yahweh loved Israel, which is made apparent by his military actions. It is also political. Yahweh could not show his supremacy over other deities without showing his power over their peoples as well. While we continue to try to understand this feature of the OT, we must always allow Israel to be at home in the ancient Near Eastern world. It is not fair to apply our twenty-first-century sensibilities to their ancient context, and thus we leave the topic unsettled and must live with the tension.

---

* For a thorough discussion and an exploration of answers, see pages 74–89 of Pitkänen in "Where to Find More" in this chapter.

---

apostasy illustrates the principle repeated in this portion of the book, "all the people did what was right in their own eyes" (Judges 17:6).

The Problem with the Promise – What about the Land Today?

The idea that the land of Canaan rightly belongs to Israel is at the heart of the books of Joshua and Judges. Yahweh promised it to their ancestors, Israel is entitled to it, and now is the time for Israel to take it. We have enough problems with the violence

of the conquest narratives, but this sense of land entitlement raises another issue. Before moving on to the next chapter, we must acknowledge a question that continues to beg for answers after all these centuries: to whom does the land belong today?

This question is a perennial issue that plagues the political process in the Middle East today. There has been no sustainable peace in the land for over six decades.[10] Jewish, Christian, and Muslim readers of the OT all have their own responses to

10 For a survey of this history, see pages 89–99 of Pitkänen in "Where to Find More" in this chapter.

the dilemma. Most Jewish readers will argue that the establishment of the modern state of Israel in 1947–48 was reasonable reparation in the immediate wake of the Holocaust. Most Muslim readers counter that the United Nations Partition Plan of 1947, dividing Palestine into two states, was illegitimate, should bear no international authority, and continues to incite hostilities across the region. Christian readers are divided. Some Christians have a certain affinity with the modern state of Israel, and for reasons related to their **eschatology** (end-times theology) believe that Christians should support Israel. Other Christians have an affinity for the plight of the Palestinians, believing that a violent injustice has been committed, and assume that Christians should support the Palestinians for ethical reasons in efforts to find a just resolution.

There is no simple political or diplomatic solution to this problem. For our purposes, it is enough to say that we should not use the OT books of Joshua and Judges in this debate. Readers may accept the OT as authoritative truth, or the "word of God," as we saw in Chapter 2. But that is not the same as saying God's promises to ancient Israel have direct application to Jews, Christians, or Muslims today. The OT may have spiritual meaning and even theological authority, but its promises and directives require interpretation and translation from that ancient culture to ours. All believing readers of the OT will have to agree to disagree on the significance of Joshua and Judges for the crisis in the Middle East today. And all can agree to pray for peace and justice.

WHERE TO FIND MORE

Commentaries: The best technical and advanced commentaries on **Joshua** and **Judges** are Pekka Pitkänen, *Joshua* (Nottingham/Downers Grove, Ill.: Apollos/InterVarsity Press, 2010); Richard D. Nelson, *Joshua: A Commentary* (Old Testament Library; Louisville, Ky.: Westminster John Knox Press, 1997); Richard S. Hess, *Joshua: An Introduction and Commentary* (Tyndale Old Testament Commentaries 6; Downers Grove, Ill.: IVP Academic, 2008); Robert G. Boling, *Joshua* (Anchor Bible 6; Garden City, N.Y.: Doubleday, 1982); Trent C. Butler, *Joshua* (Word Biblical Commentary 7; Waco, Tex.: Word Books, 1983); J. Alberto Soggin, *Judges, A Commentary* (2nd ed.; Old Testament Library; London: SCM Press, 1987); and Joseph E. Coleson, Lawson G. Stone, and Jason Driesbach. *Joshua, Judges, Ruth* (Cornerstone, Carol Stream, Ill.: Tyndale House, 2012).

Coogan, Michael D., ed. *The Oxford History of the Biblical World.* New York: Oxford University Press, 1998.

Two helpful chapters in Coogan related to the historical questions raised in this chapter are "Forging an Identity: The Emergence of Ancient Israel" by Lawrence E. Stager (pp. 90–131), and "'There Was No King in Israel': The Era of the Judges" by Jo Ann Hackett (pp. 132–64). See especially Stager on the three hypotheses used to explain Israel's appearance in Iron Age I (pp. 94–105).

King, Philip J., and Lawrence E. Stager. *Life in Biblical Israel*. Library of Ancient Israel. Louisville, Ky.: Westminster John Knox Press, 2001.

Mazar, Amihai. *Archaeology of the Land of the Bible, 10,000–586 B.C.E.* Anchor Bible Reference Library. New York: Doubleday, 1990.

Rainey, Anson F., and R. Steven Notley. *The Sacred Bridge: Carta's Atlas of the Biblical World*. Jerusalem: Carta, 2006.

On the rise of Iron I camplike settlements in the central highlands and for an extensive bibliography, see pages 111–12. See pages 125–29 for more on the complex geographical details of the books of Joshua and Judges.

CHAPTER 13

Kings

OLD TESTAMENT READING: 1 AND 2 SAMUEL

First and Second Samuel narrate Israel's transition from a tribal confederation to a dynastic monarchy, beginning with the leadership of the prophet Samuel. Saul is anointed Israel's first king, and although eventually rejected, his reign functions to define kingship under Yahweh, including submission to Torah and to the authority of Yahweh's prophets. David becomes Israel's second king and eventually the "ideal" for all kings in the OT. We will also observe during David's leadership an emerging understanding of Yahweh as "God of Israel."

Since early Israel was a theocracy under Yahweh, we will explore the issues surrounding Israel's need for and the legitimacy of a human king, the person and role of a suitable king, and finally, the importance of the prophet in assessing the king. Although Israel's transition to statehood is somewhat difficult to reconstruct historically (ca. 1050–970 BCE), we will examine evidence for similar transitions in other cultures. Archaeological evidence from Hazor, Megiddo, and Gezer suggests the notion of a state and its correlating centralized administration.

Until now, Israel has been led by a variety of leaders. First came the lawgiver, Moses, and then the courageous military general, Joshua. There followed a series of charismatic judicial authorities, the judges. There had been no king, for no king was needed. In fact, the idea "Yahweh is king" was central to Israel's theological self-understanding, as we will see later in this chapter.

Our stroll through ancient Israel's library brings us now to books that explain a change in Israel's leadership. The next two books of the Primary History — 1 and 2 Samuel — give an account of Israel's transition from tribal confederation under the leadership of judges to a dynastic monarchy. These books continue Israel's story from the period of the judges in the early Iron Age I period to the rise of its first kings, Saul and David. The switch from tribal alliance to nation-state obviously involved social and institutional changes. But the narrative of 1–2 Samuel is most interested in the religious implications of the rule of kings in ancient Israel.

"THE SCEPTER SHALL NOT DEPART FROM JUDAH"

The Torah hints that there would be kings in Israel's future. Yet the OT has mixed emotions about Israel's kings. The book of Judges represents one position: without a king to provide stability in the land, chaos and anarchy are inevitable because everyone does what is "right in their own eyes." This position favors having a king with a strong central authority.

On the other hand, the voice of the prophet Samuel represented those in Israel who believed that it was wrong to desire a human king (1 Samuel 8:6–7 and 12:12). Much of the material in 1–2 Samuel is driven by a need to defend and justify the presence of Israelite kings, especially David and his sons. The need to write the story of David in this way shows that some in ancient Israel disagreed with Samuel and opposed the Davidic dynasty. They believed that to cry for a human king was an insult to Yahweh's rule. There thus was a struggle in early Israel between theocracy – God rule – and a limited monarchy, in which the king was subject to the authority of the Torah. Eventually, the monarchists (those favoring a king) won the day. The

rule of Yahweh as King continued, however, as an important theological metaphor.

The hints we have in the Pentateuch reflect this struggle to a limited degree. According to the Torah story, Israel began as a family, led by patriarchs and matriarchs living in tents and trusting God to sustain them. No thought was given to kingship during this ancestral era. Yet even here, Jacob's deathbed blessing of Judah contains indirect references to future kings from the tribe of Judah.

> Judah, your brothers shall praise you; . . . your father's sons shall bow down before you. . . . The scepter shall not depart from Judah, nor the ruler's staff from between his feet, until tribute comes to him; and the obedience of the peoples is his. (Genesis 49:8–10)

And the editor who added the list of Edom's kings wrote from a perspective of the time when a king "reigned over the Israelites" (Genesis 36:31).

Later, when Moses led Israel out of Egypt, they had become twelve tribes united by a common covenant with Yahweh. In their covenant symbolism, Yahweh himself was their king (Exodus 15:18), who inhabited a throne, the "ark of the covenant," in a throne room in the sanctum of the tabernacle (Exodus 25:10–22). The last book of the Torah warns of the problems with human kingship (Deuteronomy 17:14–20). The "law of the king" anticipates Israel's request in 1 Samuel 8 and warns the Israelites not to ask for a king "like all the nations" around them (Deuteronomy 17:14). The law makes provisions for a king, which Yahweh himself must choose. This Israelite king must not accumulate personal wealth, or turn to Egypt for aid, or marry many wives, but instead must submit himself to the Torah like other Israelites. Such limitations on human kingship in Israel mark the institution as dramatically different from other ancient Near Eastern kings, and anticipates the crisis of 1 Samuel.

THE BOOKS OF FIRST AND SECOND SAMUEL

The two books of Samuel were originally one composition. We will see later that the same is true for 1–2 Kings and 1–2 Chronicles. The reasons for dividing these compositions into separate books is not immediately obvious. We often assume that they were divided on the basis of content, but breaks are not always at points that make sense literarily. It seems more likely they were divided for the simple and practical reason that the size of scrolls was necessarily limited in the ancient world (Chapter 2). Translation of the works into Greek (the Septuagint), which requires more space than Hebrew, resulted in division of each into two parts. Decisions about where to break off one book and begin another were probably made based on both content and space.

The opening portions of 1 Samuel assume the same historical context as that of the book of Judges and continue the story from the Judges period. The book then describes the rise and fall of Israel's first king, Saul, and the rise of David as his successor. The book of 2 Samuel is devoted to the reign of David. Both books raise and answer questions about Israel's new monarchy. Is it legitimate for Israel to have a king? If so, what is the nature and purpose of Israel's new monarchy? Who can serve suitably as king of Israel?

In general, the question about the nature and legitimacy of Israel's kingship is addressed in 1 Samuel 1–15, culminating in the fall of the tragic figure King Saul. Whoever else may eventually

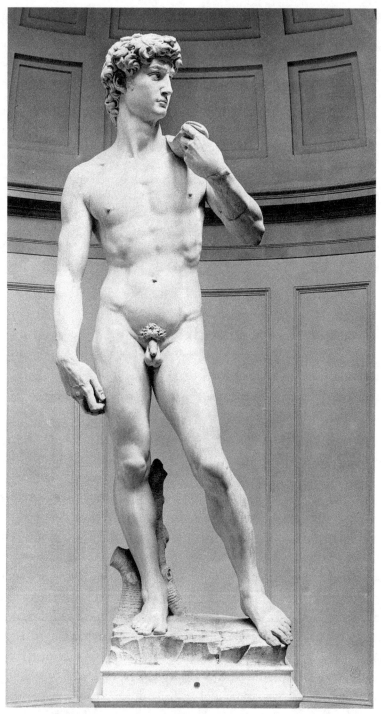

13.1. Michelangelo's *David*. Michelangelo's sculpture of David, created between 1501 and 1504, is one of the most famous sculptures in the world. Most art historians believe that the artist's intent was to depict David moments before his battle with the giant Goliath. (Photo: Alinari / Art Resource, N.Y.)

become king must certainly not be like him! Then the books move to the question, who can serve suitably as Israel's king? The towering figure of King David here and throughout the rest of the OT answers the question. Anyone who wants to be king must be like him! So, through negative example (Saul) and positive example (David), the books of 1–2 Samuel provide the models for judging Israel's kings.

Israel's Need for a King (1 Samuel 1–7)

The story of Micah's private worship center illustrates Israel's religious unfaithfulness during the judges period (Judges 17). The makeshift worship site, which was relocated to the northern city of Dan (Judges 18), came complete with idol, sanctuary ("house of God"), and a family priesthood. By contrast, the legitimate worship site at this time was at Shiloh in the territory of Ephraim (see Map 12.5). Shiloh had a sanctuary built around the ancient tabernacle that housed the ark of the covenant (1 Samuel 3:3; 4:3). Worship at the Shiloh sanctuary was supervised by the priestly family of Eli, whose family line went back to the priesthood of Aaron, brother of Moses (1 Samuel 1:3). The Shiloh sanctuary was also the site of an annual pilgrimage festival (Judges 21:19; 1 Samuel 1:3,21). Other sanctuaries were allowed during the judges period, but Shiloh was an important center of Yahweh worship during this time.

The Shiloh worship site is the backdrop for the first three chapters of 1 Samuel. Together with the book of Judges, these chapters portray Israel in the period immediately prior to the rise of kings as a tribal confederation centered on the priesthood at Shiloh, and supported by the system of judges for security. Although Yahweh was faithful in delivering Israel from all manner of threats, the priestly family of Eli was corrupt (1 Samuel 2:12–17), and the people grew weary of the constant military threats and instability. The devotion and simple trust of a single individual and his family, Elkanah of Ephraim, set up a striking contrast with the corruption of Eli's family (1 Samuel 1). The holy events surrounding the birth of the boy Samuel into Elkanah's family legitimize him as a great prophet of Israel. From early childhood, Samuel's righteousness and devotion to Yahweh prepare him for a leadership role in Israel's future. His character also emphasizes that the Elide priesthood at Shiloh had failed, and that Israel's social and religious institutions were crumbling.

The narrative then traces the fortunes of the ark of the covenant from its capture by the Philistines and its sojourn in Philistia to its eventual return to the land of Israel (1 Samuel 4–7). With or without Israel's armies, Yahweh's power is displayed in the ark of the covenant, and he is victorious over Israel's enemies. Although the ark is eventually retrieved, the narrative is included in 1 Samuel to show the extent of Israel's problems. The religious institutions at Shiloh and elsewhere were crumbling, and the capture of the ark illustrates that the military and political institutions were failing as well. Samuel's leadership role is increasingly highlighted. In this critical moment of transition for Israel, Samuel leads the nation in repentance and recovery (1 Samuel 7). Yet Israel's religious and political systems remain in shambles. Were it not for the prophet Samuel, Israel would have no hope.

13.2. Portrait of a captured Philistine. This image from the main temple of Ramses III (1184–1153 BCE) at Medinet Habu, Thebes, illustrates the distinctive "feathered" headress marking the Philistines from other Sea People warriors. The Philistines settled and inhabited the southwestern coastal region of the Southern Levant, and became ancient Israel's enemy for over two centuries. (Photo: Erich Lessing / Art Resource, N.Y.)

The Rise and Fall of Saul, Israel's First King (1 Samuel 8–15)

Samuel would not live forever. That much was clear. And his sons were not righteous like their father but were more like Eli's sons, greedy and prone to take bribes (1 Samuel 8:1–3). So this raises the question again, Where would Israel's legitimate leadership come from? The materials in the next several chapters express differing opinions about the role of monarchy, some positive and others negative. This unit generally narrates the rise of the Israelite monarchy, but also the failure of Israel's first monarch, Saul.

Three chapters relate the rise of Saul as king (1 Samuel 9–11), and they are framed by two chapters speculating on the nature of that kingship (1 Samuel 8 and 12). The Israelites realized that they could not count on the aged Samuel much longer. Not trusting his sons, they demanded a king. Samuel objects to their request, but Yahweh concedes, announcing ominously that their request

means they have rejected Yahweh as their king (8:7). The passage implies that the problem was the motivation behind their request. The Israelites wanted a king to govern them so that they would become "like other nations" (8:5). At first, King Saul is blessed and successful, leading a victorious attack against the Ammonites, which appears to vindicate his right as king (1 Samuel 11).

Defense against the Philistines was the primary reason the Israelites requested a king (9:16). Saul had modest success against the Philistines initially (1 Samuel 13–14). But he failed to accept the religious limitations of Israel's monarchy by neglecting the role of the prophet Samuel (13:13–14), and so Saul's dynasty was a failure, although he was allowed to continue as king for a while. When a second indiscretion was deemed a rejection of the "word of Yahweh," Saul's personal rulership was also rejected (8:26–28). The repudiation of King Saul helps define Israelite monarchy by explaining its narrow powers based on prophetic assessment, unlike kingship among "other nations." Israel had requested a king like other nations, and King Saul was well on his way to becoming an ancient Near Eastern despot. But Israel was not permitted such an institution, as we will see.

The Rise of David (1 Samuel 16–2 Samuel 4)

The anointing of David by the prophet Samuel is a turning point (1 Samuel 16:1–13). David receives the spirit of Yahweh, marking him as the legitimate king, while Saul loses the spirit of Yahweh and begins to be tormented by an injurious "evil spirit from Yahweh" (16:13–14). Israel now has two anointed ones (messiahs)! The rest of 1 Samuel

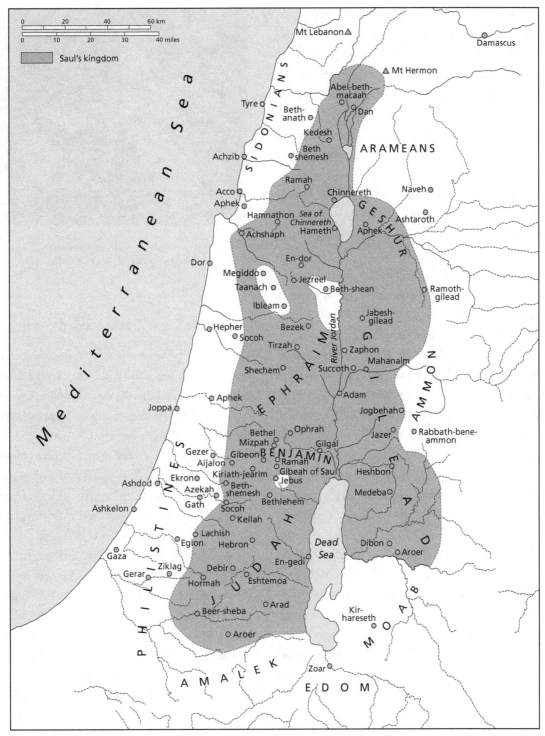

Map 13.1. Saul's kingdom

relates the shift of spiritual and political power from Saul to David. The two kings are on opposite trajectories. As Saul declines, he proves he is not adequate as a model for Israelite monarchs. David, on the other hand, slowly becomes the ideal king.

The famous story of David and Goliath is about more than a dramatic victory over a terrifying enemy (1 Samuel 17). Saul, who was anointed to provide deliverance from the Philistines, is paralyzed by the crisis, whereas David is fearless. David's clever leadership and courage mobilize the Israelite army and result in a rout of the Philistines (17:52–53). This military victory validates David's anointing as the king of Israel and shows that Saul is king in name only. Saul becomes insanely jealous of David and cannot decide whether to embrace him or kill him (1 Samuel 18–19). Ultimately, David becomes a fugitive. The two, Saul and David, cross paths on more than one occasion. David passes up two opportunities to kill Saul even though Saul is attempting to destroy him (1 Samuel 24 and 26). Meanwhile, the continued threat from the Philistines reminds the reader that King Saul has failed to function as the legitimate king of Israel. After all, the stated reason for requesting a king was so that he would fight Israel's battles (1 Samuel 8:20). King Saul was specifically chosen as the instrument for defeating the Philistines (1 Samuel 9:16). While the king spends his time tracking down David, the Philistine threat only grows worse. Saul's death on Mount Gilboa, ironically at the hands of the Philistines, confirms that Saul had become an illegitimate ruler (1 Samuel 31). After Saul's death, there was civil war between the remnants of his dynasty in the north and David in the south (2 Samuel 2–4).

13.3. Caravaggio's *David*. David has been a favorite subject of art for centuries. In this example, Michelangelo Merisi de Caravaggio (1573–1610) depicts David showing Goliath's head (1605). (Alinari / Art Resource, N.Y.)

The Rule of David (2 Samuel 5–20)

David consolidates his power as the king of Israel, first by assuming royal authority over all Israel (2 Samuel 5:1–5) and then by establishing a new capital city, Jerusalem, building a new royal palace, driving the Philistines from Judah's heartland, and introducing religious reforms in the capital (5:6–6:23). He transformed the new capital into a religious and political center. For the rest of the OT, the image of King David is closely associated with the powerful symbol of the "city of David/Jerusalem/Zion."

With all his successes, David sets out to build a temple for Yahweh, a permanent sanctuary to replace the older tent dwelling of Israel's tribal confederation (2 Samuel 7:1–3). But Yahweh has other plans for David. God informs the king through the prophet Nathan that instead of allowing David to build a house for him, Yahweh himself will build a permanent house for David, a perpetual royal dynasty (7:4–12). David's line will not end, and Yahweh will

Map 13.2. David's kingdom

SIDEBAR 13.2. THE ORIGINAL SOURCE KNOWN AS DAVID'S "COURT HISTORY"

The materials now found in 2 Samuel 9–20 and 1 Kings 1–2 have long been identified by scholars working on the OT as an original source, presumably written to explain why Solomon succeeded David as king. This older document is considered by some a contemporary document, written perhaps during Solomon's reign, and therefore among the oldest historical literature ever written. Its infrequent references to Yahweh's intervention in human affairs and suspenseful plot lead many to assume that it was written for its entertainment value as well as to legitimize Solomon's rule. Differences over its central themes have resulted in alternative names for the source. Some prefer "Succession Narrative," affirming the central question of David's successor as the focus, while others believe that the original intent was more generally a "Court Narrative" or "Court History."

The isolation of the Court History as a separate older source in the 1920s was a clue used by scholars, beginning in the 1940s, to reconstruct the Deuteronomistic History. It was accepted as one of the original documents used by the historian to write an overarching narrative from the plains of Moab to the fall of Jerusalem (Sidebar 9.5). In more recent years, some have expressed doubts about the Court History. Why is it so difficult to determine the beginning or ending of the original source? And parts of it are incomprehensible without materials found elsewhere. So, for example, how are we to understand David's gracious treatment of Mephibosheth (2 Samuel 9) without the material about the end of Saul's family (2 Samuel 2:8–4:12)? Despite these uncertainties, the theory of the Court History or Succession Narrative continues to be one of the most logical explanations of how these books were written.*

* See pages 9–13 in McCarter in the commentaries in "Where to Find More" in this chapter.

---

become a father to David's descendants (7:13–16). This relationship between Yahweh and David is known elsewhere in the OT as a "covenant" (e.g., 1 Kings 8:23–24; Psalm 89:3–4). And David's willingness to defer to the voice of the prophet is essential to the difference between him and Saul.

David's victories against Israel's enemies in the Transjordan and his mercy to the remnants of Saul's family only add to the portrait of him as an ideal king (2 Samuel 8–9). Just when the reader feels comfortable that David is nearly perfect, the narrative of the Ammonite wars reveals a disappointing side to him (2 Samuel 10–12). In David's sexual abuse of Bathsheba and the murder of her husband, Uriah, he has become exactly like any typical Near Eastern despot. The Israelite king has officially become what Samuel warned he would become – a taker not a giver (see 1 Samuel 8:11–18). Yet even in his moment of crime, David quickly and sincerely repents when confronted by the prophetic rebuke (12:7–14). David's actions are disappointing, but his genuine response in the face of the prophet's reprimand is what makes David the ideal king.

The rest of this unit traces the consequences of David's crimes (Bathsheba and Uriah), and the judgment pronounced as a result of his actions: "the sword shall never depart from [his] house" (2 Samuel 12:10). One of David's sons rapes a half-sister (2 Samuel 13–14), and another conspires to seize the throne and incites civil war (2 Samuel 14–20). David's private and personal failures have become public and violent. And the structure of 2 Samuel ties these events together with David's personal moral crisis in a cause-and-effect sequence. David's problems, and the problems in his kingdom, are a direct result of his crimes and personal failures.

Appendixes to David's Rule (2 Samuel 21–24)

The final four chapters of 2 Samuel collect diverse materials in a kind of closing note for 1–2 Samuel. Other portions of the books contain a continuous narrative thread, while these last chapters have little chronological or literary connection to the whole. The final editor of 1–2 Samuel considered these materials necessary in order to present a complete portrait of David as the ideal king of Israel.

WHAT REALLY HAPPENED?

The books of 1–2 Samuel cover events that fit into the last portion of the Iron Age I period, approximately 1050–970 BCE. We have seen that scholars today are not agreed on a historical reconstruction of this period of Israel's history (Chapter 11). Those elevating archaeology as the final authority in the debate sometimes conclude that Saul and David were fictional characters; the United Monarchy simply disappears. Others elevate the biblical evidence and tend to ignore or minimize the lack of archaeological evidence, simply repeating the story as we have it in the biblical texts. Most strive for a balance between these extremes, although such balance is elusive.

Reconstructing what happened in this period of Israel's history is complicated. We lack precise archaeological evidence, the OT's account of the story is idealized and has mostly religious motives, and the process is made even more complicated by

the high emotions and ideologies (and religious convictions) of scholars working on this topic. I don't want simply to tell you what you should think. Rather, I will outline a few pieces of information that should provide limits to our skepticism about the existence of King David or, more generally, about the existence of a United Monarchy in Israel.

From Tribes to Statehood

The narrative as told in 1–2 Samuel traces Israel's changes from the tribal structure of the judges period to an established state, with a standing army and centralized authority. Such a transition involves numerous additional changes in a society, and from today's perspective, we have problems even defining terms such as "tribe" and "state" in ancient cultures. Whatever else we may say about Israel's history during this period, Saul traces his descent to the tribe of Benjamin (1 Samuel 9:1–2), and appears to have had an administrative center at his hometown of Gibeah (1 Samuel 22:6). Similarly, David was of the tribe of Judah (1 Samuel 17:12), and established a new central capital at Jerusalem (1 Samuel 5:6–9). But we are not able to be certain about either the other social changes that would have occurred or how quickly such a transition happened.

Our understanding of how ancient tribes develop into primitive states is limited. Some assume a simplistic evolutionary development over a long period of time, in which case the account in 1–2 Samuel is nearly impossible because it occurs so quickly. Others believe that tribes and states are mutually exclusive, or at least always in tension. In this way, power shifts back and forth between tribes and states in a region, depending on which is more powerful at any given time. The OT's description of Israel's United Monarchy in 1–2 Samuel and 1 Kings could fit a number of different models defined by anthropologists and sociologists: city-states, chiefdoms, territorial states, and so forth.[1]

On the other hand, we now have a rather amazing parallel to the OT's description of Israel's statehood. At the city of Mari on the Euphrates River, a "tribal state" is attested in thousands of written documents, in which leaders of a tribe took over a city capital and adapted an administrative structure as a mature state, all rather quickly (find Mari on Map 3.2). No gradual progression was needed. And the new kings retained their tribal identity while ruling from an administrative and religious center. They appear to have integrated systematically the older tribal structures into a city-based state or kingdom. One such group of the several tribes at Mari is even known as Benjaminites ("sons of the right hand," or "Yaminites").[2] While there is no direct connection between Israel and the Mari tribal state, the comparisons suggest something similar is happening in David's sudden appearance as king of Israel from a center at Jerusalem.

Evidence of Hazor, Megiddo, and Gezer

Any discussion of the OT's account of the United Monarchy must take note of the archaeological evidence, especially that of three cities: Hazor, Megiddo, and Gezer. David's son and successor, King Solomon, was the last king of the United Monarchy according to the OT; the kingdom fell into northern Israel and southern Judah immediately after Solomon's death. The account of 1 Kings 9:15–17 attributes significant building activities to Solomon, and we have evidence pointing to a rise in monumental architecture in the tenth century BCE. These three cities are specifically mentioned in the text, and excavations have revealed defense systems exhibiting nearly identical fortification patterns; specifically, their impressive casemate walls and city gates of a common style (see Map 13.3 for the location of these cities).[3]

Many have concluded that this is a rare instance of text and tell matching perfectly. The sudden transformation of these three cities from ruin heaps in need of repair to impressive fortified government centers required a centralized authority with the means to build such a system. It has, in fact, been suggested that we would have needed to invent David and Solomon as conqueror and administrator, respectively, had the OT not already given us their names.[4]

But the connection between text and tell as it relates to Hazor, Megiddo, and Gezer has been denied by some. The architectural features thought to be characteristic of Solomon's building activities may, in fact, have been more common for a

---

1 See pages 105–15 of Grabbe in "Where to Find More" at Chapter 11.

2 For more, see Fleming in "Where to Find More" in this chapter.

3 For more on this, see pages 380–87 in Mazar in "Where to Find More" at Chapter 11.

4 John S. Holladay, Jr., "The Kingdoms of Israel and Judah: Political and Economic Centralization in the Iron IIA-B (ca. 1000–750 B.C.E.)," in *The Archaeology of Society in the Holy Land* (ed. Thomas E. Levy; New York: Facts on File, 1995), 368–98.

SIDEBAR 13.3. THE EVIDENCE OF THE TEL DAN INSCRIPTION

13.4. The Tel Dan Inscription. In 1993 and 1994, excavations conducted by Hebrew Union College at the northern city of Dan retrieved these three fragments from a large basalt monument. The inscription written on the monument appears to mention King Jehoram of Israel and King Ahaziah of Judah in a broken portion, but on another portion it clearly contains the first extrabiblical mention of the "house of David." ("House of David" inscribed on a victory stele, Tel Dan [basalt], Iron Age [ninth century BC] / Private Collection / photo: © Zev Radovan / The Bridgeman Art Library)

In the late 1980s and early 1990s, researchers studying Israel's United Monarchy got into a heated debate over whether King David was historical. A minority of scholars alleged that we cannot know anything about David because of a lack of archaeological evidence, or they denied his existence entirely, comparing him to the legendary King Arthur. (Review the dangers of elevating archaeology over the evidence of the OT text, or the OT text over archaeology; Chapter 11). On July 21, 1993, an important archaeological discovery changed the debate. That day, workers at Hebrew Union College's excavation at the northern city of Dan found a fragment of a broken stela (large stone or slab, often with a sculptured surface) on which an Old Aramaic inscription of the mid-ninth century BCE was carved. The next year, they found two more fragments of the stela. We cannot be sure how large the unbroken stela was. The inscription was considerably longer than what is preserved on our three fragments, and we can only guess at the content of the majority of the text. But what we *can* read has caused quite a commotion in the scholarship.

The following boast made by an Aramean ruler whose name is lost in the inscription can be reconstructed: "and my father lay down and went to his ancestors (place of the dead), and the king of Israel came up against my father's land. Then the storm-god Hadad made me king. And Hadad marched before me and I set out." The next lines are difficult to reconstruct, but the Aramean king claims to have led his forces in a great victory over numerous kings. Although the lines are broken, there appear then to be references to "Jehoram son of Ahab, king of Israel" and "Ahaziah son of Jehoram, king of the house of David."* Many interpretations of the inscription are possible, but the reference to the "house of David" is the first extrabiblical evidence for the existence of King David (see Sidebar 15.3 for another reference to the "House of David"). This inscription, then, presents evidence from the ninth century BCE, just a century after the United Monarchy, for the historical existence of the founder of the dynasty, King David. Some scholars have offered contrasting interpretations of the Tel Dan inscription, challenging its relevance in the debate about the tenth century. But most admit that it at least establishes limits to our skepticism.

* For more on this inscription, see Shmuel Ahituv, *Echoes from the Past: Hebrew and Cognate Inscriptions from the Biblical Period* (trans. Anson F. Rainey; Jerusalem: Carta, 2008), 466–73; Christopher A. Rollston, *Writing and Literacy in the World of Ancient Israel: Epigraphic Evidence from the Iron Age* (SBLABS 11; Leiden/Boston: Brill/SBL, 2011), 51–53.

wider period of time. Others question whether the strata of evidence among the three cities are really synchronistic, implying that the physical features in view came from slightly different periods of time. Still others have attempted to "downdate" the archaeological evidence from these cities to nearly a century later, making it irrelevant to the OT's account of the United Monarchy (see Sidebar 11.2 on the so-called low chronology). Readers in these categories usually identify David as a bandit from an insignificant village in the south, Jerusalem, and Solomon as a tribal chief, if they were historical at all. But they deny anything like the OT's picture of the United Monarchy.

Jerusalem

The OT's portrait of the United Monarchy includes the capture of the Canaanite city of Jebus and its transformation into the city of David as an important moment in the establishment of the United Monarchy (2 Samuel 5–6). And yet we have little evidence from Jerusalem itself that it served as a capital city of a territorial state in the tenth century BCE. Some have exaggerated the problem, suggesting that the city was completely unoccupied in the Late Bronze Age, which ignores the letters written by its ruler during the Amarna era (Sidebar 3.3).

In reality, construction and (re)building in Jerusalem during later Persian, Greek, and Roman times repeatedly cleared the site down to bedrock. And in any case, the city has been continuously settled for centuries, making extensive excavation impossible. Most archaeologists admit that Jerusalem bears evidence of some occupation during the tenth century, and even of the introduction of modest monumental structures at least on the eastern slope of the city of David. But it was not a thriving city until centuries later. During the late ninth and early eighth centuries, Jerusalem expanded considerably and we have evidence of it serving as an administrative center. It seems

reasonable to conclude that Jerusalem remained a modest, even neutral city as long as the United Monarchy existed. It was only after the division of the kingdom into northern Israel and southern Judah that the motivation for neutrality was lost, and the city was expanded under later kings of Judah, especially Hezekiah.[5]

Our goal is always to compare text and tell on questions of historical reconstruction (Chapter 11). When it comes to Israel's United Monarchy, we may lack definitive answers. But we're not left without *any* answers. The OT's account is a theologically driven picture of a great kingdom founded by David and expanded by Solomon. True enough! The sociological and archaeological evidence we have considered suggests that their kingdom was not as large or impressive as we might think it. But it also suggests that that the United Monarchy grew gradually from the modest chiefdom of Saul, with a royal court meeting under a tree (1 Samuel 22:6), to David's tribal state, with a new capital city at Jerusalem, and finally to a genuine territorial state under Solomon. The best approach assumes that late in David's reign, he consolidated his power and authority to something like the United Monarchy we read about in the OT.

RELIGIOUS EXPRESSION IN THE UNITED MONARCHY

Israel's social transition from tribes to statehood is not easy to reconstruct historically. We have evidence for similar transitions in other cultures that

---

5 For this reconstruction, see pages 417–30 of Vaughn in "Where to Find More" in this chapter.

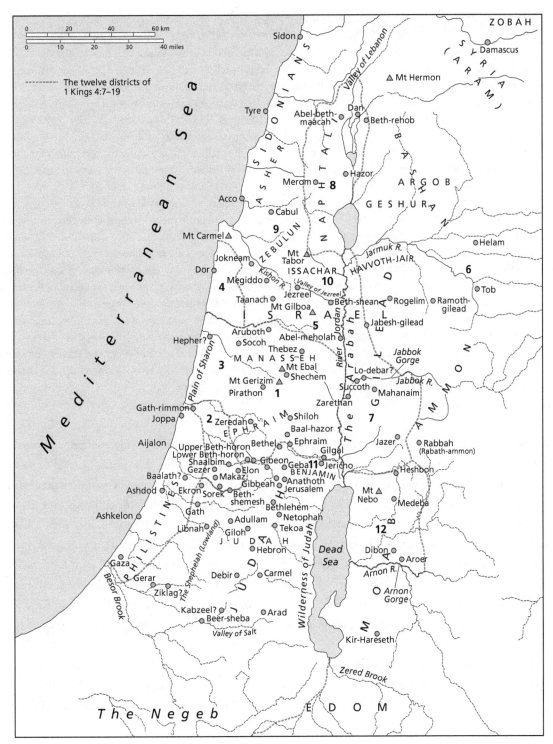

Map 13.3. Solomon's kingdom

SIDEBAR 13.4. THE STRANGE CASE OF 1 SAMUEL 28 – DEATH CULTS IN ANCIENT ISRAEL?

As you were reading through 1–2 Samuel, you probably paused over the strange case of 1 Samuel 28. King Saul, aware that he is about to go into battle with superior Philistine forces, visits a necromancer (a mantic specialist who communicates with the spirits of the deceased) to call up the dead prophet Samuel. Such divinatory practices were forbidden in the Torah (Leviticus 19:31; 20:6,27; Deuteronomy 18:11), and King Saul himself had banned such mediums earlier in his reign (1 Samuel 28:3,9). This passage casually avows that the dead Samuel did, in fact, return from the dead to have a conversation with Saul. The account plays a role in the overall message of 1 Samuel by showing how far Saul has fallen. He gradually moved from a king who outlawed the "dark arts" to a panicked and desperate man pathetically using those very arts to get approval and advice from the deceased prophet. So the passage contrasts Saul with King David. David sponsored the worship of Yahweh in united Israel, whereas Saul stooped to the most unorthodox magic practices.

This text raises the question: Did ancient Israelites practice necromancy? It seems that some did, otherwise the Torah would not have explicitly condemned the practices, and this narrative in 1 Samuel 28 would make no sense. Texts from elsewhere in the ancient Near East, especially from the port city of Ugarit in the Northern Levant, have shown that the dead were not perceived as simply cut off from the living. The dead were thought of as continuing to exist in the underworld, and they could be consulted on behalf of the living to grant blessings or for information. You should not think of this as standard theology for the ancient Near East, however. The various cultures of Egypt, Mesopotamia, and Syria-Palestine held complex theories on these points, and there was no single approach in the ancient world to necromancy or the other mantic cults. But we may conclude that, at least at certain times in OT history, *some* Israelites practiced such techniques. So the authors of the Pentateuch condemned these practices, and the editors of 1 Samuel used it to show how hopeless Saul had become.

---

can serve as models to show that religion can and often does serve as a unifying principle, providing the glue that holds different groups together in the new state.[6] We have seen so far in this textbook that monotheism is not yet such a unifying ideology. But now, in 1–2 Samuel, David is portrayed as a firm supporter of Yahweh and the worship of Yahweh. At his coronation as king over all Israel, David's devotion to Yahweh is mentioned by the northern tribes as one reason for their allegiance to him (2 Samuel 5:1–3).

David and his royal court are said to have transferred the principal center for the worship of

Yahweh from Shiloh to Jerusalem (2 Samuel 5–6). It is also possible that during David's reign, various Canaanite practices began to coalesce into the worship of Yahweh, especially features associated with the creator-father god, El. The Yahweh of earlier traditions – mountain God, warrior God, storm God – was combined with local images of Canaanite El, portraying Yahweh as cosmic creator, and perhaps even as the Great King. David seems to have encouraged this new depiction of Yahweh as the Lord of all levels of Israelite society, the "God of Israel" (2 Samuel 7:27). As we will see later, this process likely continued long after David, culminating in the reigns of Hezekiah and Josiah.

6 See pages 118–22 of Grabbe in "Where to Find More" in Chapter 11.

We have other evidence suggesting the growing importance of the worship of Yahweh in the United Monarchy. In order to explain this, I need to introduce some rather technical information about the nature of personal names in ancient Hebrew. Israelite names, and indeed ancient Semitic names in general, often use a verbal idea in the person's name together with the name of a god as a noun in an implied sentence; these are called **theophoric** names. So, for example, the name Elijah means "Yahweh is my God," the *-jah* ending being an abbreviated form of "Yahweh." Scholars have studied these names from ancient inscriptions as well as the OT's many names as evidence for discerning which deities were most popular at various times in ancient Israel. In other words, the god names that parents used in naming their children suggests which deities were worshipped at a given point in time. One count found 557 Yahweh-type names in the inscriptions, 44 El-type names, and a handful of Baal-type names.[7]

While this approach reconstructs only an approximation of naming preferences and while much of it comes from later than the United Monarchy, the overall effect suggests a number of conclusions related to the Iron Age I period. First, a number of deities occur in these names, along with a large portion of Yahweh names. Early Israel was not monotheistic, yet Yahweh was already present as an important deity in the highlands of Iron Age I. Second, since we do not believe Yahweh was a deity native to Canaan but rather was brought

into the highlands from the south (Chapter 10), it seems likely that the worship of Yahweh was introduced to the area by the newcomers in the region in Iron Age I. Finally, in the late Iron Age I period, the time of Israel's United Monarchy, Yahweh-type names become the most popular ones by far. An overwhelming majority of Israelite names have Yahweh as the **theophoric** element, suggesting the spread of Yahweh worship in the time of David. From the United Monarchy onward, Yahweh names are preferred by parents naming children.

One additional comment is needed here on Israel's new monarchy. We have explained that 1–2 Samuel set out to define the new institution of Israel's kingship, and to limit its power. Israelite kings must never be like kings of the other nations, despite the initial request of the people ("like other nations"; 1 Samuel 8:5). Israel's kings will be subject to the word of Yahweh as delivered by the prophets, and to the laws of Yahweh as given by Moses. The tension caused by the very presence of an Israelite human king is because Israel's covenant understanding of Yahweh is that Yahweh himself is the Great King. He sits enshrined on the ark of the covenant, his divine throne, in a tabernacle-like palace. The idea that Yahweh is king is at the core of Israel's self-identity as the nation of Israel, sealed by the Mosaic covenant binding Yahweh, the Great King, to Israel, the submissive vassal. "Yahweh is king" is the theological expression of Israel's relationship to Yahweh at the heart of the Torah, and it becomes important elsewhere in the OT as well (e.g., the so-called royal psalms, Psalms 47, 93, 96, 98, 99, and 100).

In this light, the very presence of a human king living in a royal palace is a threat to Israel's

7 The foundational study in this area is that of Jeffrey H. Tigay, *You Shall Have No Other Gods: Israelite Religion in the Light of Hebrew Inscriptions* (HSS 31; Atlanta, Ga.: Scholars Press, 1986).

SIDEBAR 13.5. WAS ISRAEL AN ANCIENT AMPHICTYONY?

In the nineteenth century, scholars began noticing similarities between Israel's premonarchic society and certain Classical Greek and Roman parallels. In such examples, sacral tribal leagues of twelve, or sometimes six, members were responsible for the care of a common sanctuary, based on a twelve-month rotating schedule. Known as an **amphictyony** (or "next neighbors"), the most famous such league was located in Delphi. Religion and worship traditions unified the members of the league. Throughout much of the twentieth century, scholars assumed that Israel's early history was just such an amphictyonic tribal confederation devoted to the worship of Yahweh. So it was assumed that various tribal groups from diverse locations and traditions were merged under the banner of Yahweh worship, and that a new political entity, "Israel," was created.

We must admit that this hypothesis is attractive. But we must also admit that we have no proof early Israel functioned in such an amphictyonic league – either that the twelve tribes of Israel met regularly or that they individually provided for a central sanctuary. Anthropologists have also explored parallels with other ancient Near Eastern Semitic tribes, which are closer neighbors than ancient Greece and Italy, and which show no such formal amphictyonic arrangement. The concept need not be completely abandoned, and it will no doubt continue to be explored in the future. But at this point, it seems unlikely to have been the way the tribes of early Israel perceived themselves.

---

religious understanding of the nature of Yahweh. The degree to which the king in Jerusalem expands his role, inching closer and closer to acting like an ancient Near Eastern despot, the further removed Israel will be from Yahweh. Another new institution, the "prophet of Yahweh" (which we will talk about more in Chapter 19) emerges as an important counterbalance to the king's authority. Israel's king, unlike any other in the ancient world, must submit himself to prophetic critique and respond positively to the preaching of God's word. Otherwise, king and people will go down together. This unique tension between king and prophet will come up again often, as we continue our stroll through Israel's library.

WHERE TO FIND MORE

Commentaries: The best technical and advanced commentary on **1 and 2 Samuel** is P. Kyle McCarter, *I Samuel* and *II Samuel* (Anchor Bible 8 and 9; Garden City, N.Y.: Doubleday, 1980 and 1984). See also Walter Brueggemann, *First and Second Samuel* (Interpretation; Louisville, Ky.: John Knox Press, 1990); Hans Wilhelm Hertzberg, *I and II Samuel: A Commentary* (Old Testament Library; Philadelphia: Westminster Press, 1964); and David Toshio Tsumura, *The First Book of Samuel* (New International Commentary on the Old Testament; Grand Rapids, Mich.: Eerdmans, 2007).

Day, John. *Yahweh and the Gods and Goddesses of Canaan*. JSOTSup 265. London: Sheffield Academic Press, 2002.

On the coalescence of local Canaanite religious practices into the worship of Yahweh, see pages 13–34.

Fleming, Daniel E. *Democracy's Ancient Ancestors: Mari and Early Collective Governance*. Cambridge: Cambridge University Press, 2004.

For advanced readers, this volume gives all the evidence for the tribal state of ancient Mari.

Halpern, Baruch. *David's Secret Demons: Messiah, Murderer, Traitor, King*. Grand Rapids, Mich.: Eerdmans, 2001.

Argues that the United Monarchy "grows" late in David's reign (pp. 259 and 382–91). Advanced and technical discussion of the archaeological evidence related to Hazor, Megiddo, and Gezer (pp. 427–50). For a more general discussion, see pages 380–87 of Mazar in the "Where to Find More" section in Chapter 11. For a critique of the low chronology, downdating the archaeological evidence from the tenth century to nearly a century later, see pages 451–78.

Knoppers, Gary N. "The Vanishing Solomon: The Disappearance of the United Monarchy from Recent Histories of Ancient Israel." *Journal of Biblical Literature* 116/1 (1997): 19–44.

Helpful survey and critique of the approaches that call into question the existence of a United Monarchy in ancient Israel.

Lemche, Niels Peter. *Prelude to Israel's Past: Background and Beginnings of Israelite History and Identity*. Peabody, Mass.: Hendrickson, 1998.

On tribes and states in the ancient world, see pages 99–101.

McKenzie, Steven L. *King David: A Biography*. New York: Oxford University Press, 2000.

Mettinger, Tryggve N. D. "YHWH SABAOTH – The Heavenly King on the Cherubim Throne." Pages 109–38 in *Studies in the Period of David and Solomon and Other Essays: Papers Read at the International Symposium for Biblical Studies, Tokyo, 5–7 December, 1979*. Edited by Tomoo Ishida. Winona Lake, Ind.: Eisenbrauns, 1982.

Vaughn, Andrew G., and Ann E. Killebrew, eds. *Jerusalem in Bible and Archaeology: The First Temple Period*. SBLSymS 18. Leiden: Brill, 2003.

Especially see the chapters by Cahill and Vaughn for interpretation of the archaeological evidence from Jerusalem.

CHAPTER 14

More Kings

OLD TESTAMENT READING: 1 AND 2 KINGS

First and Second Kings continue the stories of monarchic rule. Textual sources from the Assyrian and Babylonian Empires aid us considerably in the historical reconstruction of these centuries, but we will quickly observe that a religious agenda is central. First, the narrative accounts are connected by a recurring literary formula that evaluates each king – not primarily on political and military achievements but on the basis of that king's faithfulness to Yahweh. Insertions of the so-called Elijah and Elisha cycles further demonstrate a concern to emphasize prophetic authority, which demands exclusive loyalty to Yahweh.

Second, content bears out the overriding religious motivation. For example, Solomon is associated with the great wisdom tradition in Israel. Nevertheless, for these biblical authors success is measured by obedience to Yahweh, and Solomon's devotion to Yahweh is compromised because of his many wives and religious unfaithfulness. His downfall is also Israel's – the United Monarchy is divided into the northern kingdom of Israel and the southern kingdom of Judah. Religious unfaithfulness, exhibited by most of the kings, accounts for the fall of Israel to the Assyrians in 722 BCE and of Jerusalem (Judah) to the Babylonians in 586 BCE.

*I*srael wanted a king. So they got Saul and David, the first of which was a negative example and the second a positive example of what kings could become. Saul was precisely the kind of king the Israelites were not permitted to have, whereas David was the kind of ruler they could always hope for.

Once Israel started having kings, they couldn't stop. The next books in our collection read like an avalanche of kings, which of course explains the

226

name, 1–2 Kings. As we have seen, the first major portion of the OT, the Primary History, has nine books narrating events from the creation of the universe to the fall of Jerusalem and the loss of the temple in 586 BCE (Chapter 4). The books of 1–2 Kings (counted as one) trace the kings of Israel from Solomon, the last to rule over a United Monarchy, through the many kings of northern Israel and southern Judah. They cover over three centuries of history, and a bewildering number of rulers and historical events. Through it all, the primary focus is on which kings were faithful to the covenant with Yahweh. Unfortunately, too few of Israel's and Judah's kings were like David.

THE BOOKS OF FIRST AND SECOND KINGS

As with 1–2 Samuel, so, too, were the books of 1–2 Kings originally one composition. (This is why we count Samuel and Kings as two books instead of four in the Primary History.) They were probably divided into separate books when they were translated from Hebrew into other languages for use in various faith communities. The division after 1 Kings 22 is based on the size of scrolls as much as it is on content.

The books of 1–2 Kings pick up the story from the time when King David is advancing in years. It relates the reign of King Solomon as the last ruler of a unified kingdom of Israel. At Solomon's death, the kingdom divides into northern Israel and southern Judah, and the rest of the narrative is devoted to tracing what happens to them. The north has a succession of mostly flawed royal dynasties, nine in all, over two centuries. The northern kingdom of Israel falls to the Assyrians in 722 BCE. The south, by contrast, has twenty kings in a single dynasty, that of the line of King David. But even these rulers are not faithful to the covenant, with a few exceptions, so that eventually the southern kingdom of Judah falls to the Babylonians in 586 BCE.

The Reign of Solomon (1 Kings 1–11)

Who would become king of Israel after David? This question had driven the narrative of David's Court History (2 Samuel 9–20). Two successive crown princes, Amnon and Absalom, obvious choices in many ways, would not follow their father on the throne. The opening chapters of 1 Kings return to this topic to relate how a third crown prince, Adonijah, was eliminated, and how Solomon became king instead. The narrative of 1 Kings 1–2 was likely the original conclusion to the source we identified as the "Court History" (Sidebar 13.3). Since it also relates the death of King David (2:10–12), the authors and editors of the books of Kings used it here to introduce their story. This shows that their account in the books of Kings is not as much a thorough history of Israel and Judah as it is a theologized or religious history of the dynasty of King David from his death to the last monarch of the line of David.[1]

Solomon's request to Yahweh for "an understanding mind" and the ability to discern "between good and evil" (1 Kings 3:9) begins a long section that emphasizes the positive accomplishments of King Solomon. His proverbs and wisdom sayings on nearly every topic of life were legendary around the world (1 Kings 4:29–34), and thus King

---

1 For this distinction, see page 6 in Sweeney in the commentaries in "Where to Find More" in this chapter.

The historical books were originally part of the Deuteronomistic History, which incorporated older pre-Deuteronomistic materials. We have seen that in the book of Joshua, these older materials were thoroughly revised for inclusion in the history, while in the book of Judges, earlier sources were framed and introduced, but with less directly intrusive editing (Sidebar 12.2). We have also explained that the books of Samuel are based on five older narrative sources, which have been edited in various ways by the Deuteronomistic Historian (Sidebar 13.1). What about 1–2 Kings?

Like the authors and compilers of Joshua, Judges, and 1–2 Samuel, the authors responsible for the books of Kings depended on older sources. In this case, those earlier works listed the kings of Israel and Judah. The titles of these sources are even cited in 1–2 Kings: "the Book of the Acts of Solomon" (1 Kings 11:41), "the Book of the Annals of the Kings of Israel" (1 Kings 14:19, 15:31, etc.), and "the Book of the Annals of the Kings of Judah" (1 Kings 14:29, 15:7, etc.). We don't have copies of any of these older resources. But from the contents implied by these references to them in 1–2 Kings, we may assume that they were chronicles of royal activities, probably sponsored, collected, and preserved by scribes and scholars of the royal courts of ancient Israel and Judah. We also have references in the historical books to royal "secretaries" and "recorders" serving in the courts of David, Solomon, and Hezekiah (2 Samuel 8:16–17 and 20:24–25; 1 Kings 4:3; 2 Kings 18:18). These were most likely chroniclers or historians, and they may well have been responsible for the older sources used in the composition of 1–2 Kings, providing the skeletal outline for the histories of Israel and Judah.

These sources and several others appear to have been framed and introduced for inclusion by the historian, with less intrusive editing in a manner similar to the book of Judges. In this way, the books of Kings were intentionally written as the concluding chapters of the Deuteronomistic History. The last recorded event in 2 Kings is the release of King Jehoiachin from prison in exile in 561 BCE (2 Kings 25:27–30). Ancient authors typically bring their narratives down to their present day, so it seems likely the books of Kings received something like their final form shortly after that date. Before the mid-sixth-century exilic version, scholars have also identified a late-seventh-century edition of the Deuteronomistic History, including 1–2 Kings, from the time of Josiah. Others have proposed even earlier editions of the Deuteronomistic History in the late eighth century (time of Hezekiah). With regard to 1–2 Kings more narrowly, some have proposed an early-eighth-century edition (time of Jehu), and even a tenth-century edition from the time of Solomon.*

---

* As an example, see pages 3–32 of Sweeney in the commentaries in "Where to Find More" in this chapter.

Solomon becomes the fountainhead and source of Israel's wisdom traditions (Proverbs 1:1, 10:1, 25:1). In a sense, this role for Solomon completes the picture of three great leaders of early Israel, each standing as the figurehead of three great literary traditions: Moses the lawgiver, David the hymn writer, and Solomon the wisdom king.

King Solomon is also the temple builder (1 Kings 5–8). This first temple for Yahweh built in Jerusalem officially replaces the wilderness tabernacle as Yahweh's abode among his people (8:4). The king's prayer of dedication (8:22–53) is a beautiful expression of Israelite theology that we will consider later. Solomon also expands the

SIDEBAR 14.2. EXCERPTS FROM *THE INSTRUCTION OF PTAHHOTEP*

Solomon asked God for "an understanding mind," or, more literally translated, a "hearing heart" (1 Kings 3:9). Ancient Egyptian wisdom traditions have a similar concept, shedding light on what Solomon was asking. The Middle Kingdom *Instruction of Ptahhotep* (composed sometime between the twentieth and seventeenth centuries BCE) focuses on the importance of listening for one's education and character formation. The following excerpt is typical of sentiments found frequently in Egyptian wisdom literature.

> Useful is hearing to a son who hears;
> If hearing enters the hearer,
> The hearer becomes a listener,
> Hearing well is speaking well....
> Hearing is better than everything else,
> It creates good will....
> He who hears is beloved of God,
> He whom God hates does not hear.[*]

Solomon's "hearing" or "listening heart" is thus a request to become an obedient king, discerning of Yahweh's guidance, and acceptable to God.

The context of Solomon's request in 1 Kings 3, however, indicates that it goes beyond the Egyptian parallel. The *Instruction of Ptahhotep* is primarily focused on individual and personal ethics, so the learner/listener may advance in Egyptian society. Solomon is particularly focused on his responsibility to the people of Israel, and his need to govern them well. The maternity dispute between two prostitutes, narrated in the next paragraphs, illustrates that Solomon's wisdom was put to good use (1 Kings 3:16–28). Each woman claimed to be the mother of the living son while the other was the mother of the dead boy. Solomon ordered the living boy be cut in two pieces in order to see which woman would object, revealing the mother of the living child. Solomon's request was to become the kind of king who will govern Yahweh's people wisely because of an ethical and discerning character.

[*] Adapted from Miriam Lichtheim, *Ancient Egyptian Literature: A Book of Readings* (3 vols.; Berkeley: University of California Press, 1973–1980), 1:74.

royal palace and constructs many other buildings in Jerusalem (1 Kings 7). These chapters of 1 Kings are focused only on the glory of King Solomon's accomplishments, which may be summarized as follows: the people of Israel grew numerous, had plenty to eat, and were content, and the kingdom was peaceful and sovereign over an extensive portion of the Levant, even including Israel's traditional enemies, the Philistines (4:20–21). Under King Solomon, all was well, and life was good (on the extent of Solomon's kingdom, see Map 13.3).

However, the grandeur and spectacular wealth of Solomon's reign were conditioned on his obedience to God, as stressed in Yahweh's second appearance to the king (9:1–9; Gibeon was his first appearance, 3:3–15). Yahweh states without qualification, "If you will walk before me, as David your father walked, with integrity of heart and uprightness, ... then I will establish you royal throne over Israel forever." But he also warns, "If you turn aside from following me, ... then I will cut Israel off from the land" (1 Kings 9:4–5,6–7). This warning anticipates 1 Kings 11, which tells how King Solomon allowed himself to be drawn away from Yahweh because of his many wives. Political marriages were not uncommon in the ancient Near East, and Solomon had relied on such arrangements to solidify his reign. The text announces coldly that Solomon's wives "turned away his heart after other gods; and his heart was not true to Yahweh his God, as was the heart of his father David" (11:4). In the wake of this disappointment, the text also reveals that Solomon had threats within and without: Jeroboam, son of Nebat, within his own kingdom (11:26–28) and the Edomites and Arameans without (11:14–25).

The Kingdoms of Israel and Judah (1 Kings 12 – 2 Kings 17)

Next, the books of Kings cover the period when the people of God coexisted as two separate nations, Israel in the north and Judah in the south. As we have seen many times before in the Primary History, this is not history writing pure and simple, but history written with a particular religious point of view, or a theologized history. This is especially obvious in this unit, which mingles long narrative cycles devoted to the prophets Elijah and Elisha into the national histories.

Upon the death of King Solomon, Israel is torn in two – Israel in the north, comprised of ten tribes, and Judah in the south – as predicted by the prophet Ahijah (11:29–39). We are to assume that the twelfth tribe is Levi, which has no land allotment (although a parallel passage gives a different accounting of the tribes; 2 Chronicles 11:1). In order to keep his new kingdom from returning to the south, Jeroboam I of the north immediately establishes sanctuaries at Bethel and Dan to rival that of Jerusalem, as well as alternative religious festivals (1 Kings 12:25–33). The authors and editors of the books of Kings condemn these practices bluntly ("this thing became a sin"; 12:30), and in Jeroboam I they discover their quintessential bad king, just as David is the model for a good king. Future kings in the list will compare to one or the other, to Jeroboam as an evil king or to David as a good king.

The kings of each kingdom are now presented systematically, relying on a literary formula that introduces each king in a relatively parallel manner. This may remind you of a similar cyclic formula used to introduce the six major judges in the book of Judges (Chapter 12). In fact, this framework is similar to that one in Judges and has been edited in a similar way for use in the Deuteronomistic History. We may assume that it required little adaptation by the editors but was used as an overarching framework for summarizing the lengthy story to be told.

Using this cyclic literary formula, each king, with a few exception, is introduced like this. First comes a *synchronistic sentence*, identifying the new king's accession year with a specific year of the monarch in the other kingdom: "Now in the eighteenth year of King Jeroboam son of Nebat [*of Israel*], Abijam began to reign over Judah" (1 Kings 15:1). Second comes either the monarch's *age* at the time his reign

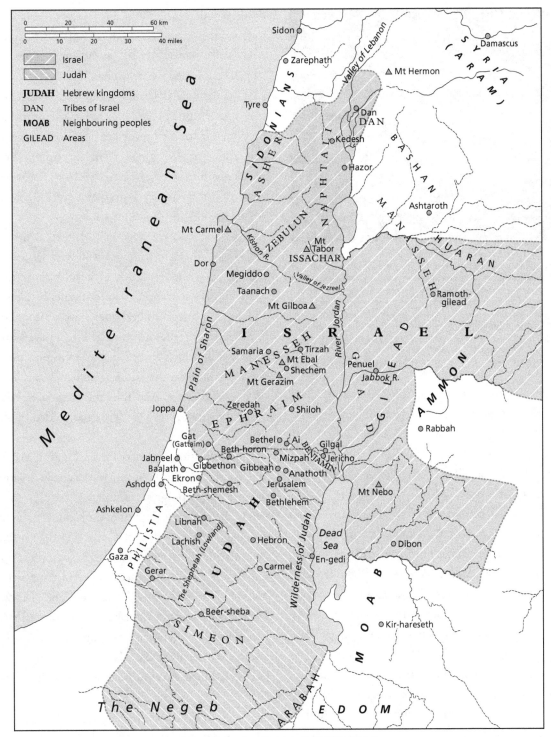

Map 14.1. Israel and Judah in the Southern Levant

14.1. Seal inscribed with "[Belonging] to Shema, the servant of Jeroboam." Found at Megiddo in 1904, the seal's mention of a certain "Jeroboam" is intriguing. Scholars are divided about whether the owner,
Shema, was a government official for Jeroboam I in the tenth century,
Jeroboam II in the eighth century, or some other unknown individual
named Jeroboam. If dated to the tenth century, as recent archaeological analysis suggests, this little seal would be the oldest extrabiblical
reference to the existence of the state of Israel of the tenth century BCE.
(Photo: Erich Lessing / Art Resource, N.Y.)

begins or his *length of reign*: "He [Abijam] reigned
for three years in Jerusalem" (15:2). Third, we have
the king's mother's name, although this is listed
only for the kings of Judah: "His mother's name
was Maacah daughter of Abishalom" (15:2). This
much so far is introductory.

The fourth component of the literary formula is
an *evaluation sentence* of the king's performance as to
whether he kept Yahweh's covenant and was faithful
to the law: "He [Abijam] committed all the sins that
his father did before him; his heart was not true to
Yahweh his God, like the heart of his father David"
(15:3). The fifth element is the citation to one of the
original resources available to the authors of 1–2
Kings, offering more information about the king in
question: "The rest of the acts of Abijam, and all that
he did, are they not written in the Book of the Annals
of the Kings of Judah?" (15:7). Sixth, there follows a

death announcement: "Abijam slept with his ances-
tors, and they buried him in the city of David" (15:8).
And finally, we have a note on the king's successor:
"Then his son Asa succeeded him" (15:8).

This formula is flexible. Editors of 1–2 Kings
could interrupt the list, after either the introductory or evaluation sentences, to provide more detail
about a particular king's reign. At times, these
inclusions are quite extensive, such as the insertions of the Elijah cycle into the story of King
Ahab (1 Kings 17–19 and 21; 2 Kings 1–2), and the
Elisha cycle into the accounts of several northern kings (Ahaziah, Jehoram, Jehu, and Jehoahaz;
2 Kings 2–9 and 13). Such inclusions show that
1–2 Kings is about more than the events of Israel's
and Judah's history. The books have a prophetic
and essentially religious agenda. The miracles and
messages of Elijah and Elisha are as important if
not more so than the building activities and wars
of powerful kings. And thus the kings are evaluated on their devotion to Yahweh as guided by the
prophets.[2]

The evaluation sentences for the kings of northern Israel accumulate in an increasingly negative
manner as one progresses through 1–2 Kings, since
nearly all "did what was evil in the sight of Yahweh,
walking in the way of Jeroboam and in the sin that
he caused Israel to commit." This besetting sin culminates in the fall of Israel to the Assyrians, when
Yahweh "removed Israel out of his sight" and the
ten tribes of the northern king went into exile (2
Kings 17:22–23). The city of Samaria, the last of
a series of northern capitals, and the land of the
northern kingdom were repopulated with people

---

2 This also helps explain why the books are considered
"Former Prophets" in the Jewish canon (Chapter 2).

SIDEBAR 14.3. THE ROLE OF JOSIAH IN ISRAEL'S HISTORY AND IN OLD TESTAMENT LITERATURE

One of the best rulers of either the northern or southern kingdom was King Josiah of Judah (640–609 BCE). He was inspired by a newly discovered copy of "the book of the law" (*sēper hattôrâ*) found by his high priest (2 Kings 22–23), which was most likely an early version of the book of Deuteronomy. Motivated by what he learned in the book, Josiah set out to reform Judah's religious practices. One edition of the Deuteronomistic History (the so-called Josianic edition) most certainly found hope in Josiah's prospects. He appeared able to turn things around and lead Judah in a great period of restoration and religious reform. When he was killed in battle unexpectedly, his reforms ended, and with them, the hopes of the authors of the Deuteronomistic History.

It seems likely King Josiah intentionally sought to become the "anointed one" (or messiah) of a restored united kingdom of Israel.* While his failure on the battlefield ended his dream of reuniting northern Israel and southern Judah, it apparently gave birth to other dreams carried forward by the authors and editors of the OT. A great variety of books and passages of the OT reflect this Josianic model for a restored Davidic monarchy with Jerusalem as its center: Hosea, Amos, Micah, Isaiah 1–39, Jeremiah, Nahum, Habakkuk, Zephaniah, and especially the Deuteronomistic History.

* For more on this, see Sweeney in the commentaries in "Where to Find More" in this chapter.

---

from a variety of areas, who combined the worship of Yahweh with the religions of other gods (17:24–41).

The Kingdom of Judah Alone (2 Kings 18–25)

The remainder of the books of Kings relates the account of the southern kingdom of Judah alone, after the fall of Israel to the Assyrians. Unlike its northern neighbor, Judah has a few kings who are evaluated positively, reaching back as far as Asa, who "did what was right in the sight of Yahweh, as his father David had done" (1 Kings 15:11). Similar assessments are recorded for Jehoshaphat (1 Kings 22:43), Jehoash (2 Kings 12:2), Amaziah (2 Kings 14:3), Azariah (also known as Uzziah; 2 Kings 15:3), and Jotham (2 Kings 15:34). Yet even these good kings failed to remove the "high places" for sacrificial worship outside Jerusalem (2 Kings 15:35). In

this regard, the kings Hezekiah and Josiah receive a special place in the evaluation of the books of Kings, for they succeeded in removing the detestable "high places" (2 Kings 18:4–6 and 23:19).

Nevertheless, eventually Judah could not overcome the sins of certain bad kings, and especially highlighted in this category is Manasseh (2 Kings 24:3–4). Nebuchadnezzar and the Babylonian army came at Yahweh's bidding to remove Judah from his sight, as he had had Israel removed before. Jerusalem was captured, the temple destroyed, and the people carried off into exile, leaving only the poorest to remain on the land as farmers (2 Kings 25:11–12). The long line of Davidic kings ruling God's people from Jerusalem came to an end. But the concluding paragraph hints that this is not yet the end of our story, since the former king, Jehoiachin, survives in Babylonian exile (25:27–30).

What Really Happened?

Reconstructing the histories of Israel and Judah is not an easy task. To the usual evidence of text and tell, we now add occasional information from the empires of Assyria and Babylonia. These empires frequently came into contact with political entities in the Levant, often leaving textual references to Israel or Judah, and at times even iconographic (i.e., pictoral) evidence. It is rare to have a single historical event attested in more than one or two sources. But occasionally we have biblical, archaeological, and textual materials illuminating the same event. While these do not always make it possible to reconstruct precisely the details of an event, the different depictions of it give us a certain depth of perception and greater understanding. For example, Nebuchadnezzar's capture of the city of Jerusalem in 597 BCE is attested in the Babylonian Chronicles, making it possible to reconstruct the events in some detail.

From an earlier period, Assyrian king Sennacherib's campaign in 701 BCE against Jerusalem and other localities in the Levant is attested in multiple sources. We have the biblical account in 2 Kings 18:13–19:37 (with parallels in 2 Chronicles 32 and Isaiah 36–37). This is corroborated by archaeological evidence from an important city of Judah, Lachish, which uncovered Sennacherib's siege ramp as well as artifacts like armor and weaponry illuminating the siege (find Lachish on Map 14.1). In addition, we have the sculptured reliefs from Sennacherib's palace at Nineveh, showing the Lachish siege in all its gory detail (see Plate IX), including images of captured Israelites impaled on stakes near the city walls, and others stripped and flayed.[3] The OT is clear that the

3 For more on these impressive reliefs, see John Malcolm Russell, *Sennacherib's Palace without Rival at Nineveh* (Chicago: University of Chicago Press, 1991), 200–205.

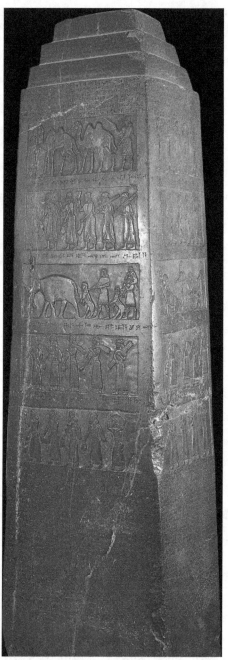

14.2. The Black Obelisk of Shalmaneser III of Assyria (858–824 BCE). Six and a half feet tall, this black limestone obelisk from ancient Kalhu, a capital of Assyria, was erected in 825 BCE, with panels of relief sculptures glorifying the achievements of the Assyrian king during thirty-one years of military campaigns. One of its panels shows Israel's King Jehu bowing before Shalmaneser (see Plate XI and discussion in Sidebar 14.5). (Photo: © The Trustees of the British Museum / Art Resource, N.Y.)

SIDEBAR 14.4. EXCERPT FROM THE BABYLONIAN CHRONICLES

The Babylonian king Nebuchadnezzar led his army against the city of Jerusalem in 597 BCE, seizing Judah's king, Jehoiachin, and appointing Zedekiah as his replacement (2 Kings 24:10–17; 2 Chronicles 36:9–10; Jeremiah 22:24–30, 24:1; Ezekiel 17:12). This excerpt is adapted from one of the Babylonian Chronicles (number 5), which covers events from the early years of Nebuchadnezzar II (605–595 BCE). The end of the chronicle is poorly preserved. It appears to record more military campaigns in the west by the Babylonian army, and we may assume that it likely recorded the Babylonian destruction of Jerusalem in 586 BCE. What we have here makes it possible to date tentatively this particular siege of the "city of Judah" (Jerusalem), beginning in late November or early December 598 BCE, and ending in the fall of the city on the second day of the month Adad, which would have been March 15 or 16, 597 BCE.

> In the month of Kislev [November/December 598 BCE], the king of Akkad [Nebuchadnezzar of Babylon] called up his armed forces and went to the land of Hatti [to the Levant]. He encamped against the city of Judah [Jerusalem]. On the second day of the month of Adar [March 15/16, 597 BCE], he captured the city and defeated its king [Jehoiachin]. He appointed a king of his own choosing in it [Zedekiah]. Nebuchadnezzar took away Jerusalem's heavy tribute and brought it back to Babylon.*

* Adapted from Bill T. Arnold, "The Neo-Babylonian Chronicle Series," page 417, in Chavalas in "Where to Find More" in this chapter.

city of Jerusalem itself did not fall to the Assyrians in 701 BCE, suggested also by Sennacherib's Prism Inscription claiming only to have confined King Hezekiah inside Jerusalem "like a caged bird."[4] All of this corroborating evidence makes the campaign of the Assyrian King Sennacherib in Judah one of the best attested events in ancient Near Eastern history.

Still, there are whole stretches of history during these centuries from Solomon to Jehoiachin that we cannot know much about. And this is true, of course, because the OT is not *primarily* interested in those historical details. As we have seen, even the OT's so-called historical books are focused

14.3. Execution of Israelite prisoners of war at Lachish. This image of Assyrian soldiers empaling Israelite prisoners after conquering Lachish in 701 BCE is one portion of a larger sculpture relief from the palace of Sennacherib in Nineveh. See also Plate IX. (Photo: Erich Lessing / Art Resource, N.Y.)

on whether this king or that judge was faithful to Yahweh. At times, we have surprisingly little information about an otherwise important king's political or military activities.

4 For more on Sennacherib's Prism Inscription, see Sarah C. Melville in Chavalas in "Where to Find More" in this chapter.

The showcase example of what I mean is the OT's coverage of King Omri, a ruler of northern Israel. Omri's reign (873–869 BCE) is summarized in a mere six verses (1 Kings 16:23–28). From these verses we learn only that he acquired the city of Samaria and built it as a new capital for the northern kingdom (v. 24). We also know from the preceding paragraphs that Omri somehow managed to seize power during a time of turmoil and uncertainty, and that he unified the northern kingdom (vv. 15–22). Other than the standard introductory and concluding statements, we know nothing else from the biblical account.

But evidence from elsewhere suggests that King Omri was far more significant politically than this. Archaeological evidence confirms that what had previously been a simple family estate was transformed by Omri and his successors into a cosmopolitan royal city, complete with fortification walls, a palace, and other public buildings.[5] Excavations at Hazor and Megiddo suggest that the reigns of Omri and his successors were a time of economic prosperity and expansion. In addition, King Omri is mentioned in extrabiblical inscriptions. The identification of King Jehu as "son of Omri" in the Black Obelisk reflects the Assyrian impression that Omri was the founder of the nation Israel. Similarly, in the inscription of the **Moabite Stone**, King Mesha of Moab considers a long period of time in which Omri "oppressed" Moab, occupying a portion of Moab's territory (Sidebar 15.3). All of this suggests that Omri was an energetic ruler who came to power amid civil strife; built an impressive

new capital; expanded the borders of his kingdom, demanding the attention of the Assyrians in Mesopotamia and the Moabites in the Transjordan; and established a dynasty in northern Israel, even if short-lived.

The authors of Kings were not much interested in Omri's royal activities, impressive as they seem. They were much more interested in Omri's son, Ahab, who is identified as the one who compromised the worship of Yahweh. Partly under the influence of Ahab's Phoenician wife, Queen Jezebel (echoing Solomon's problems), Ahab promoted a syncretistic worship of Canaanite Baal alongside Yahweh. This heresy was the real interest of our authors! So while Omri's reign takes up a mere six verses, the authors of 1–2 Kings break open Ahab's literary frame after its evaluation sentence (1 Kings 16:30) and insert an expansive narrative devoted to this theological conflict. Israel must necessarily choose between those who worship Yahweh alone (the path urged by the prophet Elijah) and those who attempt to worship Yahweh and Baal together (1 Kings 17–22; concluding sentences of Ahab's framing formula are not picked up until 22:39–40). Historically, Omri was one of Israel's greatest kings. But because he was the father of Ahab, and married his son to the Phoenician princess Jezebel, he is discounted quickly as just another king who "did what was evil in the sight of Yahweh" and who did even "more evil than all who were before him" (1 Kings 16:25).

The books of Kings present a broad general outline of a history of Israel and Judah. But as before, we are left with the delicate task of sifting through archaeological evidence, and now extrabiblical evidence, especially from Assyria and Babylonia, in

5 See page 124 of Grabbe in "Where to Find More" in Chapter 11.

SIDEBAR 14.5. THE BLACK OBELISK

The Black Obelisk is an impressive Assyrian royal stela carved on black limestone (see Figure 14.2 and Plate XI). It has a text of 190 lines inscribed around the obelisk and five panels of relief artwork, depicting scenes of conquered subjects presenting tribute to King Shalmaneser III of Assyria (858–824 BCE). Set up in the Assyrian city of Nimrud (ancient Kalhu), the stela's text glorifies the achievements of the Assyrian king, relating his military activities until his thirty-third year (826 BCE; so we presume it was erected around 825). Above and below the five panels of reliefs are Akkadian captions, although these do not necessarily correspond in every case with the images.

Above the second panel on one side is a caption mentioning "Jehu son of Omri" (Akkadian *Iaua mār Ḫumri*). The image in all probability portrays Israel's King Jehu on his knees, submitting to the Assyrian king (see Plate XI). The caption in full reads as follows.

> *I received the tribute of Jehu, the son of Omri: silver (items), gold (items), a gold bowl, a gold goblet, gold cups, gold buckets, tin (items), a staff of the king's hand, spears.*[*]

The irony, of course, is that Jehu was certainly not a "son of Omri" but a usurper who attempted to wipe out Omri's line (2 Kings 9–10). But from the Assyrian perspective in the eastern Fertile Crescent, certain kingdoms in the west were known by the names of their founders. King Omri was a prominent ruler of the northern kingdom, so that "son of Omri" implies simply that Jehu is an Israelite.

[*] For more on the translation, see Brent A. Strawn, "Black Obelisk," page 291–93 in Chavalas in "Where to Find More" in this chapter.

---

order to reconstruct the history as best we can. Portions of that history are illuminated brilliantly, while others remain somewhat obscure because of the theological agenda of the authors of 1–2 Kings.

Religious Expression Embedded in the Account of Israel's Monarchy

The books of Kings portray a gradual degeneration from Solomon's worship of Yahweh in the new temple to religious apostasy sponsored by later kings of Israel and Judah. One is orthodox and acceptable to Yahweh, leading to blessing and life. The other is contemptible and leads only to death. In this section, we will first consider Solomon's speeches as an example of Israel's acceptable orthodoxy from

the official position of the OT authors, and then explore how 1–2 Kings describe the heresy that resulted in the fall of both kingdoms.

Solomon's Speeches and Prayers at the Dedication of the Temple (1 Kings 8)

At the dedication of the temple, Solomon conveys in exquisite language some of the most beautiful expressions of OT faith. At a national convocation before the new temple, Solomon gives four speeches: first, a dedication of the new building as a place for Yahweh's eternal dwelling (1 Kings 8:12–13); second, a blessing of Israel in which Solomon emphasizes Yahweh's faithfulness to David as seen now in this new temple (8:14–21);

third, a prayer acknowledging Yahweh's incomparability and listing a series of petitions (8:22–53); and finally, another blessing of Israel in which God's promises to Moses and the ancestors are highlighted (8:54–61). These prayers and blessings are carefully phrased by the authors and editors of the books of Kings to teach approved Israelite doctrines about Yahweh (and are often considered Deuteronomistic in origin).

We cannot agree on the specific date for the composition of these addresses. But at least two themes make an exilic or postexilic date nearly impossible for the chapter, at least for its broad outlines. First, the narrator's references to the poles of the ark being visible "to this day" imply that the temple was still standing at the time of the writing of this text (v. 8; hence prior to 586 BCE). Second, Solomon's emphasis on the continued line of David on the throne makes little sense if written after the Davidic kings no longer ruled Jerusalem (v. 25).[6] The location of these speeches here, at the center and height of Solomon's power and accomplishments, represents the best of Israel's theology. Since they appear to be preexilic, these addresses provide great insight into the official understanding of Yahweh prior to the fall of Jerusalem in 586 BCE.

Yahweh is now officially "the God of Israel" (8:15). While not yet an explicit statement of monotheism, this name for God recognizes Yahweh as the unifying single deity of all the tribes of Israel, prohibits any syncretisms with Baal or other deities, and relates to the universalism of Yahweh as taught by the

eighth-century prophets (see Chapters 19 and 20). Yet the point of "God of Israel" in Solomon's first blessing is the faithfulness of Yahweh in fulfilling his promises to David by providing this newly constructed temple, a place for the ark and its precious covenant.

Solomon's prayer is especially helpful in understanding 1–2 Kings' officially approved theology (1 Kings 8:22–53). Solomon begins with an explicit statement of monolatry (review Chapter 1 for definitions), acknowledging that Yahweh, "God of Israel," is one of a kind; there is no god like him in heaven or earth (v. 23). Yahweh's uniqueness can be seen in his covenant-making and covenant-keeping character. What he promises with his mouth he accomplishes with his hands (v. 24). Yahweh is not contained or confined in a physical location, even in such a magnificent temple as Solomon's, but he hears the prayers of his faithful servants (vv. 27–30). He has the power to reverse misfortune, whether plague, famine, or enemy assault, answering the plea of his people (vv. 37–39). In the future, if Yahweh's people sin and lose the land, he is able to bless them in captivity and give them compassion in the eyes of their captors (vv. 46–51).

Solomon's final blessing contains a rare statement of practical and exclusive monotheism, reminiscent of Deuteronomy (Chapter 9). Solomon's desire is for all peoples of the earth to learn what Israel confesses, that Yahweh is God, and "there is no other" (v. 60). While few other kings after Solomon grasped so much, the righteous King Hezekiah also acknowledges that "Yahweh, the God of Israel" alone is God (2 Kings 19:15). Such orthodoxy disappears as we progress through 1–2 Kings, and its recurrence with Hezekiah only emphasizes

---

6 For more on this, and for the idea that the chapter was at least edited from a Josianic and Hezekian perspective, see page 130 in Sweeney in "Where to Find More" in this chapter.

the depth and severity of the heresy described else-where in the kingdoms of Israel and Judah.

The Blame Game: Whose Fault Is It?

The authors of the books of Kings have a dilemma. They believe Yahweh is faithful to his covenant. On the other hand, the political real-ities "on the ground" (so to speak) require an explanation. Both Israel and Judah fell to interna-tional powers from Mesopotamia, and Jerusalem was destroyed along with its Yahweh temple. The authors of 1–2 Kings cannot blame Yahweh. Who is at fault? They have an answer, and so they set out to explain the loss of the Hebrew kingdoms, first Israel to the Assyrians and then Judah to the Babylonians.

As we have said, the books of Kings systemati-cally assess each of Israel's and Judah's kings based on whether they are like Jeroboam I or David. In this way, they offer an explanation of what went wrong. We'll start with the northern kingdom, Israel. The culprit here was Jeroboam I, who estab-lished worship sites at Dan and Bethel to compete with the Jerusalem temple, placing golden calves in the Israelite cities for his people to worship (1 Kings 12:28–29). In the ancient world, deities were often perceived as standing on an animal. These calves were not likely intended as actual depictions of Yahweh but as supports for his invisible pres-ence. They were symbols of his presence in a way similar to the ark of the covenant in Jerusalem, where Yahweh was perceived as sitting enthroned between the cherubim.

But the authors of 1–2 Kings did not recog-nize such subtle distinctions. They condemned Jeroboam's golden calves as idols, breaking the First Commandment, and thought of them as equivalent to Israel's sinful worship of Aaron's golden calf in the desert (Exodus 32:1–6). This was idolatry's slippery slope, and Jeroboam is the guilty party. When Samaria fell to the Assyrians and Israel was sent into exile, it was Jeroboam who was to blame.

> *The people of Israel continued in all the sins that Jeroboam committed; they did not depart from them until Yahweh removed Israel out of his sight, as he had fore-told through all his servants the prophets. So Israel was exiled from their own land to Assyria until this day. (2 Kings 17:22–23)*

For the authors of 1–2 Kings, Israel's foundational heresy is located in the "sin of Jeroboam," which was perpetuated from father to son until the king-dom was lost.

Along the journey through time from Jeroboam I to Hoshea, things only got worse. Omri's son Ahab took deviant worship practices to a new level. After the standard evaluation sentence in which it is said Ahab "did evil in the sight of Yahweh," the authors of Kings give more detail.

> *And as if it had been a light thing for him to walk in the sins of Jeroboam son of Nebat, Ahab took as his wife Jezebel daughter of King Ethbaal of the Sidonians, and went and served Baal, and worshiped him. He erected an altar for Baal in the house of Baal, which he built in Samaria. Ahab also made a sacred pole [asherah]. Ahab did more to provoke the anger of Yahweh, the God of Israel, than had all the kings of Israel who were before him. (1 Kings 16:31–33)*

Later, King Jehu gave the order to destroy "the pillar of Baal" (*maṣṣēbat habbāʿal*; 2 Kings 10:27) in the temple, which leads us to conclude that the Baal temple in Samaria had the three traditional elements of worship: altar, stone stela, and sacred tree. Baal was the god of storm and lightning, rider of the clouds, and provider of fertility for the soil. He was prevalent throughout the Levant, and sometimes depicted materially in the form of a standing stone (see Figures 5.4 and 10.3). This takes idolatry to the next level because the deity is not *invisibly* represented as resting on a throne or calf but is thought to be *physically* present in the stone. Asherah is the Mother Goddess, sometimes wife of Canaanite El, and is usually associated with sacred trees or poles.[7] The word "asherah" in Hebrew is sometimes the name of the goddess, but in the context of Ahab's activities, it is a noun for the sacred wooden pole, as in the preceding translation.

These references in 1–2 Kings to the gradually degenerating religion(s) of the northern kingdom are confirmed by the picture emerging from archaeological and inscriptional evidence of Israelite practices during the ninth to seventh centuries BCE. Many Israelites worshipped Yahweh as the primary deity, but they also worshipped alongside him Asherah as his female consort, or Baal in the standing stones.[8] The conflict between Yahweh and Baal reflected in the books of Kings is a struggle for divine supremacy; namely, Who will be chief deity in Israel, Baal or Yahweh?

7 Certain archaeological evidence suggests that some Israelites worshipped her as the consort of Yahweh.
8 For more on this, see pages 648–58 in Zevit in "Where to Find More" in Chapter 10.

The authors of 1–2 Kings included the prophetic narrative cycles of Elijah and Elisha to combat such syncretism and to refute the idea that Israel could worship both. The motto of their ministries was "How long will you go limping with two different opinions? If Yahweh is God, follow him; but if Baal, then follow him" (1 Kings 18:21). Elijah's victory at Mount Carmel resulted in a new confession of Israelite monolatry (18:39): "Yahweh indeed is God; Yahweh indeed is God." This is a theological victory. And combined with the military coup of King Jehu, it brought the Omri dynasty to an end and settled the crisis between the worship of Yahweh versus the worship of Baal: "Thus Jehu wiped out Baal from Israel" (2 Kings 10:28). The message of the prophets – namely, exclusive loyalty to Yahweh alone – was the answer and could have saved the nation. But even after Jehu, the besetting sin of Jeroboam I continued to have its devasting effects, until the Assyrians marched into northern Israel as Yahweh's agent of punishment.

The story for the southern kingdom, Judah, isn't much better. Judah had intermittent good kings and bad kings, although most were bad. In the figure of King Manasseh (687–642 BCE), the authors found the culmination of all that was evil in Judah's monarchy (2 Kings 21:1–16). He promoted the worship of Baal and Asherah as King Ahab of the northern kingdom had done (v. 3). Manasseh followed a Mesopotamian practice by adopting the worship of the stars of heaven (vv. 3 and 5). He led Israel into crimes that were even worse than those committed by the nations Yahweh drove out of Canaan to give it to the Israelites (vv. 2 and 11). He practiced

TABLE 14.1. CHRONOLOGY FOR THE KINGS OF ISRAEL AND JUDAH (DATES FOR SAUL, DAVID, AND SOLOMON ARE APPROXIMATE; ALL DATES ARE BCE)*

Saul, 1020–1000
David, 1000–961
Solomon, 961–922

Kings of Israel	Kings of Judah
Jeroboam I, 922–901	Rehoboam, 922–915
Nadab, 901–900	Abijam, 915–913
Baasha, 900–877	Asa, 913–873
Elah, 877–876	
Zimri, 876	
Tibni, 876–873	
Omri, 873–869	Jehoshaphat, 873–849
Ahab, 869–850	
Ahaziah, 850–849	Jehoram, 849–842
Jehoram, 849–842	Ahaziah, 842
Jehu, 842–815	Athaliah, 842–837
Jehoahaz, 815–801	Jehoash, 837–801
Joash, 801–786	Amaziah, 800–783
Jeroboam II, 786–746	Uzziah/Azariah, 783–742
Zechariah, 746–745	Jotham, 750–742
Shallum, 745	
Menahem, 745–738	
Pekahiah, 738–737	
Pekah, 737–732	Ahaz, 735–715
Hoshea, 732–724	
	Hezekiah, 715–686
	Manasseh, 687–642
	Amon, 642–640
	Josiah, 640–609
	Jehoahaz, 609
	Jehoiakim, 609–598
	Jehoiachin, 598
	Zedekiah, 597–586

* *Note*: Several other chronological schema are possible; for justification of the one presented here, see Hayim Tadmor, "The Chronology of the First Temple Period: A Presentation and Evaluation of the Sources," in J. Alberto Soggin, *An Introduction to the History of Israel and Judah* (2nd ed.; Valley Forge, Pa.: Trinity Press International, 1993), appendix 2, 394–417.

various sorts of forbidden magic, and most appallingly, he appears to have practiced human sacrifice (although the meaning of "pass through the fire" is uncertain; v. 6). This was simply too much to overcome! Eventually, the authors of 1–2 Kings place the blame for the fall of Jerusalem at Manasseh's feet (2 Kings 24:1–4). His crimes are the culmination of all that is wrong in Judah's monarchy and are well deserving of Yahweh's punishment.

The books of Kings have these two pictures: young Solomon, on the one hand, and the deviations of Jeroboam, Ahab, and Manasseh, on the other. Israel's religious extremes are both here, from the Deuteronomistic ideal of the righteous king, who promotes and defends the worship of

Yahweh, to the compromises of Jeroboam I, resulting in the further heresies of Ahab and Manasseh. And yet even Solomon is not really a righteous king, at least not in the mold of David, because Solomon fails to live up to his own articulation of the service of Yahweh; he allows his heart to follow other gods (1 Kings 11:4). In this movement from Solomon to Manasseh, the books of Kings wrap up the reasons for the fall of Israel and Judah: it was because of the religious unfaithfulness of their kings. It's a sad and tragic tale, but one that argues implicitly for maintaining and defending the worship of Yahweh as defined in the speeches and prayers of King Solomon, which is the OT's Deuteronomistic ideal.

WHERE TO FIND MORE

Commentaries: The best technical and advanced commentaries on **1–2 Kings** are Marvin A. Sweeney, *I and II Kings: A Commentary* (Old Testament Library; Louisville, Ky.: Westminster John Knox Press, 2007); Mordechai Cogan and Hayim Tadmor, *II Kings: A New Translation* (Anchor Bible 11; Garden City, N.Y.: Doubleday, 1988); Mordechai Cogan, *1 Kings: A New Translation with Introduction and Commentary* (Anchor Bible 10; New York: Doubleday, 2001). See also Walter Brueggemann, *1 and 2 Kings* (Smyth and Helwys Bible Commentary; Macon, Ga.: Smyth & Helwys, 2000), and Iain W. Provan, *1 and 2 Kings* (New International Biblical Commentary: Old Testament; Peabody, Mass./Carlisle, Cumbria: Hendrickson Publishers/Paternoster, 1995).

Beckman, Gary M., and Theodore J. Lewis, eds. *Text, Artifact, and Image: Revealing Ancient Israelite Religion* (Brown Judaic Studies 346; Providence, R.I.: Brown Judaic Studies, 2006).

Contains several chapters on these topics; see especially Mark S. Smith on the perceptions of deity at Ugarit and Israel (pp. 38–63), Elizabeth Block-Smith on the significance of standing stones (pp. 64–79), Ziony Zevit on the role of kings in Israel and Judah in the religious cult (pp. 189–200), and Nili S. Fox on the question of monotheism in Israel (pp. 326–45).

Chavalas, Mark W., ed. *The Ancient Near East: Historical Sources in Translation* (Malden, Mass.: Blackwell, 2006).

Provides helpful translations and dicussions of the Assyrian and Babylonian texts related to the reconstruction of the histories of Israel and Judah. See especially Brent A. Strawn on the Black Obelisk (pp. 291–93), Sarah C. Melville on Sennacherib's Prism Inscription (pp. 345–49), and Bill T. Arnold on the Babylonian Chronicles (pp. 407–26).

Cogan, Mordechai. *The Raging Torrent: Historical Inscriptions from Assyria and Babylonia Relating to Ancient Israel.* Jerusalem: Carta, 2008.

Helpful translation and discussion of the Assyrian and Babylonian resources used in the reconstruction of the history of Israel and Judah.

Hayes, John Haralson, and Paul K. Hooker. *A New Chronology for the Kings of Israel and Judah and Its Implications for Biblical History and Literature.* Atlanta, Ga.: John Knox Press, 1988.

Sweeney, Marvin A. *King Josiah of Judah: The Lost Messiah of Israel.* Oxford: Oxford University Press, 2001.

CHAPTER 15

History Revisited

OLD TESTAMENT READING: 1 AND 2 CHRONICLES AND EZRA-NEHEMIAH

In addition to the OT's Primary History, we have a Chronistic History comprised of 1–2 Chronicles and Ezra-Nehemiah. The two histories contain some of the same materials. We will see that the Chronistic History, however, includes events of the postexilic community down to the late fifth century BCE. With the Persian Empire as the background, we will note also a different perspective, characterized by different themes, stylistic devices, portions written in Aramaic, and particular emphases on the Davidic dynasty and Israel's religious practices associated with Jerusalem.

Chronicles and Ezra-Nehemiah are sequenced differently in various canons, indicating independent collections, but we will see that they are linked literarily by the edict of King Cyrus. This historical event marked the return of Israelite exiles from Babylon to Jerusalem, now part of the Persian province Yehud, and the subsequent restoration and rebuilding of a community. Indeed, these books are significant in the OT for the way in which they confirm the postexilic community as the legitimate successor of preexilic Israel.

Israel's library to this point combines early writings of history in a comprehensive "Primary History," tracing events from the creation of the universe to the fall of Jerusalem (Chapter 4). Now we come to the last OT historical books, which were written in a later period of Israel's history. These are the books 1–2 Chronicles, Ezra, and Nehemiah. In the Christian canon, Ezra and Nehemiah are listed as two separate books (Chapter 2). For reasons we'll cover later, I will refer to them together as one volume, Ezra-Nehemiah.

Like the Primary History, the books of 1–2 Chronicles relate events from the first human, Adam, to the destruction of Jerusalem, but present

---

SIDEBAR 15.1. WHERE IS THE BOOK OF ESTHER?

You are probably wondering why I'm not including the book of Esther in this chapter. If you're using a standard Christian translation of the OT, you will see that Esther comes immediately after Ezra-Nehemiah in the Protestant canon, and only three books afterward in the Catholic canon (review Figure 2.3 and Sidebar 12.1). The Christian canonical lists group Esther together with Ezra-Nehemiah among the last of the OT historical books. So why have we reserved it for Chapter 23?

In the Jewish canon, Esther is among the "scrolls" (Hebrew *megillôt*), that also includes Ruth, Song of Songs, Lamentations, and Ecclesiastes. The Jewish canon lists these together because of their relatively small size and their use in the synagogues at specific times in the liturgical calendar. Their location elsewhere in the standard Christian Bible (following the Septuagint and Vulgate) has perfectly reasonable historical and literary rationales. There is no right or wrong order for these books, but I am treating them all together in Chapter 23 for convenience.

---

them from a different perspective and for a later generation of readers. Ezra-Nehemiah continues that story beyond the fall of Jerusalem in order to cover the restoration of God's people in the post-exilic period. The community living in and around Jerusalem during the Persian period was smaller and less powerful than Israel's United Monarchy. These last historical books set out to confirm the Persian-period community as the legitimate successor to preexilic Israel.

A New History for Postexilic Times

The books of 1–2 Chronicles and Ezra-Nehemiah taken together may be called the **Chronistic History**. I don't mean by this title that they were written together by the same author at the same time, or even that they have the same themes. We will see that we cannot be quite so confident about the way these books were written. I simply mean that taken together these books offer an updated and revised history when compared to the Primary History. The authors and editors of the Chronistic

History admired the older historical work (Genesis to 2 Kings); they did not intend to replace it but to provide an alternative perspective on the past. They believed that their readership in the postexilic community needed an up-to-date history in light of the particular circumstances in the Persian period. You might think of the Chronistic History as "a second national epic."[1]

The Chronistic History has one particular theme that sets it apart from the Primary History. It focuses on King David and his dynasty, as well as on the institutions of worship established in Jerusalem by David. These were included in the Primary History, of course, but the central focus there was the exodus from Egypt and the law of Moses. These are not mutually exclusive themes but a matter of emphasis.

The Chronistic History is obviously much smaller than the nine books of the Primary History. It has two distinct portions – the books of 1–2

---

1 For this assessment and discussion of the genre of 1–2 Chronicles, see pages 129–34 in Knoppers in the commentaries in "Where to Find More" in this chapter.

15.1. The city of David, viewed from the south, with the Old City of Jerusalem in the background. The city of David is thought to be the place where King David built his palace, established a new capital, and formalized the worship of Yahweh, the latter being a primary focus of the Chronistic History. (Photo: © Zev Radovan / The Bridgeman Art Library)

Chronicles, on the one hand, and Ezra-Nehemiah, on the other. These two share a few common literary features, such as the use of genealogies, lists, and common phrases and vocabulary. But these features are probably typical of literature from the Persian period, or at least were common among Jewish authors interested in worship of Yahweh at the Jerusalem temple. More important are the several themes and composition techniques that distinguish the parts from each other.

As you read through these books, you may have noticed several differences between 1–2 Chronicles and Ezra-Nehemiah. So, for example, the books of Chronicles read as though they were written by a single author, relying on speeches and prayers to draw comparisons between leading characters and to show the significance of events. Ezra-Nehemiah, in contrast, reads like a compilation of sources, such as correspondence to and from Persian kings, lists, the Ezra Memoirs, and the Nehemiah Memoirs. Stylistically, these are all quite different.

Another difference you may have noticed is the way these books refer to inhabitants of the territories belonging to the former northern kingdom of Israel, the northerners. Exactly how should the people who now lived in the north relate to the restoration community in Jerusalem, which includes those who had returned from exile? The books of Chronicles are conciliatory toward northerners, accepting them as true Israelites and longing for a restoration of "all Israel." But Ezra-Nehemiah is more cautious, assuming that the northerners are not true Israelites but descendants of foreigners. The vision for the people of God in the restoration community in Ezra-Nehemiah is "Judah and Jerusalem" or "Judah and Benjamin" rather than "all Israel."[2]

A third difference is in the books' reliance on prophecy. The books of Chronicles give prophecy an important role, whereas Ezra-Nehemiah give it little attention. And perhaps related to this one is a fourth difference: their relatively different theological outlook. The books of Chronicles are more comfortable with the doctrine of immediate retribution, which, as we have seen. characterizes much of the Primary History (especially the Deuteronomistic History; Chapter 9). Ezra-Nehemiah, on the other hand, considers the consequences of faith and obedience in a more nuanced way. Again, these are not mutually exclusive theologies, but relative emphases.

There may be other explanations for the differences between 1–2 Chronicles and Ezra-Nehemiah, but it seems likely they were not from the same author. This question of the authorship of the Chronistic History is not an easy one to answer. Essentially, we have three options for how these books were formed. First, the view that 1–2 Chronicles and Ezra-Nehemiah were written by the same author was the leading theory for most of the nineteenth and twentieth centuries. This approach emphasizes their literary similarities and shared objectives, assuming 1–2 Chronicles and Ezra-Nehemiah were written as a single continuous historical work. In this case, we would then refer to the "Chronicler's History," rather than a less-defined "Chronistic History."

2 See pages 24–26 in Williamson (1982) in the commentaries in "Where to Find More" in this chapter.

Second, a view gaining in popularity since the 1960s and 1970s argues that based on the linguistic evidence and the contents of the books 1–2 Chronicles and Ezra-Nehemiah were originally independent of each other. This "different authors" approach emphasizes the differences we have just considered. I hinted earlier that we should take the common literary features and phraseology as characteristic of the time and genre of these books, not of authorship. The other distinctions are too hard to ignore. The connections between the two are strongest at the editorial level, not the author level. In fact, one leading approach takes Ezra 1–6 as an editorial combination of several sources intentionally to introduce and nuance the other Ezra and Nehemiah materials, which had already been linked together, and to unite them with 1–2 Chronicles.[3]

A mediating third position assumes that 1–2 Chronicles and Ezra-Nehemiah were two independent works but were written by the same author. This minority position attempts to explain both the differences and the similarities between them. In addition to these three approaches, several readers have offered theories of multiple editors to explain the complexity of the Chronistic History, or the possibility that a Chronistic school or tradition produced these books.[4] But since 1–2 Chronicles and Ezra-Nehemiah are written anonymously, and edited together by anonymous editors, we have to be content with the uncertainty.

3 On this second view, which I favor, see the commentaries of Japhet and Williamson in "Where to Find More" in this chapter.
4 For complete discussion, see pages 72–117 in Knoppers in the commentaries in "Where to Find More" in this chapter.

What is clear is that these authors and editors wanted to comfort their readership in the restoration community in Jerusalem, and they did so by highlighting David's dynasty, the legitimacy of Yahweh worship in Jerusalem's temple, and the legitimacy of the community itself as the continuation of preexilic Israel. These authors assumed the truthfulness of Israel's older historical works, now collected and preserved in the OT's Primary History, Genesis to 2 Kings. The earlier historical works were their point of departure. The Chronistic History may even emulate those earlier works to some degree. As Israel's new national epic, the Chronistic History reminds the reader of Israel's grand and glorious past through the Davidic monarchy, and reassures the reader that the restoration community is, in fact, a legitimate continuation of that glorious past. For these historians, the postexilic Jewish community united around the rebuilt temple in Jerusalem during the Persian period *is* the restored community of ancient Israel.

THE BOOKS OF FIRST AND SECOND CHRONICLES AND EZRA-NEHEMIAH

The sequence of the books of Chronicles and Ezra-Nehemiah in the canon is puzzling. The Christian canons have them in the order of the stories they tell; Chronicles, with its account down to the fall of Jerusalem, followed by Ezra-Nehemiah with its account of the postexilic community. The Jewish canon has the order reversed, placing 1–2 Chronicles as the concluding books of the OT, preceded immediately by Ezra-Nehemiah. The situation is actually more complicated than this, because the sequence of 1–2 Chronicles and

Ezra-Nehemiah is not consistent in various early collections of Jewish writings.[5] Such various sequences in different canons confirms what we have been saying about 1–2 Chronicles and Ezra-Nehemiah as independent of each other originally. They appear to have been written and preserved separately before they were collected and tied to each other.

Regardless of who wrote these books or their sequence in the different canons, it is clear that their final editors wanted us to read them together. I say this because of a link between them embedded at the conclusion of 2 Chronicles and the beginning of Ezra – the edict of King Cyrus the Persian (2 Chronicles 36:22–23 and Ezra 1:1–4). This royal edict commissions the (re)building of Yahweh's temple in Jerusalem and releases the Jews from exile to build it. Such an important edict deserves repetition, serving as it does as a turning point in OT history. But the editor has also used it as a literary hinge, like a cross-reference, intentionally tying 1–2 Chronicles to Ezra-Nehemiah. The reader should think, "Oh, now that I've finished 2 Chronicles, I should start Ezra."

The use of Cyrus's decree to tie these books together creates one comprehensive history from two independent narratives. This is why we refer to 1–2 Chronicles and Ezra-Nehemiah as the Chronistic History, and why we read them together. And like other OT historiography, the Chronistic History is more than an antiquarian enterprise. It uses the stuff of the past to create homily, inviting the reader to accept the historian's views of Yahweh and his people (see Sidebar 4.1).

5 See pages 135–36 in Knoppers in the commentaries in "Where to Find More" in this chapter.

From Adam to David (1 Chronicles 1–9)

The use of genealogies quickly condenses vast periods of history, collapsing it into the barest of details from creation to the appearance of King David. After telescoping events in the book of Genesis in this way, 1 Chronicles turns immediately to the tribes of Israel (1 Chronicles 2–8). Names are selected to highlight the tribes of Levi and the Levitical priesthood, as well as that of Judah with its Davidic monarchy.

The United Monarchy (1 Chronicles 10 – 2 Chronicles 9)

The three kings of Israel's United Monarchy – Saul, David, and Solomon – become models of behavior, both negative and positive, for the rest of the books of Chronicles. The books assume the retribution theology prevalent in the Deuteronomistic History, the prophets, and elsewhere in the OT: faithfulness to Yahweh results in blessing, while neglect of, or deviation from, the worship of Yahweh results in curse. For these three kings, the key is whether they support the legitimate worship of Yahweh at the Jerusalem temple, and specifically whether they devote themselves to "seeking Yahweh" (i.e., consulting him or asking him for guidance).

Saul's reign is summarized briefly because the king was unfaithful to Yahweh, and "did not seek guidance from Yahweh" (1 Chronicles 10:13–14). In this way, King Saul becomes a prototype of the exilic situation for the books of Chronicles. Saul represents the pattern of unfaithfulness that recurs throughout Israel's history and is therefore

---

SIDEBAR 15.2. DAVID, SOLOMON, AND THE CITY OF ZION

David's capture of "the stronghold of Zion, now the city of David" (1 Chronicles 11:5) is retold in the books of Chronicles, along with an account of David's residence in the new capital, the placement of the ark of the covenant there, and of course, Solomon's building of the temple. The images of king and city – David/Solomon and Jerusalem/Zion – are forever linked and are among the most powerful in ancient Israel's worldview. These historical events lead to one of the most enduring convictions of Israelite thinking, sometimes today known as "**Zion theology**."

Expressed in a variety of ways in the OT, this theology makes three assumptions. First, Yahweh is the Great King, sovereign over all nations. Second, David and his descendants are human representatives on earth of the Great King. The Davidic ruler was considered the son of Yahweh. And third, Yahweh has chosen Jerusalem/Zion as his earthly dwelling place. These themes are particularly prevalent in certain psalms, and they even became the obsession of overzealous opponents of Jeremiah. We will have an opportunity to return to this topic later.

---

an example not to follow.[6] His unfaithfulness leads to his exile.

On the other hand, King David becomes a prototype of restoration. The authors include much more here than we have in 1–2 Samuel, giving in great detail David's preparations for building the temple (1 Chronicles 21–29). And the account of Solomon's reign includes more than 1 Kings on the religious institutions supporting the worship of Yahweh at the temple (2 Chronicles 3–4). Another expansion is Yahweh's night appearance to Solomon in which he assures the king that he has heard his prayer (2 Chronicles 7:12–22). The parallel text in 1 Kings 9 does not include the familiar words of 2 Chronicles 7:13–14, which are key verses for 1–2 Chronicles.

When I shut up the heavens so that there is no rain, or command the locust to devour the land, or send

6 For more on the two prototypes, see pages 92–95 and 225–26 in Williamson (1982) in the commentaries in "Where to Find More" in this chapter.

pestilence among my people, if my people who are called by my name humble themselves, pray, seek my face, and turn from their wicked ways, then I will hear from heaven, and will forgive their sin and heal their land. (2 Chronicles 7:13–14)

This system of humble repentance and forgiveness confirms the prototype of salvation and restoration. Saul represents the exilic situation (prototype of unfaithfulness), which too often finds parallels in the history of Israel. David and Solomon represent the pattern for restoration from exile, which Israel must follow in order to become once again the people of God in the postexilic community.

The Davidic Dynasty (2 Chronicles 10–36)

Kings of the southern kingdom are covered in rapid succession in 2 Chronicles. The Jerusalem temple, supported by the Davidic monarchy, was the real "Israel" in the books of Chronicles. The north is mentioned only when it relates to this

SIDEBAR 15.3. THE EVIDENCE OF THE MOABITE STONE

15.2. Victory Stela of Mesha, King of Moab. Mesha set up this stela, over four feet tall, around 830 BCE, to commemorate the construction of a sanctuary and to express gratitude to Chemosh, the god of Moab, for victories over Israel.(Photo: Erich Lessing / Art Resource, N.Y.)

The Aramaic inscription from Tel Dan dated to the ninth century BCE changed the debate about the historicity of King David (see Sidebar 13.3). While the Tel Dan Inscription was only discovered in 1993, we have known since 1868 of another important monument from further south, at Dhiban, or biblical Dibon in ancient Moab (Numbers 21:30). This stela has no less than thirty-four lines of text written in the ancient Moabite language. The inscription commemorates the achievements of the Moabite king who commissioned the work, King Mesha, especially his successes in border disputes between Moab and Israel during the time of Israel's King Omri and his son Ahab (mid-ninth century BCE).

In a fascinating human interest story (and one considerably too complicated to tell here), the stone was shattered into many fragments sometime in the 1870s, before many of the pieces were reassembled and put on display in the Louvre in 1875.* Fortunately, just prior to this event, squeezes had been made (facsimile impressions on wetted paper) so that most of the inscription could be reconstructed. The text has many interesting connections with OT history, language, and religion, including what appears to be the oldest unequivocal use of the divine name YHWH, Yahweh, outside the OT: Mesha claims to have confiscated "the vessels of Yhwh" when he recaptured the city of Nebo from Israel (lines 17–18). The Moabite Stone yielded even further historical details after the 1993 discovery of the Tel Dan Inscription. The century-old squeezes in the Louvre were reexamined in order to reconstruct the final lines of the inscription, and after careful work, another reference to the "House of David" was found there. The reconstructed lines near the conclusion of the Moabite inscription read as follows:

Now as for the town of Hauronen, the House of David lived in it ... But [the Moabite god] Kemosh said to me, "Go down and fight against Hauronen," so I went down and [fought against the city and took it] and Kemosh returned it in my days.[†]

As you can see, the Moabite Stone has many instructive features relating to the OT, including evidence that the Moabite language had a living prose dialect in the mid-ninth century BCE, with numerous parallels to the OT's Hebrew. The inscription also gives credit to the Moabite deity, Kemosh (Chemosh in the OT; Numbers 21:20), for his benevolent guidance and protection, not unlike Israel's understanding of Yahweh.

* For more on this story, which reads like a spy novel during the Franco-Prussian War, see pages 90–91 in McCarter in "Where to Find More" in this chapter.
[†] Adapted from Brian B. Schmidt, "Moabite Stone," page 313, in Chavalas in "Where to Find More" in this chapter.

overarching interest in Yahweh's temple. Following David and Solomon in the pattern of restoration, 2 Chronicles highlights those kings who properly "sought Yahweh/God" or otherwise promoted seeking Yahweh among the people: Asa (14:4), Jehoshaphat (17:4 and 19:3), Uzziah (26:5), Hezekiah (31:21), and Josiah (34:3). Negative examples did not "seek Yahweh," which is occasionally even noted, as with Rehoboam (12:14). Ultimately, it was the failure of the kings, the leading priests, and the people that resulted in the destruction of the temple, because there "was no remedy" (36:14–16). The pattern of exile had been chosen, and the Babylonians were Yahweh's instrument of retribution (36:17).

The account of Hezekiah's Passover reflects the ideal of the authors and editors of 1–2 Chronicles. They envisioned an audience of Israelites that encompassed "all Israel," including the inhabitants of the former northern kingdom of Israel (2 Chronicles 30:1–12). The Passover was announced from Beersheba to Dan, including the northernmost tribes of Asher and Zebulun (vv. 10–1;, see Map 12.5). In a similar way, the telling of Josiah's reforms is focused on "all the land of Israel" and "the remnant of Israel" (2 Chronicles 34:7,9). The authors and editors of 1–2 Chronicles are thus inviting readers from the north to participate in the people of God, centered in the old capital of Jerusalem.

In the Deuteronomistic History, the fall of Jerusalem to the Babylonians is imagined as the result of accumulated sin that had increased gradually over the course of a line of bad kings and had culminated in one especially bad king, Manasseh. By contrast, in the books of Chronicles, each generation is responsible for its own righteousness or sin.[7] In a sense, each generation determines its own fate. As we shall see, Chronicles shares this doctrine of individual accountability with the prophets of the exilic and postexilic periods (especially Ezekiel; Chapter 20).

Initial Return from Exile and the
Rebuilding of the Temple (Ezra 1–6)

Ezra-Nehemiah was sewn together as a single composition using a number of earlier sources. We have both internal and external evidence pointing in this direction. Internally, the books assume the notion that the rebuilding work of Ezra and Nehemiah was to be taken as a unity; the work of these men was a continuous flow (Nehemiah 12:26). Externally, Jewish tradition is universal that Ezra and Nehemiah were originally one book, and that together they were to be considered as separate from other books. Jewish copies of the Bible only separated them in the Middle Ages, probably because of the Christian canon.[8]

The first six chapters of Ezra-Nehemiah combine quite an interesting array of sources, including the previously mentioned edict of King Cyrus (1:2–4) and what appears to be authentic Persian letters preserved in Aramaic. The compiler of Ezra 1–6 chose to leave these letters in Aramaic, connected by Hebrew (4:8–22, 5:6–17, and 6:3–12), showing that his readership could use both languages. This is one of two examples of bilingualism in the OT, interspersing Hebrew with Aramaic; the other of example is Daniel (Chapter 22).

After their initial return from Babylon, the Jews set up an altar, reestablish the worship of Yahweh in Jerusalem, rebuild the temple, and celebrate Passover. All these activities establish a new generation as the community of God in the Persian province of Yehud, and show continuity between the former exiles and the former ancient Israelites. It

---

7 For more on this, see pages 160–64 in Japhet (1997) in "Where to Find More" in this chapter.

8 For more on the evidence of the unity of Ezra-Nehemiah, see pages xxi–xxii in Williamson (1985) in "Where to Find More" in this chapter.

seems likely Ezra 1–6 was composed after the Ezra Memoirs (Ezra 7–10; Nehemiah 8, and perhaps 9–10) were already combined with the Nehemiah Memoirs (Nehemiah 1–7, and parts of Nehemiah 12–13). The goal was to show that the reforming work of the two men was a single event theologically, even if the men were separated by many years historically. The editor may also have been arguing for the legitimacy of the new temple in Jerusalem and at the same time arguing *against* a new temple built in Samaria at Mount Gerizim.[9]

Ezra Memoirs (Ezra 7–10)

The word "memoirs" is used somewhat loosely here since these chapters are not strictly autobiographical reminiscences of Ezra. But you will find "memoirs" used widely in the scholarship on Ezra-Nehemiah to highlight the fact that these chapters combine quite a lot of first-person and third-person accounts.

Ezra was a skilled scribe with a long and impressive genealogy (7:1–6). He led another return, a second one, of nearly two thousand Jews to Jerusalem from Babylonia. The question of mixed marriages (Ezra 9–10) was of concern to Ezra in a way hard for us to understand, especially since other OT texts have no problem with it (Joseph had an Egyptian wife [Genesis 41:45], Moses a Midianite wife [Exodus 2:21], and Boaz a Moabite wife [Ruth 4]). Yet the OT had also long acknowledged the danger of intermarrying with Canaanites, which leads almost invariably to religious apostasy (Exodus 34:11–16; Deuteronomy 7:1–4). A case can be made

that the issue for Ezra as a component of his religious reforms was not *ethnically* mixed marriages, but one of religious faithfulness.

Nehemiah Memoirs (Nehemiah 1–13)

How much of Nehemiah 1–13 was part of Nehemiah's actual "memoirs" (or his personal account of events) is difficult to say. The first seven chapters are from Nehemiah himself, but it seems likely that Nehemiah 8–9 were originally part of Ezra's memoirs, and they have been placed here by the editor for greater effect. Other parts of Nehemiah 10–13 have been collected and edited from a variety of sources. One leading theory has it that the clearest portion of the book belonging to Nehemiah's memoirs (i.e., Nehemiah 1–7) was written by Nehemiah originally in Aramaic as a report to the Persian king Artaxerxes I a year or at most two years after Nehemiah's return to Jerusalem. These chapters were subsequently revised and expanded in Hebrew.[10]

Nehemiah was cupbearer for King Artaxerxes I of Persia (465–424 BCE), a position of honor and influence. The king granted Nehemiah permission and the resources to return to Jerusalem and rebuild the city's collapsed walls. Against all odds, Nehemiah successfully completed the restoration of the city's defensive walls. Through his leadership, he overcame the opposition of people of the north who felt threatened by a rejuvenated Jerusalem and the discouragement of the small and impoverished population in and around Jerusalem. Nehemiah also instituted

9 For more on this approach, see pages xxxiii–xxxv in Williamson (1985) in "Where to Find More" in this chapter.

10 See pages xxiv–xxviii in Williamson (1985) in the commentaries in "Where to Find More" in this chapter.

reforms to develop the city's administrative infrastructure and population as a means of establishing the physical and political conditions to make Jerusalem a genuine regional capital in the Persian Empire.

The political and social reforms in Jerusalem having been completed by Nehemiah, the scribe Ezra now returns to the scene to complete the religious reforms (Nehemiah 8). The "book of the law of Moses, which Yahweh had given to Israel" was most likely an early form of our Pentateuch.[11] The Feast of Tabernacles (or Succoth, "booths") was celebrated, followed by a day of national prayer and confession. Ezra-Nehemiah closes with an account of the repopulation of Jerusalem, the provision of a list of clergy (Levites, priests, and gatekeepers) with an unbroken continuity of ordination, the dedication of the city walls, and other reforms. The overall impression of the work is that of two extraordinary men, Ezra and Nehemiah, who, at great personal sacrifice, lead God's people in establishing a new community of faith on the ruins of old Israel.

BACKGROUND OF THE CHRONISTIC HISTORY

The historical background of the Chronistic History is complicated. We need to say more here about the Persian Empire, which I mentioned briefly in the overall picture of ancient Near Eastern history (Chapter 3). Here I will offer a brief survey, along with a few other items needed for your reading of 1–2 Chronicles and Ezra-Nehemiah.

Jerusalem of the District of Yehud in the Persian Empire

The Persian Empire is also known as the Achaemenid Empire after the supposed founder of its ruling dynasty, "Achaemenes."[12] The Achaemenid dynasty ruled for more than two hundred years (550–330 BCE), creating the largest empire the world had ever seen until it was conquered by Alexander the Great of Macedon. At its peak, the Persian Empire reached as far west as Egypt and the Hellespont (where Europe and Asia meet at the Aegean Sea) and across the ancient Near East to as far east as northern India. Such an enormous area was administered by its division into provinces, called "satrapies." Each province was governed by a "satrap" (governor), who was frequently a Persian official ruling from a capital city used as an administrative center for the province.

Soon after defeating the Babylonians, the Persians established a province called "Beyond the River," lying west of the Euphrates and running westward to the Egyptian frontier. The satrapy "Beyond the River" was thus made up of the polities and peoples of the Levant. But this province was subsequently divided into districts, including Samaria governed by the local family of Sanballat, and Yehud (Aramaic for Judah) governed from Jerusalem. Such close proximity explains the suspicion between these two districts in Ezra-Nehemiah, in which the province name "Beyond the River" occurs frequently (e.g., Ezra 4:10). This also puts in perspective Nehemiah's interest in making Jerusalem a worthy administrative center for the district of Yehud.

---

11 See pages 1–2 of Freedman in "Where to Find More" at Chapter 4.

12 And named in the Greek historian, Herodotus (*Hist.* 1.125).

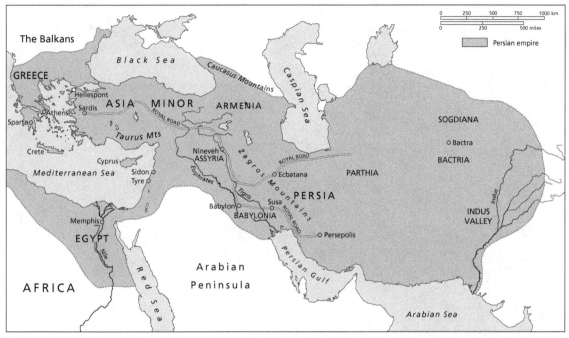

Map 15.1. Extent of the Persian Empire

It is often assumed that the Persians were religiously tolerant of subjugated peoples, and that this explains their release of the Jews from their exile in Babylonia and support of the new Yahweh temple in Jerusalem. The edict of King Cyrus may make it appear they were tolerant, but this should not be overstated. The Persian kings fostered whatever political mechanisms made it possible for the provinces to pay taxes to the central state, but they were *not* lenient about the taxes. It is more likely they simply adopted a relatively tolerant approach to governing the provinces as a practical matter. It was more effective as a means of controlling such vast territories: contented subjects were submissive subjects, or so they assumed. Regardless of their motivation, such Persian policies made it possible for the citizens of Yehud to retain their sacred laws and priestly hierarchy (evident from Ezra's freedom

to work), and to be self-governed to a limited extent. Yehud was not a reconstituted kingdom of Israel or Judah, but a Persian district centered on a religious institution in Jerusalem and permitted a certain degree of self-rule.

The Edict of King Cyrus of Persia

What do we make of the edict of King Cyrus in 2 Chronicles 36:22–23 and Ezra 1:1–4? Cyrus announces that Yahweh himself gave him the commission to build the temple in Jerusalem. In both Ezra and 2 Chronicles, the edict is introduced by a narrative claiming that Yahweh stirred up the spirit of Cyrus to make the proclamation. Remarkably, we have the words of the king himself in the Cyrus Cylinder (Sidebar 11.4), announcing the release of the citizens of Babylon from their

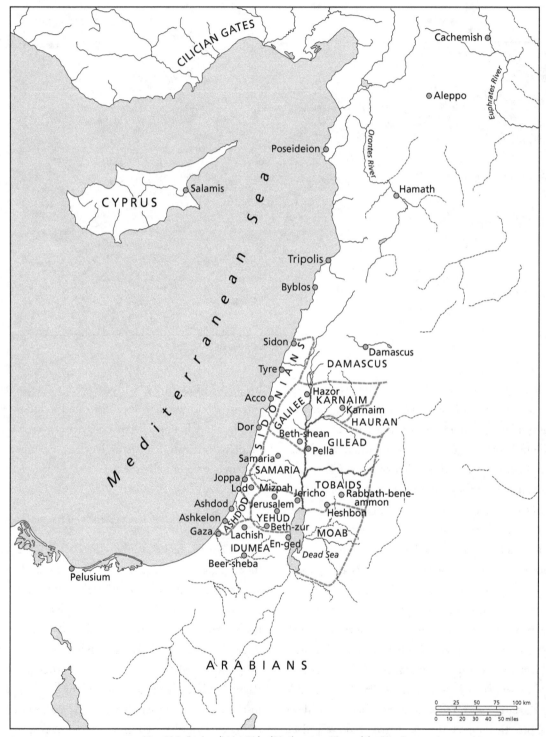

Map 15.2. Persian district "Yehud" in the satrap "Beyond the River"

SIDEBAR 15.4. KINGS OF ANCIENT PERSIA

The Persian king was said to be king of kings and ruler of all the world. He had absolute power over an elaborate imperial machinery. He was not himself subject to the law but believed himself to be divinely equipped to distinguish right from wrong.

The most important Persian kings for OT history are the following:

Cyrus the Great, 559–530 BCE
Cambyses II, 530–522 BCE
Darius I, 522–486 BCE
Xerxes I, 486–465 BCE
Artaxerxes I, 465–424 BCE

servitude, and the return of their divine images to their shrines and sanctuaries, which had been neglected and abused by Cyrus's predecessor. Even more remarkably, his words in the Cyrus Cylinder are also prefaced by a narrative, at least similar to the biblical decree, that declares the god of Babylon, Marduk, "sought and looked through all the lands, searching for a righteous king whose hand he could grasp." The narrative of the Cyrus Cylinder asserts that Marduk himself ordered Cyrus to capture his city, setting it free of its previous oppressors and making proper worship possible again.

These parallel edicts – the Cyrus Cylinder and the OT edicts of Ezra and 2 Chronicles – do not necessarily mean that Cyrus released *all* subjugated peoples to rebuild *all* cult shrines in the empire. But both Babylon and Jerusalem have such royal proclamations, and it is possible Cyrus employed local theologians in both cities to write versions of the declaration. So from the Babylonian perspective, Marduk was responsible, and from the perspective of the community in Yehud, Yahweh was responsible. One anonymous prophet of the exile took Cyrus to be a messiah, or anointed deliverer (Isaiah 45:1; Chapter 20). The edict preserved in 2 Chronicles and Ezra is most likely a paraphrased version. But we have no reason to doubt such a decree was issued by King Cyrus.

The Chronological Order of Ezra and Nehemiah

Earlier I mentioned a Persian king named Artaxerxes I (465–424 BCE). He had a grandson by the same name, Artaxerxes II, who reigned 405–359 BCE. This has led to some debate about the timing of Ezra's journey to Jerusalem, which is dated to the seventh year of Artaxerxes (Ezra 7:7–8). The OT doesn't indicate which Artaxerxes it means, first or second. So did Ezra arrive in Jerusalem in 458 or 398 BCE? Nearly everyone agrees that Nehemiah's journey to Jerusalem was under Artaxerxes I (Nehemiah 2:1–10), for a number of reasons, which puts him in Jerusalem at 445 BCE. So one theory has Ezra arriving over a decade *before* Nehemiah, and another has him coming nearly five decades *after* Nehemiah.

15.3. Cyrus Cylinder, from Babylon, southern Iraq, ca. 539–530 BCE. Written in the Babylonian dialect popular at the time, the text is a declaration of good kingship. It describes not only Cyrus's victory over Babylon but also his policy of tolerance toward conquered peoples and the reconstruction of their religious sanctuaries. (Photo: © The Trustees of the British Museum / Art Resource, N.Y.)

The sequence assumed in the books of Ezra and Nehemiah seems straightforward enough: Ezra arrived in 458 BCE followed by Nehemiah in 445 BCE. Yet the text has a number of historical anachronisms and confusing references, leading some to reverse the order. The complex way in which the original sources of Ezra-Nehemiah were combined is a better explanation for those anachronisms, and the Ezra-first sequence is preferable.[13]

13 For discussion, see pages xxxix–xliv in Williamson (1985) in the commentaries in "Where to Find More" in this chapter.

The "Empty Land" Question

The OT gives the impression that the Babylonians destroyed Jerusalem completely and carried off all survivors (2 Kings 25:1–21; 2 Chronicles 36:15–21; and compare Jeremiah 39 and Zechariah 7:7,14). Some readers doubt this picture, suggesting instead that none but a few actually went into captivity and that there was little or no distinction between a preexilic and postexilic Judah. After the Babylonian conquest of Jerusalem, life basically went on as before. The idea of the "empty land" was fabricated, in this view, by later authors in order to identify the arrival of "returnees" as true Israelites and to justify their actions in confiscating land and assuming power in the newly created district of Yehud. This view believes that the Chronistic History minimizes contributions of those who remained in Judah by fabricating the "myth of the empty land."

The OT texts undoubtedly use hyperbole to stress the extent of the destruction. In point of fact, we have references indicating that the poorest remained in the land to work as farmers (2 Kings 25:12; Jeremiah 39:10, 52:16), while the upper classes were deported. Archaeological evidence confirms that the land was left without leadership until the exiles returned from Babylonia, which does not mean, however, it was completely empty.[14] Ezra-Nehemiah may have exaggerated the extent to which Judah was desolated. But no fabrication of details was needed. Demographic studies based on excavations and surface surveys suggest population estimates for Judah in the late preexilic period at just over 32,000. During the years immediately following the fall of Babylon in 539 BCE, that number had dropped to just under 11,000, and increased again during the missions of Ezra and Nehemiah to 17,000. The population of Jerusalem itself has been estimated as a tiny 500 before Ezra's return, but more like 1,750 afterward.[15] These numbers are only estimates, but they are suggestive nonetheless. And they explain Nehemiah's passion to see the city repopulated (Nehemiah 11).

14 See Bustenay Oded in Lipschits and Blenkinsopp, "Where to Find More" in this chapter.

15 For these demographic estimates, see pages 289–90 in Mary Joan Winn Leith's chapter of Coogan in "Where to Find More" in Chapter 11.

Monotheism in the Chronistic History?

The Chronistic History begins with the first human, Adam (1 Chronicles 1:1). It concludes with the foundation of God's people as Yehud in the Persian Empire (Ezra-Nehemiah). Thus it covers virtually all of OT history down to the late fifth century BCE. Since the most explicit statements of monotheism in ancient Israel are from sixth-century Isaiah (Chapter 20), we might have expected to find explicit statements of monotheism in the Chronistic History. But the historians who gave us 1–2 Chronicles and Ezra-Nehemiah relate events; they are showing their theology rather than saying it. These are narratives focused on religious faithfulness as understood in henotheistic monolatry. Monotheism may be understood (as perhaps in 1 Chronicles 33:13), but it is seldom articulated here.

On the other hand, the Chronistic History, like the Deuteronomistic History before it, preserves speeches that reflect its theology. We saw an explicit statement of monotheism in 1–2 Kings expressed through the words of Solomon on the occasion of the dedication of the first temple (2 Kings 8:60; Chapter 14). Similarly here, Ezra's prayer on the day of national confession begins with this important saying: "You are Yahweh, you alone" (Nehemiah 9:6). Ezra's prayer continues by acknowledging Yahweh's uniqueness as seen in creation, and in Yahweh's call and covenant with Abraham, the exodus from Egypt, and the rest of Israel's history. Like so many other expressions in the OT, this may not be explicit monotheism. Indeed, from the context, it appears to be *more than* a simple denial of the existence of other deities. Rather, Ezra here affirms Yahweh's uniqueness and calls for greater commitment to him among his servants.

WHERE TO FIND MORE

Commentaries: The best technical and advanced commentaries on **1–2 Chronicles** are Sara Japhet, *I and II Chronicles: A Commentary* (Old Testament Library; Louisville, Ky.: Westminster John Knox Press, 1993); Gary N. Knoppers, *I Chronicles: A New Translation with Introduction and Commentary* (2 vols.; Anchor Bible 12; New York: Doubleday, 2004); H. G. M. Williamson, *1 and 2 Chronicles* (New Century Bible; Grand Rapids, Mich.: Eerdmans, 1982). The best technical and advanced commentaries on **Ezra-Nehemiah** are Leslie C. Allen and Timothy S. Laniak, *Ezra, Nehemiah, Esther* (New International Biblical Commentary, Old Testament, 9; Peabody, Mass.: Hendrickson Publishers, 2003), Joseph Blenkinsopp, *Ezra-Nehemiah: A Commentary* (Old Testament Library; Philadelphia: Westminster Press, 1988), and H. G. M. Williamson, *Ezra, Nehemiah* (Word Biblical Commentary 16; Waco, Tex.: Word Books, 1985).

Chavalas, Mark W., ed. *The Ancient Near East: Historical Sources in Translation.* Blackwell Sourcebooks in Ancient History. Malden, Mass.: Blackwell, 2006.

See Brian B. Schmidt on the Moabite Stone (pp. 311–16), and Piotr Michalowski on the Cyrus Cylinder (pp. 426–30).

Duke, Rodney K. *The Persuasive Appeal of the Chronicler: A Rhetorical Analysis.* JSOTSup 88. Sheffield, Eng.: Almond Press, 1990.

Like Japhet (1997), also explores the individual responsibility of each generation in 1–2 Chronicles, applying the principle to readers in the exile where "seeking Yahweh" has the potential to reverse their situation (pp. 66–74).

Japhet, Sara. *The Ideology of the Book of Chronicles and Its Place in Biblical Thought.* 2nd rev. ed. Beiträge zur Erforschung des Alten Testaments und des antiken Judentum 9. Frankfurt am Main: P. Lang, 1997.

Lipschits, Oded, and Joseph Blenkinsopp, eds. *Judah and the Judeans in the Neo-Babylonian Period.* Winona Lake, Ind.: Eisenbrauns, 2003.

Contains several important chapters related to topics in this chapter, but see especially pages 55–74 by Bustenay Oded, the "Myth of the Empty Land."

McCarter, P. Kyle. *Ancient Inscriptions: Voices from the Biblical World.* Washington, D.C.: Biblical Archaeology Society, 1996.

Roberts, J. J. M. "Zion in the Theology of the Davidic-Solomonic Empire." Pages 93–108 in *Studies in the Period of David and Solomon and Other Essays: Papers Read at the International Symposium for Biblical Studies, Tokyo, 5–7 December, 1979.* Edited by Tomoo Ishida. Winona Lake, Ind.: Eisenbrauns, 1982.

Excellent summary of "Zion theology."

Stern, Ephraim. "The Persian Empire and the Political and Social History of Palestine in the Persian Period." Pages 70–87 in *The Cambridge History of Judaism. Vol. 1, Introduction; The Persian Period.* Edited by W. D. Davies and Louis Finkelstein. Cambridge and New York: Cambridge University Press, 1984.

See also the chapter "The Jewish Community in Palestine in the Persian Period" by Peter Ackroyd (pp. 130–61).

CHAPTER 16

More Books

OLD TESTAMENT READING: GENESIS 49, DEUTERONOMY 32, AND JUDGES 5

In this chapter we turn from the Primary and Chronistic Histories to the books that make up roughly the second half of the OT. We will observe a dramatic shift in content from historical narrative to largely poetry. Furthermore, these books are much less linked editorially to one another. Rather, we will discover that superscriptions and content help us to group them literarily and, in most cases, to relate them chronologically to one another and to the Primary History.

Because of the preponderance of poetry, we will spend time in this chapter on the nature and characteristics of ancient Hebrew poetry. There are certain aspects that we do not know, such as original pronunciation or meter. However, we will readily observe one major feature – that of parallelism. This "symmetry of thought" is recognizable in three primary types: synonymous, antithetical, and synthesizing parallelisms. We will explore examples, and discover along the way that ancient Hebrew poetry is rich in content and artistic skill.

The books of the OT library have two literary types, prose and poetry. This is a convenient way to categorize the books of Israel's library, although it is imprecise. For example, the books we have covered thus far, which are mostly historical prose, also contain legal material, parables, lists and royal annals, and a variety of other types of literature. We can only use "prose" to describe the Primary and Chronistic Histories if we understand the term in a broad and general way.

Even these mostly prose books have poetry embedded in them at times, like Genesis 49,

Deuteronomy 32, and others. For the rest of the OT books, we have the reverse situation. We turn now to books in Israel's library that have mostly poetry, with prose interspersed occasionally. A few of these remaining books have a nearly equal blend of prose and poetry, such as the prophet Jeremiah. So we will need to take a detour in this chapter to explore the nature and characteristics of OT poetry.

The distinction between prose and poetry is not always helpful. First of all, poetry is difficult to define. It can be like beauty; it's in the eyes of the beholder. Most of us recognize it when we see it, but we're not sure how to explain what it is. Second, much of the OT's prose is a sophisticated and elevated level of prose, almost like an art form. In this sense, the OT's prose is sometimes more like poetry than we might imagine. Finally, as we just said, prose and poetry are often blended in the OT, so the distinction does not help in categorizing the various books. We might think of the first half of the OT as roughly prose (the Primary and Chronistic Histories) and the second half as roughly poetry. While this is a helpful way to categorize the OT, please remember there will be many exceptions to the rule.

Since we cannot think of the rest of the OT books as poetry exclusively, I want you to think of the way they relate to the books we've studied so far. In a real sense, you have reached a turning point in your walk through Israel's library. The rest of the books are generally independent self-contained books in a way the books in the first half of the OT were not. So first I invite you to think about the rest of the OT as the second floor of the library. There are different sorts of books on this floor.

They are as much a part of the OT library as the books on the ground floor. But the way these other books were collected and included in the canon is slightly different.

Before getting into the nature of Israelite poetry, this chapter will introduce the remaining OT books and explore how they relate to the Primary and Chronistic Histories. Then we will consider the nature of poetry, as a way to prepare you for reading the rest of the OT – the books on the second floor.

ALL THE REST, AND HOW THEY RELATE TO THE PRIMARY AND CHRONISTIC HISTORIES

We have called the first nine books of the OT the Primary History and explained that they have been sewn together in an editorial unity. Each book of the Pentateuch begins with a link to the previous book, and similar connecting links continue through Joshua, Judges, the books of Samuel, and the books of Kings. These nine books of the Primary History have few titles or superscriptions labeling them.[1] Each simply picks up the story line from the previous book, as was observed more than three hundred years ago by Benedict de Spinoza (Sidebar 4.4). Thus, the first nine books of the OT form a continuous history from creation to the fall of Jerusalem, the "First Bible."

Then we saw how a second national epic was written later, the Chronistic History. This

[1] The book of Deuteronomy has a superscription (1:1–5) that places the content of that book in relationship to the narrative that precedes it in Exodus and Numbers; the one-verse superscription in Genesis is distinctive because of the unique subject matter.

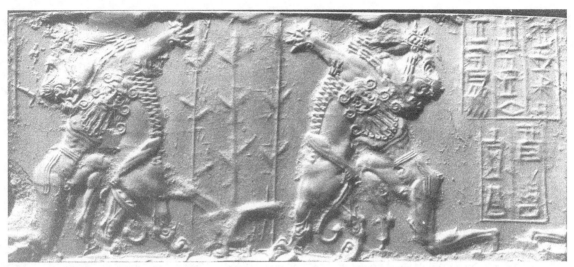

16.1. Cylinder seal depicting "contest scene." This fight scene from a third millennium seal shows a deity or human (sometimes identified with Gilgamesh) wrestling with a lion. The inscription names the son of Abilum, a scribe, a rare feature in ancient texts (see Sidebar 16.1). (Photo: Werner Forman / Art Resource, N.Y.)

continuous history is much shorter, with only two parts instead of nine – the books of Chronicles and Ezra-Nehemiah. But these were also interconnected intentionally. The link was even more obvious: the royal edict at the conclusion of Chronicles and at the beginning of Ezra. These books thus form a new and continuous history from the first human, Adam, down to the Jewish community clustered around the newly rebuilt temple in Jerusalem. Members of this community, according to the Chronistic History, are no less than the people of God, the restored community of ancient Israel. The Primary History and the Chronistic History make up approximately half the OT library. We now turn to the rest of the books of the OT, those we have imagined on the second floor.

Spinoza's simple observation was revolutionary for its time. He noted in a work written in 1670 that the Primary History was the work of a single individual, whom he identified as Ezra.[2] We might disagree with his attribution of the whole to one author, but his emphasis on the interconnectedness of the nine books of the Primary History was brilliant. Spinoza studied 1–2 Chronicles and Ezra-Nehemiah separately from the Primary History and with different results, but as we have seen here (Chapter 15), they can similarly be understood as a single work of history because of the editorial links between them.

Now we come to our big turning point: the rest of the OT books have no such continuous thread or interconnectedness. Think of the rest of the OT books as characterized by two features. First, they are introduced with superscriptions or descriptive titles, rather than narrative links connecting each to the previous book(s). There are a few exceptions to

2 Benedictus de Spinoza, *Complete Works* (ed. M. L. Morgan; trans. S. Shirley; Indianapolis, Ind.: Hackett Publishing, 2002), 477–78.

SIDEBAR 16.1. TITLES AND AUTHORS OF ANCIENT COMPOSITIONS

Most authors in the ancient world were anonymous; they simply did not leave behind their names. (Review our discussion of "books" in Chapter 2). Sometimes we have names of editors or scribes who copied and preserved the text. But these were not the actual authors. When these scribes' names are preserved, we find them in superscriptions ("titles," or "rubrics," at the beginning), or in Mesopotamia especially, in colophons (scribal notes at the end). So, for example, we don't have the names of the authors of great literary works like the *Enuma Elish* or the Gilgamesh Epic, although at times we do have the name of a scribe who copied certain texts.*

Similarly, most ancient compositions have no official title, as we normally think of such things. Instead, they are most often known by their opening words. So even our title *Enuma Elish* is taken from the opening words of the composition, "When on high." In Israel's library, the books of the OT are usually called by their opening words or by the main protagonists of that book. So the ancient Hebrew names for the books of the Torah are "In the beginning" (Genesis), "Names," (for Exodus, which begins "These are the names of"), and so forth. The historical books like Joshua, Samuel, and Ezra-Nehemiah are named for their leading characters, while others are named for the group of characters, such as Judges or Kings. Our English titles are mostly from the Greek Septuagint translation, which has a different origin.

So this is a distinction between the two halves of the OT. The Primary History has few superscriptions or titles. Its books are linked together instead by narrative connectors that create a continuous narrative thread. Even where introductory paragraphs are used (Deuteronomy), these are intended to link the new book to the narrative flow that precedes it. The same can be said for the Chronistic History. By contrast, the remainder of the OT books have a variety of superscriptions that intentionally connect them, not to each other in a continuous flow but to the narrative thread created by the Primary and Chronistic Histories.

* For more on this, see pages 37–39 in van der Toorn in "Where to Find More" in Chapter 2.

this observation, but we will point those out as we go along. These introductory titles usually direct the reader to some event or time period known from the Primary History. Instead of strung together in a narrative thread, these books point back to the narrative thread we have already studied in order to add something. Second, each of the books we will now examine was intended to be read as a self-contained whole, and most typically is homiletical (or sermonic), hymnic, or prophetic in nature. These books often come closer to what you and I think of as a "book" than do those we've studied so far.

In general then, the rest of Israel's library — those books on the second floor — are linked less

to each other in a continuous thread than to the books on the ground floor — the Primary and Chronistic Histories. They are to be read in light of the history told there. You will encounter lots of variety in the books on the second floor, and many of them will be full of mysterious poetry. Israel's ideas are expressed here with great passion and artistry, illustrating in vivid detail the contributions of ancient Israelite religious thought.

The first two books we will consider are *Job* and *Proverbs* (in the next chapter).[3] I introduce them

3 For this discussion, review the list of books in the OT canon in Figure 2.3.

together because they belong to a subcategory known as "wisdom literature," which I will define later. In its title, the book of Proverbs connects its various sayings with King Solomon (Proverbs 1:1) and later with King Hezekiah (Proverbs 25:1). The book also mentions other sources for its proverbs, but these two historical benchmarks remind the reader of 1–2 Kings and 1–2 Chronicles, linking the book to the narratives of Israel's history. In this way, Proverbs illustrates how these books relate to the Primary and Chronistic Histories.

Job, however, is something of an exception. Its opening lines are hardly the same as a title or superscription: "There was once a man in the land of Uz whose name was Job." We must admit, we have no idea how this book relates to Israel's histories in the first half of the OT. We'll explain the unique features of this fascinating book in the next chapter. For the meantime, we simply observe that Job is disconnected from any narratives of Israel's history, is clearly a self-contained book, and stands uniquely on its own.

The book of *Psalms* has titles and superscriptions on different levels (Chapter 18). In a sense, the first two psalms are titles for the whole. The first psalm speaks only in general terms about choosing between two ways of life, while the second uses references to King David and the Davidic dynasty. It mentions Yahweh's "anointed" (or "messiah," Psalm 2:2) and Yahweh's king on Mount Zion (2:6), and in an imagined speech between Yahweh and the unnamed Davidic king, Yahweh declares his fatherhood of the king: "you are my son; today I have begotten you" (2:7). This psalm prepares one to read the book of Psalms in light of the monarchy of Davidic kings in Israel's history.

Many of the psalms have additional superscriptions or titles at their beginnings. For example, Psalm 3 has the words "A Psalm of David, when he fled from his son Absalom." Most English Bibles have these titles set apart before the first verse, as a prenumbered notation. We will discuss these superscriptions in Chapter 18, especially their origins and how we should think about them. But whatever their value, they serve to connect the psalms, individually and as a whole, with the historical narratives of the first half of the OT.

Most of the OT prophets begin with a title or superscription of some sort (see Chapters 19–21). These titles are not always titles for a whole book. For example, Isaiah begins with a title at Isaiah 1:1 putting the ministry of Isaiah in the reign of four kings of Judah in the eighth and early seventh centuries BCE (the time of the kings Uzziah, Jotham, Ahaz, and Hezekiah). So this places the book of Isaiah in perspective in light of Israel's historical narrative. However, not all the oracles and sermons of the *book* of Isaiah are from this eighth-century *prophet* Isaiah, as we shall see. Similarly, not all the psalms in the book of Psalms come from the time of King David. So in general, we learn that these titles place the additional books of the OT in perspective in relation to the Primary and Chronistic Histories, but that they are not strictly claiming the origins for the books they introduce.

Thus the introductory title of the book of *Isaiah* places the first collection of sermons and oracles of that book in the eighth and early seventh centuries BCE. The same can be said of the book of *Hosea*, where we have a similar title referencing the same four kings. This means the superscriptions of these two books make the prophets Isaiah and

Hosea contemporaries. And these two prophetic books can be read in light of events described in 2 Kings and 2 Chronicles relating to the kings Uzziah, Jotham, Ahaz, and Hezekiah. In this way, most of the OT prophets can be placed in a general chronological sequence. So the books of *Amos* and *Micah*, are also eighth-century prophets. I will introduce these eighth-century prophets – Isaiah, Hosea, Amos, and Micah – in Chapter 19. It will be helpful to consider their themes together in light of eighth-century Israel.

In a similar way, the book of *Jeremiah* opens with a title associating his prophecies with the kings of Judah from 640 BCE down to the fall of Jerusalem in 586, and just beyond that date (Jeremiah 1:1–3). This particular book contains numerous other titles introducing individual sermons and associating them with specific historical contexts in the late seventh and early sixth centuries BCE. For example, "In the ninth year of King Zedekiah of Judah, in the tenth month" (Jeremiah 39:1). So this book has several historical anchors giving us more detailed connections than any other with the Primary History. The title of the book of *Zephaniah* tags its prophecies to King Josiah, placing it also in the seventh century BCE. The books of *Nahum* and *Habakkuk* have indefinite titles, but on the basis of content, they should be grouped with other seventh-century prophecies.

The book of *Ezekiel* has a title locating its prophecies in the early sixth century during the exile. The book of *Joel* has a general title, but it is one that gives no specific indication of when Joel preached the sermons collected in the book. Based on the content of the first two chapters, we can probably place the book in the sixth century BCE. The same can be said for the book of *Obadiah*.

The books of *Haggai* and *Zechariah* have titles with a precise date in the Persian period of Israel's history (520 BCE), which associates them with the events described in Ezra 1–6. The book of *Malachi* has an indefinite title, but on the basis of content, its prophecies are to be located in the fifth century. We will group it together with Haggai and Zechariah as the closing prophets of the OT canon from the Persian period.

Relying on these superscriptions, the OT prophecies may be collected and studied chronologically according to Israel's history. The eighth-century prophets are Isaiah 1–39, Hosea, Amos, and Micah. They were active during the period when Israel and Judah were coming to terms with their relationship with the Assyrian Empire (we'll take them together in Chapter 19). The seventh- and sixth-century prophets were Jeremiah, Ezekiel, Zephaniah, and most likely also Obadiah, Nahum, and Habakkuk. These were either anticipating or reacting to the Babylonian crisis (and so are together in Chapter 20). The Persian period prophets of the late sixth and fifth centuries are Haggai, Zechariah, and Malachi (Chapter 21).

The book of *Jonah* has a general title associating it with a historical figure mentioned in 2 Kings 14:25. As we will see, this little prophecy has literary features marking it as unique among the OT prophets. While its title gives the book of Jonah a historical location (eighth century BCE), its content makes it something of a handbook for reading the other OT books of prophecy. We will consider it in Chapter 21, after our survey of Israel's prophetic books.

The book of *Daniel*, is also a very different kind of prophet. So different, in fact, that the Jewish canon doesn't include it among the prophets at all, while the Christian canon collects it with the major prophets (after Isaiah, Jeremiah, and Ezekiel).[4] Daniel also opens with an introductory title, associating its message with King Jehoiakim and the Babylonian king Nebuchadnezzar (Daniel 1:1). Other chapters have their own introductions, locating specific portions of the book in the Persian period (Daniel 6 and 9–10). We will see that the book of Daniel is the OT example of a literary genre known as **"apocalyptic,"** and therefore requires a bit more explanation (in Chapter 22).

This leaves only five relatively brief books collected together in the Jewish canon near the end and preserved as a collection of "scrolls" (Hebrew *mĕgillôt*). The book of *Ruth* has an introductory title associating it with the events described in the book of Judges. The title for the book of *Esther* makes mention of the ruler Ahasuerus (i.e., the Persian king Xerxes I; 486–465 BCE), serving to put its narrative in proper perspective with the Chronistic History especially. The books of *Ecclesiastes* and *Song of Solomon* (or *Song of Songs*) begin with titles associating their sayings with Solomon, "the son of David," placing them in the context of Israel's United Monarchy. The book of *Lamentations* is an exception, since it includes no specific title or superscription. Its content, however, is without doubt to be linked to the fall of the city of Jerusalem. There is no right or wrong order for these five books of the "scrolls," and I will treat them together in Chapter 23 for a variety of reasons.

As you can see, the rest of the OT books complement the extended historical narratives of the Primary History and Chronistic History. Each of

4 We will return to this topic when we consider the definition of "prophecy" in Chapter 19.

them, with a few exceptions, is specifically linked, not to each other in a continuous flow but to the larger narrative complex of the Primary History and, to a lesser extent, the Chronistic History. These remaining books contain more poetry than the extended historical narratives we have studied thus far. And this may have been part of the process of their collection and preservation. So in all canonical groupings, Job, Psalms, and Proverbs were probably attracted to each other by their common use of poetry. We therefore need to consider next the distinctive features of Israelite poetry.

THE CHARACTERISTICS AND QUALITIES OF OLD TESTAMENT POETRY

We often think of poetry as older than prose. We tend to think this because of the way literature developed in English and most European cultures. Similarly, poetry appeared in literature before prose in the older long-standing cultures of the ancient Near East. But Israel was not one of those old long-standing cultures; ancient Israel was a relative newcomer on the scene. And in the case of early Hebrew literature, it appears that poetry and prose were developed almost side by side.

Poetry in any language is a difficult thing to define. In English, and in most European languages, we perceive poetry as characterized by meter and rhyme. But these, too, are not always easy to define, even for languages we use in everyday speech. When trying to understand these features in Israelite poetry, we encounter complications. Not only are we uncertain how ancient Hebrew was pronounced but our OT text has been overlaid through the centuries with accent and pronunciation marks that sometimes obscure poetic features,

---

SIDEBAR 16.2. IS POETRY A DISTINCT OLD TESTAMENT LITERARY CATEGORY?

The idea of poetry as characterized by parallelism is itself somewhat controversial. Some have raised questions about whether the OT has anything like our idea of poetry, assuming rather that we have foisted our own notions of poetry on the Israelite literature. To this way of thinking, the very distinction between prose and poetry is foreign to the OT. The idea of parallelism is said to be present in prose as well, and therefore ancient Hebrew literature exhibits a continuum of many different types, in which poetry and prose both participate. It is possible that parallelism itself is simply an all-purpose literary type, in which the second line performs the sole function of heightening or seconding the idea of the first line. If so, it may be much more widely present in prose than previously thought.*

It is true that some elevated prose is more lyrical than we might expect, especially in the artfully written narratives of the Deuteronomistic History. And so the differences between prose and poetry can be overstated. However, most scholars have come to accept the fact that poetry simply cannot be reduced to a heightened and intensified version of prose. Poetry as a distinct literary form in the OT is marked in a number of ways. Beyond the linguistic and stylistic features discussed in this chapter, poetry is more personal and intimate than prose, which maintains a certain distance between the writer and reader. Such intimacy is more suited for expressions of worship, exhortation, or philosophical speculation about life, such as we find in the OT poetic books. Furthermore, prose narrative assumes sequential time, whereas poetry is often timeless. Prose most often addresses the mundane everyday affairs of life, whereas poetry has the potential to soar above these. And poetry more than prose is prone to metaphor, addressing topics more obliquely but also more eloquently. Parallelism remains the best formal explanation for OT poetry's distinctive features, but these other differences are important to remember as well.

* The leading thinker in this category is James L. Kugel. For his approach, and for the objections listed here, see Kugel's book and the article by Landy in "Where to Find More" in this chapter.

---

especially meter. We're almost certain that rhyming was rare and usually a by-product of the way nouns and verbs were formed in ancient Hebrew.[5] The question of whether Israelite poetry has meter is (believe it or not) a big debate among scholars. Some believe that meter can be traced by focusing on accented syllables alone, while others believe that an alternating system of accented and unaccented syllables reveals meter (not unlike iambic or trochee poetry in European languages). Others simply leave the topic unresolved.

Whatever the case with meter and rhyme, we can be confident that these are not the determining features of Israelite poetry. Instead, the single most important characteristic of OT poetry is a symmetry of thought, which we call parallelism. The poetry you are most familiar with balances *sounds* in a symmetical way, usually rhyme, rhythm, or meter, or a combination of these. OT poetry may *occasionally* do this, but only rarely. The type of poetry we will encounter in the OT balances *ideas* in a kind of conceptual rhyming. So we find here a symmetry of thought instead of symmetry of sounds. Because

5 This has to do with suffixes that were often repeated in a series of lines and therefore created a rhyming pattern. If you know Hebrew, it will help to see the examples in pages 229–234 in Watson in "Where to Find More" in this chapter.

this is so very different from the poetry you are used to, we need to explore the various types of parallelism found in the rest of the OT books. You will want to refer back to this discussion to understand better the poetry you read from this point forward.

Israelite poetry is intended to be artistic, compelling, powerful in expression, imaginative, poignant in few words, and at times even playful. OT poetry doesn't always follow the rules of communication familiar in prose. It omits connecting words such as "therefore" and "because," and it invites you to move slowly over the words and draw out their meanings on your own. Israelite poems use short clauses or phrases of approximately the same number of words, grouped together usually in stanzas of two or three lines or clauses (sometimes more). It is the tight symmetry of thought among these parallel lines in a stanza that distinguishes Hebrew poetry. The second line of a stanza advances the thought of the first line in one of a number of ways.

Synonymous Parallelism

In synonymous parallelism (also called repetitive parallelism), the second line of the poem may express the same idea as the first in synonymous terms. This is no mere mechanical repetition of the idea in different words, but rather the second line contributes to the depth and richness of the idea of the first line.

(1) The earth is Yahweh's and all that is in it,
   the world, and those who live in it;
(2) for he has founded it on the seas,
   and established it on the rivers.
(3) Who shall ascend the hill of Yahweh?

And who shall stand in his holy place?
(4) Those who have clean hands and pure hearts,
   who do not lift up their souls to what is false,
   and do not swear deceitfully. (Psalm 24:1–4)

In this example, the terms "earth" and "world" are parallel (v. 1). The second line omits "is Yahweh's" which is implied. Right away, you see that Hebrew poetry is flexible; it doesn't follow any particular rules rigidly. The parallel verbs "founded" and "established" (v. 2) show how Hebrew theologians add richness to their understanding of God's creation of the world, by nuancing one word with another. Multiform understandings begin to accumulate as you read along. The "hill of Yahweh" is parallel to "his holy place" (v. 3), adding nuanced layers of meaning to the author's perspective of the Temple Mount in Jerusalem. The worshipper is privileged to "ascend" and "stand" in Yahweh's presence there, showing progression of movement from approaching to arriving. A repeating line may contribute clarity to a previous line, as in verse 4. What does it mean to have "clean hands and pure hearts"? Such belong to individuals who do not "lift up their souls to what is false." In this case, an additional line is added; verse 4 has three lines, showing again how flexible poetry can be. The cleanhanded and purehearted also "do not swear deceitfully." The use of three lines instead of two adds emphasis to the statement in verse 4.

(1) The heavens are telling the glory of God;
   and the firmament proclaims his handiwork.
(2) Day to day pours forth speech,
   and night to night declares knowledge. (Psalm 19:1–2)

In this example of synonymous parallelism, the phrase "glory of God" is a general expression and does not yet make the author's point specifically. In the parallel line, we learn that the "handiwork" of God – that is, the grandeur and beauty of creation itself – is, in fact, his glory. We also see from this how careful we must be in reading poetry. One would be mistaken to think of two separate speakers: (a) the heavens, and (b) the firmament. This would then lead to the idea that they are speaking of separate things: (a) God's glory, and (b) God's handiwork. As you can see, this would lead one into serious misreadings. Poetry demands slow, deliberate, and careful interpretation. You can't read these books quickly!

Antithetical Parallelism

In antithetical parallelism (also called adversative parallelism), the second line of the poem may express a contrasting idea from the first line. Often the two lines are positive and negative expressions of the same thought.

> for Yahweh knows the way of the righteous,
>> but the way of the wicked perishes. (Psalm 1:6; my
>> translation)

In this example, the "way of the righteous" in the first line is parallel to "the way of the wicked" in the second line. The verbs used with each are suggestive. While it may be unclear what it means for Yahweh to "know" one's way (or life journey), it becomes clear from the contrasting parallel that being known of Yahweh is life itself.

> Contrasting parallelism is common in the book of Proverbs.

> Hear, my child, your father's instruction,
>> and do not reject your mother's teaching.
>> (Proverbs 1:8)

The "father's instruction" is paralleled in the second line by the "mother's teaching." The ideas in the two lines are made to contrast with each other by the positive command ("hear") and the negative prohibition ("do not reject").

> The fear of Yahweh is the beginning of knowledge;
>> fools despise wisdom and instruction. (Proverbs 1:7)

The "beginning of knowledge" is paralleled in the second line by "wisdom and instruction." The contrasting elements in the lines give insight into the enigmatic expression "the fear of Yahweh." In a sense, the whole book of Proverbs (and all the wisdom literature; see Chapter 17) is written to explain what the fear of Yahweh is. In this theme verse, we learn from the contrasting parallelism that whatever else "fear of Yahweh" may be, it is the opposite of the foolish act of despising Yahweh's instruction. Put positively, then, those who fear Yahweh pay especially close attention to his instruction.

Synthesizing Parallelism

In synthesizing parallelism (also called constructive or formal parallelism), the second line of the poem may express an idea that synthesizes the previous line, or otherwise supplements or carries forward the idea of the first line. In a sense, this is a broad category of diverse types of parallelism, often given a variety of names. The following are only a few examples. A synthesizing parallel line of poetry may serve to complete the idea of the first line, in *completion* parallelism.

> *"I have set my king*
> *on Zion, my holy hill." (Psalm 2:6)*

The two lines are not synonymous or antithetical. The second line carries the idea of the first along to completion.

> *Better is a dinner of vegetables where love is*
> *than a fatted ox and hatred with it. (Proverbs 15:17)*

At first, this may appear like simple antithetical parallelism so common in the book of Proverbs. In a sense, it is. The "dinner of vegetables" is contrasted with "fatted ox," and "love" and "hatred" are obviously contrasted. But the comparative terms "better" and "than" at the beginning of each line clearly mark this as *comparison* parallelism.

> *Do not answer fools according to their folly,*
> *or you will be a fool yourself. (Proverbs 26:4)*

In this example of *substantiation* parallelism, the second line gives the reason for the idea of the first line. Such cause and effect may move in the other direction, as in this example of *causation* parallelism.

> *A gossip reveals secrets;*
> *therefore do not associate with a babbler. (Proverbs*
> *20:19)*

The English word "therefore" is implied by the causal movement of the two lines of poetry.

Another form of synthesizing parallelism is *climactic* parallelism (also called stairstep parallelism).

In this case, the first line is itself incomplete in some way, and the second line picks up some of its exact words or phrases and carries the idea to completion.

> *Ascribe to Yahweh, O heavenly beings,*
> *ascribe to Yahweh glory and strength. (Psalm 29:1)*

The two lines begin with exact repetitive parallelism. Then the vocative "heavenly beings" of the first line is replaced with "glory and strength" in the second, completing the object of the imperative verb "ascribe."

I should warn you that these examples do not exhaust the way Hebrew poetry uses parallelism. Far from it. There are numerous ways in which these three types – synonymous, antithetical, and synthesizing parallelism – are nuanced and adapted in subtle ways to say something more complex than these illustrations may lead you to believe. Learning to read more sophisticated forms of parallelism comes only with practice.

So parallelism is the fundamental characteristic of OT poetry. Beyond that, you should also be aware that Israelite poets had a highly developed appreciation for the texture of words. What I mean by this is that they were gifted artists with energetic and stylish imaginations, using words to arouse the emotion or images desired in the poem. The poetry of the OT is filled with examples in which the sounds of the Hebrew language are used creatively to add emphasis or flair to expression (at the phonetic level). The most popular such techniques are alliteration, assonance, word play (formally known as paronomasia), and the use of words that sound like what they describe (onomatopoeia). I'll illustrate a few of these, although most are invisible in English translation.

Perhaps the favorite such phonetic technique is the use of alliteration, or the repetition of the same or similar sounds at the beginning of words or in stressed syllables. So, for example, the familiar words "pray for the peace of Jerusalem" use both the *sh* and *l* consonants in such a way (*ša'ălû šelôm yerûšalaim*; Psalm 122:6).[6] Such techniques were popular in riddles and oral wisdom traditions, as is apparent in the use of the *m* sound in the questions: "What is sweeter than honey? What is stronger than a lion?" (*mah-mātôq midbāš ûmeh 'az mē'ārî*; Judges 14:18).

Another phonetic technique in OT poetry is assonance, or the repetition of identical or similar vowel sounds, especially in stressed syllables. So the recurrence of the *o* vowel intensifies the forlorn quality of the prophet's indictment (Isaiah 1:4): "Ah, sinful nation, people laden with iniquity." Similarly in the same poem, the urgency of Yahweh's appeal is stressed by the recurrence of *i* and *e* vowels (Isaiah 1:18): "Come now, let us argue it out, says Yahweh: though your sins are like scarlet, they shall be like snow; though they are red like crimson, they shall become like wool." This technique is especially common where the same suffix occurs repeatedly on nouns and verbs in close proximity, as in Jeremiah's complaint (Jeremiah 15:10): "Woe is me, my mother, that you ever bore me, a man of strife and contention to the whole land!"

Word play (formally called paronomasia) may also be used in OT poetry to add impact to or otherwise dramatize what is described. Yahweh coaxed from Amos the word for "summer fruit" (*qāyiṣ*), and then announced to the prophet "the end [*qēṣ*, or "hour of doom"] has come upon my people Israel" (Amos 8:2).[7] Similarly, Yahweh prompted Jeremiah to say the word "almond tree" (*šāqēd*), before affirming that he is "watching over" (*šōqēd*) his word to ensure it becomes reality. These are only the most obvious examples; many more could be listed. In fact, certain features of the Hebrew language make it particularly adaptable for word play in the hands of such gifted poets.

As in other languages, Hebrew poets could use words that imitate the sounds associated with the thing they're describing (formally known as onomatopoeia). The best example of this in the OT is found in Judges 5.

> *Then loud beat the horses' hoofs*
> *with the galloping, galloping of his steeds.*
> *(Judges 5:22)*

Even in English, you can almost hear the clip-clopping of horses' hooves. In Hebrew the repeated and alternating use of short *a* sounds echoes the galloping horses, especially the graphic *dahărôt dahărôt* ("galloping, galloping"). Israelite poets used onomatopoeia vividly to describe the swelling of seawaters (Psalm 93:4), the gasping and sighing of a woman undergoing childbirth (Isaiah 42:14), and others.

As you can see, Hebrew poetry is flexible in its parallel structures, and rich in techniques to

---

6 I illustrate in transliteration of the Hebrew sounds the first couple of examples here. But if you are familiar with Hebrew, you should look up the verses indicated in the other examples in a Hebrew Bible to see and hear how the phonemes indicated in the discussion are used. Pronounce them out loud and imagine the impact such techniques would have in oral delivery.

7 Two words nearly indistinguishable in some dialects of ancient Hebrew; Shalom M. Paul, *Amos: A Commentary on the Book of Amos* (Hermeneia—A Critical and Historical Commentary on the Bible; Minneapolis, Minn.: Fortress Press, 1991), 253–54.

SIDEBAR 16.3. ACROSTIC STRUCTURES IN POETRY

You may be aware that English poetry can be used artfully so that the lines of a poem form a shape suggestive of the subject. For example, George Herbert (1593–1633) wrote a "pattern poem" called "Easter Wings," in which the lines on the page symbolize birds in flight. The words carry meaning, but so does the playful and gifted way they are used. The lines of the poem appeal to the eye as much as they appeal to the ear.

Hebrew poetry occasionally uses something similar, which is at least as impressive for its literary and artistic skill. Certain poems in the OT are acrostics, in which the first letter of each line follows a distinct pattern using the letters of the alphabet. In the case of Psalm 111, the poem has twenty-two lines exactly following the sequence of the twenty-two letters of the Hebrew alphabet. (If you know the Hebrew alphabet, look up Psalm 111 in a Hebrew Bible and imagine how much skill it would take to write a hymn in such a fashion.) This pattern could be expanded considerably, so that Psalm 119 uses an arrangement of eight lines, each beginning with the same letter of the alphabet in a long acrostic. But the pattern is also flexible, so it could use only half the alphabet, or could omit or transpose certain letters.

We have acrostic structures in Psalms 9–10, 25, 34, 37, 111, 112, 119, and 145; Proverbs 31:10–31; Lamentations 1–4; and Nahum 1:2–8, and occasionally scholars explore the possibility of acrostics elsewhere.* We can only speculate about why ancient Hebrew poets used acrostic structures. But it probably emphasized the extent of the treatment, showing that the poet has covered the subject completely because he used every letter of the alphabet. And, of course, the presence of an acrostic outline also highlights the poet's skill.

* For discussion of this topic, see pages 190–200 in Watson in "Where to Find More" in this chapter.

emphasize and dramatize the poets' messages. Beyond these linguistic details, OT poetry also uses images and metaphors lavishly, which we would expect in almost any poetry. When reading these OT books of poetry, do not be surprised to see that streams can "clap their hands" (Psalm 98:8), and fields can "exult" and trees of the forest "sing for joy" (Psalm 96:12). And, of course, we all know the famous metaphor that compares one's relationship with Yahweh to that of a sheep with its shepherd (Psalm 23:1–4): "Yahweh is my shepherd, I shall not want." Or similes may be used to characterize righteous believers who are "like trees planted by streams of water," whereas the wicked are "like chaff that the wind drives away" (Psalm 1:3–4). Such profound poetry allows the Israelite theologian to explore the way in which men and women naturally long for God, "as a deer longs for flowing streams" (Psalm 42:1–2).

Poetry in most languages is that literary style or form best suited for the expression of human sentiments and passions. In these ancient Israelite patterns of parallelism and other linguistic techniques, poetry becomes even more powerful and expressive. Other forms of literature are more suited for explaining the way things are or should be, as we see in the use of the OT's narrative prose, legal exhortations, or lists of genealogies. But Israelite poetry is perfect for giving expression to the passion and quality of urgency in prayers, psalms, prophetic sermons, and wisdom speeches. For more discussion on OT poetry, you should consult the resources in "Where to Find More" for this chapter. The overview in this chapter hopefully gives you enough to get started reading OT poetry.

WHERE TO FIND MORE

Alter, Robert. *The Art of Biblical Poetry*. New York: Basic Books, 1985.

Berlin, Adele. *The Dynamics of Biblical Parallelism*. Rev. and exp. ed., with the addition of "The Range of Biblical Metaphors in *Smikhut*" by Lida Knorina. Grand Rapids, Mich.: Eerdmans, 2008.

Freedman, David Noel. *Pottery, Poetry, and Prophecy: Studies in Early Hebrew Poetry*. Winona Lake, Ind.: Eisenbrauns, 1980.

Has several helpful chapters on topics covered here; see especially pages 1–76 on words, accents, acrostics, and syllable counting in Hebrew poetry.

Koch, Klaus. *The Prophets*. 2 vols. Philadelphia: Fortress Press, 1983.

Helpful survey of the OT prophets, taking them in the chronological sequence we are suggesting here: Assyrian period, Babylonian period, and Persian period prophets.

Kugel, James L. *The Idea of Biblical Poetry: Parallelism and Its History*. New Haven, Conn.: Yale University Press, 1981. Repr., Baltimore: Johns Hopkins University Press, 1998.

Landy, Francis. "Poetics and Parallelism: Some Comments on James Kugel's The Idea of Biblical Poetry." *JSOT* 28 (1984): 61–87.

For discussion and critique of the approach of James L. Kugel, especially pages 71–72.

O'Connor, Michael Patrick. *Hebrew Verse Structure*. Winona Lake, Ind.: Eisenbrauns, 1980.

For the most impressive arguments against the presence of meter in Israelite poetry.

Petersen, David L., and Kent Harold Richards. *Interpreting Hebrew Poetry*. Guides to Biblical Scholarship. Minneapolis, Minn.: Fortress Press, 1992.

Watson, Wilfred G. E. *Classical Hebrew Poetry: A Guide to Its Techniques*. London: T & T Clark, 2005.

CHAPTER 17

Israel's Wisdom

OLD TESTAMENT READING: JOB AND PROVERBS

Having examined the nature of OT poetry, we will now explore two books by way of example. Proverbs and Job are unique in that they belong to the OT's wisdom tradition. Wisdom literature was a highly valued and enduring literary form, well attested across the ancient Near East. Materials from Egypt's tradition represent primarily "standard wisdom," a literary type characterized by proverbial sayings. These aphorisms represent predictable patterns born of everyday life experience and observation. From Mesopotamia, we have a second type that is generally more speculative and less optimistic, and willing to wrestle with the difficult question of theodicy.

The OT book of Proverbs is a collection of standard wisdom, presented as an educational curriculum and commonly based on the principle of retribution theology. The book of Job is a literary masterpiece representative of speculative wisdom. Although it displays a critique of retribution theology, Job's message honors the tension between a loving God, a righteous individual, and retributive justice. In Israel's wisdom literature we will observe in particular a distinctive moral and ethical dimension that results from Israel's relationship to Yahweh.

Now we come to two books in Israel's library that are unique. It isn't just their literary category or style that make them different, although these are somewhat distinctive, too. Both are written in poetry almost exclusively, as we observed in the previous chapter. While the poetry found here has features somewhat different from that of Psalms or the prophets, it isn't the kind of poetry alone that makes Job and Proverbs unique.

So what makes these two books different? We encounter here for the first time books in Israel's library centered on a common interest in the concept of "wisdom" (Hebrew ḥokmâ). This concept is almost impossible to define in a concise way. It is more than intellectual knowledge or brain capacity. The wisdom offered here is the capacity to live one's life well, to live in a way that shows insight into how Yahweh's world works. This kind of wisdom is *related* to intellectual ability as it shows an aptitude for right decisions, which means that we are also talking about character development and formation. Knowledge and experience contribute to wisdom; they inform the wise person about the ways of the world and encourage him or her to make right choices. In this sense, OT wisdom is about ethics.

Books centered on this kind of wisdom make no mention of Israel's exodus from Egypt, the Davidic dynasty, or the covenant with Yahweh. This is literature focused narrowly on ethical behavior and decision making. Before getting into the details of the books of Job and Proverbs, I'll introduce you to this topic in the ancient world more generally.

WISDOM LITERATURE IN THE ANCIENT NEAR EAST

Israel was not alone in the production of wisdom literature. As a matter of fact, numerous compositions fitting into the category "wisdom literature" are found across the entire ancient Near East; we have samples from Mesopotamia, Egypt, Syria-Palestine, and Asia Minor. And wisdom literature was valued in the ancient world for an astonishingly long period of time. Consider this: the length of time between the earliest and the latest such compositions from the ancient world is greater than

the interval between the latest and our own time.[1] It should not surprise us then, that wisdom literature has a variety of subcategories. The OT has examples of all of them.

Simple proverbial sayings or aphorisms could be used by themselves embedded in all kinds of literature in the ancient world. As early as the third millennium BCE, these were being gathered into anthologies (or collections of collections) and grouped by topic or style or any number of arrangements. These collections, which you might think of as *standard wisdom* or advice literature, accept the idea that regular and predictable patterns of life can be observed and recorded for future generations. The authority of these proverbs is the result of common cultural experience and is rooted in observation. Those who learn these patterns (i.e., those who listen to the advice given in the collections) improve their chances of success in life. Those who turn from the advice of the collections, through neglect or active rebellion, put themselves at risk in the world. You can see that this standard advice literature is based on the principle of retribution theology so important in other places of the OT (Chapter 9).

A second type of ancient Near Eastern advice literature may be called *speculative wisdom*.[2] At times presented in a drama setting, these materials are typically dialogues or general reflections on the meaning of life and are not as optimistic as the proverbial collections. Speculative wisdom may at times challenge or call into question the truthfulness and

1 As observed by Weeks (p. 9) in "Where to Find More" in this chapter.
2 For discussion and bibliography, see pages 56–83 of Sparks and pages 169–97 of Walton, both in "Where to Find More" in this chapter.

17.1. The goddess Ma'at. The Egyptian concept of cosmic order also has ethical dimensions and can be rendered as "truth," "righteousness," or "justice" personified as the goddess Ma'at, daughter of Re. She is most often shown wearing a large feather on her head, or the feather alone may represent her. Here the goddess Ma'at spreads wings for protection (see Plate X). (Photo: © DeA Picture Library / Art Resource, N.Y.)

validity of standard retribution thinking. You might even consider examples of speculative wisdom as pessimistic, in contrast to standard wisdom. The authority of speculative wisdom is rooted in the credentials of an individual with whom the advice is associated. The speeches of a famous individual noted for a long and successful life are passed down to subsequent generations, usually father to sons. Names for these two types of ancient Near Eastern advice literature – standard and speculative – are based on their content. If you think of literary

form rather than content, you might take these two as *instruction wisdom* and *dialogue wisdom*.

Mesopotamia and Egypt, the two oldest, leading cultures of the ancient world, had both standard and speculative advice literature. In a most general way, however, you might think of Egypt as having produced more standard instructional wisdom. In the Egyptian worldview, the concept of *ma'at* was established by divine power at the creation of the world and symbolizes a harmonious balance of both "justice" and "truth." *Ma'at* represents order and stability in Egyptian culture and was highly valued. Egyptian advice literature is based on the assumption that success will accompany the one who learns to live in adherence with *ma'at*.

Most of this advice literature from the ancient Near East was produced by a class of scribal scholars, who were sometimes organized around temples but more often served in royal courts. The Egyptian instructional category especially educated young protégés in how to live according to *ma'at*, and often prepared them for service in the royal court. The oldest example we have is the *Instruction of Ptahhotep* from the Old Kingdom, in which a vizier handed wisdom down to his son (see Sidebar 14.2). In the *Instruction of Amenemhet* from the Middle Kingdom, a deceased pharaoh instructs his son posthumously on how to avoid assassination (which the father had failed to do), and how to succeed in life. As we will see, a portion of this text has close parallels with the book of Proverbs.

We also have from Egypt a few compositions of the speculative category, which throw doubt on *ma'at*'s principles. Conversely, Mesopotamian advice literature is more likely to be of the speculative variety. We have a few proverbial compositions from Mesopotamian scholars, which assume something similar to the retribution principle we have seen in Egypt and in the OT. Such standard advice literature, passing along practical suggestions on all sorts of topics, has roots in early Sumerian culture and was copied by later scribes for centuries. But by and large, the harsh realities of life in Mesopotamia led people to look for answers about death and why innocent people sometimes suffer. A simple retributive principle assigning good things for good people and bad things for bad people didn't satisfy

Mesopotamian philosophers, and so the speculative type of advice literature is more common here.

The great dilemma addressed in speculative advice literature from Mesopotamia is the question of **theodicy**, broadly defined. Theodicy may be defined in theology and philosophy as the attempt to vindicate the goodness and justice of God (or the gods) in the face of the existence of evil and suffering in the world. How should one understand the character of God/gods when so many bad things happen? The Mesopotamian speculative literature is not setting out to vindicate the gods necessarily. But these works are at least raising the question, and they offer a variety of answers.

In the earliest Mesopotamian example, the Sumerian composition *Man and His God*, the sufferer does not challenge the justice of his god but complains that he is unaware of the causes for his suffering. He arrives at an answer that embraces the orthodoxy of retribution theology: "Never has a sinless child been born to its mother."[3] He eventually confesses his sin, in which case he is not a "righteous sufferer" but one previously unaware of the sin causing his distress. Similarly, in the later composition known as the *Babylonian Job*, the sufferer appeals to the god Marduk, who eventually responds, sending an exorcist to expel the demons causing the problems. So again, the suffering is not unmerited, and the solution is to encourage the reader to trust in Marduk, who heals and restores.

On the other hand, the work known as the *Babylonian Theodicy* challenges directly the retribution theology so widely accepted in the ancient world (see

---

3 Jacob Klein, "Man and His God," in *The Context of Scripture* (3 vols.; ed. W. H. Hallo; Leiden: Brill, 1997–2002), 1.179:573–75.

SIDEBAR 17.1. EXCERPTS FROM *THE POEM OF THE RIGHTEOUS SUFFERER*

The Poem of the Righteous Sufferer, at times called the *Babylonian Job*, is the most extensive treatment of the theme of theodicy from Mesopotamia. It is more accurately known by its name taken from the first line, "I will praise the lord of wisdom" (*Ludlul Bēl Nēmeqi*). The composition preserves the reflections of one Shubshi-meshre-Shakkan, who may also have been the author of part of the poem. The text is a monologue framed with hymns, in which the sufferer recounts how he fell from prosperity and honor to disgrace and disease. He can give no reason for his fall, except that he was driven to it by his god Marduk. Two sides of divine character are explored, anger and forgiveness, and the sufferer has no recourse but to accept the will of the god, which is beyond comprehension. The "Righteous Sufferer" in the title is not quite right, because this author is not as confident as Job is of his own innocence.*

> *From the day the lord Marduk punished me,*
> *And the warrior god Marduk became furious with me,*
> *My own god threw me over and disappeared,*
> *My goddess [Marduk's wife, Sarpanitum] broke rank and vanished.*
> *The benevolent angel who walked beside me split off,*
> *My protecting spirit retreated, to seek out someone else.*
> *My vigor was taken away, my manly appearance became gloomy,*
> *My dignity bolted and leapt for cover.*
> *Terrifying signs beset me.*
> *I was forced from my house, I wandered outside.*
> *…*
> *I called to my god, he did not show his face,*
> *I prayed to my goddess, she did not raise her head.*
> *…*
> *I, for my part, was mindful of supplication and prayer,*
> *Prayer to me was the natural recourse, sacrifice my rule.*
> *…*
> *What seems good to one's self could be an offense to a god,*
> *What in one's own heart seems abominable could be good to one's god!*
> *Who could learn the reasoning of the gods in heaven?*
> *Who could grasp the intentions of the gods of the depths?*
> *Where might human beings have learned the way of a god?*

* Excerpts adapted from Benjamin R. Foster, *Before the Muses: An Anthology of Akkadian Literature* (3rd ed.; Bethesda, Md.: CDL Press, 2005), 396–99.

Sidebar 17.4). The sufferer, like the OT character Job, insists on his own innocence. His friend counters that the principle of retributive justice cannot be denied, whereas the sufferer complains that it doesn't work in his case. He is innocent, at least of crimes meriting such suffering. Ultimately, both the sufferer and his friend affirm the inscrutable nature of the gods, who are responsible for justice in the world but who

SIDEBAR 17.2. AND ECCLESIASTES MAKES THREE

We cover only two OT books in this chapter, but a third book, Ecclesiastes, also belongs in this category. You should think of these three as the OT's books of wisdom literature: Job, Proverbs, and Ecclesiastes. The book of Job uses the narrative framework of a story to explore divine justice (or the lack of it) through long poetic discourses by the story's characters. The book of Proverbs is a collection of sayings (or a collection of collections of sayings) offering advice about how the world works and how to live successfully in it. The book of Ecclesiastes also offers advice, but in the form of long monologues that are less optimistic than Proverbs, at times even questioning whether success or human accomplishment is possible (see Chapter 23).

Wisdom teaching in the OT is not limited to these three books. The scribes who gave us these books were not narrowly focused only on wisdom themes, nor were the other authors of the OT books restricted from writing about wisdom topics. Indeed, these three wisdom books are part of a broader theological tradition or stream of thought in Israel that found expression in many other parts of the OT. So we will encounter a number of psalms that may be categorized as wisdom psalms, several of the books of prophecy have wisdom passages, and the Song of Songs is often identified as another wisdom book (we will return to this topic in Chapter 23).

Beyond such specific passages sprinkled throughout the OT, we find wisdom themes (creation, justice, retribution, and ethics) deeply embedded in a number of other OT books. For example, Deuteronomy, Amos, Hosea, and Isaiah are not wisdom books per se, but they do bear the marks of heavy influence from the wisdom tradition. We may also find wisdom influences in the Yahwist's narrative in the Pentateuch, the Joseph narrative, and the history of David's court in 2 Samuel and 1 Kings. Scholars of the OT debate whether such influence was the result of something like a Solomonic Enlightenment. Regardless, we can be confident that a wisdom theological tradition as a stream of thought was broad and influential in ancient Israel. As we discuss other portions of the OT poetic books, I will point out here and there these wisdom themes as we encounter them.

have placed some humans in unjust circumstances. Practical experience shows that sometimes bad things happen to good people, in which case the causes are simply not discernible in this life. The gods are not at fault, nor is the concept of retributive justice at fault. Humans suffer, and the reasons for such suffering are buried in the misdeeds of humans, even if those misdeeds are unknown to the sufferer.

THE BOOKS OF JOB AND PROVERBS

The books of Job and Proverbs are Israel's advice literature. They have similarities in both form and content with the ancient Near Eastern literature we have just considered, as we shall see. Beyond these similarities with other advice literature, Job and Proverbs belong together because they share an understanding of the advice they offer as "wisdom" (ḥōkmâ, and it synonyms). This wisdom found in the OT's advice literature has precise moral and ethical features. It is wisdom emerging from religious principles, and it is perceived as a result of Israel's relationship with Yahweh, as can be seen in the similarity of these theme verses.

"The fear of Yahweh, that is wisdom (ḥōkmâ); and to depart from evil is understanding." (Job 28:28)

"The fear of Yahweh is the beginning of knowledge; fools despise wisdom (ḥōkmâ) and instruction." (Proverbs 1:7)

And so Job and Proverbs belong together as Israel's wisdom books. But they also have obvious differences from each other. In general, the book of Proverbs is the OT example of standard ancient Near Eastern advice literature, is generally optimistic, and resembles in form and style other instructional literature. The book of Job is the OT version of speculative advice literature, is critical of retribution theology, and resembles especially the Mesopotamian examples we have already considered.

The Book of Job

The book of Job is highly regarded as among the best poetical works of world literature. Taken by itself, it stands as a literary masterpiece. Taken together with other speculative advice literature from the ancient world, the book of Job represents the culmination of that literature. It sharpens the focus on theodicy and offers a slightly different answer from that of Mesopotamian speculative thought.

The name of the book's hero generated speculation for years. Then, in the early twentieth century, other examples of this personal name were found in ancient Near Eastern texts from the second millennium BCE, making it likely that "Job" means "Where is the [divine] father?"[4] Such a name is appropriate for the suffering hero, whose message is summarized as a pointless cry, "Where is God

---

[4] For details, see pages 5–6 of Pope in the commentaries in "Where to Find More" in this chapter.

my Maker?" (Job 35:10). Job's name may also be reflected in his exchange with one of his so-called friends, Eliphaz, who asks, "Is not God high in the heavens?" Job responds, "Oh, that I knew where I might find him!" (Job 22:12 and 23:3).

The book of Job consists of a series of dialogues in poetry framed by a prologue (Job 1–2) and epilogue (Job 42:7–17) in narrative prose. A character by the name of Job is known elsewhere as a paragon of virtue from far distant days (Ezekiel 14:14, 20). Not only so, but he is apparently not an Israelite; he resides instead as a man of considerable wealth and honor among the "people of the east" in the "land of Uz" (Job 1:1–3). The inability to place this character in any particular period of Israel's history or even among other characters geographically gives the book a certain timeless quality. One suspects that this is intentional, highlighting the ageless quality of the book's message.

The prologue perfectly sets up the drama of the speeches. The Accuser (or "the Satan") raises a challenge against Job's character, and Yahweh gives him permission to afflict Job with the loss of everything. We as readers are allowed to witness events in the heavenly reaches, which explains what is happening to poor Job on earth. But our hero has no idea why these things are happening to him. Impressively, he pushes on with his faith, even in the face of devastating losses. In a second round of demonic affliction, Job's suffering touches his physical well-being. Faced with his wife's advice to "curse God, and die," Job does not allow such horrible words to pass his lips (Job 2:9–10). With this background, Job's three friends, Eliphaz, Bildad, and Zophar arrive on the scene to comfort him in his misery. But when they

SIDEBAR 17.3. JOB'S LIVING REDEEMER

Perhaps the most famous of Job's speeches is his assertion that he has a living redeemer (Job 19:25). This comes after a wistful statement that he wishes his words could be preserved permanently so that eventually his position could be shown to be true and he would stand vindicated (19:23–24). Then, in one of the most profound statements of faith in the OT, Job turns from such wishful thinking to express his one certainty: he knows that his living redeemer will eventually vindicate him.

> "For I know that my Redeemer lives,
> and that at the last he will stand upon the earth;
> and after my skin has been thus destroyed,
>   then in my flesh I shall see God,
> whom I shall see on my side,
>   and my eyes shall behold, and not another." (Job 19:25–27)

We are unsure from the context who Job's kinsman-redeemer is. Perhaps Job is identifying God himself as his redeemer, explaining the capitalization of "Redeemer" in the NRSV and many modern translations. Another possibility is that this redeemer is the heavenly witness that Job believes will testify on his behalf (see 16:19). This creates an ironic reading, since we've been told Job has an adversary speaking against him in heaven rather than an advocate-redeemer (Job 1:9). Whoever it is in view, Job has confidence that such a "living" redeemer bearing witness on his behalf is better than his dead words perserved on cold stone (19:23–24).

Readers of the early Christian church often took this statement to be a doctrine of resurrection, taking "redeemer" as the Messiah who will stand on the earth and enable Job to "see God" even after death. This interpretation has been immortalized in the magnificent soprano aria beginning part three of Handel's oratorio *Messiah*. Yet Job has expressly rejected the hope of resurrection elsewhere (Job 14:10–12). And were resurrection the answer offered here, it would make the rest of the book seem unnecessary. Here would be the ultimate answer to the book's questions, and perhaps the climactic closure to the book.

But Job is not asserting so much, and indeed, the OT rarely has explicit statements of resurrection (*perhaps* Daniel 12:2–3). Nonetheless, even in the midst of suffering and injustice, Job has faith in God as just, and he awaits a day when God himself will identify with his sufferings and vindicate or redeem his life. In this sense, Job's confession contributes to that line of thought eventuating in a doctrine of resurrection in early Judaism and Christianity.

see the disfigured and pitiable Job, they are shocked speechless for a week (Job 2:11–13).

The silence is broken by Job's first speech, in which he curses the day of his birth (Job 3). This is followed by a series of exchanges between Job and his three friends (Job 4–27). These speeches have a general progressive flow in logic, in which Job's three friends, each in his own way, tries to console Job but also accuses him of wrongdoing and encourages him to confess his sins. Job, through it all, maintains his innocence and at times gives voice to remarkable expressions of faith. This section culminates in Job's beautiful hymn in praise of wisdom, in which he acknowledges the exploits of

17.2. Mesopotamian Leviathan (third millennium BCE). As early as Sumerian times, the image of a flaming monster with seven serpent heads appears in the iconography of ancient Mesopotamia. On this plaque, a deity battles the monster. "Leviathan" is the name given in the west (Ugaritic and Hebrew) for the mythical monster associated with the sea and often the paradigmatic creature of chaos and evil. As such, Leviathan engages in combat with creator gods and threatens to tip the cosmic order to disastrous effect. But in Yahweh's answer to Job, God explains that Leviathan is merely a creature of his design, although Job could not possibly hope to subdue the monster himself (Job 41). (Photo: Z. Radovan / Bible Land Pictures)

humans while admitting that only God knows the way of wisdom (Job 28).

One final long discourse closes Job's case, in which he maintains his innocence again and challenges God to give an answer (Job 29–31). Unexpectedly, another character is introduced at this point, Elihu, who is angry at Job and his friends but waits his turn to speak because he is younger (Job 32:1–5). Yet his long speech clearly adds nothing to the arguments of Job's three friends (Job 32–37). Elihu finishes with the idea that "God thunders wondrously," but his voice and deeds are incomprehensible. Humans cannot find God and should stop looking (37:23–24). No one would have been more surprised than Elihu at God's appearance in the next chapter.

Yahweh finally answers Job "out of the whirlwind" (Job 38:1). God appears on the scene, not to condemn Job but to put in proper perspective the human understanding of the majesty of God (Job 38–41). The answer is at least partly wrapped in the doctrine of creation (38:4): "Where were you when I laid the foundation of the earth?" The size and grandeur of the created order is more than Job and his friends could possibly understand. And as the Creator of such a universe, the reality of God transcends their pitiful debates about justice in this life. Their grand claims to understand and explain the way things work are simply wrong. God illustrates the wondrous and mysterious ways of his creation, implying that he has not ordered the world in a mechanical way along the lines of a simplistic retribution theology. The fundamental premise of their debates is just false. Job responds with appropriate humility (42:1–6), essentially saying, "I didn't know what I was talking about; now I understand." In the prose epilogue, Job is vindicated (42:7–17).

The book of Job is an attempt to address the problem of suffering, especially the undeserved suffering of innocents. We often use the term "theodicy" for Job's content, although technically, Job does not attempt to vindicate God's justice in light of the world's violence and evil. Rather, Job is a critique of simplistic approaches to retribution

---

SIDEBAR 17.4. EXCERPTS FROM *THE BABYLONIAN THEODICY*

The Babylonian Theodicy relates a debate between two friends about divine justice. One, the sufferer, observes poverty and illness among the godly while those who pay no attention to the gods prosper. His friend counters that he is speaking from his own circumstances, and that he is wrong to question the unfathomable will of the gods. The sufferer challenges the gods to take pity on him and to care for him as they should.

The composition is closest to the OT book of Job in form and content. The poem itself is an elaborate acrostic (see Sidebar 16.3), not based on the alphabet since Akkadian is not alphabetic, but based on the first syllable of each opening line. In this way, the poem spells out the name of the author and defends him against any charges that might arise from such an unorthodox theological position: "I am Saggil-kinam-ubbib the exorcist, a worshipper of god and king."*

> Sufferer: *I am without recourse, heartache has come upon me.*
> *I was the youngest child when fate claimed my father,*
> *My mother who bore me departed to the land of no return,*
> *My father and mother left me, and with no one my guardian!*
>
> Friend: *Considerate friend, what you tell is a sorrowful tale,*
> *My dear friend, you have let our mind harbor ill....*
> *Of course our fathers pay passage to go death's way,*
> *I too will cross the river of the dead, as is commanded from of old....*
> *He who looks to his god has a protector,*
> *The humble man who reveres his goddess will garner wealth....*
>
> Sufferer: *Let me put one matter before you:*
> *Those who seek not after a god can go the road of favor,*
> *Those who pray to a goddess have grown poor and destitute.*
> *Indeed, in my youth I tried to find out the will of my god,*
> *With prayer and supplication I besought my goddess.*
> *I bore a yoke of profitless servitude:*
> *My god decreed for me poverty instead of wealth....*
>
> Friend: *O just, knowledgeable one, your logic is perverse,*
> *You have cast off justice, you have scorned divine design....*
> *Divine purpose is as remote as innermost heaven,*
> *It is too difficult to understand, people cannot understand it.*

* Excerpts adapted from Benjamin R. Foster, *Before the Muses: An Anthology of Akkadian Literature* (3rd ed.; Bethesda, Md.: CDL Press, 2005), 914–20.

---

theology. The book does not reject retribution theology, which as we have seen is prevalent in Deuteronomy and throughout much of the OT. Rather, the book of Job nuances it to provide balance in Israel's theology.

One helpful way to undertand the message of Job is to think of three principles equally valued by Job and his friends throughout their discourse: (1) a loving God, (2) a righteous Job, and (3) retributive justice. The tension that builds as the book moves forward shows the impossibility of holding these three together as equally true. One of them must go. Job's friends toss out Job as a righteous man, holding to God and retribution theology. Job maintains his innocence and the truth of retributive justice, all but giving up on God. But at the end, God arrives to affirm Job's character and to eliminate retribution theology as it was simplistically interpreted by Job and his friends.[5]

The Book of Proverbs

The book of Proverbs is Israel's equivalent of *standard* ancient Near Eastern advice literature, as opposed to Job's *speculative* type. The book is a collection of collections, and it best represents Israel's school of wisdom thought. As we have said, much of the advice literature from the ancient world was produced by a class of scribal scholars serving in royal courts and official government circles. And so we are not surprised to see the book of Proverbs associated first with King Solomon (Proverbs 1:1). Indeed, Solomon's wisdom was said to be renowned throughout the world, and he compiled proverbs on a wide variety of topics (1 Kings 4:29–34). The superscription for the book of Proverbs locates at least its first major portion in the United Monarchy of ancient Israel: "The proverbs of Solomon son of David, king of Israel."

Many of the proverbs and aphorisms found in the book were likely from conventional and popular kinship experiences, perhaps even tribal society.

These then would have been gathered together and supplemented by official court scribes once Israel was organized in a monarchic state, with scribes, priests, and historians or chroniclers serving the needs of a central government. These scribes presumably were teachers, and the content of the book of Proverbs was evidently part of the standard curriculum for an Israelite education. Egyptian instructional literature provided an education narrowly focused on training young men in the service of the royal court. But Israel's curriculum appears to address the youth of all classes. The book has several references most at home in an educational context: "Hear, my child, your father's instruction, and do not reject your mother's teaching" (Proverbs 1:8).

After the general superscription (1:1), the book opens with a lengthy introduction or prologue sounding its central themes (1:2–7). A series of five purpose clauses (infinitives construct of purpose, in Hebrew grammar) explain why the proverbs of Solomon have been collected: "[In order] to learn ..., to understand ..., to gain instruction ..., to teach ..., to explain ..."[6] From the outset, the collection is centered on "wisdom" (*ḥokmâ*), and its many associated ideals: instruction, insight, righteousness, justice, equity, shrewdness, knowledge, prudence, learning, and skill. This introduction climaxes in the book's theme verse, in contrastive parallelism: the first step in the attainment of wisdom is a proper relationship with Yahweh, but fools don't even want wisdom and instruction and by implication do not honor Yahweh (v. 7). Thus the book is set forward as an educational curriculum

---

5 For this interpretation, see pages 1–37 in Tsevat in "Where to Find More" in this chapter.

6 This is my literal translation to illustrate the point; the NRSV and other translations will vary widely.

for character formation, and it assumes that the reader is mature enough to understand the value of attaining wisdom.

This prologue in 1:2–7 has been placed at the beginning of two large collections of the proverbs of Solomon, as introduced separately at 10:1 and 25:1. The second collection is "other proverbs" of Solomon gathered by officials of King Hezekiah's court. In this way, the book reflects the centuries-old tradition of proverbs being collected, copied, studied, and handed down by officials at the royal court.

The first portion of the proverbs of Solomon is a string of connected lessons introducing wisdom itself and encouraging the student to embrace wisdom enthusiastically (Proverbs 1–9). The lengthy collection in Proverbs 10–22 gives instruction on numerous topics, including promoting obedience to parents, respect for the place of women, prudent speech, treasured friendships, and care for the poor and underprivileged, and warning against sexual promiscuity. The principle of divine retribution bestowing blessing for obedience and curse for disobedience undergirds the whole.

At the conclusion of this second lengthy collection (Proverbs 10–22), we have an introduction for a new smaller collection (22:17–24:22): "the words of the wise." This group of proverbs is identified as "thirty sayings of admonition and knowledge" (22:20), and the first portion of this collection (22:17–23:11) is an adaptation of the "thirty chapters" of an earlier Egyptian document, *The Instruction of Amenemope*. The inclusion of this material in the book of Proverbs illustrates the international quality of advice literature and demonstrates that Israel was comfortable using the conventional wisdom it

saw in the literature of its neighbors. Of course, the only divine name in Israel's adaptation is "Yahweh," which is the most obvious editorial change in the materials borrowed from the Egyptian source text. Another small collection is appended to the proverbs of Solomon, the "sayings of the wise," in Proverbs 24:23–34.

To the proverbs of Solomon collected by Hezekiah (Proverbs 25–29) are appended two additional collections: the "words of Agur son of Jakeh" (30:1–9), a miscellaneous collection of aphorisms (30:10–33), and the "words of King Lemuel" (31:1–9). This is followed by the book's conclusion in the acrostic poem praising the "woman of strength" (31:10–31). In a book often focused on wisdom for young men, it is significant that Proverbs concludes with the ideal woman, who is in every respect really an ideal person.

REVELATION, MONOTHEISM, AND THE PROBLEM OF EVIL

As you can see, Israel's wisdom literature has a distinctive theological perspective. Other portions of the OT that we have studied so far – the Primary History and the Chronistic History – focus on what we may think of as "salvation history." God has intervened in history to reveal himself, and to create and save his people Israel. Central events of this salvation history include the call of Israel's ancestors and God's covenant with them, the exodus from Egypt, the Sinai covenant, the conquest of the promised land, and the founding of the Davidic dynasty.

The books of Job and Proverbs have none of this. Their message does not contradict the salvation

SIDEBAR 17.5. EXCERPTS FROM *THE INSTRUCTION OF AMENEMOPE*

The author or compiler of the "words of the wise" in Proverbs 22:17–24:22 arranged the material into "thirty sayings" (22:20).* This organizing principle reveals a dependence on the Egyptian document *The Instruction of Amenemope*, dating from New Kingdom Egypt (1550–1069 BCE), although many of its ideas were present in earlier Egyptian instruction literature.

The thirty chapters of *Amenemope* focus on two basic themes, around which the rest revolve: (1) the ideal, "silent" man versus the "heated" man, and (2) the contrast between honesty and dishonesty. The compiler of the "words of the wise" in the OT book of Proverbs was dependent on this document, and bits and pieces of it were directly included in the collection. The following excerpts are adapted from *The Instruction of Amenemope* and are intended to illustrate this literary dependence; read them together with the indicated parallels to the book of Proverbs.†

> *Give your ears, hear the sayings,*
>   *Give your heart to understand them;*
>   *It profits to put them in your heart. (Proverbs 22:17–18)*
> *Beware of robbing the oppressed,*
>   *Of attacking the disabled. (Proverbs 22:22)*
> *Do not move the markers on the borders of fields,*
>   *Nor shift the position of the measuring-cord.*
>   *Do not be greedy for a cubit of land,*
>   *Nor encroach on the boundaries of a widow. (Proverbs 23:10)*
> *Do not strain to seek increase,*
>   *What you have, let it suffice you.*
>   *If riches come to you by theft,*
>   *They will not stay the night with you.*
>   *Comes day they are not in your house,*
>   *Their place is seen but they're not there; …*
>   *They made themselves wings like geese,*
>   *And flew away to the sky. (Proverbs 23:4–5)*
> *Do not covet a poor man's goods,*
>   *Nor hunger for his bread;*
>   *A poor man's goods are a block in the throat,*
>   *It makes the gullet vomit …*
>   *The big mouthful of bread – you swallow, you vomit it,*
>   *And you are emptied of your gain. (Proverbs 23:6–8)*
> *The scribe who is skilled in his office,*
>   *He is found worthy to be a courtier. (Proverbs 22:29)*
> *Look to these thirty chapters,*
>   *They inform, they educate;*
>   *They are the foremost of all books,*
>   *They make the ignorant wise. (Proverbs 22:20–21)*

* For discussion of the thirty sayings specifically as they relate to *The Instruction of Amenemope*, see pages 707–33 in Fox (2009) in the commentaries in "Where to Find More" in this chapter.

† Excerpts adapted from Miriam Lichtheim, *Ancient Egyptian Literature: A Book of Readings* (3 vols.; Berkeley: University of California Press, 1973–1980), 2:146–63.

history but complements it. This gives the OT a complex theological profile. The OT is not simply a one-dimensional library of books, claiming to be a revelation of God through history alone. The wisdom literature embodies another mode of divine revelation, one based on observations of everyday life and human experience.

Many readers of the OT have speculated that the origins of the book of Proverbs were essentially secular and nontheological. Some have even suggested that early versions of the book do not represent the normative religion of ancient Israel and that God in the earliest collections of proverbs has virtually none of the characteristics of Israelite religion.[7] Whether or not that is true, we may never really know. But as the book stands now in our OT canon, it clearly makes distinctive contributions to Israel's theology. In fact, you should think of wisdom literature generally as counterbalancing a narrow theology that views deliverance in historical terms. The doctrine of creation is central in this wisdom understanding of God.

> Yahweh by wisdom founded the earth;
>   by understanding he established the heavens;
> by his knowledge the deeps broke open,
>   and the clouds drop down the dew. (Proverbs 3:19–20)

This core understanding of divine revelation stands at the center of a wheel with numerous spokes, such as justice, retribution, morality, and ethics, moving outward from the center, completing the picture.

7 See pages 126–30 in Dell in "Where to Find More" in this chapter.

Related to God's creation of the universe in Israel's wisdom literature is another important idea expressed implicitly and almost by default — monotheism. We have no explicit statements of monotheism, like those in Deuteronomy or Second Isaiah (chaps. 40–55). But Israel's wisdom literature exhibits a kind of presupposition of monotheism. Not only are no other deities mentioned besides Yahweh but wisdom literature thinks of a single God behind all things, creating, directing, and instructing. The single God makes possible the order of creation, encompassing everything from the extravagant diversity of the animal kingdom, the plants, the stars, and everything else observable to human beings. The singularity of God explains the stunning diversity and plurality of human existence. God is one, and this explains a lot.

This idea of orderliness is satisfying. The monotheism presumed by wisdom literature provides the unifying principle beneath the diversity of human experiences. And yet this same monotheism presents a problem. The authors of ancient Israel's wisdom literature also held to the belief that not only is God one but God also is good and loving. How then does one explain the presence of evil and suffering in light of the one unifying principle beneath all human experiences?

Polytheism is easier. If you are trying to look beyond the experiences of life to explain why things are the way they are, it helps to have multiple divine forces at work to account for everything. In polytheistic religions, there is no problem of evil. Theodicy, or the attempt to defend the justice of God (or the gods), either is ignored in polytheistic religions or is treated in a simpler way. Bad things happen when power among the gods is not balanced between benevolent gods and malevolent gods.

But for the monotheist, explanations of evil and suffering must take into account the singularity of the one Creator God. Jewish, Christian, and Muslim readers of the OT also accept the goodness of God, and so evil cannot be placed at the feet of a malevolent Yahweh. Such will never do in light of the OT's portrait of the loving and merciful character of Yahweh. And so the book of Job is the OT's jewel in a crown of wisdom literature. Here the problem is addressed in beautiful and compelling poetry, its answer calling for faith beyond one's ability to comprehend the ways of God (Job 38:4–7). God is both all-powerful and loving. Job is righteous, and retribution theology must not be applied too rigidly. Sometimes we have no explanation for why suffering occurs. Yet the book of Job affirms that God's ways with humanity are nevertheless trustworthy and true.

WHERE TO FIND MORE

Commentaries: The best technical and advanced commentaries on the book of **Job** are David J. A. Clines, *Job 1–20, Job 21–37*, and *Job 38–42* (Word Biblical Commentary 17, 18A, and 18B; Dallas/Nashville: Word/Thomas Nelson, 1989, 2006, and 2011); Marvin H. Pope, *Job* (3rd ed.; Anchor Bible 15; Garden City, N.Y.: Doubleday, 1973); and John E. Hartley, *The Book of Job* (New International Commentary on the Old Testament; Grand Rapids, Mich.: Eerdmans, 1988). The best technical and advanced commentaries on the book of **Proverbs** are Michael V. Fox, *Proverbs 1–9 and Proverbs 10–31* (Anchor Bible 18A and 18B; New York: Doubleday, 2000 and 2009), and Bruce K. Waltke, *The Book of Proverbs* (2 vols.; New International Commentary on the OT; Grand Rapids, Mich.: Eerdmans, 2004 and 2005).

Brown, William P. *Character in Crisis: A Fresh Approach to the Wisdom Literature of the Old Testament*. Grand Rapids, Mich.: Eerdmans, 1996.

Day, John, Robert P. Gordon, and H. G. M. Williamson, eds. *Wisdom in Ancient Israel: Essays in Honour of J. A. Emerton*. Cambridge: Cambridge University Press, 1995.

Important essays on a number of topics covered in this chapter.

Dell, Katharine J. *The Book of Proverbs in Social and Theological Context*. Cambridge: Cambridge University Press, 2006.

See pages 125–38 on the "presupposition of monotheism" in Israel's wisdom literature.

Gese, Hartmut. "Wisdom Literature in the Persian Period." Pages 189–218 in *The Cambridge History of Judaism. Vol. 1, Introduction; The Persian Period*. Edited by W. D. Davies and Louis Finkelstein. Cambridge and New York: Cambridge University Press, 1984.

Sparks, Kenton L. *Ancient Texts for the Study of the Hebrew Bible: A Guide to the Background Literature*. Peabody, Mass.: Hendrickson Publishers, 2005.

Pages 56–83 have a thorough introduction to the ancient Near Eastern wisdom literature and an excellent bibliography.

Tsevat, Matitiahu. *The Meaning of the Book of Job and Other Biblical Studies: Essays on the Literature and Religion of the Hebrew Bible*. New York: Ktav, 1980.

Walton, John H. *Ancient Israelite Literature in Its Cultural Context: A Survey of Parallels between Biblical and Ancient Near Eastern Texts*. Grand Rapids, Mich.: Zondervan, 1989.

Pages 169–97 introduce ancient Near Eastern wisdom literature; pages 183–85 present a helpful discussion of Mesopotamian speculative solutions to theodicy.

Weeks, Stuart. *An Introduction to the Study of Wisdom Literature*. London: T & T Clark, 2010.

CHAPTER 18

Israel's Hymnal

OLD TESTAMENT READING: THE BOOK OF PSALMS

In this chapter, we will explore Israel's book of worship – Psalms. These "songs," collected over hundreds of years, nevertheless convey timeless expressions of Israel's faith. This OT collection has been organized into five books, and many of the individual psalms have titles, musical notations, or historical details.

Scholarship in the discipline of form criticism has furthered our understanding of how the original materials (sources behind the present texts) may have functioned in Israel's life situations (German, *Sitz im Leben*). In general, we can identify larger categories of praise and lament, and of individual and corporate psalms. Specific forms include hymns, communal and individual laments, thanksgiving songs, and royal psalms. Thus, for example, the form of lament corresponds to a crisis situation; a royal psalm form is situated in events surrounding the king. These forms, preserved and presented as the collected psalms, represent an overview of Israel's religious worldview. We will not necessarily observe statements of strict monotheism, but we will hear Israel "sing" of Yahweh, who alone is worthy of praise.

According to the books of Chronicles, King David instituted worship for the new temple to be built by his son Solomon. Worship in the temple included various types of sacrifices on an altar outside the temple, while the ark of the covenant was inside. At that time, it is said, King David appointed certain priests of the tribe of Levi to serve in the temple with harps, lyres, cymbals, and trumpets, in regular praise and thanksgiving to Yahweh (1 Chronicles 16:1–6). And, also at the same time, it is claimed that David ordered the place of music in Israel's worship.

> *O give thanks to Yahweh, call on his name,*
>> *make known his deeds among the peoples.*
> *Sing to him, sing praises to him,*
>> *tell of all his wonderful works. (1 Chronicles 16:8–9)*

Accompanied with numerous instruments, Israel's hymns were of several types, expressing thanksgiving to Yahweh, recounting his saving acts, and numbering his blessings.

Music and singing were an important part of everyday life in ancient Israel. The OT mentions harvest songs (Judges 9:27; Isaiah 16:10), victory songs after military successes (Judges 5; Exodus 15; and see 1 Samuel 18:6–7), mocking songs (Isaiah 14:4–21), and songs of lament or mourning after a death (2 Samuel 1:17–27, 3:33–34; Amos 5:1–2), not to mention the many types of praise songs and thanksgiving songs that we will discuss in this chapter. We also know from archaeological and comparative sources that people in ancient Syria-Palestine during the Iron Age played a wide variety of instruments, including hand drums (tambourines without the modern metal jingles hooked to their sides), cymbals, pipes and other wind instruments, lyres and other stringed instruments, and trumpets made of rams' horns, silver, or conch shells.

And so it should not surprise us that Israel's library includes the book of Psalms. This book is a collection of the Israelites' favorite hymns used in the worship of Yahweh. You might think of it as their hymnal or songbook for worship. "Psalm" is the Greek word for "song, hymn" and is used for the book title because the Septuagint's name for this collection is *psalmoi*, "songs sung to the accompaniment of instruments." In these songs, some of Israel's loftiest conceptions of Yahweh, faith, and religion converge in some of the most beautiful literature ever produced.

The Book of Psalms

The book of Psalms is placed together with other books of poetry in the Christian canon, usually between Job and Proverbs. The Jewish canon usually lists the book at the head of the third section of the canon, the "Writings," although this sequence is somewhat flexible (see Figure 2.3).

The Psalter (another name for the book of Psalms) has been organized by its final editors into five books of unequal length. Most English translations mark this five-part arrangement by spaces on the page, or even designations as follows:

Book One: Psalms 1–41
Book Two: Psalms 42–72
Book Three: Psalms 73–89
Book Four: Psalms 90–106
Book Five: Psalms 107–150

The Hebrew text marks these five divisions by ending each set of psalms with a doxology or expression of praise in a distinctive and formulaic pattern. Psalm 150 concludes the fifth book, and the entire Psalter itself. It seems likely this editorial arrangement was superimposed on the collection by analogy to the five-part division of the Pentateuch, although there is no formal correspondence of content between the five books of the Torah and the Psalms.

It is clear that this five-book arrangement is late, evidently provided by the final editorial stage of the Psalter, and is somewhat artificial. In some ways, this arrangment of the psalms actually conflicts with what must have been the original organizing principle of the collection. In fact, we're not sure what the original organizing principle might have been. It's important to remember that these psalms were likely gathered over hundreds of years, perhaps as much as a thousand years of Israelite history. The collection itself probably went through several stages, in which the organizing principle may have changed more than once.

Authorship appears to have been an organizing principle at one point, so that psalms attributed to David (see Psalm 72:20), Moses (Psalm 90:1), the "sons of Korah" (Psalms 42–49), and quite a number of other authors gave the collection shape. At another point in time, function must have served as an organizing principle, so that the "songs of ascent," for example, are collected as a group (Psalms 120–134). These were probably songs enouraged for use when the worshipper was traveling to the temple in Jerusalem on a religious pilgrimage. At some point, a common theme or content could attract a group of psalms into a subcategory, such as songs devoted to Yahweh as king of the universe (Psalms 93 and 95–99).

Beyond the somewhat artificial five-book format in the book of Psalms, we should not expect too much from the book by way of an all-inclusive organizing principle. We can discern themes developing within portions of the book among certain psalms, but in general we still have in the book of Psalms, a collection of collections. At this point, it's enough for you to think of the first two psalms simply as a general introduction for the whole, and of Psalm 150 as a way of wrapping the book up and tying the various themes together. Psalm 1 is a wisdom poem, which offers two ways in life, one leading to contentment and fulfillment through one's relationship with Yahweh, and the other resulting in a meaningless death. Psalm 2 moves immediately to introduce the topic of the kingship of Yahweh and the legitimacy of Yahweh's anointed ones through the Davidic line (2:6): "I have set my king on Zion, my holy hill." These two psalms thus prepare the reader for the rest of the Psalter by encouraging a life of submission to the law of Yahweh, and accepting the sovereignty of the king of heaven and his messiah, the son of David. Psalm 150 is the concluding praise hymn, in which all of creation ("everything that breathes") breaks forth in praise of Yahweh. In this way, Psalms 1–2 and Psalm 150 frame Israel's life of faith as expressed in the psalms.

When reading the psalms, you will also notice that many of them (all but 34, in fact) have a title or superscription set off from the first verse, often

in a smaller font.[1] Many of these are musical notations giving instructions to the choirmaster or
music director, calling for stringed instruments or
flutes to be used with a particular song (Psalms 4
and 5, for example). Others have brief historical
notations, associating a particular song with some
event known from the OT historical books, as when
David "feigned madness before Abimelech, so that
he drove him out, and he went away" (Psalm 34).[2]

Nearly half of the psalms are marked in these
superscriptions as psalms "of David," which *may*
indicate authorship "by David," but may also be simply *"about David,"* or *"according to* the Davidic style"
of playing or singing the music. Two such psalms
are "of Solomon" (Psalms 72 and 127), and one
is "of Moses" (Psalm 90). While these superscriptions were not a part of the original compositions
of the songs, they were known by the translators
of the Septuagint and thus included in the Greek
versions. They therefore represent quite early Jewish
traditions about the individual psalms.

It should be obvious by now that we cannot
associate the book of Psalms with any one specific
period of Israel's history. Indeed, we have reason to
believe that this collection includes poems, prayers,
and hymns from both the earliest and the latest
periods of OT history. For example, based on content, Psalm 137 was written during the exile:

> By the rivers of Babylon —
>> there we sat down and there we wept
>> when we remembered Zion.

On the willows there
> we hung up our harps.
For there our captors asked us for songs,
and our tormentors asked for mirth, saying,
> "Sing us one of the songs of Zion!"
How could we sing Yahweh's song
> in a foreign land? (Psalm 137:1–4)

By contrast, the repetitive parallelism of Psalm 29,
as well as other stylistic and content indications,
leads us to think it is quite old, probably an adaptation of an old Canaanite poem dedicated to the
storm god Hadad-Baal.

> Ascribe to Yahweh, O heavenly beings,
> ascribe to Yahweh glory and strength.
> Ascribe to Yahweh the glory of his name;
> worship Yahweh in holy splendor. (Psalm 29:1–2)

Similarly, Psalm 104 has undeniable parallels in
phraseology, theology, and sequence of ideas with
the Egyptian *Great Hymn to the Aten* from the Late
Bronze Age (Sidebar 10.3), whether or not we think
the two texts have a direct literary dependence.

Despite the general historical references in some
of the psalms and psalm titles, one gets the feeling
that this collection is not *supposed* to be tied down
to any one particular historical period of Israel's
history. These psalms are timeless. Some are quite
old, such as Psalms 29 and 68, and others definitely
have an exilic context, such as Psalms 126 and 137.
But for the most part, we are not able to locate
individual psalms in particular historical settings.
Given the nature of these songs as worship litur-
gies, such a lack of context is intentional. These
are intensely personal and emotional expressions
of faith, intended to be embraced and shared by

---

1 The Hebrew Bible counts each superscription as part or all
of verse 1, leaving us with different verse enumerations in
English than in the original Hebrew.
2 Although the king in 1 Samuel 21:10–15 is Achish instead of
Abimelech.

SIDEBAR 18.2. THE POWER OF MUSIC

18.1 Jug with lyre player and cymbals. This pictorial jug from eleventh-century BCE Megiddo displays a lyre player and a procession of animals. In the foreground is a pair of Iron Age I cymbals made of bronze. (Photo: Erich Lessing / Art Resource, N.Y.)

Consider for a moment the power music has over us, even in our contemporary world of high technology. Like the ancient Israelites, we use music in worship in almost all churches and synagogues. In mosques, music can be heard in the chanting of the Qur'an. But we also use music – whether classical, heavy metal, pop, rap, or countless others – to sell commercial products, to intensify our level of entertainment in movies and television programs, and to elevate artistic expression in its own right. Music can also be a powerful educational tool, serving as a mnemonic device helping us to remember elementary things like our ABCs.

In the ancient world, music seemed to hold a magical spell over people. They were more aware than we, perhaps, of music's therapeutic benefits (1 Samuel 16:16,23). The blast of a ram's horn could seem almost supernatural to the Israelites (Exodus 19:13; Joshua 6:4–9). Certain musical instruments were considered so powerful that they were perceived as fueling ecstatic prophecy (1 Samuel 10:5; 2 Kings 3:15).

The texts of the psalms were thus to be sung with musical instruments, enhancing their educational impact and making it possible for Israel to learn Yahweh's "wonderful works." Music also enhanced the texts' emotive impact, perhaps made more powerful by the parallel poetry of the psalms, repeating, restating, or otherwise seconding the truth of each assertion (on parallelism in Hebrew poetry, review Chapter 16). The collection of psalms contains several references to the way these songs were intended to be sung with instrumental music.

Praise Yahweh with the lyre;
* make melody to him with the harp of ten strings.*
Sing to him a new song;
* play skillfully on the strings, with loud shouts. (Psalm 33:2–3)*

Make a joyful noise to Yahweh, all the earth;
* break forth into joyous song and sing praises.*
Sing praises to Yahweh with the lyre,
* with the lyre and the sound of melody.*
With trumpets and the sound of the horn
* make a joyful noise before the King, Yahweh. (Psalm 98:4–6)*

Sing to Yahweh with thanksgiving;
* make melody to our God on the lyre. (Psalm 147:7)*

Praise Yahweh!
Sing to Yahweh a new song,
* his praise in the assembly of the faithful.*

Let Israel be glad in its Maker;
    let the children of Zion rejoice in their King.
Let them praise his name with dancing,
    making melody to him with tambourine and lyre. (Psalm 149:1–3)

Praise him with trumpet sound;
    praise him with lute and harp!
Praise him with tambourine and dance;
    praise him with strings and pipe!
Praise him with clanging cymbals;
    praise him with loud clashing cymbals! (Psalm 150:3–5)

all in any generation. The reader is thus invited to enter into the worship, accepting his or her role in ancient Israel's life of praise, lifting a voice or playing an instrument, in an unending chorus of praise.

FORM CRITICISM AND PSALM TYPES

So far in our study of OT books, I have introduced a scholarly approach most often identified as *literary* or *source criticism*. This approach focuses on the underlying sources of the present text. It resulted in the late nineteenth century in a hypothesis on the origins of the Pentateuch, known as the "Documentary Hypothesis." This hypothesis identified four sources in the Torah: J, E, D, and P (Sidebars 4.3 and 6.2). The second half of the twentieth century saw numerous challenges to the Documentary Hypothesis, and scholars continue to debate the content, date, and even existence of some of the sources. But by and large, some variation of this hypothesis continues to offer the best explanation for the Pentateuch's composition.

This is not the whole story, of course. Another influential approach, *form criticism*, examines the reconstructed literary, preliterary, and even oral stages of the sources prior to their composition. This approach assumes that ancient Near Eastern authors relied on stock material arising from popular tradition, with fixed literary genres or types having preset formal characteristics. Most of these literary "forms" functioned in a specific "situation in life" (*Sitz im Leben*, in German), or social setting, such as the temple, cultic festivals, or law court. Many such formal types of literature have been identified from the ancient world: priestly instruction, prophetic judgment speech, prophetic salvation speech, court complaint, and mourner's lament among them.

Beginning with the work of Hermann Gunkel (1862–1932) in the early twentieth century, scholars studied the Pentateuch and OT historical books from the perspective of form criticism. Preliterary forms behind the books of the Primary History were thought to be folk traditions, narratives, etiologies (stories told to explain the origins of something), legends, myths, liturgical instructions,

SIDEBAR 18.3. OTHER METHODS BEYOND SOURCE AND FORM CRITICISM

Source and form criticism are not the only methodologies employed by scholars of the OT, but these two are foundational for all others. Source criticism identifies the earliest literary sources, while form criticism attempts to peer behind the sources to explore the smaller oral traditions used in their composition. The principles and theories of source and form approaches were established by the late nineteenth and early twentieth centuries. During the twentieth century, these methods were refined and additional approaches were developed based on them.

Redaction criticism is devoted to an investigation of the editorial process ("redact" is another word for "edit"). It studies the way the early sources were selected, arranged, expanded, and combined into the final form we have today in the OT. Redaction criticism is not necessarily limited to exploring the written sources; at times scholars also consider how older oral versions of these materials were edited. But for the most part, you should think of redaction criticism as accepting the results of source criticism, and taking it further. It attempts to move from the early sources to the final form, examining the process in which the sources were brought together. Some have expressed doubt that editors were involved in the process of textual composition in the ancient world. But we have several examples from ancient Near Eastern literature that demonstrate the way scribes and ancient editors did their work, validating the need for redaction criticism.

Tradition criticism is an all-encompassing endeavor devoted to an investigation of the way older texts have been taken up, (re)interpreted, and incorporated in newer texts. This may involve cases in which both the older and newer texts are preserved in the OT, such as the intertextuality between 1–2 Chronicles and the books of Samuel and Kings. Or it may involve a study of the way an OT book's final form relates to its earlier sources. Tradition criticism focuses on the specific literary and oral processes that led up to the OT book in its present form. This approach also serves as a subcategory of *historical criticism*, which attempts to reconstruct the events and history behind the OT text as much as possible.

Rhetorical criticism is a more recent approach that focuses on the OT as an organic literary whole, exploring its artistic integrity as a literary creation. Sometimes known as *synchronic criticism*, this approach gives less attention to the historical background of the oral or literary sources of the text and attempts to explore instead the intentionality of structure and the literary unity of OT books. Most rhetorical critics assume a deliberate literary structure for the books, which they often assert is the only empirical object for study. Yet another approach, sometimes called *canonical criticism* (though this designation is refuted by others) is related to rhetorical criticism and attempts to interpret the OT in light of the way that it has been shaped so as to serve as Scripture in a believing or worshipping community. Most readers in this camp look for the meaning of a text or book based on how it has been embedded in the canonical context, and they often draw theological or religious significance from the readings.

Sometimes these approaches are viewed as competing with each other. In particular, the early proponents of rhetorical criticism rejected the results of source and form criticism, and perceived themselves as independent from earlier scholarship. Most today speak of a need for a holistic, inclusive approach that considers the contributions of each methodology. Indeed, the nature of the particular text or OT book under investigation may dictate which method or combination of methods is preferable. So, for example, form criticism has been indispensable for scholars working on the book of Psalms.

18.2. Hermann Gunkel, 1862–1932. Gunkel is the father of form criticism. He defined and bequeathed to later scholarship the method for identifying the form of each individual traditional unit, classifying it, and attempting to associate it with specific historical and sociological settings.

covenant formulas, and so on. But the development of form criticism launched an especially fruitful era of research on the psalms and the OT prophets, as we shall see.

Form criticism as it relates to the book of Psalms seeks the origin of individual songs and poems in their function rather than in their history. This approach was fruitful because the historical "situations in life" of the psalms are nearly impossible to identify anyway, as we have said. In a kind of scholarly detour, many scholars speculated for decades about whether certain psalms originated in specific festivals or in celebrations of worship (often reconstructed in theory) in the temple. Much of this we simply cannot know.

Still, form criticism has been helpful in identifying two contrasting categories for thinking about the psalms. First, you should think in terms of the extremes of human experiences, joy and sorrow. Joy issues forth before God in praise, sorrow in the form of lament. These polar opposites – praise and lament – permeate the other types of songs in the book of Psalms. Second, think in terms of a contrast between individual/personal and corporate/

communal. Scholars of form criticism have rightly identified characteristics of both individual and corporate psalms, and a number of other types or subcategories of psalms fit within these broad patterns. It will enrich your reading of the psalms to keep the following genres or forms in mind.[3]

Hymns or Praise Songs

Praise psalms often begin with an imperative plural, calling on all worshippers to praise God/Yahweh. Reasons for praise usually include God's character or his wondrous works.

> *Praise Yahweh, all you nations!*
> *Extol him, all you peoples!*
> *For great is his steadfast love toward us,*
> *and the faithfulness of Yahweh endures forever.*
> *Praise Yahweh!* (Psalm 117)

Such praise hymns may be embedded in longer songs of different categories, or the reasons for praise may dominate throughout in a sort of proclamation of praise (Psalm 46). At other times, the summons to praise God may dominate throughout (see Psalms 146–150).

Certain praise hymns are devoted to extolling God's kingship, and are sometimes categorized as **"enthronement psalms."**

> *Clap your hands, all you peoples;*
> *shout to God with loud songs of joy.*
> *For Yahweh, the Most High, is awesome,*
> *a great king over all the earth.* (Psalm 47:1–2)

3 Most commentaries on the book of Psalms will include some variation of this list, which ultimately goes back to Gunkel and his students.

A small group of enthronement/praise hymns (Psalms 93 and 95–99) appear as a minor collection centered on the exclamation, "Yahweh is king!" Perhaps related to this category are the "songs of Zion" celebrating Yahweh's choice of Mount Zion in Jerusalem as his holy abode (see Sidebar 15.2).

> Great is Yahweh and greatly to be praised
>   in the city of our God.
> His holy mountain, beautiful in elevation,
>   is the joy of all the earth,
> Mount Zion, in the far north,
>   the city of the great King.
> Within its citadels God
>   has shown himself a sure defense. (Psalm 48:1–3)

Songs in praise of Mount Zion may describe the joy of traveling to the city (Psalm 122) or of walking around the city walls (48:12–14).

Songs of Thanksgiving

Related to praise hymns, the thanksgiving psalm is more particularly connected to a specific act of deliverance, usually salvation from one's enemies or healing from sickness. The Hebrew word "thanksgiving" (*tôdâ*) is common in these psalms, as in "I will praise the name of God with a song; I will magnify him with thanksgiving" (Psalm 69:30). The verb, however, is not always present in English translations, where it is sometimes "extol" or "praise."

Thanksgiving songs revolve around the telling of God's act of deliverance.

> I will extol you, O Yahweh, for you have drawn me up,
>   and did not let my foes rejoice over me.
> O Yahweh my God, I cried to you for help,
>   and you have healed me.

> O Yahweh, you brought up my soul from Sheol,
>   restored me to life from among those gone down to the Pit.
>   (Psalm 30:1–3)

By recounting God's saving acts, the worshipper is stirred to express resolute confidence in God's power to save and deliver: "O taste and see that Yahweh is good; happy are those who take refuge in him" (Psalm 34:8). Sometimes the account of God's deliverance is expanded considerably (Psalm 18:4–19,31–45).

Many thanksgiving psalms are expressed in the voice of an individual, but we have community thanksgiving psalms as well: "We give thanks to you, O God; we give thanks; your name is near" (75:1). Corporate thanksgiving may have been particularly appropriate in times of blessing for a good harvest.

> The earth has yielded its increase;
>   God, our God, has blessed us.
> May God continue to bless us;
>   let all the ends of the earth revere him. (Psalm 67:6–7)

Songs of Lament or Prayer

Songs of lament or prayer arise from times of crisis in which the speaker feels abandoned by God, has been attacked by enemies, or carries some particular affliction or sorrow. These may be individual songs phrased in the first-person singular voice (Psalm 3), or communal laments in which the corporate voice of the people is raised (Psalm 80). In either case, the songs of lament have a particular, although flexible, structure or outline. The components in the following list may occur in different sequences, and parts may be expanded considerably or omitted altogether. I will illustrate the components with

18.3. The Psalms at Qumran cave 11. A portion of the Psalms Scrolls discovered at Qumran in 1947, dated probably to around 30–50 AD (parchment). (Photo: The Israel Museum, Jerusalem, Israel / The Bridgeman Art Library)

excerpts from Psalm 54, an individual complaint against one's enemies.

Songs of lament open with (a) an address or invocation, which is usually "O God" or "O Yahweh" but may also be stated emphatically, "My God, my God," as in Psalm 22:1.

> Save me, O God, by your name,
> and vindicate me by your might. (Psalm 54:1)

The address is followed by (b) a petition or request for God to take action and deliver the psalmist from distress (the petition frequently comes third in the structure, after the complaint). And often, the petition intermingles with the address, as in this example in Psalm 54, where verse 1 anticipated the request with "save me" and "vindicate me."

> Hear my prayer, O God;
> give ear to the words of my mouth. (Psalm 54:2)

The petition is often followed by (c) a complaint, in which the speaker names the problem.

> For the insolent have risen against me,
> the ruthless seek my life;
> they do not set God before them. (Psalm 54:3)

Often the complaint takes the form of a somber question, as in Psalm 13:2: "How long must I bear pain in my soul, and have sorrow in my heart all day long?" The question may even be directed to

SIDEBAR 18.4. WHAT KIND OF POEM IS PSALM 23?

The iconic Psalm 23 is perhaps the most famous portion of the OT. But what is it, exactly? As beautiful and familiar as it sounds in our ears, we aren't quite sure how to classify it in this list of psalm types. Is it a royal hymn? Does it fit into a subcategory of thanksgiving hymns? As we have said, these types often blend together, and we cannot place each psalm neatly in a narrowly defined category. You should probably think of Psalm 23 as an expansion of the "affirmation of trust" component of a song of lament. In this case, the affirmation stands alone.

> (1) Yahweh is my shepherd, I shall not want.
> (2) He makes me lie down in green pastures;
> he leads me beside still waters;
> (3) he restores my soul.
> He leads me in right paths
> for his name's sake.
> (4) Even though I walk through the darkest valley,
> I fear no evil;
> for you are with me;
> your rod and your staff –
> they comfort me.
> (5) You prepare a table before me in the presence of my enemies;
> you anoint my head with oil;
> my cup overflows.
> (6) Surely goodness and mercy shall follow me
> all the days of my life,
> and I shall dwell in the house of Yahweh
> my whole life long.

The psalm relies on two powerful metaphors for God, that of shepherd (vv. 1–4) and that of gracious host (vv. 5–6). It speaks in a deeply personal voice ("my shepherd," "my soul," "my head," "my life"), giving Psalm 23 an intimate quality that we find in many of Israel's psalms. This is partly what makes the OT book of Psalms so abiding and accessible for every generation of readers.

God, as in Psalm 22:1: "My God, my God, why have you forsaken me?"

The expression of complaint, however, is never the main point of a lament psalm. The complaint serves to buttress the call for God to intervene, whether it precedes the request in the structure or follows it. After the petition and complaint, the lament psalm generally moves to (d) an affirmation of trust in God/Yahweh.

> But surely, God is my helper;
> Yahweh is the upholder of my life.
> He will repay my enemies for their evil.
> In your faithfulness, put an end to them. (Psalm 54:4–5)

This affirmation may be expanded to recount God's wondrous acts of salvation from the past (Psalm 44:1–7) or to highlight God's character as the holy God (Psalm 22:3), the strength of his people (Psalm 28:6–9).

Most songs of lament conclude in (e) a vow to praise God/Yahweh when the crisis or threat is passed.

> With a freewill offering I will sacrifice to you;
>> I will give thanks to your name, O Yahweh, for it is good.
> For he has delivered me from every trouble,
>> and my eye has looked in triumph on my enemies.
>> (Psalm 54:6–7)

Such vows may involve singing directly to Yahweh (13:6) or announcing his saving actions to others (22:22–24).

Royal Psalms

Royal psalms have no fixed literary pattern or outline but are focused on particular events connected with the earthly king in Jerusalem. Some of these songs are apparently related to a coronation ceremony, or in celebration of a coronation's anniversary.

> Yahweh says to my lord,
>> "Sit at my right hand
>> until I make your enemies your footstool." (Psalm 110:1; cf.
>> Psalm 2)

Such songs were at times prayers on the king's behalf (Psalms 20 and 72) or psalms of thanksgiving in the words of the king himself (18). Another was a special song composed for a royal wedding (Psalm 45).

Wisdom and Instruction Psalms

A number of psalms in the collection appear to have come from the same philosophers and theologians who gave us the wisdom literature (Chapter 17). Rather than prayers, hymns, or songs of lament and thanksgiving, these psalms focus on the themes of Israel's instruction literature, that is, the promises and pitfalls of life, and advice for living in a way that pleases God and results in success. Above all else, these psalms emphasize God's Torah or "instruction, law," and all its many synonyms (underscored in the following example).

> The law of Yahweh is perfect,
>> reviving the soul;
> the decrees of Yahweh are sure,
>> making wise the simple;
> the precepts of Yahweh are right,
>> rejoicing the heart;
> the commandment of Yahweh is clear,
>> enlightening the eyes;
> the fear of Yahweh is pure,
>> enduring forever;
> the ordinances of Yahweh are true
>> and righteous altogether.
> More to be desired are they than gold,
>> even much fine gold;
> sweeter also than honey,
>> and drippings of the honeycomb. (Psalm 19:7–10)

Psalm 119 is an impressive acrostic (Sidebar 16.3); the longest psalm in the book, it focuses on the instruction of Yahweh, which makes possible an upright and acceptable walk of life by means of reflection on Torah. Similarly, Psalm 1 urges the contemplative life, meditating constantly on Yahweh's Torah (1:2).

A few instructional psalms even share the condensed proverbial style of the book of Proverbs and cover themes familiar from that material, such as family life, work, and personal piety (Psalms 127, 128, 133). Many others serve didactic purposes, explaining how best to deal with old age (Psalm 37:25–26), wealth (49), the joys of fearing and serving Yahweh (Psalm 112), and a host of other issues. Inclusion of these wisdom psalms makes the book of Psalms a kind of synopsis of the entire OT. It has songs devoted to creation, Israel's ancestors, the exodus, the Sinai covenant, the conquest of the promised land, the Davidic dynasty, and even this practical material from Israel's instruction literature. The book of Psalms is a miniature OT.

Be careful with these literary psalm categories. Many of the psalms are combinations of one or more of these formal types, some of them mixing and matching the genres, or moving back and forth between styles of songs. The founder of form criticism, Hermann Gunkel, gave us five basic categories – hymns, communal laments, individual laments, thanksgiving songs, and royal psalms – and with the few changes and alterations in this list that I have given, his categories are still useful today. But you should be aware that some psalms do not easily fit into one particular genre or category.

IMAGES OF YAHWEH/GOD IN THE BOOK OF PSALMS

We have seen that the book of Psalms is a miniature OT, or at least that it offers a synopsis of the OT's themes and worldview. Most of the themes and religious ideas found so far in Israel's collection of books are also found here in beautiful poetry and song. This includes, of course, many of Israel's conceptions of Yahweh/God.

Lament songs often portray God as the source of security in times of distress; he is a shepherd, a rock, a fortress or strong refuge, a shelter, a shield, and others. In one such affirmation of trust, the psalmist declares the incomparable quality of God's character.

> Your way, O God, is holy.
>> What god is so great as our God?
> You are the God who works wonders;
>> you have displayed your might among the peoples.
> With your strong arm you redeemed your people,
>> the descendants of Jacob and Joseph. (Psalm 77:13–15)

The surpassing nature of Israel's God is manifest in his holiness, his wondrous works among the nations, and his redemption of his people, Israel.

Hymns of praise and songs of thanksgiving also celebrate God's surpassing and incomparable character. He is Creator of the universe (Psalms 8 and 33), who also blesses and sustains the world (104). He is Ruler/King of all nations (Psalms 47 and 95), who judges all peoples (96:10) and rules over heaven and earth (103:19–22). God's work in history is cause for praise and celebration, as recounted in certain praise hymns that recount God's mighty acts of salvation in Israel's past (Psalms 78, 105, and 106). In songs, hymns, and prayers, the Psalter repeats and celebrates Israel's understanding of Yahweh as Creator, Sustainer, Deliverer, and Lord, and frequently as a God unlike any other.

We must be careful not to read into these statements of praise and affirmations of trust the strict monotheism we have come to attribute to the OT. Many of the psalms are closest to monolatrous henotheism, in that they teach and encourage devotion to Yahweh/God as supreme over all other deities (review the definitions of monolatry and henotheism in Chapter 1). It is possible to understand the incomparability of Yahweh/God in the Psalms as Israel's *implicit* monotheism.

> Who is like Yahweh our God,
>> who is seated on high,
> who looks far down
>> on the heavens and the earth?[4] (Psalm 113:5–6)

But even here we should be cautious about assuming that this is strict monotheism.

What we find in the book of Psalms is therefore similar to religious expression elsewhere in the OT. Israelite authors were less concerned with negative statements denying the existence of other deities, and more concerned with defining God positively. They wrote history, law, and poetry always to invite their readers to worship and serve Yahweh exclusively; that is, Yahweh alone, at the exclusion of other deities. As elsewhere in the OT, we should consider their statements strict monotheism only when they claim that Yahweh "alone" is deity (as a positive assertion), or when they deny the reality of other deities (a negative assertion). We have seen that such *explicit* statements of monotheism are rare in the OT, and yet they do occur. The same is true of the book of Psalms.

Perhaps the most explicit statement we have is Psalm 86, an individual lament. The psalm's affirmation of trust begins with the idea of God's incomparability, as we have seen elsewhere in the Psalter: "There is none like you among the gods, O Lord, nor are there any works like yours" (Psalm 86:8). But then the poem goes further.

> For you are great and do wondrous things;
>> you alone are God. (Psalm 86:10)

This last clause is not simply a call to monolatrous faithfulness, worshipping God alone. Here we find an explicit assertion that Israel's God alone is deity. In the context of the book of Psalms, you might think of this as Israel's "rhetoric of praise," since the statement is a prayer instead of a philosophical treatise on monotheism.[5] The worshipper who wrote this poem took a step beyond the incomparability of God to embrace the idea that God alone is God.

On rare occasions, we have negative statements in the OT denying the existence of other deities. In the book of Psalms, the clearest such example is Psalm 96, a praise hymn extolling the majesty of Yahweh as king.

> For great is Yahweh,
>> and greatly to be praised;
>> he is to be revered above all gods.
> For all the gods of the peoples are idols,
>> but Yahweh made the heavens. (Psalm 96:4–5)

Here again the worshipper moves beyond declaring Yahweh's incomparability ("above all gods"),

4 See similar questions in Psalms 18:31; 35:9–10, and 89:5–8.

5 On the presence of monotheism in prayers as the "rhetoric of praise," as opposed to Deuteronomy 4:35 as "the rhetoric of persuasion," see pages 151–52 in Smith (2001) in "Where to Find More" for Chapter 1.

this time to a denial that other deities exist (they "are idols"). The denial itself is a playful alliterative wordplay: "the gods" (*'ĕlōhê*, a form of *'ĕlōhîm*) are "idols" (*'ĕlîlîm*; see Chapter 16 for these techniques in OT poetry). The term "idols" is "worthless things, nothings," so the poet is cleverly saying the *elohim* are *elilim*, the gods are nothings! As with Psalm 86, this poem is part of the Psalter's "rhetoric of praise," in which the character of Yahweh as the only God elicits adoration.

Another negative way of denying the existence of other deities is to announce their deaths. One particularly striking example from the Psalter is Psalm 82, which is unlike other genres. This poem has often been identified as a mythology, perhaps because of the opening verse.

> God has taken his place in the divine council;
> in the midst of the gods he holds judgment. (Psalm 82:1)

As in a few other examples of early Israelite poetry, God takes his place among other divine beings in a heavenly council (see the "heavenly beings" of Psalm 29:1, and see "the gods" in Deuteronomy 32:8). Other deities are thought to exist, but they cannot be compared to Yahweh/God. Eventually, the Israelites came to deny their existence altogether, emptying the heavens of all deities other than Yahweh and, in the process, yielding completely new understandings of God, the universe, and human-divine relations.

Psalm 82 may be said to conceptualize Israel's transition to strict monotheism.[6] In the first verse of the poem, God is the leader of a divine council. He condemns the other gods as inadequate

6 See pages 83–85 in Frymer-Kensky in "Where to Find More" for Chapter 4.

because of the way they govern the universe (82:2–5). Finally, God proclaims that the other deities are mortal, that they will die like humans.

> I had thought to myself, "You are gods,
> children of the Most High, all of you.
> However, you will die like humans,
> fall like any prince." (Psalm 82:6–7, my translation)

In a sense, this poem traces the progression from old polytheism to a new Israelite understanding of God as the only deity. But the transition to monotheism required a complete reconfiguration of the Israelites' worldview. The universe itself was now conceived in a new unified and unifying principle, reflecting the character of the one Creator God. The Israelite God, Yahweh, expanded to absorb all features and characteristics of deity formerly attributed to numerous other gods. Religious institutions were transformed to reflect a new cosmic constant, a uniform and harmonious universe of unvarying repetitions instead of an unpredictable cosmos filled with whimsical deities. In this new way of thinking, all was transformed – ideas of deity, humanity, and nature – according to the unique and singular character of Yahweh.

In Israelite monotheism, the one and only Yahweh was sufficient for all one's needs. By means of a covenant relationship with his people Israel, Yahweh became a personal deity, intimately involved in their national life. He was all they would need. Their hymns of praise and thanksgiving reflect this new understanding, even if they explicitly state their monotheism only rarely. As we shall see, this is Israel's enduring contribution. Their concept of monotheism changed the world forever.

WHERE TO FIND MORE

Commentaries: The best technical and advanced commentaries on the **Psalms** are Leslie C. Allen, *Psalms 101–150* (Word Biblical Commentary 21; Nashville: Thomas Nelson, 2002); Peter C. Craigie, *Psalms 1–50* (Word Biblical Commentary 19; Nashville: Thomas Nelson, 2005); John Goldingay, *Psalms* (3 vols.; Baker Commentary on the Old Testament Wisdom and Psalms; Grand Rapids, Mich.: Baker Academic, 2006 and 2008); Hans-Joachim Kraus, *Psalms* (2 vols.; Continental Commentary 19a and 19b; Minneapolis, Minn.: Augsburg Fortress, 2000); Frank Lothar Hossfeld and Erich Zenger, *Psalms 2 and Psalms 3* (Hermeneia 19; Minneapolis, Minn.: Fortress Press, 2005 and 2011); Marvin E. Tate, *Psalms 51–100* (Word Biblical Commentary 20; Nashville: Thomas Nelson, 2005).

Barton, John. *Reading the Old Testament: Method in Biblical Study*. Rev. ed. Louisville, Ky.: Westminster John Knox Press, 1996.

Provides more information on the various methodologies introduced in Sidebar 18.3.

Braun, Joachim. *Music in Ancient Israel/Palestine: Archaeological, Written, and Comparative Sources*. Translated by Douglas W. Stott. Grand Rapids, Mich.: Eerdmans, 2002.

See pages 113–88 for discussion of musical instruments of Syria-Palestine during the Iron Age. For more on the role of music in ancient Israel, see pages 285–300 in King and Stager in "Where to Find More" for Chapter 3.

Westermann, Claus. *Praise and Lament in the Psalms*. Translated by Keith R. Crim and Richard N. Soulen. Atlanta, Ga.: John Knox Press, 1981.

Explores the polar experiences of human life, joy and sorrow, as fundamental themes in the book of Psalms.

Whybray, R. Norman. *Reading the Psalms as a Book*. Journal for the Study of the Old Testament, Supplement Series 222. Sheffield, Eng.: Sheffield Academic Press, 1996.

Israel's Prophets: The Maturing Period

We have already encountered prophets in the historical books. We will look now at four of the OT's writing prophets: Amos, Hosea, Micah, and Isaiah. Eighth-century Israel witnessed increased accessibility to writing and an expanded role for the prophet. The recurrent phrase, "Thus says Yahweh" (messenger formula), epitomizes the primary role of the prophet as a messenger speaking on behalf of God.

Sources from Mari in the eighteenth century BCE and others from seventh-century Assyria verify the antiquity of divination practices, of which prophecy is a type. Israel demonstrated opposition to certain divination practices, but its prophets consistently delivered messages from Yahweh, distinguished by their ethical and moral vision. These books have three basic types of OT prophetic speech: prophecies are the most common and represent messages to an individual or corporate entity; utterances are the confessions or prayers of the prophet to God; and narratives offer historical details corresponding to the prophet. Two important features will become evident as we explore the content of these books: covenant loyalty to Yahweh and the international extent of Yahweh's authority.

We come now to a separate collection of books in Israel's library. The OT's books of prophecy make up a subset of the whole. Our first task will be to define Israel's understanding of prophecy, which as you will see, is probably not what you may think it is. Then we will introduce the contents of four of these books, reserving the remainder for later. This is a large (sub) collection of books and an important topic. So we will devote three chapters to a study of the prophets.

SIDEBAR 19.1. WRITING IN ANCIENT ISRAEL

The question of when Israelites began to write Hebrew texts in the OT period is a complicated issue and hotly debated among scholars. Some argue that literacy was widespread from the tenth century onward because of the alphabetic script used for Hebrew (as opposed to the hieroglyphic and cuneiform scripts used in Egypt and Mesopotamia, respectively). Others assume that literacy in ancient Israel was extremely limited because our epigraphic evidence from the Iron Age (Old Hebrew texts preserved usually on potsherds, stone, or animal skins) is hardly more than notes and economic lists – certainly not literature! Recent studies have shown that societies with alphabetic scripts are no more likely to be literate than societies with complex writing systems. On the other hand, our body of Hebrew epigraphic texts from the Iron Age are enough to demonstrate that professional scribes were present in ancient Israel and that they received some type of formal training in the scribal arts, probably under the direction of the state.* Furthermore, widespread literacy is not needed to produce literature, since much could be produced by a small group of priestly or royal administrative scribes.

There is no reason to doubt, based on the epigraphic evidence, that scribes in ancient Israel were writing throughout Iron Age II (ca. 930–539 BCE). It is impossible to trace the origins and composition of Israel's Torah and historiographical materials during this period with precision. But the rise of the prophet-scribe, or secretaries working with them, made it possible to preserve the actual thinking of the eighth-century prophets (their "very words," if you will). In numerous prophecies and utterances of these OT books of prophecy, we actually hear for the first time the voices of these ancient Israelite theologians. In these writings, their ideas and convictions are boldly preserved, unfiltered by the royal historiographers of the more official Primary History. When you hear the passion of their voices and read the depth of their insights, you realize why their texts were preserved for all ages. The OT prophetic message is timeless, as pertinent for modern readers as it was for ancient Israel.

* For more on this, and what follows here, see pages 127–35 in Rollston in "Where to Find More" in this chapter.

Take a moment now to review the Jewish and Christian canons in Figure 2.3. The OT includes fifteen books of written prophecy. There are three so-called *major* prophets: Isaiah, Jeremiah, and Ezekiel. (The Christian canon includes in this list Daniel, which we have reserved for Chapter 22 because it is a different literary genre or type of book altogether.) We then have twelve *minor* prophets in the list. The terms "major" and "minor" have to do with the relative size of these books. There is nothing less important about the minor prophets; their books are simply shorter than the others.

These fifteen are the "written prophets" to distinguish them from other prophets in ancient Israel, such as Samuel, Nathan, Gad, Elijah, and Elisha. These other prophets were active earlier in Israel's history but did not leave behind books in the OT containing their sermons, exhortations, prayers, and so forth. We know about these other prophets because of their actions described in the historical books, which were probably preserved by the official royal courts. But in the eighth century BCE, writing became generally more widespread in ancient Israel, providing a means for preserving the

19.1. The Khirbet Qeiyafa Inscription (tenth century BCE). An Early Alphabetic (or "proto-Canaanite") text of five lines discovered in 2008 in Israel's heartland. The inscription is not completely decipherable, although it appears to contain the words "servant / serving," "judge / judging," "king," "God / gods," "widow," "immigrant," and others known to be Semitic words. Some have concluded that the inscription is a simple list of personal names. (Photo: Khirbet Qeiyafa Expedition, produced at Megavision Laboratory)

19.2. Rendition of the Khirbet Qeiyafa Inscription. The drawing of the inscription shows how archaic its letters are. The direction of the writing appears to be **dextrograde** (from left to right, like English) and unlike Hebrew, which is written **sinistrograde** (from right to left). Whether the text is an early and primitive form of Hebrew is debated today. We are divided over the significance of the inscription, which some have argued reveals a high level of social ethics in the United Monarchy while others deny it has anything to do with ancient Israel. (Photo: A rendition of the Khirbet Qeiyafa Ostracon by Michael Netzer for illustration purposes, based on photographs of the potsherd by the Khirbet Qeiyafa project at the Hebrew University of Jerusalem)

actual words of the prophets. There are other reasons why Israel's prophets or their aides began preserving their preaching in writing, as we will see.

For a variety of reasons, it is helpful to take these fifteen books in three separate groups, instead of in the canonical order. We will begin in this chapter with the prophets of the eighth century BCE: Isaiah of Jerusalem, Hosea, Amos, and Micah.

WHAT IS "PROPHECY"?

What do you think of when you hear the word "prophecy"? We use the English term in a variety of ways but seldom with the same meaning it has in the OT. So we will need first to explore what prophecy was in ancient Israel.

When you use the words "prophet" and "prophecy" you probably have something in mind that relates to predicting future events. But in the OT, prophets were perceived primarily as speaking on behalf of God. A prophet was a spokesperson for God's message, which occasionally related to the future but not always. As you will see, the basic content of the OT books of prophecy is not primarily about future events.

In addition to the books' contents, two other features of the OT prophets highlight their role as speaking on behalf of God. The first is the frequent use of a messenger formula borrowed from the literary forms of ancient letters. We have thousands of such letters from the ancient world, often beginning with an announcement to the addressee and stating the name of the author or sender: "speak to Mr. so-and-so; thus says Mr. such-and-such." But the one who carries the letter to the addressee and reads the contents is not the author, merely the messenger speaking on behalf of the sender. The messenger reads out the exact words of the author of the letter. In a similar way, the OT prophets merely represent God and announce

In addition to "prophet" (*nābî'*), the OT has other words to describe its prophets. These terms are found in the historical books and occasionally are sprinkled in the books of prophecy themselves. They suggest that different labels were used early in Israel's history to designate a variety of types of prophets. Elijah, who was certainly known as a prophet, is also called a "man of God" (2 Kings 1:9), as is Moses (Deuteronomy 33:1). This designation assumed a prophet showed certain characteristic behaviors, especially as one who manifested divine power through miracles, or who possessed a prophetic gift such as healing or divination. It could also be used for an anonymous prophet, an indefinite and mysterious "man of God," who appears unannounced, acts and performs signs, pronounces a prophecy, and leaves at once (1 Samuel 2:27–36; 1 Kings 13:1–10).

The OT also uses the terms "seer" (*rō'eh*) and "visionary" (*ḥôzeh*, which can also mean simply "seer"). These are usually individuals who might be consulted for a specific discernment from God (1 Samuel 9:5–8). These terms were of long-standing usage. We even have an editorial insertion explaining that "seer" (*rō'eh*) is the older word for prophet, in case the reader might be confused by the outdated terminology (1 Samuel 9:9). As the English implies, a "visionary" is a prophet who experiences visions or dreams and derives an interpretive word of God from them. But by far the most frequent technical term is simply "prophet," and in time, these other terms were used less commonly.

God's messages: "Thus says Yahweh" (Amos 1:3). By implication, they are not personally responsible for the contents of their sermons. They are merely articulating the exact words of God, the author of the message. A second feature that points in the direction of their representative, messenger status is the Hebrew noun "prophet" (*nābîḥ*). We cannot be certain of its original meaning, but it likely indicates "one who is called." In this way, the prophets are called by God to represent him in addressing the king or the people of Israel.

Prophecy is a subcategory of a broader phenomenon known as divination, or the consultation of the divine for the purposes of discerning the divine will. Most forms of divination use purposely prescribed observations – such as the movement of stars, the entrails of a sacrificial animal, or the movement of oil in water – to read or deduce the divine will. Instead, prophecy is a distinctive branch of divination, using no prescribed observations but setting up the human prophet as a transmitter of divine messages.[1]

divine sender → message → human transmitter → recipient(s)

More than other forms of divination, prophecy is direct revelation of the divine will mediated through a human agent. As we shall see, other peoples of the ancient Near East had many forms of divination, including prophecy. By contrast, the OT generally opposes deductive forms of divination and relies almost entirely on prophecy. Yahweh's will is thought of as revealed to the prophet, who then serves as God's mouthpiece. The four components of prophecy in ancient Israel look like this.

1 See pages 1–2 of Nissinen in "Where to Find More" in this chapter.

SIDEBAR 19.3. ANCIENT NEAR EASTERN PROPHECIES

Dozens of prophetic texts have been discovered among the nearly twenty-five thousand documents found at ancient Mari, or Tell Ḥarīri in modern Syria (see Map 3.2). Most of these are prophetic oracles embedded in letters from the time of King Zimri-Lim of Mari (ca. 1774–1760 BCE). These are not prophecies preserved alone in a single text but copies of correspondence in which the speaker quotes the words of a prophet for the benefit of the addressee. Typically, these are messages conveyed to the king by means of a trusted ally rather than directly from the prophet.

> Abiya, prophet of the god Adad, lord of the city of Aleppo, came to me and said: "Thus says Adad: 'I have given the whole country to Yahdun-Lim.'"*

In the prophecy, the deity Adad recites his history of grace and benevolent kindness to Zimri-Lim, recounting how he eventually took the land from Yahdun-Lim and other rulers and granted it to Zimri-Lim. By means of this prophecy, the god Adad then urges Zimri-Lim to rule justly and to always seek an oracle from Adad before going into battle.

From much later, we have a collection of texts from the Neo-Assyrian period in which oracles of nine women and four men are addressed, usually to a king of Assyria, either Esarhaddon (681–669 BCE) or Assurbanipal (668–627 BCE). In a few cases, we even have multiple oracles collected in a single document, arranged systematically in a way that reminds us of OT books of prophecy. These may be prototypes of prophetic compositions, illustrating the movement from oral to written preservation and arrangment. On the other hand, we have nothing like the full-scale literary compositions of the OT prophecies among these ancient Near Eastern texts. In addition to prophetic texts proper, several other Neo-Assyrian documents refer to the prophets and their activities, providing a fascinating picture of their roles in that society.

* Adapted and excerpted from page 21 of Nissinen in "Where to Find More" in this chapter. See also J. J. M. Roberts, *The Bible and the Ancient Near East: Collected Essays* (Winona Lake, Ind.: Eisenbrauns, 2002), 166–69.

Yahweh/God → word of Yahweh/God → prophet → Israel

So the OT understands its prophets to be individuals called by God to serve as mediators and preachers of divine revelation. They serve up the "word of God." The messages of these divine-word transmitters encourage the Israelites to a deeper personal experience with God based on the ancient covenant between Yahweh and early Israel, call for faithfulness to that covenant commitment, and stress an ethical-religious message.

Israel wasn't the only society in the ancient Near East with prophets. In fact, prophecy was known throughout the region for nearly two millennia. Yet we have a concentration of prophetic sources from the city of Mari in the eighteenth century BCE and from the Neo-Assyrian period in the seventh century BCE. The OT even preserves the tradition of a certain Balaam, prophet of Pethor on the Euphrates, who is known from ancient inscriptions (Numbers 22–24). So although there were definitely other prophets at work in the ancient Near East, the Israelite prophets were distinguished by their ethical-moral message, which they delivered with passion and specific application to the Israelites. None of the prophecies in other societies of the ancient Near East were anything quite as monumental and lasting as those contributions made by the OT prophets.

ISRAEL'S BOOKS OF PROPHECY

The books of prophecy introduced here (and in Chapters 20 and 21) contain three basic types of prophetic speech: prophecies, utterances, and narratives. These three types are distinguished from each other by their intended recipients. The *prophecies* are sermonic speeches of a prophet delivered originally to an individual (usually a king), or to the Israelite people at large or to a particular group of them. The *utterances* are prayers or confessions directed by the prophet to God, often reflecting on the burden of the prophetic task and the pain of delivering God's message. The *narratives* are historical materials about events or circumstances surrounding a particular prophet, typically collected and written down by someone else, such as the prophet's followers or disciples. Narrative stretches are most prominent in Jeremiah, but other prophetic books have narrative portions as well, such as Isaiah, Hosea, and Amos.[2] Jeremiah also contains a collection of utterances. But prophetic speeches (the first of these three types) are far and away the largest portion of the OT books of prophecy.

The prophecies, or sermonic speeches, may occur in brief and condensed sayings or in long

sermons exploring a particular theme. Short pithy sayings are in some passages collected in a string making up a particular homily. Scholars studying the OT prophets from the perspective of form criticism have been able to identify two basic types of prophetic speech: announcements of judgment and announcements of salvation (similar to the work done on the Psalms; see Chapter 18). The announcements of judgment usually come with an accusation, and may be addressed to an individual or to the nation at large. The following example is a judgment speech against an individual (Amaziah, representing King Jeroboam II of Israel) with four elements: summons to hear, accusation, messenger formula, and announcement proper.

> (16) *"Now therefore hear the word of Yahweh.*
> *You say, 'Do not prophesy against Israel,*
>   *and do not preach against the house of Isaac.'*
> (17) *Therefore thus says Yahweh:*
> *'Your wife shall become a prostitute in the city,*
> *and your sons and your daughters shall fall by the sword,*
>   *and your land shall be parceled out by line;*
> *you yourself shall die in an unclean land,*
>   *and Israel shall surely go into exile away from its land.'"*
>
>   (Amos 7:16–17)

The accusation derisively points to the guilty party's own words ("you say …," v. 16) followed by the messenger formula and the judgment itself in verse 17. This same basic structure of the prophetic announcement of judgment was flexible and often expanded in certain ways when applied to the people of Israel or Judah.

The OT books of prophecy include a variety of forms for speeches of salvation. This may be a simple *assurance of salvation*, usually marked by a

---

2 Especially Isaiah 6–8 and 36–39, Jeremiah 36–45, Hosea 1, Amos 7:10–17, and perhaps Jonah could be included in this category.

second-person address speaking of salvation that is already complete even if it has to be worked out in the near future.

> But now thus says Yahweh,
>> he who created you, O Jacob,
> he who formed you, O Israel:
> Do not fear, for I have redeemed you;
>> I have called you by name, you are mine. (Isaiah 43:1)

Or the salvation speech may take the form of a *declaration of salvation* about to be accomplished in the immediate future, reversing some particular situation that appears otherwise hopeless. This type of announcement is often marked by a "sign" and is conditioned on the faithfulness of God's people.

> (16) Thus says Yahweh,
>> who makes a way in the sea,
>> a path in the mighty waters,
> (17) who brings out chariot and horse,
>> army and warrior;
>> they lie down, they cannot rise,
>> they are extinguished, quenched like a wick:
> (18) Do not remember the former things,
>> or consider the things of old.
> (19) I am about to do a new thing;
>> now it springs forth, do you not perceive it?
>> I will make a way in the wilderness
>> and rivers in the desert.
> (20) The wild animals will honor me,
>> the jackals and the ostriches;
>> for I give water in the wilderness,
>> rivers in the desert,
>> to give drink to my chosen people,
> (21) the people whom I formed for myself
> so that they might declare my praise. (Isaiah 43:16–21)

Yet another type of salvation speech is the *portrayal of salvation*, which focuses on salvation in the distant future in a blessed period beyond the present age. These speeches promise a period of peace for all creation, transforming present historical realities. This type of salvation speech shares with apocalyptic literature a focus on eschatology (an interest in final, ultimate things in a far distant future time somehow discontinuous from the present reality; see Chapter 22).

> (17) For I am about to create new heavens and a new earth;
>> the former things shall not be remembered or come
> to mind.
> (18) But be glad and rejoice forever in what I am creating;
>> for I am about to create Jerusalem as a joy,
>> and its people as a delight.
> (19) I will rejoice in Jerusalem, and delight in my people;
>> no more shall the sound of weeping be heard in it,
>> or the cry of distress.
> (20) No more shall there be in it an infant that lives but a
>> few days,
>>> or an old person who does not live out a lifetime;
>> for one who dies at a hundred years will be considered a
> youth,
>> and one who falls short of a hundred will be considered
> accursed.
>> (Isaiah 65:17–20)

We have already seen how prophets drew on the language of ancient letters to symbolize their messenger role: "Thus says Yahweh." Now we need to explore how Israel's prophets drew on many other literary images and forms known to them and their audiences from everyday life experiences and customs, all of which could be used in any of the three speech types – prophecies, utterances, or narratives. The OT prophets were quite creative in their adaptation and use of these images, the most common of which were borrowed from shared life experiences or from religious expressions and ideas practiced in worship. For example, they borrowed from funeral laments to address people whom they perceived as condemned to die.

> *Ah, you who call evil good and good evil,*
>> *who put darkness for light and light for darkness,*
>> *who put bitter for sweet and sweet for bitter!*
>> *(Isaiah 5:20, and continuing in vv. 21–24; compare*
>> *Amos 5:18)*

Or similarly, a dirge or funeral hymn could be used to sing over the death of Israel itself.

> *(1) Hear this word that I take up over you in lamentation,*
>> *O house of Israel:*
> *(2) Fallen, no more to rise,*
>> *is maiden Israel;*
>> *forsaken on her land,*
>> *with no one to raise her up. (Amos 5:1–2)*

At other times, the OT prophets drew on the experience of court cases or legal settings. Yahweh brings an indictment against Israel; he is the plaintiff as well as the judge in such contexts.

> *(1) Hear the word of Yahweh, O people of Israel;*
>> *for Yahweh has an indictment against the inhabitants of*
>> *the land.*
> *There is no faithfulness or loyalty,*
>> *and no knowledge of God in the land.*
> *(2) Swearing, lying, and murder,*
>> *and stealing and adultery break out;*
>> *bloodshed follows bloodshed.*
> *(3) Therefore the land mourns, and all who live in it languish;*

> *together with the wild animals and the birds of the air,*
>> *even the fish of the sea are perishing. (Hosea 4:1–3)*

The use of powerful rhetorical questions was probably not directly related to court settings, but rather reflected everyday controversies or perhaps a form of disputation known among wisdom scholars.

> *(3) Do two walk together unless they have made an appointment?*
> *(4) Does a lion roar in the forest, when it has no prey?*
>> *Does a young lion cry out from its den,*
>> *if it has caught nothing?*
> *(5) Does a bird fall into a snare on the earth,*
>> *when there is no trap for it?*
> *Does a snare spring up from the ground,*
>> *when it has taken nothing?*
> *(6) Is a trumpet blown in a city,*
>> *and the people are not afraid?*
> *Does disaster befall a city,*
>> *unless Yahweh has done it?*
> *(7) Surely the Lord GOD does nothing,*
>> *without revealing his secret to his servants the prophets.*
> *(8) The lion has roared; who will not fear?*
> *The Lord GOD has spoken; who can but prophesy? (Amos 3:3–8)*

It also seems likely that the prophets drew occasionally on everyday priestly instruction for worship in the temple, as in the following example using sarcasm to scold the Israelites' attitude toward worship.

> *(4) Come to Bethel — and transgress;*
>> *to Gilgal — and multiply transgression;*
>> *bring your sacrifices every morning,*
>> *your tithes every three days;*
> *(5) bring a thank offering of leavened bread,*

and proclaim freewill offerings, publish them;

for so you love to do, O people of Israel!

says the Lord GOD. *(Amos 4:4–5)*

THE BOOKS OF AMOS, HOSEA, MICAH, AND ISAIAH

Before we get too far into the contents of the books of Amos, Hosea, Micah, and Isaiah, I should say a word about the subtitle of this chapter and those of the next two. By the use of "The Maturing Period," I mean to introduce you in this chapter to the earliest of the writing prophets, all of them from the eighth century BCE. The second half of the century is when prophecy emerged as a written enterprise, with themes and messages fully developed for Israel and Judah. The role and function of Israel's earlier prophets (Samuel, Elijah, etc.) have now matured into the messages of these written books of prophecy. We might call these "the prophets of Israel's monarchy," but some of the other prophets we will discuss in the next chapter also lived prior to the loss of the monarchy in 586 BCE. Another label for these prophets might be "prophets of the Assyrian period,"[3] which is another helpful way of thinking about the books of prophecy covered in this chapter. Yet it isn't quite as helpful for the rest of the books of the prophets, which then must be put into the Babylonian and/or Persian periods. Classification isn't always as simple as when a prophet lived and preached.

In reality, these books of prophecy overlap with those discussed in the next chapter, and likewise

to some extent with those covered in Chapter 21. Moreover, some of these prophetic books cannot be dated with any degree of confidence. Like so many of the psalms, a few of the minor prophets are impossible to put into a specific historical time slot. We will take the prophets in three separate groups not so much because they are precisely from three periods of Israel's history, but because each of the three groups shares numerous themes in common, and you will find it more helpful to keep them in the following sequence, even if it is not strictly chronological.

Chapter 19 – Israel's Prophets: The Maturing Period
(Amos, Hosea, Micah, and Isaiah of Jerusalem)
Chapter 20 – Israel's Prophets: The Crisis and Beyond
(Jeremiah, Obadiah, Nahum, Habakkuk, Zephaniah, Ezekiel, and Isaiah of the exile)
Chapter 21 – Israel's Prophets: The Restoration
(Haggai, Zechariah, Malachi, Joel, and Jonah)

The Book of Amos

The book of Amos is the oldest of Israel's writing prophets. Because of both the specifics of the superscription (1:1) and the narrative telling how he was thrown out of the northern kingdom of Israel (7:10–17), we know more about the man Amos than we do about many of the other prophets. Amos was a farmer from a southern village named Tekoa, near Bethlehem. He claims to have been called by Yahweh from tending sheep and cultivating sycamore trees to prophesy Yahweh's message of doom against the northern kingdom. Don't let Amos's

---

3 As is done in the two-volume study by Koch, see "Where to Find More" in this chapter.

Map 19.1. Southern Levant during the eighth-century prophets

unassuming background deceive you. The prophecies and utterances that make up the book of Amos are sophisticated literary creations, marked with passionate rhetoric and reflecting a thoughtful prophet well versed in Israel's traditions and literary arts. You may have noticed that many of the examples I used in previous paragraphs illustrating the literary types of Israel's books of prophecy come from the book of Amos.

For a brief period in the eighth century, most likely for only a year sometime in the 750s BCE, Amos left his occupation in the south and preached a message of imminent doom against the northern kingdom Israel. The only narrative portion of the book comes as an insertion into a list of five utterances near the end, in which we are told of a conflict between Amaziah, the priest of Bethel, who represented King Jeroboam II of Israel (786–746 BCE; Amos 7:10–17). In the third of these utterances, Amos announces that Yahweh's judgment against northern Israel is imminent and impossible to avoid. Its worship centers – "high places" and "sanctuaries" – are about to be destroyed and its king, Jeroboam, removed by violence (7:9). This was all that Amaziah (and presumably Jeroboam) could tolerate. Amos was forbidden from continuing to preach against Israel, although this is not the conclusion of the book.

The first six chapters of the book of Amos preserve his prophecies of judgment against the northern kingdom. The prophecies "against the nations" in chapters 1–2 introduce a category of prophetic oracle that we will see again in Isaiah, Jeremiah, and Ezekiel. Israel's and Judah's immediate neighbors are addressed in these prophecies (Damascus, Gaza, Tyre, etc.), but the prophecies were not actually preached to be heard by those nations and cities. Instead, they serve a literary function in moving toward a climactic condemnation of the northern kingdom of Israel (2:6–16). This in turn prepares readers for the heart of the book (chaps. 3–6), which is a series of blistering prophecies against northern Israel, highlighting the nation's social ills, especially its mistreatment of the poor, and its worship practices, which had been perverted into mere formalities. This portion of the prophet's message is summarized aptly in the memorable words of Amos 5:24: "Let justice roll down like waters, and righteousness like an ever-flowing stream."

The book concludes with five utterances in the form of prophetic visions, each beginning with an object lesson instigating a prophecy of judgment: locusts (7:1–3), consuming fire (7:4–6), a plumb line (7:7–9), a basket of summer fruit (8:1–3), and Yahweh standing beside the altar (9:1–4). These visionary conversations between Yahweh and Amos build on each other to create a sense of hopelessness due to the impending and unavoidable doom hanging over northern Israel. The prophet intercedes on behalf of Israel in the first two instances, and Yahweh has mercy on them. But with the third – the plumb line – and the remaining visions, no amount of intercession works because the people Israel are beyond redemption. Judgment is unavoidable. Concluding the book (9:11–15) are brief prophecies of salvation that were probably added later. The historical Amos was likely a prophet of unmitigated doom, whereas the final form of the book of Amos offers the possibility of hope even in the midst of certain doom.

The Book of Hosea

The pre-writing prophets included Elijah and Elisha in the north in the ninth century BCE. In contrast, most of the fifteen writing prophets were from the south. Hosea is the exception. He appears to have come from the north originally, and he was active in and around Samaria for most of his ministry (find Samaria in Map 19.1). He delivered his prophecies some time shortly after Amos, his older contemporary, probably around 750–730 BCE. He may have been associated with priestly circles at the sanctuary at Shechem who were loyal Yahwists, and who later fled to Jerusalem after the fall of the northern kingdom, taking Deuteronomistic theology with them. At some point later, the book of Hosea was updated for readers in Judah, as a number of additions and insertions suggest, such as the added clause at Hosea 5:5, "Judah also stumbles with them" (and consider Hosea 1:7,11; 3:5; 6:11).

The focus of Hosea's speeches is the worship of the Canaanite god Baal blended with the worship of Yahweh in the northern kingdom of Israel, and the appalling social conditions resulting from the moral laxity of Israel's kings, priests, and people. In the face of these religious and social failures, Hosea issues an unadulterated call to return to the covenant that Yahweh established with Israel in the desert (Hosea 6:7 and 8:1). He believed that the solution was to be found in the knowledge of God as offered in Yahweh's law and as illustrated by Yahweh's love (especially in the tender imagery of 11:1). Hosea is the "prophet of love," who always held out hope for the "return" (or "repentance") of the people to Yahweh's side. This emphasis grows to a crescendo in the book, culminating in the final chapter's recurring plea to "return to Yahweh" (Hosea 14:1–3).

The identity of the two women in chapters 1 and 3 is hard to sort out. In Hosea 1, the prophet is commanded to take a wife named Gomer, who becomes a prostitute ("take for yourself a wife of whoredom" in 1:2 is proleptical, meaning that she wasn't a prostitute at first but the command collapses the facts of her behavior into a single reality). Hosea and Gomer have three children, whose symbolic names encapsulate Hosea's prophetic message for Israel.[4] Then in Hosea 3, the prophet is commanded to purchase an adulterous woman, who symbolizes Israel's unfaithfulness in Hosea's preaching. Some readers assume that the two women are, in fact, the same. In this case, Hosea paid her price and purchased Gomer back after she left him, turned to prostitution, and ended up destitute. A more likely interpretation is that Hosea's wife Gomer was unfaithful, which sadly provided a parallel for Israel's unfaithfulness to Yahweh. A second woman, the unnamed adulteress of Hosea 3, did not become the prophet's wife but was simply a symbol of Israel's need to be faithful to Yahweh and abstain from relationships with other gods.

The Book of Micah

The superscription in the book of Micah names Moresheth as Micah's hometown, which is confirmed by Jeremiah 26:18 (find Moresheth on Map 19.1). Some of Micah's speeches seem to have

---

4 These were not their real names, of course, and the use of symbolic names for the children of OT prophets will come up again in Isaiah 7–8.

SIDEBAR 19.4. THE HISTORY OF PROPHECY IN ANCIENT ISRAEL

According to references in the Primary History, Israel had other prophets long before the eighth century BCE. In fact, Abraham and Moses are called prophets (Genesis 20:7 and Deuteronomy 34:10), although this can only mean they were messengers of God's word in the most general sense. Deborah also is called a prophetess (Judges 4:4). The prophet Samuel, as a transitional figure from the judges period to Israel's monarchy, was the paradigmatic prophet for ancient Israel (1 Samuel 3:19–21). Samuel's activities and messages were truly the beginning of the prophetic traditions in ancient Israel. Nathan served as prophet in David's court, and we have references to many other such prophets in the early years of the monarchy.

The imposing figures of Elijah and Elisha are also part of Israel's long history of prophets we might call "pre-writing prophets," but whose activities are recorded in the Primary History (1 Kings 17–19, 21; 2 Kings 1–7). They challenged religious syncretism, called for covenant faithfulness, and performed dramatic miracles confirming their legitimacy as Yahweh's prophets. The focus of these prophets was primarily the royal courts of Israel. In other words, they primarily directed their messages to the kings of Israel. Indeed, the history of prophecy in ancient Israel from Samuel in the tenth century to the eighth century was intimately tied to the rise of Israel's monarchy. The appearance of kings in early Israel was accompanied by the rise of the office of the prophet. Israel's king was always and forever to be attentive to the word of God spoken through the prophets (Deuteronomy 18:15–22). The rise and accessibility of writing in the eighth century, together with the new and increasingly serious threat of Assyria, produced a new urgency in the prophetic witness. The message was democratizied, by which I mean that the prophets were no longer preaching to the king of Israel or Judah but instead were appealing directly to the people for repentance and covenant faithfulness.

The fifteen prophetic books of the OT canon are called the "writing prophets" because their messages have been written down and preserved in books rather than embedded in historical narratives of the Primary History, which further distinguishes them from Samuel, Elijah, and Elisha. But you should be careful not to think of these fifteen as authors of the books bearing their names. Their sermons and speeches were almost exclusively oral at first and were written down by others. Most of these prophetic books show evidence of heavy editing and the addition of supplementary materials. Some are more like collections of diverse prophetic material *related* to a particular prophet. Most of the contents of these books reach back to the preaching of the prophets whose names they bear (see Sidebar 20.3).

On the other hand, when you think of the composition of Israel's books of prophecy, you should think in terms of "attributed authorship."* None of these books is anonymous. They have each one been attributed to a specific named prophet in their superscriptions. And the superscriptions are the works of editors. It appears that most of the prophets had scribes or disciples who helped with the writing of their speeches, and in the case of Jeremiah, we know his name: Baruch, son of Neriah (Jeremiah 36:4). Rarely did a prophet write his own prophecies, although the prophet we know as Deutero-Isaiah is an exception (see the next chapter). And as a rule, prophetic materials had to be attributed to an identifiable prophet, so that anonymous prophecies were added to another known collection (as in the book of Isaiah; again, see the next chapter). As a result, all Israelite prophecies are attributed to a particular prophet, and in the case of Malachi, it may be that an editor has even manufactured a name (see Chapter 21).

* For more on this, see pages 36–39 in van der Toorn in "Where to Find More" in Chapter 2.

this region specifically in mind (Micah 1:13–16), and the passion he felt for his kinsfolk in the region may be heard in the plaintive use of "my people" (Micah 1:9). Most of his prophecies appear to have been delivered in the decades following his older contemporaries, Amos and Hosea, probably in the mid-720s and for a decade or so afterward.

The book opens with a compelling prophecy of judgment, which will fall upon Samaria, Jerusalem, and the region around Lachish, including Micah's home territory (Micah 1). The heart of the book attacks the social elite, who oppress the poor and distort justice (Micah 2–5), with a few prophecies of salvation mixed among these harsher attacks. The final two chapters open with Yahweh's legal dispute against Israel (6:1–8), announce his ruling of condemnation of the city of Samaria (6:13), and conclude by urging hope and trust for salvation in the future (7:7 and 11–13). The question "Who is a God like you?" (7:18) is a play on the prophet's name, Micah, an abbreviation of Michaiah, "Who is like Yahweh?"

Those made uncomfortable by Micah's message respond with a conviction justifying their behavior, one that we will encounter again with Jeremiah (Sidebar 20.2). We'll call this "Zion theology," although the name isn't perfect. The idea is that the covenant with God guarantees salvation. They believe that Jerusalem and the sacred Temple Mount, Zion, are incapable of falling to the enemy because Yahweh has committed himself to preserving them forever. Micah warns that Yahweh's promises are conditioned upon righteousness and do not extend indefinitely for those who oppress the poor. Jerusalem is not, in fact, inviolable. It will be held accountable for the sins of its inhabitants.

Micah's adversaries object: "Surely Yahweh is with us!" and "No harm shall come upon us." To them he announces, "therefore because of you Zion shall be plowed as a field" (Micah 3:11–12).

Micah's impassioned plea for justice and righteous treatment of the poor is forever preserved in his immortal words.

> He has told you, O mortal, what is good;
>   and what does Yahweh require of you
> but to do justice, and to love kindness,
>   and to walk humbly with your God? (Micah 6:8)

The Book of Isaiah

The Israelite editors of the fifteen OT books of prophecy collected the speeches related to a particular prophet, in some cases supplemented and expanded them, and then attributed the whole collection to that prophet in an opening superscription. In some cases, we may assume that the largest portion of each book actually goes back to the prophet named in the superscription. But not in every case. While it was the practice of these editors to assign the name of an individual prophet to each collection, sometimes other prophetic sayings gravitated to a collection of speeches. If homilies or prophetic sayings were worth preserving in writing, the editors routinely attributed them to a named prophet. They were not normally free to leave a group of prophetic sayings anonymous.

In the case of the book of Isaiah, the editorial supplements and expansions grew over many years to such a size that we are probably justified in speaking of an Isaianic group of prophets, or a "school" of writers and thinkers following in the footsteps of the great eighth-century prophet by the name of Isaiah son of Amoz from Jerusalem (Isaiah 1:1). Most of the prophecies of salvation collected in the second half of the book can be attributed to one of these followers, who is unnamed but usually called "Deutero-Isaiah" or "Second Isaiah." We will come to that portion of the book of Isaiah containing his work in the next chapter. For now, we will consider him as the anonymous editor/author from the time of the exile who was responsible for editing the first thirty-nine chapters of our current book of Isaiah, and for composing the second major portion. Deutero-Isaiah is exceptional because he appears to have actually written most of his prophecies, as opposed to delivering them orally and having them written down by someone else. He is also exceptional because he remained anonymous. To distinguish this exilic author/editor from the eighth-century prophet, Isaiah son of Amoz, we will refer to him as "Isaiah of the exile."

As you can see, the book of Isaiah has a complex literary history. Its structure reveals a "collection of collections," almost like the Psalms or Proverbs, in three parts. First, Isaiah 1–39 contain prophecies of the eighth-century prophet, Isaiah son of Amoz, although his work has been expanded considerably. This portion of the book is sometimes called "Proto-Isaiah" or "First Isaiah." We will refer to this portion of the book simply as "Isaiah of Jerusalem." Then we have Isaiah 40–55, containing prophecies of salvation coming from the period of the exile, preserved intentionally in writing it appears by Deutero-Isaiah. Finally, we have Isaiah 56–66, containing prophecies from the postexilic period and usually referred to as "Trito-Isaiah" or

"Third Isaiah." We will consider this final portion of the book together with Deutero-Isaiah in the next chapter.

Although containing very different types of prophecies, the three parts of the book of Isaiah are related to each other. The best theory for how the book was formed is the idea that Deutero-Isaiah was responsible for editing and shaping chapters 1–39 as the message of the eighth-century prophet. Then he wrote chapters 40–55 as an intentional update or amendment, providing prophecies of salvation from the perspective of the exile. The final chapters, Isaiah 55–66, were contributed some time later as a continuation of the prophecies of Deutero-Isaiah.[5] While the book in its final form is composed of three portions, it nevertheless has a definite unity.

Isaiah of Jerusalem

The prophetic ministry of Isaiah son of Amoz took place in Jerusalem. Given the ease with which he interacted with the kings of Judah, he was apparently at home in the royal court (Isaiah 7:3, 37:5–7, etc.). His preaching reflects intimate knowledge of temple worship in Jerusalem and the priesthood, but also of the political circumstances of Judah and the royal house of David. We will see that others of the writing prophets testify to a specific call to prophetic service (e.g., Jeremiah and Ezekiel). Isaiah's call occurred in the year King Uzziah died, which was around 742 BCE (6:1). Together with references in the book's superscription, we may assume that

---

5 For a presentation of this theory, see Williamson in "Where to Find More" in Chapter 20.

Isaiah of Jerusalem was active from the 740s to the end of the century.

After five chapters of introduction and Isaiah's call in chapter 6, the book presents prophecies and narratives surrounding the Assyrian crisis (Isaiah 7–12). A new king took the throne in Assyria in 745 BCE, Tiglath-pileser III, and quickly revived the once proud empire from a north Mesopotamian base. In response to the growing threat from Assyria in the east, a coalition emerged in the Levant led principally by Aram-Syria of Damascus and the king of northern Israel at Samaria. This coalition of Syria and Israel (or "Ephraim," for short) aimed to remove Ahaz by force and place a puppet ruler on the throne in Jerusalem who would support their cause. The ensuing conflict is known as the Syro-Ephraimite War (Isaiah 7:1–2), pitting Judah against its neighbors to the north, Israel and Syria.

The question is whether the young King Ahaz of Judah would side with the Syro-Ephraimite coalition or would turn to the enemy itself, Assyria, for deliverance. The prophet Isaiah saw these international events as an opportunity. It was time for Ahaz to decide what he really believed. Ahaz had only recently assumed the throne after the death of his father, Jotham (see 2 Kings 15:29–38). Isaiah considered this moment of personal and national crisis a question of faith. Whom would Ahaz trust? Would he turn to Tiglath-pileser and the might of Assyria, or would he trust in Yahweh?

Like Hosea before him, Isaiah used the symbolic names of his children in his proclamations. His sons, Shear-jashub ("a remnant shall return"; 7:3) and Maher-shalal-hash-baz ("the spoil speeds, the prey hastens"; 8:3–4), are constant reminders that salvation is to be found in Yahweh alone. It is

possible the child named Immanuel ("God is with us"; 7:14) was also a son of Isaiah, although the text is not clear. Of course, Immanuel was to become a powerful messianic figure in biblical literature (Matthew 1:23). The prophet relentlessly urged Ahaz to rely on Yahweh to get through the crisis. All the nations threatening Judah were only temporarily empowered by Yahweh. Their fall was imminent. And afterward, a Davidic prince would arise to establish a time of tranquil peace and security (11:1–9). Isaiah's portrait of a royal redeemer, with memorable salvific names ("Everlasting Father, Prince of Peace"; 9:6) is a classic prophecy of salvation for all time.

To the disappointment of the prophet, Ahaz turned to Tiglath-pileser for help. The Assyrians defeated Damascus in 732 BCE and Samaria in 722 BCE, which was seen as confirmation of Isaiah's preaching. The book, in virtual silence about Ahaz's failures, turns immediately to a condemnation of the world's nations in a prophetic genre we have seen already in Amos: prophecies against the nations (Isaiah 13–23). Beginning with Babylon in the east and sweeping across the ancient Near Eastern map, Isaiah condemns ten nations, illustrating that none of them merits trust or the faith of kings in Jerusalem. By highlighting Babylon (13:1–14:23) the book anticipates the rise of Judah's next great threat.

The next unit of the book, Isaiah 24–27, exhibits an apocalyptic style, with themes and prophecies of universal scope envisioning an eschatological period of doom and salvation (see Chapter 22). Most readers assume that these chapters, the Isaiah Apocalypse, were added to the prophecies of Isaiah of Jerusalem much later. Their location after the prophecies against the nations suggests a stance that gives up on the possibility of salvation in the circumstances of the near future and longs instead for an ultimate and final day of salvation in the distant future.

The next major unit, Isaiah 28–35, contains several prophecies and utterances from later in Isaiah's life. Amid numerous prophecies of judgment, there are also glimmers of hope for a remnant of believers who remain faithful to Yahweh. This first portion of the book of Isaiah closes with narratives, Isaiah 36–39, thought to be borrowed from 2 Kings 18–20, although the direction of literary dependency is uncertain. The historical circumstances have now moved on to King Hezekiah (715–686 BCE), whose piety and faithfulness are implicitly contrasted with the failure of Ahaz in Isaiah 7. By raising the specter of the Babylonians in Isaiah 39, these chapters also serve as a literary bridge between the Assyrian context of Isaiah 1–39 and the Babylonian exile as context for Isaiah 40–55.

Religious Contributions of the Eighth-Century Prophets

There are no explicit statements of monotheism in the prophecies that we've studied from the eighth century BCE. Yet these prophets were Israel's leading thinkers of the day, and they made distinct contributions to the monotheism that eventually emerged in the pages of the OT. Two features in particular are clear: (1) the role of the covenant, with its call for exclusive loyalty to Yahweh, as early as the eighth century BCE, and (2) the prophetic emphasis on the international extent of Yahweh's authority.

First, we have seen how important the concept of *covenant* is in Deuteronomy and in the religion of Moses generally (Chapters 9 and 10). It was once thought that the idea arose quite late in Israel's history. But the eighth-century prophet Hosea considered Israel's covenant with Yahweh the primary way of understanding the nation's relationship with God (Hosea 2:18, 6:7, and 8:1). And the monotheistic principle in Israel almost certainly emerged from (or, at least *with*) this concept of covenant with its call for exclusive devotion to Yahweh alone. By means of his metaphor of marriage (Yahweh the groom, Israel the bride) as well as his emphasis on covenant, Hosea championed monolatrous devotion to Yahweh (and compare Micah 4:5). The call to obey only one God led eventually to the conviction that this God is the only God.

Second, in addition to this preaching on the exclusive worship of Yahweh alone, the eighth-century prophets also advanced the idea that Yahweh's power and authority extended beyond the borders of Israel. They understood for the first time that Yahweh's authority was international or even universal. In the ancient world, a deity's influence was thought to extend only to the borders of its territories, much like an ancient king's rulership was bounded by his nation's borders. But even Israel's pre-writing prophets of the ninth century, Elijah and Elisha, already understood that Yahweh was not like other deities. His presence was thought to be felt and known beyond the traditional borders of ancient Israel (1 Kings 17:8, 18:10, and 19:15; 2 Kings 8:7–15).

With the writing prophets of the eighth century, the international extent of Yahweh's power and authority is articulated in a new way. Their prophecies "against the nations," for example (Amos 1–2 and Isaiah 13–23), show Yahweh's obvious control of far distant lands and peoples. Egypt, Babylonia, and Assyria are mere instruments in Yahweh's hands to accomplish his purposes. The prophet Amos asserts that the Israelites are not the only people Yahweh has transplanted from one location to another. As he brought Israel out of Egypt, Yahweh also brought the Philistines out of Caphtor and the Arameans out of Kir (Amos 9:7).

According to the eighth-century prophets, Yahweh is in control of all nations, everywhere and always. This conviction surely contributed to the emerging monotheism of the OT. The next logical step was to call into question the very existence of the deities in those other nations. Indeed, these theological contributions of the eighth-century prophets made possible the survival of Israelite Yahwism once Jerusalem and its monarchy were destroyed and the people taken into exile in a foreign land.

WHERE TO FIND MORE

Commentaries: The best technical and advanced commentaries on the eighth-century prophets are: **Amos** – Shalom M. Paul, *Amos: A Commentary on the Book of Amos* (Hermeneia; Minneapolis, Minn.: Fortress Press, 1991); **Hosea** – J. Andrew Dearman, *The Book of Hosea* (New International Commentary on the Old Testament; Grand Rapids, Mich.: Eerdmans, 2010); Francis I. Andersen and David Noel Freedman, *Hosea: A New Translation with Introduction and Commentary* (Anchor Bible 24; Garden City, N.Y.: Doubleday, 1980); **Micah** – Francis I. Andersen and David Noel Freedman, *Micah: A New Translation with Introduction and Commentary* (Anchor Bible 24E; New York: Doubleday, 2000); **Isaiah** – Brevard S. Childs, *Isaiah* (Old Testament Library; Louisville, Ky.: Westminster John Knox Press, 2001); and H. G. M. Williamson, *A Critical and Exegetical Commentary on Isaiah 1–27, vol. 1, Isaiah 1–5* (International Critical Commentary; New York and London: T & T Clark, 2006).

Cook, Stephen L. *The Social Roots of Biblical Yahwism*. Society of Biblical Literature Studies in Biblical Literature 8. Atlanta, Ga.: Society of Biblical Literature, 2004.

Argues that the eighth-century prophets were purveyors of a stream of theological tradition, which Cook terms "Sinai theology," calling for exclusive allegiance to a single divine Yahweh; also explores the prophets' role on the periphery of Israelite and Judahite society until the reforms of Hezekiah and Josiah.

Koch, Klaus. *The Prophets. Vol. 1, The Assyrian Period*, and Vol. 2, *The Babylonian and Persian Periods*. Philadelphia: Fortress Press, 1983 and 1984.

Nissinen, Martti. *Prophets and Prophecy in The Ancient Near East*. SBLWAW 12. Atlanta, Ga.: Society of Biblical Literature, 2003.

The introduction in pages 1–11 surveys ancient Near Eastern examples of prophecy, followed by translations and discussions of numerous such texts.

Petersen, David L. *The Prophetic Literature: An Introduction*. Louisville, Ky.: Westminster John Knox Press, 2002.

Rollston, Christopher A. *Writing and Literacy in the World of Ancient Israel: Epigraphic Evidence from the Iron Age*. Society of Biblical Literature Archaeology and Biblical Studies 11. Leiden/Boston: Brill/SBL, 2010.

Westermann, Claus. *Basic Forms of Prophetic Speech*. Louisville, Ky.: Westminster John Knox Press, 1991 [1967].

Westermann, Claus. *Prophetic Oracles of Salvation in the Old Testament*. Louisville, Ky.: Westminster John Knox Press, 1991.

See both Westermann volumes for a thorough presentation of the three types of prophetic speech: prophecies, utterances, and historical narratives.

CHAPTER 20

Israel's Prophets: The Crisis and Beyond

OLD TESTAMENT READING: JEREMIAH, OBADIAH, NAHUM, HABAKKUK, ZEPHANIAH, EZEKIEL, AND ISAIAH 40–66

In this chapter, we will expand our prophetic coverage, exploring the books of Jeremiah, Obadiah, Nahum, Habakkuk, Zephaniah, Ezekiel, and the second portion of Isaiah. Lengthy books like Jeremiah and Ezekiel are considered "major," whereas the shorter books, such as the single-chapter Obadiah, are deemed "minor prophets." Some books include personal details about the prophet, whereas others like Nahum are virtually devoid of such information. However, all of these writing prophets articulated Yahweh's messages in the seventh century BCE and through the crises leading up to the destruction of Jerusalem in 586 BCE and the ensuing exile.

We will note how the traumatic events of Israel's changing world impacted the urgency, tone, and even theological emphases of the prophets. For example, Second Isaiah contains one of the most explicit OT statements of monotheism. In Ezekiel, we will observe the first focus on the role of individual responsibility for sin, along with an especially personal tone by means of the first-person voice. Finally, we will encounter the concept of the "Day of the Lord," which represents Israel's move toward eschatology.

Jerusalem fell to the Babylonians in 586 BCE. In one moment, the Judeans lost their city, their king, and their temple and priesthood. Their leadership was taken away into exile. This was obviously a turning point in Israelite history. Beyond the crisis itself, the exile lasted until 539 BCE, when the Persians captured Babylon and released the Judeans shortly thereafter. The period

326

of the exile was likewise an important moment in history.[1]

The trauma of these events left an unmistakable mark on the pages of the OT. In fact, it is possible to view these historical events – the destruction of Jerusalem and the beginning of the Babylonian exile – as the center point of the OT canon. The first half of the OT is the Primary History approximately (using the Jewish canon; Figure 2.3), which concludes with these events (2 Kings 25). Similarly, the same events stand near the center of the fifteen writing prophets collected in the OT, assuming that Jeremiah 52, with its account of the destruction of Jerusalem, represents the approximate midway point of the collection of prophets. Remarkably, the same can be said for "the writings" (again, using the Jewish canon), where we have the book of Lamentations at its center, with its vivid and emotional response to the fall of the city of Jerusalem. In this type of symmetrical literary arrangement, the center point reflects the most important themes of the texts. Thus the excruciating events of 586 BCE and the years immediately after stand quite literally at the center of the OT, and even at the center of its constituent parts.[2]

The conceptual impact of the fall of Jerusalem cannot be denied. The collection of OT books of prophecy covered here reflects that impact. Israel's prophetic consciousness matured in the eighth century. In the seventh century leading up to the crisis, the prophetic witness grew more intense. Social conditions in Judah were not improving.

1 Review Chapter 13 for the way these events fit into OT history generally.
2 For this attempt to explain the organization of the entire OT around this event, see Freedman in "Where to Find More" in Chapter 4.

20.1. Exile scenes from Sennacherib's palace in Nineveh. This relief art from Sennacherib's palace shows prisoners being led into exile carrying their baggage with them. These prisoners were certainly from the Levant being driven into exile in the east, and some believe that they were Israelite or Judahite exiles. (Photo: Erich Lessing / Art Resource, N.Y.)

The inhabitants' leadership appeared to have learned nothing from the collapse of the northern kingdom, Israel, to the Assyrians in 722 BCE. The dominant power was shifting from Assyria to Babylonia; the world was changing, and God's people were in jeopardy again. Several prophets spoke of this situation, and it is to their writings that we now turn.

THE BOOKS OF JEREMIAH, OBADIAH, NAHUM, HABAKKUK, ZEPHANIAH, EZEKIEL, AND "ISAIAH OF THE EXILE"

I have arranged in rough chronological order (as best as we can know it) the OT books of prophecy coming from the period leading up to and including the Babylonian crisis. In this section, we consider the books individually. You may want to review the list in Figure 2.3 to keep in mind the order in which they have been collected in the OT.

SIDEBAR 20.1. WHERE IS THE BOOK OF LAMENTATIONS?

You may be wondering why I haven't included the book of Lamentations in this chapter, in light of its close association with Jeremiah. If you are using a standard Christian translation of the OT, you will see that Lamentations comes immediately after Jeremiah in the Christian canons (Figure 2.3). So why have we reserved it for Chapter 23?

In the Jewish canon, Lamentations is among the five "scrolls" (Hebrew *mĕgillôt*) collected near the end of the OT. As we have seen, each of these five scrolls was read in the synagogues of early Judaism at specific times in the liturgical calendar (see Sidebar 12.1). Lamentations in particular was read in commemoration of the destruction of the temple, or the Ninth of Ab. For a variety of reasons, I find it useful to treat these five books together, and so the Megilloth will be studied as a group in Chapter 23.

The Book of Jeremiah

In addition to prophecies of judgment and salvation, we have quite a lot of narrative material in the book of Jeremiah. In fact, because of all this narrative we know more about the life and person of Jeremiah than about any other OT prophet. Jeremiah was from a priestly family from the Levitical town of Anathoth of Benjamin, only about three miles northeast of Jerusalem (Jeremiah 1:1; compare Joshua 21:18). The origins of these priests are unclear. They were perhaps among those who migrated south after the fall of Samaria in the north in 722 BCE.

Jeremiah was called to become a prophet in the thirteenth year of King Josiah (627/626 BCE; Jeremiah 1:2, and compare 25:3 and 36:2). We know that Josiah initiated his religious reforms around 621 (2 Kings 22–23). As the new king of Judah in the south, he appears to have perceived himself as the "anointed one" (or messiah) of a restored united kingdom of Israel, reuniting the north kingdom with Judah in a new age of strength and independence (see Sidebar 14.3). When he was killed in battle, his dream of a united Israel was thwarted. But this Josianic model of a restored Davidic monarchy with Jerusalem at its center inspired many, including the prophet Jeremiah. And yet, Jeremiah was relatively silent about Josiah's attempts at reform. Most of Jeremiah's prophetic speeches and other activities relate to the period after Josiah's tragic death in 609 BCE.

We may safely assume, then, that Jeremiah was relatively silent between 622 and 609 BCE mostly because he was confident that Josiah was on the right track and optimistic about the outcome of the reform efforts. When the good king lost his life in battle at Megiddo, everything changed. Josiah's successors were not faithful to the covenant or to his attempts to reform the religious practices of the nation. As a result, Jeremiah's prophecies grew increasingly strident in their judgments. He was probably born mid-seventh century and was active until about 580 BCE.

Jeremiah appears to have been influenced by the prophecies of his predecessor, Hosea. Several common themes between the two books have led readers to speculate that they may both have had connections to prophetic-Levitical groups from northern Israel, who in Jeremiah's case, had migrated to

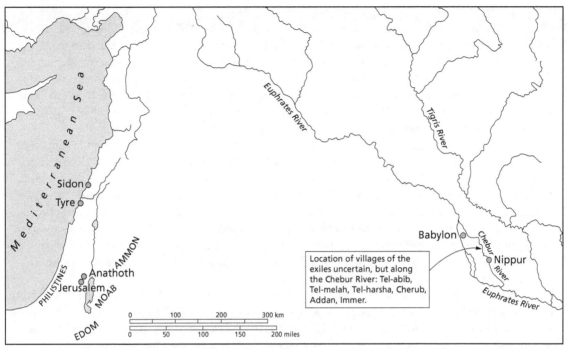

Map 20.1. The world of the seventh- and sixth-century prophets

the south (or as far as Anathoth) after the fall of Samaria in 722 BCE. Jeremiah is the OT prophet who personally experienced the most devastating losses of the ancient Israelites. He is the "weeping prophet" (9:1 and 13:17) because he witnessed the fall of Jerusalem to the Babylonians (586 BCE) and because he was persecuted for his prophecies of the coming destruction (Jeremiah 15:10, 20:1–2, and 37:15). Little wonder, then, that the OT book of Lamentations, a vivid account of the destruction of Jerusalem, has long been ascribed to the prophet Jeremiah (Chapter 23).

The book of Jeremiah may be studied in five subunits. The first is a collection of his prophecies of judgment against Judah and Jerusalem (Jeremiah 1–25), including his earliest speeches in the first six chapters. The book's first chapter is essentially

Jeremiah's call to prophetic ministry, complete with visions and assurances that Yahweh will be with the young prophet during the difficult days ahead (1:8,19). Jeremiah was called primarily "to pluck up and to pull down, to destroy and to overthrow," although along the way there will also be opportunity "to build and to plant" (1:10). Owing to the circumstances around him, his prophecies will be almost entirely ones of judgment, although it may be comforting that *even* Jeremiah contains a few prophecies of salvation and hope.

This first unit of the book contains Jeremiah's "confessions," a collection of utterances directed to Yahweh depicting in emotional language the agony of his situation (spread throughout Jeremiah 12–20). We also have here Jeremiah's "Temple Discourse," in which he took his message

SIDEBAR 20.2. THE PROPHETIC STRUGGLES AGAINST ZION THEOLOGY

Jeremiah's ranting against those who take confidence in the presence of the temple in Jerusalem may seem hard to understand (Jeremiah 7 and 26). Similarly, Ezekiel's vision of Yahweh's glory departing from Mount Zion is difficult to relate to our contemporary setting. To get the full weight of these prophecies, you need to remember something of the history of Israel's theological development, including something we call "Zion theology," or the "Zion tradition." Derived from the southeastern slope of the city, the name "Zion" is an old synonym for Jerusalem, sometimes also known as the "City of David."

Under the United Monarchy of David and Solomon, a three-pronged idealogy emerged in support of Israel's new political and social reality. First, the concept of Yahweh as God of the ancestors was replaced with titles such as "Great King" and "Most High," reflecting Yahweh's suzerain or supreme status on earth. Suitable for Israel's new political strength, Yahweh became a more international deity, which eventually emerges in the universalism of the eighth-century prophets. Second, David and his dynastic line of rulers were chosen by Yahweh as his human representatives on earth. Third, Yahweh also chose Zion/Jerusalem as his abode on earth. This confluence of theological traditions was assumed by Isaiah of Jerusalem, and it eventually became an important means of legitimizing the ideal Judean state with its Davidic dynasty centered in Jerusalem (review Sidebar 15.2).

By the time of Jeremiah, however, this Zion tradition had become a problem. Cherished beliefs had become hardened and uncompromising dogma. The inhabitants of Jersulem had come to believe that they were secure in an impregnable city, untouchable because of Yahweh's unconditional commitment to David and Jerusalem. Even with the Babylonian army knocking at their door, they had the capacity blithely to assume they had nothing to fear. Therefore, Jeremiah pointed to Shiloh, the first place chosen for Yahweh's sacred abode (and functioning as a Yahweh holy site, as at 1 Samuel 1–3). Just as Yahweh had abandoned Shiloh, so he would do to Jerusalem (Jeremiah 7:12–15 and 26:6). Ezekiel similarly imagined the unthinkable. Yahweh's sacred presence could be taken from Zion (Ezekiel 1 and 10).

to the heart of Judahite religion, the temple itself, warning people against blind faith in the idea that Yahweh's temple is still standing while they regularly break the Ten Commandments (Jeremiah 7:1–15). Yahweh announces through Jeremiah that he will destroy this temple as he destroyed his earlier sacred house at Shiloh. A narrative account of this event is probably preserved in Jeremiah 26:1–6, dating it to 609 BCE and likely representing the initiation of Jeremiah's public ministry. Jeremiah 21–25 contain his prophecies of judgment against Jerusalem during the days of King Zedekiah (597–586 BCE).

The second unit of the book offers narratives about Jeremiah's experiences (Jeremiah 26–35), as distinct from the words he preached. This includes an account of a letter Jeremiah sent to Jewish expatriates who had been taken to Babylonia in 597 by Nebuchadnezzar (Jeremiah 29). He advises them to settle in the land because their exile would last seventy years (29:10). But Jeremiah also encourages the Jews in exile, saying that Yahweh still has "plans" for them; Yahweh will visit them after their seventy-year exile and provide for them "a future with hope" (29:10–11). This announcement then leads to chapters containing prophecies of salvation

SIDEBAR 20.3. THE PRODUCTION OF A BIBLICAL BOOK

The book of Jeremiah reveals a clue about the way an OT book of prophecy might have been composed, at least in this one example. Take a moment now and read Jeremiah 36. The prophet's personal secretary, Baruch son of Neriah, wrote on a scroll a portion of Jeremiah's preaching "from the day" Yahweh first spoke to him (presumably 627/626 BCE) "until today," which was the fourth year of King Jehoiakim's rule (or 605 BCE). This scroll was read aloud twice in one day, first by Baruch publicly in the temple precincts and then by a royal official named Jehudi in the presence of Jehoiakim and his court officials (36:10,21). This scroll contained at least three columns but was brief enough to be read in one hearing. It was dictated to Baruch by the prophet, or "from the mouth" of the prophet himself.

Scholars have attempted to reconstruct the contents of this "primitive" Jeremiah scroll by relying on contents elsewhere in the current book of Jeremiah. While we cannot know precisely what was on this "first scroll" of Jeremiah (v. 28), the message of its contents was that the king of Babylon would soon destroy Judah because of its sins (v. 29). King Jehoiakim, offended by its message, destroyed this first scroll as it was being read to him (vv. 20–23). Subsequently, the words of this scroll were dictated onto another scroll, which was expanded with "many similar words" (v. 32).

This process may well illustrate how our current OT books of prophecy were composed (also on this topic, see Sidebar 19.4). The prophet was personally responsible (at times, through a secretary) for the initial writing of the contents of his originally oral speeches. Since much of the material in the current book of Jeremiah is third-person narrative about the prophet's activities, we may safely assume that these early written prophecies were then expanded, either by the same secretary or by a group of the prophet's followers. In this way, an initial "scroll" would evolve and develop along a number of potential routes, touched by many hands as editors or even coauthors, until each prophet's activities and speeches took the shape of the books we now have preserved in our OT.

and hope that are in striking contrast to the rest of the book (Jeremiah 30–31). The prophet is commanded to "write in a book all the words" of comfort (30:2), promising restoration of both northern Israel and southern Judah in the future.

The third section of the book is sometimes called the "Memoirs of Baruch" (Jeremiah 36–45). These are narratives in the third person recounting events in the life of Jeremiah, including his reliance on a personal secretary and scribe, Baruch, who served as his chronicler. These narratives include the prophet's confrontations with Kings Jehoiakim and Zedekiah, his imprisonment, and his forced exile into Egypt after the fall of Jerusalem. The

unit closes with Jeremiah's personal prophecy for Baruch, who suffered alongside his mentor.

The fourth section of the book of Jeremiah contains prophecies against the foreign nations (Jeremiah 46–51), a distinct literary form of prophecy we have already seen in Amos and Isaiah of Jerusalem (Chapter 19).[3] The fifth and final section of the book is a single chapter (Jeremiah 52), in

3 The Septuagint not only locates these oracles against the nations in a different place (after Jeremiah 25:13a) but also gives them a different arrangement. These and other differences between the Hebrew text and the Septuagint of Jeremiah again illustrate that these biblical books evolved in diverse ways.

which the fall of Jerusalem is recounted (mostly paralleling the account of 2 Kings 24–25). We learn here that, in addition to the massive exile of 586, Nebuchadnezzar also deported Jews from Judah to Babylon in 597 and later in 581 BCE (52:28–30).

The Book of Obadiah

The diminutive book of Obadiah, with its only twenty-one verses, comes from a prophet about whom we know virtually nothing. The "vision" of Obadiah (whose name means "servant of Yahweh") is a prophecy of judgment against Judah's neighbor to the southeast, Edom (see Map 20.1), a symbol of human arrogance and unjust oppression.

This prophetic speech probably comes from shortly after the fall of Jerusalem in 586 BCE. The prophecy condemns the Edomites, a people considered fraternal relatives of the Israelites (Genesis 36). The Edomites responded to the devastation in Judah with gloating and rejoicing, taking advantage of the devastation by looting the city and conspiring with the Babylonians for personal gain. The passion and emotive language of the speech implies that the prophet was an eyewitness to these events and spoke against the opportunistic Edomites as a word of comfort for the shattered occupants of the city of Jerusalem.

The Book of Nahum

We know practically nothing about the prophet Nahum, whose name means "comforter" or "(God) comforts." Because his prophecy against the nation Assyria was delivered prior to the fall of its capital city, Nineveh (according to the superscription, 1:1), we may assume that his prophetic activities

occurred before 612 BCE when Nineveh fell to a Medo-Babylonian coalition. The book of Nahum also has references suggesting that the oracles were delivered prior to the collapse of Assyrian might, sometime in the 650s or 640s BCE (see Nahum 1:12 and 2:13).

The prophet's name, Nahum, was common enough at that time. While it may have been a symbolic name (a pseudonym), it was nevertheless appropriate because the prophet's message was intended to provide comfort for the people of Judah suffering under Assyrian oppression. The oracles contained here were similar to the distinct literary genre we have seen elsewhere in Amos, Isaiah, and Jeremiah, as prophecies against a foreign nation (Chapter 19). In this way, Judah was encouraged to remain faithful to Yahweh because Assyria's days were numbered.

The Book of Habakkuk

The speeches of Habakkuk are utterances arranged in a dialogical interchange between the prophet and Yahweh. The prophet's name is most unusual. Its closest parallel is an Assyrian garden plant, which seems a far stretch. Attempts have been made to derive his name from the verb "to embrace," but perhaps we should just admit that its meaning is impossible to determine. Similarly, we cannot know much about when Habakkuk lived. The content and language of the book imply that these prophecies come from around 600 BCE, likely during the rule of Jehoiakim of Judah (609–598 BCE).

The prophet is tortured by the pervasive injustice in Judahite society and clings tenaciously to the conviction that Yahweh is a just God. But how can Yahweh silently tolerate the suffering of the people of Judah (1:2–4)? Yahweh's answer assures the prophet that an invincible Babylonian army will accomplish justice by invading Judah (1:5–11). The prophet objects that justice at the hands of the wicked and idolatrous Babylonians is hardly satisfying. Besides, this is not what Habakkuk had in mind (1:12–17)! Believing that he has made an impressive case, he stations himself as a sentinel watching for the messenger, awaiting Yahweh's reply (2:1).

While waiting in his watchtower (symbolically), Habakkuk is given a revelation from Yahweh that he is to write on tablets plainly and clearly so that all who are able to read can do so without misunderstanding. This divine response includes a saying as impressive for its profundity as for its simplicity: "the righteous live by their faith" (2:4; and see the use of this phrase in the New Testament, Romans 1:17, Galatians 3:11, and Hebrews 10:38).[4] Yahweh assures Habakkuk that the Babylonians will have their turn at being punished. But for the meantime, they will be Yahweh's instruments for chastening Judah.

The final chapter of the book of Habakkuk is a prayer (3:1) in which the prophet details a vision he received, apparently some time later. It portrays God's journey from the south, and his ultimate victory over the wicked (3:2–16). The book's concluding verses of trust and joy, maintaining faith in Yahweh despite disappointing life circumstances, remains a classic of religious literature.

> (17) Though the fig tree does not blossom,
>> and no fruit is on the vines;
>> though the produce of the olive fails,
>> and the fields yield no food;

> though the flock is cut off from the fold,
>> and there is no herd in the stalls,
> (18) yet I will rejoice in Yahweh;
>> I will exult in the God of my salvation.
> (19) Lord Yahweh is my strength;
>> he makes my feet like the feet of a deer,
>> and makes me tread upon the heights. (Habakkuk 3:17–19)

The Book of Zephaniah

According to the superscription in the first verse of the book that bears his name, the prophet Zephaniah was active during the reign of King Josiah (640–609 BCE), and was therefore a contemporary of Jeremiah.[5] His name means "Yahweh has protected." His prophecies proclaim judgment for Jerusalem and Judah, while also turning to the familiar judgment "against the nations" category (2:4–15). Ultimately, however, there will be hope for "daughter Zion" (3:9–20).

Central to this book's message is the concept the "day of Yahweh" (Zephaniah 1:7–18, 2:1–3, and 3:8–20). You may have noticed this idea in other prophets that we've covered thus far (Amos, Isaiah, and Obadiah), and it will come up again (Malachi and Joel in the next chapter). In general, the "day of Yahweh" is a period of time in the future when Yahweh arrives to establish his decisive rule on earth, vindicating the faithful remnant and punishing the wicked.[6] We are unable to trace the origins of this concept. But the prophets used it to good effect to push the hopes of final victory

---

4 The Hebrew term for "faith" is just as easily "faithfulness."

5 His great, great grandfather, Hezekiah, is likely another nobleman by the same name, *not* King Hezekiah of Judah (715–686 BCE).

6 See pages 27–28 of Arnold in "Where to Find More" for Chapter 22.

and ultimate peace into the future. The Sinai covenant and Davidic expectations may be temporarily
suspended because of Judah's failure and the fall
of Jerusalem. But ultimately, on that great day of
Yahweh in the future, all will be made right. This is
Israel's step in the direction of eschatology, or theories of final or end things. We will return to this
topic in Chapter 22.

The Book of Ezekiel

The prophet Ezekiel, whose name means "God
strengthen [this child]," was among the exiles
taken from Judah to Babylon in 597 BCE when
Nebuchadnezzar captured the city. The book's
superscription in Ezekiel 1:1–3 reveals that
Ezekiel's prophetic ministry began in 593 BCE
and continued at least until 571 (the date of an
oracle recorded in Ezekiel 29:17). From his perspective in exile, Ezekiel predicted not only the
complete destruction of Jerusalem and the collapse of Judahite society but also the restoration
of the temple complex and of Yahweh worship.
Ezekiel's prophecies reveal an especially sensitive
individual, who often wrapped his interpretations
of Judah's experiences together with his own.
When his wife died during the siege of Jerusalem,
he compared his own stunned grief with the effect
that the fall of Jerusalem would have on God's
people (24:15–24).

Ezekiel served as a prophet, but he came from
the ranks of Judah's priests (1:3). As a result, his
prophecies focus on the Jerusalem temple and the
worship of Yahweh prescribed there. Scholars have
identified the style and vocabulary of the book of
Ezekiel with other priestly writings of the OT,
especially the priestly and holiness source(s) of the
Pentateuch.

The book is made up of prophecies and narratives that are the personal experiences of the
prophet. (Remember the three types of prophetic
speeches are *prophecies*, *utterances*, and *narratives*; review
Chapter 19.) All of this material has a distinct
autobiographical feel, since it's all in the first-person
voice: "I was among the exiles by the river Chebar"
(1:1).[7] The only exception to the first-person presentation is in the superscription at Ezekiel 1:2–3.

The prophecies of this priest in exile are organized in three parts. The first portion of the book
(Ezekiel 1–24) presents prophecies of judgment
concerning Jerusalem and Judah prior to 586 BCE.
The opening chapters are a dramatic recasting of
Ezekiel's call to prophetic ministry, in which the
reader is drawn into his tortured conclusion that
the spirit of Yahweh has departed Jerusalem and
the city's fate is irreversible. The ensuing prophecies draw a straight line from the fall of Jerusalem
back to the sins of God's people, with no allow-
ances, exceptions, or qualifications. With compelling clarity, the prophet Ezekiel assumes the
corporate guilt of the people, but also, for the first
time, he makes clear the individual responsibility
for sin and misconduct (Ezekiel 18). There is no
evading the truth: there was enough guilt to go
around for everyone.

---

7 The "river Chebar" was a canal of the Euphrates River
near which a settlement of Judean exiles resided in southern Babylonia. One such settlement of exiles was known
as Tel-Abib (3:5). This canal was part of the "waters of
Babylon" by which the Judean exiles wept over the fall of
Jerusalem (Psalm 137:1).

SIDEBAR 20.4. SEQUENCE OF EVENTS DEFINING "THE EXILE"

Events surrounding the fall of Jerusalem and the beginning of the exile are central to the OT message. It is not surprising then that the books of prophecy are so intimately related to the events leading up to and including the exile. Here are event dates that you will need to remember as you read the prophets. Details and specific dates come from biblical references, combined with ancient Near Eastern resources, especially the Babylonian Chronicles.*

640–609 BCE – Reign of King Josiah.

626 BCE – Call of Jeremiah the prophet (Jeremiah 1:2).

621 BCE – Josiah begins his reforms (2 Kings 22–23).

609 BCE – Death of King Josiah, and the loss of Jeremiah's hopes for reform of Judahite society

609–598/597 BCE – Reign of King Jehoiakim, who initially submits to Babylonia (but see 601 BCE).

605 BCE – As a result of the battle of Carchemish, Nebuchadnezzar ousts Egypt from the Levant.

601 BCE – The Babylonians suffer a setback in their attempt to invade Egypt and are forced to withdraw to Babylon. Against the advice of the prophet Jeremiah, King Jehoiakim of Judah decides at this time to cast his lot with the pro-Egyptian party.

598 BCE – During the siege of the city of Jerusalem, King Jehoiakim dies and his son Jehoiachin assumes the throne.

598 BCE – Reign of King Jehoiachin.

598 BCE – In December, the Babylonians march west to campaign against Judah.

597 BCE – On March 16, the Babylonians capture Jerusalem and sieze Jehoiachin, taking him into exile with members of the royal household. Zedekiah, his uncle and the last son of Josiah to become king, is placed on the throne by the Babylonians.

597–586 BCE – Reign of King Zedekiah.

593 BCE – Call of Ezekiel the prophet (Ezekiel 1:2).

589 BCE – Renewed strength of Egypt provokes King Zedekiah to throw off the Babylonian yoke and to rely once again on support from Egypt.

587 BCE – In January, Jerusalem is put to siege again by the Babylonians.

586 BCE – The walls of Jerusalem are finally breached in mid-July. The next month, the city is burned and the temple razed. The exile begins.

539 BCE – Persian forces defeat the Babylonian army north of the city on October 10 and advance on the city of Babylon itself. It falls with little resistance, and Cyrus the Persian enters triumphantly on October 29, marking the end of the exile.

* Especially Chronicles 5 and 7; see Bill T. Arnold, "The Neo-Babylonian Chronicle Series," in *The Ancient Near East: Historical Sources in Translation* (ed. Mark W. Chavalas; Blackwell Sourcebooks in Ancient History; Malden, Mass.: Blackwell, 2006), 416–20.

The second portion of the book presents Ezekiel's oracles against the foreign nations, mostly Judah's immediate neighbors: Ammon, Moab, Edom, the Philistines, Tyre, Sidon, and Egypt (Ezekiel 25–32). As we have seen with other prophets, this was a common literary genre in the OT prophets that was intended to comfort God's people. Someday, all of Judah's enemies will be punished by God.

The last part of the book of Ezekiel is devoted to Israel's future reunification and salvation (Ezekiel 33–48). Just as Ezekiel had been stationed as a watchman or sentry, to be on the lookout for news of judgment (3:17), so now God sets him as a sentry to watch for and announce the coming restoration of God's people (33:7). Israel will be revived; it will rise again from the dry dust of death, as in the famous valley of the dry bones (37:1–14). The people of God, formerly divided into two nations, Israel and Judah, will be reunited as a single nation (37:15–28). This restoration of Israel will take place despite the opposition of powerful human forces, personified cartoonishly as Gog of Magog, most likely a depiction of Nebuchadnezzar of Babylon.[8] The Babylonians are noticeably missing in Ezekiel's oracles against the nations in chapters 25–32. It is no surprise that Ezekiel, as a prophet living in the Babylonian heartland, speaks of Nebuchadnezzar in apocalyptic codes when addressing the downfall of the mighty Babylonian Empire (on apocalyptic literary forms, see Chapter 22).

Themes in these restoration chapters are related to Ezekiel's particular concerns as a priest. In the day of salvation, Yahweh promises to cleanse and purify the people, to empower Israel with a new sensitivity to the statutes and ordinances of the Torah, and to restore the ancient ancestral covenant in which Yahweh will be their God and they shall be God's people.

8 Countless attempts have been made to identify Gog of Magog, and my interpretation is by no means the majority opinion. I take "Magog" as a cipher of Babylon, and "Gog" thus stands for Nebuchadnezzar, its chief prince. Whatever we conclude about this, Gog of Magog stands for the archetypal enemy from the north, symbolically representing the forces of evil opposing God and God's people.

(25) I will sprinkle clean water upon you, and you shall be clean from all your uncleannesses, and from all your idols I will cleanse you. (26) A new heart I will give you, and a new spirit I will put within you; and I will remove from your body the heart of stone and give you a heart of flesh. (27) I will put my spirit within you, and make you follow my statutes and be careful to observe my ordinances. (28) Then you shall live in the land that I gave to your ancestors; and you shall be my people, and I will be your God. (Ezekiel 36:25–28)

This portrait of restoration and hope is concluded with Ezekiel's grand vision of the ideal "blueprint" for a rebuilt temple (Ezekiel 40–48), where Yahweh once again dwells in the midst of his people, the priests are restored to leadership, the Torah is taught and enthusiastically observed, festivals and feast days are kept, and life-sustaining water flows from the Temple Mount restoring everything in the land, bringing to life even the waters of the Dead Sea, transforming it into a Sea of Life! (See Plate XII.)

Isaiah of the Exile

The prophecies of Isaiah of the exile were never a separate book in their own right (Isaiah 40–55). From the beginning, they were written in order to envelop the earlier prophecies of Isaiah of Jerusalem, incorporating and expanding the message of the eighth-century prophet (as we discussed in the previous chapter, relating to Isaiah 1–39). This author considered the writings of eighth-century Isaiah sealed until a time when God's judgment was ended (based partly on Isaiah 8:16–22) and a new day of salvation arrived. Writing from a later period, the poet of chapters 40–55 considered himself the herald of this new age of salvation. He was an editor of the eighth-century Isaiah's prophecies, but also the *author* of his own prophecies in a new sense for OT books. Since we do not know his name, scholars today refer to him with a technical designation, Deutero-Isaiah or Second Isaiah. I am also calling him "Isaiah of the exile" because his historical location can be identified between the fall of Jerusalem in 586 BCE and the fall of Babylon in 539 BCE, locating his prophetic ministry squarely in the exile.[9]

Isaiah of the exile was a gifted poet. His call to speak to the people of God opens his writings (40:6–11) and may be compared to the prophetic calls of Jeremiah, Ezekiel, and Isaiah of Jerusalem (see Jeremiah 1, Ezekiel 1–3, and Isaiah 6).[10] He describes the fall of the city of Babylon to King Cyrus of Persia, which occurred in 539 BCE, as a future event (Isaiah 47), and the fall of Jerusalem in 586 BCE as a past event (51:17–20). He expects the complete destruction of the city of Babylon (which did not occur, since it fell without a fight to the Persians), and he probably formulated much of what we read in these prophecies shortly before Cyrus captured Babylon (Cyrus is specifically mentioned in 44:28 and 45:1,13). Deutero-Isaiah was an author

who had firsthand experience with Babylonian craft techniques, probably as an eyewitness to the manufacture of idols (40:18–20, 44:9–20, and 46:5–7). His description of the making and use of idols is at home in the Babylonian practices of the 550s and 540s BCE. In sum, Isaiah of the exile was responsible for editing the first thirty-nine chapters of our current book and for composing the next major section of the book (Isaiah 40–55) a decade or so prior to the fall of Babylon in 539 BCE.

Isaiah of the exile is a prophet of comfort, a note sounded by the opening words: "Comfort, O comfort my people, says your God" (40:1). The time for prophecies of judgment is past, and the people of God now need comforting words of salvation. The plural verbs in 40:1–2 may portray God addressing the heavenly council or a group of prophetic disciples, calling for a time of pronouncing hope and restoration rather than judgment and destruction. Another voice calls for the making of a miraculous highway and removal of all natural obstacles so that Yahweh's glory may lead the return of God's people home from exile (40:3–5). Isaiah of the exile responds in the first person, "What shall I cry?" The reassuring reply is a theme for his ministry (40:6–8): "the word of our God will stand forever." What follows in Isaiah 40–55 are some of the most impressive poems of the OT. The prophet uses literary forms borrowed in part from the practices of ancient Israelite worship as oracles of salvation, in which a worship leader would respond with comforting words to an individual's prayer or cry of lamentation. These beautiful poems now stand in the book of Isaiah in near symmetrical balance to the prophecies of judgment in Isaiah 1–39.

9 Attempts to attribute all of the book of Isaiah to the son of Amoz of the eighth century are possible but not likely.
10 I am using masculine pronouns to refer to "him" for convenience of discussion, although, of course, he may have been a woman. We have no evidence either way, except we know that schools of prophets were restricted to men for the most part and that he evidently came from a school of Isaiah's disciples (see 8:16).

Isaiah of the exile expresses faith in Yahweh as Creator of heaven and earth, who can be trusted to save and restore his people Israel. While relying on the prophecies of Isaiah of Jerusalem, this poet also emphasizes the uniqueness and incomparability of Yahweh. No other gods exist besides him (45:5): "I am Yahweh, and there is no other; besides me there is no god." Such explicit monotheism was a distinguishing characteristic of the exiled Judeans, living as they did among the nations.

An important subcategory of these prophecies are the "Servant Songs," or Songs of Yahweh's Servant (42:1–4, 49:1–7, 50:4–9, and 52:13–53:12). Israel is named as the servant in 49:3, a personification of the people of God awaiting Yahweh's intervention and salvation. At other times in these hymns, we are not always able to determine who is being identified as Yahweh's servant. Elsewhere in Deutero-Isaiah, Cyrus the Persian functions as the anointed one (44:1 and 45:1). The prophet seems to have a particular individual in view in the final servant song of Isaiah (52:13–53:12), although this also could be a personification of the people. Important theological contributions of this last song, in particular, include the idea that the servant is a righteous, innocent individual, and that he suffers on behalf of others, providing them a means of forgiveness for their own sins (especially 53:10–12). Readers often take this individual as a personification of an "Ideal Israel," a righteous remnant of God's people suffering as a surrogate for others. It is not surprising, of course, that early Christians took these Servant Songs as messianic prophecies, and identified Jesus as the suffering servant (Acts 8:32–35).

The remaining portions of the book of Isaiah (Isaiah 56–66) are sometimes called Trito-Isaiah or Third Isaiah. But this designation gives the wrong impression, almost as though these chapters stood as a separate book at some point. I would not encourage you to think of these chapters as ever existing as an independent document, or even as coming from the hand of a single author or editor. Rather, it's more likely that these last eleven chapters of the book of Isaiah were added as an update or amendment. They give every evidence of being included in the years immediately after the exile ended. Babylon is not mentioned in Isaiah 56–66, and yet the temple has not been rebuilt (Isaiah 66:1). Rather, these prophecies of salvation are focused on rebuilding and reestablishing Jerusalem/Zion as the city of God, and they do so from a perspective after the return from exile yet before the reconstruction of the temple, so between 539 and 520 BCE.

The prophecies of Isaiah 56–66 have in view the salvation speeches we know as Deutero-Isaiah, and they refer to them frequently. The grand vision of Deutero-Isaiah has not become a reality, even after the exile ends. These prophecies renew and extend that agenda for the exaltation of Jerusalem and God's people into the future. Standing squarely in the ancient prophetic tradition, this closing unit opens with a call for maintaining justice and righteousness (56:1). Eventually, the light of Yahweh's glory will shine upon Jerusalem, which will be repopulated and will draw all nations to it for peace (60). In the "year of Yahweh's favor," all those who mourn in Zion will be comforted, captives will be liberated, and the oppressed will be delivered, and together they will rebuild the "ancient ruins," perhaps a reference to the temple (60:1–4). The new and resplendent Jerusalem is really only part of the "new heavens and a new earth" in which former things will be forgotten (65:17) and which picks up and continues the concerns of Deutero-Isaiah (42:9,10; 43:19, and 48:6).

RELIGIOUS CONTRIBUTIONS OF THE PROPHETS OF THE CRISIS

The eighth-century prophets focused on (1) the exclusive worship of Yahweh alone in covenant faithfulness, or monolatry, and (2) the international extent of Yahweh's authority as God of all nations rather than of Israel alone, or universalism (Chapter 19). These two themes in Israel's first writing prophets – Amos, Hosea, Micah, and Isaiah of Jerusalem – contributed to the emerging monotheistic principle in ancient Israel. The ideas of monolatry and universalism are certainly present in the speeches of the prophets leading up to the crisis of 586 BCE. But the changing world in which the prophets lived and preached, together with the traumatic events they witnessed, result in important innovations in their theology.

The old concept of Yahweh/El, God of the ancestors in Genesis, had eventually become Yahweh, God of all Israel in the monarchy. The eighth-century prophets began to see that Yahweh was also the God of the whole earth. Ruling from his throne in the Jerusalem temple, Yahweh reigns over all nations. Now Jeremiah and Ezekiel take this universalism in a new direction. Yahweh may abandon the temple in Jerusalem because of the iniquity of his people, but his sovereign power will not be diminished (Jeremiah 7; Ezekiel 1). Yahweh's

power is not limited to a specific location at Mount Zion, nor to his chosen people, Israel. Yahweh is free and sovereign to rule the cosmos regardless of the events occurring in Judah.

Explicit statements of monotheism are still rare in the preexilic prophets. But at times, they use rhetoric that reflects an emerging monotheism.[11]

> (19) *O Yahweh, my strength and my stronghold,*
>   *my refuge in the day of trouble,*
>   *to you shall the nations come*
>   *from the ends of the earth and say:*
>   *Our ancestors have inherited nothing but lies,*
>   *worthless things in which there is no profit.*
> (20) *Can mortals make for themselves gods?*
>   *Such are no gods! (Jeremiah 16:19–20)*

In this prayer, the prophet himself (apparently) asserts that the nations of the earth will someday acknowledge their worship of other gods as a lie. Humans cannot make for themselves gods; such creations are no gods at all!

With Isaiah of the exile, we come to the most explicit and undeniable statements of monotheism of the OT (i.e., Isaiah 40–55). The universalism of God begins to merge in Deutero-Isaiah with Yahweh's role as Creator.

> (18) *For thus says Yahweh,*
>   *who created the heavens*
>   *(he is God!),*
>   *who formed the earth and made it*

---

11 For more on "monotheistic rhetoric" in the late monarchy, and on explicit monotheistic theology of the exile, which we will discuss later, see pages 149–94 in Smith in "Where to Find More" in Chapter 1.

(he established it;

he did not create it a chaos,

he formed it to be inhabited!):

I am Yahweh, and there is no other. (Isaiah 45:18; compare 44:6,8)

In Deutero-Isaiah's prophecies of salvation, these themes of universalism, creation, and monotheism are intertwined.

(5) I am Yahweh, and there is no other;

besides me there is no god.

I arm you, though you do not know me,

(6) so that they may know, from the rising of the sun

and from the west, that there is no one besides me;

I am Yahweh, and there is no other.

(7) I form light and create darkness,

I make weal and create woe; I Yahweh do all these

things. (Isaiah 45:5–7)

And if Yahweh is the sovereign, Creator God of the universe, he is also the only hope for salvation.

(21) Declare and present your case;

let them take counsel together!

Who told this long ago?

Who declared it of old?

Was it not I, Yahweh?

There is no other god besides me,

a righteous God and a Savior;

there is no one besides me.

(22) Turn to me and be saved,

all the ends of the earth!

For I am God, and there is no other. (Isaiah

45:21–22; compare 43:11)

Here in Isaiah of the exile, Yahweh is exalted as the only God of the universe, just as Judah is politically

reduced to desolation. This is a remarkable contribution of the OT to the history of religious expression.

Some readers deny this is monotheism. Instead, it is argued, we have too wide a gap between our Enlightenment-era definitions of monotheism, or the "belief that there is only one God" (review Sidebar 1.3), and ancient Israel's conceptions of the oneness or singularity of Yahweh. Some have even questioned whether we can fully understand what the ancients meant by "god" from our contemporary context. Is it possible that Israel's understanding of Yahweh's oneness is so far removed from our modern theological and philosophical conceptions that we are comparing apples to oranges? Perhaps it would be better to admit that the OT's assertions about Yahweh's character, including Deutero-Isaiah's denial of the existence of other gods, are not the same thing as our concept of monotheism. The OT's rhetorical expressions denying the existence of other deities need careful nuancing and have different connotations in antiquity than we may imagine.[12] Anything more is to impose on the text of the OT our own preconceived theological notions, and to make the OT say more than it really does.

On the other hand, such an approach may put too fine a point on the whole discussion. For the purposes of this textbook, we have explained that monotheism has many nuances and that the OT seldom uses explicit statements that we would take as strict philosophical monotheism (Chapter 1). Yet OT passages specifically denying the reality of other gods should be accepted as a mark of

12 For such a recent approach to Isaiah, see MacDonald in "Where to Find More" in this chapter.

monotheism. Think of this as two sides of the same coin, with "heads" representing positive assertions about the unique qualities and characteristics of Israel's God, Yahweh, and "tails" representing the explicit denial that other gods exist at all. A flip of the OT coin almost always lands on "heads," but the coin is still real. The passages we have studied in Deutero-Isaiah (as well as in Deuteronomy and a few in the Psalms) are best understood as Israel's monotheizing texts.

WHERE TO FIND MORE

Commentaries: The best technical and advanced commentaries on the prophets covered here are: **Jeremiah** – William L. Holladay, *Jeremiah: A Commentary on the Book of the Prophet Jeremiah* (Hermeneia; 2 vols.; Philadelphia: Fortress Press, 1986 and 1989); **Nahum, Habakkuk, Zephaniah** – J. J. M. Roberts, *Nahum, Habakkuk, and Zephaniah: A Commentary* (Old Testament Library; Louisville, Ky.: Westminster John Knox Press, 1991); **Ezekiel** – Daniel I. Block, *The Book of Ezekiel* (New International Commentary on the Old Testament; 2 vols.; Grand Rapids, Mich.: Eerdmans, 1997 and 1998); and **Isaiah** – John N. Oswalt, *The Book of Isaiah, Chapters 40–66* (New International Commentary: Old Testament; Grand Rapids, Mich.: Eerdmans, 1998).

MacDonald, Nathan. "Monotheism and Isaiah." Pages 43–61 in *Interpreting Isaiah: Issues and Approaches*. Edited by David G. Firth and H. G. M. Williamson. Nottingham, Eng./Downers Grove, Ill.: Apollos/IVP Academic, 2009.

Roberts, J. J. M. "Solomon's Jerusalem and the Zion Tradition." Pages 163–70 in *Jerusalem in Bible and Archaeology: The First Temple Period*. Edited by Andrew G. Vaughn and Ann E. Killebrew. SBLSymS 18. Leiden: Brill, 2003.

For details on the "Zion tradition."

Williamson, H. G. M. *The Book Called Isaiah: Deutero-Isaiah's Role in Composition and Redaction*. Oxford: Clarendon Press/Oxford University Press, 1994.

For the best articulation of the theory that Isaiah 40–55 never stood as an independent work but was from the start intended as a continuation of Isaiah of Jerusalem.

CHAPTER 21

Israel's Prophets: The Restoration

OLD TESTAMENT READING: HAGGAI, ZECHARIAH, MALACHI, JOEL, AND JONAH

This final chapter on Israel's writing prophets highlights those whose messages supported postexilic restoration during the Persian period. As in earlier chapters, we will need to consider the conditionality of prophecy as well as its "forthtelling" rather than "foretelling" nature.

In 539 BCE, the Persian king Cyrus allowed the first group of Israelite exiles to return to Jerusalem, now part of the administrative province of Yehud. The prophets Haggai and Zechariah serve to inspire this rebuilding process, particularly of the temple. We will observe in Zechariah growing evidence of a messianic hope in a future Davidic king as well as a literary shift from eschatology to apocalyptic forms. Malachi, dated around 470 BCE, builds on earlier OT prophetic themes of purity and covenant faithfulness. Much harder to date is Joel, as it contains sections indicative of two entirely different periods of Judah's history; however, we will note the "day of Yahweh" theme in Joel, portrayed this time as a terrible day of reckoning for the nations. Jonah is unique as a narrative, conveying through rather humorous form the serious concern of Yahweh for all peoples.

After the exile ended in 539 BCE, Judah and Jerusalem were restored as a Persian administrative district known as Yehud. The last group of writing prophets comes from this period. We have gaps in our knowledge of this period of Israel's history, which sometimes makes it difficult to read these books of prophecy. Yet some of the most important concepts of the OT emerged during this time and are preserved in these books of prophecy from the Persian period.

Events surrounding the return of the Judeans from exile and the restoration of Jerusalem are important to remember when reading the books of prophecy presented in this chapter. Here are a few of the most important dates to keep in mind. Details and specific dates come from biblical references and from precise ancient Persian sources, as well as from references in the Greek historians.

539 BCE – Persian forces defeat the Babylonian army on October 10 north of the city, and advance on the city of Babylon. It falls with little resistance, and Cyrus the Persian enters triumphantly on October 29, marking the end of the exile.

538 BCE – First return of Judeans to Jerusalem, under Sheshbazzar (Ezra 1:1–11); altar is rededicated and worship restored on the Temple Mount (Ezra 3:1–6).

520 BCE – Work on the temple resumes, inspired by the prophesies of Haggai and Zechariah and authorized by King Darius of Persia.

515 BCE – Completion of work on the Second Temple in Jerusalem.

460–454 BCE –Egypt, supported by the Greeks, revolts against Persia.

458 BCE – Ezra arrives in Jerusalem.

445 BCE – Nehemiah arrives in Jerusalem.

THE RESTORATION OF JERUSALEM AND JUDAH (YEHUD) IN THE PERSIAN PERIOD

The following sketch of the postexilic period will be helpful as you read these last books of prophecy (see the overview of this period in Chapter 15, especially Sidebar 15.4 on the kings of ancient Persia). We have mentioned previously the turning point represented by Cyrus's conquest of Babylonia in October 539 BCE, including the fall of the city of Babylon itself. The official decree of King Cyrus releasing Jewish exiles and allowing them to return to Jerusalem most likely occurred in 538 BCE (Ezra 1:1–11). This event is paralleled in the Cyrus Cylinder, a native Persian source highlighting Cyrus's actions in restoring and rebuilding Babylon (Sidebar 11.4), much as his decree in the Ezra text indicates his intention to rebuild Jerusalem. Leadership at this time was provided by a certain Sheshbazzar, the first in a series of governors of the Persian (sub)

province of Yehud (Ezra 1:8 and 5:14). Because we have so little further information about this first return, Sheshbazzar simply disappears from the record and we don't know more about him.

This first group of returnees under Sheshbazzar was likely a small number and not responsible for any significant rebuilding of the city.[1] We know very few details, but we assume that only a tiny portion of Babylonian Jews returned to Jerusalem at this time. The first-century Jewish historian Josephus states that most were "unwilling to leave their possessions" (*Antiquities* 11.1.3, para. 8). Those who did return and establish a meager community lacked resources to fulfill the dream of rebuilding the temple, although they may have made preparations for its reconstruction and may have rededicated the altar in order to

[1] This is so despite the assertion in Ezra 5:16 that they began laying the foundations of the new temple. The foundation was completed a year or two later (Ezra 3:7–13), but the work was halted by outside interference (Ezra 4:4–5).

21.1. Darius I, also known as Darius the Great (522–486 BCE). Relief from the treasury of the palace in Persepolis, approximately 491–486 BCE, showing King Darius giving audience.(Photo: SEF / Art Resource, N.Y.)

restore the worship of Yahweh at the site (Ezra 3:1–6). All attempts to rebuild the temple during the reigns of the Persian kings Cyrus and Cambyses failed.

Their successor, King Darius I (522–486 BCE), restructured the empire, instituting administrative reforms, which may have contributed to the conviction that the time was right to begin rebuilding the temple in Jerusalem. The enterprise was reauthorized by Darius in 520 BCE (Ezra 4:24), supported by the governorship of Zerubbabel and the high priesthood of Joshua, and inspired by the prophecies of Haggai and Zechariah. Zerubbabel was the grandson of Jehoiachin, the captive king (Ezra 3:2; Nehemiah 12:1; 1 Chronicles 3:19), and as a descendant of the line of David, his presence in the early restoration community was a cause for great hope that the Davidic monarchy would be restored (Haggai 2:23).[2] The high priest Joshua was the son of Jehozadak, the last preexilic chief priest (1 Chronicles 6:15; and see Ezra 3:2, where the

2 Zerubbabel may have been a subordinate to Sheshbazzar in the first return in 538 BCE, although the connection between the two is uncertain.

names have variant spellings Jeshua and Jozadak). These two – Zerubbabel and Joshua – were powerful figures during the reign of Darius I. Zerubbabel as governor ran secular affairs, and Joshua supervised matters of ritual. Like Sheshbazzar, both Zerubbabel and Joshua disappear from the biblical record with hardly a trace.

The new temple was completed in early 515 BCE, and it was dedicated for service with great joy by the people (Ezra 6:14–16). Nevertheless, Yehud was really only a small district of the Persian satrapy known as "Beyond the River" (Abar Nahara; Ezra 4:10–11, 5:3, and 8:36; Nehemiah 2:7), stretching from the upper Euphrates River westward across the Levant (see Map 15.2). Yehud was poorer and less populated than many other areas, the city of Jerusalem consisting only of the original city of David and the Temple Mount. A few towns north of Jerusalem, such as Gibeon and Bethel, faired somewhat better according to archaeological evidence and biblical references.

Estimates of population size based on archaeology surveys and OT references are impossible to verify, and we should use them cautiously. Nevertheless, they illustrate with modest confidence the diminished size and importance of Yehud. We suspect that Judah prior to the exile had well over 100,000 inhabitants; some would say as many as 200,000.[3] Population estimates for Yehud in the first portion

3 These are tentative estimates, of course, and for the issues surrounding these numbers and others offered here, see Ziony Zevit, "Text Traditions, Archaeology, and Anthropology: Uncertainties in Determining the Populations of Judah and Yehud from ca. 734 to ca. 400 BCE," in *"Up to the Gates of Ekron": Essays on the Archaeology and History of the Eastern Mediterranean in Honor of Seymour Gitin* (ed. Sidnie White Crawford et al.; Jerusalem: W. F. Albright Institute of Archaeological Research and Israel Exploration Society, 2007), 436–43.

of the Persian period covered here, approximately 538–450 BCE, have been suggested as low as 11,000, although probably this is much too low. Similarly, a population of around 17,000 has been suggested for Yehud in the second portion of the Persian period, approximately 450–332 BCE. Jerusalem itself is thought to have had as few as 500 residents during the first part of the Persian period, and only 1,750 in the second part, in contrast to as many as 24,000 in the seventh century BCE. While these population levels are just guesses, they illustrate the dramatic reduction of political influence in the region for Jerusalem and Judah/Yehud.

We have little information about the Jewish community in Yehud from the time the temple was rebuilt until the coming of Ezra and Nehemiah (ca. 515–458 BCE). The books of Ezra and Nehemiah indicate that there was conflict between the returned exiles, who thought of themselves as true Israelites, and the indigenous populations, including especially the nonexiled Judeans, and the Samarians in the north. The returned exiles were comparatively well-to-do (Ezra 2:68–69; Zechariah 6:9–11). They believed that Yahweh's presence left Jerusalem during the exile and took up residence instead with them in Babylonia. The collection of materials in Ezra 4–6 leading up to the construction of the temple reflects this conflict between the returned exiles and the indigenous Jewish groups.

As we have seen, Zerubbabel simply disappears from the record, and no governor of Yehud is mentioned again until Nehemiah. In general, we are probably right in assuming that Persia was simply not interested in the tiny, backwater province, Yehud, and so neither the Bible nor Persian sources

mentioned its governors by name. King Darius was preoccupied for most of his rule with various wars with the Greeks. His successors Xerxes I (486–465) and Artaxerxes I (465–424) were forced to deal with rebellions in Babylon and Egypt. In fact, it was an Egyptian revolt of 460 BCE, supported by the Greeks, that eventually became a turning point in Persian policies regarding Yehud. Under Cyrus's son Cambyses (530–522 BCE), the Persians had achieved their goal of conquering Egypt in 525 BCE. But with the resurgence of both Egypt and Greece, the Persians now needed a secure ally in the Levant, and a rejuvenated, stronger Jerusalem would serve that purpose. The missions of Ezra and Nehemiah may be seen as part of a new policy for controlling the region.

The last portion of the Persian period (ca. 450–332 BCE) was an important moment in Jewish self-identification. Ezra arrived in Jerusalem in 458 BCE (Ezra 7:7–8).[4] His religious reforms took written form in much of what we have in the OT today. According to later Jewish tradition, Ezra's work in establishing the Torah was more important than rebuilding the temple (b. Megilla 16b).[5] Nehemiah was appointed governor of Yehud and arrived in Jerusalem in 445 BCE. He rebuilt the city's walls, built a governor's residence, put administrative systems in place, and worked to increase the city's population. The complementary works of Ezra and Nehemiah created in Yehud a resilient community of faith, capable of withstanding the seismic political and cultural changes about to occur in the ancient Near East.

4 For the likelihood of 458 BCE as the date of his return, see Chapter 15.
5 Ezra was also credited with creating Judaism (m. Abot 1.1).

21.2. Yehud coin. Small silver coins, the first-known Jewish coins, were minted near Jerusalem in the late Persian period some-time around 350 BCE. This one has a bird, perhaps a falcon or hawk, with the word "Yehud" written in archaic paleo-Hebrew script ("YHD"). The reverse side of the coin has a simple lily or fleur-de-lis pattern, symbol of purity and beauty in ancient Israel. (Photo: Z. Radovan / Bible Land Pictures)

The Books of Haggai, Zechariah, Malachi, Joel, and Jonah

The first three books covered in this section make up something of a subcategory of OT writing prophets: Haggai, Zechariah, and Malachi. These three prophets (or perhaps four, as we will see), and their respective collections of writings, come from the postexilic community in and around Jerusalem. They use language and images similar to the prophets who came before them, and they considered themselves squarely within the prophetic tradition. The "word of Yahweh" came to all three (Haggai 1:1; Zechariah 1:1; Malachi 1:1), and both Haggai and Zechariah are called prophets.

The Book of Haggai

Haggai, whose name probably means "born on the feast day" or "festival child," is an obscure figure. While we know almost nothing about him personally, this is compensated somewhat by the precise dates of his speeches. He delivered his messages

from Yahweh between August 29 and December 18, 520 BCE, early in the reign of Darius I of Persia (Haggai 1:1; 2:1,10,20).

Haggai's messages were solely focused on the reconstruction of the temple in Jerusalem. Four separate speeches embedded in the book attempt to motivate the people, and especially the leadership of Yehud (Zerubbabel and Joshua), so as to reinvigorate the rebuilding project. The work was at a standstill because of economic conditions and discouragement. Yet Haggai (1:4) objects: "Is it time for you yourselves to live in your paneled houses, while this house lies in ruins?" It was a matter of priorities. The prophet alleges that the people have prospered sufficiently and that it is time to give attention to the proper maintenance of worship in the restoration community. He makes his case by turning around the economic argument. Hardships among the restoration community have been caused by their lackadaisical approach to Yahweh's house (Haggai 1:9–11), and Yahweh's blessings will come to Yehud *after* the reconstruction of the temple (2:6–9 and 2:15–19). In a twist on today's movie quote, "if you build it, Yahweh will come."

The prophet Haggai has great hopes that Zerubbabel, a direct descendant of King David, will fulfill the messianic expectations of the old monarchic ideal. Relying on the image of the ideal king from before the exile, the "signet ring" (Jeremiah 22:24), Haggai considers Zerubbabel God's servant and chosen one (Haggai 2:23). Sadly, as we know, the great expectations of Haggai did not come to fruition with the completion of the temple in 515 BCE. There was not superabundance from heaven, nor did the nations of the earth submit to a revived monarchic Judah (2:21–22). Zerubbabel did not become the hoped for messianic ruler. It seems likely, therefore, that the preaching of Haggai was collected in something like its present arrangement prior to the completion of the temple in 515 BCE.

The Book of Zechariah

Of the speeches collected in the book of Zechariah, the visions and prophecies of chapters 1–8 are from the same time as the speeches of Haggai. And like Haggai's, they focus on the reconstruction of the temple in Jerusalem. By contrast, the speeches in Zechariah 9–14 are undated oracles containing no mention of the rebuilding of the temple, nor of Zerubbabel and Joshua. These and many other differences have resulted in a conventional distinction between Zechariah 1–8 as "proto-Zechariah," and Zechariah 9–14, often referred to as Deutero-Zechariah or Second Zechariah. The distinction is a helpful one, even if we are unable to trace specifics of the book's composition history.

On the other hand, the constituent parts of the book of Zechariah share certain ideas and have distinctive literary connections. The book stands as a prophetic composite, at the heart of which are a series of original night visions offering comfort and hope to the restoration community (1:7–6:15). This nucleus is expanded by an introduction (1:1–6) and a call for deeper and more sincere repentence (7:1–8:23). Because chapters 7 and 8 were added two years into the building program (518 BCE, according to 7:1), the implication is that they offer slight corrective to the night visions. The unconditional salvation of the visions in chapters 1–6 are nuanced in chapters 7–8 by the assertion that continuance in Yahweh's blessings is dependent on obedience to Yahweh's will and on taking care of the needy (7:9–10). Finally, the book is topped off with speeches in which the optimism of the night visions is gone, salvation is defined differently, and hope for fulfillment is pushed into a distant eschatological era.

The prophet named Zechariah, "Yahweh remembers," was a contemporary of Haggai. Based on the dates given for some of Zechariah's visions, their ministries overlapped. Zechariah's prophecies began no later than autumn 520 BCE (Zechariah 1:1) and extended at least until December 518 BCE (Zechariah 7:1). The eight night visions may have occurred in a single night, on February 15, 519 BCE (Zechariah 1:7). By means of the visions, Yahweh declares his intention to restore what has been lost. City, temple, and king will be restored in line with the older Zion theology of preexilic times (see Sidebar 20.2).

Yet Zechariah is more reserved than Haggai about the role of the Davidic king, represented by the governor Zerubbabel (Zechariah 3:8, 4:6–10, and 6:12–13). He envisions a joint messiahship of prince and priest, a sort of diarchy, in which the two will rule a fully restored, peaceful, and reunified Israel. Even here, the real power resides with the priest. After all, the new temple has no adjacent royal palace, as in preexilic days. The loss of Israel's kingship and even the gradual decline of the power of the Persian governors reflect the diminishing role of the prophets and the growing power of the high priesthood. Unlike his older contemporary, Haggai, the prophet Zechariah puts his hopes for the fulfillment of the Zion messianism on a future Davidic king together with the high priest, rather than on Zerubbabel.

Announcements of new oracles introduced with "the word of Yahweh" at Zechariah 9:1 and 12:1 give the distinct impression of something different happening in these last portions of the book compared to Zechariah 1–8. The literary forms are distinct, but so, too, are the theological themes. For example, chapters 9–14 envision messianic salvation through a triumphant future king (9:9–10), whereas no mention is made of a high priest nor a joint rulership of priest and king, such as the diarchy so central to the preaching of the first portion of the book. These last six chapters of the book of Zechariah rely on trusted prophetic traditions of old Israel – Zion theology, the coming messiah, the divine warrior motif, and so forth – to announce the coming of a new era of salvation in Jerusalem's future. The move from eschatology to apocalyptic is one we will return to in Chapter 22.

The Book of Malachi

Little is known about the prophet named "Malachi" ("my messenger"). In fact, the Greek Septuagint translation takes "Malachi" in the superscription as "his messenger" instead of as a personal name. Some have suggested we take these few prophecies as anonymous, assuming that the title Malachi is derived from the statement in Malachi 3:1: "See, I am sending *my messenger* to prepare the way before me." But this argument cuts both ways, since the speeches could just as easily be playing on the prophet's name, in the same way personal names have been used in other OT prophecies (Hosea 1:3–8; Isaiah 7:14 and 8:3–4). While we cannot know much about the individual behind these prophecies, the book's position as last among the writing prophets, together with hints in some of the content of these prophecies, suggests a date in the early fifth century, probably around 470 BCE.

Building on themes of earlier OT prophecies, the book of Malachi puts the love of Yahweh for his people at the foundation of everything else (1:2–5). These speeches are also interested in liturgical purity and covenant faithfulness. We have here an announcement that the day of Yahweh is about to dawn, marked by the appearance of God's messenger to prepare the way (3:1–2 and 4:1).[6] In Malachi, the judgment day distinguishes between the righteous and wicked, with Yahweh providing righteous sunlight to shine for his people, who will inflict judgment upon his enemies (3:16–4:3). The final verses of the book (4:4–6) may have been added to tie together the writing prophets, or even to tie together all the historical books with the prophets, as the former and latter prophets of the Jewish canon (Figure 2.3). In any case, the connection between Moses and Elijah, as one who gave the Torah to Israel and another who applied the Torah to his generation, makes for a fitting closure.

6 On the "day of Yahweh," review Chapter 20.

For the Christian canon too, this connection suitably concludes the entire OT (and prepares for the appearance of Moses and Elijah on the Mount of Transfiguration; Mark 9:2–8).

The Book of Joel

I have reserved the book of Joel for this chapter because of its blended character. Like so many other prophets in the collection we call "minor prophets," we know practically nothing about the man Joel ("Yahweh is God"). The book bearing his name has two portions from very different periods of Judah's history. The first is a prophetic speech from before the exile (1:1–2:27), while the second portion of the book draws lessons from the earlier speech but comes from a much later period, probably around 400 BCE (2:28–3:21). This second portion especially draws on the prophecies of Ezekiel and Malachi, presupposes the Babylonian exile, and stands between classical prophecy and apocalyptic literature (see Chapter 22).[7]

The opening speech uses a specific historical event from Judah's history: a catastrophic locust plague that also resulted in years of drought and economic ruin (2:25). We don't know from other references when this event took place, but the temple was still standing in Jerusalem (1:13). The prophet takes the occasion as a mark of the "day of Yahweh," which initiates the utter destruction of the people of God in Jerusalem and Judah (1:15 and 2:1–2,11). In a text that sums up the prophetic message of repentance, the prophet calls for an organized fast in which the nation laments its sins and returns to Yahweh (2:12–14). Yahweh responds to their corporate repentance by restoring what was lost in the plague (2:18–27).

The second part of the book of Joel develops the ideas and themes of the first part for a new situation. The prophetic speeches in Joel 2:28–3:21 envision a future in which God's spirit empowers all the people with gifts of prophecy. The day of Yahweh is changed from a day of judgment against Judah and Jerusalem to a terrible day of reckoning for the nations. Mount Zion and Jerusalem become a means of escape, the only source of salvation for humanity (2:31–32). Just as the plague in Judah's earlier history became a time for repentance and trust, so, too, can the discouraged and impoverished postexilic community take heart in the promises of future abundance and salvation.

The Book of Jonah

As with the book of Joel, I have reserved the book of Jonah for this chapter, this time because of the book's uniqueness. Jonah is unlike other books of prophecy collected in the OT because it is not a collection of prophetic speeches at all. Instead, we have here a narrative *about* the prophet, whose name was Jonah ("dove"). A prophet by this name is mentioned in 2 Kings 14:25. However, the book of Jonah's superscription (also like Joel) contains no references to particular kings of Israel or Judah, and therefore no dates for these narratives. Numerous features of the book of Jonah indicate a much later date, probably the fifth or fourth century BCE.

You are probably familiar with the story of the book of Jonah, or at least with the central event: the protagonist was swallowed by a whale. In reality, the text says only that Yahweh assigned a "large

---

7 For the view that the book of Joel is a literary unity with late apocalyptic origins, and not just 2:28–3:21, see Wolff's commentary in "Where to Find More" in this chapter.

fish" especially for the task (1:17). It seems likely that the entire book, but especially the first chapter, would have been uproariously funny for its first readers. The very idea of a prophet of Yahweh objecting to the message he receives and running in the opposite direction, "to Tarshish," would surely have been met with laughter.[8] What a silly prophet! At least we can assume that this book would have been especially enjoyable to read for a number of reasons. It uses comedy to make what is otherwise a serious point: God is passionate about human lives, even those of Israel's enemies, and this takes priority over everything else.

The book is divided into two portions by the repetition of the simple command to go immediately to Nineveh and do what prophets do: to announce a message of judgment in the hopes of arousing repentance (Jonah 1:2 and 3:2). Jonah doesn't like the Ninevites very much, and the juvenile prophet runs away in a pathetic attempt to avoid "the presence of Yahweh" (1:3). But Jonah discovers that Yahweh's presence follows him to the Mediterranean Sea. A great storm threatens to destroy his ship on its way to Tarshish, and the Phoenician sailors prove to be more devout than the Israelite prophet. The irony continues when Jonah identifies himself to the sailors as a Hebrew, who worships "Yahweh, the God of heaven and earth, who made the sea and the dry land" (1:9). He calmly tells them what they must do to save themselves and the ship: toss him overboard (1:12). They reluctantly agree to do so, and immediately became

devout worshippers of Yahweh themselves, offering sacrifices and vows (Jonah 1:16).

The many delicious ironies of this scene continue when Jonah surprisingly survives being consumed by the "large fish." He prays to Yahweh from the belly of the fish, composing an eloquent psalm about the values of worship at Yahweh's "holy temple" (Jonah 2:4,7) and concluding that "deliverance belongs to Yahweh" (2:9). Having observed what looks like Jonah's change of heart, Yahweh commands the fish to spit the prophet out upon dry land.

But has Jonah really learned his lesson? When Yahweh commands him a second time to announce judgment against Nineveh, Jonah appears at first to obey without hesitation (Jonah 3:2–3). To his surprise, his preaching works! Nineveh's king and his nobles lead the people of the city in genuine repentance, and Yahweh decides to spare them. Jonah's displeasure, even anger, at Yahweh's gracious forgiveness frames the unexpected concluding chapter of the book. Jonah's actions may be described as shockingly immature or as selfish. But the point of the narrative is the inexplicable character of Yahweh, who is free to forgive and restore whomever he wants.

Jonah may have been motivated by a nationalistic hatred for the Assyrians of Nineveh, or by personal embarrassment that his prophecies were not fulfilled. In any case, all such considerations are secondary and trivial compared to the truth of Yahweh's love and mercy. Through the farcical prophet Jonah, the book teaches that Yahweh's loving grace cannot be limited to Israel alone. God would always rather show mercy than execute judgment, even if he has already announced judgment

---

8 Tarshish was in the extreme west of the ancient Near East, whereas Jonah had been commanded to go east to Nineveh.

by his prophets. And in this sense, the book is a corrective to simplistic approaches to prophecy. It teaches that the call to prophetic ministry cannot be avoided, but divine judgment can.

We have said that Jonah is not a book of prophecy like others. But this raises a question we have trouble answering: Exactly what kind of literature is this book? Is it a parable? A satire? A midrash?[9] Biography? Novel? The fact is, the book of Jonah doesn't fit any of these literary categories perfectly. We have in this story a kind of object lesson, written to be enjoyed because of its humorous and subtle ironies. But also written to make an important point.

That point is supported by numerous allusions and even quotations from earlier OT passages. The most obvious example is Jonah's complaint about Yahweh's forgiving character.

You are a gracious God and merciful, slow to anger, and abounding in steadfast love, and ready to relent from punishing. (Jonah 4:2)

Jonah is appealing to Israel's orthodox understanding of Yahweh, as defined in Exodus 34:6–7, which gives the fullest explanation for the name "Yahweh." The irony, of course, is that Jonah is unhappy about all this. He would prefer a God who wipes out Israel's enemies regardless of whether they respond to the prophetic message of repentance. Jonah's concerns and passions are not in line with Yahweh's.

Even the king of Nineveh knows that Yahweh may turn aside from imminent punishment if the Ninevites would only "turn from their evil ways"

9 Midrash is a type of Jewish interpretation or commentary on the Scriptures, usually the Torah.

(3:8). Ironically, the Assyrian king appears to be well aware of Jeremiah's theology, even if the prophet Jonah is not (Jeremiah 18:7–8,11 and 26:3,13,19). And Jonah's act of running away and his request to die (4:8) reminds one of Elijah's flight from Jezebel (1 Kings 19:4). Similarly, the psalm of thanksgiving in Jonah 2 has many connections with the book of Psalms (e.g., Psalms 31:7,23; 42:8). These reminders of earlier OT passages contribute to the irony: both the Phoenican sailors and the Assyrian king understand Yahweh better than the prophet Jonah does. They also understand Israel's theology better. The prophet may be using the right words, "I am a Hebrew" and "I worship Yahweh," but his actions and attitudes indicate that he doesn't understand at all.

And so the book offers powerful lessons about Yahweh and the way Yahweh relates to his prophet and to his prophetic word. It also emphasizes Yahweh's care and compassion for all peoples of the earth, and his ability to extend mercy and forgiveness to whomever he chooses. As messenger of God's word, the prophet must constantly guard against personal attitudes and actions that take ownership of that word to seek vengeance or vindication. This is part of what it means for a prophet to be a "servant" of Yahweh, a lesson that Jonah had forgotten (Jeremiah 7:25; and frequently in Jeremiah; Amos 3:7; Zechariah 1:6).

Use and/or Abuse of the Old Testament Prophets

Just as the prophet Jonah misunderstood Yahweh's word, so, too, do many readers misappropriate the OT prophets today. We cannot cover in this textbook all the cautions necessary for you as a reader of the OT prophets. Yet it may be helpful to keep the following warnings in mind.

This chapter is the last of three devoted to the OT books of prophecy. Take a moment to reflect now on the opening comments at the beginning of Chapter 19. We noted that these prophets were spokespersons for Yahweh, whose message occasionally related to the future but not always so. An easy way to remember this is to picture the OT prophets as *"forth*tellers" of Yahweh's message rather than as *"fore*tellers" of the future. In some of their speeches, these prophets envisioned the future, even at times the distant future. But they did not do this as often as you might think, and not nearly as much as did those Israelite authors who gave us apocalyptic literature (covered in the next chapter). The future in view for these OT prophets is now past. In other words, they predicted events that were in Israel's future but not in our own. To see how their prophecies were fulfilled, we look back to history and to how events played out in the life of ancient Israel.

This leads to another warning about the way to read the OT prophets. Some readers assume that every predictive prophecy contained in these books relating to Israel's immediate future must find some particular fulfillment in time and space. In other words, some make the mistake of assuming that if a certain prophecy or prediction in the OT hasn't occurred in Israel's past, it must be pushed into a future still ahead of us today. But that misses a central truth about these OT prophetic speeches. Their predictions about Israel's immediate future were conditional. If a prophet warns Israel that punishment is coming but Israel repents and returns to Yahweh, the prophecy of punishment is no longer applicable. The story of Jonah illustrates

the point. Nineveh genuinely repents, and Yahweh forgives even those dreaded Assyrians! Similarly, promises of blessing are conditioned on maintaining the relationship with Yahweh. OT prophecy directs behavior; it does not necessarily require literal, physical fulfillment (see Jeremiah 18:1–11).

This leads finally to the warning that these OT books of prophecy require greater care in interpretation than we often give them. They cannot be read casually as though they were written first for us today. Of course, *all* ancient books (modern ones too) require interpretation, which is an entire discipline of reading with the purpose of moving from the ancient text to a contemporary significance (a discipline known as **hermeneutics**, which establishes theories and methods for interpretation). These books of prophecy carry profound messages of personal and social responsibility. Most readers through the centuries have understood the importance of those messages. Unfortunately, readers have also at times layered the prophetic message with additional, extraneous interpretations related to "end times," or eschatological meanings. Nearly every generation has its examples of well-meaning readers who use these materials to set dates for the end of the world or to predict some cataclysmic world event that they claim is foretold in the OT prophets (including the apocalyptic materials covered in the next chapter). Such readings fail to grasp the fundamental nature of OT books of prophecy.

Religious Contributions of the Prophets of the Restoration

The prophets of the postexilic period assumed and built on the central themes of their predecessors: (a) the exclusive monolatrous worship of Yahweh alone in covenant faithfulness, and (b) the international extent of Yahweh's authority as God of all nations (Chapters 19 and 20). These two themes – monolatry and universalism – contributed to the emerging monotheistic principle in ancient Israel, as illustrated by these postexilic prophets as well. The OT prophets of the Persian period focused almost exclusively on positive oracles of salvation and hope for their times. The needs of the dejected faith community in Yehud were obviously quite different from those of preexilic Judah or those of the Babylonian exile.

One particularly interesting text in these prophets is found near the conclusion of the book of Zechariah.

And Yahweh will become king over all the earth; on that day Yahweh will be one and his name one. (Zechariah 14:9)

The assertion that Yahweh will become king of the entire world is not necessarily surprising. We have seen this idea of the universal scope of Yahweh's sovereign kingship (even while Judah's own kingship, the line of David, has ceased to rule in Jerusalem) as important in a number of psalms (Psalms 93, 96, 97, and 99), as well as occasionally in the prophetic literature (e.g., Jeremiah 3:17). This continues the earlier prophetic concept of the international reach of Yahweh's rulership. In Zechariah, the "day of Yahweh" is the time when his kingship becomes unambiguously universal.

Another theme in this verse sounds vaguely familiar: "Yahweh will be one and his name one." Here the concept of "oneness" returns in a way reminiscent of the Shema in Deuteronomy 6:4 (Sidebar 9.1). This term itself cannot support the weight of monotheism per se, especially as it is used in the Shema. Yet its use in Zechariah 14:9 seems to build on and assume the Shema, and implies "the only one."[10] The emphasis here is the future realization of the exclusive and singular reign of Yahweh over all the earth; Yahweh is the only deity who will rule. The difference is that the Shema proposes the simple fact ("Yahweh is one"), whereas Zechariah envisions a future in which Yahweh *will be one.* If this is a more explicit statement of monotheism, it envisions a time in the future when Yahweh will rule as king of the universe with no rivals.

These books of prophecy offer a few other texts pertinent to our survey of monotheism in the OT. Malachi 2:10 also uses the term "one" in the expression, "Has not one God created us?" In the surrounding context, this may refer simply to the creation of Judah as a singular people (see especially 2:11). However, a statement in Joel is without doubt an assertion of monotheism, and uses the same terminology we have seen in Isaiah of the exile (as in Isaiah 45:5; Chapter 20).

You shall know that I am in the midst of Israel, and that I, Yahweh, am your God and there is no other. And my people shall never again be put to shame. (Joel 2:27)

As with Isaiah of the exile, Joel merges the saving role of Yahweh with Yahweh's character as the only deity of the universe. And so here again, we admit that the OT prophets have arrived at the concept that transformed world thought – that of the sole existence of their deity, Yahweh.

10 See pages 153–54 of Smith in "Where to Find More" in Chapter 1.

WHERE TO FIND MORE

Commentaries: The best technical and advanced commentaries on the prophets covered here are: **Joel** – Hans Walter Wolff, *Joel and Amos: A Commentary on the Books of the Prophets Joel and Amos* (Hermeneia; Philadelphia: Fortress Press, 1977); **Haggai and Zechariah** – Carol L. Meyers and Eric M. Meyers, *Haggai, Zechariah 1–8* and *Zechariah 9–14* (Anchor Bible 25B and 25C; New York: Doubleday, 1987 and 1993); **Malachi** – Andrew E. Hill, *Malachi: A New Translation with Introduction and Commentary* (Anchor Bible 25D; New York: Doubleday, 1998); *and Malachi* (Old Testament Library; Louisville, Ky.: Westminster John Knox Press, 1984 and 1995); **Jonah** – Jack M. Sasson, *Jonah: A New Translation with Introduction, Commentary, and Interpretation* (Anchor Bible 24B; New York: Doubleday, 1990); David L. Petersen, *Haggai and Zechariah 1–8* and *Zechariah 9–14*.

Leith, Mary Joan Winn. "Israel among the Nations: The Persian Period." Pages 276–316 in *The Oxford History of the Biblical World*. Edited by Michael David Coogan. New York: Oxford University Press, 1998.

Pages 282–302 present a helpful summary of the historical issues covered in this chapter, with particular attention given to the biblical references.

Stern, Ephraim. *Archaeology of the Land of the Bible: The Assyrian, Babylonian, and Persian Periods, 732–332 BCE*. Anchor Bible Reference Library. New York: Doubleday, 2001.

For the geographical and historical background of the satrapy Abar Nahara (the Aramaic name; but also Eber Hanahar in Hebrew), see pages 366–72. For an archaeological survey of Yehud, see pages 428–43, and for a survey of the history of the period, pages 576–82. See also the chapter by Ephraim Stern in the Cambridge History of Judaism *in "Where to Find More" for Chapter 15.*

CHAPTER 22

Israel's Apocalyptic Message

OLD TESTAMENT READING: DANIEL

The OT book of Daniel will be the focus of our attention in this chapter, and thus we will consider the literary genre of apocalyptic writing. In general, there are two subcategories of apocalyptic writing: historical and otherworldly. The latter is characterized by the transcendence of space and a celestial setting.

We have many apocalyptic compositions dating from the mid-second century BCE through the second century CE. As we examine the style and characteristics of this unique form of communication, we will observe that the concept of apocalyptic writing manifests a marked distinction between the spiritual and the physical worlds. Reading such literature appropriately, we will observe its primary purpose of encouraging the reader in faithful endurance and patience, assured that God will ultimately triumph and care for his righteous followers. Although monotheism is not explicitly stated in Daniel's apocalypse, we will note that his God is the sole deity of the universe.

---

*I*n addition to the OT's fifteen books of prophecy covered in Chapters 19–21, Israel's library also includes a distinct type of literature called "apocalyptic." As we will see, this literature is not altogether different from prophecy. In fact, many readers believe that they are related, one (apocalypticism) as emerging from the other (prophecy). Nevertheless, apocalyptic literature is different enough to require a chapter devoted entirely to it. And the OT includes one book in its repertoire that contains in its chapters a fully developed **apocalypse** – the book of Daniel. This chapter will introduce the topic of ancient apocalyptic literature and will explore the OT's examples of such literature, giving special attention to the book of Daniel.

What Does "Apocalyptic" Mean?

Our word "apocalypse" comes from the Greek word *apokálypsis* (meaning "revelation"). The book of Revelation in the New Testament begins with this word as a title, "The Revelation of Jesus Christ" (Revelation 1:1). Its use there probably indicates that "apocalypse" was understood as a literary genre, even in antiquity. For this reason, the book of Revelation became the benchmark for identifying the characteristics and themes of apocalyptic literature.

But not all apocalyptic books or literature carry this title. In fact, it was only in the nineteenth century that a critical mass of books from antiquity were discovered and compared, and scholars began to realize that such a distinct literary type existed. And what exactly characterizes this genre? It is both easy and difficult to define. It seems easy to define because apocalyptic literature exhibits a convergence of several characteristics marking it as a distinctive literary genre. But it is difficult to define because it takes a variety of literary forms and the convergence of characteristics is not always obvious.

It was only in the late 1970s that scholars were able to agree on a definition of a literary type "apocalypse." The following is an adaptation of that definition, which is widely accepted today.

A type of literature that self-consciously reveals divine truth, often in a narrative framework. The revelation is explained by a celestial being or "angel" to the human recipient. Such divine revelation makes known a reality that transcends present experience, with regard to both time and space: time, because it promises salvation in the far distant future or even at the end of time; and space, because ultimate reality is located in another, supernatural world.[1]

At times, the recipient of the revelation may be carried into the other world for a heavenly journey to receive insight. At other times, angels or celestial messengers represent the supernatural world, giving explanation to the revelation. The presence of angelic interpreters is characteristic of a literary subcategory, the "historical apocalypse," for which the OT book of Daniel is our prime example.

Apocalyptic literature thus has a unique manner of communicating, usually with all or most of the following stylistic features or characteristics. *First*, this type of literature believes that divine knowledge is being communicated to human recipients. It is self-consciously revelatory. *Second*, most apocalyptic books are visionary, containing initial revelations that are highly symbolic and mysterious. These visions are impossible for the human to understand properly without divine guidance, which leads to, *third*, the presence of heavenly mediators to interpret the visions. *Fourth*, most of these writings use a literary technique known by the Latin expression **vaticinium ex eventu**, "prophecy after the fact." This is essentially hindsight prediction, in which an historical event known to the author is described in future predictive language. And *fifth*, the name of the author, if stated in the document, is often a pseudonym,

---

[1] Adapted from John J. Collins, "Introduction: Towards the Morphology of a Genre," in *Apocalypse: The Morphology of a Genre* (ed. J. J. Collins; Semeia 14; Missoula, Mont.: Scholars Press, 1979), 1–20, esp. 9.

assuming the identity of a venerated hero of the past (in Jewish apocalyptic literature, we have the names Enoch, Abraham, and Isaiah so used).

In addition to these stylistic characteristics, apocalyptic writings typically have certain conceptual features that mark them as distinctive. The apocalyptic worldview reflects a keen awareness of the distinction between the spiritual world and the material or physical world. This leads further to a fully developed angelology, in which angels or heavenly messengers (or demons) represent the spiritual world. Alternatively, the human recipient of the vision may be transported into the supernatural world on an otherworldly journey, in which they discern the truth of the revelation.

Regardless of the medium, time and space are both transcended in order to achieve the revelation. Thus we have two distinct but overlapping subcategories of apocalyptic texts. In the so-called *historical apocalypse*, time is the central focus, in which the march of human history culminates in a final period of divine sovereignty. Usually in historical apocalypses, the divine messenger or angel condescends to earth with the interpretation. By contrast, the *otherworldly journey* is an apocalyptic text in which space is transcended, and the visionary is transported to the celestial setting.

Another common conceptual feature in apocalyptic texts is the periodization of history, in which a consecutive series of earthly epochs culminates in a final eschatological (or "end-times") moment of final judgment. In most fully developed apocalypses, this final period is a time of reward for the righteous and punishment for the wicked in a life beyond death.

Our attempts to understand the style and characteristics of apocalyptic texts will help as you read the book of Daniel, as well as when you run across occasional passages in the prophets that share these features. Just be aware that the lines around apocalyptic literature are not always clearly drawn. Yet the nature of this type of material leads me to say, "You'll know it when you see it." When you read of mysterious animals arising from the sea, or of animal horns with human eyes and a mouth that speaks, or of angels that come to interpret dreams, or of a future day when the sun turns to darkness and the moon turns to blood – you'll know.

And knowing that you are reading apocalyptic literature alerts you to this fact: you can ask or expect only so much from these texts. Don't expect accurate and explicit details of a historical timeline, either of past historical events or of predicted events in the future. Just as you cannot read zoological precision into the animals of Daniel 7 and 8, so you cannot read "end-time" precision into the prophecies of Daniel's visions. The purpose of apocalyptic is to assure the reader that God will one day reverse the current injustices and sufferings of his righteous followers. The objective is encouragement for faithfulness, endurance, and patience. Reading these materials for more will result in misreading them.

Where Did Apocalyptic Literature Come From?

We have as many as seventeen ancient compositions in the category of apocalyptic literature, counting both the Jewish apocalypses of the Second Temple period and the early Christian apocalypses.[2] These range in dates from the mid-second century BCE to the second century CE. The OT has one fully developed apocalypse, found in the second half of the book of Daniel (chaps. 7–12). But the OT also has other passages and collections of prophetic speeches that share many of these apocalyptic features, especially Isaiah 24–27, Zechariah 9–14, and Joel 3–4. We might call these other collections of prophecies *early* or *proto*-apocalypses. What you call these other collections of apocalyptic-*like* prophecies depends to some degree on whether you think they are related to the apocalypse of Daniel 7–12. Did Daniel's apocalyptic visions *emerge* from OT prophecy? What about apocalyptic literature generally? Did it somehow evolve from OT prophecy? Where does this distinctive literary genre come from?

Scholars have expended a great deal of energy trying to discover the origins of apocalyptic literature. Three options present themselves. First, many have assumed that Jewish apocalypticism emerged (and with it, later Christian apocalypticism) under Persian influence, especially the dualism of Zoroastrianism. Second, Israelite apocalypticism may have been an evolutionary transformation of OT prophecy. On the one hand, the apocalyptic features of some OT prophetic texts (again, Isaiah 24–27, Zechariah 9–14, and Joel 3–4) would naturally lead us to assume a genetic relationship between later Israelite prophecy and apocalypticism. On the other hand, the fact that we have parallel examples of apocalypticism in *older* non-Israelite ancient Near Eastern texts rules out a simple, direct evolution from Israelite prophecy to later Jewish apocalyptic literature (for these older Mesopotamian examples, see Sidebar 22.1). Third, Jewish apocalypticism may have been a development of OT wisdom traditions. Daniel is certainly portrayed as a wisdom specialist (Daniel 1:17), and the book of Daniel itself has many wisdom themes.

It's best to admit that we cannot be certain about this. In reality, all three of these possibilities may have played a role, with none of them being dominant. In other words, we must leave open the possibility that early Jewish apocalypticism, including the book of Daniel, appeared on the scene as a new phenomenon. Many factors may have contributed, including Israel's wisdom traditions, prophecy, and Persian dualism, in different degrees. And there may have been other influences beyond these, and beyond our knowledge. Rather than a single line of influence evolving and resulting in the appearance of apocalypticism, we should think of numerous influences like tributaries flowing into a single new flow of thought. The book of Daniel represents that new development in ancient Israel's library.

THE BOOK OF DANIEL

The book of Daniel deserves separate treatment for at least two reasons. First, this book is the youngest of the books in Israel's library, most likely the last to be added to the collection.[3] Second, Daniel is not a book of prophecy in the same way as the fifteen writing prophets we have studied thus far.

---

2 In addition to more among texts from the Judean Desert; see pages 37–38 in Russell in "Where to Find More" in this chapter.

3 See pages 78–100 in Freedman in "Where to Find More" of Chapter 2.

The ancient world prior to the composition of Jewish and Christian apocalypses also produced texts that should be identified as apocalyptic. We have examples from Egypt and Persia, and even some from Greece.* But we have five in particular from Mesopotamia that appear to be the earliest predecessors to Jewish apocalyptic: the Marduk prophecy, the Shulgi prophecy, the Uruk prophecy, the Dynastic prophecy, and a fragmented text called simply "Text A."

These Akkadian texts date from the twelfth century BCE to the fourth or third centuries BCE. They make "predictions" of events that had already occurred, providing us today with empirical examples of the way hindsight prophecy (*vaticinium ex eventu*) worked. Each text sets out initially to establish the speaker's (or text's) credibility by predicting a series of kings who would arise and listing a few deeds of each, although these "predictions" had already in fact occurred. This is followed by a genuine prediction legitimizing a final king or institution at the end of the series.

For example, one of these texts is from the twelfth century BCE, and claims to be a revelation given to a famous king named Shulgi (ca. 2094–2047 BCE). The king himself predicts the history of Babylonia, and his prophecies are punctuated with datable historical events down to the twelfth century. These hindsight prophecies are then followed by a genuine prediction of the region's restoration, bringing events right up to the author's time.

In another example, the revelation is given by the Babylonian god Marduk himself. The deity traces his early history over Babylonia, including his travels throughout the world. He spent time in the west among the Hittites, in the north in Assyria, and even in the land of Elam to the east. In this case, the text does not use *vaticinium ex eventu* leading up to the culmination, but rather ends the historical survey with such a hindsight prophecy. After the survey of his travels, Marduk "predicts" that a good king will arise in Babylon who will bring his cult statue home again and restore the city to its former glory, including the main temple of Marduk. Babylon will once again flourish under Marduk's watchful benevolence. This "prediction" was composed to legitimize the reign of Nebuchadnezzar I (1126–1105 BCE), and his "future" actions that in fact had already taken place.†

* For an overview of these ancient Near Eastern parallels, including the ones from Mesopotamia discussed here, see pages 240–51 in Sparks in "Where to Find More" in Chapter 5.
† For details of the "Shulgi Prophecy" and the "Marduk Prophecy," see Benjamin R. Benjamin, *Before the Muses: An Anthology of Akkadian Literature* (3rd ed.; Bethesda, Md.: CDL Press 2005), 357–59 and 388–91, respectively.

This book is the OT's version of apocalyptic literature, which is why I have reserved it for treatment in this chapter of our textbook. As one of the earliest examples of the subgenre "historical apocalypse," the book of Daniel has much in common with Israel's older prophetic traditions as well as with later Jewish apocalyptic literature, which it greatly influenced.

The final form of the book of Daniel took shape after the OT's collection of fifteen writing prophets had been closed in a fixed canon. More to the point, the man Daniel is not called a "prophet" (*nābîʾ*) in the OT. Nor do we find the book of Daniel among the prophets in the Jewish canon, but rather collected together with other later books in the final section of the canon, the "Writings"

(Figure 2.3). In part, this reflects an understanding of prophets as primarily focused on *forthtelling* God's word as spokespersons for Yahweh rather than on *foretelling* future events. The book's location in the Jewish canon reflects this understanding of Daniel as an apocalyptic visionary rather than as a prophet in the classic sense.

Yet most English translations of the OT include the book of Daniel with the prophets immediately after Ezekiel and before the twelve minor prophets, following the arrangement of the Greek Septuagint and the Latin Vulgate. This tradition is possible and perfectly logical as one that takes Daniel as a prophet.[4] Prophecy is understood in a slightly different way in this case, taking it as primarily focused on *foretelling* future events. Since the second half of the book is almost exclusively visionary predictions of the future, one can easily see how the book of Daniel came to be collected among the prophets in this canonical arrangement of OT books.

The book of Daniel consists of two clearly defined and distinct symmetrical halves. The first half, Daniel 1–6, contains narratives from the life of Daniel and his friends in exile during the Babylonian and Persian periods. These narratives, written in the third person about Daniel and his friends, emphasize their uncompromising devotion in the face of overwhelming religious oppression and persecution. The second half of the book, Daniel 7–12, contains apocalyptic visions. These chapters are the most clearly apocalyptic materials in the OT. We have here visions attributed to Daniel, and with the exception of two introductory phrases (Daniel 7:1

and 10:1), they are presented in the first-person voice of Daniel. Together, the narratives and visions teach that God is sovereign over world history, including the most arrogant and oppressive human power structures, and that, eventually, God will overturn all such power structures in establishing a permanent kingdom of peace on earth.

The Narratives (Daniel 1–6)

The first chapter of the book of Daniel gives necessary background for the rest of the book. Daniel and his three friends, Shadrach, Meshach, and Abednego, are introduced as especially gifted by God, and Daniel, in particular, has abilities in dream and visioninterpretation. They are also young men unwilling to compromise when it comes to their faith (Daniel 1:8). The opening superscription for the book locates the historical context as 605 BCE, when Nebuchadnezzar laid siege to Jerusalem and took these four young men captive into Babylonia (1:1). Although this particular event is not mentioned elsewhere in the OT, we do have Babylonian sources telling of Nebuchadnezzar's campaign through the Levant in that year.[5]

The next three chapters are narratives in which King Nebuchadnezzar represents worldly power in its rawest and seemingly most invincible forms. But these narratives teach that raw human power is no match for the simple faith of God's servants, as long as they humbly believe and submit to God's will. Gradually even Nebuchadnezzar learns

---

4 As is done in the New Testament (Matthew 24:15) and the Jewish historian Josephus (*Antiquities* 10.11.7, §266–268).

5 Bill T. Arnold, "The Neo-Babylonian Chronicle Series," *The Ancient Near East: Historical Sources in Translation* (ed. Mark W. Chavalas; Blackwell Sourcebooks in Ancient History; Malden, Mass.: Blackwell, 2006), 416.

that his power is only a temporary and derivative authority from the "Most High God," who is God of gods and Lord of kings (2:47 and 4:2). In the first narrative, Daniel is the only expert in Babylon who is able to both discern the king's dream and give its interpretation (Daniel 2). The message of the dream is that Nebuchadnezzar's is only the first of a series of world empires, which will all eventually be destroyed and replaced by God's new and everlasting kingdom (2:44–45).

The next narrative involving Nebuchadnezzar features Daniel's three friends, Shadrach, Meshach, and Abednego (Daniel 3). They refuse to worship before a new idol commissioned by Nebuchadnezzar, risking their lives in the process. When given a second chance to compromise their faith in order to save their lives, they announce unambiguously that they consider the powerful Babylonian king, and the threat he represents, to be basically insignificant and irrelevant. They're indifferent to his threats. They stand firm: they will not compromise and worship his statue. Indignant, Nebuchadnezzar throws them into a fiery furnace, as promised. When he sees that God sends a messenger to deliver them from death in the furnace, he is sufficiently impressed with the power of their God, and he decrees that everyone in his kingdom should respect this deity.

The final story featuring Nebuchadnezzar is another dream-vision (Daniel 4). The tree in the king's dream symbolizes Nebuchadnezzar himself. Once proud and seemingly invincible, the Babylonian king will be cut down at the command of the Most High God and be humiliated beyond recognition. The lessons of Daniel's interpretation (and of these narratives) is that the power and

grandeur of human structures is only illusory. It is not real, and certainly not permanent. The readers of these narratives are obviously suffering under oppressive political powers. They need the assurance that God will eventually turn things around. And if God can overturn Nebuchadnezzar, and bring him down, then anything is possible. They have no greater symbol of reprehensible human power than Nebuchadnezzar until, that is, they meet the king in the book's next chapter.

King Belshazzar of Babylon takes the image of pride and oppressive human power to a new level — the level of blasphemy (Daniel 5). While his kingdom is only hours away from destruction at the hands of the approaching Persian army, he indulges himself and his followers in senseless revelry (5:1–4). Shockingly, Belshazzar uses the sacred vessels from Yahweh's temple in Jerusalem — taken as war trophies by his predecessor Nebuchadnezzar and housed in the Babylonian treasury (Daniel 1:2) — as drinking glasses at his extravagant party. When the fingers of a human hand suddenly appear and begin writing something on the wall of the royal palace, everything comes to a halt (5:5). Only Daniel is able to interpret the mysterious writing. The words *mene, mene, tekel,* and *parsin* use an elaborate wordplay to announce immediate and certain doom for Belshazzar and his empire (5:24–28).[6] That very night Belshazzar is killed and his kingdom passes to another, illustrating once again the ephemeral nature of arrogant human power.

6 Opinions differ as to specifics, but the words probably use three levels of meaning, based on (1) scale weights, (2) sound-alike verbs ("reckoned," "weighed," and "assessed"), and (3) outcomes ("paid out," "too light," and "Persia"). See Al Wolters, "The Riddle of the Scales in Daniel 5," *Hebrew Union College Annual* 62 (1991): 155–77.

22.1. *Belshazzar's Feast* by Rembrandt, about 1635. Rembrandt attemped to capture the moment in which Belshazzar and his guests became aware of the divine hand writing a message on the wall. For the form of the Aramaic letters, Rembrandt relied on the work of his contemporary Menasseh ben Israel. The artist wrote the letters in columns instead of right to left, perhaps relying on a theory that the words were a mystery to all but Daniel because they were written vertically. Rembrandt also got the last letter wrong, confusing *n* in "parsin" for *z*. (Photo: © National Gallery, London, Great Britain / Art Resource, N.Y.)

The final narrative portion of the book is set in a much later period, during the reign of the Persian king Darius I (522–486 BCE). Daniel would of necessity be viewed in this chapter as quite elderly, possibly in his nineties or older. His political enemies, driven by bitter jealousy, attempt to end his career but can find no fault or weakness in him other than his faith (6:5). Using trickery and deception, they trap King Darius, who has no alternative but to send his friend Daniel to certain death in the den of lions. God's salvation reverses the circumstances, sending Daniel's enemies to a torturous death instead (6:19–24). The Persian king, similar to Nebuchadnezzar before him, promotes the worship of the God of Daniel throughout his empire (6:26–28).

The Visions (Daniel 7–12)

The rest of the book of Daniel consists of four dreams or visions. In the narratives of Daniel 1–6,

the young man Daniel is divinely gifted with the ability to interpret the dreams of others, while in Daniel 7–12, he himself becomes the recipient of divine revelation in apocalyptic visions. In the narratives, he had the ability to "read" the meaning of revelation encoded in dream-visions (Daniel 2 and 4) or in sacred writings (Daniel 5). In the visions of Daniel 7–12, this idea that Daniel is able to discern the future through revealed wisdom is appropriated for the apocalyptic vision of the future. The narratives predicted the near future for Babylon and Persia, whereas time and eternity are blended in the visions of Daniel 7–12, encompassing all of human history in an eschatological culmination of that history.

Together with the narratives, these visions tell the story of what happens to an evil oppressor of God's people. The visions are thematically related to the narratives of Daniel 1–6 and build especially on Nebuchadnezzar's dream in chapter 2. The four sequential earthly kingdoms of Nebuchadnezzar's dream are symbolized in Daniel's first vision by four awe-inspiring animals (Daniel 7). Thus, human governments will be replaced by the single kingdom of God who will rule over all.

The human kingdoms in Daniel 2 pass away, replaced by a stone cut "not by human hands" (2:34). The four beasts of Daniel's first vision arise from the Mediterranean Sea aroused by four winds of heaven. The four creatures are impossible to describe precisely. So the visionary compares them by approximation with known creatures: *like a* lion, *like a* bear, and *like a* leopard. The appearance of the terrifying fourth beast is beyond all known approximates. Each beast is more terrible and threatening than the last. They symbolize increasing arrogance and blasphemy of human kingdoms, building as in a crescendo against the holy ones of the Most High. All four will be destroyed, and their greatness and dominion given over to "the people of the holy ones of the Most High" (7:27). In the process, Daniel is permitted a glimpse into the celestial realm, where he sees "the Ancient of Days" (God) granting all dominion and kingship to "one like a son of man" (or better, "like a human being"; 7:13–14). This "one like a human being" represents the "people of the holy ones of the Most High" (7:27). The image of the future, apocalyptic role of the "son of man" was influential in early Christian traditions about Jesus.[7]

Daniel's second vision (Daniel 8) identifies two of the kingdoms by name: the two-horned ram symbolizes the Medo-Persian Empire, and the goat is Greece (8:20–21). In so doing, this vision connects these kingdoms more directly to the time of the author of the visions. The horn between the goat's eyes is Alexander III of Macedon (better known as Alexander the Great). After his death, Alexander was succeeded by four rival states, one of which was the Seleucid kingdom. The "beautiful land" of Judah was included in the Seleucid's territory (8:9). One of its kings, "another horn," was Antiochus IV Epiphanes, who desecrated the temple and attacked the religion of the Jews in Jerusalem. The angel Gabriel explains the vision for Daniel, that the persecution will last only for a brief time, a little over three years (8:14).

The vision of Daniel 9 is instigated by Daniel's study of the sacred writings of the prophet Jeremiah (9:1–2), which leads to one of the greatest prayers of confession in the OT (9:3–19). Jeremiah's "seventy years" prophecy (Jeremiah 25:11–12 and 29:10) gives Daniel hope, even an expectation, that the exile is about to end (assuming his location in Babylon prior to the Persian conquest in 539 BCE).[8] Speaking on behalf of the people of God in exile, Daniel repents and calls for God to cause his face to "shine upon [his] desolated sanctuary" in Jerusalem (9:17). Gabriel appears again, this time to reinterpret the "seventy years" so that it applies both to the end of the exile in 539 BCE and to the end of the desolation of another far distant time (for Daniel) in the 160s BCE.

The final vision is a new revelation, in which hundreds of years of Persian and Greek history are summarized for Daniel by an angel (Daniel 10–12). This particular vision is not so much a vision like the others as it is a lesson from "the book of truth" (10:21). The angel summarizes two hundred years of Persian history (11:2) and the conquests of Alexander the Great (11:3–4) and then moves quickly to the long struggle between the kings of the north and south, those of the Seleucid and Ptolemaic kingdoms, respectively. Most of the message is reserved for Antiochus IV Epiphanes, the contemptible and arrogant oppressor anticipated in the visions of Daniel 7 and 8 (11:21–45). Not only is Antiochus responsible for the "abomination that makes desolate" (11:31), he is also the king who set his heart "against the holy covenant" and acted against it (11:28,30). After initial successes, even this oppressor will meet his downfall

---

7 For a summary of the complex issues surrounding Daniel 7:13 and its use in the New Testament, see Adela Yarbro Collins, "The Influence of Daniel on the New Testament," especially pages 90–105 in John J. Collins (1993) in "Where to Find More" in this chapter.

8 Counting from Nebuchadnezzar's triumphant conquests of Syria-Palestine in 609 BCE until the fall of Babylon in 539 BCE.

SIDEBAR 22.2. MACCABEAN PERIOD HISTORY

The events of history predicted by means of prophecy *ex eventu* in the visions of Daniel 7–12 were considerably later than most of OT history. Since these historical events are beyond the OT history we have covered so far, they require a bit more background. In order to understand these chapters, it will be necessary to keep this summary in mind.

Born in 356 BCE, Alexander the Great succeeded his father as king of Macedonia in 336, and crossed into Asia Minor in 334 BCE to renew the wars with Persia. He defeated the last Persian king in 331 and marched his troops eastward as far as northern India. The spread of Greek culture (or Hellenism) across the ancient world began at this time, marking the end of ancient Near Eastern history and the beginning of Greco-Roman history.

After extending his control to nearly impossible limits, creating the largest empire the world had known, Alexander returned to the old prestigious capital, Babylon, in order to consolidate his rule. He died shortly afterward in 323 BCE, apparently of fever perhaps related to a battle wound he received in India. Since he left no designated successor, his expansive empire immediately broke into four territories: the Macedonian and Greek homeland, Thrace, Syria and the east, and Egypt (the "four prominent horns" of Daniel 8:8, and see 8:22 and 11:3–4). Members of his family ruled temporarily, but his generals (known as the *Diadochi*, "successors") and their heirs warred over the next forty years to gain control of the fragmented empire.

Eventually by 280 BCE, the result was a threefold division of the empire into the Ptolemies in Egypt; the Seleucids over much of Asia Minor, Syria, and the eastern regions of the empire; and the Antigonids over mainland Greece and Thrace. Judah fell under Ptolemaic control for most of the third century BCE. Because the Seleucid rulers felt that southern Syria-Palestine rightfully belonged to them, the region was the object of a series of "Syrian wars" throughout much of the century. Finally, in 200 BCE, the Seleucid rulers defeated Ptolemaic Egypt and gained control of all Syria-Palestine, including Judah.

Life for Judah under Seleucid rule does not appear to have changed immediately. However, everything changed under the Seleucid king Antiochus IV Epiphanes (175–164 BCE). Through a complex sequence of events and for reasons that are not entirely clear, Antiochus eventually instituted a series of attacks on Judaism itself: circumcision was forbidden, copies of the ancient Torah scrolls were destroyed, a pagan altar was built on the temple altar, and most shocking of all, swine were sacrificed in the temple. This is the "abomination that desolates" in the visions of Daniel (9:27, 11:31, and 12:11). The result was a Jewish revolt led by the Maccabean family and recorded in the books of Maccabees. The Maccabean rulers (also known as Hasmonean rulers, named for an ancestor, Hasmon) recaptured Jerusalem and brought the "abomination that desolates" to an end, establishing Jewish independence for a century, from 164 BCE until the Roman conquest in 63 BCE.

during "the time of the end" (11:40–45). And the great prince, Michael, will protect the people of God, who will be delivered because they are found "written in the book" (12:1).

Daniel 11 is the best example of the apocalyptic principle of prophetic hindsight (or *vaticinium ex eventu*). The histories of the Persian Empire and Greece and the Seleucid Empire are "foretold" with detailed accuracy. By contrast, the end of the rule

of Antiochus IV Epiphanes, described in Daniel 11:40–45, is only vaguely predicted and without the benefit of historical hindsight. The transition from *ex eventu* prophecy to real predictive prophecy can be traced in Daniel 11 to this portrait of Antiochus. The visionary is speaking before the end of Antiochus's rule, but he is just as confident of its outcome. The purpose in this technique is not deception. This is an acceptable literary means

22.2. Antiochus IV Epiphanes (175–164 BCE). A tetradrachm (silver coin valuing four drachms) with the image of Antiochus IV Epiphanes, the Seleucid king who attacked Judaism as a means of controlling the southern portion of his realm. (Photo: Erich Lessing / Art Resource, N.Y.)

of encouraging readers to understand that history is in God's hands. Events of recent history are on a trajectory of God's design, culminating eventually in the salvation of God's people and their liberation from the suffering of this world. They must remain faithful, awaiting God's timing for the fulfillment of all things.

The closing paragraphs refer to the resurrection of the righteous dead (12:2), although not as a fully developed belief in resurrection, as we have later in the Pharisees and Christianity.[9] The seer has in mind glimpses of a restored people of God in line with Isaiah 26:19 and 66:24, and perhaps Ezekiel 37. The idea in Daniel goes further, however, by

imagining a resurrection not only of the righteous, who will awaken to "everlasting life," but also of others who will awaken to "shame and evelasting contempt." And it applies to Daniel individually, who is encouraged to live out his remaining years in confidence; even though he may not live to see the vindication of God's people himself, he will rise for his "reward at the end of days" (12:13). This is the clearest such assertion in the OT, and it is likely the origin for later ideas and convictions about resurrection (see 1 Corinthians 15).

Composition of the Book

One interesting – perhaps even odd – feature of the book of Daniel is its bilingualism: it has six

9 See pages 306–8 and 316–19 in Goldingay in "Where to Find More" in this chapter.

chapters in Aramaic and six in Hebrew. This in itself isn't odd. Bilingualism can be a powerful rhetorical tool in cultures with easy access to multiple languages.[10] What makes the use of two languages in Daniel odd is the lack of symmetry matching the book's contents. As we have seen, the book is equally divided between six chapters of narrative (1–6) and six of visions (7–12). But the languages, although almost equal in quantity of text, are asymmetrical: chapter 1 in Hebrew, chapters 2–7 in Aramaic, and chapters 8–12 back to Hebrew.[11] The reasons for this are likely related to the way the book of Daniel was written, or more precisely, to the way it evolved over time.

The narrative chapters of Daniel are marked by disjointed stops and starts, and even some confusing contradictions. For example, where has Daniel gone in chapter 3, after he was so prominent in chapters 1–2? He became ruler of the province of Babylon and chief prefect of all the wise men of Babylon in Daniel 2:48. But he isn't even mentioned in the next chapter, which is especially perplexing after Nebuchadnezzar summons all the officers and prefects of his kingdom to be present at the statue's dedication (3:2). We have other tensions in the narratives of Daniel 2–6, which probably indicate that these chapters circulated independently as separate traditions before being collected together in their present arrangement. Most readers assume that they were written in Babylon by an exilic author using Aramaic as the international

language. The first chapter would then have been written intentionally as an introduction for the collection of narratives. While we don't have enough evidence to speculate more about these traditions prior to the time when they were collected, we suspect that they were written sometime during the third century BCE.

Daniel 7, written also in Aramaic but in the apocalyptic visionary style, was added later, perhaps to round out the older narratives. In this sense, chapter 7 is transitional from the narratives to the visions. Chapters 8–12 are fully developed apocalyptic visions, relying, as we have said, on the themes of chapters 1–6, especially the series of earthly kingdoms replaced by one eternal kingdom of God. Presumably these visions were written in Jerusalem and added at the time of the crisis caused by Antiochus IV Epiphanes, around 167–165 BCE.[12] They were likely written in Hebrew instead of Aramaic because of the renewed nationalistic spirit of the Maccabean period. Aramaic created more of an international flavor for chapters 2–7, while Hebrew revived the language of old Israel and of the covenant with Yahweh.

CONTRIBUTIONS OF ISRAEL'S APOCALYPTIC MESSAGE

The religious faith expressed in the pages of the OT evolved over a thousand years of history. The worship of a deity known as Yahweh originated south of Syria-Palestine in Iron Age I, probably

---

10 I have explained the use of two languages here and in the book of Ezra as a rhetorical feature; Bill T. Arnold, "The Use of Aramaic in the Hebrew Bible: Another Look at Bilingualism in Ezra and Daniel," *Journal of Northwest Semitic Languages* 22/2 (1996): 1–16.

11 Technically, the Aramaic portion is 2:4b–7:28.

12 The final editor of the book appears not to have known about the reversal of the "abomination that desolates," the cleansing of the temple, and the death of Antiochus in 164 BCE.

in the Sinai Peninsula or the southern Negeb.[13] Although we do not have evidence for these earliest stages, Yahwism eventually developed into an Israelite henotheistic monolatry; Yahweh became the exclusive deity of national Israel. The religious reforms of King Josiah in the late seventh century solidified the monolatrous faith of Israel in written form (see Sidebar 14.3), and it is possible that the first articulation of monotheism comes from this period.

During and after the Babylonian exile, this monolatrous faith was transformed into a universal monotheism. The international scope of Yahweh's authority had become important in the preaching of Israel's prophets as early as the eighth century BCE (see Chapter 19). But the crisis of 586 BCE resulted in new formulations of this concept of the universal rule of Yahweh among the prophets of the exile and afterward. By the mid-sixth century BCE, especially with Isaiah of the exile, the transformation of Israel's monolatry into monotheism was complete. Israel's monolatrous devotion to Yahweh had given birth to monotheism. And the pages of the OT reflect this journey.

Just as the OT's fifteen writing prophets contribute to this religious development, Israel's apocalyptic message adds to the flow of thought culminating in monotheism. We don't have explicit monotheistic statements here, as are found in Deutero-Isaiah, for example. But the apocalyptic imagination (claiming for itself the status of divine revelation) is but one of several streams of postexilic thought contributing to the explicit monotheism of Judaism and the worship of a universal

God.[14] The vivid imagery of Daniel's apocalyptic visions revives and reuses older mythic imagery in a new monotheistic configuration. Myth itself was rejected or suppressed throughout much of the OT. Israel preferred to talk of Yahweh in narrative forms instead. But this older ancient Near Eastern mythic imagery survived, and it appears in Israel's library in isolated passages. Then, here in this youngest of OT books, the visions of Daniel bring back the old mythic imagery in a new monotheistic formulation of God's culminating victory at "the end of days" (Daniel 10:14). Monotheism is assumed here and permeates the whole.

Beyond this general undercurrent of monotheism in the apocalyptic, there is one other feature of the book of Daniel you should consider. When reading Daniel, you may notice that God is often "Most High," or simply "God of heaven." In fact, the use of "Most High" in early Judaism is a means of communicating with non-Jews, because it could also refer to Greek Zeus, to a leading Phoenician deity, or to other gods worshipped by non-Jews.[15] This is a fascinating reversal, since "Most High God" was one of the early ancestral names for God that came to be replaced by the revelation of "Yahweh" in Mosaic religion (see Chapter 10). Now, however, it returns as a

---

13 Review our discussion of this early period in Chapter 10.

14 On the concept of four dominant voices combining in a single witness to the new vision of one and only one deity (priestly, deuteronomic, wisdom, and apocalyptic), see pages 167–94 of Smith in "Where to Find More" in Chapter 1. For more on this discussion of the reuse of older mythic imagery in apocalyptic, see Smith's pages 173–78.

15 For some of this history, see pages 117–26 in Lemaire in "Where to Find More" in Chapter 10. This name for God is also used in the New Testament, especially in Luke-Acts: "he … will be called the Son of the Most High" (Luke 1:32).

convenient way of communicating with non-Jews, especially with foreign rulers in the narratives of Daniel 1–6.

In fact, the confessions and royal decrees of Nebuchadnezzar and Darius in these narratives are remarkable statements of what might otherwise be orthodox Israelite religion. Nebuchadnezzar begins by acknowledging that Daniel's God is "God of gods and Lord of kings" (2:47). Then he proclaims to his subjects that the "Most High God" has a kingdom that is everlasting and that "his sovereignty is from generation to generation" (4:1–3). Nebuchadnezzar moves from acknowledging God, to proclaiming God, and eventually to submitting to and worshipping God.

> I blessed the Most High,
> > and praised and honored the one who lives forever.
> For his sovereignty is an everlasting sovereignty,
> > and his kingdom endures from generation to generation.
> All the inhabitants of the earth are accounted as nothing,
> > and he does what he wills with the host of heaven
> > and the inhabitants of the earth.
> There is no one who can stay his hand
> > or say to him, "What are you doing?" (Daniel 4:34–35)
>
> Now I, Nebuchadnezzar, praise and extol and honor the King of heaven,
> > for all his works are truth,
> > and his ways are justice;

> and he is able to bring low
> > those who walk in pride. (Daniel 4:37)

The decree of King Darius is no less remarkable for a foreign potentate.

> I make a decree, that in all my royal dominion people should tremble and fear before the God of Daniel:
> > For he is the living God,
> > > enduring forever.
> His kingdom shall never be destroyed,
> > and his dominion has no end.
> He delivers and rescues,
> > he works signs and wonders in heaven and on earth;
> > for he has saved Daniel
> > from the power of the lions. (Daniel 6:26–27)

Taken together, these confessions present a portrait of earth's rulers moving from idolatrous polytheism to a recognition of the God of heaven, and eventually to submission to and even worship of the "Most High." This is the book's way of envisioning the same universalism of the writing prophets. Yahweh, otherwise known as the "God of heaven" or the "Most High," is over all and through all, and worthy of everyone's praise. While not denying the existence of other deities (explicit monotheism), these poems and confessions certainly imply that Daniel's God – whom we otherwise know as Yahweh – is the sole deity of the universe, even for Babylonians and Persians.

WHERE TO FIND MORE

Commentaries: The best technical and advanced commentaries on the book of **Daniel** are John J. Collins, *Daniel: A Commentary on the Book of Daniel* (Hermeneia; Minneapolis, Minn.: Fortress Press, 1993); John Goldingay, *Daniel* (Word Biblical Commentary; Dallas: Word, 1989).

Arnold, Bill T. "Old Testament Eschatology and the Rise of Apocalypticism." Pages 23–39 in *The Oxford Handbook of Eschatology*. Edited by Jerry L. Walls. Oxford and New York: Oxford University Press, 2008.

For a general introduction to many of the topics treated in this chapter; and, in the same volume, the chapter by John J. Collins covers the options on the origins of apocalyptic literature (pp. 40–55).

Collins, John J. *The Apocalyptic Imagination: An Introduction to Jewish Apocalyptic Literature*. 2nd ed. Biblical Resource Series. Grand Rapids, Mich.: Eerdmans, 1998.

See pages 23–37 on the quest for the origins of Jewish apocalypticism.

Grabbe, Lester L. "Israel under Persia and Greece." Pages 440–57 in *The Biblical World*, vol. 1. Edited by John Barton. London: Routledge, 2002.

Helpful survey of historical events needed for reading Daniel 7–12, especially pages 447–56 for the Maccabean period.

Hengel, Martin. "The Political and Social History of Palestine from Alexander to Antiochus III (333–187 BCE)." Pages 35–78 in *The Cambridge History of Judaism, vol. 2, The Hellenistic Age*. Edited by W. D. Davies and Louis Finkelstein. Cambridge and New York: Cambridge University Press, 1989.

A number of essays in this volume are especially helpful background for the topics discussed in this chapter, including "Antiochus IV" by Otto Mørkholm (pp. 278–91), "The Hasmonean Revolt and the Hasmonean Dynasty" by Jonathan A. Goldstein (pp. 292–351), and "The Book of Daniel" by H. L. Ginsberg (pp. 504–23).

Oswalt, John N. "Recent Studies in Old Testament Apocalyptic." Pages 369–90 in *The Face of Old Testament Studies: A Survey of Contemporary Approaches*. Edited by David W. Baker and Bill T. Arnold. Grand Rapids, Mich.: Baker Books, 1999.

Russell, D. S. *The Method and Message of Jewish Apocalyptic, 200 BC–AD 100*. OTL. Philadelphia: Westminster Press, 1964.

Will, Édouard. "The Succession to Alexander." Pages 23–61 in *The Cambridge Ancient History, vol. 7, pt. 1, The Hellenistic World*. Edited by F. W. Walbank, A. E. Astin, M. W. Frederiksen, and R. M. Ogilvie. 2nd ed. Cambridge and New York: Cambridge University Press, 1984.

Several other chapters of this volume deal with the centuries immediately following Alexander's death.

CHAPTER 23

The Scrolls

OLD TESTAMENT READING: SONG OF SONGS, RUTH, LAMENTATIONS, ECCLESIASTES, AND ESTHER

With this chapter, we arrive at five final books in our OT collection. They have been brought together in the Jewish canon as the "five scrolls," related by their use in the Jewish liturgical calendar.

Our survey will begin with the Song of Songs, a collection of Israel's love poetry. We have other ancient parallels, but we will note in these the particular imagery drawn from everyday life in Syria-Palestine. Second, Ruth is an exquisite narrative about ordinary Israelites. Their uncommonness is on display in their exemplary characters and their genealogical connection to Israel's beloved King David. A third book, Lamentations, is a collection of five poems presented in acrostic form. Recounting the tragedies incurred in Jerusalem's destruction, the poetry nevertheless exhibits some of the OT's most glorious expressions of Yahweh's mercy. Ecclesiastes, another unique poetry collection with ancient Near Eastern parallels, offers reflections on the human experience. Finally, we will examine Esther. God is never mentioned in the book, yet this story merited inclusion in the canon, and we will note its subtle but important contribution to OT theology.

We have reserved for this chapter five relatively brief books that round out the rest of Israel's library. Known as the "five scrolls" or the "Megilloth" (měgillôt is Hebrew for "scrolls"), these books are collected together in the "Writings" of the Jewish canon and included immediately following Psalms, Proverbs, and Job (see Figure 2.3 for this discussion).[1] In the Christian traditions, these five scrolls are scattered among other books of the OT, based loosely on literary type. Two are included among the historical books because they are narratives (Ruth and Esther). Two are included with Job, Psalms, and Proverbs because of their poetic nature (Ecclesiastes and Song of Songs). Lamentations is grouped with Jeremiah because of the tradition that associates the book with that prophet.

Each of these books makes its own distinctive contribution to the OT message. At various stages in the canonical process, each one was considered profound enough to be included in the list of sacred books. Much later, Jewish readers associated each book with a particular time of the liturgical calendar for reading in the synagogues: Song of Songs at Passover, Ruth during the Festival of Weeks, Ecclesiastes during the Festival of Tabernacles (Succoth), Lamentations on the Ninth of Ab (a fast commemorating the destruction of the temple), and Esther at Purim. Apparently these books were read in the synagogues at each event from parchment scrolls, which may explain why they came to be known simply as "the scrolls."

THE MEGILLOTH, OR THE FIVE SCROLLS

The five books of the Megilloth are collected together in modern Hebrew editions of the OT, but not always in the same sequence. In fact, the

order and arrangement of the Megilloth was flexible as late as the twelfth century CE, at which time a sequence emerged based on the chronological order of their liturgical use in synagogues: Song of Songs, Ruth, Lamentations, Ecclesiastes, and Esther. Alternatively, the five books are arranged in some editions of the Hebrew text even today according to the presumed age of the scrolls: Ruth, Song of Songs, Ecclesiastes, Lamentations, and Esther. I will introduce them here in the first option, according to the order of their use in the liturgy.

The Song of Songs

The title of the book, "Song of Songs," comes from the first two Hebrew words of the superscription (šîr haššîrîm), the superlative implying this is the greatest song of all. The book is also known as the Canticle of Canticles, or simply Canticles, from the Latin version, and Song of Solomon, also based on the superscription, in which King Solomon is mentioned as somehow related to the Song. The superscription itself is not making a claim to authorship, however, and it can be taken as "concerning or about Solomon," or "belonging to Solomon" (Song of Songs 1:1). The book was associated with King Solomon because of the Israelite traditions about him as a collector of proverbs and songs (1 Kings 4:32). The references to the young man of the poems as "the king" should not be taken as referring to Solomon.

The Israelites loved to sing, and music was an important part of their lives (Chapter 18). Most of the songs we have preserved in the OT originated in religious contexts, but the songs collected in the eight chapters of the Song of Songs seem to be

---

1 These three — Job, Proverbs, and Psalms — were taken together by Jewish readers as the "Book of Truth." The Hebrew word "truth" has three Hebrew consonants, serving as an acronym based on the initial letter of each book. Thus the three books of "truth" were followed by the five Megilloth.

23.1. Megillat Esther. The term "megillah" is appropriate for all five scrolls, but most often occurs for the book of Esther alone, as in Megillat Esther ("the scroll of Esther") or simply "Megillah" (the "scroll," i.e., Esther). The middle panel of this illuminated Megillah has a selection from Esther 2–3. (Photo: Erich Lessing / Art Resource, N.Y.)

secular love poetry. Indeed, the nonreligious character of this book led to intense debates in both early Judaism and early Christianity about whether to include the Song in the OT canon. Many could accept the book only by taking its explicit sexual content as an allegory of Yahweh's love for Israel (in Judaism) or of Christ the bridegroom's love for the church, the bride. Yet it is not at all clear that the poets and first authors of these poems saw them as *anti*-religious or antithetical to faith. Indeed, it seems more likely that the Israelite philosophers who gave us these beautiful poems believed that their faith impacted every part of their lives, even their most intimate relationships.

Like the books of Psalms and Proverbs, the Song of Songs is a collection. These are Israel's love songs, beautifully composed with luscious description and rich imagery. The Israelites were not alone in celebrating sensuous love in poetry. Love and lovemaking have been the focus of gifted poetics in nearly all cultures across the ancient Near East, Sumerian, Akkadian, Syro-Palestinian,

and, especially, Egyptian.[2] The Song of Songs represents Israel's version of this literature – secular love songs – and it is among the most sophisticated poetry of the Bible.

The Song's love poems focus on the lovers' intense longing for each other, often detailing their physical attractiveness in rich imagery taken from agriculture, flora and fauna, architecture, or even the military. Her eyes are like doves, and her hair is like a flock of goats (4:1); his head is fine gold, and his lips are lilies (5:11–13). While such images may seem strange today, they draw on all that was pleasant and enjoyable in Syro-Palestinian life to describe the desire of these lovers for each other.

The fact that the book is a collection makes it difficult to know how much structure and unity we have here. Some portions of the Song come from preexilic times, but others reflect a Persian influence, meaning that the book evolved over a long period of time. We cannot know when it was finally composed. Attempts have been made to see the Song of Songs as a drama (some suggest that there were three speakers in a love triangle) or as the reenactment of a sacred wedding in cultic celebration.[3] None of these explanations is satisfying. You should think of the book more simply as an anthology of Israelite love poems, arranged according to repeated words and phrases, and a portrayal of two leading characters along a loose narrative frame.[4]

2 Compare, for example, the Egyptian love poetry with Song of Songs; see Miriam Lichtheim, *Ancient Egyptian Literature: A Book of Readings* (3 vols.; Berkeley: University of California Press, 1973–1980), 2:179–93.

3 For these options and others, see pages 454–56 in Vriezen and van der Woude in "Where to Find More" in Chapter 2.

4 See pages 209–22 in Fox (1985) in "Where to Find More" in this chapter.

The Song of Songs is not alone among literary celebrations of human love in the ancient Near East. We find similar such literary types from Egyptian, Sumerian, Akkadian, and Ugaritic collections. Whereas the Mesopotamian and Ugaritic texts of this literary type served a cultic purpose, Egyptian love poems seem to have reflected a secular obsession with this subject. The Egyptians may have produced love poems earlier in their history. But our examples come from the New Kingdom period.

The following is an excerpt from the so-called Papyrus Chester Beatty I, which presents the alternating voices of a young man and a young woman pondering their passion for each other.[*]

> The One, the sister without peer,
> The handsomest of all!
> She looks like the rising morning star
> At the start of a happy year.
> Shining bright, fair of skin,
> Lovely the look of her eyes,
> Sweet the speech of her lips,
> She has not a word too much.
> Upright neck, shining breast,
> Hair true lapis lazuli;
> Arms surpassing gold,
> Fingers like lotus buds.
> Heavy thighs, narrow waist,
> Her legs parade her beauty;
> With graceful steps she treads the ground,
> Captures my heart by her movements.
> She causes all men's necks
> To turn about to see her;
> Joy has he whom she embraces,
> He is like the first of men!

Like the OT's Song of Songs, this selection, and most Egyptian love poetry, has only a general story line but assumes a loosely arranged chronology. Unlike certain other ancient Near Eastern parallels, these poems do not suggest borrowing or literary dependence in either direction. Instead, these texts remind us that Israel was but one nation among others reflecting on many of the same mysteries of life, yet each with its own distinctive voice.

[*] Adapted from Miriam Lichtheim, *Ancient Egyptian Literature: A Book of Readings* (3 vols.; Berkeley: University of California Press, 1973–1980), 2:182.

The Book of Ruth

The four-chapter narrative of the book of Ruth tells an amazing story, with a surprise ending. You will find here literary artistry as sophisticated as that of any narrative in the Primary History. The style is concise and quick moving, with subtle wordplays and nuanced ironies that make important contributions to OT theology.

There once was a man named Elimelech, who lived in Bethlehem. Because their land was experiencing severe drought, Elimelech, his wife Naomi, and their two sons have no choice but to move to neighboring Moab, across the Jordan River (see Map 12.5 for Moab in relation to Judah). Sadly, Elimelech dies in Moab, leaving the family stranded. Both sons take Moabite wives. But after ten years, the two sons also die, leaving Naomi in a helpless situation (Ruth 1:1–5). Having heard that the famine at home was ending, Naomi decides to go back to Bethlehem. She insists that her daughters-in-law, Orpah and Ruth, return to their families in Moab, where they might begin again and have brighter futures. Orpah finally agrees to go back home. But Ruth stubbornly and surprisingly refuses to abandon Naomi and says as much in what has become a classic statement of one person's committing totally and unconditionally to another.

> "Where you go, I will go;
>
> where you lodge, I will lodge;
>
> your people shall be my people,
>
> and your God my God.
>
> Where you die, I will die – there will I be buried.
>
> May Yahweh do thus and so to me, and more as well,
>
> if even death parts me from you!" (Ruth 1:16–17)

Ruth's upstanding character is revealed here for the first time. She will continue to show herself to be a laudable figure of the OT. Her prominence in the story is surprising since Ruth is (1) a woman, (2) not an Israelite, and (3) not connected to a royal, priestly, or prophetic personage. Indeed, the book's story is about average citizens, "Joe and Sally Israelite" if you will, unlike most of the other narratives of the OT.

When Naomi and Ruth arrive back in Bethlehem, they are destitute and apparently without hope of sustaining themselves (1:19–22). In an effort to provide food for them both, Ruth, the younger of the two women, volunteers for a menial task (2:2). According to Israelite law, during harvest the poorest of the poor could glean in the fields for scraps (Leviticus 19:9–10 and 23:22; Deuteronomy 24:19–22). Chapter 2 is the account of Ruth's "chance" encounter with Boaz, a wealthy member of Naomi's family, while gleaning the fields during barley harvest. In chapter 3, with Naomi's guidance, Ruth reminds Boaz of his obligation to Naomi as next of kin according to Israelite tribal custom. He declares himself more than willing to help under the condition that a nearer kinsman be given the right of first refusal.

In the concluding chapter, the unnamed next of kin declares himself unable to help Naomi and Ruth, leaving Boaz free to intervene. All the legal particulars having been properly observed, the kinsman-redeemer obligation is transferred to Boaz, who marries Ruth. The narrative is especially careful to point out that all the characters are righteous people, even in circumstances in which we might expect them to mistreat each other or to act selfishly. Not these Israelites! Nor this Moabitess, Ruth. These are exemplary characters in the OT, and their conduct contrasts greatly with the behavior of the kings, priests, and prophets we have met in other narratives.

The marriage of Boaz and Ruth is blessed with a child, which reverses Naomi's traumatic losses in Moab. Naomi is more a surrogate mother than a grandmother to the lad (4:16); the pain of losing her own two boys is lessened (1:5). The tender picture of Naomi nursing the newborn might have been the end of the story. But when Naomi's friends name the baby, we have a real surprise. They name him Obed. It turns out that this baby will grow up to be the grandfather of none other than King David himself! The closing genealogy drives the point home (4:18–22). Through the lives of these good people, doing the best they can in terrible circumstances and trusting Yahweh along the way, God has guided history.

The role of providence in the narrative is clear enough in retrospect. The field where Ruth gleaned just happened "by chance" to belong to Boaz (2:3). Details of the story reflect the Israelite conviction that Yahweh will bless those who react responsibly to the circumstances of life (2:12). And the surprise ending – identifying the Moabitess as the great-grandmother of King David – refutes other voices in ancient Israel who were much less accepting of foreign associations among God's people (Deuteronomy 23:3; Ezra 9–10; Nehemiah 13).

The Book of Lamentations

The title of the book of Lamentations has several variations. The Hebrew expression "how!" (*'êkâ*) occurs three times in the book to introduce the beginning of a cry of desperation or extreme distress (Lamentations 1:1, 2:1, and 4:1). In these contexts, the word takes the connotation "how is it possible that?" or "surely it's not possible that!" or, by extension, "Oh, how terribly!" The prominence of this term, then, means that it serves as the book's superscription, and it became the first Hebrew title of the book. Other early Jewish sources refer to the book as *qînôt*, "lamentations, elegies, dirges,"

referring to funeral songs or chants. This is the idea behind the Septuagint's name for the book, *thrēnoi*, "dirges," and the Vulgate's expanded subtitle, "The Lamentations of Jeremiah."

The book of Lamentations consists of five poems giving a vivid account of the horrors of 586 BCE, when Jerusalem was destroyed by the Babylonians. The literary style of most of these poems is characterized by a *qînah*-dirge meter of three plus two beats known from elsewhere in the OT. In addition, the first four of the poems are acrostics (Lamentations 1–4), each verse beginning with the next letter of the Hebrew alphabet (see Sidebar 16.3). Remarkably, the third poem devotes three verses to each of the twenty-two letters of the Hebrew alphabet for a perfectly constructed sixty-six-line poem. (If you know the Hebrew alphabet, have a look and appreciate fully how gifted this poet must have been.) The acrostics hint that these funeral songs cover the the topic thoroughly. Every letter of the alphabet is used; the pain of the loss of Jerusalem is complete.

There is nothing in the five poems themselves that would associate the book with Jeremiah. The poems were attributed to Jeremiah quite early, since the Septuagint translation adds a lengthy introduction, detailing that Jeremiah sat and wept over the city, and uttered these lamentations after Israel was taken captive and Jerusalem destroyed. But many internal pieces of evidence argue against this identification of the author. The book of Lamentations, like so many other portions of the OT, is anonymous. Its author(s) witnessed the fall of the city and represented the people of Israel in commemorating the utter despair of the moment with funeral songs.

The Book of Ecclesiastes

The English title for the book of Ecclesiastes comes from the Septuagint translation of the opening line: "The words of the *ekklēsiastou* (genitive of *ekklēsiastēs*, "preacher") the son of David." This title was followed by the Latin Vulgate and was adopted in most English translations. The Hebrew word so translated is *qōhelet*, a noun known nowhere else in the OT and therefore not entirely clear in meaning. It appears to be a title for an official responsible for calling the community together in sacred assembly, and occasionally speaking to them.[5] In this case, the English terms "preacher" and "teacher" are not entirely appropriate. Contemporary scholarship often uses "Qoheleth" as a title for the book to avoid the imprecision of the English title.

The book of Ecclesiastes has a unique but vital role to play in Israel's library collection. There's nothing else quite like it in the OT. It shares certain literary and thematic features with the book of Job, and it is most certainly written by a scribe at home in Israel's wisdom traditions (Ecclesiastes 12:9–10). As we have seen for the book of Psalms, the book of Proverbs, and the Song of Songs, this book also is a collection of poems. But this is no simple collection of wisdom aphorisms. Qoheleth is a thinker, a wisdom philosopher, who offers in these twelve chapters personal reflections on the human experience.[6] The book exhibits little structure or intentional literary arrangement. Yet the sayings are unified by a single idea.

Vanity of vanities, says Qoheleth,[7]
vanity of vanities! All is vanity. (Ecclesiastes 1:2)

With this salvo, Qoheleth announces that everything in this life is meaningless and temporary, a theme that opens and closes the book (Ecclesiastes 12:8) framing the whole.

The book of Ecclesiastes has no mention of Israel's salvation history, so central to the message of the Primary History. Nor do we find here any mention of God's will revealed in the sacred law, or Torah (except perhaps an allusion in the epilogue; Ecclesiastes 12:13). And unlike Israel's traditions of prophecy, wisdom, or apocalyptic visionaries, Qoheleth finds no meaning or significance in world events. He finds no profit or benefit for those who work hard "under the sun" (1:3). The most powerful king among us searches in vain for wisdom and meaning in life (chaps. 1–2).[8] Everyday experiences in the cycles of life are useless, and we can only hope to enjoy our work and food (chaps. 3–4, and especially 3:13 and 22). Long life and riches are equally of no value; old age and death await us all (12:1–7). These themes are explored in detail in Qoheleth's long monologue in the main body of the book (1:12–12:8), framed with an introduction and epilogue by a final editor (1:1–11 and 12:8–14).

Some assume that Qoheleth was a true skeptic, whose musings were critiqued and corrected by a more orthodox Israelite editor (the critique begins in earnest at 12:8). On the other hand, Qoheleth's faith itself seems solid (3:14). I prefer not to think

---

5 The word may even be a personal name, Qoheleth, although otherwise unattested and not likely.
6 The book may be a collection from late in Israel's history, combining the work of several authors.
7 NRSV has "says the Teacher."
8 First-person passages of chapters 1–2 identifying Qoheleth with the king in Jerusalem (see 1:12) gave rise to the tradition that Solomon wrote the book, but nothing in chapters 3–12 supports such a claim.

SIDEBAR 23.2. MESOPOTAMIAN PARALLELS TO ECCLESIASTES

We have numerous texts from ancient Egypt and Mesopotamia that compare to Ecclesiastes. As with other comparisons of ancient Near Eastern wisdom traditions and those of the OT, the parallels are at times so striking that literary dependence in one direction or the other seems likely, although we cannot tell which direction (Chapter 17).* One collection of Mesopotamian wisdom sayings, preserved in Sumerian and Akkadian copies and fragments, is devoted to the theme of life's futility and vanity. The materials are structured by a recurring line.†

> Regulations were laid down at the command of the gods. From days of old there has been vanity (literally "wind").

Elsewhere, the philosopher warns, "the whole of life is but the twinkling of an eye; the life of humankind does not [last] forever." The context of these quotes surveys the great accomplishments of kings of the past, whose achievements are now forgotten, and so were in vain. Unlike other parallels from ancient Near Eastern texts, these quotes illustrate not an interest in theodicy especially, but the sheer vanity of human existence.

In *The Dialogue of Pessimism*, a master and his servant consider what activities are right to do. The master proposes one activity, and the servant quickly concurs. The master proposes the opposite, and the servant agrees with that too.‡

> Servant, listen to me.
> Yes, master, yes.
> I will fall in love with a woman.
> So, fall in love, master, fall in love. The man who falls in love with a woman forgets sorrow and care.
> No, servant, I will certainly not fall in love with a woman.
> Do not fall in love, master, do not fall in love. A woman is a pitfall, a pitfall, a hole, a ditch, a woman is a sharp iron dagger that slashes a man's throat.
>
> …
>
> Servant, listen to me.
> Yes, master, yes.
> Quickly bring me water to wash my hands, give it to me so I can sacrifice to my god.
> Sacrifice, master, sacrifice. The man who sacrifices to his god makes a satisfying transaction, he makes loan upon loan.
> No, servant, I will certainly not sacrifice to my god.
> Do not sacrifice, master, do not sacrifice. You will train your god to follow you around like a dog. He will require of you rites or a magic figurine or what have you.

* For discussion and bibliography, see pages 56–83 in Sparks in "Where to Find More" in Chapter 4.
† Quotes of this little studied material are from W. G. Lambert, "Some New Babylonian Wisdom Literature," *Wisdom in Ancient Israel: Essays in Honour of J. A. Emerton* (ed. John Day, Robert P. Gordon, and H. G. M. Williamson; Cambridge: Cambridge University Press, 1995), 30–42.
‡ Quotes adapted from Benjamin R. Foster, *Before the Muses: An Anthology of Akkadian Literature* (3rd ed.; Bethesda, Md.: CDL Press), 923–26.

SIDEBAR 23.2. (CONTINUED)

Among other activities the master considers are going for a chariot ride, having dinner, starting a revolution, and becoming a moneylender. When he proposes something altruistic for the sake of his country, the slave responds with a resolute conviction that history will not know the difference: "Go up on the ancient ruins and walk around, look at the skulls of the lowly and great. Which was the doer of evil, and which was the doer of good deeds?" Around and around this goes until eventually, the master falls into utter hopelessness over the futility of life. When he asks whether anything is worth doing, the slave offers death as the only suitable end to this meaningless life.

> Servant, listen to me.
>
> Yes, master, yes.
>
> What, then, is good?
>
> To break my neck and your neck and throw us in the river is good. Who is so tall as to reach to heaven? Who is so broad as to encompass the netherworld?
>
> No, servant, I will kill you and let you go first.
>
> Then, my master will certainly not outlive me even three days!

Comparisons with Qoheleth end here. The *Dialogue* concludes that death is the only fitting conclusion to this miserable life, while Qoheleth affirms that, transient as they are, life's joys are worth the effort as is especially faithful service to Yahweh.

of the body of the book as the rantings of a skeptic, agnostic, or deranged individual. It is precisely because of his faith that he feels compelled to evaluate this life honestly, if not less cheerfully than other Israelite thinkers.

The Book of Esther

The book of Esther is a remarkable narrative full of political intrigue, high drama, and suspense. It also makes an important but exceedingly subtle contribution to OT theology. In some ways, the presence of this little book is surprising in Israel's library. God is not mentioned here. Nor are there references to the worshipping life of the Jews living in Jerusalem, or to the requirements of the Torah. Instead, the book of Esther has all the markings of

a secular novel about Jews continuing to live in exile in the Persian Empire.

It is not surprising that both Jewish and Christian believers debated whether to include the book in the OT canon. In the end, the book's subtle portrait of the *Deus absconditus*, the hidden God, working and moving mysteriously through the actions of others, was accepted as an undercurrent throughout the narrative. Both traditions eventually recognized in the book of Esther a degree of interconnectedness with the rest of the OT, and it achieved canonical status.

One of the heroes of the story, Mordecai, had no idea that his act of kindness to the Persian king would result in protection for his life and the lives of others. Esther had no idea that her rise in the Persian king's harem would put her in a position to risk her life to save her people. But by the providence of God, Mordecai and Esther were used by God to save the Jews.

The original readers of the book were probably Jews still living in exile in Persia, late during the empire's history. The book encourages faithfulness among those living among the Persians far away from Jerusalem, away from the new temple with its sacrificial benefits, and seemingly far away from the blessings of Torah instruction and supervision. They certainly offered no threat to the might of the Persian Empire. Yet their unique religious convictions drew attention to the Jews as a distinct entity. Whether or not they were strict monotheists, their monolatry or exclusive worship of one God resulted in certain cultural differences that aroused the jealousy and even hatred of some Persians (see Esther 3:2–4). Although we have no historical specifics, we may assume that this novel is loosely based on an attempted pogrom against the Jews that took place late in the Persian period.

To get the point of the story, we must begin at its end, with the institution of the feast of Purim (Esther 9:18–10:3). The origins of this festival are obscure, but we may assume that it genuinely commemorates the reversal of a threat of annihilation against the Jews in Persia; it is celebrated on the fourteenth and fifteenth of Adar. The term *purim*, "lots," is derived from the Akkadian term *puru*, "lot," and refers to the lots cast by Haman in the story (3:7 and 9:24). The narrative then is told to explain the origins of the threat, the miraculous deliverance of the Jews, and therefore the origins of Purim.

The story begins with the rejection of Queen Vashti by King Ahasuerus (Xerxes, 486–465 BCE). As her replacement, the king chooses beautiful

Esther, an orphan who was the cousin and adopted daughter of Mordecai (2:7). Mordecai himself is portrayed as holding some official position in the royal palace, although we are given no details.[9] He learns of an assassination plot against the king (again the details of how he learns this are inconsequential) and passes the information to Ahasuerus through Esther (2:21–23). Mordecai essentially saves the life of King Ahasuerus, a detail that is then recorded in the royal annals, and presumably forgotten.

Mordecai, son of Kish from the tribe of Benjamin (2:5), represents Israel's first king, Saul (1 Samuel 10:21).[10] His nemesis in the book is Haman, the senior minister in the royal court, who is ironically identified as "the Agagite" (3:1). Jewish readers of the exile would have identified Haman immediately with King Agag of the Amalekites, the archenemies of ancient Israel (Exodus 17:8–16; Deuteronomy 25:17–19). King Saul had failed to take Yahweh's vengeance against the Amalekites and thereby lost his kingdom (1 Samuel 15:1–35). Now, these many centuries later, Mordecai, through his loving and devoted adopted daughter Esther, would be given another opportunity to defend God's people against adversaries.

When Mordecai refuses to pay homage to Haman, the latter plots to exterminate the Jews (3:6). Mordecai learns of the plot and advises Esther to intervene. In one of the classic speeches of OT literature, Mordecai explains that although Esther's secret identity as a Jewish woman will perish with

9 He sits "at the king's gate" (2:19,21; 3:2; and several more occurrences), and lived "in the citadel of Susa" (2:5) rather than simply in the city of Susa.
10 Saul also had a relative named Shimei (Esther 2:5 and 2 Samuel 16:5).

her, salvation for the Jews "will rise" from some other source (implying that God would still ensure the Jews' safety, while Esther herself would perish). In essence, this is an opportunity for Esther to be used by divine providence to save her people.

> *"Do not think that in the king's palace you will escape any more than all the other Jews. For if you keep silence at such a time as this, relief and deliverance will rise for the Jews from another quarter, but you and your father's family will perish. Who knows? Perhaps you have come to royal dignity for just such a time as this." (Esther 4:13–14)*

Esther agrees. By means of an elaborate ruse, she leads Haman to think that he is about to be honored by the king and queen. Meanwhile, Haman continues to be consumed by hatred of Mordecai and the Jews, and he orders the construction of a special gallows on which he plans to hang Mordecai (Esther 5).

The night before the morning on which Mordecai is to be hanged, King Ahasuerus has insomnia. He orders the royal annals to be read to him in order to lull him to sleep. It so happens that the portion of the annals read to him that night remind him that Mordecai had never been rewarded for saving the king's life from the assassination plot. On waking, King Ahasuerus asks his trusted prime minister, Haman, what honors should be bestowed on someone especially deserving of royal recognition and gratitude. Haman, thinking he was about to be honored even further by Ahasuerus, lists a number of attractive suggestions whereupon the king orders him to give them all to Mordecai (Esther 6).

The irony continues. Queen Esther finally reveals to Ahasuerus the plot against the Jews about to be carried out by Haman, and she pleads for her life and the life of her people. When Ahasuerus realizes what is happening, he orders Haman to be hanged on the very gallows Haman had constructed for Mordecai (Esther 7). While this at first appears to resolve all the tensions of the narrative, there remains one problem. The edict of Haman ordering the extermination of the Jews is a Medo-Persian law, which cannot be revoked (Esther 8:8; compare 1:19 and Daniel 6:8). Instead, King Ahasuerus grants Mordecai and the Jews freedom to defend themselves on the thirteenth of Adar (8:9–14). On the appointed day, a great victory is won against all the enemies of the Jews, including the ten sons of Haman (9:1–17). This victory is followed by a great celebration across the empire, instituting the Feast of Purim on the fourteenth of Adar in the countryside and on the fourteenth and fifteenth in the city of Susa (9:18–10:3).

When we turn to find historical details in the story, we encounter problems immediately, beginning with the identity of Queen Vashti. According to the Greek historian Herodotus, the wife of Xerxes was Amestris, and no mention is found of Vashti or Esther in the records (Herodotus, *hist.* 7.114; 9.109–112). While there are other puzzling historical features of the book, all become nearly insurmountable when we consider the likelihood that a Persian king would promote civil war within his own empire (Esther 8:8 and 9:11–12). We should probably read the book of Esther as a historical novel, a literary type in which enough historical details are given (such as the name of King Ahasuerus/Xerxes, and a possible pogrom at that time) to establish the fictive characters in time and place.

23.2. Ruins of Apadana Palace, Persepolis, Iran. The great palace begun by Darius the Great and completed by his son Xerxes thirty years later; it was used by the Persian king for official audiences. (Photo: © Arazu / Dreamstime.com)

Contributions of the Megilloth to Old Testament Faith

We don't have explicit statements of monotheism in the Megilloth. Yet these five scrolls combine to create an impression, which itself makes a well-defined contribution to the OT's religious expression of faith. That impression is simply that no aspect of life as experienced and explored by the Israelites was perceived as outside the bounds of faith. Whether one is examining the puzzling ambiguities of life (Ecclesiastes), or the joy of the Purim celebration (Esther), or sexual intimacy (Song of Songs), or sorrow (Lamentations), all are incorporated into life with God.

Beyond this impression, we might explore further the subtle way divine providence is assumed in the books of Ruth and Esther. In the book of Ruth nothing in human affairs occurs as mere chance (Ruth 2:3). Chance, or the occurrence of accidental happenings with no observable or contrasting causes, is easier to explain in a polytheistic context. But for the book of Ruth, no chance happenings are observed at all. We look in vain for an explicit statement of monotheism here. Yet the singularity of Israel's worship of Yahweh makes the occurrence of chance an ironic feature of the book's rhetoric.

Divine providence also comes to the foreground in the book of Esther, which does not even use the word "God" or "Yahweh." Mordecai providentially intervened in the assassination plot against the Persian king, which eventually made it possible for him to intervene on behalf of God's people when they were threatened with extermination. His compelling speech to Esther at the turning point in the book articulates the belief that salvation would arise for the Jews from some other quarter, if not from Esther or himself (4:14). The narrator implicitly sides with providence by asserting that it was the *very night* before Mordecai's scheduled execution that Ahasuerus was unable to sleep, and the selection of readings from the royal annals *just happened* to include the portion about Mordecai's heroic efforts to save the king (6:1). The assumption that divine providence is at work is not the same as monotheism. Yet the presence of monotheism, or at least monolatrous henotheism, results in a more emphatic conviction about divine providence in these books than we would expect otherwise.

WHERE TO FIND MORE

Commentaries: The best technical and advanced commentaries on these books are, for **Song of Songs**: Tremper Longman, *Song of Songs* (New International Critical Commentary on the Old Testament; Grand Rapids, Mich.: Eerdmans, 2001), Roland E. Murphy, *The Song of Songs: A Commentary on the Book of Canticles or the Song of Songs* (Hermeneia; Minneapolis, Minn.: Fortress Press, 1990); for the book of **Ruth**: Robert L. Hubbard, *The Book of Ruth* (New International Critical Commentary on the Old Testament; Grand Rapids, Mich.: Eerdmans, 1988), Jack M. Sasson, *Ruth: A New Translation with a Philological Commentary and a Formalist-Folklorist Interpretation* (JHNES; Baltimore: Johns Hopkins University Press, 1979); for the book of **Lamentations**: F. W. Dobbs-Allsopp, *Lamentations* (Louisville, Ky.: John Knox Press, 2002); for the book of **Ecclesiastes**: Michael V. Fox, *A Time to Tear Down and A Time to Build Up: A Rereading of Ecclesiastes* (Grand Rapids, Mich.: Eerdmans, 1999), Tremper Longman, *The Book of Ecclesiastes* (New International Commentary on the Old Testament; Grand Rapids, Mich.: Eerdmans, 1998), C. L. Seow, *Ecclesiastes: A New Translation with Introduction and Commentary* (Anchor Bible 18C; New York: Doubleday, 1997); for the book of **Esther**: Frederic W. Bush, *Ruth, Esther* (Word Biblical Commentary 9; Dallas: Word Books, 1996), Jon D. Levenson, *Esther: A Commentary* (Old Testament Library; Louisville, Ky.: Westminster John Knox Press, 1997).

Fox, Michael V. *The Song of Songs and the Ancient Egyptian Love Songs*. Madison, Wis.: University of Wisconsin Press, 1985.

Lambert, W. G. "Some New Babylonian Wisdom Literature." Pages 30–42 in *Wisdom in Ancient Israel: Essays in Honour of J. A. Emerton*. Edited by John Day, Rorbert P. Gordon, and H. G. M. Williamson. Cambridge: Cambridge University Press, 1995.

Important discussion of the Dialogue of Pessimism, pages 36–42.

Lambert, W. G. *Babylonian Wisdom Literature*. Winona Lake, Ind.,: Eisenbrauns, 1996 [1960].

CHAPTER 24

The Old Testament Today

In this final chapter, we will summarize the OT and explore its lasting contributions to world history, society in general, and the monotheistic religions of Judaism, Christianity, and Islam. Specifically, we will explore four particular aspects of the OT, and examine how each functions to create a cohesive and living whole.

This overview in turn will remind us that the OT's central message communicates, in a host of ways, what it perceives as Israel's life in covenant relationship with God, obeying God's Torah, and living morally and ethically in right relationship with other human beings. Within this overarching concern of the OT, we have already observed the continual thread of a monotheistic worldview in process. The development of the OT's conviction of the singularity of God is indeed among the most enduring contributions to human history.

Similarly, the OT's contribution to civil society cannot be underestimated. Thus, in conclusion, we will explore three core values in particular that are rooted, not in secularization as often is assumed, but in the rich and enduring legacy of the OT.

So we have come to the end of our walk through ancient Israel's library. The books of this library, collected as they are in the OT, constitute one of the most important documents of all time. The OT is an essential resource for our understanding of ancient history. It provides rich insight into human civilization before the Greco-Roman period (i.e., before Classical antiquity), and of course, the OT is especially important for a study of the history of religious thought and expression.

The OT's historical importance is just the beginning. It would be naïve to think of the OT as an archaeological artifact, some relic from the distant past reflecting only a dead civilization. That would limit its significance to a narrow study of history. But the OT has another significance that makes it current, and relevant for the world in which we live today. Millions of readers around the globe continue to accept the OT as the word of God, which gives it a timeless relevance that we cannot ignore.

I said in the first sentence of this textbook, that "what you think about God – if you think about God at all – affects nearly everything else you believe to be true." This is why the OT is such a monumental document of religious significance. Much of what people believe about God was expressed first in the OT, and is foundational for the rest. Whether you are a believer of the Jewish, Christian, or Muslim traditions, a secularist, or not sure what you think, the message of the OT continues to be relevant for the world in which you live. This chapter will summarize what we've studied in the OT and then will offer a few final reflections on the relevance of the OT for you today.

ANATOMY OF THE OLD TESTAMENT

As you know by now, the diverse materials of the OT cannot be summarized in a brief paragraph or two. One helpful analogy is to consider the various anatomical systems of a living organism, such as the human body. Our bodies are made of a skeletal system, a nervous system, a cardiovascular system, and several others. In many ways, the OT is like a living organism with several anatomical systems, so I'll use these as a way to summarize the content and message of the OT.

The *skeletal system* is the scaffolding providing support for the rest of the organism. It is also helpful to remember that the skeleton determines the overall shape and scope of the organism. When we consider how this relates to the OT, we might think of the Primary History as the OT's skeletal system. The metanarrative from Genesis to 2 Kings provides the historical framework on which the rest is formed. Israel's story begins with the ancestral narratives, prefaced by the creation of the cosmos and primordial events. The story concludes in the restoration period of Persian history.

The metanarrative of the Primary History includes both the actions of Yahweh in Israel's national story and the instruction of Yahweh for Israel's life with him; both Torah story and Torah instruction (Chapters 7–8). The story recounts Israel's history, its land and kings, its successes and failures, and its reformulation as the province of Yehud in the Persian period (Chapters 12–15). This is the foundational structure for the whole OT. Such a grand sweep of history does not attempt to explain directly what Israel thinks about God. Instead, the individual narrative stories and the extended metanarrative they create *show* rather than *tell* us about God. They provide the shape and scope for the rest.

The *nervous system* is the location of thinking and coordinates all the actions of the organism. The brain and spinal cord serve as the body's control center for the nervous system, transmitting signals throughout the body. An organism's nervous system provides guidance and direction by means of electrochemical impulses throughout the rest of the body. You might find it helpful to think of certain creeds or explicit assertions about the character of Yahweh as the OT's nervous system. These creeds are found throughout the OT, and they essentially present the cumulative wisdom of ancient Israel about God based on the actions of God in Israel's history.

Most of these creeds seem to go back to an original affirmation of faith found in Exodus 34:6–7, an assertion about the very nature of God.

> (6) Yahweh, Yahweh,
> a God merciful and gracious,
> slow to anger,
> and abounding in steadfast love and faithfulness,
>
> (7) keeping steadfast love for the thousandth generation,
> forgiving iniquity and transgression and sin,
> yet by no means clearing the guilty,
> but visiting the iniquity of the parents upon the children
> and the children's children,
> to the third and the fourth generation. (Exodus 34:6–7)

This ancient creed highlights Yahweh's attributes. His grace and compassionate forgiveness (v. 6) are balanced by retributive justice (v. 7). This profound text summarizes what Israel has learned about Yahweh, and their authors return to this affirmation frequently in other sermons and assertions elsewhere in the OT.[1] This might be considered the official thinking about God — the orthodox theological conviction — providing guidance and direction for the whole. These first two components of the OT — the metanarrative and the creeds, or the skeletal and nervous systems — can be observed grammatically as well, through the use of verbs and adjectives. The

narrative conventionally uses verbs to narrate the actions of Yahweh, and the creeds use adjectives to explain his character.[2]

An organism's *cardiovascular system* provides its lifeblood through the heart and a network of arteries and veins. You should think of the speeches of Moses in the book of Deuteronomy as the heart of the OT, especially the general exhortations of Deuteronomy 5–11 (review Chapter 9). These speeches create a new relational ethic for the ancient Israelites, urging them to love Yahweh and fear him, to remember, follow, and serve him, and to cling to him, swearing by his name and worshipping him. In this way, all one's emotions and personal resources are combined in a singular and focused commitment to Yahweh, to live according to his commands and treat others with respect and compassion.[3] And as we have seen, this relational ethic is memorably summed up in the Shema's command: "Love Yahweh your God with all your heart, and with all your soul, and with all your might" (Deuteronomy 6:5; review Chapter 9).

This ethical dimension of Israel's covenant relationship with Yahweh pulsates throughout the rest of the OT. These are the moral values of the Sinai covenant, defining Israel's relationship with Yahweh in terms of integrity and right conduct. The first two features of our summary — the metanarrative and creeds of the OT — focus on Israel's understanding of God. These are intellectual convictions

---

1 For the way these verses have been revised and interpreted in other OT texts, see pages 335–50 in Fishbane in "Where to Find More" in this chapter.

2 This way of thinking about OT theology has been explored in pages 145–228 in Brueggemann in "Where to Find More" in this chapter.

3 For the way these commands to love and fear Yahweh, etc., combine to define Israel's covenant relationship with God, see Bill T. Arnold, "The Love-Fear Antinomy in Deuteronomy 5–11," *Vetus Testamentum* 61 (2011): 551–69.

about God's essential nature and personal characteristics. But this third component, the heart of the
OT, explores the practical and behavioral aspects
of relating to Yahweh. What difference should it
make to live in covenant relationship with a God
understood in this way? This ethical lifeblood of
the OT is Israel's answer.

Our bodies have several other anatomical systems. The final one to consider in this summary of
the OT is the *muscular system*, which makes it possible for an organism to move through life. Muscles
in the body provide strength, balance, and motion
by responding to impulses in the nervous system.
In a sense, the rest of the OT is a collection of
Israel's responses through centuries of experiences
based on their theological and ethical understanding of God. The authors move, adapt, and respond
according to the creeds and ethical demands of the
Sinai covenant.

The prophets affirm Israel's early creedal convictions about God and apply the ethical demands of
their relationship with God to numerous life situations. Israel's theology is in motion in the books of
prophecy (Chapters 19–21). Each prophet applies
the truths of the Torah to new circumstances of
history, sometimes deriving new meanings and
moving Israel's understanding in new directions.
Eventually, the prophets (or perhaps wisdom sages
under Persian influence) were responsible for push-
ing the ultimate meaning of their understanding
of God into the distant future in a new literary
form, apocalypticism (Chapter 22). The OT's
other "writings" (wisdom literature, Chapter 17;
psalms, 18; and the Megilloth, 23) are further ways
in which OT authors fleshed out their theology in
the affairs of everyday life. They were unafraid to

move into any and every aspect of life with their
convictions about Yahweh. Israelite theology, as
preserved in the pages of the OT, was all-inclusive
in its agenda for life with God.

ENDURING CONTRIBUTIONS OF THE OLD TESTAMENT

We have seen that the OT is not expressly a monotheistic document. We did not find the idea of
monotheism expressed in its overarching structure
(the skeleton outline of the Primary History). Nor
is monotheism stated in Israel's central theological
tenets (the creedal nervous system), nor in the ethical convictions of the Sinai covenant (the heartbeat of the OT). Yet the *origins* of monotheism
are clearly present in all these places in the form
of Israel's monolatrous henotheism. Eventually,
monotheism itself was articulated by the prophets,
especially Isaiah of the exile, as Israel moved forward into its later history.[4]

The Israelite thinkers and writers who gave us
the OT were focused on the relational aspects of
life with God. Their primary concern was developing faithful devotion to Yahweh, the God of Israel,
among fellow Israelites, at the exclusion of all other
deities. They simply had no need until late in their
history to articulate the concept of monotheism.
In this way, the OT's message is *more than* a philosophical formulation of monotheism. It arrives at
the conclusion that only one God exists, but this
isn't the OT's central message. Rather, the OT is
more interested in understanding what it means to

---

4 And we found a few other expressions of monotheism,
especially in Deuteronomy and selected Psalms.

live in covenant relationship with God, obeying his laws, nurturing and safeguarding the relationship, and living ethically with other humans, especially "foreigners, widows, and orphans," those vulnerable in their society. This message is its contribution to faith communities flowing from the OT itself, among Jewish, Christian, and Muslim believers.

The OT legacy in our times goes beyond even this central message. Its conviction about the singularity of God is a contribution to world history important for all of us to remember, irrespective of our faith positions. Everyone in today's world, whether Jew, Christian, Muslim, Buddhist, Hindu, secularist, or undecided, is impacted by the concept that only one God exists. At the beginning of our study, I called monotheism "Israel's gift to the world," one to be compared to Greece's legacy in philosophy, Egypt's in art and architecture, or Babylon's in astronomy and literature (Chapter 1). In fact, we have seen how Israel's monotheism was a linchpin development in world history during a "time of spiritual genius" known as the Axial Age (ca. 800–200 BCE).[5] Israel came to understand God as alone in his divinity – the One God – which was a decisive insight of the Axial Age. Israel's contribution changed the world, and continues to nourish human thought and development.

It can be reasonably argued that monotheism is the single most significant innovation in human history.[6] The social consequences of

monotheism – both good and bad – cannot be denied. Contrary to what you might think, and most likely to what you have been taught, modern science emerged in sixteenth-century Europe precisely *because* of the contributions of Judeo-Christian monotheism, not in spite of them. Science was not born, as is often assumed, when modern thinkers finally threw off the blinders of religious ignorance. Quite the contrary. In fact, science is a direct result of theological assumptions unique to Judeo-Christian formulations in Europe, explaining why science was born only in Europe. As it turns out, science and religion are not incompatible after all, but have always been inseparable. Ironically, today's debate pitting religion and science against each other misses entirely this historical link between monotheism's heirs in Europe and the birth of science. Monotheism is Israel's gift to the world, and science is its delayed benefit.

And that's not all. Until recently, we have completely underestimated the impact of the OT in constructing our contemporary world. Consider three values we most often assume to be central and foundational for civil society: (1) the notion of individual rights and liberties; (2) the conviction that people have the right to govern themselves without a monarch or dictator; and (3) the separation of church and state, which ensures religious tolerance. These three are features of modern political thought. Few among us would debate their importance.

We usually assume, and are often taught, that we arrived at these great values through a process of secularization. Medieval and Renaissance Europe were incapable of such advances, we are told, because they were so thoroughly religious,

---

5 Review Armstrong in "Where to Find More" in Chapter 3. The identification of the Axial Age as a time of "spiritual genius" is her assessment (p. 397).

6 This has, in fact, been the argument of Rodney Stark in a two-volume work; see Stark in "Where to Find More" in this chapter.

especially Christian. Then, in the sixteenth and seventeenth centuries, the birth of science was part of a philosophical separation in which religion was partitioned and excluded from the exploration of political theory and the investigation of most other topics. This separation, we are led to believe, eventually produced our modern values, implying that liberty, freedom, and tolerance are only possible when religion is suppressed. One might easily conclude that secularization saved modern society from the straightjacket of religion itself.

Most of us are not aware of how profoundly we have accepted this story. But an important recent study has proven that the story is completely false.[7] Ironically, the values of our modern societies are not the result of secularization but rather the result of deep reflection on the OT itself. The values we embrace so heartily are the result not of a *separation from* religion but of a *reformation of* religion. As a result of the Protestant Reformation, Christian scholarship in Europe turned to the OT for guidance on the way modern states should be governed. The sixteenth and seventeenth centuries witnessed a revival of the Hebrew language, and scholars sought to understand the text of the OT through investigation of the Hebrew and Aramaic manuscripts. For help in the process, Christian scholars turned to Jewish rabbinical interpreters with their centuries-long tradition of OT exegesis. Such interaction and dependence on the OT and Jewish resources for interpreting the OT changed the way scholarship was done in Europe.

The new Christian scholarship relied on Jewish interpretation of OT texts to conclude that Israel's request for a king in 1 Samuel 8 was sinful idolatry. This eventually led to the conclusion that all monarchies were undesirable and that republics were the only legitimate form of government. This was no less than "a crucial turning point in the history of European political thought."[8] Further reflection by Christian scholars of this period on the OT's plan for fairness in land use and wealth distribution in ancient Israel transformed the way people thought about the right of a state to limit private wealth in order to ensure the fair distribution of wealth. Others explored the OT and rabbinic interpretations of biblical laws allowing unbelievers and strangers to live in the land undisturbed, so long as they agreed to follow certain laws and regulations, which resulted in a commitment to religious tolerance in open societies. Our concept of religious tolerance emerged from deeply held religious study of the OT text. Secularization was not required.

Given this understanding of the OT's role in European Christian scholarship of the sixteenth and seventeenth centuries, it is more likely that the values of the world we live in today were called into being not by the suppression of religion but by deeply held religious convictions. In this way, the "traditional narrative" that our contemporary values are based on secularization "will have to be significantly revised, if not discarded."[9] In this process, the role of the OT will need to be remembered, not only in its legacy of monotheism for the faith communities of the world but also for its contributions to nearly every aspect of our lives together.

7 The important work to which I refer here is that of Nelson in "Where to Find More" in this chapter.

8 Page 3 of Nelson in "Where to Find More" in this chapter.
9 The quote is from page 5 of Nelson in "Where to Find More" in this chapter.

24.1. Old Testament (Photo: Bill T. Arnold)

As I said at the beginning of this chapter, the OT is not an archaeological artifact, as though it represents some relic from a dead civilization. It continues to be a foundational document for the religious convictions of millions of people. Beyond this, the OT's expression of monotheism changed the world in ways that we are continuing to explore. Its influence on the birth of science and modern political theory are relatively new areas of investigation. Whatever else you think about ancient Israel's library, it continues to demand our attention after all these centuries.

WHERE TO FIND MORE

Berman, Joshua. *Created Equal: How the Bible Broke with Ancient Political Thought.* Oxford and New York: Oxford University Press, 2008.

Brueggemann, Walter. *Theology of the Old Testament: Testimony, Dispute, Advocacy.* Minneapolis, Minn.: Fortress Press, 1997.

The verbs in Israel's narrative portrayal of Yahweh's character include "creating," "making promises," "saving," "commanding," and "leading" (pp. 145–212); the creedal adjectives repeated frequently in the OT stem from Exodus 34:6–7 (pp. 213–28).

Fishbane, Michael A. *Biblical Interpretation in Ancient Israel.* Oxford: Clarendon Press, 1988.

Nelson, Eric. *The Hebrew Republic: Jewish Sources and the Transformation of European Political Thought.* Cambridge, Mass.: Harvard University Press, 2010.

Explains the processes followed by Christian political thinkers and theorists of sixteenth- and seventeenth-century Europe. The Protestant Reformation heightened the importance of turning to OT texts in their original languages of Hebrew and Aramaic. To understand the text better, these authors relied on the Jewish community, especially in Holland, where the influence of rabbinic exegesis was felt most profoundly. The result was a revolution in political thinking, in which the OT had a profound influence on the foundations of modern democracies.

Stark, Rodney. *One True God: Historical Consequences of Monotheism*. Princeton, N.J.: Princeton University Press, 2001.

Stark, Rodney. *For the Glory of God: How Monotheism Led to Reformations, Science, Witch-hunts, and the End of Slavery*. Princeton, N.J.: Princeton University Press, 2003.

This second volume of Stark's two-volume work shows how monotheism made possible the birth of science in sixteenth-century Europe and led eventually to the abolition of slavery. His work clearly traces also how a number of the same reasonable leaders who argued against slavery engaged in violent witch-hunting. His first volume (2001) outlines the nature and rise of monotheism, and its earlier social consequences.

GLOSSARY

Amphictyony refers to a league or confederation of tribes organized around a deity's shrine. It is sometimes used to refer to the league of Israelite tribes during the OT period of Judges. (See Sidebar 13.5.)

Apocalyptic (apocalypse) describes a type of literature that self-consciously reveals divine truth, often in a narrative framework. The English word "apocalypse" comes from the Greek word *apokálypsis*, meaning "revelation." The revelation is explained by a celestial being or angel to the human recipient. Such divine revelation makes known a reality that transcends present experience with regard to both time and space.

Apocrypha is from a Greek word meaning "hidden things" and refers to a group of noncanonical (or deuterocanonical) books. Fourteen such books were considered valuable early Jewish literature but were excluded from the Masoretic Text of the Hebrew Bible. They were included in the Greek Septuagint and Latin Vulgate translations, and are still contained in certain canonical traditions.

Asherah is the Mother Goddess and sometimes wife of the Canaanite El or the female consort of Baal. Asherah is commonly associated with sacred trees of poles. The word "asherah" in Hebrew is sometimes the name of the goddess, but it also occurs as a noun for the sacred wooden pole.

Axial Age is an era from approximately 800 to 200 BCE, also referred to as the Mythical Age. It is especially identified as a period of spiritual development in human history – even a turning point.

Baal was the god of storm and lightning, rider of the clouds, and provider of fertility for the soil. The Canaanite-Phoenician term *baal* means "lord" or "master."

Bronze Age designates a period of history that is further divided into the Early (3300–2000 BCE), Middle (2000–1550 BCE), and Late (1550–1200 BCE) Bronze Ages. It is preceded by the Chalcolithic (Copper-Stone) Age and followed by the Iron Age.

Canonical criticism is an approach related to rhetorical criticism and attempts to interpret the OT in light of the way it has been shaped to serve as Scripture in a believing or worshipping community. Those who use the approach tend to seek the meaning of a text or a book based on the way it has been embedded in the canonical context, and they often draw theological or religious significance from the readings.

Chronistic History refers to a collection of Israel's historical writings and is comprised of 1–2 Chronicles and Ezra-Nehemiah. It represents an updated and revised history from that of the **Primary History**. The author(s) is often referred to as the Chronicler.

Cisjordan is a designation for the territory west of the Jordan River in the land of Canaan that was occupied by nine and one-half tribes of Israel.

Cosmogony is a designation for a tradition of the origin or birth of the universe. Ancient Near East examples locate the universe's origin in a great conflict between old and young gods. The younger gods win, and kingship and cosmic order are established.

Cosmology is a theory or specific model for understanding the structure and dynamics of the physical universe. The content of Genesis 1–11 is an expression of Israel's cosmology.

Court History, also called the "Succession Narrative," refers to materials found in 2 Samuel 9–20 and 1 Kings 1–2 (accounts of David's reign and Solomon's succession to the throne) and is identified as an original source by OT scholars.

Covenant, at a basic level, is defined by bilateral agreements between parties that are not symmetrical in their requirements, that is, they do not require the same obligations for both parties. The agreements are intended to bind two parties intimately together in a relationship perceived as mutually exclusive. The concept is central to the OT for understanding the relationship between Yahweh and Israel.

Cuneiform is a wedge-shaped script found in ancient Mesopotamia, originating in Sumer around 3000 BCE.

Cyrus Cylinder is a Persian source that dates to approximately 539–530 BCE and highlights the actions of King Cyrus. Written in a Babylonian dialect of the time, the text is a declaration of good kingship. It describes Cyrus's victory over Babylon, as well as his policy of tolerance toward conquered peoples and the reconstruction of their religious sanctuaries.

Deutero-Isaiah, also known as Second-Isaiah, is the term commonly used to refer to Isaiah 40–66 (or just 40–55), which exhibit a different historical location and time than chapters 1–39. Scholars have long recognized elements of literary and thematic continuity as well as discontinuity between the two parts.

Deuteronomistic History is the name given to a so-called second history that begins with Deuteronomy, thus the name, and covers the series of books Deuteronomy, Joshua, Judges, 1 and 2 Samuel, and 1 and 2 Kings. Deuteronomy establishes the themes and theological agenda that stretch across the entire series of books/narrative, namely, covenant theology.

Dextrograde denotes the direction of writing from left to right, like English and unlike Hebrew.

Documentary Hypothesis is based on the theoretical existence of four separate sources or documents in the formulation of the Pentateuch, referred to by the letters *J, E, D,* and *P.*

Elohist is the name given to one of Israel's historians, whose writing is distinctive for its use of the Hebrew term *Elohim* to refer to God. The Elohist's writing may have been combined with that of the Yahwist. There is some current doubt as to whether an Elohist source existed as an independent document.

Enneateuch refers to the nine books (Greek *ennea* is "nine" and *teuchos*, "scroll") included in the **Primary History.**

Enthronement psalms is a category of praise hymns in the book of Psalms extolling God's kingship.

Enuma Elish is the Akkadian title (from its opening words, "when above") for the Babylonian creation epic. Its central theme is the exaltation of Babylon's patron god, Marduk.

Epigraphy refers to ancient texts that have been preserved – usually on potsherds, stone, or animal skins. (See Sidebar 19.1.)

Eschatology denotes a theory of final or end things.

Fertile Crescent is an arch-shaped, arable swath of land that stretches from Mesopotamia westward and south through the Levant and down to Egypt.

Form criticism is the study of small literary units that are classified according to their genre and function in a specific sociological setting, or "situation in life" (German, *Sitz im Leben*). Hermann Gunkel is considered the "father" of form criticism. (See Figure 18.2.)

Gilgamesh Epic, a poem from ancient Iraq, describes the adventures of its hero, Gilgamesh. Its twelve tablets represent the longest, and perhaps greatest literary composition from Mesopotamia, comparable in literary grandeur to Homer's *Odyssey*. (See Plate IV.)

Hermeneutics refers to the discipline that establishes theories and methods for interpretation.

Hieroglyphics is a system of writing using pictorial symbols, often combined with alphabetic elements such as that used in ancient Egypt, to represent meaning or sounds, or combinations of meaning and sounds.

Iron Age is the era in history from approximately 1200 to 539 BCE; it can be furthered divided in Iron I, IIA, IIB, and IIC. (See Table 3.1.)

Levant refers to the western region of the Near East, including the modern countries of Syria, Lebanon, Israel, Palestine, and Jordan.

Mari is a city on the Euphrates River, in which many texts of the second millennium have been discovered.

Masoretic Text is the traditional medieval text of the Hebrew Bible. It is named for the Masoretes, who meticulously preserved and worked through the sacred texts.

Merneptah Stela dates from approximately 1207 BCE and is named for the Egyptian pharaoh who is commemorating the defeat of several Canaanite nations. It includes the earliest mention of "Israel" and thus seems to confirm their presence in Canaan during Iron Age I.

Messiah derives from the Hebrew word meaning "anointed one." OT kings (e.g., David; 1 Samuel 16:1–13) and priests were "anointed" (with oil) to set them apart for their roles.

Moabite Stone, or Victory Stela of Mesha, king of Moab (ca. 830 BCE), commemorates the construction of a sanctuary and expresses gratitude to Chemosh, the god of Moab, for victories over Israel. The inscription includes a reference to the house of David. (See Figure 15.2 and Sidebar 15.3.)

Monolatrous henotheism expresses Torah's call for an exclusive commitment to serve one God, while not denying the existence of other gods.

Monotheism, as generally used today, expresses the belief in only one God and denies the existence of multiple deities. (See Sidebar 1.3.)

Nomism denotes the establishment of ethics based on moral law.

Pantheism refers to a system in which God is equated with the universe itself.

Pentateuch denotes the first five books of the Bible, also known as the Torah, or the books of Moses.

Persian Empire (also known as the Achaemenid Empire) was ruled by the Achaemenid dynasty for more than two hundred years (550–330 BCE). It represented the largest empire the world had ever seen until it was conquered by Alexander the Great of Macedon, reaching as far west as Egypt and the Hellespont (where Europe and Asia meet at the Aegean Sea), across the ancient Near East to northern India in the east. Administratively, it was divided into provinces governed by Persian officials known as satraps.

Postexilic Chronistic History is the OT's third extended historical narrative. Composed after the exile, it thus seeks to justify the restoration of Israel and encourage the inhabitants of the former land of Israel – now the Persian province Yehud. It focuses primarily on the importance of worship in the newly rebuilt temple and seeks to establish the restored Israel as a continuation of the old, and as legitimate heir and successor of preexilic Israel.

Primary History consists of the nine-book account of Israel's story from the creation to the exile. Sometimes considered "The First Bible," it includes the books of Genesis, Exodus, Leviticus, Numbers, Deuteronomy, Joshua, Judges, 1–2 Samuel (as one book), and 1–2 Kings (as one book). The collective term is based on intentional interconnections between the books and an overall unifying theme.

Primeval History is the term for the content of Genesis 1–11.

Primogeniture denotes a social practice of inheritance whereby a family's accumulated wealth and status is passed down to the eldest son.

Redaction criticism is a methodology devoted to an investigation of the editorial process for the biblical text. Its concern is the way early sources may have been selected, arranged, expanded, and combined into the final form we have today in the OT. (See Sidebar 18.3.)

Retribution theology is a foundational concept of the Deuteronomistic History that maintains, in relationship to Deuteronomy's covenant theology, that rejection of God and failure to keep the covenant results in death and despair. It is also a characteristic of some of Israel's wisdom literature.

Rhetorical criticism focuses on the OT as an organic whole, exploring its artistic integrity as a literary creation. Sometimes known as *synchronic criticism*, this approach gives less attention to the historical background of the oral or literary sources of the texts and attempts to explore instead the intentionality of structure and literary unity of OT books. (See Sidebar 18.3.)

Septuagint is the Greek translation of the Hebrew OT. It is the oldest and most important translation of the OT, and began with a translation of the Pentateuch translated by Jewish scholars in Alexandria, Egypt, in the third century BCE. Commonly abbreviated as LXX, the name *Septuagint* comes from a legend asserting that about seventy scholars translated the Pentateuch into Greek. Translations of the other books occurred over the following two centuries.

Shiloh refers to a place in the territory of the Israelite tribe of Ephraim. It was considered the legitimate center of Yahweh worship during the early years of Israel's life, prior to the monarchy (during the period of the judges).

Sinistrograde is the term for the direction of writing from right to left, as in Hebrew.

Source criticism is a methodology that focuses on the underlying literary sources of the present text. The assumption is that ancient literary compositions often combined or absorbed other, older texts; thus, it divides the book into its component parts and attempts to identify the relative dates of these parts.

Tanak is the acronym based on the three parts of the Hebrew Bible: the Torah (Pentateuch), the Neviim (the Prophets), and the Ketuvim (the Writings).

Targum is the Aramaic, interpretive translation made of the Hebrew texts.

Ten Commandments are also known as the Decalogue and refer to the collection of ten laws that Yahweh inscribed on stone tablets and gave to Moses. (Cf. Exodus 20:1–7; Deuteronomy 5:6–21.)

Textual criticism is an important methodology concerned with the process of text transmission and the reconstruction, as much as possible, of the literary product standing at the beginning of the transmission process.

Theocracy means literally a "rule by God," and it generally refers to a society or state in which the priests or authorities govern in the name of a deity. The classic statement of Israel's official theocracy occurs in the words of Gideon: "I will not rule over you, and my son will not rule over you; Yahweh will rule over you" (Judges 8:23).

Theodicy is defined in theology and philosophy as the attempt to justify the goodness of God (or the gods) in the face of evil and suffering in the world.

Theogony is a type of creation account that explains the universe by recounting the birth and succession of the gods, especially those gods perceived as ancient and influential at the beginning.

Theophoric (names) among ancient Semitic names often use a verbal idea in the person's name together with the name of a god as a noun in an implied sentence. For example, Elijah means "Yahweh is My God," the *–jah* ending being an abbreviated form of "Yahweh."

Tradition criticism is an all-encompassing endeavor devoted to an investigation of the way older texts have been taken up, (re)interpreted, and incorporated in new texts. It is a subcategory of *historical criticism*, which attempts to reconstruct the events and history behind the OT text as much as possible. (See Sidebar 18.3.)

United Monarchy refers to Israel's monarchy under its first three kings, Saul, David, and Solomon. After Solomon's reign, the monarchy was divided between the northern kingdom of Israel and the southern kingdom of Judah.

Universalism when used in OT studies refers to the idea that Yahweh's authority as God extends to all nations, not just to Israel alone.

Vaticinium ex eventu is a Latin expression meaning "prophecy after the fact." It refers to a literary technique that is characteristic of apocalyptic literature in which a historical event known to the author is described in future predictive language. Daniel 11 best exemplifies this type of "prophetic hindsight" in the OT.

Vulgate is a Latin translation of the Bible that was completed by Jerome in 405 CE. It became the standard edition of the Bible for a thousand years.

Yahweh represents a pronounced form of Israel's name for God, which is represented in the Hebrew Bible almost seven thousand times as YHWH (the *tetragrammaton*).

Yahwist is the name given to the author/compiler of that part of Israel's history distinguished by its use of "YHWH," or "Yahweh," as the sacred name for God. The so-called first Israelite historian (the oldest stratum in the Pentateuch) may have originated in the southern kingdom of Judah in the eighth or ninth century BCE. The work of this author is referred to as the *Yahwistic History*, and "J" is used for the original Yahwist's source.

Yehud is the name of the Persian province that included Jerusalem and the Levant region, and to which the community of Jews returned from their exile in Babylon.

Zion theology, also known as the "Zion tradition," makes three assumptions: Yahweh is the Great King, David and his descendants are human representatives of Yahweh on earth, and Yahweh has chosen Jerusalem/Zion as his earthly dwelling place. In the OT, those who held this position maintained that the covenant with God guaranteed salvation and believed that Jerusalem and the sacred Temple Mount, Zion, were incapable of falling to the enemy because Yahweh committed himself to preserving them forever. The name "Zion" is an old synonym for Jerusalem itself. (See Sidebar 15.2.)

BIBLIOGRAPHY

So much has been written about the Old Testament that no bibliography can be thought of as complete. Instead, you will find here a brief list of additional resources you might find helpful for going deeper in your study of the Old Testament. A few of these books have been included in this textbook under sections called "Where to Find More." Others are recommended here for the first time.

1. Translations

Common English Bible (CEB). Nashville: Common English Bible, 2011.

New Revised Standard Version (NRSV). New York: Division of Christian Education of the National Council of the Churches of Christ in the USA, 1989.

Pietersma, Albert., and Wright, Benjamin G., eds. A New English Translation of the Septuagint: And the Other Greek Translations Traditionally Included Under That Title. New York and Oxford: Oxford University Press, 2007.

Tanakh: A New Translation of the Holy Scriptures according to the Traditional Hebrew Text. Philadelphia: Jewish Publication Society, 1985.

2. Introductory Matters

Soulen, Richard N., and R. Kendall Soulen. Handbook of Biblical Criticism. 4th ed. Louisville, Ky.: Westminster John Knox Press, 2011.

Tate, W. Randolph. Interpreting the Bible: A Handbook of Terms and Methods. Peabody, Mass.: Hendrickson Publishers, 2006.

Vriezen, T. C., and A. S. van der Woude. Ancient Israelite and Early Jewish Literature. Translated by Brian Doyle. Leiden and Boston: Brill, 2005.

3. Geography

Aharoni, Yohanan. The Land of the Bible: A Historical Geography. 2nd ed. Philadelphia: Westminster, 1979.

Pritchard, James B. The HarperCollins Concise Atlas of the Bible. San Francisco: HarperSanFrancisco, 1997.

Rainey, Anson F., and R. Steven Notley. The Sacred Bridge: Carta's Atlas of the Biblical World. Jerusalem: Carta, 2006.

4. Archaeology

Levy, Thomas Evan, ed. The Archaeology of Society in the Holy Land. New York: Facts on File, 1995.

Mazar, Amihai. Archaeology of the Land of the Bible, 10,000–586 B.C.E. Anchor Bible Reference Library. New York: Doubleday, 1990.

Meyers, Eric M., ed. The Oxford Encyclopedia of Archaeology in the Near East. New York: Oxford University Press, 1997.

Stern, Ephraim. *Archaeology of the Land of the Bible: The Assyrian, Babylonian, and Persian Periods, 732–332 BCE*. Anchor Bible Reference Library. New York: Doubleday, 2001.

5. History: The Ancient Near East

Edwards, I. E. S., and John Boardman, eds. *The Cambridge Ancient History*. 3rd ed. 14 vols. Cambridge: Cambridge University Press, 1970.

Kuhrt, Amélie. *The Ancient Near East, C. 3000–330 BC*. London: Routledge, 1994.

Sasson, Jack M., ed. *Civilizations of the Ancient Near East*. 4 vols. New York: Scribner, 1995.

6. History: Ancient Israel

Arnold, Bill T., and Richard S. Hess, eds. *Ancient Israel's History: An Introduction to Issues and Sources*. Grand Rapids, Mich.: Baker, 2014.

Coogan, Michael D., ed. *The Oxford History of the Biblical World*. New York: Oxford University Press, 1998.

Grabbe, Lester L. *Ancient Israel: What Do We Know and How Do We Know it?* London and New York: T & T Clark, 2007.

7. History: Everyday Life

Averbeck, Richard E., Mark W. Chavalas, and David B. Weisberg, eds. *Life and Culture in the Ancient Near East*. Bethesda, Md.: CDL Press, 2003.

Borowski, Oded. *Daily Life in Biblical Times*. Society of Biblical Literature Archaeology and Biblical Studies. Atlanta, Ga.: Society of Biblical Literature, 2003.

King, Philip J., and Lawrence E. Stager. *Life in Biblical Israel*. Library of Ancient Israel. Louisville, Ky.: Westminster John Knox Press, 2001.

8. Ancient Near Eastern Texts: Introduction

Ehrlich, Carl S., ed. *From an Antique Land: An Introduction to Ancient Near Eastern Literature*. Lanham, Md.: Rowman & Littlefield, 2009.

Sparks, Kenton L. *Ancient Texts for the Study of the Hebrew Bible: A Guide to the Background Literature*. Peabody, Mass.: Hendrickson Publishers, 2005.

Walton, John H. *Ancient Near Eastern Thought and the Old Testament: Introducing the Conceptual World of the Hebrew Bible*. Grand Rapids, Mich.: Baker Academic, 2006.

9. Ancient Near Eastern Texts: Translations

Chavalas, Mark W., ed. *The Ancient Near East: Historical Sources in Translation*. Blackwell Sourcebooks in Ancient History. Malden, Mass.: Blackwell, 2006.

Foster, Benjamin R. *Before the Muses: An Anthology of Akkadian Literature*. 3rd ed. Bethesda, Md.: CDL Press, 2005.

Hallo, William W., and K. Lawson Younger, eds. *The Context of Scripture*. 3 vols. Leiden and Boston: Brill, 1997–2002.

Lichtheim, Miriam. *Ancient Egyptian Literature: A Book of Readings*. 3 vols. Berkeley: University of California Press, 1973–1980.

Simpson, William Kelly, ed. *The Literature of Ancient Egypt: An Anthology of Stories, Instructions, Stelae, Autobiographies, and Poetry*. 3rd ed. New Haven, Conn.: Yale University Press, 2003.

10. Methodology

Baker, David W., and Bill T. Arnold. *The Face of Old Testament Studies: A Survey of Contemporary Approaches*. Grand Rapids, Mich.: Baker Books, 1999.

Barton, John. *Reading the Old Testament: Method in Biblical Study*. Rev. ed. Louisville, Ky.: Westminster John Knox Press, 1996.

LeMon, Joel M., and Kent Harold Richards, eds. *Method Matters: Essays on the Interpretation of the Hebrew Bible in Honor of David L. Petersen*. Society of Biblical Literature: Resources for Biblical Study. Atlanta, Ga.: Society of Biblical Literature, 2009.

Mays, James Luther, David L. Petersen, and Kent Harold Richards, eds. *Old Testament Interpretation:*

Past, Present, and Future. Essays in Honor of Gene M. Tucker. Nashville, Tenn.: Abingdon Press, 1995.

11. Bible Dictionaries

Alexander, T. Desmond, and David W. Baker, eds. *Dictionary of the Old Testament: Pentateuch.* Downers Grove, Ill.: InterVarsity Press, 2003.

Arnold, Bill T., and H. G. M. Williamson, eds. *Dictionary of the Old Testament: Historical Books.* Downers Grove, Ill.: InterVarsity Press, 2005.

Boda, Mark J., and J. G. McConville, eds. *Dictionary of the Old Testament: Prophets.* Downers Grove, Ill.: IVP Academic, 2012.

Freedman, David N., ed. *Anchor Bible Dictionary.* 6 vols. New York: Doubleday, 1992.

Longman, Tremper, and Peter Enns, eds. *Dictionary of the Old Testament: Wisdom, Poetry and Writings.* Downers Grove, Ill., and Nottingham, Eng.: IVP Academic/InterVarsity Press, 2008.

Sakenfeld, Katharine Doob, ed. *The New Interpreter's Dictionary of the Bible.* 5 vols. Nashville: Abingdon Press, 2006.

INDEX

Aaron, 101, 162, 180, 190, 211
Abdi-Heba, 44, 45, 175
Abraham
    covenant with, 31, 47, 48, 60, 62, 84, 85, 88, 103, 151, 168,
        187, 259
    historicity of, 91, 174
    in Islam, 5, 85
    journeys of, 87
Abraham cycle, 86, 89, 92
Abram. See Abraham
Achaemenid Empire. See Medo-Persian Empire;
    Persian Empire
Adam, 70, 71, 72, 74, 77, 78, 79, 81, 82, 244, 249, 259, 263
    in Islam, 5
Akhenaten, 44, 45, 157, 158
Akkad, 42, 234
Akkadian
    culture, 42, 43, 372
    language, 44, 52, 76, 127, 128, 237, 284, 359, 373, 377, 379
Albright, W. F., 90
Alexander the Great, 46, 254, 363, 364
alphabet, 17, 44
    Akkadian, 284
    Hebrew, 273, 375
Amarna Letters, 44, 45, 220
Amenophis III, 44
Amenophis IV, 44, 45, 157
Ammon, 39, 335
Ammonites, 194, 212
Amon-Min, 17
Amorites, 43, 204

Amos
    book of, 140, 233, 266, 280, 307, 312, 315, 317, 322, 331, 332, 333
    the prophet, 55, 181, 266, 272, 307, 309, 315, 317, 318, 320, 339
Amphictyony, 211, 224
Amurru, 43
Anatolia, 127, 128. See Asia Minor
ancestral narratives, 69, 78, 84, 85, 86, 87, 88, 91, 92, 94, 96, 100,
    143, 148, 152, 155, 156, 384
ancient Near East, 90
    archaeology of, 106
    creation accounts of, 73, 74
    cultures of, 12, 40, 44, 45, 46, 49, 52, 63, 73, 82, 85, 110, 121, 148,
        202, 204, 224, 267, 310, 311
    geography of, 40
    history of, 41, 46, 168, 169, 176, 235, 254, 364
    kingship of, 209, 212, 224
    literature of, 40, 56, 62, 75, 77, 78, 79, 80, 81, 82, 83, 86, 92, 98, 116,
        126, 127, 128, 130, 161, 167, 222, 281, 296, 297, 335, 358, 367, 370
    poetry of, 372, 373
    political marriages of, 230
    prophecy of, 311, 324
    region of, 32, 34, 35, 37, 41, 44, 52, 67, 80, 95, 170, 176, 254, 322,
        345, 350
    religions of, 15, 17, 28, 46, 53, 95, 113, 148, 152, 156, 161, 179
    treaties of, 137, 142, 147, 151, 180
    wisdom literature of, 275, 276, 277, 278, 280, 281, 285, 289,
        290, 377
animism, 11, 46
Antiochus IV Epiphanes, 363, 364, 365, 366
antiquarianism, 53
anti-Semitism, 2

apocalyptic literature, 313, 349, 352, 355, 356, 357, 358, 359, 369, 395
Apocrypha, 23, 25, 30
Arabah, 39
Arad, 124, 125
Aramaic, 5, 26, 27, 137, 219, 244, 251, 252, 253, 254, 354, 361, 362, 366, 388, 390
Aramaic Bible (Peshitta), 5
archaeology, 90, 89, 162, 168, 169, 171, 197
Ark of the Covenant, 104, 113, 129
Artaxerxes I, 253, 257, 345
Aryan, 2
Asher
    tribe of, 252
Asherah, 154, 163, 164, 180, 240
Ashurbanipal, 138
Asia Minor
    region of, 17, 37, 364
    wisdom literature of, 276
Assyria, 34, 46, 138, 181, 234, 236, 237, 239, 307, 311, 319, 322, 324, 327, 332, 359
Astruc, Jean, 56
Aten, 10, 44, 46, 157, 158
atheism, 7
    definition of, 7, 11
    narrow, 7
    wide, 7
Axial Age, 15, 31, 32, 49, 52, 69, 110, 111, 128, 130, 156, 164, 387

Baal, 77, 78, 111, 154, 159, 160, 161, 163, 165, 181, 223, 236, 238, 239, 240, 318
    of Lightning, xiii
Baal Cycle, 77, 161
Babylon
    city of, 43, 46, 128, 159, 182, 234, 244, 252, 255, 257, 258, 322, 331, 335, 336, 338, 345, 361, 362, 363, 364, 387
    fall of, 46, 177, 259, 326, 337, 343, 363
    province of, 366
    religion of, 2, 9, 46, 76, 158, 159, 359
Babylonian Chronicle, 177, 234, 242, 335
Babylonian exile, 16, 20, 21, 26, 163, 233, 323, 327, 332, 334, 349, 353, 367
Babylonian Job, 278, 279. See Poem of the Righteous Sufferer
Babylonian Noah. See Utnapishtim
Babylonian Talmud, 28
Babylonian Theodicy, 278, 284
Bashan, 39
Beersheba, 95
Benjamin
    tribe of, 48, 217, 247, 328, 379

Bethel, 95, 134, 179, 197, 198, 230, 239, 314, 317, 344
Book of the Covenant, 116, 118, 122, 126, 128, 132, 133, 139, 151
Book of the Dead, xii, 43, 278
Book of the Law. See Torah
Books of Moses, 56, 116. See Pentateuch, Torah
Byzantine Empire, 28

canon, 16, 21, 23, 24, 167, 248, 262, 264, 266, 288, 292, 319, 327, 359, 370, 372, 378
    Christian, 23, 244, 252, 267, 292, 308, 349
    definition of, 21
    development of, 21, 22
    Jewish, 22, 23, 25, 185, 189, 232, 245, 248, 266, 267, 292, 327, 328, 348, 359, 360, 370
    Protestant, 23, 25, 26, 245
    Roman Catholic, 22, 25, 26, 245
canonical criticism, 297
Chemosh, 250, 251
Chinnereth. See Sea of Galilee
Chronicles
    book of, 20, 23, 55, 57, 64, 209, 244, 245, 247, 248, 249, 250, 252, 254, 257, 260, 263, 265, 266, 291, 297, 392
Chronistic History, 57, 244, 245, 246, 247, 248, 249, 254, 259, 262, 264, 267, 286
Cicero, 54
City of David, 214, 220, 232, 245, 246, 250, 330, 344
Classical Period, 32
cosmogony, 67, 73, 74, 76, 82
cosmology, 73, 80
Council of Jamnia, 21, 22, 23
Court History, 216, 227
Covenant Code, 126, 127, 128, 145
cuneiform, 17, 75, 76, 127, 128, 177, 308
Cyrus Cylinder, 178, 255, 257, 258, 260, 343
Cyrus II, 46, 178

Dan
    city of, 180, 195, 211, 219, 230, 239, 251, 252
    tribe of, 195
Daniel
    book of, 23, 25, 252, 266, 308, 355, 356, 357, 358, 359, 360, 362, 365, 366, 367, 369
    the sage, 355, 358, 360, 361, 362, 363, 367, 368
Darius I, 257, 344, 346, 362
Darius the Great. See Darius I
David
    anointing of, 63, 212, 214
    court history of, 216, 280
    covenant with, 60, 81, 216, 237, 238, 330

date of, 208, 241

dynasty of, 49, 176, 219, 227, 245, 248, 265, 344, 347, 353

historicity of, 168, 175, 217, 218, 219, 220, 251

kingdom of, xiv, 215, 220

as a model king, 239

as model king, 207, 216, 217, 226, 227, 230, 232, 233, 250

united monarchy of, 40, 47, 168, 176, 225, 249, 330, 395

Day of Yahweh, 333, 334, 342, 348, 349, 353

Dead Sea, xii, 26, 27, 39, 92, 144, 187, 336

Dead Sea Scrolls, 12, 13, 26, 28, 30

Deborah, 63, 193, 194, 319

Decalogue. *See* Ten Commandments

Delitzsch, Friedrich, 2

Deutero-canonical. *See* Apocrypha

Deutero-Isaiah. *See* Second Isaiah

Deuteronomic Code, 126, 145

Deuteronomistic History, 56, 57, 58, 59, 62, 140, 145, 146, 175, 189, 190, 201, 209, 216, 227, 228, 230, 233, 247, 249, 252, 259, 268

Deuteronomy

book of, 12, 55, 56, 57, 58, 59, 62, 64, 69, 106, 110, 131, 132, 133, 135, 137, 138, 139, 140, 141, 142, 143, 144, 145, 147, 149, 151, 152, 156, 162, 168, 185, 189, 233, 238, 262, 264, 280, 284, 288, 323, 341, 385, 392, 394

Dialogue of Pessimism, Akkadian composition, 377

divine assembly, 9

divine council, 9, 15, 81, 305

Documentary Hypothesis, 56, 91, 296

Dynastic prophecy, 359

Ecclesiastes

book of, 64, 185, 245, 267, 280, 281, 292, 370, 371, 376, 377, 381

Eden, 55, 70, 71, 79, 185

Edom, 39, 162, 163, 201, 208, 332, 335

Egypt

apocalyptic literature of, 359

Brook of, 187

country of, 22, 26, 29, 34, 37, 40, 42, 43, 44, 45, 46, 48, 60, 72, 86, 94, 96, 100, 101, 105, 106, 108, 157, 158, 176, 187, 189, 254, 287, 324, 331, 335, 343, 345, 364

culture of, 40, 41, 42, 43, 44, 163, 222, 387

exodus from, 47, 60, 101, 103, 107, 112, 113, 142, 144, 162, 168, 174, 177, 179, 200, 208, 245, 259, 276, 286

history of, 31, 54

literature of, 1, 17, 44, 45, 73, 74, 75, 156, 162, 163, 201, 286, 287, 294, 308, 372, 373, 377

love poetry of, 372, 373

religion of, 2, 7, 8, 10, 43, 46, 48, 68, 69, 99, 157, 158, 277

slavery in, 47, 48, 60, 89, 99, 101, 107, 124, 157

wisdom literature of, 229, 275, 276, 277, 278, 285

Ehud, 63, 193

Eichhorn, Johann G., 56

El, 6, 44, 77, 94, 96, 111, 143, 153, 154, 155, 159, 161, 163, 187, 222, 223, 240, 339

el-Amarna, 44, 157, 158

Elijah, 181, 223, 236, 308, 310, 315, 318, 319, 323, 348, 351, 395

Elijah cycle, 226, 230, 232, 240

Elisha, 181, 230, 308, 318, 319, 323

Elisha cycle, 226, 232, 240

Eloah, 6

Elohim, 6

Elohist, 57, 121

Enkidu, 77, 82

Enneateuch, 60, 62, 64, 65, 85, 189

Enuma Elish, 76, 77, 80, 159, 161, 264

Ephraim

tribe of, 89, 94, 192, 195, 196, 211, 394

Epic of Atrahasis, 75

Epic of Creation, 76

Esarhaddon, 137, 138, 311

Esau, 47, 92

Esther

book of, 23, 25, 185, 244, 245, 267, 370, 371, 378, 381, 382

Queen, 378, 379, 380

Euphrates River, 34, 35, 111, 187, 218, 254, 311, 334, 344

Eve, 70, 71, 77, 79, 81

Exodus

book of, 20, 27, 43, 55, 58, 60, 61, 62, 69, 94, 99, 100, 101, 102, 103, 106, 107, 110, 111, 114, 116, 120, 123, 132, 133, 135, 139, 140, 143, 152, 162, 168, 191, 262, 264, 394

Ezekiel

book of, 252, 266, 267, 308, 317, 326, 327, 334, 336, 339, 360

the prophet, 182, 266, 315, 321, 330, 334, 335, 336, 337, 349

Ezra

book of, 22, 23, 55, 57, 64, 178, 244, 245, 247, 248, 249, 252, 253, 254, 257, 258, 259, 260, 263, 264, 366, 392

the scribe, 22, 178, 253, 254, 255, 257, 259, 263, 343, 345

father's house, 84, 93, 179

Fertile Crescent, 31, 34, 44, 46, 74, 161, 237

First Isaiah, 321

First Testament. See Old Testament

form criticism, 92, 291, 296, 297, 298, 300, 303, 312

definition of, 296

Gad

tribe of, 192, 193

Galilee, 2, 195, 198

genealogy, 71, 72, 74, 79, 86
   of Ezra, 253
   priestly, 71
   of Ruth, 375
Genesis
   book of, 27, 55, 58, 60, 67, 69, 70, 74, 78, 82, 84, 85, 86, 87, 88,
      89, 92, 96, 97, 99, 100, 126, 139, 145, 148, 152, 154, 155, 156,
      165, 168, 179, 187, 189, 245, 248, 249, 262, 264, 339, 384, 394
Genesis (1–11), 60, 67, 68, 69, 70, 73, 74, 78, 79, 80, 81, 84, 85, 88,
      152, 155, 392, 394
Genesis (12–50), 60, 67, 69, 84, 85, 86, 94, 96, 152, 155
Gezer, 95, 108, 175, 207, 218, 225
Gideon, 63, 193, 194, 395
Gilead, 39, 95
Gilgamesh, 82, 263, 264
Gilgamesh Epic, 4, 77, 264
God, names for
   El, 94
   El Elohe Israel, 94
   El Elyon, 94
   El Olam, 94
   El Roi, 94
   Elohim, 88
   El-Shaddai, 94
   God of heaven, 367
   LORD of Hosts, 6
   Most High God, 367
   Yahweh, 88
   YHWH Sabaoth, 6
Great Hymn to the Aten, 157, 294
Greece
   country of, 32, 34, 40, 45, 220, 224, 345, 363, 364
   culture of, 44, 224, 364, 387
   history of, 54, 176, 254, 343, 363, 364, 380
   literature of, 3, 116, 128, 359
   religion of, 367
Greek Bible. *See Septuagint*
Greek, language, 6, 21, 22, 23, 25, 26, 27, 34, 60, 61, 62, 71, 73, 118,
      132, 209, 264, 292, 294, 348, 356, 360, 391, 392, 394
Gunkel, Hermann, 296, 298, 300, 303

Habakkuk
   book of, 233, 266, 326, 327, 332
   the prophet, 266, 315, 332, 333
Hadad-Baal, 294
Hagar, 47, 85, 96
Haggai
   book of, 266, 342, 346
   the prophet, 177, 266, 315, 342, 343, 344, 346, 347
Hammurabi, 43, 122, 127, 128, 159

Harnack, Adolf von, 2
Hazor, 95, 105, 175, 194, 197, 198, 200, 207, 218, 225, 236
Hebrew Bible. *See* Old Testament
Hebrew Scriptures. *See* Old Testament
Hebrew, language, 5, 6
Hebron, 92, 95, 134, 179, 198
henotheism, 9, 12, 14, 18, 128, 163, 164
   definition of, 9
   development of, 11
henotheistic monolatry, 259, 367
Herodotus, 52, 54, 176, 254, 380
Hexateuch, 189
Hezekiah, 21, 146, 181, 220, 222, 228, 233, 235, 238, 241, 251, 252,
      265, 266, 286, 323, 324, 333
high chronology, 175, 176
historical apocalypse. *See* apocalypse
historical narrative, 52, 55, 57, 61, 62, 100, 106, 130, 145, 146, 189,
      261, 265
historiography, 51, 53, 54, 110, 195, 249
Hittites, 37, 44, 52, 53, 108, 127, 137, 204, 359
   king of, 136
Holiness Code, 126, 151
Horeb. *See* Mount Horeb
Hosea
   book of, 110, 140, 233, 265, 280, 307, 312, 315, 318
   the prophet, 110, 163, 180, 181, 266, 307, 309, 315, 318, 320, 322,
      323, 328, 339
house of David, 219, 220, 251, 321, 393
Hurrians, 136
Hyksos, 43, 44

Instruction of Amenemope, 286, 287
Instruction of Ptahhotep, Egyptian composition, 227, 229
Instructions to Merikare, 75
Irenaeus, 29
Isaac, 47, 69, 92, 95, 96, 97, 187
   historicity of, 91
Isaac interlude, 86, 87
Isaiah
   book of, 12, 13, 140, 259, 265, 267, 280, 308, 312, 315, 317, 320,
      321, 326, 332, 333, 336, 337, 338, 340, 367, 392
   of the exile, 315, 327, 336, 337, 338, 339, 340, 353, 367, 386
   son of Amoz, 21, 55, 307, 309, 315, 321, 322, 330, 331, 337, 339, 357
Ishmael, 47, 96, 97
Islam, 1, 3, 4, 6, 11, 12, 14, 16, 23, 28, 29, 30, 47, 84, 96, 129, 164, 166, 383
Israel Stela. *See* Merneptah Stela

Jabneh. *See* Jamnia
Jacob, 47, 69, 84, 86, 88, 89, 94, 95, 96, 100, 134, 187, 208
   historicity of, 91

Jacob cycle, 86, 87, 89, 92

Jamnia, 21, 22

Jephthah, 63, 193, 194

Jeremiah
  book of, 20, 55, 140, 233, 266, 267, 272, 308, 312, 317, 320, 326,
    327, 328, 329, 331, 332, 339, 371
  the prophet, 15, 21, 145, 250, 262, 266, 272, 315, 319, 321, 328,
    329, 330, 333, 335, 337, 351, 363, 375

Jeroboam I, 230, 232, 239, 240, 242

Jerome, 23, 25, 27

Jesus, 2, 5, 23, 29, 85, 96, 164, 338, 356, 363
  in Islam, 4, 5, 29

Jewish Bible. *See* Old Testament

Job
  book of, 22, 264, 265, 267, 275, 276, 280, 281, 283, 284, 285,
    286, 289, 292, 370, 371, 376
  the character, 279, 281, 282, 283

Joel
  book of, 266, 333, 342, 346, 349, 353
  the prophet, 266, 315

Jonah
  book of, 266, 312, 342, 346, 349, 351, 352
  the prophet, 315, 350, 351

Jordan River, 39, 57, 106, 132, 139, 163, 171, 187, 191, 192, 193, 198,
    201, 374

Joseph, 89, 94, 101, 106, 168, 192, 253
  narrative of, 20, 60, 69, 84, 86, 89, 94, 100, 280

Joshua
  book of, 47, 55, 57, 58, 62, 63, 94, 106, 145, 146, 167, 168, 173,
    174, 184, 185, 187, 189, 190, 192, 193, 195, 197, 200, 201, 202,
    204, 205, 206, 209, 228, 262, 264, 392, 394
  son of Nun, 19, 48, 62, 171, 175, 190, 191, 193, 194, 200, 202,
    207, 344

Josiah, 21, 139, 140, 146, 181, 222, 228, 233, 241, 251, 252, 266, 324,
    328, 333, 335, 367

Judah
  kingdom of, 47, 48, 55, 57, 64, 140, 168, 175, 176, 178, 181, 218,
    219, 220, 226, 227, 230, 232, 233, 234, 236, 237, 239, 240, 242,
    243, 255, 266, 312, 315, 322, 327, 329, 331, 333, 334, 335, 336, 340,
    347, 349, 395
  region of, 40, 195, 214, 231, 332, 334, 342, 343, 344, 353, 363, 364, 374
  son of Jacob, 208
  tribe of, 48, 89, 217, 249

Judges
  book of, 55, 57, 58, 62, 63, 94, 146, 167, 175, 180, 184, 185, 187,
    189, 190, 193, 194, 195, 197, 201, 202, 204, 205, 206, 208, 209,
    211, 228, 230, 262, 264, 267, 272, 391, 392, 394

Khirbet Qeiyafa, 309

King's Highway, 40

Kings
  book of, 23, 55, 57, 59, 64, 94, 145, 146, 167, 176, 181, 207, 209,
    218, 226, 227, 228, 230, 232, 233, 236, 237, 238, 239, 240, 242,
    245, 248, 250, 259, 262, 264, 265, 266, 280, 297, 384, 392, 394

Koran. *See* Qur'an

Lachish, 170, 198, 234, 235, 320

Lamentations
  book of, 185, 245, 267, 327, 328, 329, 370, 371, 375,
    381, 382

Latin Bible. *See* Vulgate

Latin, language, 4, 25, 26, 27, 149, 150, 356, 360, 371, 376

law codes, 116, 122, 126, 127, 128, 130

Leah, 47

Letter of Aristeas, 26

Levant, 35, 37, 38, 39, 43, 44, 45, 46, 53, 161, 162, 168, 197, 229, 234,
    235, 240, 254, 322, 327, 335, 344, 345, 360, 393, 395
  Northern, 37, 111, 222
  Southern, 37, 40, 48, 49, 57, 62, 107, 163, 174, 175, 176, 178, 182,
    195, 197, 200, 201, 211, 212, 230, 231, 315, 316

Levi
  tribe of, 94, 101, 192, 230, 249, 291

Leviticus
  book of, 55, 58, 61, 69, 100, 116, 120, 129, 133, 394

low chronology, 175, 176, 225

Ludlul Bēl Nēmeqi, 279. *See* Poem of the Righteous Sufferer

LXX. *See* Septuagint

Malachi
  book of, 266, 319, 333, 342, 346, 348, 349
  the prophet, 266, 315, 348

Man and His God, Sumerian composition, 278

Manasseh
  tribe of, 89, 94, 192, 193

Marduk, 9, 10, 46, 76, 77, 158, 159, 161, 178, 257, 278,
    279, 359

Marduk prophecy, 359

Mari, 91, 111, 218, 225, 307, 311

Masoretes, 26

Masoretic Text, 26, 28

Mediterranean Sea, 32, 34, 40, 109, 187, 350, 362

Medo-Persian Empire, 46, 363

Megiddo, 140, 153, 155, 175, 207, 218, 225, 230, 232, 236, 295,
    296, 328

Megillot, 185, 328

Memphite Theology, Egyptian inscription, 74

Merneptah, xiii, 107, 108, 163, 174

Merneptah Stela, 108, 178, 197

Mesha, King of Moab, xiv, 236, 251
  Victory Stela, 250, 251

Mesopotamia
  apocalyptic literature of, 359
  calendar from, xii, 17
  cultures of, 40, 41, 42, 43, 45, 91, 127, 163, 222
  history of, 54
  iconography of, 283
  literature, origins of, 75, 76, 77, 156, 264, 308, 358, 377
  region of, 1, 17, 31, 34, 35, 37, 40, 42, 44, 46, 47, 72, 86, 88, 127,
    178, 236, 239
  religions of, 10, 68, 69, 158, 159
  wisdom literature of, 275, 276, 277, 278, 279
Messiah, 28, 29, 49, 140, 233, 257, 265, 293, 328, 348
Micah
  book of, 233, 266, 307, 315, 318
  the prophet, 181, 266, 307, 309, 315, 318, 320, 339
Middle Kingdom, Egyptian history, 43, 229, 278
Min (Egyptian deity), 7, 8
Miqra. *See* Old Testament
Mishnah, 28, 164
Moab, 39, 133, 139, 146, 163, 191, 201, 236, 250, 251, 335, 374
Moabite Stone, 236, 250, 251, 260
monolatrous henotheism, 10, 14, 46, 53, 69, 73, 74, 80, 96, 99, 103,
    113, 114, 121, 152, 202, 304, 382, 386
monolatry, 9, 12, 14, 18, 134, 142, 143, 147, 163, 181, 182, 238, 240,
    304, 323, 339, 352, 353, 367, 379
  definition of, 9, 147
monotheism, 7, 10, 11, 12, 14, 15, 18, 52, 99, 103, 125, 128, 134, 142,
    143, 152, 155, 157, 162, 164, 222, 223, 242, 259, 304, 305, 340,
    353, 382, 386
  affective, 10
  of Akhenaten, 44, 46, 157
  in apocalyptic literature, 367
  Babylonian, 46
  Biblical, 10, 163
  definition of, 10, 11, 14, 15, 147, 165
  development of, 10, 11, 12, 14, 18, 31, 32, 114, 163, 165, 182, 305,
    323, 324, 339, 353, 367, 383
  emergent, 10
  ethical, 179
  exclusive, 238
  explicit, 10, 12, 131, 133, 142, 143, 238, 259, 323, 326, 338, 339, 367,
    368, 381
  impact of, 1, 3, 6, 12, 14, 49, 53, 69, 81, 82, 110, 164, 387, 389, 390
  implicit, 10, 11, 12, 73, 80, 96, 143, 164, 288, 304, 355, 367
  in Judaism, Christianity, and Islam, 3, 4, 6, 12, 14, 15, 16, 28, 29,
    84, 148, 152, 164, 383
  in wisdom literature, 286, 288, 289
  legacy of, 6, 17, 51, 388
  narrow, 180

  practical, 143, 146, 148, 152
  rhetoric of, 339
  strict, 11, 291, 303, 304, 305
  universal, 165, 367
Moses
  birth of, 101
  covenant with, 47, 60, 111, 133, 168
  death of, 57, 59, 131, 135, 144, 145
  in Islam, 4, 5, 29, 85
  law of, 22, 43, 132, 190, 191, 245, 254
  religion of, 148, 149, 151, 152, 154, 155, 156, 161, 162, 164, 165, 323
  speeches of, 62, 106, 131, 132, 134, 135, 138, 139, 141, 142, 143, 145, 385
Mot (god of death), 77
Mount Ebal, 133, 135
Mount Gerizim, 133, 135, 253
Mount Horeb, 48, 103, 104, 132, 179, 181. *See* Horeb; Mount
    Sinai; Sinai
Mount Sinai, 9, 18, 59, 60, 61, 81, 99, 103, 104, 107, 110, 111, 112, 113,
    118, 121, 125, 151
Muhammad, 4, 5, 29, 85
Muslim, 5, 12, 96, 184, 204, 289, 384, 387
myth, 10, 54, 66, 67, 74, 76, 78, 79, 80, 83, 85, 159, 180, 259, 296
Mythical Age, 32

Nabonidus Chronicle, 177
Nahum
  book of, 233, 266, 326, 327, 332
  the prophet, 266, 315, 332
Naomi, 374
Nathan, the prophet, 214, 308, 319
Nebuchadnezzar II, 46, 234, 360, 362, 363
Neco, Pharaoh of Egypt, 140
Negeb, 40, 162, 187, 195, 367
Nehemiah
  book of, 22, 23, 55, 57, 64, 177, 244, 245, 247, 248, 249,
    252, 253, 254, 257, 258, 259, 260, 263, 264, 345, 392
  the cupbearer, 178, 253, 257, 343, 345
New Kingdom, Egyptian history, 7, 8, 43, 44, 101, 102, 157,
    287, 373
New Testament, 4, 25, 26, 29, 156, 164, 333, 356, 360, 363
Newer Testament. See Old Testament
Nile River, 34, 35, 101, 112, 189
Noah, 55, 71, 74, 86, 155, 204
  covenant with, 60, 81, 85, 87, 103, 151
  in Islam, 5
Novum Testamentum. See New Testament
Numbers
  book of, 55, 58, 61, 62, 69, 99, 100, 106, 114, 116, 120, 132, 133, 135,
    139, 143, 185, 189, 191, 262, 394

Obadiah
    book of, 266, 326, 327, 332, 333
    the prophet, 266, 315, 332
Old Babylonian Period, 43
Old Kingdom, Egyptian history, 42, 43, 278
Old Testament (names for), 1, 4, 21
Older Testament. *See* Old Testament
Origen, 29
OT. *See* Old Testament
Othniel, 63, 193, 194

Palestine, 25, 32, 35, 37, 163, 205, 260
Palestinian Talmud, 28
pantheism, 46, 81
pantheon, 113, 156
    of Babylon, 76, 178
    of Canaan, 153, 155
    of Egypt, 7, 8, 99, 101, 157
    of Israel, 9
    of Mesopotamia, 159
    of Syria-Palestine, 161
    of Ugarit, 77, 111, 154, 161
Papyrus Chester Beatty I, 373
patriarchs, 67, 85, 92, 141, 154, 179, 208
Pentateuch, 56. *See* Torah
    definition of, 23
Persian Empire, 37, 53, 54, 178, 244, 254, 255, 259, 260
Persians, 46, 54, 177, 178, 254, 255, 326, 337, 345, 368, 379
Petrie, Sir Flinders, 90
Philistines, 37, 63, 194, 211, 212, 214, 229, 324, 335
Phoenicia, xiii, 17, 18, 105, 111, 236, 350, 367
Poem of the Righteous Sufferer, Akkadian composition, 278, 279
polytheism, 1, 6, 7, 12, 17, 73, 148, 156, 288, 381
    definition of, 11, 147
    development of, 11, 46, 163, 179, 305, 368
    of Canaan, 163
    of Israel, 9, 163, 180
    in the Old Testament, 6, 9, 11
Priestly Code, 126
Primary History, 20, 22, 51, 55, 58, 59, 61, 62, 64, 65, 78, 85, 144,
    155, 167, 184, 185, 189, 207, 227, 230, 244, 245, 247, 248, 261,
    262, 263, 264, 266, 267, 286, 296, 308, 319, 327, 373, 376,
    384, 386
Primeval History, 69, 70, 71, 73, 74, 76, 77, 78, 79, 83, 85, 88, 152,
    155, 156
    Biblical, 79, 80, 81
primogeniture, 92
Prism Inscription, 235, 242
Proto-Isaiah. *See* First Isaiah

Proverbs
    book of, 22, 264, 267, 270, 271, 275, 276, 278, 280, 281, 285,
    286, 287, 288, 289, 292, 303, 321, 370, 371, 372, 376
Psalms
    book of, 19, 22, 27, 55, 117, 265, 267, 275, 291, 292, 293, 294,
    295, 297, 298, 299, 300, 301, 302, 303, 304, 306, 312, 321, 341,
    351, 353, 370, 371, 372, 376, 386, 392
Ptah (Egyptian god), 74
Pyramid Texts, 43

Qoheleth. *See* Ecclesiastes
Qumran, 26, 27, 141, 299, 300
Qur'an, 4, 5, 23, 29, 96, 164, 295

Rachel, 47
Ramses II, 52, 101, 102, 108
Ras Shamra, 154, 161
Rebekah, 47, 85
Red Sea, 34, 40, 103, 107, 110, 114, 174
redaction criticism, 297
Reed Sea, 107, 112, 114. *See* Red Sea
Reshep, 7, 8
retribution theology, 57, 64, 141
Reuben
    tribe of, 192, 193
rhetorical criticism, 297
Rome, 3, 22, 23, 25, 26, 27, 32, 40, 42, 54, 123, 130, 149, 150, 169,
    220, 224, 364, 383
Ruth
    book of, 58, 59, 64, 185, 245, 267, 370, 371, 373, 381
    the Moabitess, 19, 374, 375

Samaria
    city of, 46, 49, 57, 64, 70, 134, 176, 232, 236, 239, 240, 253, 320,
    322, 328, 329
    district of, 2, 254, 318
Samson, 63, 193, 194, 272
Samuel
    book of, 23, 55, 57, 58, 63, 94, 145, 167, 185, 195, 207, 209, 211,
    217, 222, 223, 224, 227, 228, 250, 262, 264, 280, 297,
    392, 394
    the prophet, 19, 62, 63, 208, 212, 308, 315, 319
Sarah, 47, 60, 85, 87
Sarai. *See* Sarah
Saul
    date of, 208, 241
    historicity of, 168, 175, 217
    kingdom of, xiv, 213
    united monarchy of, 47, 168, 176, 220, 249, 395

Sea of Galilee, 39

Sea Peoples, 45

Second Intermediate Period, Egyptian history, 43

Second Isaiah, 11, 165, 182, 288, 319, 321, 326, 337, 338, 340, 341

Second Temple Period, 58, 358

Second Testament. See Old Testament

Septuagint, 22, 23, 25, 26, 27, 28, 71, 107, 132, 185, 209, 245, 264, 292, 294, 331, 348, 360, 375, 376

Shalmaneser III, 234, 237

Shasu, 162, 163, 201

Shechem, 62, 92, 95, 133, 179, 180, 193, 194, 202, 318

Shiloh, 180, 181, 202, 209, 211, 222, 330

Shulgi Prophecy, Akkadian text, 359

Sidon, 187, 335

Sinai. *See* Horeb; Mount Horeb; Mount Sinai

Sinai Peninsula, 35, 43, 48, 60, 103, 104, 107, 162, 187, 367

Solomon

    building projects of, 218, 228

    date of, 241

    historicity of, 168, 175, 218

    kingdom of, xiv, 220, 221

    as sage, 226, 229, 265, 267, 285, 286

    temple of, 104, 111, 250, 291

    united monarchy of, 47, 48, 168, 176, 249, 330, 395

Song of Solomon

    book of, 185, 245, 267, 280, 292, 370, 371, 372, 373, 376, 381, 382

Song of Songs. *See* Song of Solomon

source criticism, 56, 296, 297

Spinoza, Benedict de, 59, 64, 262, 263

Stele of Qadesh, xii, 7, 8

Sumer, 42, 392

Sumerian, 127, 283

    language, 127, 128

    literature, 31, 42, 77, 278, 372, 373, 377

Suppiluliuma I, 136

Syria-Palestine

    cultures of, 45, 108, 222, 292, 306, 370

    geography of, 37, 158, 170

    literature of, 77, 156, 161

    region of, 1, 17, 31, 34, 35, 37, 43, 44, 46, 107, 151, 155, 363, 364, 366

    religions of, 159, 162

    wisdom literature of, 276

Table of Nations, 72

Talmud, 22

Tanak. See Old Testament

Targumim, 27

Tel Dan Inscription, 219, 220, 251

Ten Commandments, 10, 48, 59, 60, 100, 103, 116, 118, 121, 122, 123, 126, 128, 130, 133, 202, 330

Tertullian, 4

tetragrammaton, 6

textual criticism, 26, 27, 30

theogony, 67, 73, 74, 76, 82

Third Isaiah, 321, 338

Thomsen, Christian J., 41

Tiamat, 76, 77, 159, 161

Tiglath-pileser III, 46, 322

Tigris River, 34, 35, 177

Torah, 4, 19, 116, 131, 167, 364, 378. *See* Pentateuch

    authorship of, 19

    books of, 264

    canonization of, 21

    core of, 120

    definition of, 28

    in Ezra, 345

    in Islam, 29

    instruction, 116

    origin of, 144

    priestly legal materials of, 126

    sources of, 100, 296

    story, 99

Tower of Babel, 72, 85

tradition criticism, 297, 395

Transjordan, 39, 40, 193, 200, 201, 216

Trito-Isaiah. *See* Third Isaiah

Tyre, 105, 317, 335

Ugaritic

    language, 77, 154, 283, 373

    pantheon, 111, 161

Ur, 42, 72, 128

Uruk, 17, 42, 77

Uruk prophecy, 359

Utnapishtim, 77

vaticinium ex eventu, 356, 359, 364

Vetus Testamentum. See Old Testament

Via Maris, 40

Vulgate, 23, 25, 28, 86, 107, 149, 150, 185, 245, 360, 375, 376

Way of the Sea. *See Via Maris*

Wellhausen, Julius, 91, 111, 126

Witter, H. B., 56

Xerxes I, 257, 267, 345, 379, 380, 381

Yahweh War, 192
Yahwist, 55, 121, 280
Yahwistic History, 55, 56, 57, 58, 59, 70, 79
Yamm (sea god), 77

Zebulun
    tribe of, 252
Zechariah
    book of, 266, 342, 346, 347, 353
    the prophet, 177, 266, 315, 342, 343, 344, 347

Zephaniah
    book of, 233, 266, 326, 327, 333
    the prophet, 266, 315, 333
Zimri-Lim, 311
Zion
    city of, 214, 249, 250, 265, 271, 293, 299, 330, 338, 339,
        349, 395
Zion theology, 250, 260, 320, 330, 341, 347,
        348, 395
Zion Tradition. *See* Zion theology

CPSIA information can be obtained
at www.ICGtesting.com
Printed in the USA
LVHW06s2106280818
588401LV00004B/75/P

9 780521 705479